Lecture Notes in Artificial Intelligence   8773

Subseries of Lecture Notes in Computer Science

Lecture Notes in Artificial Intelligence 8714

Subseries of Lecture Notes in Computer Science

LNAI Series Editors

Randy Goebel
University of Alberta, Edmonton, Canada
Yuzuru Tanaka
Hokkaido University, Sapporo, Japan
Wolfgang Wahlster
DFKI and Saarland University, Saarbrücken, Germany

LNAI Founding Series Editor

Joerg Siekmann
DFKI and Saarland University, Saarbrücken, Germany

Andrey Ronzhin   Rodmonga Potapova
Vlado Delic (Eds.)

Speech and Computer

16th International Conference, SPECOM 2014
Novi Sad, Serbia, October 5-9, 2014
Proceedings

 Springer

Volume Editors

Andrey Ronzhin
St. Petersburg Institute for Informatics and Automation of
the Russian Academy of Sciences
Speech and Multimodal Interfaces Laboratory
St. Petersburg, Russia
E-mail: ronzhin@iias.spb.su

Rodmonga Potapova
Moscow State Linguistic University
Institute of Applied
and Mathematical Linguistics
Moscow, Russia
E-mail: rkpotapova@ya.ru

Vlado Delic
University of Novi Sad
Faculty of Technical Sciences
Novi Sad, Serbia
E-mail: vdelic@uns.ac.rs

ISSN 0302-9743   e-ISSN 1611-3349
ISBN 978-3-319-11580-1   e-ISBN 978-3-319-11581-8
DOI 10.1007/978-3-319-11581-8
Springer Cham Heidelberg New York Dordrecht London

Library of Congress Control Number: 2014948674

LNCS Sublibrary: SL 7 – Artificial Intelligence

Typesetting: Camera-ready by author, data conversion by Scientific Publishing Services, Chennai, India

Printed on acid-free paper

Springer is part of Springer Science+Business Media (www.springer.com)

Preface

The Speech and Computer International Conference (SPECOM) is a regular event organized since the first SPECOM in 1996 that was held in St. Petersburg, Russian Federation. It is a conference with a long tradition that attracts researchers in the area of computer speech processing (recognition, synthesis, understanding etc.) and related domains (including signal processing, language and text processing, multi-modal speech processing or human-computer interaction for instance). The SPECOM international conference is an ideal platform for know-how exchange especially for experts working on the Slavic and other highly inflectional languages and also know-how exchange between these, usually less-resourced languages and standard, well-resourced languages.

In the long history of the SPECOM conference it was organized alternately by the St. Petersburg Institute of Informatics and Automation of the Russian Academy of Sciences (SPIIRAS) and the Moscow State Linguistic University (MSLU) in their home cities. But there were cases when SPECOM was organized in different locations to stimulate the international nature of the conference. Thus, it was organized in 1997 by the Cluj-Napoca Subsidiary of Research Institute for Computer Technique (Romania), in 2005 by the University of Patras (Greece), in 2011 by the Kazan (Privolzhsky) Federal University (Russian Federation, Republic of Tatarstan), and in 2013 by the University of West Bohemia (UWB), Faculty of Applied Sciences, Department of Cybernetics in Plzen (Pilsen), Czech Republic. This year (2014) the decision was made to prolong the tradition and SPECOM place is chosen closer to the western border of the community of Slavic languages, the place where speech processing research has a long tradition and good results, bridge between two formerly separated political regions, the place which can be seen as a bridge between different groups of languages.

The SPECOM 2014 was the 16th event in the series. It was our great pleasure to host the SPECOM 2014 conference in Novi Sad, Serbia, organized this time by the Faculty of Technical Sciences (FTN) - University of Novi Sad, in cooperation with Moscow State Linguistic University (MSLU) and St. Petersburg Institute for Informatics and Automation of the Russian Academy of Science (SPIIRAS). The conference was held in the Congress Centre of the Hotel Park during October 5–9, 2014. Moreover, the SPECOM 2014 conference was organized in parallel with the 10th conference DOGS 2014 (Digital Speech and Image Processing), a bi-annual event traditionally organized by the Faculty of Technical Sciences, University of Novi Sad. Organization of two separated conferences allowed the continuity of their traditions and their independence, while organization of them at the same venue and at the same time allowed participants to attend sessions of both conferences according to their interests. Experienced researchers and professionals in the speech processing and related domains as well as newcomers found in the SPECOM 2014 conference a forum to communicate with people sharing similar interests.

Instead of competing between the two conferences for invited plenary talks, the decision was made to share them. Thus, the participants of both conferences could enjoy very interesting invited talks of Alexander Petrovsky (Head of Computer Engineering Department, Belarusian State University of Informatics and Radioelectronics), Andrew Breen (Director of Speech Synthesis Innovation, Nuance), Geza Nemeth (Head of the Speech Communication and Smart Interactions Laboratories, Department of Telecommunications and Media Informatics, Budapest University of Technology and Economics) on the newest achievements in the relatively broad and still unexplored area of highly inflected languages and their processing. Invited papers are published as a first part of the SPECOM 2014 proceedings.

This volume contains a collection of submitted papers presented at the conference, which were thoroughly reviewed by members of the conference reviewing team consisting of around 60 top specialists in the conference topic areas. A total of 56 accepted papers out of 100 submitted, altogether contributed by 142 authors and co-authors, were selected by the Program Committee for presentation at the conference and for inclusion in this book. Theoretical and more general contributions were presented in common (plenary) sessions. Problem oriented sessions as well as panel discussions then brought together specialists in limited problem areas with the aim of exchanging knowledge and skills resulting from research projects of all kinds.

Last but not least, we would like to express our gratitude to the authors for providing their papers on time, to the members of the conference reviewing team and Program Committee for their careful reviews and paper selection and to the editors for their hard work preparing this volume. Special thanks are due to the members of the Local Organizing Committee for their tireless effort and enthusiasm during the conference organization. We hope that you benefitted from the event and that you also enjoyed the social program prepared by members of the Local Organizing Committee.

July 2014   Andrey Ronzhin

Organization

The conference SPECOM 2014 was organized by the Faculty of Technical Sciences, University of Novi Sad (UNS, Novi Sad, Serbia), in cooperation with the Moscow State Linguistic University (MSLU, Moscow, Russia) and the St. Petersburg Institute for Informatics and Automation of the Russian Academy of Science (SPIIRAS, St. Petersburg, Russia). The conference website is located at: http://specom.nw.ru/.

Program Committee

Etienne Barnard, South Africa
Laurent Besacier, France
Denis Burnham, Australia
Vlado Delić, Serbia
Christoph Draxler, Germany
Thierry Dutoit, Belgium
Peter French, UK
Hiroya Fujisaki, Japan
Slobodan Jovicic, Serbia
Jean-Paul Haton, France
Rüdiger Hoffmann, Germany
Dimitri Kanevsky, USA
Alexey Karpov, Russian Federation
Michael Khitrov, Russian Federation
George Kokkinakis, Greece
Steven Krauwer, The Netherlands
Lin-shan Lee, Taiwan
Boris Lobanov, Belarus
Benoit Macq, Belgium
Roger Moore, UK

Heinrich Niemann, Germany
Dimitar Popov, Italy
Vsevolod Potapov, Russian Federation
Rodmonga Potapova, Russian Federation
Josef Psutka, Czech Republic
Lawrence Rabiner, USA
Gerhard Rigoll, Germany
Andrey Ronzhin, Russian Federation
John Rubin, UK
Murat Saraclar, Turkey
Jesus Savage, Mexico
Tanja Schultz, Germany
Milan Sečujski, Serbia
Pavel Skrelin, Russian Federation
Viktor Sorokin, Russian Federation
Yannis Stylianou, Greece
Luboš Šmídl, Czech Republic
Christian Wellekens, France
Miloš Železný, Czech Republic

Local Organizing Committee

Nikolay Bobrov
Vlado Delic (Chair)
Nikola Janicijevic
Liliya Komalova
Alexey Maslov
Irina Podnozova

Rodmonga Potapova
Alexander Ronzhin
Andrey Ronzhin
Anton Saveliev
Milan Sečujski
Miloš Železný

Acknowledgements

Special thanks to the reviewers who devoted their valuable time to review the papers and thus helped to keep the high quality of the conference review process.

Sponsoring Institutions

University of Novi Sad
International Speech Communication Association, ISCA
AlfaNum Speech Technologies Ltd
Speech Technology Center Ltd

About Novi Sad

Novi Sad is the second largest city in Serbia and the capital of the Autonomous Province of Vojvodina. The city has a population of 336,000 inhabitants. It is located in the southern part of Pannonian Plain, on the border of the Bačka and Srem regions, on the banks of the Danube river and Danube-Tisa-Danube Canal, facing the northern slopes of Fruska Gora mountain. The city was founded in 1694, when Serb merchants formed a colony across the Danube from the Petrovaradin fortress, a Habsburg strategic military post. In the 18th and 19th centuries, it became an important trading and manufacturing center, as well as a center of Serbian culture of that period, earning the nickname Serbian Athens. Today, Novi Sad is an industrial and financial center of the Serbian economy, as well as a major cultural center.

The University of Novi Sad (UNS, `www.uns.ac.rs`) was founded on 28 June 1960. Today it comprises 14 faculties located in the four major towns of Vojvodina: Novi Sad, Subotica, Zrenjanin, and Sombor. The University of Novi Sad is now the second largest among six state universities in Serbia. The main University Campus, covering an area of $259,807m^2$, provides the University of Novi Sad with a unique and beautiful setting in the region and the city of Novi Sad. Having invested considerable efforts in intensifying international cooperation and participating in the process of university reforms in Europe, the University of Novi Sad has come to be recognized as a reform-oriented university in the region and on the map of universities in Europe.

The Faculty of Technical Sciences (Fakultet Tehničkih Nauka, FTN, `www.ftn.uns.ac.rs`) with 1,200 employees and more than 11,000 students is the largest faculty at UNS. FTN offers engineering education within 71 study programmes. As a research and scientific institution, FTN has 13 departments and 31 research centers. FTN also publishes 4 international journals and organizes 16 scientific conferences on various aspects of engineering, including the conference DOGS which is dedicated to the area of speech technologies where FTN has the leading position in the Western Balkan region.

Table of Contents

Invited Talks

Conference Papers

Creating Expressive TTS Voices for Conversation Agent Applications

Andrew Breen

Nuance Communication, Norwich, United Kingdom
abreen@nuance.com

Abstract. Text-to-Speech has traditionally been viewed as a "black box" component, where standard "portfolio" voices are typically offered with a professional but "neutral" speaking style. For commercially important languages many different portfolio voices may be offered all with similar speaking styles. A customer wishing to use TTS will typically choose one of these voices. The only alternative is to opt for a "custom voice" solution. In this case, a customer pays for a TTS voice to be created using their preferred voice talent. Such an approach allows for some "tuning" of the scripts used to create the voice. Limited script elements may be added to provide better coverage of the customer's expected domain and "gilded phrases" can be included to ensure that specific phrase fragments are spoken perfectly. However, even with such an approach the recording style is strictly controlled and standard scripts are augmented rather than redesigned from scratch. The "black box" approach to TTS allows for systems to be produced which satisfy the needs of a large number of customers, even if this means that solutions may be limited in the persona they present.

Recent advances in conversational agent applications have changed people's expectations of how a computer voice should sound and interact. Suddenly, it's much more important for the TTS system to present a persona which matches the goals of the application. Such systems demand a more flamboyant, upbeat and expressive voice. The "black box" approach is no longer sufficient; voices for high-end conversational agents are being explicitly "designed" to meet the needs of such applications. These voices are both expressive and light in tone, and a complete contrast to the more conservative voices available for traditional markets. This paper will describe how Nuance is addressing this new and challenging market.

Keywords: Expressive text-to-speech, voice talent selection, conversational style.

1   Introduction

The commercial importance of Text-to-Speech (TTS) systems has been steadily growing year on year, with systems being deployed in a wide variety of markets ranging from low-end embedded devices such as toys and cell phones, to in-car solutions for navigation, and finally deployed as large scale systems for Enterprise solutions

A. Ronzhin et al. (Eds.): SPECOM 2014, LNAI 8773, pp. 1–14, 2014.
© Springer International Publishing Switzerland 2014

used for directory assistance, customer care and most recently a host of novel domains such as news reading and information query. Each market has specific demands on the technology; on embedded devices TTS systems must compete for limited "real estate", while large server based systems must be computationally efficient and able to service hundreds of simultaneous requests in real-time while providing high quality synthesis.

The success of TTS in these different markets has been due to a combination of factors, most notably the development and adoption of the right technology for a given market and an understanding of how to make the technology work effectively for commercial applications. TTS in the market place must be robust to a broad range of input material while offering an "acceptable" level of performance and quality.

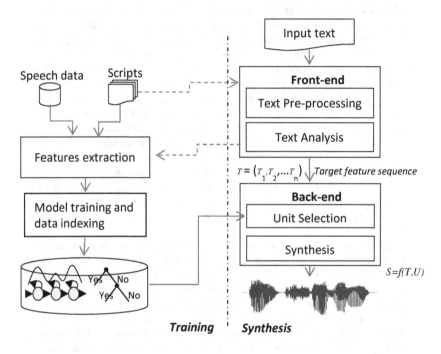

Fig. 1. Diagram of the training and synthesis phases in speech synthesis; during training a dbase of indexed units is created. During synthesis the search function $S=f(T,U)$ is used to obtain an sequence of units which optimally matches each target with units in the inventory.

Text-to-speech (TTS) systems have developed over years of research [1,2], resulting in a relatively standardized set of components as shown in Figure 1. The Front-end (FE), which derives information from an analysis of the text, and the Back-end (BE), which uses this information to search an indexed knowledge base of pre-analysed speech data. Indexed data most closely matching the information provided by the front-end is extracted and used by a speech synthesizer to generate synthetic speech. The pre-analysed data may be stored as encoded speech or as a set of parameters used to drive a model of speech production or as in hybrid systems a combination of both. It can be argued that recent commercial deployments of TTS have forced the pace of development in the back-end more than the front-end, although as this paper will discuss, this situation may now be changing. Back-end developments have consolidated into two broad categories; unit selection followed by waveform concatenation and unit selection followed by parametric synthesis, each approach having specific benefits. Waveform concatenation [4,5,6] currently offers the highest segmental speech quality but such systems are large and inflexible. Parametric synthesis systems [7] are robust to data compression, flexible and produce a more consistent quality, but currently suffer from a "synthetic" speech quality. At the moment, waveform concatenation methods are the most widely deployed solutions, parametric systems being limited to deployments which have strict computational and memory constraints.

This practical approach to development has lead to what some call the "encoding of ignorance" within modern commercial systems. Such systems have focused on the production of an overall solution, deploying methods which afford improvements in quality leading to great technology adoption, but do not attempt to offer significant insights into the underlying mechanisms of speech production. This pressure to feed the increasing demands of applications has resulted in a technological cul-de-sac, which is forcing researchers to re-evaluate well-established methods.

The paper is divided into 7 sections, each section describing in detail the steps taken by Nuance to address one aspect of this growth in demand; the creation of "characterful" synthesis systems for conversational agent applications. Section 2 will review an often overlooked but important element in successful system design: the selection of the voice talent. Section 3 provides an overview of the steps taken in creating an appropriate recording script used to build the synthesis voice. Section 4 discusses the importance of prosody in expressive voices and how it is used within these systems. Sections 5 and 6 describe the different synthesis methods investigated. Finally Section 7 provides results and conclusions.

2   The Voice

As previously stated in Section 1, commercial systems have focused on developing techniques which improve the adoption of synthesis. For a system to be deployed it must meet the acceptance criteria of a customer. This includes objective metrics such as pronunciation accuracy, but it also includes subjective metrics such as how pleasant the voice is and how well it matches the persona being designed within the whole application. Section 4 will discuss in detail the technical challenges facing TTS systems when asked to produce specific speaking styles. This section will focus on the interaction between the characteristics of the voice of the recording talent and the demands of a specific speaking style.

Traditional TTS applications have been dominated by basic information retrieval and confirmation applications. This is in part because of the demand for such services in the broader speech market, but also because the limitations of the technology have played well in these domains. Directory, banking and booking services have preferred personas which are mature, conservative and relatively slow paced. Voice selection and creation processes have been tuned over the years to cater for these markets, with large "portfolios" of voices being developed in many languages. Where customers have requested a specific voice talent, such talents have be tutored to produce recordings in a specific style which works well with traditional TTS technologies. Portfolio voices are a combination of speaker, style and script and are designed to cater for the widest possible use case. The constraints imposed by technology in script design are considered in Section 3. "Custom voices" are a useful supplement to the portfolio model. In such cases in addition to the choice of voice talent, systems may be tailored in script design to ensure that a particular customer's domain is well represented by the voice. The ultimate expression of this is "gilded phrases", where specific recordings are stored and reproduced by the TTS system unadulterated. The application of gilded phrases in the development of expressive voices is discussed in Section 6.

The choices of speaker and style, as with many other commercial topics, are subject to changes in fashion. Recently a trend has emerged for more lively, youthful and dynamic personas that do not work well with the traditional methods of synthesis which have been heavily tailored to the pre-existing market. In order to better understand this relationship between speaker and speaking style a series of extensive MOS evaluations were conducted. Figure 2 shows the results of a MOS evaluation which compared a high quality portfolio voice, recorded in the standard portfolio style, with an example of a voice designed for the conversational agent market. 23 native US subjects were asked to score on clarity of pronunciation, naturalness, and overall impression. Scores were measured on a 5 point scale with 5 being the highest score. In order to evaluate the significance of different types of text material on subjective preference, two tests were conducted: one test composed of short length material e.g. navigation and prompt domain, and another using longer "passage" length material e.g. news. The experiments suggest that there is a marked preference for the conversation style in the shorter material, and a slight preference for the traditional style in the longer material.

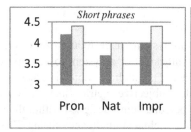 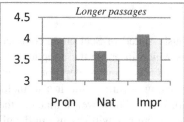

Fig. 2. Results from two MOS evaluations comparing different speakers and speaking styles on two types of text material: short phrases and longer passages. The results for the portfolio voice appear as "solid fill" bars while the results for the conversational style are shown as "no fill" bars. The results suggest that for shorter material in particular there is a strong preference for a more youthful speaker and dynamic style.

These experiments strongly suggested that in order to meet the demands of conversational agent applications, a more youthful voice is needed. A short list of 3 voices talents were selected from 25 candidates. An extensive MOS evaluation was then conducted to determine which of the shortlisted candidates met the requirements of pleasantness, dynamism and friendliness. As a baseline the same portfolio voice used in the previous experiment was included. Evaluations were conducted using 40 native US subjects. Subjects were asked to rate the voices on pleasantness and ease of listening. Each voice talent recorded 5 passages of 15-20 seconds. The material was randomised and two questions were presented to the subjects: a) *"how pleasant do you find this voice based on this sample?"* b) *"would it be easy to listen to this voice for long stretches of time?"*. The results of these tests are shown in figure 3.

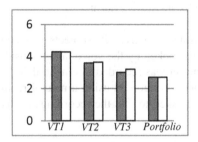

Fig. 3. Plot showing MOS evaluation comparing different voice talents and a reference portfolio voice ("Solid fill" bar denotes pleasantness, "no fill" bar denotes the ease of listening). The plot shows a clear preference for VT1 compared to the other voice talents. The speaker and speaking style of the portfolio voice again being least preferred.

A further evaluation using 42 native US subjects was conducted to elicit the prominence of important characteristics in each of the voice talent recordings. Each voice talent recorded 5 passages of 15-20sec. The samples were randomized. In order to streamline the evaluation, the following options were provided to listeners to describe the characteristics of the voice talents: *Spontaneous, Friendly, Lively, Reserved, Competent, Professional, Relaxed, Extravert, Attractive, Successful, Natural, Modern, Sexy, Boring, Slow and Fast*. In addition, the listeners could provide free form description of the audio samples. Figure 4 shows the results for two voice talents, VT1 and the portfolio voice. The results show that the primary characteristics of VT1 are *Friendly, Lively, Professional, Attractive and Natural*. While the primary characteristics for the portfolio voice are *Professional, Boring, Slow, Reserved* and *Competent*. These results nicely summarize the expected response to the voice talent recordings. The portfolio voice has been recorded to meet the demands of traditional customers, looking for a clear professional voice, while also meeting the demands of the technology which require the voice talent to speak in a neutral style. In contrast, the voice talent recordings were designed to meet the needs of conversational agents and come across as friendly and lively. However, in these recordings fewer constraints were placed on the speaker. They were asked to produce a "natural" read reflecting the content of the text. This also comes through in the results.

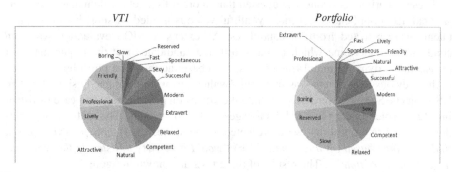

Fig. 4. Two pie charts of results for the "characteristics" experiments. The effects of the different speakers and speaking styles are clearly evident.

One final evaluation using 10 native US subjects was conducted. In this experiment two sets of recordings spoken by the voice talent considered to be the best candidate were evaluated. One set was recorded in a neutral style similar to that adopted for portfolio voices and one set recorded using a natural reading style appropriate to the material. Subjects were asked to rate the recordings on listening effort, pleasantness and naturalness.

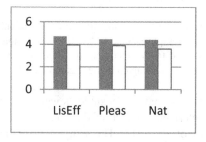

Fig. 5. Plot showing the effects of reading style on subject preference. The "solid fill" bars represents natural read, "no fill" bars neutral read.

Figure 5 clearly shows that speaking style affects all three metrics and confirms that the voice talent selection alone is not enough to produce the desired results. The implications of these findings will be discussed in more detail in Sections 4 and 5.

3   The Scripts

As shown in Fig. 1, concatenative synthesis uses a database of indexed coded audio samples. The encoding may be simple or complex but in either case, there is a fundamental limitation on the size of the unit inventory, the design of which can have a profound effect on performance and quality. In the absence of a particular customer or target application, scripts tend to focus on two properties in their design. These are basic phonetic coverage and common domains. Basic phone coverage is a fundamental requirement when creating a concatenative TTS system. However, the definition of complete coverage is not as clear as it may first appear to be. Early concatenative systems were designed on the principle of diphone units. The theoretical justification for which was that coarticulation effects between phonemes were captured in the diphone unit, leaving segmental joins to be made in the relatively stable mid-phone point, leading to improved segmental clarity and smoothness. Prosody in such systems was predicted through a prosodic model and applied using signal processing such as PSOLA [2]. The size and completeness of the phone database was determined by the number of phonemes and by basic features such as lexical stress. However, researchers recognised that overall quality could be improved if larger units were stored, and specifically larger units which covered common domains e.g. dates, times. It was also recognised that prosodic models were limiting the naturalness of synthesis systems. Often high quality could be achieved through selecting a mixture of units where prosody was included as a selection feature and not predicted and post applied. These trends lead to what are termed "pure selection" synthesis systems [4,5,6]. Such developments resulted in an explosion in the number of features used to select units and consequently significant growth in the size of the unit database. It also had the effect of breaking the simple definition of database completeness. The growth of features means that even the largest practical database suffers from unit sparsity.

Script design as well as the voice talent and the recording style influence overall acceptability. The more a script can be targeted to the application, the higher the chance of units matching the input can be found in the database and the higher the chance of longer unit sequence being selected leading to improved synthesis.

In order to design a voice to meet the specific demands of conversational agent applications a new approach to creating scripts was considered. This approach is summarised in Fig 6. In this approach conversational agent applications were considered to consist of a series of overlapping domains. These domains were classified into closed and open depending on factors such as the complexity of the language and the likelihood of seeing a large number of out of vocabulary (OOV) items. For example, telephone numbers would be considered a closed domain, as it consists of a well specified syntax and a defined word set. In contrast news is both structurally complex and likely to contain OOV items.

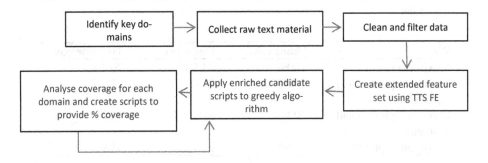

Fig. 6. Steps involved in creating a script optimised for conversational agent applications

Table 1 lists the top domains identified in conversational agent applications. Data from each of these domains was collected and filtered. Finally an iterative script creation process was performed where a "master" script was created through progressively refining coverage of units in each of the key domains. Using this approach, coverage of key phones and features for each domain could be calculated and combined to provide a master script which was tuned to the overall application.

The script creation process cannot hope to accommodate all the features used in modern unit selection. Some features are assumed to be "implicitly captured" through the text selection in combination with the recording process. No attempt was made to include fine grained prosodic features as part of script creation. However, in order to capture gross prosodic traits, features which could be robustly extracted from the text were included in the script creation process to supplement the traditional phonemic features. The combination of phonemic and orthographic cues was termed the enriched candidate set. Examples of these orthographic cues are shown in Table 2.

Table 1. Top domains identified in conversational agent applications

Domains	Description
Dialogue	General discourse e.g. "hello"
Knowledge	"What is a ..."
Entertainment	"Who is..."
Weather	"What is the weather ..."
Navigation	"Where is ..."
Number	"How much..."
Calendar	"When is ..."

Table 2. Examples of features used to create an enriched set for script creation

Boundary type	Orthographic cue
Document Initial/Final boundary	Degenerate
Paragraph Initial/Final boundary	Identified by TTS FE
Sentence Initial/Final boundary	. ! ?
Within sentence Initial/Final boundary	, ;
Parenthetical Initial/Final boundary	() [] {} " ' - _

Table 3 shows the percentage of enriched features covered in a specific domain for a pre-defined number of script entries.

Table 1. Percentage of enriched features covered in a specific domain for a pre-defined number of script entries

Weather	Phone cov.	Diphone cov.	Triphone cov.
Maximum phones	100%	73.5%	70.1%
Maximum phones and diphones	100%	98.4%	95.8%
Maximum phones and triphones	100%	97%	95.6%
Maximum diphones	99.5%	98.4%	95.9%

As described above, domains are defined in terms of whether they are open or closed. This is clearly not a binary classification; rather domains can be seen as having an "openness" property, which can be described in terms of the number of sentences needed to cover a specified number or percentage of enriched features in the scripts. Figure 7 shows the data collected for weather and navigation domains. Navigation has greater openness. This metric is highly dependent on the sampled data. A flowery description of the weather will have very different properties to a terse description. Navigation phrases which do not include place names will have very different properties from a data set which does.

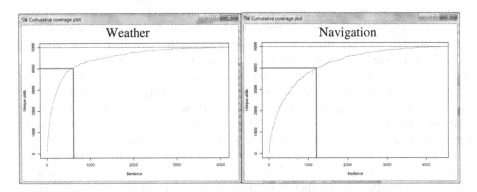

Fig. 7. Two diagrams showing how different domains have different "openness" properties

Earlier in this section it was mentioned that for practical computational reasons fine grained prosodic features, while used in the unit selection process during synthesis, are not explicitly considered in script creation. It is assumed that characteristic prosodic patterns will be captured as part of the recording style. This assumption also highlights the issues raised in Section 1, which considered the influence of style on acceptance. The next section considers these prosodic factors in more detail.

4   Prosody

Prosody can be viewed as the rhythm, stress and intonation of speech, and is fundamental in communicating a speaker's intentions and emotional state [3]. In TTS systems the prosody prediction component produces symbolic information (e.g. stress patterns, intonation and breath groups) which may or may not be augmented with parametric information (e.g. pitch, amplitude and duration trajectories). Combined, these features are used to define the prosodic realization of the underlying meaning and structure encoded within the text, and are used as feature constraints in unit selection.

There are two fundamental challenges to generating natural synthetic speech; the first challenge is to match the predictive power of the FE with the granularity of labelling of the speech data. The FE must identify and robustly extract features which closely correlate with characteristics observed in spoken language. These same features must be identified and robustly labelled in the unit database. A unit database labelled with too few features matched to a powerful FE will lead to poor unit discrimination during selection, while a weak FE which can only produce a limited set of features will lead to inaccessible units when matched with a richly labelled database. In other words, the expressive power of the FE must match the expressive power of the labelling. The second challenge is that of data sparsity. As already discussed, the unit database is finite, in order to produce high quality synthesis, sufficient examples must exist to adequately represent the expressive power of the features produced by the FE. As prosody is used in selection, the audible effects of sparsity increase as the style of speech becomes more expressive. One way to control these effects is to limit the number and weight of prosodic features. However, such an approach only works well if matched with recordings where prosody is strictly controlled. Weak prosody control during selection when coupled with an expressive database leads to unnatural prosody and segmental "glitching". Another motivation for controlling the style is database size. A neutral prosody will result in a substantially smaller database than one which attempts to capture expressive speech. These two reasons are why the majority of TTS systems strictly control the prosody during recording. Unfortunately, these constraints also limit the acceptability of conversational style synthesis.

Figure 8 shows how expressive speech has greater pitch variability and range compared to a relatively neutral style. This increase must be constrained through selection, while controlling the number of added features, which fragment the search space and exacerbate the problem of unit sparsity. Understanding and controlling sparsity is an active research area [9,10]. As described in Section 3 the traditional features were augmented with additional document and prosody features. An example of the type of symbolic prosodic features considered is shown in Table 4.

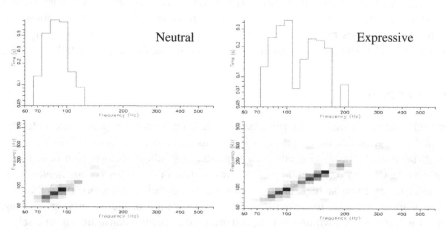

Fig. 8. (a) Two plots [8] (neutral style and expressive styles) showing (a) A histogram of all glottal periods (elapsed time, logarithmic scale), (b) a scatter-plot between adjacent glottal periods on a grey-scale.

As previously stated, in order to appreciate the benefit of a richer feature set, good FE prediction and accurate labelling must go hand in hand. A method of automatically labelling the speech data with the type of features shown in Table 4 has been produced, and matched with a "lazy learning" technique for prediction. Accuracy rates of above 75% across all the features investigated have been achieved.

Table 2. Description of prosodic features produced by the FE

Label	Description
Word Prominence Level	Reduced: typically function words, no lexical stress, no pitch movement.
	Stressed: stressed syllable in (content) word.
	Accented: stressed syllable in (content) word has salient pitch movement.
	Emphasized: stronger than accented.
Prosodic Phrase Boundary	Word
	Weak: intonation phrase.
	Strong: Major phrase.
Sentence	Phrase type (Prototypical Phrase Intonation Contour).

This section and the previous sections have described how a speech database tailored for conversational agent applications has been recorded, designed, and labeled. The next section describes the synthesis method used to produce smooth and compelling synthesis using this data.

5   Synthesis

Expressive speech requires a synthesis process complex enough to control the greater prosodic variability found. Nuance has been working for many years on a method of selection and synthesis capable of supporting expressive speech. The method, called Multi-form synthesis (MFS) is a statistically motivated hybrid approach which combines the segmental quality benefits of concatenative systems with the flexibility and trainability of model based approaches. A detailed description of this approach can be found in [11]. Hybrid methods have been shown to be robust to sparsity which, as discussed above, is one of the side effects of expressive speech. However in order to produce compelling results, MFS must be combined with the rich prosody prediction discussed in Section 4. Without such prosodic control, synthetic speech may sound smooth but with unnatural prosody.

Figure 9 diagrammatically shows the key processes of MFS synthesis. In this diagram, input text is analysed to create feature vectors. These may be complex features as described in Section 4. A search is then performed matching the phonetic and prosodic context vectors to the HMMs model in inventory M, from which a sequence of model segments Om is obtained. These model segments are used to direct a search of template candidates O_T in the template inventory T. Om is also used to generate (Pgen PI) a first set of parameter trajectories p.

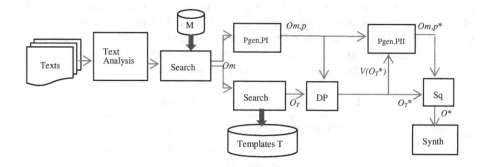

Fig. 9. Multi-Form Synthesis (MFS)

The model segments, parameter trajectories and template candidates are input into a dynamic programming algorithm (DP). As a result, the best template segment sequence O_T^* is obtained. The variance of parameter trajectories of the best template sequence is fed into a second parameter generation algorithm (Pgen PII) which regenerates the parameters p^*. The result of this process is a sequence of speech parameter trajectories Om,p^* with variance reassembling the variance of the best template segments. This is done to combine seamlessly template segments with model segments. Finally, the best models and template segments are sequenced. This sequence O^* of "multiform" segments is sent to the synthesizer-concatenator. The parameter trajectories are converted to synthetic speech and concatenated with the template segments, which yields the speech output waveform.

6   One Last Trick

So far this paper has concentrated on how to create material for expressive voices and how to use this material within a TTS system. As previously mentioned, there are limits to the degree of expressivity which can be accommodated within a TTS system, even one designed to support expressive speech. In addition, para-linguistic sounds such as laughing, crying, exclamations etc. do not fit easily into traditional linguistic analyses. Fortunately there is a simple pragmatic approach which can be used to support highly expressive and para-linguistic elements. In this approach, shown in figure 10, key idiomatic phrases ("gilded phrases") are recorded and sit alongside traditional unit selection synthesis. During synthesis, orthographic pattern matching is used to identify fragments in the text. When such fragments are identified, a gilded phrase (pre-recorded phrase fragment) is selected instead of a full FE analysis and BE synthesis. Such an approach can be highly effective for domains such as dialogue prompts which consist of frequently re-occurring highly expressive phrase patterns.

Gilded phrases can be identified as separate elements during script design, or as shown in Fig. 10, they can be automatically constructed from an analysis of the standard script elements and used to supplement or augment the main unit inventory.

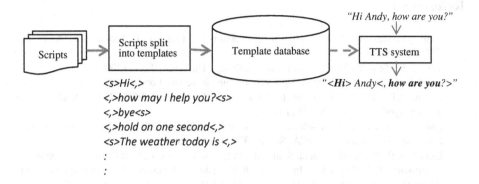

"Hi Andy, how are you?"

<s>Hi<,>
<,>how may I help you?<s>
<,>bye<s>
<,>hold on one second<,>
<s>The weather today is <,>
:
:

"<Hi> Andy<, how are you?>"

Fig. 10. Diagram showing the construction and use of "gilded phrases"

7   Results and Conclusions

This paper has focused on the creation of a specific type of speech synthesis, expressive conversational speech. The early part of the paper demonstrated the importance of matching the recoding talent and style to the target domain. The later sections described why expressive speech places additional demands on traditional concatenative systems, and briefly described how Nuance addresses these challenges. Figure 11 shows the results of a MOS evaluation which compared our latest expressive system with a reference conversational agent application. It can be seen that the new system outperforms the reference both for a closed domain and an open domain.

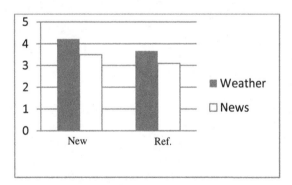

Fig. 11. MOS evaluation against a reference system

Acknowledgments. The work described in this paper is not solely the work of any one individual but represents the combined efforts of the Nuance TTS R&D team. I would like to take this opportunity to thank the team for all their hard work and dedication.

References

1. Klatt, D.: Review of text-to-speech conversion for English. J. Acous. Soc. Amer. 82, 737–793 (1987)
2. Taylor, P.: Text-To-Speech Synthesis. Cambridge University Press (2009)
3. Ladd, D.R.: Intonational Phonology. Cambridge University Press (1996)
4. Breen, A.P.: The BT Laureate Text-To-Speech System. In: ESCA/IEEE Workshop on Speech Synthesis, pp. 195–198 (1994)
5. Hunt, A., Black, A.: Unit selection in a Concatenative Speech Synthesis System using a Large Speech Database. In: ICASSP, pp. 373–376 (1996)
6. Donovan, R.: Trainable Speech Synthesis, PhD Thesis, University of Cambridge (1996)
7. Yoshimura, T., Tokuda, K., Masuko, T., Kobayashi, T., Kitamura, T.: Simultaneous Modelling of Spectrum, Pitch and Duration in HMM-Based Speech Synthesis. In: Eurospeech 1999, pp. 2374–2350 (1999)
8. SFS "Speech Filing System", http://www.phon.ucl.ac.uk/resource/sfs/
9. Chen, L., Gales, M.J.F., Wan, V., Latorre, J., Akamine, M.: Exploring Rich Expressive Information from Audiobook Data Using Cluster Adaptive Training. In: Interspeech 2012 (2012)
10. Zen, H., Senoir, A., Schuster, M.: Statistical Parametric Speech Synthesis using Deep Neural Networks. In: ICASSP, pp. 7962–7966 (2013)
11. Pollet, V., Breen, A.P.: Synthesis by Generation and Concatenation of Multi-form Segments. In: ICSLP 2008 (2008)

Gaps to Bridge in Speech Technology

Géza Németh

Department of Telecommunications and Media Informatics (TMIT),
Budapest University of Technology and Economics, (BME) Hungary
nemeth@tmit.bme.hu

Abstract. Although recently there has been significant progress in the general usage and acceptance of speech technology in several developed countries there are still major gaps that prevent the majority of possible users from daily use of speech technology-based solutions. In this paper some of them are listed and some directions for bridging these gaps are proposed. Perhaps the most important gap is the "Black box" thinking of software developers. They suppose that inputting text into a text-to-speech (TTS) system will result in voice output that is relevant to the given context of the application. In case of automatic speech recognition (ASR) they wait for accurate text transcription (even punctuation). It is ignored that even humans are strongly influenced by a priori knowledge of the context, the communication partners, etc. For example by serially combining ASR + machine translation + TTS in a speech-to-speech translation system a male speaker at a slow speaking rate might be represented by a fast female voice at the other end. The science of semantic modelling is still in its infancy. In order to produce successful applications researchers of speech technology should find ways to build-in the a priori knowledge into the application environment, adapt their technologies and interfaces to the given scenario. This leads us to the gap between generic and domain specific solutions. For example intelligibility and speaking rate variability are the most important TTS evaluation factors for visually impaired users while human-like announcements at a standard rate and speaking style are required for railway station information systems. An increasing gap is being built between "large" languages/markets and "small" ones. Another gap is the one between closed and open application environments. For example there is hardly any mobile operating system that allows TTS output re-direction into a live telephone conversation. That is a basic need for rehabilitation applications of speech impaired people. Creating an open platform where "smaller" and "bigger" players of the field could equally plug-in their engines/solutions at proper quality assurance and with a fair share of income could help the situation. In the paper some examples are given about how our teams at BME TMIT try to bridge the gaps listed.

Keywords: Gaps in speech technology, domain-specific applications, open platform, user preferences.

1   Introduction

Speech technology has gained widespread use during my 30+ years in the area. From the appearance of modern personal computers there were exaggerating marketing

A. Ronzhin et al. (Eds.): SPECOM 2014, LNAI 8773, pp. 15–23, 2014.

predictions for exponential growth of speech technology (Fig. 1). This has never come true and although some people with vision such as Steve Jobs have seen the difficulties [2], it led to a roller-coaster type of investments and downgrading of speech R&D in the last three decades. There has been rather a linear increase of performance and acceptance of real-life applications in several countries worldwide.

	1981	1982	1983	1984	1985	AAGR (%) 1981-1985	1985 % OF TOTAL
SPEECH RECOGNITION							
Devices (Chips)	1	2	4	10	30	134%	20%
Products (Board Level)	10	17	36	70	100	78%	67%
Systems	4	6	9	13	20	50%	13%
Subtotal	$15	$25	$ 49	$ 93	$150	88%	100%
SPEECH SYNTHESIS							
Devices (Chips)	15	35	80	160	320	115%	65%
Products (Board Level)	5	12	25	50	100	111%	20%
Systems	3	9	20	40	75	124%	15%
Subtotal	$23	$56	$125	$250	$495	115%	100%
TOTAL	$38M	$81M	$174M	$343M	$645M	103%	

Source: Strategic, Inc.

Fig. 1. Speech technology market growth prediction between 1981-1985 [1]

Recently more realistic business predictions are presented [3] and some widely used applications are available in several countries (e.g. navigation systems, Apple's Siri, etc.). But there is still a long way to go in order to provide speech technology solution in most of the areas where human speech communication is used. Even in the most developed language and market (English) there are huge areas (e.g. language learning [4]) where the performance of current systems is not satisfactory. In this position paper I will introduce some of the gaps that I regard important to bridge in order to create systems that are more acceptable for the final judges, the end users.

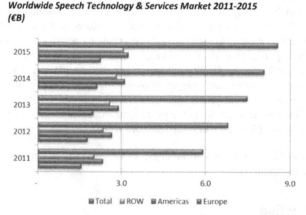

Fig. 2. Speech technology market growth prediction between 2011-2015 [3]

2   "Black-Box" Thinking

Perhaps the biggest gap to bridge for widespread use of speech technology is the education of both software developers/system integrators and end users. Both of them frequently consider TTS as a direct replacement of a "standard output device" (screen, printer or a human announcer) and ASR as a direct replacement for a "standard input device" (keyboard/mouse or a human typist). It is often ignored that typing errors are easy to detect when reading but when the mistyped text is read by a TTS system it may be very hard to comprehend. Similarly if the user mistypes something, a spell-checker may help. But a badly pronounced or out-of-vocabulary pronunciation cannot be corrected by the ASR module. There is an incredible amount of information that we use in human-human communication that is typically neglected in a speech technology application scenario. We know among others the age, education level, communication context, history of earlier communication, expertise, speaking rate of our partner and we can quickly adapt to all of these. So humans change both "their ASR and TTS" features significantly. Even during a single communication session we may request reading style change (e.g. ask for syllabification or spelling).

We have partially covered these needs in an e-mail reading application [5] by introducing three user levels (beginner, intermediate and expert) besides the chance to select the speaking rate. The verbosity of the menu system was adapted to the user level. Users also appreciated multiple system voices. In this e-mail reader application about 30% of the users changed the default male system prompt voice to a female alternative. In a reverse directory application [6] (input: phone number output: customer name and address is read out) the adaptation concept was implemented by three readout modes:

- continuous reading of the directory record (fast, overview mode)
- extended syllabification reading of the customer name (e.g. Bodó: Bo – Do with a long o) and continuous reading of the address (medium speed, supporting the detection of the exact written form of the customer name)
- spelling of the customer name character by character (slow, but very precise operation)

Users also prefer if the TTS system is not deterministic (i.e. not providing exactly the same waveform output for the same text input). We have found that such a solution can be implemented based on prosodic samples in various TTS technologies [7] with a definite user preference (c.f. Fig. 3). Our tests were performed for Hungarian and we are looking for interested partners to test the concept in other languages. It is important to note that speaking styles depend on voice timbre in addition to prosody, as well. So modelling voice timbre features (e.g. glottalization) is also an important topic [8].

Speech technology experts should be aware of and call the attention of the other contributing parties to these aspects and "educate" them about the optimal use of the available technology.

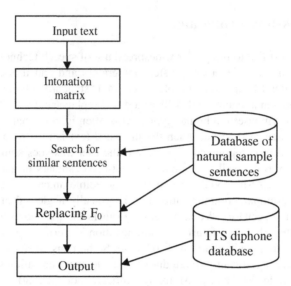

Fig. 3. The concept of generating TTS prosodic variability based on prosodic samples [7]

3   Generic vs. Domain Specific Solutions

Just as there is no single shoe type for everyone there is no single ASR or TTS system for all applications as long as we have no unified model of human communication suitable for engineering implementation. In the meantime the best approach is to create domain specific systems. It is not even sure that we should always strive for human-like performance. That may lead to the "uncanny valley" effect well known from robotics. Maybe in most cases our talking applications should behave rather in a way that resembles to special pets. This approach paves the way to the so-called eto-informatics.

Unfortunately for the time being there is not even a generic, standardized classification about the communicative contexts/speaking styles. ASR systems are still very much dependent on both the acoustic conditions and a priori knowledge about the recognition domain. More or less each research group develops its own alternatives. Associating the right application context to a particular technological solution may be critical from the end-users point of view. For example hyper-articulated script recordings may be optimal for intelligibility but may sound arrogant for the end-user. The most important factors for a given technology may also be domain/user dependent. For example to my great surprise several Hungarian blind users still prefer our 15 year-old diphone/triphone ProfiVox TTS system [9] as the Hungarian voice of the Jaws for Windows screen reader although there are other, newer Hungarian engines of international vendors. They have given the following justification:

- highly variable speech rate while maintaining good intelligibility
- fast response time (may be in the 10ms range)
- several voices (both male and female)
- optimized abbreviation handling.

The same system is also very well accepted as the voice of a humanoid robot [10]. But this system was completely unacceptable when presented as a mockup of a price-list reader over the telephone for a major telecom operator [11].

In the latter case the main requirement is that the output of the TTS system should not be easily distinguished from a recorded prompt and should be based on the voice talent of the company. A similar requirement applies to railway station announce-ments [12], and weather news reading [13]. In this case several hours of speech (in one of our applications more than 50 hours) has to be recorded and annotated in a corpus-based system in order to meet these requirements. This trend is expressed in the provisioning of several different system voices in the latest car navigation sys-tems. Besides different voice timbre, dialects and various social speaking styles even with very harsh wording are provided as alternative speech output modalities. Re-cently in-car smart(phone) applications have gained a momentum after nearly 10 years of experimentation [14].

If the occasional clicks and glitches of corpus-based systems in case of out-of-domain text input is not acceptable or quick adaptation and creation of new voices is required than statistical parametric approach (usually HMM) is a trivial alternative. This solution can make use of already available tools and data created for waveform concatenation systems [15]. The output of the HMM system may be combined with higher quality elements of a corpus-based system so that this hybrid solution may only detected by expert evaluation. It is worthwhile to consider age related features as that may influence user preference as well [16]. TTS based expressive sound events –spemoticons– may offer a good link between objective and subjective aspects of sound perception [17].

4   "Large/Small" Languages

Of the 7106 known living languages of the world only 393 have more than one mil-lion first-language speakers [18]. There are only 23 languages with at least 50 million first-language speakers. According to the META-NET White Paper series on Eu-rope's Languages in the Digital Age [19] English is the only European language having good (not excellent) support in language and speech technology tools and resources. Central- and Eastern European languages mostly fall in the *fragmentary/weak/no support* with some *moderate* cases. During my Internet search I found less than 50 languages with TTS and less than 100 languages with ASR support worldwide. That does not include the domain specific alternatives that have been argued for in the previous sessions. So there is an incredible amount work that should be performed to provide proper solutions at least to several non-English speaking societies. There is a lack of readily available tools and data with specific information about language dependent and language independent features. Currently there is both lack of resources and multiplication of efforts to create the same (or similar) tools and resources.

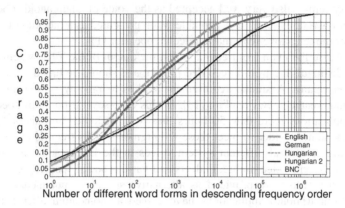

Number of different word forms in descending frequency order

Fig. 4. Corpora coverage by the most frequent words (logarithmic horizontal scale) of standard texts [20]

A good illustration of this problem can be seen in Fig. 4. That study [20] investigated the number of different word forms (between space characters) appearing in various size of English, German and Hungarian corpora and the coverage that a given number of most frequent words can provide. It can be seen that the relatively small English corpus (3.5 million tokens) needs the least elements for a certain level of coverage. Hungarian has by far the largest number of words. That phenomenon trivially influences the vocabulary size for ASR systems but it is also exhibited in corpus-based TTS solutions. For example, in Hungarian more than 5.000 sentences were needed for proper coverage of the weather news domain which can be covered with about 1.000 sentences in English. A further problem for Hungarian is the relatively free word order.

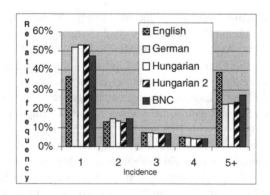

Fig. 5. Frequency of occurrences [20]

Figure 5 "illustrates a very problematic aspect –data scarcity- of corpus based approaches. It is clear, that even for English, which contained only 62.000 different word forms in a 3.5 million corpus, nearly 40% of the 62.000 different units (at least 20.000 words) appeared only once in the corpus. So even if one collects a huge corpus for training a system, in case of a real-life application there is a very great probability that quite a few new items (related to the training corpus) will appear. If the corpus is large enough -such as the BNC for English- a very large ratio of rare items will appear only once. For Hungarian the problem is even harder. In a practically convincing case one should collect either such a big corpus, that all items should fall in the rightmost column (i.e. appearing at least five times in the corpus) or apply rule-based or other (non-word-based) approaches. Often the combination of several techniques may provide the best solutions."

The situation is very similar for Slavic languages, as well.

5   Closed and Open Platforms

It can be seen from the previous sections that no single company has the chance to cover at least the over 1million first-language speaker languages. Not to mention the several domain-specific adaptations, required for successful real-life applications. The only chance would be to use open platforms which allow the inclusion of new languages and domains for all respective application areas and provide quality assurance. Unfortunately currently there is a trend that operating systems manufacturers and systems integrators want to solve everything on their own or with some key partners. This approach prevents innovative academic groups, SME-s and non-profit civil organizations from developing new concepts that could be tested in real-life scenarios.

There is a great need for a really open environment where speech and language technology components can be efficiently integrated into new smart devices and environments. Experimenting with new solutions for disabled people is a critical factor because they may be highly dependent on an innovative engineering solution. For this reason they are ideal test subjects often with outstanding patience and thorough feedback. Current technological and policy limitations hinder advancement in several areas. The trend of the virtualization of services in infocommunication networks may open up new possibilities in this direction.

6   Conclusions

Although there has been enormous progress in speech technology during the last three decades there is still a long way to go. Due to the high dependence of speech communication on cognitive processes there is a very small probability of generic solutions for basic speech technology components in the foreseeable future. It seems to be more promising to create well-tailored engines for practically important applications. In order to be able to port solutions across platforms and languages it is important to define common scenarios (e.g. reading weather, scientific news, celebrity news, user manuals, directory services, subtitling of official vs casual conversations) and communicative contexts (e.g. informal-formal). For example both the health and the vehicle infotainment industries could be a good starting point. In an optimal case that could be implemented in an open testbed that would also provide quality assurance and testing. Due to a basically common cultural background with significant linguistic and social variation Central- and Eastern Europe could be an optimal location for such an experiment. The BME TMIT team is open for co-operation from basic research to practical applications in any speech technology area.

Acknowledgments. The views expressed in the paper are those of the author. The research results mentioned and presented in the paper have been achieved by the co-operation of the Speech Communication and Smart Interactions Laboratory team at BME TMIT. They have been supported among others by the BelAmi, TÁMOP-4.2.1/B-09/1/KMR-2010-0002, CESAR (ICT PSP No 271022, EU_BONUS_12-1-2012-0005), PAELIFE (AAL_08-1-2011-0001), and the EITKIC_12-1-2012-0001 projects with support from the Hungarian Government, the Hungarian National Development Agency, the Hungarian National Research and Innovation Fund and the EIT ICT Labs Budapest Associate Partner Group.

References

1. Voice Synthesis Nearing Growth Explosion, Computerworld (August 31, 1981)
2. Brown, M.: The "Lost" Steve Jobs Speech from 1983; Foreshadowing Wireless Networking, the iPad, and the App Store. In: Talk by Steve Jobs at International Design Conference in 1983, October 2 (2012) (retrieved July 2014)
3. The Global Language Technology Market, LT-Innovate, p. 11 (October 2012)
4. Handley, Z.: Is text-to-speech synthesis ready for use in computer-assisted language learning? Speech Communication 51(10), 906–919 (2009)
5. Németh, G., Zainkó, C., Fekete, L., Olaszy, G., Endrédi, G., Olaszi, P., Kiss, G., Kiss, P.: The design, implementation and operation of a Hungarian e-mail reader. International Journal of Speech Technology 3/4, 216–228 (2000)
6. Németh, G., Zainkó, C., Kiss, G., Olaszy, G., Fekete, L., Tóth, D.: Replacing a Human Agent by an Automatic Reverse Directory Service. In: Magyar, G., Knapp, G., Wojtkowski, W., Wojtkowski, G., Zupancic, J. (szerk.) Advances in Information Systems Development: New Methods and Practice for the Networked Society, pp. 321–328. Springer (2007)
7. Németh, G., Fék, M., Csapó, T.G.: Increasing Prosodic Variability of Text-To-Speech Synthesizers. In: Interspeech 2007, Antwerpen, Belgium, pp. 474–477 (2007)
8. Csapó, T.G., Németh, G.: Modeling irregular voice in statistical parametric speech synthesis with residual codebook based excitation. IEEE Journal on Selected Topics In Signal Processing 8(2), 209–220 (2014)
9. Olaszy, G., Németh, G., Olaszi, P., Kiss, G., Gordos, G.: PROFIVOX - A Hungarian Professional TTS System for Telecommunications Applications. International Journal of Speech Technology 3(3/4), 201–216 (2000)
10. Csala, E., Németh, G., Zainkó, C.: Application of the NAO humanoid robot in the treatment of marrow-transplanted children. In: Péter, B. (ed.) 2012 IEEE 3rd International Conference on Cognitive Infocommunications (CogInfoCom), Kosice, Slovakia, pp. 655–658 (2012)
11. Németh, G., Zainkó, Cs., Bartalis, M., Olaszy, G., Kiss, G.: Human Voice or Prompt Generation? Can They Co-Exist in an Application? In: Interspeech 2009: Speech and Intelligence, Brighton, UK, pp. 620–623 (2009)

12. Klabbers, E.A.M.: High-Quality Speech Output Generation through Advanced Phrase Concatenation. In: COST Telecom Workshop, Rhodes, Greece, pp. 85–88 (September 1997)
13. Nagy, A., Pesti, P., Németh, G., Bőhm, T.: Design issues of a corpus-based speech synthesizer. HÍRADÁSTECHNIKA LX:(6), 6–12 (2005)
14. Németh, G., Kiss, G., Tóth, B.: Cross Platform Solution of Communication and Voice/Graphical User Interface for Mobile Devices in Vehicles. In: Abut, H., Hansen, J.H.L., Takeda, K. (eds.) Advances for In-Vehicle and Mobile Systems: Challenges for International Standards, pp. 237–250. Springer (2005)
15. Tóth, B., Németh, G.: Hidden Markov Model Based Speech Synthesis System in Hungarian. Infocommunications Journal LXIII:(7), 30–34 (2008)
16. Zainkó, C., Tóth, B.P., Bartalis, M., Németh, G., Fegyó, T.: Some Aspects of Synthetic Elderly Voices in Ambient Assisted Living Systems. In: Burileanu, C., Teodorescu, H.-N., Rusu, C. (eds.) Proceedings of the 7th International Conference Speech Technology and Human-Computer Dialogu, Cluj-Napoca, Romania, pp. 185–189. IEEE, New York (2013)
17. Németh, G., Olaszy, G., Csapó, T.G.: Spemoticons: Text-To-Speech based emotional auditory cues"m. In: ICAD 2011, Budapest, Magyarország, pp. 1–7. Paper Keynote 3 (2011)
18. Ethnologue, SIL International (retrieved July 2014)
19. META-NET White Paper series on Europe's Languages in the Digital Age (2013), http://www.meta-net.eu/whitepapers/key-results-and-cross-language-comparison (retrieved July 2014)
20. Németh, G., Zainkó, C.: Multilingual Statistical Text Analysis, Zipf's Law and Hungarian Speech Generation. Acta Linguistica Hungarica 49:(3-4), 385–405 (2002)

Instantaneous Harmonic Analysis: Techniques and Applications to Speech Signal Processing

Alexander Petrovsky and Elias Azarov

Belarusian State University of Informatics and Radioelectronics,
Department of Computer Engineering, Minsk, Belarus
{palex,azarov}@bsuir.by

Abstract. Parametric speech modeling is a key issue in various processing applications such as text to speech synthesis, voice morphing, voice conversion and other. Building an adequate parametric model is a complicated problem considering time-varying nature of speech. This paper gives an overview of tools for instantaneous harmonic analysis and shows how it can be applied to stationary, frequency-modulated and quasiperiodic signals in order to extract and manipulate instantaneous pitch, excitation and spectrum envelope.

Keywords: Speech processing, instantaneous frequency, harmonic model.

1 Introduction

There are many speech processing applications that require parametric representation of the signal. One of the most popular multipurpose approaches for flexible speech processing is hybrid stochastic/deterministic parameterization [1,2]. According to it the signal is decomposed into two parts of different nature: stochastic part (unvoiced speech) can be modeled as a random process with given power spectral density, while deterministic part (voiced speech) is a quasiperiodic signal that can be represented using harmonic modeling. The harmonic model assumes that the signal is a sum of sines with slowly varying parameters.

In this paper we briefly describe some methods for harmonic parameters estimation that can be applied for speech analysis. To be consistent with term 'instantaneous' it is assumed that the signal is a continuous function $s(t)$ that can be represented as a sum of P harmonic components with instantaneous amplitude $A_p(t)$, frequency $\omega_p(t)$ and phase $\varphi_p(t)$ [3]:

$$s(t) = \sum_{p=1}^{P} A_p(t)\cos\varphi_p(t),$$

where $\varphi_p(t) = \int_0^t \omega_p(t)dt + \varphi_p(0)$ and $\omega_p \in [0, \pi]$ (for discrete-time signals π corresponds to the Nyquist frequency). In speech processing it is assumed that frequency trajectories of separate harmonics are close to integer multiples of pitch

A. Ronzhin et al. (Eds.): SPECOM 2014, LNAI 8773, pp. 24–33, 2014.

(or fundamental frequency), i.e. $\omega_p(t) \approx p\omega_1(t)$. Since parameters of the model vary slowly it is possible to assume that each component is narrow-band.

An alternative to instantaneous modeling is frame-based modeling, i.e. when harmonic parameters are assumed to be stationary over whole analysis frame. The simplest way to show the difference between these two approaches is to extend the modeling signal beyond analysis window as shown in figure 1. In frame-based modeling analysis frame is repeated while in the other case the signal is extended according to the parameters corresponding to a specified moment of time.

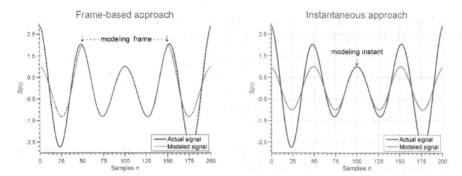

Fig. 1. Signal extension using frame-based and instantaneous modeling

An issue of frame-based approach is aliasing that emerges during synthesis stage. A classical overlap and add method applied in different speech processing systems [4,5] reduces amount of aliasing noise by using concatenation windows. However this effect is not avoided completely because the method cannot ensure that each harmonic is a narrow-band component. Instantaneous harmonic modeling allows filtering and manipulating of each harmonic and therefore can be theoretically more beneficial for voiced speech synthesis.

The present work gives a review of recent approaches to instantaneous harmonic analysis of voiced speech. Despite that we consider input signal as a continues-time function all the analysis techniques presented in the paper can be applied to discrete-time signals as well. We also present some approaches to pitch and spectral envelope extraction based on the harmonic model.

2   Estimation of Instantaneous Harmonic Parameters of Speech

2.1   The Fourier and Hilbert Transform

Most of the analysis techniques require separation of individual harmonics before extraction of instantaneous components. A combination of the Fourier and Hilbert transform can do both separation and extraction. Let us assume that harmonic components do not intersect in frequency domain and therefore can be separated by narrow-band filtering. A good practical approach is to use linear phase filters that can be implemented as a filter bank. Let ω_1 and ω_2 are normalized frequencies from range $[0, \pi]$ that specify bottom and top edges of a pass-band. Then continuous impulse response of the correspondent filter $h(t)$ can be derived as follows:

$$h_{\omega_1,\omega_2}(t) = \frac{1}{\pi} \int_0^{\omega_2} e^{-j\omega t} d\omega - \frac{1}{\pi} \int_0^{\omega_1} e^{-j\omega t} d\omega =$$

$$= \frac{e^{-j\omega t}}{-jt\pi} \Big|_0^{\omega_2} - \frac{e^{-j\omega t}}{-jt\pi} \Big|_0^{\omega_1} = \frac{e^{-j\omega_1 t} - e^{-j\omega_2 t}}{jt\pi}.$$

Substituting ω_1 and ω_2 with center frequency ω_c and wideness of the pass-band $2\omega_\Delta$ i.e. $\omega_1 = \omega_c - \omega_\Delta$ and $\omega_2 = \omega_c + \omega_\Delta$ the equation becomes:

$$h_{\omega_1,\omega_2}(t) = \frac{e^{-j\omega_c t} e^{j\omega_\Delta t} - e^{-j\omega_c t} e^{-j\omega_\Delta t}}{jt\pi} = \frac{e^{-j\omega_c t}(e^{j\omega_\Delta t} - e^{-j\omega_\Delta t})}{jt\pi} =$$

$$2\frac{\sin(\omega_\Delta t)}{t\pi} e^{-j\omega_c t}.$$

If the output of the filter is a one periodic component with time-varying parameters then it can be written in the following way:

$$s_{\omega_1,\omega_2}(t) = s(t) * h_{\omega_1,\omega_2}(t) = A(t)e^{j\varphi(t)},$$

where $A(t)$ is instantaneous amplitude, $\varphi(t)$ – instantaneous phase and $\omega(t)$ – instantaneous frequency. Considering that $s_{\omega_1,\omega_2}(t)$ is a complex analytical signal its parameters can be calculated directly using the following equations:

$$A(t) = \sqrt{R^2(t) + I^2(t)},$$

$$\varphi(t) = \arctan\left(\frac{-I(t)}{R(t)}\right),$$

$$\omega(t) = \varphi'(t),$$

where $R(t)$ and $I(t)$ are real and imaginary parts of $s_{\omega_1,\omega_2}(t)$ respectively.

To get an impulse response with finite length it is possible to use window tion $w(t)$:

$$h_{\omega_1,\omega_2}(t) = 2\frac{\sin(\omega_\Delta t)}{t\pi} w(t)e^{-j\omega_c t}.$$

The method that has been shortly described above applies Hilbert transform to each subband signal. If the filters are uniform (which is generally the case for quasi periodic signals) in real-life applications analysis routine can be implemented very efficiently using fast Fourier transform (FFT). That makes this approach very popular for speech processing applications [6,7].

The accuracy of harmonic separation significantly degrades in case of pitch modulations. The technique requires long analysis window that results in spectral smoothing when frequencies of harmonics change too fast. One of possible solutions to the problem is to use the filter with frequency-modulated impulse response:

$$h_{\omega_1,\omega_2}(t) = 2\frac{\sin(\omega_\Delta(t - t_0))}{(t - t_0)\pi}w(t - t_0)e^{-j\varphi_c(t,t_0)},$$

where $\varphi_c(t,t_0) = \int_{t_0}^{t} \omega_c(t)dt$ and t_0 – the instant of harmonic parameters extraction. In real-life applications required trajectory of center pass-band frequency $\omega_c(t)$ can be estimated from pitch contour. Direct recalculation of impulse response for each estimation instant and each subband is computationally inefficient. Another way to get a similar effect of improving frequency resolution for pitch-modulated signals is to use time-warping. A warping function is applied to the input signal:

$$s_{wrp}(t) = s(\varphi_c^{-1}(t,0)),$$

which adaptively warps time axis of the signal and eliminates pitch modulations [8,9]. Since pitch becomes constant it is possible now to apply an efficient FFT-based analysis scheme that has been described above.

2.2   Energy Separation Algorithm and Prony's Method

Energy Separation Algorithm

The Hilbert transform that has been used in the previous subsection for harmonic parameters extraction is not the only one possible option. Another popular approach is the energy separation algorithm (ESA) [10] which is based on the nonlinear differential Teager-Kaiser Energy Operator (TEO) [11]:

$$\Psi[s(t)] \triangleq \dot{s}^2(t) - s(t)\ddot{s}(t),$$

where $\dot{s}(t) = ds(t)/dt$.

According to ESA two TEO's outputs are separated into amplitude modulation and frequency modulation components. As shown in [12] the third-order energy operator

$$\Upsilon_3[s(t)] \triangleq s(t)s^{(3)}(t) - \dot{s}(t)\ddot{s}(t),$$

where $s^{(3)}(t) = d^3s(t)/dt^3$, can be used for estimating damping factor.

Considering that for a periodical signal with constant amplitude and frequency $s(t) = A\cos(\omega t + \theta)$ the following equations are true:

$$\Psi[s(t)] = A^2\omega^2,$$

$$\Psi[\dot{s}(t)] = A^2\omega^4,$$

instantaneous frequency and absolute value of amplitude can be obtained as follows:

$$\omega(t) = \sqrt{\frac{\Psi[\dot{s}(t)]}{\Psi[s(t)]}},$$

$$|A(t)| = \frac{\Psi[s(t)]}{\sqrt{\Psi[\dot{s}(t)]}}$$

These equations constitute energy separation algorithm for continuous signals.

Prony's Method for Continuous-Time Signals

Despite the fact that Prony's method is originally intended for discrete-time data it is possible to apply it to continuous-time signals as well. Let us consider a continuous signal $s(t)$ which can be represented as a sum of damped complex exponents:

$$s(t) = \sum_{k=1}^{p} h_k z_k^t,$$

where p is the number of exponents, $h_k = A_k e^{j\theta_k}$ is an initial complex amplitude and $z_k = e^{\alpha_k + j\omega_k}$ is a time-dependent damped complex exponent with damping factor α_k and normalized angular frequency ω_k. Then let us introduce a time shift t_0 and obtain n-th order derivatives of $s(t)$ [13]:

$$s^{(n)}(t) = \left(\sum_{k=1}^{p} h_k z_k^{t-t_0} \right)^{(n)} = \sum_{k=1}^{p} h_k (\alpha_k + j\omega_k)^n z_k^{t-t_0} = \sum_{k=1}^{p} l_k(t) y_k^n,$$

where (n) denotes order of derivative, $l_k(t) = h_k z_k^{t-t_0} = A_k e^{\alpha_k(t-t_0)+j(\theta_k+\omega_k(t-t_0))}$, $y_k = (\alpha_k + j\omega_k) = e^{(\ln|y_k|+j\arg(y_k))}$.

According to the equation for any fixed moment of time $t = t_0$ series of derivatives $s, \dot{s}, \ddot{s}, \dots, s^{(n)}$ can be represented as a sum of damped complex exponents with initial complex amplitudes $l_k(t_0) = h_k$, damping factors $\ln|y_k|$ and normalized angular frequencies $\arg(y_k)$. The required parameters of the model h_k and y_k can be found using original Prony's method as it is briefly summarized below.

In order to estimate exact model parameters $2p$ complex samples of the sequence are required. The solution is obtained using the following system of equations:

$$\begin{pmatrix} y_1^0 & y_2^0 & \cdots & y_p^0 \\ y_1^1 & y_2^1 & \cdots & y_p^1 \\ \vdots & \vdots & & \vdots \\ y_1^{p-1} & y_2^{p-1} & \cdots & y_p^{p-1} \end{pmatrix} \begin{pmatrix} h_1 \\ h_2 \\ \vdots \\ h_p \end{pmatrix} = \begin{pmatrix} s \\ \dot{s} \\ \vdots \\ s^{(p-1)} \end{pmatrix}.$$

The required exponents $y_1, y_2, \dots, y_p$ are estimated as roots of the polynomial

$$\psi(z) = \sum_{m=0}^{p} a_m z^{p-m}$$

with complex coefficients a_m which are the solution of the system

$$
\begin{pmatrix}
s^{(p-1)} & s^{(p-2)} & \cdots & s \\
s^{(p)} & s^{(p-1)} & \cdots & \dot{s} \\
\vdots & \vdots & & \vdots \\
s^{(2p-2)} & s^{(2p-3)} & \cdots & s^{(p-1)}
\end{pmatrix}
\begin{pmatrix}
a_1 \\
a_2 \\
\vdots \\
a_p
\end{pmatrix}
= -
\begin{pmatrix}
s^{(p)} \\
s^{(p+1)} \\
\vdots \\
s^{(2p-1)}
\end{pmatrix}
$$

and $a_0 = 1$. Each damping factor α_k and frequency ω_k are calculated using the following equations:

$$
\alpha_k = \mathrm{Re}(y_k), \omega_k = \mathrm{Im}(y_k).
$$

Using the extracted values of $y_1, y_2, \ldots, y_p$ the initial system is solved with respect to $h_1, h_2, \ldots, h_p$. From each of these parameters initial amplitude A_k and phase θ_k are calculated as:

$$
A_k = |h_k|, \theta_k = \arctan\left[\frac{\mathrm{Im}(h_k)}{\mathrm{Re}(h_k)}\right].
$$

For real-valued signals the solution gives pairs of complex conjugate exponents. In order to identify parameters of b real-valued sinusoids we should calculate $4b - 1$ derivatives.

Considering $s(t)$ as a single real-valued damped sinusoid it is possible to identify its parameters using its actual value and three derivatives. Using the equations that have been given above we can formulate the following estimation algorithm.

1) Calculate three derivatives of the signal: $\dot{s}, \ddot{s}, s^{(3)}$;

2) Calculate coefficients of the polynomial:

$$
a_1 = \frac{s s^{(3)} - \dot{s}\ddot{s}}{\dot{s}^2 - s\ddot{s}} = \frac{Y_3[s]}{\Psi[s]},
$$

$$
a_2 = \frac{\ddot{s}^2 - \dot{s}s^{(3)}}{\dot{s}^2 - s\ddot{s}} = \frac{\Psi[\dot{s}]}{\Psi[s]};
$$

3) Calculate roots of the polynomial:

$$
y_{1,2} = \frac{1}{2}\left(-a_1 \pm \sqrt{a_1^2 - 4a_2}\right) = -\frac{Y_3[s]}{2\Psi[s]} \pm \sqrt{\frac{Y_3^2[s]}{4\Psi^2[s]} - \frac{\Psi[\dot{s}]}{\Psi[s]}};
$$

4) Calculate initial complex amplitude:

$$
h = \frac{s y_2 - \dot{s}}{y_2 - y_1} = \frac{1}{2}\left(s + \frac{\frac{Y_3^2[s]}{2\Psi[s]}s + \dot{s}}{\sqrt{\frac{Y_3^2[s]}{4\Psi^2[s]} - \frac{\Psi[\dot{s}]}{\Psi[s]}}}\right);
$$

5) Calculate required parameters of the sinusoid:

$$\alpha = \text{Re}(y_1) = -\frac{Y_3[s]}{2\Psi[s]},$$

$$\omega = \text{Im}(y_1) = \sqrt{\frac{\Psi[\dot{s}]}{\Psi[s]} - \frac{Y_3^2[s]}{4\Psi^2[s]}},$$

$$A = 2|h|, \qquad \theta = \arctan\left[\frac{\text{Im}(h)}{\text{Re}(h)}\right].$$

Note that the resulting equation for damping factor is exactly the same as given in [12] and the equation for frequency can be derived from the case of cosine with exponential amplitude discussed in [10]. The equations show how ESA and Prony's method are connected in the case of one real-valued sinusoid.

3 Estimation of Pitch and Spectral Envelope from Instantaneous Harmonic Parameters

In this section we show how high-level speech characteristics such as pitch and spectral envelope can be estimated from instantaneous harmonic parameters.

3.1 Instantaneous Pitch Estimation

The most popular approach for period candidate generating is autocorrelation-based functions such as normalized cross-correlation function (NCCF). Let $s(m)$ be a discrete-time speech signal, z – step size in samples and n – window size. The NCCF $\phi(x, k)$ of K samples length at lag k and analysis frame x is defined as [14]:

$$\phi(x, k) = \frac{\sum_{i=m}^{m+n-1} s(i)s(i + k)}{\sqrt{e_m e_{m+k}}}, k = 0, K - 1; \ m = xz; \ x = 0, M - 1,$$

where $e_i = \sum_{l=i}^{i+n-1} s^2(l)$. Instantaneous parameters of harmonic model give a spectral representation of the current instant $s(t)$ that can be utilized in order to estimate momentary autocorrelation function $R_{inst}(t, \Delta t)$. Using the Wiener-Khintchine theorem:

$$R_{inst}(t, \Delta t) = \frac{1}{2} \sum_{p=1}^{P} A_p^2(t) \cos(\omega_p(t)\Delta t).$$

$R_{inst}(t, \Delta t)$ corresponds to the autocorrelation function calculated on infinite window of periodic signal generated with specified harmonic parameters. As far as analysis window is infinite there is no difference between autocorrelation and cross-correlation functions. Considering this fact it is possible to propose the instantaneous version of NCCF $\phi_{inst}(t, \Delta t)$ in the following form:

$$\phi_{inst}(t, \Delta t) = \frac{\sum_{p=1}^{P} A_p^2(t) \cos(\omega_p(t) \Delta t)}{\sum_{p=1}^{P} A_p^2(t)}.$$

Unlike original time-domain NCCF lag Δt does not need to be an integer, valid values can be produced for any desired frequency. Function $\phi_{inst}(t, \Delta t)$ is immune to any rapid frequency modulations in the neighborhood of t provided that estimated instantaneous harmonic parameters are accurate enough. This period candidate generating function has been used in instantaneous pitch estimator [15], based on the harmonic model.

3.2   Estimation of Instantaneous Spectral Envelope

Let us use conventional linear-prediction (LP) technique for spectral envelope estimation of continuous-time signal $s(t)$. We assume that harmonic model of the signal is specified by the correspondent set of time-varying parameters. LP model approximates given signal sample $s(n)$ as a linear combination of the p past samples that leads to the following equality:

$$s(n) = \sum_{i=1}^{p} a_i s(n - i) + Gu(n),$$

where $a_1, a_2, ..., a_p$ are prediction coefficients, $u(n)$ is a normalized excitation and G is the gain of the excitation [16]. The prediction error $e(n)$ is defined as the difference between the source and predicted samples:

$$e(n) = s(n) - \tilde{s}(n) = s(n) - \sum_{k=1}^{p} a_k s(n - k).$$

The basic problem of LP is to find the set of predictor coefficients that minimize the mean-square prediction error. Let us consider a harmonic signal with constant amplitudes and constant frequencies of components. The relative residual energy can be evaluated as the following sum:

$$E_a^2 = \sum_{k=1}^{K} A_k(n)^2 \left(\left[1 - \sum_{i=1}^{p} a_i \cos(\omega_k(n)i) \right]^2 + \left[\sum_{i=1}^{p} a_i \sin(\omega_k(n)i) \right]^2 \right).$$

In order to minimize E_a^2 it is possible to use the basic minimization approach by finding partial derivatives with respect to variables a_i and then solving the system of linear equations. Eventually the following system can be derived:

$$\sum_{i=1}^{p} a_i q(|i - j|) = -q(j),$$

where $j = 1, 2, ..., p$ and $q(l) = \sum_{k=1}^{K} A_k(n) \cos(f_k(n)l)$, $(l \geq 0)$.

It is known that LP spectral representation tends to model individual harmonic components instead of the spectral envelope when the order of prediction becomes high. Using derived transformation system it is possible to represent exactly the specified envelope as a high-order filter by using amplitude and frequency vectors of infinite dimension.

The spectral envelope can be considered as a continuous function of frequency $A(\omega)$, specified on the interval $[0, \pi]$. Then the matrix elements $q(l)$ can be derived as the following integral:

$$q(l) = \int_{0}^{\pi} A(\omega)\cos(\omega l)d\omega.$$

If $A(\omega)$ contain discontinues in points $\omega_d = (\omega_1, \omega_2, ..., \omega_l)$, then the equation can be expressed as:

$$q(l) = \sum_{i=1}^{l+1} \int_{\bar{\omega}_{d,i}}^{\bar{\omega}_{d,i+1}} A(\omega)\cos(\omega l)d\omega,$$

where $\bar{\omega}_d = (0, \omega_1, \omega_2, ..., \omega_l, \pi)$.

Continuous spectral envelope can be estimated from amplitude and frequency vectors using linear interpolation. Single segments of the envelope $f_i \leq \omega \leq f_{i+1}$, $1 \leq i \leq K - 1$ are described by linear equations of the form $A(\omega) = b_i \omega + c_i$. Parameters b_i and c_i are estimated from adjacent values of frequency and amplitudes. Finally elements of the required system can be derived in the following way:

$$q(l) = \sum_{i=1}^{K-1} D(l, i),$$

$$\text{where } D(l, i) = \begin{cases} \frac{b}{l^2}[\cos(f_{i+1}l) + f_{i+1}l\sin(f_{i+1}l)] + \frac{c}{l}\sin(f_{i+1}l) - \\ \quad - \frac{b}{l^2}[\cos(f_i l) + f_i l\sin(f_i l)] - \frac{c}{l}\sin(f_i l) & l \neq 0 \\ \frac{1}{2}bf_{i+1}^2 + cf_{i+1} - \frac{1}{2}bf_i^2 - cf_i & l = 0. \end{cases}$$

The presented technique is compared to original LP in [17] where was shown that it provides much more accurate envelope estimation compared to conventional time-domain method such as autocorrelation and covariance.

4   Conclusions

A short review of techniques for instantaneous harmonic analysis has been given in the paper. The techniques can be applied to voiced speech in order to extract time-varying parameters of each harmonic. The extracted parameters can be used for instantaneous pitch and envelope estimation.

References

1. Laroche, J., Stylianou, Y., Moulines, E.: HNS: Speech modification based on a harmonic+noise model. In: Acoustic, Speech, and Signal Processing: Proceedings of IEEE International Conference ICASSP 1993, Minneapolis, USA, pp. 550–553 (April 1993)
2. Levine, S., Smith, J.: A sines+transients+noise audio representation for data compression and time/pitch scale modifications. In: Proceedings of 105th AES Convention on Signal Processing, San Francisco, USA, p. 21 (1998) (preprint no 4781)
3. McAulay, R.J., Quatieri, T.F.: Speech analysis/synthesis based on a sinusoidal representation. IEEE Trans. on Acoust., Speech and Signal Processing ASSP-34, 744–754 (1986)
4. Moulines, E., Charpentier, F.: Pitch synchronous waveform processing techniques for text-to-speech synthesis using diphones. Speech Communication 9(5-6), 453–467 (1990)
5. Kawahara, H., Takahashi, T., Morise, M., Banno, H.: Development of exploratory research tools based on TANDEM-STRAIGHT. In: Proc. of the APSIPA, Japan Sapporo (2009)
6. Flanagan, J.L., Golden, R.M.: Phase vocoder. Bell System Technical Journal 45, 1493–1509 (1966)
7. Abe, T., Honda, M.: Sinusoidal model based on instantaneous frequency attractors. IEEE Trans. on Audio, Speech, and Language Processing 14(4), 1292–1300 (2006)
8. Nilsson, M., Resch, B.: Kim Moo-Young, Kleijn, W.B.: A canonical representation of speech. In: Proc. of the IEEE ICASSP 2007, Honolulu, USA, pp. 849–852 (2007)
9. Azarov, E., Vashkevich, M., Petrovsky, A.: GUSLAR: A framework for automated singing voice correction. In: Proc. of the IEEE ICASSP 2014, Florence, Italy, pp. 7969–7973 (2014)
10. Maragos, P., Kaiser, J.F., Quatieri, T.F.: Energy separation in signal modulations with application to speech analysis. IEEE Trans. Signal Processing 41, 3024–3051 (1993)
11. Kaiser, J.F.: On a simple algorithm to calculate the 'energy' of a signal. In: Proc. of the IEEE ICASSP 1990, Albuquerque, NM, pp. 381–384 (1990)
12. Maragos, P., Potamianos, A., Santhanam, B.: Instantaneous energy operators: applications to speech processing and communications. In: Proc. of the IEEE Workshop on Nonlinear Signal and Image Proc., Thessaloniki, Greece (1995)
13. Azarov, E., Vashkevich, M., Petrovsky, A.: Instantaneous harmonic representation of speech using multicomponent sinusoidal excitation. In: Proc. of the Interspeech 2013, Lyon, France, pp. 1697–1701 (2013)
14. Talkin, D.: A Robust Algorithm for Pitch Tracking (RAPT). In: Kleijn, W.B., Paliwal, K.K. (eds.) Speech Coding & Synthesis. Elsevier (1995) ISBN 0444821694
15. Azarov, E., Vashkevich, M., Petrovsky, A.: Instantaneous pitch estimation based on RAPT framework. In: Proc. of the EUSIPCO, Bucharest, Romania (2012)
16. Rabiner, L., Juang, B.H.: Fundamentals of speech recognition. Prentice Hall, New Jersey (1993)
17. Azarov, E., Petrovsky, A.: Linear prediction of deterministic components in hybrid signal representation. In: Proc. of the IEEE International Symposium on Circuits and Systems(ISCAS), Paris (2010)

A Comparison of Two Prosody Modelling Approaches for Sesotho and Serbian

Lehlohonolo Mohasi[1], Milan Sečujski[2], Robert Mak[2], and Thomas Niesler[1]

[1] Department of Electrical and Electronic Engineering, Stellenbosch University, South Africa
{lmohasi,trn}@sun.ac.za
[2] Faculty of Technical Sciences, University of Novi Sad, Serbia
secujski@uns.ac.rs

Abstract. Accurate prediction of prosodic features is one of the critical tasks within a text-to-speech system, especially for under-resourced languages with complex lexical prosody. For synthesized speech to have a natural-sounding intonational contour, an adequate prosodic model should be employed. This study compares the Fujisaki model and the HMM-based prosodic modeling in the context of text-to-speech synthesis, for two quite distant languages with rich prosodic systems: Sesotho, a tonal language from the Bantu family, and Serbian, a South-Slavic language with pitch accent. The results of our experiments suggest that, for both languages, the Fujisaki model outperforms the HMM-based model in the modelling of the intonation contours of utterances of human speech.

Keywords: Prosody modelling, Fujisaki model, hidden Markov models, text-to-speech synthesis, Sesotho language, Serbian language.

1 Introduction

Accurate prosodic modelling is a crucial factor in order for text-to-speech (TTS) systems to produce intelligible and natural-sounding speech. Prosodic features include the fundamental frequency (F0) contour, duration, pause and amplitude. Tone, on the other hand, is a linguistic property marked by prosodic features such as F0 and intensity. Due to the absence of prosodic marking in the written format, automatic prosody generation for text-to-speech is a challenge for most languages, particularly those with more complex lexical prosody. This holds for both tonal languages such as Sesotho [1], as well as pitch-accent languages such as Serbian [2]. In this paper, we investigate and compare two tools which comprise prosody modelling and automatic prosody generation for text-to-speech systems, and calculate their efficiencies for the two languages mentioned above. In this research we focus on the modelling and prediction of F0, which is perceptually the most important element of sentence prosody.

The first method employs the Fujisaki model [3], which is reliant on the acoustics of the uttered speech. The Fujisaki model is a manageable and powerful model for prosody manipulation. It has shown a remarkable effectiveness in modelling the F0 contours and its validity has been tested for several languages, including tonal

A. Ronzhin et al. (Eds.): SPECOM 2014, LNAI 8773, pp. 34–41, 2014.

languages such as Mandarin [4] and Thai [5]. The second method, widely used within hidden Markov model based speech synthesis (HTS), employs a set of trained statistical models (context-dependent HMMs), which are used to predict prosodic parameters such as durations of particular phonetic segments and values of log F0. Both models rely on a previously recorded speech corpus, used to train the model, i.e. to set the values of its relevant parameters.

Section 2 gives a brief background of Sesotho and Serbian, followed by the description of the two models, the Fujisaki model (Section 3) and HTS (Section 4). Preparation of data for the experiments and the subsequent surface tone transcription are explained in Sections 5 and 6 respectively. Experimental results are illustrated in Section 7 and the conclusions drawn thereof are in Section 8.

2   Background on the Sesotho and Serbian Languages

Sesotho is a Southern Bantu tonal language spoken in Lesotho as a national language and in South Africa as one of the eleven official languages. It has two tone levels: high and low, of which the high tone is the active tone. Sesotho is classified as a grammatical tone language, which means that words may be pronounced with varying tonal patterns depending on their particular function in a sentence. In order to create certain grammatical constructs, tonal rules may modify the underlying tones of the word and thus lead to differing surface tones. The underlying tone, also known as the lexical tone, is the tonal pattern of the word in isolation. The surface tone, on the other hand, is a 'spoken' tone, i.e. the tone given to a word when spoken as part of a sentence. The surface tone can be derived from the underlying tone using tonal rules.

Serbian is the standardized variety of the Serbo-Croatian language, spoken in Serbia as the official language, and in some other countries of the Balkan peninsula as well. Serbo-Croatian is the only Slavic language which uses a pitch accent, assigning it at the level of the lexicon and using it to differentiate between word meanings or values of morphological categories. Traditional grammars define the pitch accent of Serbo-Croatian through four distinct accent types, which involve a rise or fall in pitch associated with either long or short vowels, and with optional post-accent lengths. However, more recent analyses ([6], [7]) have shown that these accent types can be interpreted as tonal sequences, i.e. reduced to sequences of high and low tones, without loss of representativeness, provided that phonemic length contrast is preserved. Thus, words can be thought of as strings of syllables following tonal patterns, and the surface tone of the utterance can be derived from its underlying tone using appropriate tonal rules.

3   The Fujisaki Model

The Fujisaki model, which is formulated in the log F0 domain, analyses the F0 contour of a natural utterance and decomposes it into a set of basic components which, together, lead to the F0 contour that closely resembles the original. The components are: a base frequency, a phrase component, which captures slower changes in the F0 contour as associated with intonation phrases, and a tone component that reflects faster changes in F0 associated with high tones. The tone commands of the Fujisaki analysis are an indicator of tones in the utterance.

The method was first proposed by Fujisaki and his co-workers in the 70s and 80s [8] as an analytical model which describes fundamental frequency variations in human speech. By design, it captures the essential mechanisms involved in speech production that are responsible for prosodic structure. A chief attraction of the Fujisaki model lies in its ability to offer a physiological interpretation that connects F0 movements with the dynamics of the larynx, a viewpoint not inherent in other currently-used intonation models which mainly aim to break down a given F0 contour into a sequence of 'shapes' [9]. The Fujisaki model has been integrated into a German TTS system and proved to produce high naturalness when compared with other approaches [10]. The inverse model, automated by Mixdorff [3], determines the Fujisaki parameters which best model the F0 contour. However, the representation of the F0 contour is not unique. In fact, the F0 contour can be approximated by the output of the model with arbitrary accuracy if an arbitrary number of commands is allowed [11]. Therefore, there is always a trade-off between minimizing the approximation error and obtaining a set of linguistically meaningful commands.

Mixdorff et al. [12] and Mohasi et al. [13] found that for Sesotho, the Fujisaki captures tone commands of positive amplitudes for the high tones. For other tonal languages that have been investigated using this technique, such as Mandarin [4], Thai [5], and Vietnamese [14], low tones are captured by tone commands of negative polarity. In contrast, low tones in Sesotho were found to be associated with the absence of tone commands. It should be noted that, unlike Sesotho, so far there has been no reported research into the modelling of intonation using the Fujisaki model for Serbian.

4   Hidden Markov Model-Based Speech Synthesis (HTS)

HTS has been demonstrated to be very effective in synthesizing speech. The main advantage of this approach is its flexibility in changing speaker identities, emotions, and speaking styles. Statistical parametric speech synthesis using a hidden Markov model (HMM) as its generative model is typically called HMM-based speech synthesis. In this approach, HMMs represent not only the phoneme sequences but also various contexts of the linguistic specification. The models are trained on a speech corpus in order to be able to predict the values of prosodic and spectral parameters of speech for a given text. However, since it is impossible to prepare training data for all conceivable linguistic contexts, a number of tree-based clustering techniques have been proposed in order to allow HMMs to share model parameters among states in each cluster.

The synthesis part of the system converts a given text to be synthesized into a sequence of context-dependent labels. According to the label sequence, a sentence-level HMM is constructed by concatenating context-dependent HMMs. The duration of each state is determined to maximise its probability based on its state duration probability distribution. Then a sequence of speech parameters including spectral and excitation parameters is determined so as to maximise the HMM likelihood. Finally, a speech waveform is resynthesised directly from the generated spectral and excitation parameters by using a speech synthesis filter, for example, a mel-log spectral approximation filter for mel-cepstral coefficients or an all-pole filter for linear-prediction-based spectral parameter coefficients [15].

5   Data Preparation

The data used for the Sesotho corpus is based on a set of weather forecast bulletins obtained from the weather bureau in Lesotho, Lesotho Meteorological Services (LMS). The original data was compiled and broadcast for Lesotho TV. The original audio data was not of high quality, containing considerable background noise, as well as a large variability in speaking rate. The poor signal-to-noise ratio (SNR) in particular made this data unsuitable for eventual use in TTS development. For this reason, the sentences were re-recorded by the first author, who is a female native speaker of Sesotho. The recordings were performed in a quiet studio environment, at a sampling rate of 48 kHz. The corpus contains 40 minutes of speech and utterances are 12 seconds long on average.

The available Serbian speech corpus contains approximately 4 hours of speech, recorded in a sound-proof studio and sampled at 44 kHz. All sentences were uttered by a single female voice talent, a professional radio announcer using the ekavian standard pronunciation. General intonation in the database ranged from neutral to moderately expressive, and the effort was made to keep the speech rate approximately constant. However, in order to avoid a considerable difference in the experiment setup for Serbian and Sesotho, only a portion of the corpus corresponding in size to the entire Sesotho corpus was used for the principal experiment involving the comparison between the Fujisaki model and HMM prosody generation for both languages.

6   Surface Tone Transcription

Various studies show that the pronunciation of Sesotho lexical items can differ from one syntactic context to another. Words in isolation are pronounced differently from words in context in many languages, and therefore, there is a need to perform a surface tone transcription as part of the compilation of the corpus. The requirements for surface tone transcription are a pronunciation dictionary, a set of tonal rules, and a morphological analysis. The pronunciation dictionary for Sesotho is based on two tone-marked dictionaries, that by Du Plessis et al. [16] and Kriel et al. [17]. We used Sesotho tonal rules due to Khoali [18], whose work on Sesotho tone is the most recent. The sentences in the corpus were then annotated with underlying tones from the pronunciation dictionary, from which a surface tone transcription was deduced by means of a morphological analysis as well as tonal rules.

The sequence of tones for the Serbian corpus was determined based on the pitch accent assigned by the system for automatic POS tagging [19], with tagging errors manually corrected. Appropriate tonal rules were used to convert the underlying accent to the surface accent (or, alternatively, to convert the underlying tone to surface tone).

Once the surface tone transcription was complete for both languages, the sentences were annotated at syllable levels using Praat TextGrid editor [20]. F0 values were extracted using Praat at a step of 10ms and inspected for errors. The F0 tracks were subsequently decomposed into their Fujisaki components applying an automatic method originally developed for German [21]. Initial experiments in [13] for Sesotho have shown that the low tones in the critical words of the minimal pairs could be modelled with sufficient accuracy without employing negative tone commands. Serbian, as illustrated in Figure 1, also shows positive tone commands only. As a consequence, only high tones were associated with tone commands. Adopting this rationale, automatically calculated parameters were viewed in the FujiParaEditor [22] and corrected when necessary.

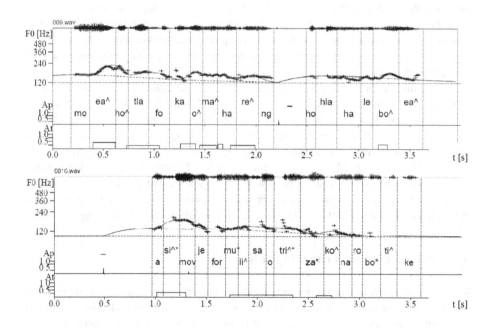

Fig. 1. Sesotho (009.wav) and Serbian (0016.wav) sentences illustrating the Fujisaki-modelled F0 contours (with crosses '+') and their surface tone labels. The high surface tones are indicated by the symbol '^', while stress is indicated by '*' for Serbian. Vertical dotted lines mark syllable boundaries. The Sesotho sentence reads *"Moea ho tla foka o mahareng, ho hlaha leboea."* – "A moderate wind will blow from the north." and that for Serbian reads *"Asimov je formulisao tri zakona robotike."* – "Asimov formulated the three laws of robotics."

7   Experiment Results

Ten utterances from each language were selected for testing by both models. The resulting synthesized data were then compared with original utterances, where root mean square error (RMSE), mean absolute error (MAE), and correlation coefficient (CC) were calculated for duration and pitch. Tables 1, 2, and 3 show the results obtained from these calculations.

Table 1. Comparison between original utterances and those resynthesized by a Fujisaki model

	Duration (ms)		Pitch (Hz)	
	Sesotho	Serbian	Sesotho	Serbian
RMSE	0.00	0.00	9.18	14.41
MAE	0.00	0.00	6.28	8.38
CC	1.00	1.00	0.89	0.63

Table 2. Comparison between original utterances and those synthesized by a HTS system

	Duration (ms)		Pitch (Hz)	
	Sesotho	Serbian	Sesotho	Serbian
RMSE	35.76	22.39	23.41	16.10
MAE	28.14	17.27	18.65	12.28
CC	0.27	0.74	0.03	0.59

Table 3. Comparison between utterances resynthesized by a Fujisaki model and those synthesized by a HTS system

	Duration (ms)		Pitch (Hz)	
	Sesotho	Serbian	Sesotho	Serbian
RMSE	35.76	22.39	23.75	17.54
MAE	28.14	17.27	19.15	14.57
CC	0.27	0.74	-0.04	0.37

In Table 1, both languages show a positive high correlation for both duration and pitch, with Sesotho presenting a closer relationship than Serbian. Duration displays perfect correlation of the value of 1 for the two languages, which suggests that the duration of the utterances was not affected during resynthesis. This is also an indication that the F0 extracted by the Fujisaki model is closely similar to that of original utterances. The RMSE and MAE values do not show any variation for duration, and the variation in pitch is quite small.

In the comparison between the original utterances and those synthesized via a HTS system [23], given in Table 2, the values here demonstrate a substantial difference from those found in Table 1. Correlation for Serbian is significant for both duration and pitch, while that for Sesotho is quite low for both instances, with almost no correlation for pitch. The RMSE and MAE variations have increased for both languages, considerably so for duration. For pitch, the increase in variation is by a small margin for Serbian, while that for Sesotho is almost three times as much.

Table 3 compares the two tools and the scores attained are the same as in Table 2 for duration. For pitch, the increase in variation values is small in comparison to values obtained in Table 2. However, correlation has decreased for both languages, with Sesotho showing a negative correlation.

In general, the Fujisaki model has a more accurate F0 modelling capability than HTS. Although the Fujisaki model performed better for Sesotho, HTS showed a significantly higher performance for Serbian. This is due to the fact that Serbian had more data available for training in HTS, whereas data for Sesotho did not meet the minimum requirements.

8   Conclusion

In this paper we have explored and compared the F0 modelling capabilities of the Fujisaki model and HTS for two distant languages, Sesotho and Serbian. Accurate F0 (prosody) modelling is crucial for a natural-sounding text-to-speech system. The results obtained show the Fujisaki model to be more accurate than HTS. The prosodic-modelling accuracy of the HTS system can be improved by training more data, preferably more than 4 hours of speech. This is our next step, especially for the Sesotho language.

Acknowledgments. The presented study was sponsored in part by the National Research Foundation of the Republic of South Africa (grant UID 71926), by Telkom South Africa, and by the Ministry of Education and Science of the Republic of Serbia (grant TR32035).

References

1. Zerbian, S., Barnard, E.: Word-level prosody in Sotho-Tswana. In: Speech Prosody (2010)
2. Sečujski, M., Obradović, R., Pekar, D., Jovanov, L., Delić, V.: AlfaNum System for Speech Synthesis in Serbian Language. In: 5th Conf. Text, Speech and Dialogue, pp. 8–16 (2002)
3. Mixdorff, H.: A novel approach to the fully automatic extraction of Fujisaki model parameters. In: IEEE Int. Conference on Acoustics, Speech, and Signal Processing, Istanbul, Turkey, pp. 1281–1284 (2000)
4. Mixdorff, H., Fujisaki, H., Chen, G., Hu, Y.: Towards the automatic extraction of Fujisaki model parameters for Mandarin. In: Eurospeech/Interspeech 2003, pp. 873–876 (2003)
5. Mixdorff, H., Luksaneeyanawin, S., Fujisaki, H.: Perception of tone and vowel quantity in Thai. In: ICSLP (2002)
6. Gođevac, S.: Transcribing Serbo-Croatian Intonation. In: S.-A. Jun (ed.) Prosodic Typology: The Phonology of Intonation and Phrasing, pp. 146–171. Oxford Linguistics, UK (2005)

7. Sečujski, M., Jakovljević, N., Pekar, D.: Automatic Prosody Generation for Serbo-Croatian Speech Synthesis Based on Regression Trees. In: Interspeech 2011, pp. 3157–3160 (2011)
8. Fujisaki, H., Hirose, K.: Analysis of voice fundamental frequency contours for declarative sentences of Japanese. Journal of the Acoustics Society of Japan (E) 5(4), 233–241 (1984)
9. Taylor, P.A.: The Rise/Fall/Connection model of intonation. In: Speech Communication, 15, 169–186 (1995)
10. Mixdorff, H., Mehnert, D.: Exploring the Naturalness of Several High-Quality Text-to-Speech Systems. In: Eurospeech 1999, pp. 1859–1862 (1999)
11. Aguero, P.D., Wimmer, K., Bonafonte, A.: Automatic analysis and synthesis of Fujisaki intonation model for TTS. In: Speech Prosody (2004)
12. Mixdorff, H., Mohasi, L., Machobane, M., Niesler, T.: A study on the perception of tone and intonation in Sesotho. In: Interspeech 2011, pp. 3181–3184 (2011)
13. Mohasi, L., Mixdorff, H., Niesler, T.: An acoustic analysis of tone in Sesotho. In: ICPhS XVII, pp. 17–21 (2011)
14. Dung, T.N., Luong, C.M., Vu, B.K., Mixdorff, H., Ngo, H.H.: Fujisaki model-based F0 contours in Vietnamese TTS. In: ICSLP (2004)
15. Masuko, T.: HMM-Based Speech Synthesis and Its Applications. Ph.D. thesis, Tokyo Institute of Technology, Japan (2002)
16. Du Plessis, J.A., et al.: Tweetalige Woordeboek Afrikaans-Suid-Sotho. Via Afrika Bpk, Kaapstad, SA (1974)
17. Kriel, T.J., van Wyk, E.B.: Pukuntsu Woordeboek Noord Sotho-Afrikaans, Van Schaik, Pretoria, SA (1989)
18. Khoali, B.T.: A Sesotho Tonal Grammar. PhD Thesis. University of Illinois, Urbana-Champaign, USA (1991)
19. Sečujski, M., Delić, V.: A Software Tool for Semi-Automatic Part-of-Speech Tagging and Sentence Accentuation in Serbian Language. In: IS-LTC (2006)
20. Boersma, P.: Praat - A system for doing phonetics by computer. Glot International 5(9/10), 341–345 (2001)
21. Mixdorff, H.: Intonation Patterns of German - Model-based Quantitative Analysis and Synthesis of F0 Contours. PhD Thesis. TU Dresden, Germany (1998)
22. Mixdorff, H.: FujiParaEditor (2012), http://public.beuth-hochschule.de/~mixdorff/thesis/fujisaki.html
23. Pakoci, E., Mak, R.: HMM-based Speech Synthesis for the Serbian Language. In: ETRAN, Zlatibor, Serbia (2012)

A Dependency Treebank for Serbian: Initial Experiments

Bojana Jakovljević[1], Aleksandar Kovačević[2], Milan Sečujski[2], and Maja Marković[1]

[1] Faculty of Philosophy, University of Novi Sad, Serbia
bjn.jakovljevic@gmail.com
[2] Faculty of Technical Sciences, University of Novi Sad, Serbia
kocha78@uns.ac.rs

Abstract. The paper presents the development of a dependency treebank for the Serbian language, intended for various applications in the field of natural language processing, primarily natural language understanding within human-machine dialogue. The databank is built by adding syntactical annotation to the part-of-speech (POS) tagged AlfaNum Text Corpus of Serbian. The annotation is carried out in line with the standards set by the Prague Dependency Treebank, which has been adopted as a starting point for the development of treebanks for some other kindred languages in the region. The initial dependency parsing experiments on the currently annotated portion of the corpus containing 1,148 sentences (7,117 words) provided relatively low parsing accuracy, as was expected from a preliminary experiment and a treebank of this size.

Keywords: Dependency parsing, dialogue systems, Serbian language.

1 Introduction

The development of speech and language technologies in the last decades has relied increasingly on machine learning systems trained on large quantities of data. Ever since the first large-scale treebank, the Penn Treebank [1], was developed, treebanks have been applied in a wide array of fields including both the engineering of human-machine communication as well as theoretical linguistics [2]. Although it has been shown that treebanks constructed automatically using appropriate parsers can be of some use in the process of training machine learning systems (e.g. in establishing the frequencies of already known parsing rules), gold-standard treebanks, containing huge quantities of manually annotated sentences, are still necessary. This can be a serious obstacle in the development of natural language processing systems, as the preparation of such treebanks is known to be an extremely time-consuming and costly process. The problem is particularly severe for under-resourced languages, including Serbian.

The beginning of the development of such corpora for Slavic languages is related to the appearance of the Prague Dependency Treebank (PDT) [3]. This treebank has introduced a complex scheme of annotation at morphological, syntactical and tecto-grammatical levels following the Functional Generative Description (FGD) [4], and as such, it has set a standard for the successive development of a number of treebanks

A. Ronzhin et al. (Eds.): SPECOM 2014, LNAI 8773, pp. 42–49, 2014.

for kindred languages. Unlike the Penn Treebank, which annotates phrase structure, PDT and all treebanks subsequently developed following its principles annotate dependency structure, defined through relations between words (heads) and their dependents. The dependency approach has a long tradition in the domain of syntactic structure of classical and Slavic languages [5], and is more suitable for languages with free word order as it does not consider a finite verb phrase constituent as a unit. The examples of dependency treebanks for languages kindred to Serbian most notably include the Slovene Dependency Treebank [6,7] and the Croatian Dependency Treebank [8]. It should be noted that a promising research direction is also towards the development of techniques aimed at transferring treebanks between languages, particularly having in mind the high degree of similarity between most languages of the South Slavic family [9].

The rest of the paper is organized as follows. The second section describes the manual effort towards the development of the Serbian dependency treebank. Experimental setup and initial results are given in Section 3, while Section 4 concludes the paper and gives an outline of the future work.

2   Development of the Serbian Dependency Treebank

Serbian is the standardized variety of the Serbo-Croatian language spoken in Serbia as the official language, and also recognized in some other countries in the region. It is also one of the under-resourced languages of Europe, with a number of specific features that make its computational processing a difficult task [10]. In terms of syntax, it belongs to SVO languages with free distribution of mobile sentence constituents. However, although many different constituent orderings can be considered grammatical, the choice of a particular one is governed by a combination of syntactic, semantic, pragmatic and stylistic factors.

The development of the dependency treebank for Serbian has been based on the following existing language resources for Serbian (Table 1.): the AlfaNum Morphological Dictionary of Serbian and the AlfaNum Text Corpus of Serbian, tagged for part-of-speech (POS), including the values of particular morphological categories, using the AlfaNum POS tagger [11]. The tagger is based on a number of hand-written

Table 1. Language resources for human-machine communication developed for Serbian and used for the development of the Serbian Dependency Treebank

Name	Modality of acquisition, source	Size	Format	Memory
AlfaNum Morph. Dictionary of Serbian	Manual; dictionaries, online texts	100,517 lexemes (3,888,407 inflected forms)	ASCII	106 MB
AlfaNum Text Corpus of Serbian	Manual; online texts	200,027 words	ASCII	13 MB

context rules whose application to a particular string of words is controlled via a beam-search algorithm. The tagger reaches the accuracy of 93,2% on a positional tag set containing 748 different POS tags. The remaining errors have been manually corrected, and the corpus has been extended with orthographical representation of non-orthographic items such as numbers, abbreviations, Roman numerals etc. A section of the corpus containing 1,148 sentences (7,117 words) has been syntactically annotated (by the first author of this publication), following the recommendations for the annotation of PDT at the analytical level [12], having in mind certain differences between Serbian and Czech. Syntactic annotation has been performed using the TrEd treebank editor v2.0 [13], which is also used for the development of PDT.

The process of annotation required a number of adjustments which were necessary in order to make the PDT formalism applicable to Serbian. The remainder of the section provides some instances of adapting the PDT formalism to the Serbian language. In order to focus on specific linguistic phenomena, the sentences used for the purpose of illustration were additionally generated and do not represent examples from the corpus.

2.1   The Treatment of Yes-No Questions and Negation

The formation of yes-no questions in Czech most often involves the use of intonation and negation is directly attached to the main verb. On the other hand, Serbian makes use of the interrogative particles *li* and *da li* in the former case and the negative particle *ne* in the latter. Considering the fact that Serbian grammars do not provide any information on the syntactic status of the interrogative particles, they are assigned the analytical function AuxY (Fig. 1a), the function which is commonly used for all the constituents which do not qualify for a straightforward label [14].The negative particle *ne* is treated in the same way (Fig. 1b). However, in the case of embedded questions, the particles *li* and *da li* behave as conjunctions and are treated as such (Fig. 1c).

2.2   The Treatment of Auxiliary Verbs

According to the PDT, auxiliary verbs are assigned the function AuxV and are directly dependent on the main verb. Serbian exhibits two types of auxiliaries. In contrast to the auxiliary verb *jesam/biti* (Fig. 2a), the auxiliary *hteti* behaves as a modal verb, requiring infinitive/the construction *da+present* as its complement. Due to the fact that the structures consisting of a finite form of a modal verb and infinitive are considered as compound verbal predicates in the PDT, we decided to treat the structures with the auxiliary verb *hteti* in the same way (Fig. 2b).

2.3   The Treatment of Cardinal Numbers

The annotation of the corpus resulted in the division of Serbian cardinal numbers into two categories. Due to the fact that it behaves as an agreeing attribute, number 1 is assigned the analytical function Atr and is dependent on a noun (Fig. 3a).

Numbers above 4 (except for those containing numbers 1-4 as their last element) assign genitive plural both to a noun and its attribute(s), which is the reason for treating them as governors (Fig. 3b). Finally, numbers 2, 3 and 4 require nominal forms which differ

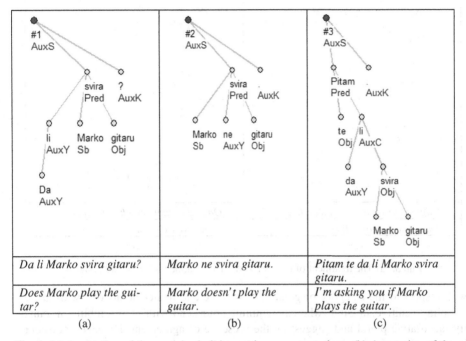

Fig. 1. (a) Annotation of the particle *da li* in matrix yes-no questions, (b) Annotation of the negative particle *ne*, (c) Annotation of the particle *da li* in embedded yes-no questions

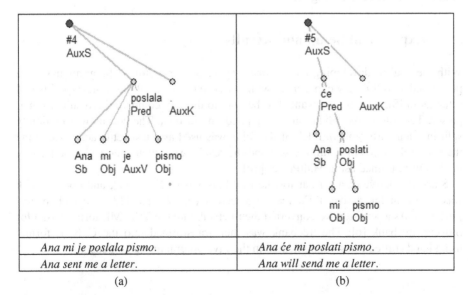

Fig. 2. (a) Annotation of the auxiliary verb *jesam/biti*, (b) Annotation of the auxiliary verb *hteti*

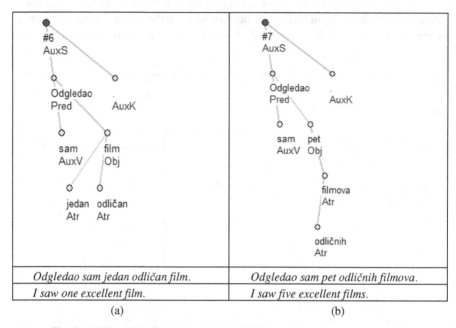

Fig. 3. (a) The treatment of number 1, (b) The treatment of numbers above 4

with respect to the category of gender. Masculine and neuter nouns end with -*a*, resembling genitive singular, whereas feminine nouns end with -*e*, resembling nominative/accusative plural and suggesting the presence of agreement. However, considering that all these nominal forms represent fossilized remnants of the category of dual [15], as well as in order to achieve uniformity, we decided to treat the entire set of numbers as governors (Fig. 4).

3   Experiment Setup and Results

With the goal of developing an automatic syntactic parser for Serbian language, we performed a preliminary experiment with our corpus. We used the same experimental setup as in [8], because we wanted to be able to directly compare the results to their parser. Ten fold cross-validation was applied on our data. The corpus was randomly split into ten parts (folds). Each of the folds was used as a test set exactly once (and the rest of the folds as a training set) and the results were then averaged. The parsing models were trained using MaltParser [16].

Since the native data format for the MaltParser is CoNLL [17], and our treebank was stored in the native TrEd feature structure (FS) format [13], we had to preprocess it. As a first step we converted the treebank into the TEIXML format, used for Slovene treebank [6]. The treebank was then transformed into the CoNLL format using hand crafted rules, implemented in the Java programming language.

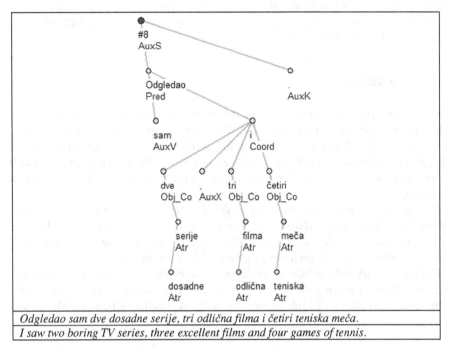

| Odgledao sam dve dosadne serije, tri odlična filma i četiri teniska meča. |
| I saw two boring TV series, three excellent films and four games of tennis. |

Fig. 4. The treatment of numbers 2, 3 and 4

MaltParser offers a variety of parsing algorithms, among which we opted to test three major groups: the Nivre standard and eager algorithms [18], the Covington projective and non-projective algorithms [19] and the Stack eager, lazy and projective algorithms [20,21]. We chose these groups because they fit into the preliminary nature of our experiment (due to their simplicity and low time complexity) and because they include a subset of algorithms used in [8]. The algorithms were applied to the training data with the default settings, without any feature modifications and fine-tuning. Evaluation was done by using MaltEval [16].

Table 2 presents the results obtained in our experiment. The best parsing accuracy was achieved using the Stack Lazy algorithm. In comparison to [8] (the first three

Table 2. The parsing accuracy of ten fold cross-validation, with the metrics provided by MaltEval. The results presented in [8] are given in brackets for comparison.

Metric	Eager	Standard	Stack proj.	Stack lazy
LAS	0.52 (0.71)	0.56 (0.68)	0.56 (0.70)	0.58
LA	0.64 (0.81)	0.66 (0.81)	0.67 (0.82)	0.69
UAS	0.63 (0.84)	0.65 (0.78)	0.64 (0.82)	0.66

columns), our models provided significantly lower scores, which was expected since our treebank is in its preliminary annotation stage and contains half as many sentences (1148) as theirs (2699).

4   Conclusion

The paper presents the current stage of the Serbian Dependency Treebank and the results of an initial experiment related to the development of an automatic syntactic parser for Serbian language. It also discusses the necessary amendments to the principles of syntactic annotations introduced in [12] for the Czech language, which are generally used as a basis for treebank development across the Slavic research community.

The automatic parser experiment was realized as ten fold cross-validation. Various algorithms included in the Malt-Parser system were tested. The obtained results were expectedly inferior to the results of similar research [8], because of the relatively small treebank size and the preliminary nature of the experiments.

The future work will include a significant enlargement of the treebank and extensive research on improving the accuracy of automatic dependency parsers, particularly by taking advantage of high degrees of syntactic similarity between Slavic languages in general.

Acknowledgments. The presented study was financed by the Ministry of Education and Science of the Republic of Serbia under the Research grants TR32035 and III 47003. The authors particularly acknowledge the contributions of Tanja Milićev and Nataša Milićević from the Department of English Language and Literature, Faculty of Philosophy, University of Novi Sad, whose advice and stimulating discussions throughout the process of annotation were immensely helpful.

References

1. Marcus, M., Santorini, B., Marcinkiewicz, M.A.: Building a Large Annotated Corpus of English: The Penn Treebank. Computational Linguistics 19(2), 313–330 (1993)
2. Han, A.L.-F., Wong, D.F., Chao, L.S., He, L., Li, S., Zhu, L.: Phrase Tagset Mapping for French and English Treebanks and Its Application in Machine Translation Evaluation. In: Gurevych, I., Biemann, C., Zesch, T. (eds.) GSCL. LNCS (LNAI), vol. 8105, pp. 119–131. Springer, Heidelberg (2013)
3. Hajič, J., Böhmová, A., Hajičová, E., Hladká, B.V.: The Prague Dependency Treebank: A Three-Level Annotation Scenario. In: Abeillé, A. (ed.) Treebanks: Building and Using Parsed Corpora, pp. 103–127. Kluwer, Amsterdam (2000)
4. Sgall, P., Hajičová, E., Panevová, J.: The Meaning of the Sentence in Its Semantic and Pragmatic Aspects. D. Reidel Publishing Company, Dordrecht (1986)
5. Nivre, J.: Inductive Dependency Parsing. Text, Speech and Language Technology, vol. 34, p. 46. Springer (2006)

6. Ledinek, N., Žele, A.: Building of the Slovene Dependency Treebank Corpus According to the Prague Dependency Treebank Corpus. In: Grammar and Corpus, Prague, Czech Republic (2005)
7. Džeroski, S., Erjavec, T., Ledinek, N., Pajas, P., Žabokrtský, Z., Žele, A.: Towards a Slovene Dependency Treebank. In: LREC, Genova, Italy (2006)
8. Berović, D., Agić, Ž., Tadić, M.: Croatian Dependency Treebank: Recent Development and Initial Experiments. In: LREC, Istanbul, Turkey, pp. 1902–1906 (2012)
9. Agić, Ž., Merkler, D., Berović, D.: Slovene-Croatian Treebank Transfer Using Bilingual Lexicon Improves Croatian Dependency Parsing, In: 15th Int. Multiconf. Information Society 2012, Ljubljana, Slovenia (2012)
10. Vitas, D., Popović, L., Krstev, C., Obradović, I., Pavlović-Lažetić, G., Stanojević, M.: The Serbian Language in the Digital Age. In: Rehm, G., Uszkoreit, H. (eds.) METANET White Paper Series. Springer (2012)
11. Sečujski, M.: Automatic part-of-speech tagging of texts in the Serbian language. PhD thesis, Faculty of Technical Sciences, Novi Sad, Serbia (2009)
12. Hajič, J., Panevová, J., Buráňová, E., Urešová, Z., Bémová, A.: Annotations at Analytical Level: Instructions for Annotators. Technical report. UFAL MFF UK, Prague (1999)
13. http://ufal.mff.cuni.cz/tred/
14. Rosa, R., Mašek, J., Mareček, D., Popel, M., Zeman, D., Žabokrtský, Z.: HamleDT 2.0: Thirty Dependency Treebanks Stanfordized. In: LREC, Reykjavik, Iceland (2014)
15. Stevanović, M.: Savremeni srpskohrvatski jezik – gramatički sistemi i književnojezička norma II. Narodna knjiga, Belgrade (1991)
16. Nilsson, J., Nivre, J.: MaltEval: An Evaluation and Visualization Tool for Dependency Parsing. In: LREC, Marrakech, Morocco, pp. 161–166 (2008)
17. http://ifarm.nl/signll/conll/
18. Nivre, J.: An Efficient Algorithm for Projective Dependency Parsing. In: The 8th International Workshop on Parsing Technologies (IWPT 2003), Nancy, France, pp. 149–160 (2003)
19. Covington, M.A.: A fundamental algorithm for dependency parsing. In: The 39th Annual ACM Southeast Conference, Athens, USA, pp. 95–102 (2001)
20. Nivre, J.: Non-Projective Dependency Parsing in Expected Linear Time. In: The Joint Conference of the 47th Annual Meeting of the ACL and the 4th International Joint Conference on Natural Language Processing of the AFNLP, Singapore, pp. 351–359 (2009)
21. Nivre, J., Kuhlmann, M., Hall, J.: An Improved Oracle for Dependency Parsing with Online Reordering. In: The 11th International Conference on Parsing Technologies (IWPT 2009), Paris, France, pp. 73–76 (2009)

A Framework for Recording Audio-Visual Speech Corpora with a Microphone and a High-Speed Camera

Alexey Karpov[1,2], Irina Kipyatkova[1], and Miloš Železný[3]

[1] St. Petersburg Institute for Informatics and Automation of RAS, St. Petersburg, Russia
[2] ITMO University, St. Petersburg, Russia
[3] University of West Bohemia, Pilsen, Czech Republic
{karpov,kipyatkova}@iias.spb.su, zelezny@kky.zcu.cz

Abstract. In this paper, we present a novel software framework for recording audio-visual speech corpora with a high-speed video camera (JAI Pulnix RMC-6740) and a dynamic microphone (Oktava MK-012) Architecture of the developed software framework for recording audio-visual Russian speech corpus is described. It provides synchronization and fusion of audio and video data captured by the independent sensors. The software automatically detects voice activity in audio signal and stores only speech fragments discarding non-informative signals. It takes into account and processes natural asynchrony of audio-visual speech modalities as well.

Keywords: Audio-visual speech recognition, multimodal system, automatic speech recognition, computer vision, high-speed video camera.

1   Introduction

At present, there are state-of-the-art studies in audio-visual speech recognition (AVSR) for a lot of languages of the world including English, French, German, Japanese, Chinese, etc. Development of automatic Russian speech recognition technologies based on audio information obtained from a microphone (or a smartphone) is carried out in some International industrial companies such as Google Inc. (Google Voice Search), Nuance (Dragon Naturally Speaking), IBM, in some Russian companies including Speech Technology Center, Stel, Auditech, IstraSoft, Poisk-IT, Cognitive Technologies, Art Brain, SpeechDrive, Kvant, Speech Communication Systems, Speereo, Sistema-Sarov, as well as in several institutes of the Russian Academy of Sciences (SPII RAS, IPU RAS), and leading Universities (SPbSU, MSU, MSLU, ITMO Universities in Russia, Karlsruhe Institute of Technology and University of Ulm in Germany, LIMSI-CNRS in France, University of Aizu in Japan, Binghamton University in USA, etc.), and some other organizations [1-4]. There exists a consortium "Russian Speech Technology" (http://speechtech.ru) that connects main developers of Russian speech recognition systems, but in last years it has been inactive because of some organizational problems.

At that it is well known that audio and visual signals of speech supplement each other very well and their joint multimodal processing can improve both accuracy and

A. Ronzhin et al. (Eds.): SPECOM 2014, LNAI 8773, pp. 50–57, 2014.

robustness of automatic speech recognition (ASR) [5-6]. There are a few of studies of visual-based speech recognition (automatic lip-reading) for Russian in Moscow State University [7], Linguistic University of Nizhny Novgorod [8], in the Higher School of Economics [9], as well as in the Institute of Cybernetics in Ukraine [10]. But at present only in SPIIRAS there are ongoing systematic studies on fusion of audio and video speech modalities for the task of Russian speech recognition [11-14]. We should notice also that recently "RealSpeaker Lab." company (resident of Skolkovo, http://www.realspeaker.net) was also founded. Software called RealSpeaker for video processing was integrated with Google Voice Search ASR and now it supports several languages of the world including Russian. However, there are no scientific papers or technical documentation (besides of advertising materials) with the description of the system that allows us to doubt that any real fusion of audio and video information in the speech recognizer is made. In this system, the free available Internet service Google Voice Search is applied for automatic speech recognition (ASR) and video processing is carried out by a software (based on the free OpenCV library) as a distraction without real integration with audio recognition results and without improving the speech recognition performance.

Stochastic modeling of acoustic and visual speech units is very important for statistical-based methods of ASR. For this purpose, speech databases (corpora) recorded in the conditions approached to the real field conditions as much as possible are needed. For training of the unimodal Russian speech recognition systems a number of speech corpora (in particular, RuSpeech, SPEECHDAT, ISABASE, SPEECON and even database of children speech InfantRU/ChildRU [1]) are already created and commercially available. Recently, a corpus of audio-visual Russian speech (RusAVSpeech-Corpus - Multimedia corpus of audio-visual Russian speech; it was registered in Rospatent in 2011 with № 2011620085) was recorded using a standard video camera (25 frames per second - fps). There is also a multimedia Russian speech corpus called MURCO [15], which is a part of the Russian National Corpus (www.ruscorpora.ru), but it is aimed for studies of emotional and gestural cues in conversational speech and does not contain phonemic and visemic levels of segmentation required for speech recognizer training.

It is important also that recently there were a few of papers reporting on results of automatic lip reading with application of a high-speed video camera [16, 17]. The given researches are focused only on the analysis of visual speech (lip articulations) without audio signal processing. These papers report also on improvement of visual speech recognition accuracy with fps rate higher than 30Hz. There is also a multimodal corpus of Dutch speech recorded by AVT Pike F032C camera with fps above 100Hz [18].

In the end of 2012, an idea was proposed to apply high-speed video cameras along with microphones for the task of audio-visual speech recognition [19]. High frequency of video frames is crucial for analysis of dynamical images, since visible articulation organs (lips, teeth, tip of tongue) change their configuration quite fast at speech production and duration of some phonemes (e.g. explosive consonants) is within 10-20ms (duration of each video at 25 fps frame is 40 ms that is too long). So recordings made by a standard camera with 25-30 fps cannot catch fast dynamics of lips movements and most of the important information is missing in these signals.

In the given paper, we present a novel software framework for recording audio-visual speech corpora with the use of JAI high-speed camera with 200 fps and a dynamic microphone.

2   Framework for Recording Audio-Visual Speech Corpora

The new software framework has been developed in order to capture and record audio-visual speech. One Oktava MK-012 microphone and one JAI Pulnix RMC-6740GE high-speed camera are used. JAI RMC-6740GE is a high-speed progressive scan CCD (charge-coupled) camera. The frame rate for a full resolution image (640x480 pixels) is 200 fps. While recording speaker's face, the camera is rotated by 90 degrees in order to have 480 pixels in horizontal and 640 pixels in vertical that better fits for human face proportions, recorded images are rotated later by the software. This camera transmits all captured raw video data via the Gigabit Ethernet interface. The main problem connected with it consists in data traffic, we use 24-bit color images with the resolution of 640x480 pixels (one uncompressed image takes 0.92MB) in 200 fps mode, and a state-of-the-art PC is not able to save these video data in the real-time mode to HDD and it skips some frames. Nevertheless, it can save whole video data without loss to RAM memory, which has limits on a regular PC and can store only 1-2 min of video data (1 min of video in such a format takes about 11 Gb RAM). It is why we have developed own software to solve this problem.

Architecture of the software framework is presented in Figure 1. The key module is an audio-based voice activity detector (VAD). Audio capturing thread gets signal from the microphone by frames (5ms long) and stores them in a memory buffer, then it checks whether it is speech or not calculating segment energy and applying logical-temporal processing (human being's speech must be longer than 20 consecutive segments and pauses for explosive consonants within a speech fragment must be shorter than 10 segments). If the VAD detects a speech signal it then sends a command to make a time stamp of speech beginning for further audio-visual signal saving.

At the same time and in parallel to this process, video frames captured from the camera are stored in a circular buffer (it is allocated in advance to store 20 sec of last continuous video data) so in any moment it has last 20 sec of visual speech. When the VAD detect end of speech-like signal (i.e. number of pause segments is quite high) then it gives a command to calculate a time stamp of speech ending. It must be noted that continuous speech phrase has to be shorter than 20 sec in other case circular buffer does not contain speech beginning. Then raw video and audio data, which are stored in the corresponding memory buffers, are flushed to the hard disk drive and saved in files. It takes time a bit more than real-time (duration of audio-visual speech). When the software flushes the data then speaker should be mute. On completion saving video and audio data, the speaker can continue the recording session and a next text phrase to read is presented to him/her on the monitor screen, which is located just below the video camera. Here the recording cycle starts from the beginning again and the VAD module waits for a speech signal. When the current speaker has pronounced all prepared phrases, the software stops audio and video capturing threads and keeps working in the off-line mode processing audio and video data stored in the files of the database.

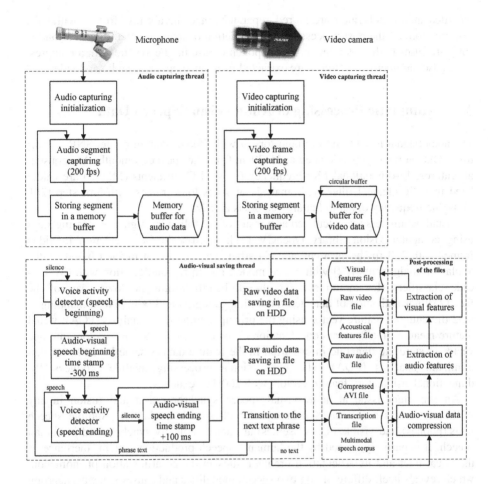

Fig. 1. Architecture of the software framework for recording audio-visual speech corpora

In our audio-visual speech corpus, each speaker has to read and pronounce 100 continuous phrases including 50 phonetically rich and meaningful phrases of the Russian State Standard No. 16600-72 "Speech transmission in radiotelephone communication channels. Requirements for speech intelligibility and articulation evaluation" consisting of 4-8 words plus 50 strings of connected digits (sequences of phone numbers) consisting of 3-7 digits. The former part of the corpus is needed for AVSR system training and the latter one is intended for its adjustment and recognition performance evaluation. An example of recorded audio-visual speech data is provided (http://www.spiiras.nw.ru/speech/JAIavi.zip).

All the recording sessions are made in a quiet office room at daylight, at that all the luminescent lamps must be turned off because they can make artifacts in visual data. Every recording session lasts 30-35 min in average that allows us to get 8-10 min of speech data from each speaker excluding pauses, which are discarded by the VAD module and time for raw data flushing to files and signal post-processing. At first the recorded audio and video are stored separately in camera's raw format without a compression. At the post-processing on completion of the main recording session the software fuses both files related to one spoken phrase in one avi file with a compression. Also parametrical features are extracted from uncompressed audio and video.

3   Automatic Processing of Audio-Visual Speech Data

The audio signal is captured in mono format with 48kHz sampling rate, SNR ≈ 30dB using Oktava microphone located at 15-20cm from the speaker's mouth. As acoustical features, 12-dimentional Mel-Frequency Cepstral Coefficients (MFCC) are calculated from 26 channel filter bank analysis of 20ms long frames with 5ms step [20]. Thus, the frequency of audio feature vectors is 200Hz.

Visual parameters are calculated as a result of the following signal processing steps using computer vision library OpenCV [21]: multi-scale face detection in video frames with 200 fps using a cascade classifier with AdaBoost method based on the Viola-Jones algorithm [22] with a face model; mouth region detection with two cascade classifiers (for mouth and mouth-with-beard) within the lower part of the face [23]; normalization of detected mouth image region to 32×32 pixels; mapping to a 32-dimentional feature vector using the principal component analysis (PCA); visual feature mean normalization; concatenation of the consecutive feature vectors into one vector to store the dynamic information in the feature data; viseme-based linear discriminant analysis (LDA). The video signal processing module produces 10-dimensional articulatory feature vectors with 200Hz frequency.

An important issue at audio-visual speech synchronization and fusion in any AVSR system is a natural asynchrony of both speech modalities. Audible speech units (phones) and visible ones (visemes) are not completely synchronized in human speech. It is partially caused by the human's speech production system. Inertance of the vocal tract and its articulation organs results in the co-articulation phenomenon, which reveals itself differently on two speech modalities and causes some asynchrony between them. Recent corpus-based studies reported [14, 24], that that visemes always lead in phone-viseme pairs as well as, at a beginning of a phrase visual speech units usually lead more noticeably (up to 150-200 ms for stressed rounded vowels) over the corresponding phonemes than in the central or ending part of the phrase.

Some studies also showed [25, 26], that degree of asynchrony of phoneme and viseme stream in the speech formation process is different for different languages and nations. For example, for Japanese lip movements and sound stream of speech are almost synchronous, therefore early method of audio-visual speech fusion shows the best results. In English (especially American English) there is rich lip articulation (even hyper-articulation) that often causes temporal disagreement between streams of the formed phonemes and visemes.

In order to take into account this phenomenon for recording audio-visual speech corpus, the software makes a time stamp of speech beginning 300 ms before the first speech segment detected by the VAD, so audio-visual speech fragment longer in 300 ms is taken in order to catch beginning of lips movements involved in audible speech production. The same audio-visual speech capturing/recording software framework can be also used for VAD and signal capturing in the on-line speech recognition mode with direct use of microphone and camera.

In order to automatically generate initial phoneme and viseme segmentations of the data, we apply hidden Markov models (HTK toolkit) with forced alignment method based on the Viterbi algorithm [20]. This method uses canonic text transcriptions of the spoken phrases made by an expert and feature vectors calculated by the system. As a result of the forced alignment, audio-visual speech signals are matched with corresponding transcriptions and optimal signal segmentations with time stamps for the audio and visual speech units are produced. After that automatically made segmentations have to be checked and corrected by an expert.

At present, we are in the process of recording our audio-visual Russian speech corpus and we have already collected of speech data from several Russian speakers having normal voice and articulation, both men and women. Multimodal data (video, audio, texts) of each speaker takes about 50–80GB, 99.8% of which are video data. After this stage we will develop an AVSR system for Russian, which can apply both the microphone and the high-speed video camera. General architecture of the AVSR system is presented in Figure 2. It will use state asynchronous Coupled Hidden Markov Models (CHMM) for stochastic modeling audio and video signals of speech [13]. Later this system will be a part of a universal assistive information technology [27].

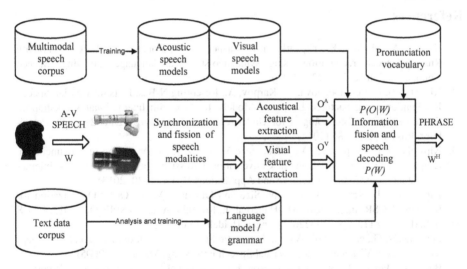

Fig. 2. General architecture of the audio-visual Russian speech recognition system (AVRSRS)

4   Conclusion and Future Work

In the paper, we have described the software framework for audio-visual speech signal recording and processing. This software helps at recording audio-visual speech corpora and uses JAI Pulnix RMC-6740 high-speed video camera (it allows capture video frames with 200 fps) and Oktava MK-012 microphone. The software framework provides synchronization and fusion of audio and video data captured by the independent microphone and video camera, it automatically detects voice activity in audio signal and stores only speech fragments discarding non-informative signals, as well as it takes into account and processes natural asynchrony of audio-visual speech modalities as well. Our software can be also used for voice activity detection and signal capturing in the on-line mode of AVSR with direct use of the audio-visual sensors. At present, we are in the process of recording our audio-visual Russian speech corpus and we have already collected of speech data from several Russian speakers. Multimodal data (video, audio, texts) of each speaker takes about 50–80GB, 99.8% of which are video data. After this stage we will develop an AVSR system for Russian that can apply both the microphone and the high-speed camera and will use state asynchronous CHMM for modeling audio and video signals.

Acknowledgments. This research is partially supported by the Russian Foundation for Basic Research (Project № 12-08-01265-a), by the Government of Russian Federation (Grant 074-U01), as well as by the European Regional Development Fund (ERDF), project "New Technologies for Information Society" (NTIS), European Centre of Excellence, ED1.1.00/02.0090.

References

1. Karpov, A., Markov, K., Kipyatkova, I., Vazhenina, D., Ronzhin, A.: Large vocabulary Russian speech recognition using syntactico-statistical language modeling. Speech Communication 56, 213–228 (2014)
2. Kipyatkova, I., Verkhodanova, V., Karpov, A.: Rescoring N-Best Lists for Russian Speech Recognition using Factored Language Models. In: Proc. 4th International Workshop on Spoken Language Technologies for Under-resourced Languages SLTU-2014, St. Petersburg, Russia, pp. 81–86 (2014)
3. Kipyatkova, I., Karpov, A., Verkhodanova, V., Zelezny, M.: Modeling of Pronunciation, Language and Nonverbal Units at Conversational Russian Speech Recognition. International Journal of Computer Science and Applications 10(1), 11–30 (2013)
4. Kipyatkova, I., Karpov, A.: Lexicon Size and Language Model Order Optimization for Russian LVCSR. In: Železný, M., Habernal, I., Ronzhin, A. (eds.) SPECOM 2013. LNCS (LNAI), vol. 8113, pp. 219–226. Springer, Heidelberg (2013)
5. Potamianos, G., et al.: Audio-Visual Automatic Speech Recognition: An Overview. Chapter in Issues in Visual and Audio-Visual Speech Processing. MIT Press (2005)
6. Bailly, G., Perrier, P., Vatikiotis-Bateson, E.: Audiovisual Speech Processing. Cambridge University Press (2012)
7. Soldatov, S.: Lip reading: Preparing feature vectors. In: Proc. International Conference Graphicon 2003, Moscow, Russia, pp. 254–256 (2003)
8. Gubochkin, I.: A system for tracking lip contour of a speaker. In: Modern Science: Actual problems of theory and practice. Natural and Technical Sciences, No. 4-5, pp. 20–26 (2012) (in Rus.)
9. Savchenko, A., Khokhlova, Y.: About neural-network algorithms application in viseme classification problem with face video in audiovisual speech recognition systems. Optical Memory and Neural Networks (Information Optics) 23(1), 34–42 (2014)

10. Krak, Y., Barmak, A., Ternov, A.: Information technology for automatic lip reading of Ukrainian speech. Computational Mathmatics. Kyiv 1, 86–95 (2009) (in Rus.)
11. Železný, M., Císar, P., Krnoul, Z., Ronzhin, A., Li, I., Karpov, A.: Design of Russian audio-visual speech corpus for bimodal speech recognition. In: Proc. 10th International Conference on Speech and Computer SPECOM 2005, Patras, Greece, pp. 397–400 (2005)
12. Cisar, P., Zelinka, J., Zelezny, M., Karpov, A., Ronzhin, A.: Audio-visual speech recognition for Slavonic languages (Czech and Russian). In: Proc. International Conference SPECOM 2006, St. Petersburg, Russia, pp. 493–498 (2006)
13. Karpov, A., Ronzhin, A., Markov, K., Zelezny, M.: Viseme-dependent weight optimization for CHMM-based audio-visual speech recognition. In: Proc. Interspeech 2010 International Conference, Makuhari, Japan, pp. 2678–2681 (2010)
14. Karpov, A., Ronzhin, A., Kipyatkova, I., Zelezny, M.: Influence of phone-viseme temporal correlations on audio-visual STT and TTS performance. In: Proc. 17th International Congress of Phonetic Sciences ICPhS 2011, Hong Kong, China, pp. 1030–1033 (2011)
15. Grishina, E.: Multimodal Russian corpus (MURCO): First steps. In: Proc. 7th Int. Conf. on Language Resources and Evaluation LREC 2010, Valetta, Malta, pp. 2953–2960 (2010)
16. Chitu, A.G., Rothkrantz, L.J.M.: The influence of video sampling rate on lipreading performance. In: Proc. SPECOM 2007, Moscow, Russia, pp. 678–684 (2007)
17. Chitu, A.G., Driel, K., Rothkrantz, L.J.M.: Automatic lip reading in the Dutch language using active appearance models on high speed recordings. In: Sojka, P., Horák, A., Kopeček, I., Pala, K. (eds.) TSD 2010. LNCS (LNAI), vol. 6231, pp. 259–266. Springer, Heidelberg (2010)
18. Chitu, A.G., Rothkrantz, L.J.M.: Dutch multimodal corpus for speech recognition. In: Proc. LREC 2008 Workshop on Multimodal Corpora, Marrakech, Morocco, pp. 56–59 (2008)
19. Karpov, A., Ronzhin, A., Kipyatkova, I.: Designing a Multimodal Corpus of Audio-Visual Speech using a High-Speed Camera. In: Proc. 11th IEEE International Conference on Signal Processing ICSP 2012, pp. 519–522. IEEE Press, Beijing (2012)
20. Young, S., et al.: The HTK Book, Version 3.4. Cambridge Univ. Press (2009)
21. Liang, L., Liu, X., Zhao, Y., Pi, X., Nefian, A.: Speaker independent audio-visual continuous speech recognition. In: Proc. Int. Conf. on Multimedia & Expo ICME 2002, Lausanne, Switzerland, pp. 25–28 (2002)
22. Viola, P., Jones, M.: Rapid object detection using a boosted cascade of simple features. In: Proc. IEEE Int. Conf. on Computer Vision and Pattern Recognition CVPR 2001, USA, pp. 511–518 (2001)
23. Castrillyn, M., Deniz, O., Hernndez, D., Lorenzo, J.: A comparison of face and facial feature detectors based on the Viola-Jones general object detection framework. Machine Vision and Applications 22(3), 481–494 (2011)
24. Feldhoffer, G., Bardi, T., Takacs, G., Tihanyi, A.: Temporal asymmetry in relations of acoustic and visual features of speech. In: Proc 15th European Signal Processing Conference EUSIPCO 2007, Poznan, Poland, pp. 2341–2345 (2007)
25. Sekiyama, K.: Differences in auditory-visual speech perception between Japanese and America: McGurk effect as a function of incompatibility. Journal of the Acoustical Society of Japan 15, 143–158 (1994)
26. Chen, Y., Hazan, V.: Language effects on the degree of visual influence in audiovisual speech perception. In: Proc. 16th International Congress of Phonetic Sciences ICPhS 2007, Saarbrücken, Germany, pp. 2177–2180 (2007)
27. Karpov, A., Ronzhin, A.: A Universal Assistive Technology with Multimodal Input and Multimedia Output Interfaces. In: Stephanidis, C., Antona, M. (eds.) UAHCI 2014, Part I. LNCS, vol. 8513, pp. 369–378. Springer, Heidelberg (2014)

A Neural Network Keyword Search System
for Telephone Speech

Kevin Kilgour and Alex Waibel

Karlsruhe Institute of Technology, IAR, Interactive Systems Lab
Adenauerring 2, 76131 Karlsruhe
http://www.kit.edu
kevin.kilgour, alex.waibel@kit.edu

Abstract. In this paper we propose a pure *"neural network"* (NN) based keyword search system developed in the IARPA Babel program for conversational telephone speech. Using a common keyword search evaluation metric, *"actual term weighted value"* (ATWV), we demonstrate that our NN-keyword search system can achieve a performance similar to a comparible but more complex and slower *"hybrid deep neural network - hidden markov model"* (DNN-HMM Hybrid) based speech recognition system without using either an HMM decoder or a language model.

Keywords: ATWV, Deep Neural Networks, Keyword Search

1 Introduction

Keyword search is a spoken language processing task in which the goal is to find all occurrences of a keyword (one or more written words) in a large audio corpus. It is sometimes also referred to as spoken term detection. In this paper we'll focus on two phase keyword search systems, where in the first phase the audio corpus in processed and indexed without any knowledge of the keywords. After the keyword list becomes known this index is queried and a prediction list is rapidly returned without re-processing the audio data.

All modern high performing keyword search systems are based on speech recognition systems [10,2,7] or on a combination of multiple speech recognition systems [9]. This requires not only an acoustic model and a language model but also that the audio has to be processed by a speech recognition decoder, which can be quite time consuming. While some work has been performed on isolated keyword detection [12] without the use of a speech recognition system, their setups generally require knowledge of the keywords before training the system.

We propose an alternative system that only uses a neural network of a complexity similar to an acoustic model and directly produces a indexable set of keyword predictions with confidences from the audio corpus. In section 2 of this paper we formally describe the keyword search task and describe how the performance of a keyword search system can be measured. After explaining the baseline speech recognition based keyword search system in section 3, we present our neural network keyword search system in section 4 and show how its output can be easily converted into an indexable format.

A. Ronzhin et al. (Eds.): SPECOM 2014, LNAI 8773, pp. 58–65, 2014.

Table 1. Overview of the provided data for the 80h Vietnamese full LP and the 10h Lao limited LP

Language Code	Name	Version	language pack	dictionary size	transcribed text
107	Vietnamese	IARPA-babel107b-v0.7	full LP	6857	∼120.000
203	Lao	IARPA-babel203b-v3.1	limited LP	4215	∼98000

The evaluation of both keyword search systems is presented and discussed in section 5 while section 6 contains a short summary and conclusion.

2 Keyword Search

In this section we'll present an overview of the keyword search task with particular focus on the IARPA Babel program, which aims to design keyword search systems *that can be rapidly applied to any human language in order to provide effective search capability for analysts to efficiently process massive amounts of real-world recorded speech* [8].

2.1 Data Overview

In order to evaluate the rapid application to new languages the Babel program concentrates on under-resourced languages like Tagalog, Vietnamese or Lao. Keyword search systems can only be trained on the provided 80 hours of transcribed audio data in the full language pack (LP) case or 10 hours in the limited LP case. A pronunciation dictionary for the transcribed words is also provided. We tested our setup on both the Vietnamese full LP case and on the Lao limited LP case (see table 1). These languages are chosen because of their low vocabularies ($<$10.000).

2.2 Actual Term Weighted Value (ATWV)

Given an audio test set (T seconds long) and a list of N keywords, a keyword search (KWS) system should produce a list of keyword occurrences, with timestamps, for each keyword. In this context the keywords do not necessary have to be single words and can instead be bi-grams or short phrases like *"the 8 o'clock bus"* or *"running rabbit"*. When the list of predicted keywords is compared to the reference, all predictions within 0.5 seconds of a reference keyword occurrences are counted as hits (N_{corr}) and the other incorrect predictions are counted as false alarms (N_{FA}). The total occurrences of a keyword in the reference is referred to as N_{true} and all keywords not detected by the keyword search system are referred to as *misses*.

The *"actual term weighted value"* (ATWV) is computed over all N keywords that occur at least once in the reference.

$$ATWV = \frac{1}{N} \sum_w \left[\frac{N_{\text{corr}}(w)}{N_{\text{true}}(w)} - \beta \frac{N_{\text{FA}}(w)}{T - N_{\text{true}}(w)} \right]$$

The balancing factor β weighs the importance of false alarms compared to misses. In the Babel program β is typically set to 999.9 and T, the length of the dev data, is about

36000s. The initial ATWV target is set at 0.3 (often written as 30%). Since $T \gg N_{\text{true}}$ we can simplify the ATWV definition to:

$$ATWV \approx \frac{1}{N} \sum_w \left[\frac{N_{\text{corr}}(w)}{N_{\text{true}}(w)} - \frac{N_{\text{FA}}(w)}{36} \right]$$

which shows us that while the penalty for a false alarm is constant at roughly $\frac{1}{36N}$, the penalty for a miss depends on the number of true occurrences of the keyword in the reference. Keywords that only occur once incur a miss penalty of $\frac{1}{N}$ (36 times its false alarm penalty), while keywords that occur 36 times have the same miss and false alarm penalty.

A KWS system that not only produces keyword predictions but also confidences associated with each prediction allows us to use keyword specific thresholds in order to minimize our expected penalty [9] .

$$thr(w) = \frac{\beta \cdot N_{\text{true}}(w)}{T + (\beta - 1) \cdot N_{\text{true}}(w)}$$

Since $N_{\text{true}}(w)$ is not known, it has to be estimated based on known information. A simple and effective method involves using the sum of the detection confidences $S(w)$.

$$\hat{N}_{\text{true}}(w) = \alpha \cdot S(w) = \sum_{d \in \text{detections}(w)} \text{conf}(d)$$

where α is a boosting factor that compensates for the fact that not all occurrences of the keyword will be present in the prediction list [17].

As an input to our indexing and keyword search tool [11] we use confusion networks that are normally generated by speech recognition systems.

3 Keyword Search using Speech Recognition

The best performing keyword search systems are based on automatic speech recognition systems (ASR) which, instead of being tuned to minimize word error rate, are tuned to generate a confusion network (or word lattice) that maximizes ATWV (see figure 1). As a baseline we use a hybrid DNN-HMM ASR system with a modular DNN acoustic model [3] and a 3gram Kneser-Ney smoothed language model [5]. The language model is trained on the audio transcripts.

Since both Vietnamese and Lao are tonal languages we decided to use pitch features [13] as well as the normal log MEL features. In the following paragraphs we describe the Vietnamese acoustic model in detail since we use its topology as the basis for our neural network keyword search system. For Lao limited LP system we used the best acoustic model that we had available.

We use 40 log MEL features augmented with the 14 pitch features as input features to the DNN acoustic model which is trained in two stages. First a normal bottleneck feature network [4] with 5 hidden layers prior to the bottleneck and 1600 neurons in

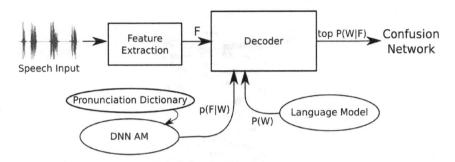

Fig. 1. Overview of a normal speech recognition based keyword search system. The confusion networks generated by the speech recognizer can by indexed and queried a later point in time.

each layer is trained on a window of 13 input features (10ms frameshift). A final hidden layer and the target layer are discarded after training. The target layer consists of 10000 neurons each corresponding to a context dependent phone-state and the bottleneck contains 42 neurons. This network can be seen as a non-linear dimensionality reduction of the 702 (13*54) dimensional input feature vector to a 42 dimensional bottleneck feature (BNF).

A 15 frame window (also 10ms frameshift) of these BNFs is used as the input to the second stage which consists of a further 5 hidden layers with 1600 neurons each and a 10000 neuron final target layer where again each neuron corresponds to a context dependent phone-state. All layers use a sigmoid activation function, except for the output layer which uses the softmax activation function.

Both stages are pre-trained layer-wise using denoising auto encoders [15] for 1 million mini-batches per layer (mini-batch size 256) with constant learning rate of 0.01. For fine-tuning the newbob learning rate schedule is used which starts of with a constant learning rate of 1 until that no longer improves the cross-validation accuracy after which the learning rate is exponentially decayed. Our training setup utilizes the Theano library [1].

Prior to decoding the audio data is segmented into utterances by using the Gaussian Mixture Models (GMM) method proposed by [6]. The decoding is performed using the IBIS single pass decoder of the Janus Recognition Toolkit (JRTk) [14] resulting in set of confusion networks from which we can generate the list of keyword predictions with confidences. After applying the keyword specific thresholds described at the end of section 2, we score the ATWV.

4   Neural Network Keyword Search System

The neural network keyword search system uses the same 40 logMEL + 14 pitch features as the speech recognition system. The topology of the neural network shown in figure 2 is almost identical to the topology of the DNN acoustic model of the speech recognition system. The bottleneck feature part of the network is the same but the BNFs are stacked over a larger window of 29 frames and the final layer contains only 6857 neurons (Lao 4215), each associated with either a word, a noise or silence. This output layer gives the occurrence probabilities for each of the 6857 known words.

out: $P(w|F_{in})$

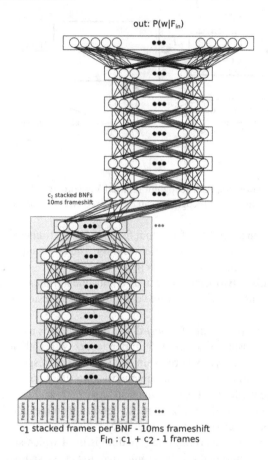

c_2 stacked BNFs
10ms frameshift

c_1 stacked frames per BNF - 10ms frameshift
$F_{in} : c_1 + c_2 - 1$ frames

Fig. 2. Neural Network Topology; the neural network consists of two subnetworks. The output of the initial DBNF network from a standard ASR system is stacked over c_2 frames and used as the input of the deep word classification network. The input feature vector to the DBNF consists of 40 log MEL features concatenated with 14 pitch features and stacked over c_1 frames. All hidden layers contain 1600 neuron except for the bottleneck layer (42) and the target layer (6800).

Training is also performed in an similar manner to the training of the DNN acoustic model with exception that a smaller initial learning rate of 0.5 is used in final fine tuning stage.

Processing the audio with the NN keyword search system involves first segmenting it into into utterances using either the GMM or the SVM method of [6] and then extracting the required features from the audio which can be passed through the neural network.

Using a frame shift of 10ms results in a our neural network generating 100 6857 dimensional probability vectors per second of audio. The fact that some utterances can be over 10 seconds forces us to deal with a large amount of data. We collect all the probability vectors of an utterances into word frame probability matrix (WFPM) where each row j represents one frame and each column i corresponds to a word.

Table 2. ATWV results and real time factors (rtf) of a standard speech recognition based keywords search systems and our proposed neural network based keyword search system on the Babel Vietnamese and Lao development sets

Language	ASR KW	NN KWS
Vietnamese full LP	27.94% ATWV / 5.3 rtf	31.35% ATWV / 3.4 rtf
Lao limited LP	24.44% ATWV / 5.7 rtf	8.62% ATWV / 3.7 rtf

4.1 WFPM Post processing

In order to perform a keyword search using keyword specific thresholds with our existing tools we convert the generated WFPM to a confusion network-like structure. As an initial step the matrix is smoothed by averaging the word probabilities across multiple frames

$$[p_{i,j}]_{k-smooth} = \frac{1}{2k+1} \sum_{j-k}^{j+k} p_{i,j}$$

and converted into a sparse matrix by setting all probabilities below a given threshold to 0.

$$[p_{i,j}]_{c-filt} = \begin{cases} p_{i,j} & \text{if } p_{i,j} > c \\ 0 & \text{otherwise} \end{cases}$$

The resolution of the WFPM is reduced from one row every 10ms to one row every $x \cdot 10$ms by only keeping rows where $\lfloor \frac{x}{2} \rfloor \equiv j \mod x$. After this the rows can be re-normalized since we lost some probability mass when going to a sparse matrix. The sparse WFPM can now be converted into a confusion network be treating each row, j, as list a transition portabilities for their associated words between nodes $j - 1$ and j.

This pseudo confusion network can be scored in the same way as the normal confusion network.

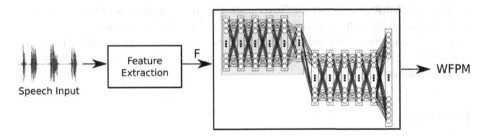

Fig. 3. Overview of the proposed neural network keyword search system

5 Evaluation

As evaluation data we used the Babel 107 Vietnamese developed set and the Babel 203 Lao development set. As can be seen in table 2 the neural network keyword search system slightly outperforms the ASR keyword search system on the Vietnamese full LP set but is far behind it on the Lao limited LP set. One reason for this is due to the fact that a relatively poor (ATWVs >50% have been reported on this set) Vietnamese baseline system was used in this setup; it was chosen because its acoustic model has a similar topology to our proposed neural network keyword search system. The poor performance of our NN keyword search system on the Leo limited LP set is in part due to the fact that we didn't tune it in towards the new language or towards the low resource condition.

The evaluation was performed on 4 16-core AMD Opteron 6276 CPUs where we measured the per-core real time factor. The fact that each Opteron only has 8 floating point units (1 for every 2 cores) reduces the real-time performance of both systems significantly. The matrix multiplication were performed with the openBLAS library [16].

6 Conclusion

This paper has introduced a neural network keyword search system based on the design of a modular DNN acoustic model used for speech recognition. On the Vietnamese full LP set our system is able to achieve a performance similar to that of a full speech recognition system and above the Babel initial goal of 30% ATWV. It also only requires $\frac{2}{3}$ the CPU time. Further work still needs to be carried out in three areas, closing the gap to current best ASR based keyword search systems ($> 50\%$ ATWV), investigating the problems with our limited LP system and dealing with the problems that occur with very large vocabularies. Until then this neural network keyword search system can only be recommended in very specific circumstances.

Acknowledgments. Supported in part by the Intelligence Advanced Research Projects Ac- tivity (IARPA) via Department of Defense U.S. Army Research Laboratory (DoD/ ARL) contract number W911NF-12-C-0015. The U.S. Government is authorized to reproduce and distribute reprints for Governmental purposes notwithstanding any copyright annotation thereon. Disclaimer: The views and conclusions contained herein are those of the authors and should not be interpreted as necessarily representing the official policies or endorsements, either expressed or implied, of IARPA, DoD/ARL, or the U.S. Government.

References

1. Bergstra, J., Breuleux, O., Bastien, F., Lamblin, P., Pascanu, R., Desjardins, G., Turian, J., Warde-Farley, D., Bengio, Y.: Theano: A CPU and GPU math expression compiler. In: Proceedings of the Python for Scientific Computing Conference (SciPy) (June 2010) Oral Presentation

2. Cui, J., Cui, X., Ramabhadran, B., Kim, J., Kingsbury, B., Mamou, J., Mangu, L., Picheny, M., Sainath, T.N., Sethy, A.: Developing speech recognition systems for corpus indexing under the iarpa babel program. In: 2013 IEEE International Conference on Acoustics, Speech and Signal Processing (ICASSP), pp. 6753–6757. IEEE (2013)
3. Gehring, J., Lee, W., Kilgour, K., Lane, I., Miao, Y., Waibel, A., Campus, S.V.: Modular combination of deep neural networks for acoustic modeling. In: Proc. Interspeech, pp. 94–98 (2013)
4. Gehring, J., Miao, Y., Metze, F., Waibel, A.: Extracting deep bottleneck features using stacked auto-encoders. In: 2013 IEEE International Conference on Acoustics, Speech and Signal Processing (ICASSP), pp. 3377–3381. IEEE (2013)
5. Goodman, J., Chen, S.: An empirical study of smoothing techniques for language modeling. Tech. rep., Technical Report TR-10-98, Harvard University (August 1998)
6. Heck, M., Mohr, C., Stüker, S., Müller, M., Kilgour, K., Gehring, J., Nguyen, Q.B., Van Nguyen, H., Waibel, A.: Segmentation of telephone speech based on speech and non-speech models. In: Železný, M., Habernal, I., Ronzhin, A. (eds.) SPECOM 2013. LNCS (LNAI), vol. 8113, pp. 286–293. Springer, Heidelberg (2013)
7. Hsiao, R., Ng, T., Grezl, F., Karakos, D., Tsakalidis, S., Nguyen, L., Schwartz, R.: Discriminative semi-supervised training for keyword search in low resource languages. In: 2013 IEEE Workshop on Automatic Speech Recognition and Understanding (ASRU), pp. 440–445. IEEE (2013)
8. IARPA: Iarpa babel program - broad agency announcement, baa (2011), http://www.iarpa.gov/Programs/ia/Babel/solicitation_babel.html
9. Karakos, D., Schwartz, R., Tsakalidis, S., Zhang, L., Ranjan, S., Ng, T., Hsiao, R., Saikumar, G., Bulyko, I., Nguyen, L., et al.: Score normalization and system combination for improved keyword spotting. In: 2013 IEEE Workshop on Automatic Speech Recognition and Understanding (ASRU), pp. 210–215. IEEE (2013)
10. Kingsbury, B., Cui, J., Cui, X., Gales, M.J., Knill, K., Mamou, J., Mangu, L., Nolden, D., Picheny, M., Ramabhadran, B., et al.: A high-performance cantonese keyword search system. In: 2013 IEEE International Conference on Acoustics, Speech and Signal Processing (ICASSP), pp. 8277–8281. IEEE (2013)
11. Kolkhorst, H.: Strategies for Out-of-Vocabulary Words in Spoken Term Detection. Undergraduate thesis (2011)
12. Kurniawati, E., George, S.: Speaker dependent activation keyword detector based on gmm-ubm (2013)
13. Metze, F., Sheikh, Z.A., Waibel, A., Gehring, J., Kilgour, K., Nguyen, Q.B., Nguyen, V.H.: Models of tone for tonal and non-tonal languages. In: 2013 IEEE Workshop on Automatic Speech Recognition and Understanding (ASRU), pp. 261–266. IEEE (2013)
14. Soltau, H., Metze, F., Fugen, C., Waibel, A.: A one-pass decoder based on polymorphic linguistic context assignment. In: IEEE Workshop on Automatic Speech Recognition and Understanding, ASRU 2001, pp. 214–217. IEEE (2001)
15. Vincent, P., Larochelle, H., Lajoie, I., Bengio, Y., Manzagol, P.A.: Stacked denoising autoencoders: Learning useful representations in a deep network with a local denoising criterion. The Journal of Machine Learning Research 9999, 3371–3408 (2010)
16. Wang, Q., Zhang, X., Zhang, Y., Yi, Q.: Augem: Automatically generate high performance dense linear algebra kernels on x86 cpus. In: Proceedings of SC 2013: International Conference for High Performance Computing, Networking, Storage and Analysis, p. 25. ACM (2013)
17. Wang, Y.: An in-depth comparison of keyword specific thresholding and sum-to-one score normalization. Tech. rep., Technical Report, Carnegie Mellon University (2014)

A Note on Feature Extraction
Based on Kanade-Shi-Tomasi Procedure
and Kalman Filters

Tatjana Grbić[1], Aleksandar Jovanović[2], Slavica Medić[1], and Aleksandar Perović[3]

[1] University of Novi Sad, Faculty of Technical Sciences
[2] University of Belgrade, Faculty of Mathematics
[3] University of Belgrade, Faculty of Transport and Traffic Engineering
{tatjana,slavicm}@uns.ac.rs,
aljosha.jovanovich@gmail.com, pera@sf.bg.ac.rs

Abstract. We present a short overview of the portion of our work in the analysis of biological, acoustic, sonar and radar signals, with particular emphasis on the feature extraction using modified Kanade-Shi-Tomasi procedure and the application of Kalman filters. Developed methodology is illustrated with several examples.

Keywords: Automatic detection of spectral features, invariants of signal features, brain-computer interface, noise elimination in radar signals.

1   Introduction

Feature detection and extraction has been a prominent topic in signal processing from its very beginnings. Our interest in this area has started in late eighties with the formulation of initial problems related to brain functionality, especially in detection of specific cognitive activities. The first success was related to detection of imagined tones in early nineties using rather meagre acquisition resources, see [2, 3]. Later our interest varied from integration of digital imaging devices with optical microscopic systems, feature extraction based on photo morphology, various standard and non-standard applications of Fourier spectroscopy, as well as analysis of different causality criteria used in contemporary study of brain functionality.

The body of the related work is rather staggering. Due to the very limited space, we are unable to offer due credit to the research that had significant impact on our work. References [1-8] are pointers to our work where the reader can found detailed presentation of the research topics that we have deal with during the last quarter of the century, while the rest of the references [9-21] contain work of some of our colleagues and collaborators and can be also used as nice reference resources.

The paper offers an overview of the part of our work published in [7] related to extraction of the dot-like objects from heavily contaminated signals. We present two extraction methods that are based on the Kanade-Shi-Tomasi procedure and the so called bank of Kalman filters. Though all testing is carried out on digital images, we

A. Ronzhin et al. (Eds.): SPECOM 2014, LNAI 8773, pp. 66–73, 2014.

believe that the offered methodology can be successfully applied in detection and extraction of any kind of features that are both narrow in band and frequency. Related to speech recognition, the offered methods may yield some promising result in automated extraction of some specific sound patterns from the signals with lots of background noise and artefacts.

2   Feature Extraction Based on Intensity Discrimination

In this section we will present the first of the two methods that we have used for the efficient extraction and recognition of dot-like objects with the diameter not greater than 10 pixels. Both methods can be applied to matrices and vectors, which can be used to handle short frequency pulses and spectral features that are stable and narrow in frequency.

The first of the mentioned two recognition/extraction procedures for small objects is based on intensity discrimination of considered pixels. The method itself is an adaptation of the procedure for the extraction of the characteristic features from a bitmap image developed by Shi, Tomasi and Kanade (see [15, 17]).

As an input we have a simple monochrome (0 = white, 255 = black) bitmap (matrix) A of a fixed format (here presented with 400×400 pixel resolution). The components of A can be signal amplitude values, or e.g. spectrogram intensities, and will be denoted by $A(x, y)$. Here x indicates the corresponding row and y indicates the corresponding column. Spatial x-wise and y-wise differences I_x and I_y are defined by

$$I_x = \frac{A(x+1,y)-A(x-1,y)}{2}, I_y = \frac{A(x,y+1)-A(x,y-1)}{2}. \tag{1}$$

The matrix G of sums of spatial square differences is defined by

$$G = \sum_{x=p_x-\omega_x}^{p_x+\omega_x} \sum_{y=p_y-\omega_y}^{p_y+\omega_y} \begin{bmatrix} I_x^2 & I_x I_y \\ I_x I_y & I_y^2 \end{bmatrix}, \tag{2}$$

where $\omega_x = \omega_y$ is the width of the integration window (the best results are obtained with values between 2 and 4), while p_x and p_y are the indices corresponding to the indices x and y such that the formula (2) is defined. Hence, all so called inner pixels, i.e. pixels for which I_x and I_y are definable, are included in the computation. The more compact form of the matrix G is given by

$$G = \begin{bmatrix} a & b \\ c & d \end{bmatrix}. \tag{3}$$

Consequently, the eigenvalues of G are given by

$$\lambda_{1,2} = \frac{a+d}{2} \pm \frac{\sqrt{(a-d)^2+4bc}}{2}. \tag{4}$$

Moreover, for each inner pixel with coordinates (x, y) we define $\lambda(x, y)$ by

$$\lambda(x,y) = \min(\lambda_1(x,y), \lambda_2(x,y)). \qquad (5)$$

Finally, for the given lower threshold T_{min} and the parameter A_{max} (in our examples $A_{max} = 255$) we define λ_{max} by

$$\lambda_{max} = \max\{\lambda(x,y) \mid (x,y) \text{ is an inner pixel}\}. \qquad (6)$$

The extraction matrix E is defined by

$$E(x,y) = \begin{cases} \frac{A_{max}}{\lambda_{max}} \cdot \lambda(x,y), & \frac{A_{max}}{\lambda_{max}} \cdot \lambda(x,y) > T_{min} \\ 0, & \frac{A_{max}}{\lambda_{max}} \cdot \lambda(x,y) < T_{min} \end{cases}. \qquad (7)$$

With two available images/spectrograms, using described method we can solve harder cases of automatic extraction. Indeed, let B and C be two images where every pixel is contaminated with noise which has a normal Gaussian distribution, in which a stationary signal is injected, objects at coordinates $(x_1, y_1), \dots (x_{10}, y_{10})$, all with an intensity of e.g. m (within $[0,255]$ interval) and fluctuation parameter p; we generate the new binary image A as follows:

$$A(x,y) = \text{abs}(B(x,y) - C(x,y))$$
$$\text{If } A(x,y) < p \text{ then } A(x,y) = 255$$
$$\text{else } A(x,y) = 0;$$

The above simple discrimination reduces random noise significantly and reveals the signals together with residual noise. By performing the procedure defined by the equations (1) thru (7), we obtain the filtered image with extracted signals. The method is adapted, using two parameters of optimization (minimax): the minimalization of the integral surface of detected objects, then the maximization of the number of the small objects.

In order to illustrate the application of the presented extraction method from the single source, we will present three sample images together with the corresponding extraction images (Fig.1-3). Initial images are formed by initial introduction of several dots (useful signals) with an amplitude of $a = 120$, and then contaminated with the random cloudlike noise.

Fig. 1. Noise reduction – first example

The images on the left side show the initial bitmap, while the images on the right side show the corresponding extraction result. In all three examples the initial setting is $A_{max} = 255$ and $T_{min} = 124$.

Fig. 2. Noise reduction – second example

In the first two examples the noise reduction was complete. However, in the last example some part of the noise remained in the extraction image (top and low right).

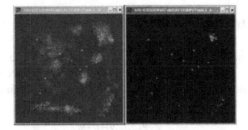

Fig. 3. Noise reduction – third example

Note that the amplitude of the target signal is lower than the chosen lower threshold in all three examples.

As we have mentioned above, described extraction procedure can be used for the extraction of heavily contaminated signals in dynamic situations provided that we have several consecutive images. The illustration example starts with the following two images (Fig.4):

Fig. 4. Noise reduction from two images – the initial setting

After the application of the extraction procedure, we have obtained the left image on Figure 5.

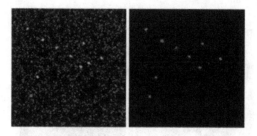

Fig. 5. Noise reduction from two images – intermediate and final stage

Note that some residual noise is present on the left image. However, after the application of the noise reduction procedure of that image, the noise reduction was complete, as it is shown on the right-side image on Figure 5.

3　Feature Extraction Based on Kalman Filters

Another method for the detection/extraction of small features is based on a so called bank of Kalman filters. After the construction of the initial sequence of images, Z_k, the bank of one-dimensional simplified Kalman filters (see [18]) is defined as follows:

$$K_k(x,y) = \frac{P_{k-1}(x,y)+Q}{P_{k-1}(x,y)+Q+R},$$

$$\hat{X}_k(x,y) = \hat{X}_{k-1}(x,y) + K_k(x,y) \cdot \left(Z_k(x,y) - \hat{X}_{k-1}(x,y)\right),$$
$$P_k(x,y) = (1 - K_k(x,y)) \cdot (P_{k-1}(x,y) + Q).$$

Initially, $P_0(x,y) = \hat{X}_0(x,y) = 0, Q = 1, R = 100$, where Q is the covariance of the noise in the target signal and R is the covariance of the noise of the measurement. Depending on the dynamics of the problem we put: the output filtered image in kth iteration is the matrix $\hat{X}_k$, the last of which is input in the procedure described by equations (1) to (7), finally generating the image with the extracted objects.

This method shows that it is not necessary to know the signal level if we can estimate the statistical parameters of noise and statistics of measured signal to some extent. In the general case, we know that its mean is somewhere between 0 and 255 and that it is contaminated with noise with the unknown variance.

The method of small object recognition, originally developed for the marine radar object tracking, works with vectors equally well. It is applicable to the automatic extraction of signals which are embedded in the noise and imperceptible (also in the spectra) in the case when we can provide at least two sources which are sufficiently linearly independent (their linear dependence on the signal components is essential for the object filtering – extraction), or in the situations when the conditions for application of Kalman filters are met.

As an illustration of the application of Kalman filters in the feature extraction, we have constructed the initial sequence of images, Z_k, of the size 200×200 pixels in the following way (Figure 6):

Fig. 6. Construction of Kalman filters

First, in each image we have introduced noise by $Z_k(x, y) = \text{randn}(0,90)$, where "randn" function generates pseudo-random numbers in the interval [0,255] using Gaussian distribution with $\mu = 0$ and $\sigma = 90$. Then, in every image we injected 10 objects (useful signals) at the same positions, each of them of a size around 10 pixels, with random (Gaussian) fluctuation of intensity around value 120 (Figure 6). After the construction of the initial sequence of images, the bank of $200 \times 200 = 40000$ one-dimensional simplified Kalman filters is defined using the iterative procedure as above. The process of noise elimination and feature extraction is shown in the images in Figure 7:

Fig. 7. Application of Kalman filters

The image on the left in Figure 7 shows the extraction result after the 21 iterations of Kalman filter bank, the central image shows the result after the 34 iterations, and the final image shows the result after 36 iterations.

4   Conclusion

This paper contains a short overview of the portion of our previous work on the problem of the automatized recognition of features in signals and their Fourier or wavelet spectra and spectrograms, see [1-8]. The algorithms sketched here use techniques developed for image processing and are suitable for morphologic investigations. These algorithms also offer possibility of localization and extraction of important features, as well as determination of their topological and geometrical characteristic invariants. Those invariants are often crucial for the representation and to classification the by application of subtle similarity measures. Small object recognition in cases of heavy contamination by noise of mainly random nature is successfully performed in rather general circumstances. Due to a modest complexity, all are real time applicable, even without the enhanced hardware.

Acknowledgements. This work is partially supported by Serbian Ministry of Education and Science through grants 174009, III41013, TR31036, TR32035 and TR36001.

References

1. Jovanović, A.: CCD microscopy, image and signal processing. CD-ROM, University of Belgrade, Faculty of Mathematics (1997)
2. Jovanović, A.: Brain signals in computer interface (in Russian, Lomonosov, Russ. Academy of Science). Intelektualnie Sistemi 3(1-2), 109–117 (1998)
3. Jovanović, A., Perović, A.: Brain computer interfaces – some technical remarks. International Journal of Bioelectromagnetism 9(3), 91–102 (2007)
4. Jovanović, A.: New-technology in biomedical research and diagnostics. E-book, Faculty of Mathematics, Un. of Belgrade (2006)
5. Spasić, S., Perović, A., Klonowski, W., Djordjević, Z., Duch, W., Jovanović, A.: Forensics of features in the spectra of biological signals. International Journal for Bioelectromagnetism 12(2), 62–75 (2010)
6. Jovanović, A., Perović, A., Klonowski, W., Duch, W., Djordjević, Z., Spasić, S.: Detection of structural features in biological signals. Journal of Signal Processing Systems 60(1), 115–129 (2010)
7. Perović, A., Đorđević, Z., Paskota, M., Takači, A., Jovanović, A.: Automatic recognition of features in spectrograms based on some image analysis methods. Acta Polytechnica Hungarica 10(2),153–172 (2013)
8. Klonowski, W., Duch, W., Perović, A., Jovanović, A.: Some Computational Aspects of the Brain Computer Interfaces Based on Inner Music. Computational Intelligence and Neuroscience (2009), doi:10.1155/2009/950403
9. Cincotti, F., Mattia, D., Babiloni, C., Carducci, F., del Bianchi, L.R.M., Mourino, J., Salinari, S., Marciani, M.G., Babiloni, F.: Classification of EEG mental patterns by using two scalp electrodes and Mahalanobis distance-based classifiers. Method of Information in Medicine 41(4), 337–341 (2002)
10. Pfurtscheller, G., Neuper, C., Guger, C., Harkam, W., Ramoser, H., Schlög, A., Obermaier, B., Pregenzer, M.: Current Trends in Graz Brain-Computer Interface (BCI) Research. IEEE Transaction on Rehabilitation Engineering 8(2), 216–219 (2000)
11. Nijboer, F., Sellers, E.W., Mellinger, J., Jordan, M.A., Matuz, T., Furdea, A., Halder, S., Mochty, U., Krusienski, D.J., Vaughan, T.M., Wolpaw, J.R., Birbaumer, N., Kübler, A.: A P300-based brain-computer interface for people with amyotrophic lateral sclerosis. Clinical Neurophysiology 119(8), 1909–1916 (2008)
12. Zatorre, R.J., Halpern, A.R.: Mental Concerts: Musical Imagery and Auditory Cortex. Neuron 47, 9–12 (2005)

13. Kroger, J.K., Elliott, L., Wong, T.N., Lakey, J., Dang, H., George, J.: Detecting mental commands in high-frequency EEG: Faster brain-machine interfaces. In: Proc. Biomedical Engineering Society Annual Meeting, Chicago (2006)
14. Pfurtscheller, G., Lopes da Silva, F.H.: Event-related EEG/MEG synchronization and desynchronization: Basic principles. Clinical Neurophysiology 110(11), 1842–1857 (1999)
15. Bouguet, J.Y.: Pyramidal Implementation of the Lucas Kanade Feature Tracker. Preprint, http://robots.stanford.edu/cs223b04/algo_affine_tracking.pdf
16. Bradski, G.: Computer Vision Tracking for Use in a Perceptual User Interface. Preprint, http://www.cse.psu.edu/~rcollins/CSE598G/papers/camshift.pdf
17. Shi, J., Tomasi, C.: Good Features to Track. Preprint, http://www.ai.mit.edu/courses/6.891/handouts/shi94good.pdf
18. Welch, G., Bisho, G.: An Introduction to the Kalman Filter, University of North Carolina at Chapter Hill, Chapter Hill, TR 95-014 (2004)
19. Sameshima, K., Baccala, L.A.: Using partial directed coherence to describe a neuronal assembly interactions. J. Neurosci. Methods 94, 93–103 (1999)
20. Vialatte, F.B., Sole-Casals, J., Dauwels, J., Maurice, M., Cichocki, A.: Bump Time-Frequency Toolbox: A Toolbox for Time-Frequency Oscillatory Bursts Extraction in Electrophysiological Signals. BMC Neuroscience 10(46) (2009), doi:10.1186/1471-2202-10-46
21. Spasić, S., Culić, M., Grbić, G., Martać, L., Sekulić, S., Mutavdžić, D.: Spectral and fractal analysis of cerebellar activity after and repeated brain injury. Bulletin of Mathematical Biology 70(4), 1235–1249 (2008)

A Robust SVM/GMM Classifier for Speaker Verification

Zoran Cirovic[1] and Natasa Cirovic[2]

[1] School of Electrical and Computer Engineering of Applied Studies, Belgrade, Serbia
zcirovic@viser.edu.rs
[2] Faculty of Electrical Engineering, University of Belgrade, Serbia
natasa@etf.bg.ac.rs

Abstract. One of the basic problems in the speaker verification applications is presence of environmental noise. State-of-art speaker verification models based on Support Vector Machine (SVM) show significant vulnerability to high noise level. This paper presents a SVM/GMM classifier for text independent speaker verification which shows additional robustness. Two techniques for training GMM models are applied, providing different results depending on the values of environmental noise. The recognition phase was tested with Serbian speakers at different Signal-to-Noise Ratio (SNR).

Keywords: SVM, GMM, classifier, speaker verification.

1   Introduction

Speaker verification is a type of speaker recognition. It is an automated process for verification of person's identity using speech signal. Based on the signal source and decision making process, speaker verification is a biometric method.

In practice, speech verification systems are often used for access control, most often together with other additional methods. These additional methods can be based on some other biometric method or cryptography mechanism for authentication. Decision methods that are applied in verification systems are of generative or discriminative type. Generative methods approximate the probability of the stochastic modeled processes. These methods include Hidden Markov Model – HMM and Gaussian Mixture Model - GMM. In case of generative type classifiers, the model is chosen depending on the nature of verification. If the text is known in advance, the system is trained for these specific speech utterances and HMM is used. If the text is not known in advance, the system is trained for unknown speech utterances, and GMM is used. Discriminative methods optimize the classifier with respect to minimization of the classification error, not regarding the nature of the process. These methods include Support Vector Machine - SVM, [1].

The basic problem in speaker verification is presence of noise, as well as high variation of accustic speech signal. Presence of environmental noise can not be avoided or disregarded in the speaker verification process. When the speech is corrupted by environmental noise, the distribution of the audio feature vectors is also damaged.

A. Ronzhin et al. (Eds.): SPECOM 2014, LNAI 8773, pp. 74–80, 2014.

This leads to misclassification and poor recognition. For a system to be of practical use in a high noise environment it is necessary to address the issue of robustness. To combat this problem, researchers have put forward several new algorithms, which assume prior knowledge of the noise, like: noise filtering techniques [2,3], parallel model combination [4,5,6], Jacobian environmental adaptation [7,8], using microphone arrays [9,10] or techniques of speech enhancement which target the modeling of speech and noise pdf [11,12], introducing additional speech modalities [13,14,15,16]. One of the noise supperession approaches is multiconditional which constructs several models that are suitable for a number of noisy environments, each constructed in the same way, [17,18,19]. This paper presents a classifier for speaker verification system that includes two models adapted in case for high or low enviroment noise conditions. The classifier can adaptively select one of the two models, based on the level of noise, achieving a total error rate that is lower than for each separate system.

2   System Description

As is well known, a typical speaker verification system has two basic parts: for model training and testing, i.e. speaker verification. Both parts use identical front-end processing and classifier, as is shown in Fig.1.

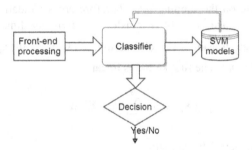

Fig. 1. Speaker verification system

Front-end processing includes transformation of audio speech signal into speaker features suitable for further processing. Speaker features should suppress the nonspeach charachteristics (noise, transmission chanel charachteristics, emotions, etc.), suppress common characteristics of speakers and enhance speaker specifics. Instead of audio speech samples, we use speaker feature vectors of Mel-Frequency Cepstral Coefficients (MFCC). Linear Prediction Cepstral Coefficients (LPCC) or some variation of these coefficients, [20].

After feature extraction, speaker specifics are further enchanced during the GMM training process. For each of speakers the GMM models $\lambda_i = \{\mu_i, \Sigma_i, w_i\}$, $i = 1,...,N_s$ is created. Model parameters w_i represents weights, μ_i mean vector and Σ_i covariance matrix. For a given training vectors and a initial GMM configuration,

parameters of the GMM are estimated using an iterative algorithm. The aim of parameter estimation is to find the model parameters which maximize the likelihood of the
GMM for training data and initial model, [21,22].

Two algorithms for estimation of parameters are implemented. Maximum A Posteriori (MAP) parameter estimation is based on a posteriori adjustments of common
GMM for each speaker. Using MAP estimation the model for each speaker is obtained by adaptation of the common GMM Universal Background Model (GMM-
UBM). Thus, this algorithm is composed in two steps. In the first step the UBM is
formed using expectation maximization (EM) estimation. In the second step UBM is
adapted for each speaker separately using MAP. The second implemented EM algorithm is maximum-likelihood (ML), and it is applied for additional model in our classifier. During each iteration of the algorithm a new model $\lambda_i^{'}$ is established such that
$P(\mathbf{X} / \lambda_i^{'}) \geq P(\mathbf{X} / \lambda_i)$, where $\mathbf{X}$ is input training vectors. New model then becomes the
initial model for the next iteration and the process is repeated until some convergence
threshold is reached.

Mean values of obtained GMM mixtures are used as inputs for modeling SVM
classifiers - supervectors. Supervectors represent high dimension vectors obtained by
modeling a stochastic process, generative models, and represent inputs for SVM classifier, which is discriminative model. In this way complementary properties of both
models are used, [1], [21]. SVM classifier is binary and linear, formed in such a way
to maximize the margin between two classes and simultaneously, minimizing the
verification error rate on the training set. Therefore cross validation implementation
was necessary. Input space of SVM is transformed to higher dimension space, more
suitable for classification using a kernel function, $K(\mathbf{x}_1, \mathbf{x}_2) = \Phi(\mathbf{x}_1)^{\mathrm{T}} \Phi(\mathbf{x}_2)$. In this
paper we used two kernel. The first kernel is linear:

$$K_{Lin}(\mathbf{X}_i, \mathbf{X}_j) = \sum_{k=1}^{M} w_k \mu_k^i \Sigma^{-1} \mu_k^j. \tag{1}$$

and the second is standard RBF kernel:

$$K_{rbf}(\mathbf{X}_i, \mathbf{X}_j) = \exp\left(-\gamma \left\| \mu_{EM}^i - \mu_{EM}^j \right\| \right). \tag{2}$$

3   Classifier

Extended block diagram of the classifier, which is implemented in the present system
is shown in Fig.2

The part (i) is based on training using linear GMM kernel, (1), and input supervectors obtained in GMM-UBM models, [21].

The part (ii) also uses mean values obtained in GMM models as input. The
K-means algorithm is used to find initial centroids for EM training. Instead of using
UBM model with several hundred centroids as in part (i), in this part we start with

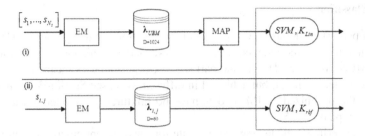

Fig. 2. Classifier block diagram for model training

much smaller number of centroids per model. We use the sensitivity of EM training to initialization and form several models per speaker whose mean values create super-vectors. In this way we gain higher statistical reliability of the system, making it more robust. The same lengths of input sequences per speaker are obtained for SVM train-ing, too. These SVM models are based on the usage of the RBF kernel, (2), [23].

4   Experimental Results

4.1   Database

The corpus consists of 50 sessions with 16 speakers with up to 4 sessions per speaker. The utterances for each session were very carefully chosen to provide a very good representation of typical Serbian language [24]. Audio signals were recorded original-ly sampled at 44 kHz. One session was used as enrollment and the remaining 49 ses-sions were used for speaker verification. This resulted in $49 * 50 = 2450$ speaker verification tests, for each level of environmental noise. These tests are repeated for 7 different levels of additive White-Gaussian noise, for $SNR = 0, 5, 10, ..., 30dB$.

4.2   Front-End Processing

The audio feature vector is formed as a collection of 14 mel-frequency cepstral coef-ficients (MFCC), plus corresponding deltas, altogether $D = 42$ coefficients per frame. MFCC are based on the uniformly-spaced triangular filterbanks from 300 to 3400 Hz. Each frame corresponds to 1024 samples, i.e. $t_W \cong 23.2ms$ time window.

The frames are overlapped to avoid the risk of losing valuable transient. In our system, frames are overlapped by one half of the frame length. After computing the MFCCs, a cepstral mean subtraction was done, [12]. To separate speech frames from silent and noise, classical voice activity detector based on energy and zero crossing-rate was applied.

Afterwards, the training of GMM models using MFCC vectors was performed. This training is done in two ways, described in the sections 3.1 and 3.2. Finally, these two kinds of input vectors are used for training the two different SVM classifiers.

4.3   Classifier

The first part (i) of classifier, $C_{1, M=1024}$, is based on training using linear GMM kernel and input supervectors obtained in GMM-UBM models. This model is characterized with M=1024 mixtures. The second part (ii), $C_{2, M=60}$, also uses mean values obtained in GMM models as input, but achieved in different way, see Section 3. In this part of classifier the optimized GMM models have 60 mixtures per model and use several models per speaker, [25].

In this experiment the testing of error rate for the different environmental noise levels was performed for two parts of classifiers separately. The obtained results are presented in Table 1 and graphically visualized in Fig. 3.

Table 1. Verification error of classifier parts

SNR, [dB]	0	5	10	15	20	25	30
$C_{1, M=1024}$	32.68	23.33	20.06	6.73	**5.26**	**2.13**	**1.4**
$C_{2, M=60}$	**15.57**	**8.93**	**7.86**	**6.5**	5.66	5.3	5.3

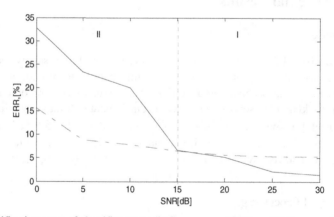

Fig. 3. Verification error of classifier parts: (i) $C_{1,M=1024}$ – solid line; (ii) $C_{2,M=60}$ – dash dot line

4.4   Noise Adaptation of Classifier

These results clearly show the different efficiency of the applied classifiers depending on the noise level. In the case of low environmental noise (SNR > 15dB), better results can be obtained by implementing the classifier C1. However, if the verification is done in the high noise conditions, then the implementation of the classifier C2 is significantly more efficient. By using the noise level detector, higher robustness is achieved, compared to using separate parts as independent classifiers.

5 Conclusion

We have demonstrated a complex SVM/GMM based classifier which can be used in a speaker verification system. Presented classifier achieves increased robustness by using additional models per speaker. Experimental results show significant reduction of verification error in noise environment, especially for SNR < 15dB. On the other hand, application of this classifier affects the rate of verification, which can be a disadvantage in practice. Depending on the specific implementation, future work can be done on speed optimization of the classifier. Also, future work should explore this classifier on more statistically-significant wider speaker populations to further validate results.

References

1. Campbell, W.M., Sturim, D.E., Reynolds, D.A.: Support vector machines using GMM supervectors for speaker verification. IEEE Signal Processing Letters 13, 308–311 (2006)
2. Ortega-Garcia, J., Gonzalez-Rodriguez, L.: Overview of speech enhancement techniques for automatic speaker recognition. In: Proc. 4th International Conference on Spoken Language Processing, Philadelphia, PA, pp. 929–932 (1996)
3. Suhadi, S., Stan, S., Fingscheidt, T., Beaugeant, C.: An evaluation of VTS and IMM for speaker verification in noise. In: Proceedings of the 9th European Conference on Speech Communication and Technology (EuroSpeech 2003), Geneva, Switzerland, pp. 1669–1672 (2003)
4. Gales, M.J.F., Young, S.: HMM recognition in noise using parallel model combination. In: Proceedings of the 9th European Conference on Speech Communication and Technology (EuroSpeech 1993), Berlin, Germany, pp. 837–840 (1993)
5. Matsui, T., Kanno, T., Furui, S.: Speaker recognition using HMM composition in noisy environments. Comput. Speech Lang. 10, 107–116 (1996)
6. Wong, L.P., Russell, M.: Text-dependent speaker verification under noisy conditions using parallel model combination. In: Proceedings of the IEEE International Conference on Acoustics, Speech and Signal Processing (ICASSP 2001), Salt Lake City, UT, pp. 457–460 (2001)
7. Sagayama, S., Yamaguchi, Y., Takahashi, S., Takahashi, J.: Jacobian approach to fast acoustic model adaptation. In: Proceedings of the IEEE International Conference on Acoustics, Speech and Signal Processing (ICASSP 1997), Munich, Germany, pp. 835–838 (1997)
8. Cerisara, C., Rigaziob, L., Junqua, J.-C.: Alpha-Jacobian environmental adaptation. Speech Commun. 42, 25–41 (2004)
9. Gonzalez-Rodriguez, L., Ortega-Garcia, J.: Robust speaker recognition through acoustic array processing and spectral normalization. In: Proceedings of the IEEE International Conference on Acoustics, Speech and Signal Processing (ICASSP 1997), Munich, Germany, pp. 1103–1106 (1997)
10. McCowan, I., Pelecanos, J., Scridha, S.: Robust speaker recognition using microphone arrays. In: Proc. A Speaker Odyssey-The Speaker Recognition Workshop, Crete, Greece, pp. 101–106 (2001)
11. Hu, Y., Loizou, P.C.: A generalized subspace approach for enhancing speech corrupted by colored noise. IEEE Trans. Speech and Audio Processing 11(4), 334–341 (2003)

12. Kundu, A., Chatterjee, S., Murthy, A.S., Sreenivas, T.V.: GMM based Bayesian approach to speech enhancement in signal/transform domain. In: Proceedings of the IEEE International Conference on Acoustics, Speech and Signal Processing (ICASSP 2008), Las Vegas, NE, pp. 4893–4896 (2008)
13. Campbell, W.M., Quatieri, T.F., Campbell, J.P., Weinstein, C.J.: Multimodal Speaker Authentication using Nonacoustic Sensors. In: Proceedings of the International Workshop on Multimodal User Authentication, Santa Barbara, CA, pp. 215–222 (2003)
14. Zhu, B., Hazen, T.J., Glass, J.R.: Multimodal Speech Recognition with Ultrasonic Sensors. In: Proceedings of the 8th Annual Conference of the International Speech Communication Association, Antwerp, Belgium, vol. 4, pp. 662–665 (2007)
15. Subramanya, A., Zhang, Z., Liu, Z., Droppo, J., Acero, A.: A Graphical Model for Multi-Sensory Speech Processing in Air-and-Bone Conductive Microphones. In: Proceedings of the 9th European Conference on Speech Communication and Technology (EuroSpeech 2005), Lisbon, Portugal, pp. 2361–2364 (2005)
16. Cirovic, Z., Milosavljevic, M., Banjac, Z.: Multimodal Speaker Verification Based on Electroglottograph Signal and Glottal Activity Detection. EURASIP Journal on Advances in Signal Processing 2010, 930376 (2010)
17. Kim, K., Young Kim, M.: Robust Speaker Recognition against Background Noise in an Enhanced Multi-Condition Domain. IEEE Transactions on Consumer Electronics 56(3), 1684–1688 (2010)
18. Zao, L., Coelho, R.: Colored Noise Based Multi-condition Training Technique for Robust Speaker Identification. IEEE Signal Processing Letters 18(11), 675–678 (2011)
19. Asbai, N., Amrouche, A., Debyeche, M.: Performances Evaluation of GMM-UBM and GMM-SVM for Speaker Recognition in Realistic World. In: Lu, B.-L., Zhang, L., Kwok, J. (eds.) ICONIP 2011, Part II. LNCS, vol. 7063, pp. 284–291. Springer, Heidelberg (2011)
20. Davis, S.B., Mermelstein, P.: Comparison of Parametric Representations for Monosyllabic Word Recognition in Continuously Spoken Sentences. IEEE Transactions on Acoustic, Speech and Signal Processing 28(4), 357–366 (1980)
21. Reynolds, D.A., Quatieri, T.F., Dunn, R.B.: Speaker verification using adapted Gaussian mixture models. Digital Signal Processing 10(1-3), 19–41 (2000)
22. Xuan, G., Zhang, W., Chai, P.: EM algorithms of Gaussian mixture model and hidden Markov model. In: Proceedings of International Conference on Image Processing, ICIP 2001, Thessaloniki, Greece, vol. 1, pp. 145–148 (2001)
23. Burges, C.: A Tutorial on Support Vector Machines for Pattern Recognition. In: Fayyad, U. (ed.) Data Mining and Knowledge Discovery, vol. 2, pp. 121–167. Kluwer Academic Publishers, Boston (1998)
24. Jovicic, S.T., Kasic, Z., Dordevic, M., Rajkovic, M.: Serbian emotional speech database: Design, processing and evaluation. In: Proceedings of the 11th International Conference Speech and Computer (SPECOM 2004), St. Petersburg, Russia, pp. 77–81 (2004)
25. Cirovic, Z., Banjac, Z.: Jedna primena SVM klasifikatora u verifikaciji govornika nezavisno od teksta. In: Proceedings of Conference Infoteh, Jahorina, Bosnia and Herzegovina, pp. 833–836 (2012)

A Sequence Training Method for Deep Rectifier Neural Networks in Speech Recognition

Tamás Grósz, Gábor Gosztolya, and László Tóth

MTA-SZTE Research Group on Artificial Intelligence
of the Hungarian Academy of Sciences and University of Szeged
Szeged, Hungary
{groszt,ggabor,tothl}@inf.u-szeged.hu

Abstract. While Hidden Markov Modeling (HMM) has been the dominant technology in speech recognition for many decades, recently deep
neural networks (DNN) it seems have now taken over. The current DNN
technology requires frame-aligned labels, which are usually created by
first training an HMM system. Obviously, it would be desirable to have
ways of training DNN-based recognizers without the need to create an
HMM to do the same task. Here, we evaluate one such method which
is called Connectionist Temporal Classification (CTC). Though it was
originally proposed for the training of recurrent neural networks, here
we show that it can also be used to train more conventional feed-forward
networks as well. In the experimental part, we evaluate the method on
standard phone recognition tasks. For all three databases we tested, we
found that the CTC method gives slightly better results that those obtained with force-aligned training labels got using an HMM system.

Keywords: connectionist temporal classification, deep neural networks.

1 Introduction

For three decades now, Hidden Markov Models (HMMs) have been the dominant technology in speech recognition. Their success is due to the fact that they
handle local (frame-level) likelihood estimation and the combination of these
local estimates into a global (utterance-level) score jointly, in a unified mathematical framework. Recently, however, it was shown that deep neural network
(DNN) based solutions can significantly outperform standards HMMs [5]. This
technology replaces the Gaussian mixtures of the HMM by a DNN, while the
utterance-level decoding is still performed by the HMM. Hence, this approach is
usually referred to as the hybrid HMM/ANN model [1]. The DNN component
of these hybrid models is usually trained only at the frame level. That is, we
generate frame-level training targets for the network, and during training we optimize some frame-level training criteria. This frame-by-frame training, however,
has several drawbacks. First, we must have frame-level labels to be able to start
the training. For very old and small databases (like the TIMIT dataset used
here) a manual phonetic segmentation is available. But for more recent corpora

A. Ronzhin et al. (Eds.): SPECOM 2014, LNAI 8773, pp. 81–88, 2014.
© Springer International Publishing Switzerland 2014

which are hundreds of hours long, manual segmentation is clearly out of question. Hence, the usual solution for obtaining frame-level labels is to train a standard HMM system, and then use it in forced alignment mode. This means that, based on the current technology, the training of a DNN-based recognizer should always be preceded by the training of a standard HMM model. This clearly makes the creation of a DNN-based system much more tedious and time-consuming, and although quite recently there have been some attempts at having the standalone training of DNN systems, these technologies are still far from complete [8].

Besides the cost of getting forced alignment labels, the frame-level training of a neural network has another, more theoretical limitation. During this training, we minimize the frame-level error cost, such as the frame-level cross-entropy between the network output and the training targets. These training targets are hard-labeled, which means that we expect the network to give an output of 1 for the correct class and 0 for the remaining ones. This is not necessarily optimal regarding the decoding process, which combines the frame-level scores. A more sophisticated method that derives "soft" training targets from the sentence-level scores can be expected to result in a better performance.

Graves et al. proposed a method that provides a solution to both the above-mentioned problems, and called it the Connectionist Temporal Classification (CTC) method for Recurrent Neural Networks (RNNs) [3]. This method requires just the transcription of the utterance, without any further label alignment information. But their architecture differs fundamentally from the standard HMM/ANN model: owing to the use of recurrent neural network classifiers, they apply the training method called *backpropagation through time* [13], making the training process much slower and more complex. The number of model parameters is also quite high. Furthermore, as frames have to be processed in strictly increasing order, decoding is much harder to parallelize. When using bidirectional recurrent networks (which are required to achieve the best performance with this approach [4]), we have to wait for the end of the utterance before we can start evaluating, making real-time speech processing impossible. Lastly, instead of using a standard language model like a phoneme n-gram, they use a special technique called prediction network, which is also based on an RNN. Thus, their approach is quite involved and quite different from the usual HMM/ANN model.

In this study we show that the CTC training scheme is not an inseparable part of the RNN-based architecture, and with a few small modifications it can also be applied to the training of HMM/ANN models. Here, we use it to train standard feed-forward deep neural nets over three different databases. The results show that the CTC method gives a consistently better performance compared to the case where the training targets are got using forced alignment with an HMM.

2   Connectionist Temporal Classification

Following the work of Graves et al. [3], first we outline the Connectionist Temporal Classification training scheme. Similar to standard frame-level backpropagation training, it is an iterative method, where we sweep through the whole

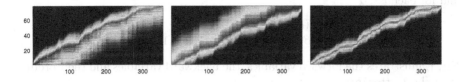

Fig. 1. The α (left), β (middle) and $\alpha\beta$ (right) values for a given utterance. The horizontal axis corresponds to the frames of the utterance, while the vertical axis represents the states (phonemes)

audio training data set several times. A speciality of this training method is that we process a whole utterance at a time instead of using just fixed-sized batches of it; however, we only need the correct transcription of the utterance, and do not require any time-alignment.

The CTC training method is built on the dynamic search method called forward-backward search [6], which is a standard part of HMM training. The forward-backward algorithm not only gives the optimal path, but at the same time we also get the probability of going through the given phoneme of the transcription for all the frames of the utterance. From this, for each frame, we can calculate a probability distribution over the possible phonemes; then these values can be used as target values when training the acoustic classifier.

2.1   The Forward-Backward Algorithm

Let us begin with the formal description of the forward-backward algorithm. First, let us take the utterance with length T, and let its correct transcription be $z = z_1 z_2 \ldots z_n$. We will also use the output vectors y^t of the neural network trained in the previous iteration. $\alpha(t, u)$ can be defined as the summed probability of outputting the u-long prefix of z up to the time index $t \leq T$. The initial conditions formulate that the correct sequence starts with the first label in z:

$$\alpha(1, u) = \begin{cases} y_{z_1}^1 & \text{if } u = 1, \\ 0 & \text{if } u \geq 2. \end{cases} \tag{1}$$

Now the forward variables at time t can be calculated recursively from those at time $t - 1$; we can remain in state z_{u-1}, or move on to the next one (z_u). Thus,

$$\alpha(t, u) = \begin{cases} y_{z_u}^t \alpha(t - 1, u) & \text{if } u = 1, \\ y_{z_u}^t \big(\alpha(t - 1, u) + \alpha(t - 1, u - 1)\big) & \text{otherwise.} \end{cases} \tag{2}$$

In the backward phase we calculate the backward variables $\beta(u, t)$, which represent the probability of producing the suffix of z having length $n - u$ starting from the frame $t + 1$. The backward variables can be calculated recursively as

$$\beta(T, u) = \begin{cases} 1 & \text{if } u = n, \\ 0 & \text{otherwise,} \end{cases} \tag{3}$$

and for each $t < T$

$$\beta(t, u) = \begin{cases} y_{z_u}^t \beta(t+1, u) & \text{if } u = n, \\ y_{z_u}^t \left(\beta(t+1, u) + \beta(t+1, u+1) \right) & \text{otherwise.} \end{cases} \quad (4)$$

Fig. 1. illustrates the forward variables, the backward variables and their product for a short utterance.

2.2   Using the $\alpha\beta$ values for ANN training

The $\alpha(t, u)\beta(t, u)$ product values express the overall probability of two factors, summed along *all paths*: the first is that we recognize the correct sequence of phonemes, and the second is that at frame t we are at the uth phoneme of z. For neural network training, however, we would need a distribution over the phoneme set for frame t. It is not hard to see that such a distribution over the phonemes of z can be obtained by normalizing the $\alpha(t, u)\beta(t, u)$ products so that they sum up to one (by which step we eliminate the probability of recognizing the correct sequence of phonemes). Then, to normalize this distribution to one over the *whole set of phonemes*, we need to sum up the scores belonging to the multiple occurrences of the same phonemes in z. That is, the regression targets for any frame t and phoneme ph can be defined by the formula

$$\frac{\sum\limits_{i:z_i=ph} \alpha(t, i)\beta(t, i)}{\sum\limits_{i=1}^{n} \alpha(t, i)\beta(t, i)}. \quad (5)$$

We can use these values as training targets instead of the standard binary zero-or-one targets with any gradient-based non-linear optimization algorithm. Here, we applied the backpropagation algorithm.

2.3   Garbage Label

Although the above training method may work well for the original phoneme set, Graves et al. introduced a new label (which we will denote by $\mathcal{X}$), by which the neural network may choose not to omit any phoneme. This label can be inserted between any two phonemes, but of course it can also be skipped. They called this label "blank", but we consider the term "garbage" more logical.

To interpret the role of this label, let us consider a standard tri-state model. This divides each phone into three parts. The middle state corresponds to the steady-state part of the given phone, whereas the beginning and end states represent those parts of the phone which are affected by coarticulation with the preceding and the subsequent phones, respectively. By introducing label $\mathcal{X}$, we allow the system to concentrate on the recognition of the cleanly pronounced middle part of a phone, and it can map the coarticulated parts to the symbol $\mathcal{X}$. Therefore, we find it more logical to use the term *garbage label* instead of *blank*, as the latter would suggest that the label $\mathcal{X}$ covers silences, but in fact this label more likely corresponds to the coarticulated parts of phones.

Formally, introducing this label means that instead of the phoneme sequence z we will use the sequence $z' = \mathcal{X}z_1\mathcal{X}z_2\mathcal{X}\ldots\mathcal{X}z_n\mathcal{X}$. The forward-backward algorithm also has to be modified slightly: the initial α values will be set to

$$\alpha(1, u) = \begin{cases} y^1_{z'_1} & \text{if } u = 1 \text{ or } u = 2, \\ 0 & \text{if } u \geq 3, \end{cases} \tag{6}$$

while for the latter labels we allow skipping the $\mathcal{X}$ states:

$$\alpha(t, u) = \begin{cases} y^t_{z'_u}\,\alpha(t-1, u) & \text{if } u = 1, \\ y^t_{z'_u}\big(\alpha(t-1, u) + \alpha(t-1, u-1)\big) & \text{if } z'_u = \mathcal{X}, \\ y^t_{z'_u}\big(\alpha(t-1, u) + \alpha(t-1, u-1) + \alpha(t-1, u-2)\big) & \text{otherwise.} \end{cases} \tag{7}$$

The calculation of the β values is performed in a similar way.

It is also possible to use the garbage label with a tri-state model: then $\mathcal{X}$ is inserted between every state of all the phonemes, while still being optional.

2.4 Decoding

When using Recurrent Neural Networks, it is obvious that we cannot perform a standard Viterbi beam search for decoding. However, when we switch to a standard feed-forward neural network architecture, this constraint vanishes and we can apply any kind of standard decoding method.

The only reason we need to alter the decoding part is that we need to remove the garbage label from the resulting phoneme sequence. Luckily, in other respects it does not affect the strictly-interpreted decoding part. This label also has to be ignored during search when we apply a language model like a phoneme n-gram. In our tests we used our own implementation of the Viterbi algorithm [6].

3 Experiments and Results

3.1 Databases

We tested the CTC training method on three databases. The first was the well-known TIMIT set [7], which is frequently used for evaluating the phoneme recognition accuracy of a new method. Although it is a small dataset by today's standards, a lot of experimental results have been published for it; also, due to its relatively small size, it is ideal for experimentation purposes. We used the standard (core) test set, and withheld a small part of the training set for development purposes. The standard phoneme set consists of 61 phonemes, which is frequently reduced to a set of 39 labels when evaluating; we experimented with training on these 61 phonemes and also on the restricted set of 39 phonemes.

The next database was a Hungarian audiobook; our choice was the collection of short stories by Gyula Krúdy [9] called "The Travels of Szindbád", presented by actor Sándor Gáspár. The total duration of the audiobook was 212 minutes. From the ten short stories, seven were used for training (164 minutes), one for

Table 1. The accuracy scores got for the three different DRN training methods

Database	Method		Dev. set	Test set
TIMIT	Monostate (39)	CTC + DRN	73.31%	**71.40%**
		Hand-labeled	72.74%	70.65%
		Forced Alignment	72.90%	71.08%
	Monostate (61)	CTC + DRN	73.93%	**72.66%**
		Hand-labeled	73.58%	72.06%
		Forced Alignment	74.08%	72.45%
	Tristate (183)	CTC + DRN	76.80%	**75.59%**
		Hand-labeled	77.25%	75.30%
		Forced Alignment	77.22%	75.52%

development (22 minutes) and two for testing (26 minutes) purposes. A part of the Hungarian broadcast news corpus [12] was used as the third database. The speech data of Hungarian broadcast news was collected from eight Hungarian TV channels. The training set was about 5.5 hours long, a small part (1 hour) was used for validation purposes, and a 2-hour part was used for testing.

3.2   Experimental Setup

As the frame-level classifier we utilized Deep Rectifier Neural Networks (DRN) [2,11], which have been shown to achieve state-of-the-art performance on TIMIT [10]. DRN differ from traditional deep neural networks in that they use rectified linear units in the hidden layers; these units differ from standard neurons only in their activation function, where they apply the rectifier function ($\max(0, x)$) instead of the sigmoid or hyperbolic tangent activation. This activation function allows us to build deep networks with many hidden layers without the need for complicated pre-training methods, just by applying standard backpropagation training. Nevertheless, to keep the weights from growing without limit, we have to use some kind of regularization technique; we applied L2 normalization. Our DRN consisted of 5 hidden layers, with 1000 rectifier neurons in each layer. The initial learn rate was set to 0.2 and held fixed while the error on the development set kept decreasing. Afterwards, if the error rate did not decrease for a given iteration, the learn rate was subsequently halved. The learning was accelerated by using a momentum value of 0.9. We used the standard MFCC+Δ+$\Delta\Delta$ feature set, and trained the neural network on 15 neighbouring frames, so the number of inputs to the acoustic model totalled 585.

We did not apply any language model, as we wanted to focus on the acoustic model. Furthermore, due to the presence of the garbage symbol in the phoneme set, including a phoneme n-gram in the dynamic search method is not trivial; of course, we plan to implement this small modification in the near future.

3.3   Results

First we evaluated the CTC training method on the TIMIT database, the results of which can be seen in Table 1. As for this data set a manual segmentation is

Table 2. The accuracy scores got for the two different DRN training methods

Database	Method		Dev. set	Test set
Audiobook	Monostate (52)	CTC + DRN	82.15%	**83.45%**
		Forced Alignment	82.24%	83.02%
	Tristate (156)	CTC + DRN	87.42%	**88.33%**
		Forced Alignment	87.53%	88.04%
Broadcast news	Monostate (52)	CTC + DRN	74.04%	**74.42%**
		Forced Alignment	74.18%	74.36%
	Tristate (156)	CTC + DRN	78.38%	**78.77%**
		Forced Alignment	77.87%	78.26%

also available, the results obtained by training using the manually given boundaries is used as a baseline. As a further comparison, the training was repeated in the usual way, where the training labels are obtained using forced alignment. We found that the results obtained using the hand-labeled set of labels were noticeably worse than the ones we got when we used forced-aligned labels. This reflects the fact that the manually placed phone boundaries are suboptimal compared to the case where the algorithm is allowed to re-align the boundaries according to its needs. The results obtained using tri-state models were always better than those got with monostate ones, on all three databases. Furthermore, the CTC DRN training model consistently outperformed the other two tested training schemes (although sometimes only slightly), when evaluated on the test set. On the development set usually the standard training strategies were better, which can probably be attributed to overfitting.

Training when using CTC was slightly slower than in the baseline cases: calculating the α and β values increased the execution times only by a very small amount, but it took a few more iterations to make the weights converge. On TIMIT, CTC used all training vectors 24-25 times, whereas it was 18-19 in the baseline cases. This is probably due to that CTC strongly relies on the acoustic classifier trained in the previous iteration, so it takes a few iterations before the training starts to converge. We think these values are not high, especially as Graves et al. reported much higher values (frequently over 100) [4].

Another interesting point is that besides the similar accuracy scores, standard backpropagation leads to a relatively high number of phoneme insertions, while when performing CTC it is common to have a lot of deletion errors. The reason is that the correct phonemes are often suppressed by $\mathcal{X}$s, which labels are then deleted from the result before the accuracy score is calculated. This behaviour, however, does not affect the overall quality of the result.

4   Conclusions

In this study we adapted a sequence learning method (which was developed for Recurrent Neural Networks) to a standard HMM/ANN architecture. Compared to standard zero-or-one frame-level backpropagation ANN training we found that networks trained with this sequence learning method always produced higher accuracy scores than the baseline ones. In the future we plan to implement a duration model, incorporate a phoneme bigram as language model, and combine the method with a convolutional network to further improve its performance.

Acknowledgments. This publication is supported by the European Union and co-funded by the European Social Fund. Project title: Telemedicine-oriented research activities in the fields of mathematics, informatics and medical sciences. Project number: TÁMOP-4.2.2.A-11/1/KONV-2012-0073.

References

1. Bourlard, H.A., Morgan, N.: Connectionist Speech Recognition: A Hybrid Approach. Kluwer Academic, Norwell (1993)
2. Glorot, X., Bordes, A., Bengio, Y.: Deep sparse rectifier networks. In: Proceedings of AISTATS, pp. 315–323 (2011)
3. Graves, A.: Supervised Sequence Labelling with Recurrent Neural Networks. SCI, vol. 385. Springer, Heidelberg (2012)
4. Graves, A., Mohamed, A.R., Hinton, G.E.: Speech recognition with Deep Recurrent Neural Networks. In: Proceedings of ICASSP, pp. 6645–6649 (2013)
5. Hinton, G., Deng, L., Yu, D., Dahl, G., Mohamed, A., Jaitly, N., Senior, A., Vanhoucke, V., Nguyen, P., Sainath, T., Kingsbury, B.: Deep Neural Networks for acoustic modeling in Speech Recognition. IEEE Signal Processing Magazine 29(6), 82–97 (2012)
6. Huang, X., Acero, A., Hon, H.W.: Spoken Language Processing. Prentice Hall (2001)
7. Lamel, L., Kassel, R., Seneff, S.: Speech database development: Design and analysis of the acoustic-phonetic corpus. In: DARPA Speech Recognition Workshop, pp. 121–124 (1986)
8. Senior, A., Heigold, G., Bacchiani, M., Liao, H.: GMM-free DNN training. In: Proceedings of ICASSP, pp. 5639–5643 (2014)
9. Tóth, L., Tarján, B., Sárosi, G., Mihajlik, P.: Speech recognition experiments with audiobooks. Acta Cybernetica, 695–713 (2010)
10. Tóth, L.: Convolutional deep rectifier neural nets for phone recognition. In: Proceedings of Interspeech, Lyon, France, pp. 1722–1726 (2013)
11. Tóth, L.: Phone recognition with Deep Sparse Rectifier Neural Networks. In: Proceedings of ICASSP, pp. 6985–6989 (2013)
12. Tóth, L., Grósz, T.: A comparison of deep neural network training methods for large vocabulary speech recognition. In: Proceedings of TSD, pp. 36–43 (2013)
13. Werbos, P.J.: Backpropagation Through Time: what it does and how to do it. Proceedings of the IEEE 78(10), 1550–1560 (1990)

Algorithms for Acceleration of Image Processing at Automatic Registration of Meeting Participants

Alexander Ronzhin[1], Irina Vatamaniuk[2], Andrey Ronzhin[1,3], and Miloš Železný[4]

[1] SPIIRAS, 39, 14th line, St. Petersburg, 199178, Russia
[2] SUAI, 67, Bolshaya Morskaia, St. Petersburg, 199000, Russia
[3] ITMO University, 49 Kronverkskiy av., St. Petersburg, 197101, Russia
[4] University of West Bohemia, Pilsen, Czech Republic
{ronzhinal,vatamaniuk,ronzhin}@iias.spb.su
zelezny@kky.zcu.cz
www.spiiras.nw.ru/speech

Abstract. The aim of the research is to develop the algorithms for acceleration of image processing at automatic registration of meeting participant based on implementation of blurriness estimation and recognition of participants faces procedures. The data captured by the video registration system in the intelligent meeting room are used for calculation variety of person face size in captured image as well as for estimation of face recognition methods. The results shows that LBP method has highest recognition accuracy (79,5%) as well as PCA method has the lowest false alarm rate (1,3%). The implementation of the blur estimation procedure allowed the registration system to exclude 22% photos with insufficient quality, as a result the speed of the whole system were significantly increased.

Keywords: face recognition, intelligent meeting room, rapid image processing, image blur estimation, local binary patterns.

1 Introduction

Currently, there is a wide range of intelligent spaces prototypes (e.g. intelligent meeting rooms [1,2,3]). For developing services of intelligent room the basic information about the room, meeting participants (number of people, their identities, location, etc.) and their interaction should be acquired. For analyzing of acquired data the methods of audio and video signal processing are used: location and tracking [4,5,6], speech recognition [7], estimation of head orientation and face recognition [8], etc. Implementation of such methods provides valuable data that can be used for annotation of meetings, as well as to provide necessary context data to build real-time support services in intelligent room [9]. Such services require identification of meetings participants without any constraints on head-pose, illumination, and other uncontrolled condition [10]. In addition, the face resolution varies and generally is low according to the distance between camera and participant. Such problem may be decided by usage of video data from multiple views, provided by several cameras.

This paper is organized as follows. Section 2 discusses the methods of biometric identification based on face recognition. Section 3 describes the specifics of the

A. Ronzhin et al. (Eds.): SPECOM 2014, LNAI 8773, pp. 89–96, 2014.

developed method of automatic registration of meeting participants. Section 4 presents the experiments, conditions and results.

2   Biometric Identification Methods Based on Face Recognition

The most common biometric identification technologies are fingerprint and retina, voice, signature, face, palm and finger geometry recognition [11]. From commercial point of view the popularity of biometric identification technology is distributed as follows [12]: fingerprint recognition takes the first place, occupying 54% of the market. Second place is taken by hybrid technology (14.4%), where several types of biometric data are simultaneously used for user recognition. Face recognition technology (11.5%) takes third place, further recognition technologies for palm geometry (10%), retinal (7.3%), votes (4.1%), and signature (2.4%), typing rhythm (0.3%) are arranged. First contactless biometric systems were based on the text-dependent methods of speaker determining, superior systems identify the speaker's voice on any phrase with duration sufficient for decision making. In multimodal biometric systems, the analysis of the speaker position, his/her head location, changing the geometry of the face, its brightness and other parameters [12] are estimated.

Face recognition technology is a well compromise between security and convenience for a user, as well as between the security and confidentiality of personal data. In most cases, at face recognition two main steps are carrying out: 1) detecting the position of the user's face in the image with a simple or complex background [13]; 2) analysis of the facial features to identify the user. Detection of the presence and position of a user's face is carried out by analyzing the pixels belong to the foreground (face area) and background of the image [14]. On images, where the background is clean, i.e. uniform and solid, not difficult to detect the area of the face, but when it is composed of several layers, which are attended by other objects, this problem becomes quite complex. Typically, methods based on identifying the key points of the face, such as eyes, nose, lips, or analyzing the color space of the image, as well as methods of using other features of the face are used for detection of a face region. After segmentation of a face region, is necessary to perform normalization of parameters such as size, orientation, brightness and other characteristics. Image normalization is important to identify the key points of the face, relative to which correction of parameters will be performed. Only after the normalization procedure the procedure for calculating features and generation of personality biometric template, which is stored in the database, be performed.

Today, the most common methods of face recognition are the principal component analysis (PCA) [15], the Fisher linear discriminate analysis (LDA) [16] and the local binary patterns (LBP) [17]. The application of the considered methods can improve the efficiency of face recognition in the case of a small number of training samples and in the processing of digital images of large size under a small sample, as well as reduce the dimension of the facial features and improve the speed of image processing.

2.1   Principal Component Analysis

The purpose of face recognition system is the division of the input signals (image files) into several classes (users) [18]. The application of such systems is relevant for a wide range of tasks: images and movies processing, human-computer interaction, identification of criminals, etc. Input signals may contain a lot of noise due to various conditions such as lighting, users pose, their emotions, different hairstyles. However, the input signals are not completely random and even more common features partly present in each incoming signal. Among the common features in input data the following objects can be observed: eyes, mouth, nose, and the relative distances between these objects. Such common features in the fields of research on face recognition are called eigenfaces [15] or principal components. The subspace of eigen features in the image is calculated by the following formula: $\hat{\Phi} = \sum_{i=1}^{M} w_i u_i, (w_i = u_i^\top \Phi)$, where Φ is an input image, $w_i u_i$ are the feature vectors; M is the total amount of images in training database.

After that, the resulting matrix $\hat{\Phi}$ is converted into the eigenvectors of the covariance matrix C corresponding to the original face images:

$$C = \frac{1}{M} \sum_{n=1}^{M} \Phi_n \Phi_n^\top.$$

Further the calculation of the Mahalanobis distance is performed by formula:

$$e^2 = \sum_{i=1}^{M} \frac{1}{\lambda_i} (w_i - w_i^k)^2,$$

where k is a number of used eigenfaces, λ is a scalar of eigenvalues.

After the calculation of e^2 value, its comparison with the pre-selected threshold is performed for the belongingness definition of the analyzed face to users faces, which are added to the training database.

2.2 Fisher Linear Discriminate Analysis

The main idea of LDA is to find such a linear transformation to separate features clusters after transformation [19], which is achieved due to the scattered matrix analysis [20]. This method selects M-class scatter for matrix S_b and S_w between- and within-classes as follows:

$$S_b = \sum_{i=1}^{M} Pr(C_i)(\mu_i - \mu)(\mu_i - \mu)^\top, S_w = \sum_{i=1}^{M} Pr(C_i) \sum i,$$

where $Pr(C_i)$ is a priori probability of class C_i, which takes the value $\frac{1}{M}$ with the assumption of equal priori probabilities; μ - the overall average vector; $\sum i$ average scatter of sample vectors of different classes C_i around their representation in the form of the mean vector μ_i.

Distribution of class features can be calculated using the ratio of the scatter matrices S_b and S_w determinants: $J(A) = \arg\max_A \frac{A S_b A^\top}{A S_w A^\top}$, where A is a matrix with size $m \times n$, where $m \leq n$.

For optimization of the previous formula the approach described in the paper [20] is used, as a result the formula becomes: $S_b A = \lambda S_w A$, where λ is the largest generalized eigenvalues of S_w.

Solution of previous equation is to calculate the inverse matrix S_w, solution of the eigenvalue problem for the matrix $S_w^{(-1)} S_b$ described in [20]. However, this method is numerically unstable since performs a direct appeal to the high dimension matrix of probabilities. In practice, the most commonly used algorithm LDA is based on finding matrix A, which can simultaneously diagonalized matrix S_b and S_w: $A S_w A^\top = I, A S_b A^\top = \Lambda$, where Λ is a diagonal matrix with elements sorted in descending order.

2.3 Local Binary Patterns

One of the first researches dedicated to texture description based on LBP is [21]. The LBP operator describes a pixel 3x3-neighborhood in the binary form. When neighbor's value is greater than the center pixel's one, its labeled "1". Otherwise, its labeled "0". This gives an 8-digit binary number. The LBP is considered uniform pattern, if it contains two or less bitwise transitions from 0 to 1 or vice versa when the bit pattern is traversed circularly. The LBP operator can be extended to use circular neighborhoods of any radius and number of pixels by bilinear interpolation of pixel values.

A histogram of the labeled image $f_l(x, y)$ contains information about the distribution of the local micro patterns, such as edges, spots and flat areas, over the whole image. It can be defined as:

$$H_i = \sum_{x,y} I\{f_l(x, y) = i\}, i = 0, 1, \ldots, n - 1,$$

in which n is a number of different labels produced by the LBP operator, and $I A$ is 1 if A is true and 0 if A is false. For efficient face representation, three different levels of locality are used: a pixel-level (labels for the histogram), a regional level (the labels sum over a small region), and a global description of the face (the regional histograms). For this purpose the image is divided into regions $R_0, R_1, \ldots, R_{(m-1)}$ and the spatially enhanced histogram is defined as:

$$H_{i,j} = \sum_{x,y} I\{f_l(x, y) = i\} I\{(x, y) \in R_j\}, i = 0, 1, \ldots, n - 1, j = 0, 1, \ldots, m - 1.$$

Obviously, some of the regions contain more information, useful for face recognition than others. Taking this into account, each region is assigned a weight depending on the importance of the information it contains. The described methods of face recognition used in conjunction with blur estimation methods in the system of preparation and support of meetings carried out in the smart room speed up the registration process.

3 Automatic Participant Registration System

The developed automatic participant registration system has two algorithms for face capture with different quality. At the first one the rapid procedure of face recognition is used. It based on capture one photo, which includes the view of all participants with low resolution and following face recognition. At this stage the image patches with participant faces has resolution around of 30x30 pixels. The faces unrecognized during the first level of processing further are separately captured by pan-tilt-zoom camera with high resolution at the second algorithm of registration system work. At that the captured face region has resolution higher than 200x200 pixels.

There are two algorithms for image capturing and processing. In the first algorithm a high-resolution image (1280x1024 pixels), which is a group photo of sitting participants in chairs, is processed for finding their faces by face detection procedure [22]:

$$D_{v\_h}^{roi} = \begin{cases} 1, \sum\limits_{n=1}^{N} a_n h_n(I) \geq \frac{1}{2} \sum\limits_{n=1}^{N} a_n, \\ 0, \text{otherwice} \end{cases}$$

where h_n is a set of features $n = 1, 2, \ldots, N$, which are used in the Haar cascades; a_n - features weight coefficient, I - input image.

To reduce image processing time for each chair area (k) with the possible appearance of a participant's face was determined. Due to the fact that chairs have a static position, this procedure is performed once for the selected configuration of the chairs, as follows:

```
{The beginning of the first algorithm}
for(k=0;k < Number_of_Chairs; k++)
    FaceRegion[k] = FaceDetection (area[k]);
    if (FaceRegion[k])
        FaceRecognition(FaceRegion);
        SaveImage(FaceRegion);
    end if
end for
{The beginning of the second algorithm}
for(i=0;i < Number_of_Unregistered_Participants; i++)
    FaceRegion = FaceDetection (InputImage);
    if (FaceRegion)
        blurriness estimation (InputImage(FaceRegion));
{The blurriness estimation procedure executes blurred photos from future processing}
        if (FaceRegion not blurred)
            FaceRecognition(FaceRegion);
            SaveImage(InputImage);
        end if
    end if
end for
```

Each founded region is processed by face recognition function, which identifies all participants with low charge of computational resource and time, because the average size of such region is around of 30x30 pixels. The second algorithm is aimed to identify unregistered participants, which faces haven't been recognized by previous algorithm. The first step of this algorithm is capturing close-up photo of participant with resolution 704x576 pixels. For blur estimation the NIQE (No-Reference Image Quality Assessment) [23] method was implemented. Such blurriness happens when participant moves in photographing moment or may be particularly closed by other participant or if camera, from which algorithm receives image, still haven't focused. If the participant hasn't been identified, then the procedure for registration of new participant is started, where his/her photo is used for focusing attention on the audiovisual speech synthesis system.

Introduction of the blur estimation procedure as preliminary stage of photo processing allows the registration system to exclude 22% photos with high resolution but insufficient quality from face recognition stage, as a result the speed of the whole system were significantly increased. Implementation of the blur estimation procedure on the first level of processing of the photos with resolution around 30x30 pixels did not give positive results, because such low resolution is insufficient to make decision about image blurriness.

4   Experiments

For the experimental evaluation of a method of automatic registration of participants during the events in the intelligent meeting room the accumulation of participants photos was produced only at the first algorithm of the system. As a result, the number of accumulated photos was more than 55,920 for 36 participants. The training database contains 20 photos for each participant. At the preparatory stage of experiments have been decided to determine the threshold for the three face recognition methods: 1) PCA; 2) LDA; 3) LBP. During this experiment threshold was calculated for each participant added to the recognition model, a maximum value of a correct recognition hypothesis for the LBP ranged from 60 to 100, for the PCA from 1656 to 3576, for the LDA from 281 to 858. As a consequence, for the further experiments were selected the minimum threshold value - 60, 1656 and 281, for these methods, respectively. Table 1 presents the average values of face recognition accuracy, as well as first (False Alarm (FA) rate) and second (Miss rate (MR)) type errors for each selected method.

Table 1. Average values of face recognition accuracy, FA and MR

Method	FA, %	MR, %	Accuracy, %
LBPH	12	8,5	79,5
PCA	1,3	23,5	75,2
LDA	19,2	7,8	73

The high value of false positives and miss rate errors was due to the fact that the photos were stored in the course of actual of events, without a prepared scenario and focusing participants on a single object. Hereupon at the time of photographing participants can move freely, according to their face in the photos could be blurred or partially hidden.

For estimation of influence of participants face size change on recognition rate was decided to divide them into several groups. Figure 1a shows distribution of participants by variety difference of their face sizes in ranges from 0 to 10, from 10 to 20, and so on. Most of participants have difference between minimum and maximum face size in range from 30 to 40 pixels. Figure 1b shows distribution of recognition rate for three methods for the groups of participants. From figure 1b it is obvious that with increasing of the

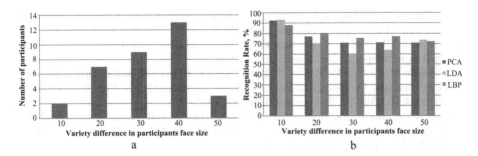

Fig. 1. Distribution of participants and recognition rate by variety difference of their face sizes

participant's face size variety difference the recognition accuracy gradually decreases, this is due to the fact that, at the normalization of images to a uniform size distortion in the certain facial features like eyes, nose, mouth may occur.

Considering the experimental conditions (different distances from the camera to a participant, lighting, movement of participants while taking pictures), influencing on quality and quantity of extracted facial features from the image, which are directly influenced on the accuracy of recognition and occurrence of false positives, we can conclude that the best results are shown by method LBP 79,5%.

5   Conclusion

Development of intelligent meeting rooms, as well as realization meetings support services based on natural and unobstructive method of interaction between users and intelligent space is a relevant subject of research. Application of biometric identification technology based on face recognition methods provides automation of registration processes of meeting participants.

During the research an algorithm for acceleration of image processing at automatic registration of meetings participants personalities based on blurriness estimation and recognition of participants faces. Experimental estimation of the face recognition methods was provided on database with more than 55 thousands photos for 36 participants. During experiments three face recognition methods LBPH, PCA and LDA were compared. The results shows that LBP method has highest recognition accuracy (79,5%) as well as PCA method has the lowest false alarm rate (1,3%).

Acknowledgments. This research is supported by the Scholarship of the President of Russian Federation (Project no. СП-1805.2013.5), Government of the Russian Federation, Grant 074-U01, and European Regional Development Fund (ERDF), project New Technologies for Information Society (NTIS), European Centre of Excellence, ED1.1.00/02.0090.

References

1. Yusupov, R.M., Ronzhin, A.L., Prischepa, M., Ronzhin, A.L.: Models and Hardware-Software Solutions for Automatic Control of Intelligent Hall. ARC 72(7), 1389–1397 (2011)

2. Aldrich, F.: Smart Homes: Past, Present and Future. In: Harper, R. (ed.) Inside the Smart Home, pp. 17–39. Springer, London (2003)
3. Nakashima, H., Aghajan, H.K., Augusto, J.C.: Handbook of Ambient Intelligence and Smart Environments. Springer, Heidelberg (2010)
4. Calonder, M., Lepetit, V., Strecha, C., Fua, P.: BRIEF: Binary Robust Independent Elementary Features. In: Daniilidis, K., Maragos, P., Paragios, N. (eds.) ECCV 2010, Part IV. LNCS, vol. 6314, pp. 778–792. Springer, Heidelberg (2010)
5. Ronzhin, A., Budkov, V.: Speaker Turn Detection Based on Multimodal Situation Analysis. In: Železný, M., Habernal, I., Ronzhin, A. (eds.) SPECOM 2013. LNCS (LNAI), vol. 8113, pp. 302–309. Springer, Heidelberg (2013)
6. Zhang, C., Yin, P., et al.: Boosting-Based Multimodal Speaker Detection for Distributed Meeting Videos. IEEE Transactions on Multimedia 10(8), 1541–1552 (2008)
7. Karpov, A., Markov, K., Kipyatkova, I., Vazhenina, D., Ronzhin, A.: Large vocabulary Russian speech recognition using syntactico-statistical language modeling. Speech Communication 56, 213–228 (2014)
8. Ekenel, H.K., Fischer, M., Jin, Q., Stiefelhagen, R.: Multi-modal Person Identification in a Smart Environment. In: Proc. of CVPR 2007, pp. 1–8 (2007)
9. Stiefelhagen, R., Bernardin, K., Ekenel, H.K., McDonough, J., Nickel, K., Voit, M., Wlfel, M.: Audio-Visual Perception of a Lecturer in a Smart Seminar Room. Signal Processing 86(12), 3518–3533 (2006)
10. Ekenel, H.K., Fischer, M., Stiefelhagen, R.: Face Recognition in Smart Rooms. In: Popescu-Belis, A., Renals, S., Bourlard, H. (eds.) MLMI 2007. LNCS, vol. 4892, pp. 120–131. Springer, Heidelberg (2008)
11. Schneiderman, H., Kanade, T.: Object detection using the statistic of parts. International Journal of Computer Vision 56(3), 151–177 (2004)
12. Abate, A.F., Nappi, M., Riccio, D., Sabatino, G.: 2D and 3D face recognition: A survey. Pattern Recognition Letters 28(14), 1885–1906 (2007)
13. Gorodnichy, M.D.: Video-Based Framework for Face Recognition in Video. In: Proc. CRV 2005, pp. 330–338 (2005)
14. Castrillón-Santana, M., Déniz-Suárez, O., Guerra-Artal, C., Hernández-Tejera, M.: Real-time Detection of Faces in Video Streams. In: Proc. of CRV 2005, pp. 298–305 (2005)
15. Turk, M.A., Pentland, A.P.: Face recognition using eigenfaces. In: Proc. of IEEE CVPR, pp. 586–591 (1991)
16. Belhumeur, P.N., Hespanha, J., Kriegman, D.: Eigenfaces vs. Fisherfaces: Recognition Using Class Specific Linear Projection. TPAMI 19(7), 711–720 (1997)
17. Ahonen, T., Hadid, A., Pietikäinen, M.: Face Recognition with Local Binary Patterns. In: Pajdla, T., Matas, J(G.) (eds.) ECCV 2004. LNCS, vol. 3021, pp. 469–481. Springer, Heidelberg (2004)
18. Georgescu, D.: A Real-Time Face Recognition System Using Eigenfaces. Journal of Mobile, Embedded and Distributed Systems 3(4), 193–204 (2011)
19. Yang, J., Yu, Y., Kunz, W.: An Efficient LDA Algorithm for Face Recognition. In: The Proc. Sixth Int. Conf. Control, Automation, Robotics and Vision (2000)
20. Fukunaga, K.: Introduction to Statistical Pattern Recognition, 2nd edn. Academic Press, New York (1990)
21. Ojala, T., Pietikainen, M., Maenpaa, T.: Multiresolution gray-scale and rotation invariant texture classification with local binary patterns. TPAMI 24, 971–987 (2002)
22. Viola, P., Jones, M., Snow, D.: Detecting pedestrians using patterns of motion and appearance. In: Proc. of IEEE ICCV, pp. 734–741 (2003)
23. Mittal, A., Soundarajan, R., Bovik, A.C.: Making a 'Completely Blind' Image Quality Analyzer. IEEE Signal Processing Letters 20(3), 209–212 (2013)

Analysis and Synthesis of Glottalization Phenomena in German-Accented English

Ivan Kraljevski[1], Maria Paola Bissiri[2], Guntram Strecha[2], and Rüdiger Hoffmann[2]

[1] VoiceINTERConnect GmbH, Dresden, Germany
[2] TU Dresden, Chair for System Theory and Speech Technology, Dresden, Germany
ivan.kraljevski@voiceinterconnect.de
{maria_paola.bissiri,guntram.strecha,
ruediger.hoffmann}@tu-dresden.de

Abstract. The present paper investigates the analysis and synthesis of glottalization phenomena in German-accented English. Word-initial glottalization was manually annotated in a subset of a German-accented English speech corpus. For each glottalized segment, time-normalized F0 and log-energy contours were produced and principal component analysis was performed on the contour sets in order to reduce their dimensionality. Centroid contours of the PC clusters were used for contour reconstruction in the resynthesis experiments. The prototype intonation and intensity contours were superimposed over non-glottalized word-initial vowels in order to resynthesize creaky voice. This procedure allows the automatic creation of speech stimuli which could be used in perceptual experiments for basic research on glottalizations.

Keywords: glottalization, speech perception, speech synthesis.

1 Introduction

In the present paper glottalization is employed as a cover term, defining two major speech phenomena: glottal stops and creaky voice. Glottal stops are produced by closing and abruptly opening the vocal folds. Creaky voice is a more frequent and perceptually equivalent phenomenon, consisting in irregular and low frequency vocal fold vibrations.

In some languages, such as Arabic, glottalizations can be phonemic, i.e. they can differentiate word meaning. This is not the case in German and in English, however in both languages glottalizations are relevant for speech communication. In German, glottalizations are very frequent at word-initial and morpheme-initial vowels [1,2], and are therefore relevant indicators of word and morpheme boundaries. In English glottalization of word-initial vowels is less frequent and more likely to occur at phrase boundaries and pitch accented syllables [3]. German learners of English could transfer their word-linking habit of frequent word-initial glottalization to their English productions, which might therefore sound jerking and overemphasizing to English native speakers [4].

The automatic analysis of glottalizations is seldom carried out [5] because large annotated speech databases and suitable algorithms are rarely available. Acoustic modeling of glottalization can improve Automatic Speech Recognition (ASR) performance [6] since glottalizations can be good cues to word boundaries. Regarding speech synthesis, glottalization modeling is considered useful in order to improve naturalness [5].

A. Ronzhin et al. (Eds.): SPECOM 2014, LNAI 8773, pp. 97–104, 2014.

Furthermore, given the different occurrences and linguistic functions of glottalizations in different languages, their appropriate realization in synthesized speech is desirable.

Inserting a sudden drop in F0 in the target vowel is sufficient to elicit the perception of glottalization [7], however, in order to synthesize glottalizations, it is preferable to manipulate also spectral tilt and the duration of the glottal pulses. HMM-based speech synthesis has been employed also for creaky voice. Csapó and Németh [8] used a synthesis model with three heuristics: pitch halving, pitch-synchronous residual modulation with periods multiplied by random scaling factors and spectral distortion. Raitio et al. [9] presented a fully automatic HMM-based system for synthesis of creaky voice.

In the present paper, pitch and intensity analysis was performed on word-initial glottalizations in a German-accented English corpus, and Principal Component Analysis (PCA) was employed to reduce the dimensionality of the analyzed intonation contours. The component vectors were classified into clusters as glottal stops and creaky voice. The cluster centroids were estimated and used for F0 and log-energy contours reconstruction. The intonational and intensity contours of glottalizations were superimposed on natural unglottalized speech and the acoustic characteristics of the resulting resynthesized speech were evaluated by means of informal listening tests and comparison of voice quality measures.

2 Acoustic Characteristics of Creaky Voice

Glottal stops are characterized by the closure of the glottal folds, visible as a silent phase in the spectrogram, followed by its abrupt opening, after which some irregular vocal fold vibrations at the onset of the following sound can appear.

Creaky voice is a mode of vibration of the vocal folds, in which they are more addicted together. This mode of vibration can affect some more adjacent segments or just part of them, e.g. a single vowel can be realized as partly creaky and partly modal voiced. Creaky voice does not significantly affect the formants of a sound, its more typical characteristics are low F0, reduced intensity and also increased period to period irregularities.

Automatic F0 and intensity measures are not always reliable indicators of creaky voice. F0 detection algorithms are well known to fail in creaky stretches of speech, and intensity can vary for other reasons besides voice quality, e.g. recording conditions or speaker's loudness level. The specific spectral structure of creaky voice can be more useful to detect it than F0 and intensity [6].

For instance, spectral tilt, i.e. "the degree to which intensity drops off as frequency increases" [10], is reported to be more steeply positive for creaky than for modal phonation. Accordingly, in creaky voice the amplitude of the second harmonic (H2) has been found to be higher than the amplitude of the first harmonic (H1) [11].

3 Speech Database

The speech database employed in the present investigation consists in BBC news bulletins read by 4 male and 3 female German native speakers, studio recorded with 44.1 KHz resolution and then downsampled to 16 kHz and 16 bit. It has a total duration of

3 hours and 13 minutes and is composed of 418 recorded sequences. In 102 of them, about 38 minutes of speech, glottalization of word-initial vowels was manually labeled by an expert phonetician (the second author).

The following categories were labeled: absence of glottalization (0), glottal stop (G), creaky voice (CR), breathy voice (H) and sudden drop in F0 (L). Since a glottal closure can be followed by a longer stretch of creaky vowel, the criterion for labeling as glottal stop was that the closure should have a duration of at least 2/3 of the whole glottalization. If the closure was shorter, the segment was categorized as creaky voice.

4   Pitch and Intensity Analysis

In the present investigation, the approach by [12] was employed to analyze pitch in the speech corpus. It is a hybrid pitch marking method that combines outputs of two different speech signal based pitch marking algorithms (PMA) where the pitch marks are combined and represented by Finite State Machine (FSM).

The most accurate pitch marks, those with the highest confidence score, are chosen in the selection stage. The pitch marking was performed for each utterance in the BBC corpus and the results were stored for further analysis.

Mel-cepstral analysis was performed with a frame rate of 5 ms and frame duration of 45 ms, with Blackman window applied, and the frequency band up to 16 KHz with 40 Mel DFT filters. The logarithm of the energy were calculated at each channel output. The zero coefficients presented the log of energy of the analyzed frame and were stored as intensity contours for each utterance for further statistical analysis.

In order to eliminate the speaker dependent variations in F0, energy and segment duration, time normalization was performed on F0 and log-energy contours of the glottalized segments in the BBC corpus. For each glottalization label, the linear time normalization was performed by producing a relative duration expressed as the percentage of the label length (100 samples). Cubic spline interpolation was used in the normalization by smoothing first and second derivatives throughout the curve. Subsequently, the observed maximum was subtracted from the linear time normalized contours. For the speech data employed, the predicted F0 value domain was set between 0-400 Hz. The F0 analysis algorithm also produced negative values indicating unvoiced frames, which were treated as absence of F0 and equaled to 0.

In this way, the mean F0 and log-energy values and their variation over the duration of each glottalized segment can be observed in Tab. 1. This analysis procedure allows the easy manipulation and generation of F0 and intensity contours for the resynthesis of glottalization phenomena.

5   Principal Component Analysis

Principal Component Analysis (PCA) as an orthonormal transformation is widely used in multivariate data analysis for dimension reduction and decorrelation. PCA is carried out to capture most of the variation between the contours using a smaller number of new variables (principal components), where each of these components represents a linear combination of the contour parameters.

Table 1. Mean and standard deviation of F0, intensity and segment duration for word-initial creaky voice (CR), glottal stops (G) and non-glottalized vowels (0)

	F0 in Hz	Intensity in dB	Duration in ms.
label counts	mean (sd)	mean (sd)	mean (sd)
CR 572	124.62 (63.48)	7.23 (0.65)	80 (31)
G 307	26.76 (25.56)	6.15 (0.72)	90 (31)
0 174	157.30 (52.48)	7.30 (0.60)	58 (19)

The number of components that should be retained is chosen according to the criterion of minimal total variance. After performing PCA on the contour set, it was observed that in both cases retaining the first 5 components is enough to cover more of 90% of the variation (for F0, 90.35% and for the log-energy 98.42%).

Figure 1 presents the relationship between the first two components. Glottalization phenomena – creaky voice, glottal stop and absence of glottalization – are clearly distinguished even by employing only the first two components.

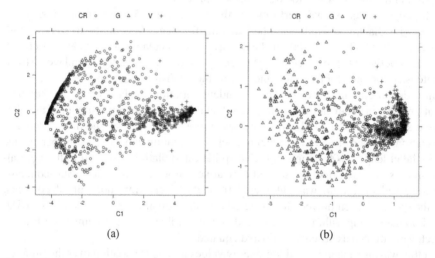

Fig. 1. PC1 vs PC2 for F0 (a) and log-Energy (b) for creaky voice (CR), glottal stops (G) and non-glottalized vowels (V)

6   Synthesis of Glottalization Phenomena

Besides PCA analysis, non-parametrical statistical tests were performed over the F0 and log-energy data sets confirming the existence of distinctive contour features between the observed glottalization phenomena. The analysis of non-glottalized word-initial vowels was included to provide comparison of the acoustic features in the annotated segments. On Fig. 2, the F0 and intensity typical contours are presented.

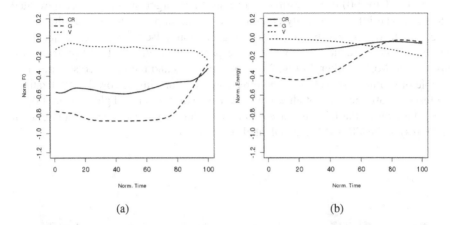

(a)   (b)

Fig. 2. F0 (a) and intensity (b) typical contours for creaky voice (CR), glottal stops (G) and non-glottalized word-initial vowels (V) used for the synthesis experiments

They are reconstructed using the centroid vectors obtained by means of the supervised clustering procedure of the PCA components. The representative vectors of the first five principal components were multiplied with the transposed transformation matrix. It can be seen that the prototype contours express the distinctive features of the glottalization phenomena.

For example, glottal closures larger than 2/3 of the segment duration are a characteristic of the G labels (glottal stops), thus producing a large relative intensity drop in the G prototype contour. In the case of CR, the pitch halving effect with small F0 variation is noticeable, while the intensity reduction is relatively small and constant. For the non-glottalized vowel, F0 and intensity are constant over the whole segment except in the vicinity of the 10% duration from the boundaries, as a result of the consistency in the manual labeling procedure.

Our main motivation to resynthesize glottalization phenomena was to automatically generate stimuli for perception experiments on glottalizations. By means of resynthesis it should be possible to create stimuli that differ only because of the presence or absence of glottalization and are identical in any other aspect. Resynthesis experiments were conducted on short speech segments from the BBC corpus. The F0 and intensity contours were superimposed on a part of an utterance selected from the BBC corpus.

The pitch analysis was performed using the hybrid method described in Sec. 4 with 10 ms shift and 45 ms frame width, and the maximal log-energy value was estimated on the right boundary of the word-initial vowel. Furthermore, in order to increase naturalness, jitter and shimmer were increased by randomly varying timing and amplitude in the synthetic contours according to the following equation:

$$y(n) = x(n) + (-1)^n \cdot a \cdot b(n) \cdot Rand(n), n = 1, ..N. \tag{1}$$

Where $x(n)$ is the value for the frame n of the prototype contour, $b(n)$ is the corresponding value of the standard deviation for a sample and $Rand(n)$ is a random number generated from a normal distribution. The intensity was modulated by random values up to $a=0.1$ (1 for F0) of the normalized value, since larger ones introduce unwanted distortions. The F0 and intensity contours were superimposed and the resulting synthetic speech was created by generating an excitation pulse train (lower frequencies) and noise (higher frequencies), which were passed through Mel Log Spectrum Approximation (MLSA) filter. In Fig. 3, the spectrograms and the averaged spectra of an example of synthetic speech with the three cases of word-initial vowel glottalizations are presented: absence of glottalization (0), creaky voice (CR), and glottal stop (G).

The duration of the label is chosen to corresponds to the estimated mean duration (80–90 ms) of the CR and G manual labels in the corpus.

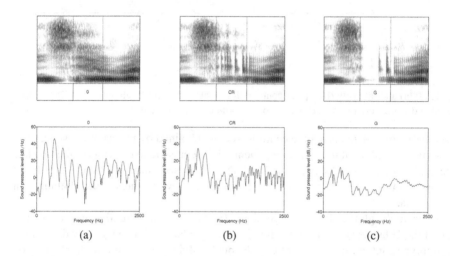

Fig. 3. Spectrograms (top) and averaged spectra (bottom) of a speech segment synthesized in three versions: with word-initial (a) non-glottalized vowel (0), (b) creaky voice (CR), and (c) glottal stop (G).

The synthesized creaky voice exhibits acoustic characteristics typical for natural creaky voice: lower energy as well as steeper spectral slope (H2-H1) than modal voice; irregular periods are also visible in the spectrogram. The synthetic glottal stop shows very low energy in its first part and a couple of irregular glottal pulses in its second part, as it occurs in natural glottal stops.

In order to support the observations from the inspection of the spectrogram, voice quality analysis was conducted using Praat. Jitter, shimmer, mean harmonics-to-noise ratio (MHNR), H1 and H2 were measured in the original non-glottalized signal, and in the corresponding synthetic signals with non-glottalized vowel, creaky voice and glottal stop (see Tab. 2). The original non-glottalized segment has increased jitter (3.2%) compared to the synthetic non-glottalized segment which indicates that the vowel in this case is produced with lower quality. The reason is the influence of the the preceding consonant, which was reduced after the resynthesis. Moreover, for accurate measurements of vowel quality parameters, it is recommended to analyze longer vowel segments.

The non-glottalized synthetic segment, thus without F0 and intensity modification, introduces lower jitter, increased shimmer and equal MHNR ratio compared to the original one. The synthetic CR has much lower values for HNR and increased shimmer,

Table 2. Voice quality analysis for the original non-glottalized vowel and for the three corresponding synthetic signals: non-glottalized vowel, creaky voice and glottal stop

	Jitter (%)	Shimmer (%)	MHNR (dB)	H2-H1 (dB)
Original (non-synthetic)	3.2	6.9	11.8	1.5
Non-glottalized vowel (0)	2.3	10.4	11.8	4
Creaky voice (CR)	2.9	21.3	6.1	7.4
Glottal stop (G)	1.1	18.2	5.8	2

which applies to the G segment as well. Informal listening tests also indicated that the synthetic glottal stops and creaky voiced vowels were easy to identify as such and sounded similar to natural ones.

The approach proposed in the present paper can effectively manipulate stretches of modal voice transforming them into glottalizations. It is just necessary to define the start and end points of the segments that need to be glottalized. These should be long enough – e.g. around 80 ms, the mean duration of G and CR labels in the corpus (see pag. 102) – otherwise too much downsampling of the F0 and intensity prototype contours would not deliver a good synthesis. This is especially valid for the synthesis of glottal stops since the glottal closure cannot be realized properly if the segment is too short. For segments of sufficient length the manipulation delivers good quality glottalizations without artifacts.

By informally comparing manipulated utterances with and without glottalization, the impression is often that the glottalization inserts a stronger phrase boundary or emphasizes the target word, as it occurs with natural glottalizations in English. The proposed method can thus create speech stimuli suitable for investigating the influence of glottalizations on speech perception.

7   Conclusions

In the present paper the analysis and synthesis of glottalization phenomena in German-accented English are presented. Glottalizations of word-initial vowels were manually annotated by a human expert in a small part of a German-accented English speech corpus. Pitch and intensity analysis were performed on the annotated subset of the corpus, and for each word-initial segment, labeled as glottal stop, creaky voice or non-glottalized vowel, time normalized F0 and intensity contours were produced. The contours describe the relative variation compared to the maximal observed values in the segment. Multivariate statistical analysis was performed on the contour data sets in order to find the principal components and to reduce the contour dimensionality (from 100 to 5). Clustering analysis of the PCs gave the centroid contours which were used in the resynthesis experiments. The prototype contours were modulated with random values in order to simulate the effects of jitter and shimmer. Such F0 and log-energy contours were superimposed on natural non-glottalized word-initial vowels chosen from the corpus. Qualitative analysis (spectrum observations and informal listening tests) as well as quantitative analysis (voice quality measurements) indicated that the synthetic utterances indeed possess the desired glottalization phenomena characteristics. This procedure could be employed for the automatic generation of speech stimuli for perceptual experiments on glottalizations.

References

1. Kohler, K.J.: Glottal stops and glottalization in German. Data and theory of connected speech processes. Phonetica 51, 38–51 (1994)
2. Kiessling, A., Kompe, R., Niemann, H., Nöth, E., Batliner, A.: Voice source state as a source of information in speech recognition: detection of laryngealizations. In: Speech Recognition and Coding. New Advances and Trends, pp. 329–332. Springer, Berlin (1995)
3. Dilley, L., Shattuck-Hufnagel, S., Ostendorf, M.: Glottalization of word-initial vowels as a function of prosodic structure. Journal of Phonetics 24, 423–444 (1996)
4. Bissiri, M.P.: Glottalizations in German-accented English in relationship to phrase boundaries. In: Mehnert, D., Kordon, U., Wolff, M. (eds.) Systemtheorie Signalverarbeitung Sprachtechnologie, pp. 234–240. TUD Press, Dresden (2013)
5. Drugman, T., Kane, J., Gobl, C.: Modeling the creaky excitation for parametric speech synthesis. In: Proc. of Interspeech, Portland, Oregon, pp. 1424–1427 (2012)
6. Yoon, T.-J., Zhuang, X., Cole, J., Hasegawa-Johnson, M.: Voice quality dependent speech recognition. In: Proc. of Int. Symp. on Linguistic Patterns in Spontaneous Speech, Taipei, Taiwan (2006)
7. Pierrehumbert, J.B., Frisch, S.: Synthesizing allophonic glottalization. In: Progress in Speech Synthesis, pp. 9–26. Springer, New York (1997)
8. Csapó, T.G., Németh, G.: A novel irregular voice model for HMM-based speech synthesis. In: Proc. ISCA SSW8, pp. 229–234 (2013)
9. Raitio, T., Kane, J., Drugman, T., Gobl, C.: HMM-based synthesis of creaky voice. In: Proc. Interspeech, pp. 2316–2320 (2013)
10. Gordon, M., Ladefoged, P.: Phonation types: A cross-linguistic overview. Journal of Phonetics 29(4), 383–406 (2001)
11. Ni Chasaide, A., Gobl, C.: Voice source variation. In: Hardcastle, W.J., Laver, J. (eds.) The Handbook of Phonetic Sciences, pp. 427–461. Blackwell, Oxford (1997)
12. Hussein, H., Wolff, M., Jokisch, O., Duckhorn, F., Strecha, G., Hoffmann, R.: A hybrid speech signal based algorithm for pitch marking using finite state machines. In: INTERSPEECH, pp. 135–138 (2008)

Annotation and Personality: Individual Differences in Sentence Boundary Detection

Anton Stepikhov[1] and Anastassia Loukina[2]

[1] Department of Russian, St. Petersburg State University,
11 Universitetskaya emb., 199034 St. Petersburg, Russia
`a.stepikhov@spbu.ru`
[2] Educational Testing Service,
660 Rosedale Rd, MS 11-R, Princeton, NJ 08541, USA
`aloukina@ets.org`

Abstract. The paper investigates the relationships between personality traits and expert manual annotation of unscripted speech. The analysis is based on the results of a psycholinguistic experiment in which the participants were asked to annotate sentence boundaries in transcriptions of Russian spoken monologues. Personality traits were measured using the Eysenck Personality Inventory and the Five Factor Personality Questionnaire. A multiple regression model showed that the traits measured by the Five Factor Personality Questionnaire along the scales 'unemotionality vs. emotionality' and 'practicality vs. playfulness' had significant effect on the average sentence length.

Keywords: sentence boundary detection, spontaneous speech, manual annotation, Russian, personality, five factor personality model, big five, Eysenck personality inventory.

1 Introduction

Expert manual annotation is usually considered to be the gold standard for sentence boundary detection in unscripted speech. These boundaries are crucial for natural language processing since a range of automatic procedures are based on this information. Nonetheless the extent of inter-annotator agreement may vary significantly [1,2,3]. For example, we earlier showed considerable disagreement in the number of boundaries and average length of sentences marked by expert annotators in Russian spontaneous speech [3]. In the present paper we explore the role of individual differences between annotators in the inter-annotator agreement.

Previous work sometimes sought to establish strict definition of a unit of segmentation as a way to increase inter-annotator agreement (cf. [4]). On the contrary, our basic assumption in this study is that sentence boundaries are inherently ambiguous and vary between speakers. This is illustrated by Russian written texts which allow substantial variability in placement of sentence boundaries. While several syntactically independent sentences may be combined into one by a semicolon or just a comma, main and subordinate clauses of the same sentence may be segmented as separate sentences. In some cases, a sentence boundary may even be placed between two syntactic

A. Ronzhin et al. (Eds.): SPECOM 2014, LNAI 8773, pp. 105–112, 2014.

constituents governed by the same head. Therefore sentence length in a written text is significantly determined by the author's individuality. We suggest that similar variability is also likely in spoken monologues and especially in expert annotations of sentence boundaries in speech since the latter can be seen as a transformation of an oral text into a written one.

Previous studies have looked into how the inter-annotator agreement may be affected by the choice of material. For example, when studying the effect of social characteristics of speaker and type of text we found higher inter-annotator agreement for texts produced by female speakers than for texts produced by male speakers and also higher agreement for more structured texts such as story telling than for descriptive texts [3].

In this paper we investigate whether the preference for different sentence length observed in previous studies may be related to the presence of different personality traits such as extraversion or neuroticism. We use two personality questionnaires to evaluate such traits: the Eysenck Personality Inventory (EPI) [5] adopted and validated for Russian by [6] and the Five Factor Personality Questionnaire, or the Big Five (FFPQ) [7] adopted and validated for Russian by [8].

We use linear regression to evaluate whether variation in sentence lengths between the annotators can partially be explained by differences in personality as measured by two personality questionnaires. The results of the analysis may be of a special interest for oral speech researchers, psycholinguists and those involved in development and adjustment of automatic sentence boundary detection models.

2   Experimental Design and Data Collection

2.1   Data

The study is based on expert manual annotation of spontaneous monologues. We used three texts taken from the corpus of transcribed spontaneous Russian monologues described in [2]. This corpus contains manual transcriptions of different types of monologues recorded by 32 native speakers of Russian. Each speaker was presented with several tasks: (1) to read a story with a plot and subsequently retell it from memory ('story'), (2) to read a descriptive narrative without a plot and retell it from memory ('description'), (3) to describe a series of pictures in a cartoon ('picture story'), (4) to describe a landscape painting ('picture description') , and finally (5) to comment on one of the suggested topics ('free comment'). All speakers were well acquainted with the person making the recording and used natural conversational style. All recordings were done in Russia.

For this study we selected 3 monologues from this corpus produced by the same male speaker. This speaker had a higher education and was 40 years old at the time of the recording. Since expert manual annotation depends on text genre [3] we included the monologues which covered three different tasks: "Description" (162 words), "Story" (225 words) and "Free comment" (312 words).

2.2   Participants

Fifty native speakers of Russian (9 male and 41 female) took part in the experiment. All participants were students or professors in linguistics and/or modern languages with a background in linguistics. The age of participants varied between 18 and 68 with a median age of 24. Forty nine participants were right-handed.

2.3 Personality Questionnaires

The participants were first asked to complete two personality questionnaires.

Eysenck Personality Inventory (EPI) consists of 57 yes/no questions and the results are interpreted along two scales: introversion vs. extraversion and stability vs. neuroticism. Each scale ranges from 0 to 24. There is also a separate lie-scale designed to identify participants who are being insincere and exclude them from the data.

Five Factor Personality Questionnaire (FFPQ) includes 75 items with five-level Likert scale (from -2 to 2 including 0). Each item has two opposite statements, and a respondent has to choose the closest score on the scale to one or another statement. The results of FFPQ are interpreted along five scales corresponding to five super-trait factors to describe personality: 1) introversion vs. extraversion, 2) separateness vs. attachment, 3) naturality vs. controlling, 4) unemotionality vs. emotionality, and 5) practicality vs. playfulness.[1] Each scale ranges from 15 to 75. Both questionnaires were administered on paper.

2.4 Sentence Boundary Annotation

After completing the questionnaires, the participants were given orthographic transcriptions of the 3 recordings described in Section 2.1 and asked to mark the sentence boundaries using conventional full stops or any other symbol of their choice (e.g. a slash). The participants did not have access to actual recordings and were asked to provide annotations based on text only. In addition, the transcriptions did not contain any punctuation or any other information that could indicate prosodic information such as graphic symbols of hesitation or filled pauses (like *eh, uhm*) or other comments (e.g. *[sigh], [laughter]*). Thus, we tried to focus on semantic and syntactic factors in boundary detection (see [2] for further discussion about the relative role of prosodic and semantic factors for this task). The experts were presumed to have a native intuition of what a sentence is and, thus, it was left undefined. There were no time-constraints.

In addition to the three main texts, the participants were also asked to annotate sentence boundaries in a control text included to make sure that the participants understood the task correctly. For this control task we selected a short written story (371 words) which had relatively simple syntax and almost unambiguous sentence boundaries. This text was processed in the same way as other monologues to remove punctuation and capitalisation and presented along with other texts.

3 Data Analysis and Results

We first computed scores for each scale of the two personality inventories giving us 7 personality scores per each participant. We also computed an average sentence length

---

[1] We follow [7] for factor names since this version of FFPQ was used as the basis for the Russian version.

in each text for every annotator. We then used multiple linear regression analysis to evaluate the effect of personality traits on average sentence length.

3.1 Inter-annotator Agreement in Control Text and Main Corpus

We first compared the inter-annotator agreement in the control text and spoken monologues. We used the method suggested in [2] to compute boundary confidence scores (BCS) for each boundary. This score reflects how many annotators agreed on the presence of a boundary at a particular location. Then the number of BCS with acceptable (60-100%) or low (less than 60%) agreement for each text was calculated.

We found that the number of positions with acceptable agreement was 2.5 times higher in the control text (60.4% of all boundaries marked by experts) than in spoken monologues (24.7% of all boundaries). Since this result was what we had expected, we concluded that all participants understood the task correctly and followed the same pattern while performing the annotation.

3.2 Descriptive Analysis of the Main Corpus

Table 1 shows the descriptive statistics for all personality traits as well as sentence length across different texts.

Table 1. Summary statistics of the acquired data ($N = 50$)

Personality scores					
Inventory	Scale	Mean	SD	Min	Max
EPI	introversion vs. extraversion	12.86	4.46	5.00	21.00
EPI	stability vs. neuroticism	14.74	4.22	5.00	22.00
FFPQ	introversion vs. extraversion	49.00	9.01	27.00	70.00
FFPQ	separateness vs. attachment	52.50	10.06	25.00	67.00
FFPQ	naturality vs. controlling	52.28	9.70	27.00	74.00
FFPQ	unemotionality vs. emotionality	53.22	10.41	22.00	70.00
FFPQ	practicality vs. playfulness	56.82	7.80	39.00	74.00
Average sentence length in different texts					
	Description	15.96	2.88	10.80	23.14
	Story	15.12	3.27	9.78	25.00
	Free comment	15.69	4.19	6.93	26.00
	Control text	14.20	2.08	10.91	21.82

The values of both scales of EPI (introversion vs. extraversion scale and stability vs. neuroticism scale) were highly correlated with the values of two corresponding scales of FFPQ – introversion vs. extraversion scale (Pearson's $r = 0.78$, $p < 0.01$[2]) and unemotionality vs. emotionality scale (Pearson's $r = 0.7$, $p < 0.01$). This shows that these two scales measure the same traits within each of the inventories. There were no correlations significant at $\alpha = 0.01$ between other traits in these questionnaires.

---

[2] All p–values in this section are adjusted for multiple comparison using Bonferroni correction.

Average sentence length across speakers varied between 7 and 26 words with an average length of about 15 words. We also observed correlations between average sentence length across different texts for the same annotator (r varied between 0.44 and 0.62, $p < 0.01$).

3.3 Multiple Regression Models

We first used multiple linear regression to model whether variability in sentence length can be explained by two personality traits measured by EPI. We used the sum of the mean values of sentence length in description, story and free comment as a response variable. This approach allowed us to estimate the effect of personality traits across texts of different types.

Upon building and examining this model, we found that the fit was unduly affected by two influential cases (Cook's $D > 4/50$). We removed these from the data. All further analyses were performed using only the data from the remaining 48 annotators.

The model based on EPI scales did not show any statistically significant association between personality traits and annotation results: multiple $R^2 = 0.006$, adjusted $R^2 = -0.04$, $F_{(2,45)} = 0.15$, $p = 0.87$ (see also Table 2).

Table 2. Raw (B) and standardised (β) coefficients, and p-values of EPI scales in a multiple regression model ($N = 48$)

Independent variable	B	Standardised β	p-value
introversion vs. extraversion	0.14	0.08	0.60
stability vs. neuroticism	0.02	0.01	0.95

In contrast, multiple linear regression built using five FFPQ scales' scores as independent variables showed significant effect of personality traits on sentence length (multiple $R^2 = 0.24$, adjusted $R^2 = 0.15$, $F_{(5,42)} = 2.61$, $p = 0.04$). Estimated β and p-values for the independent variables are given in Table 3.

Table 3. Raw (B) and standardised (β) coefficients, and p-values of FFPQ scales in a multiple regression model ($N = 48$)

Independent variable	B	Standardised β	p-value
introversion vs. extraversion	0.14	-0.03	0.84
separateness vs. attachment	0.13	0.15	0.30
naturality vs. controlling	0.00	0.02	0.92
unemotionality vs. emotionality	-0.28	-0.39	0.01*
practicality vs. playfulness	0.42	0.46	0.01*

We then modified our model excluding three insignificant variables from it. After transformation the new model achieved multiple $R^2 = 0.21$, adjusted $R^2 = 0.18$, $F_{(2,45)} = 6.05$ and $p = 0.005$ (see also Table 4). Analysis of deviance of the first and

Table 4. Raw (B) and standardised (β) coefficients, and p-values of two FFPQ scales in the modified multiple regression model ($N = 48$)

Independent variable	B	Standardised β	p-value
unemotionality vs. emotionality	-0.28	-0.39	0.01
practicality vs. playfulness	0.44	0.45	0.003

the modified models revealed that goodness of fit did not change after transformation ($p = 0.7$).

Finally, we fitted the same models to the control written text. None of the models achieved statistical significance. The model based on 'unemotionality vs. emotionality' and 'practicality vs. playfulness', which was the best performing model on spoken monologues, showed the following performance on the control text: multiple $R^2 = 0.10$, adjusted $R^2 = 0.065$, $F_{(2,45)} = 0.26$ and $p = 0.08$.

4   Discussion and Conclusions

We have examined the relationship between expert manual annotation of sentence boundaries in unscripted speech and expert personality. We found that, in agreement with previously reported results [2], the annotators differed in average sentence length. At the same time, there was a significant correlation between mean length of annotated sentences for each annotator across different texts. This suggests that there may be a tendency for each annotator to prefer sentences of a particular length which remains constant across different texts.

We modelled average sentence size in the annotations as a linear function of personality traits of annotators computed using two different personality questionnaires. Multiple regression analysis showed that about 18% of variability in sentence length can be explained by two personality traits which are described by the scales 'unemotionality vs. emotionality' and 'practicality vs. playfulness' of the Big Five. Of these two 'practicality vs. playfulness' had somewhat stronger effect than 'unemotionality vs. emotionality'.

The regression model showed that all other things being equal less emotional people tend to divide oral text into longer sentences than more emotional ones. At the same time, people who are more open to new experiences prefer longer sentences than more practical ones.

Since the absolute values of standardised regression coefficients for these scales are very close (Table 4), their mutual effect, when both scales have the same values, is close to zero; i.e. very emotional and open people annotate texts in the same way as unemotional and practical ones do. And, vice versa, the greater the difference between the scores of these scales the stronger the effect of the factor with higher scores. This would imply that very emotional but practical people divide texts into shorter sentences, and unemotional but open ones into longer utterances.

One possible explanation for the observed personality effect may be that it affects the annotator's attitude towards the task which in turn results in a difference in sentence length. For example, personality may affect the diligence with which the annotator approached the task. In this case we would expect a similar effect of personality traits on sentence length in all texts. However, our analysis showed that personality scores had no effect on sentence length in the control text with almost unambiguous syntactic boundaries. This suggests that characteristics such as attentiveness to the task which may come along with the annotator's personality, do not determine choices of boundary placement alone, but that there are more fundamental interactions between personality and segmentation in silent reading.

The use of questionnaires to measure personality has a number of drawbacks. Firstly, there is a probability of response bias due to respondent's wish to "erect a favorable social façade" [9] or possible deliberate faking. An informant may as well be unwittingly defensive or may not be sufficiently self-observant. Secondly, the five-factor model is not all-encompassing – there is a level of psychological understanding that simply cannot be reached and revealed by this approach [9]. Thus, there may be other individual traits which also influence the segmentation, e.g. divergent semantic sensibilities of annotators about the meaning of the text as a whole or their way of thought. However, these limitations do not affect the main result of our study: the variability between the annotators can partially be explained by their individual characteristics such as their responses to a personality questionnaire.

Other individual characteristics that may affect the annotation are the verbal and/or visual memory of the annotator. For example [10] showed that higher working memory capacity leads to larger implicit prosodic chunks in silent reading. This fact may be extrapolated to segmentation of a text into sentences in the process of expert manual labelling. Therefore in the future we plan to explore the relations between annotators' memory abilities and segmentation.

Acknowledgments. The paper has benefited greatly from the valuable comments of Dr. Walker Trimble. We also thank all the participants of the experiments. Finally, we would like to acknowledge Dr. Keelan Evanini, Dr. Su-Youn Yoon and the two anonymous reviewers for their comments and feedback.

References

1. Liu, Y., Chawla, V.N., Harper, M.P., Shriberg, E., Stolcke, A.: A study in machine learning from imbalanced data for sentence boundary detection in speech. Computer Speech and Language 20(4), 468–494 (2006)
2. Stepikhov, A.: Resolving Ambiguities in Sentence Boundary Detection in Russian Spontaneous Speech. In: Habernal, I., Matoušek, V. (eds.) TSD 2013. LNCS (LNAI), vol. 8082, pp. 426–433. Springer, Heidelberg (2013)
3. Stepikhov, A.: Analysis of expert manual annotation of the russian spontaneous monologue: Evidence from sentence boundary detection. In: Železný, M., Habernal, I., Ronzhin, A. (eds.) SPECOM 2013. LNCS (LNAI), vol. 8113, pp. 33–40. Springer, Heidelberg (2013)
4. Foster, P., Tonkyn, A., Wigglesworth, G.: Measuring spoken language: A unit for all reasons. Applied Linguistics 21(3), 354–375 (2000)
5. Eysenck, H.J., Eysenck, S.B.G.: Manual of the Eysenck Personality Inventory. University of London Press, London (1964)

6. Shmelev, A.G.: Test-oprosnik Ajzenka. In: Bodalev, A.A., Karpinskaya, et al. (eds.) Praktikum po Psikhodiagnostike. Psikhodiagnosticheskie Materialy, pp. 11–16. MGU, Moscow (1988) (in Russ.)
7. Tsuji, H., Fujishima, Y., Tsuji, H., Natsuno, Y., Mukoyama, Y., Yamada, N., Morita, Y., Hata, K.: Five-factor model of personality: Concept, structure, and measurement of personality traits. Japanese Psychological Review 40(2), 239–259 (1997)
8. Khromov, A.B.: P'atifactornyj oprosnik lichnosti: Uchebno-metodicheskoe posobie. Izd-vo Kurganskogo gosudarstvennogo universiteta, Kurgan (2000) (in Russ.)
9. Block, J.: The Five-Factor Framing of Personality and Beyond: Some Ruminations. Psychological Inquiry 21(1), 2–25 (2010)
10. Swets, B., Desmet, T., Hambrick, D.Z., Ferreira, F.: The role of working memory in syntactic ambiguity resolution: A psychometric approach. Journal of Experimental Psychology: General 136(1), 64–81 (2007)

Associative Mechanism of Foreign Spoken Language Perception (Forensic Phonetic Aspect)

Rodmonga Potapova[1] and Vsevolod Potapov[2]

[1] Institute of Applied and Mathematical Linguistics, Moscow State Linguistic University,
Russia, 119034, Moscow, Ostozhenka, 38, Russia
[2] Department of Philology, Lomonosov Moscow State University, Russia, 119899, Moscow,
Vorobyovy Gory, Russia
RKPotapova@yandex.ru

Abstract. The experiment involved auditory decoding of foreign spoken language material that had been especially developed and phonetically balanced. The study focuses on auditory perception conditioned by interlanguage interference. In this situation the listener has to employ different sets of perceptual samples of phonetic units. It is assumed that in the case of auditory decoding of foreign spoken language utterances, listeners construct the phonemic, syllabic, rhythmic and prosodic patterns of speech utterances of their first language, or mother-tongue. The problem of auditory spoken language perception is bound up with problems of voice and speech line-up in the field of forensic phonetics and with language competence of criminalistic experts, first of all of forensic phoneticians.

Keywords: spoken language identification, interlanguage interference, auditory perception, non-native speakers, forensic phonetics.

1 Introduction

Today in Europe, Canada and USA there are many investigations in the field of forensic linguistics in which the voice line-up method is used. The basis of this method is perceptual voice identification by ear witness [2,4,7,8,9,10,11,12,13]. From A.S. Laubsteins point of view, the problem of voice line-ups is a specific problem which arises from the fact that it is not simply a voice line-up, but a speech line-up, and there is much more content in speech than the simple sound of the voice [9, p.262]. And relatively little is known about how people are identified on the basis of their voices [9, p.264].

From our point of view there is a definitely lack in some information about ear-witness auditory perception of unfamiliar language. The investigations in the domain of spoken language line-up (not only voice and speech line up) are very perspective as additional information source in criminalistic activity.

Research on the problems of influences of a listener's native language on speaker identification is key to solving a lot of questions concerning forensic phonetics. The majority of research in this domain is dedicated to experiments involving a listener and a speaker of different native-language backgrounds [3,5,6,24].

It was determined that the native-language background of a listener has an effect on his or her identification of speakers of a foreign language. It is known that all

A. Ronzhin et al. (Eds.): SPECOM 2014, LNAI 8773, pp. 113–122, 2014.

investigations concerning forensic phonetics, where the native-language background differs between listeners and speakers, can be divided into the following main areas:

- identification of the voice quality of a speaker [1];
- identification of his or her manner of speaking (pitch, rate of articulation, rhythmical and fluency features) [1];
- identification of linguistic specification of spoken text (discourse): phonological features of units of the segmental level, communicative relevant suprasegmental units, rhythmic patterns [21].

This paper forms part of some researches, studying mechanisms of associative linguistic decoding of the speech flow in foreign languages by listeners of different native-language background. In relation to this, we need to discuss briefly the peculiarities of auditory spoken language perception. Two opposing points of view are known at present.

The first, considered traditionally to be held by linguists, is based on the postulate that the perceptual space is identical to the phonological space. The second, formed on the basis of psycho-physiological research of human perceptual capabilities, encompasses the belief that: the ability to distinguish different groups of sounds - in particular, vowels - is universal, which means that the perceptual space does not depend on the specific language phonological system (all people can differentiate between the same groups of vowels, using the same set of criteria).

The first point of view seems too categorical and vague, while the second is contradictory to many facts widely known by phonetics specialists and foreign-language teachers (students with normal hearing sometimes fail to differentiate between the vowels of their native language and of the one they are learning).

Recently, a third point of view on human perceptual abilities has been formulated, based on the available data from previous experiments. It suggests that a person is able to distinguish a greater number of sound properties than the number of phoneme properties that exist in his or her native language. The same phonetic properties of vowels may play different roles when perceived by different-language speakers. For instance, native Russian-speakers are extremely sensitive to "i"-like transitions in the initial and final phases of vowels, because these transitions are signs of palatalization of the preceding or succeeding consonant [17]. There is cause to believe that speakers of other languages do not possess such sensitivity.

The study of peculiarities of perception and imitation of sounds of non-native languages (in a phonetic experiment or in real-life learning situations) helps not only to reconsider certain traditional beliefs about the reasons for mistakes made in a non-native spoken language, but also to put forth a new interpretation of the data obtained.

First, there is no doubt that experiments do not confirm the supposedly universal nature of phoneme differentiating criteria which play an important role in the discrimination of meanings. Perception of phonetic correlates of various discriminating properties is not regulated by any universal law, but depends on the kind of phonetic correlates that are used in the phoneme system of the person's native language.

Second, the traditional beliefs about the properties of the phonemic (phonological) hearing need to be reviewed. When perceiving sounds which are absent from their native language, people do not necessarily classify them as phonemes of their native language. It is quite possible that the differentiation here is more subtle, based on (a) the qualities of the auditory processing of speech signals; (b) the knowledge of one or more foreign languages; and (c) on the person's individual associative capabilities. The phonological hearing may be even more sensitive to sounds of non-native languages. What is important though, is the fact that different groups of sounds are not influenced in the same way by the phonological hearing which has a standardizing effect. One of the most important qualities of the phonological hearing is the ability to ensure different techniques of processing native and foreign-language sounds.

The hypothetical perceptual interference phenomena, predicted from the contrasting studies of phoneme systems of various languages, often do not occur, because the general impact of speech activity grows. For instance, it is impossible to work with the phoneme level units without considering allophonic variations; just as it is to describe segment-related (sound) phenomena without taking into account suprasegmental (prosodic and rhythmic) ones [14,16,18].

Finally, the perceptual decoding abilities unique to humans are to a large extent weakened by the factor known as "language competence", which includes, along with articulation and perceptual skills, and the ability to predict the phonic organization of an utterance, the speaker's ability to express the important fragment of the reality model in a non-native language [19,22].

2   Material and Procedure of the Experiment

The experiment involved perceptual identification of material that had been specially developed and phonetically balanced. The study focuses on auditory perception conditioned by interlanguage interference. In this situation the listener has to employ different sets of perceptual samples of phonetic units. It is assumed that in the case of perceptual decoding of foreign spoken language, the listener has to construct the phonemic, syllabic, rhythmic and prosodic patterns of the speech utterance being played, depending on the extent of his or her competence in the language in question.

The experiment envisaged the auditory perception by a group of listeners (Russian native speakers) regarding languages with which they were unfamiliar, in this case, English and German. The following methods were used when working with the people taking part. Every group consisted on average of up to 20 people. The main groups were comprised of first-year students at the Moscow State Linguistic University, who did not speak these particular foreign languages.

Before the experiments, the listeners received the following instructions:

1. Listen to phonograms with foreign spoken language utterances many times.
2. Note down all perceived sounds by means of Cyrillic alphabet.
3. Try to make the segmentation of the utterances using auditory criteria including pauses.
4. Try to distinguish groups of syllables united by a single stress on the basis of increasing in loudness, length and often pitch and separate them with special markers.
5. Mark the stress locations (syllable groups) listened to.

6. Try to define degrees of stress.
7. Put different markers ($\tilde{\ }$, $´$, $`$) concerning the main, secondary, or other stress degrees.

Use additional symbols for sounds which do not have corresponding designators in Russian. For example, the duration of the sounds (a horizontal line above the corresponding letter), their nasal quality (a wave above the letter), etc.

Mark the pitch dynamics (rising, falling or even ($\uparrow \downarrow \longrightarrow$), regarding auditory sensation in terms of which a group of sounds may be defined on a scale.

The instructions were discussed with the listeners prior to the experiment and the necessary amendments were made. The spoken material included phrases which were constructed taking into account the phonetically balanced factor (all phonemes, phoneme combinations, segmentation types, rhythmic patterns, etc.).

The phrases were played to the listener with ten-second pauses between them. First, whole utterances were played; then separate fragments (approximately, syntagmas). The number of repetitions was not limited. After writing down the sounds, the listeners attempted to mark the rhythmic and melodic patterns of what they had just heard. At the end of the experiment the first utterances were played once again for an additional checking, as, considering the process of adaptation, one could expect the number of perceptual errors committed in the beginning to be removed during a repeat session.

3   Discussion of Experimental Data

Perceptual reconstruction of the English spoken language by non-native speakers
The experiment with the English-language material showed that the listeners did not encounter serious problems at the level of perception of sounds. The following graphic codes were established for two English sounds in the course of the experiments - u $\longrightarrow$ u^{ju} and th $\longrightarrow$ v. The short, mostly one-syllable words were perceived well, whereas longer, polysyllabic words, presented some problems. The listeners adapted very quickly when practising with simpler material (i.e., short words).They needed to listen to this only two or three times before writing anything down.

With more complicated text, certain polysyllabic words caused problems and had to be repeated several times. This could also be due to the higher tempo of speech in these sections. Longer phrases required many repetitions. Very often the listeners recognized the beginning and the ending of a phrase or a syntagma first, and only after that retrieved "the middle". Regarding some of the longer phrases, the listeners remarked that the tempo was slow enough for perception.

The listeners did not adapt to the perception of the material at the same pace, so, requests were made to try and work with the material individually.

The following examples are given on the basis of auditory perception of the spoken English language by Russian native speakers without English competence.

Vowels

- In some cases in monosyllabic words the front open vowel /I/ is substituted by the front close vowel.
- The front open vowel // is substituted in monosyllabic words by the front open /a/, or by the cluster VC: /er/, i.e. front close-mid united with vibrant.

- The back close short /ʋ/, or cluster /jʋ/ is perceived as a back close long vowel /u/.
- There is substitution of diphthongs /əʋ/ for monophthong /eʋ/.

Consonants

- Either voiceless plosive velar /k/, or voiceless plosive dental /t/ are perceived instead of voiceless plosive bilabial /p/ in the initial position of a word.
- The front sonorant /n/ is perceived in the initial position of a word instead of voiced plosive bilabial /b/.
- The half-voiced dental plosive /d/ is perceived in the final position of a word as palatalized dental sonorant /l/.
- The final dental sonorant (lateral consonant) /l/ is not perceived in any cases. It is substituted in its turn for non-syllabic /u/.
- The voiced fricative labiodental /v/ in the initial position of a word is at times perceived as voiced plosive velar /g/.
- The voiceless fricative dental /θ/ is perceived in the initial position of a word as the voiceless fricative labiodental /f/.
- The voiceless fricative dental /ð/ is perceived in 100% of cases in the initial position of a word as the voiced fricative labiodental /v/.
- The final position of the phonetic word [ə] is perceived as the sonorant (lateral consonant).
- In the final position of a word plosive velar /g/ is perceived instead of the nasal sonorant /n/.
- The initial vibrant is perceived in all cases as the voiced fricative dental /ʒ/.
- The bilabial consonant /w/ in the initial position of a word is perceived as the labiodental /v/ or vowel /ʋ/.
- The word man [mn] has the following variants in the process of perception: [mn]; [nm]; [np], i.e. it is metathesis of sonorants and in the final position of this word the voiceless plosive labial /p/ also appears instead of the nasal sonorant /n/.

Rhythmic structures, pitch identification
Rhythmic structure is one or several syllables united by the main word stress. This concept corresponds with the concept phonetic word [14,15].

- The three-syllable rhythmic structures: loss of one pretonic syllable.
- The four-syllable rhythmic structures: omission of one consonant resulting in one syllable formed from two.
- The four-syllable rhythmic structures: an additional syllable may appear in the final position of a word, e. g., CCVCV instead of CCVv (Vv - diphthong).
- The five-syllable rhythmic structures: listeners substitute the syllable structure resulting, e.g., in one syllable instead of two: CCVC instead of CV/CV, or the loss of one syllable in the middle part of a word, or sound regrouping in the syllable: CCV instead of CVC.
- The seven-syllable rhythmic structures: sound regrouping in the syllable: CVC instead of CCV.
- There are cases of segmenting some structures into two words.

Utterances segmentation

- As a rule, it is impossible to make a juncture segment between the words.
- It is difficult to determine the number of syllables (usually a syllable is lost).
- There is segmentation of a polysyllabic word into smaller words.
- The substitution of the initial syllable of a word for a single sound.
- The initial part of a word is identified, while the final part is not.
- Articles and prepositions are not easily identified.
- The identification of a syntagma may be characterised as "closed-in construction": initial and final parts of a syntagma are easily identified.
- The substitution of some word combinations in a sentence (a syntagma) for more frequently used phrases.
- The short syntagma (the number of syllables: 7 ± 2) is identified well and is segmented correctly.
- Normally, the pitch contour of syntagmas is reproduced correctly, i.e. the final tone falling in final parts of syntagmas and phrases is correctly identified, and also the final rising, i.e. the falling-rising intonation curve is concentrated on one syllable, combining emphasis of a word with rising final part of a syntagma in English. The falling-rising pitch curve of such stress is often preceded by an initial glide upwards.

The use of the above mentioned sound, syllable, phonetic word, syntagma, phrase units encompasses all language levels. Thus, a study of sound, syllable, and cluster allows an analysis of the perception of separate sounds and their sequences (transitions between sounds, combinability (concurrence-range) in a certain language). The transition to larger units such as word, phonetic word, and cluster allows us to examine sounds within a meaningful unit, to analyse vocabulary, and concerning perception, to start drilling the rhythmic organisation of a word (number of syllables, localisation of stress, and gradation of stresses). The transition to syntagmas and phrases involves, first of all, rhythmics (syntagmas and phrases, meaningful and relatively complete speech units) and melodies as well as basic characteristics of speech segmentation, with regard to meaning and intonation curve. Finally, large speech fragments (phonoparagraph, text) considered are also indissolubly connected with the analysis of meaning, but on the level of segmentation - to rather large blocks (it is necessary to take into account the role of the corresponding various constructions).

The question on segmentation should include two aspects in the process of training experts. The first aspect is teaching comprehension from small to large fragments (from parts or constituents to their unity). The second one is teaching segmentation of a large fragment into smaller ones (the whole - into its constituent elements).

The complex of exercises should include the following spheres of perception:

1. Auditory perception (it is possible with pronouncing, i.e. using articulatory mechanism) of speech fragments of various size.
2. Instruction in oral and written (orthographic) presentation.
3. Instruction in oral presentation and its transcription sound.
4. Instruction in written (orthographic) presentation and written presentation of sound transcription.

5. Instruction in translation elements (using oral text as the basis, as well as transcriptional and orthographic recordings).

The selection of material included in exercises should meet the following requirements:

1. To contain facts, characterising peculiarities and differences between the foreign language and the native one (in most cases this phenomenon conditions mistakes of the listeners).
2. To contain facts, distinguishing between colloquial and literary speech (the practice shows that untrained listeners encounter great difficulties in perceiving spontaneous speech). At this stage of study, the question about the peculiarities of dialect was not under consideration, though it is necessary to take them into account.
3. To present the material in accordance with possible modifications, produced by equipment, e.g., by communications. The set used in the experiment, recorded under different interferences and distortions, may be in this group. Thus, items 2 and 3 include speech stimuli, which are presented to the participants for perception in inconvenient conditions. The extent of complication may be different, e.g., may have some gradations. The instruction should move from perception of easy to more complicated units, from perception without interference and distortions to perception with such conditions.

Consequently, we have material of various quality containing the following variants:

- The literary language (full type of pronunciation);
- The colloquial language;
- The spoken language with interference and distortions.

Perceptual reconstruction of the German spoken language by non-native speakers
In the experiment reported here concerning the perception of the German spoken language by non-native speakers, the following issues were investigated.
Vowels

- There is no differentiation between long (nasal) and short (non-nasal) German vowels.
- The labialized front vowels [y:], [:], [y] and [oe] are substituted by [ju:] and [jo:] with no quantitative differences.
- The glottal stop of vowels in an open initial syllable position is not identified by the listeners.
- The diphthongs [ao] and [ɔ] are substituted by [au] and [oj], respectively.
- The long [a:] and short [a] are not differentiated.
- The long front close [e:] is substituted by the short front open [ɛ].
- The long front vowel [i:] is substituted by the short and less front [i].

Consonants

- All the voiceless aspirated consonants are substituted by voiceless non-aspirated ones.

- The German non-palatalized consonants are substituted by the corresponding palatalized ones before front vowels.
- The voiceless fricative palatalized consonant [Ç] after vowels is substituted by [ʃ] or [x].
- The voiceless consonant in the position of assimilated juncture after a voiceless consonant is substituted by the voiced consonant; and the preceding voiceless consonant by the voiced one.
- The [ŋ] sound is substituted either by the consonant cluster [n+g], or by the sound [n].
- The different vibrant types are not differentiated between.
- The vocal [ə] is not identified.
- The voiceless consonant assimilation is substituted by the voiced assimilation.
- The final [t] is often absent from the cluster [ist].
- The final [d] is omitted from the word [und].

Rhythmic Structures

- The proclitics, including articles, prepositions, etc. are broken into separate syllables, which are either clustered with the preceding word or perceived as isolated words.
- As a rule, the phonetic words are segmented incorrectly, which results in a distortion of the words rhythmic structure.
- Different gradations of stress are not identified.
- The two- and three-syllable rhythmic structures are unified to make units with a greater number of components. The number of syllables reaches 7 or 9.

Utterances

- The pitch beginning and ending of syntagmas are identified correctly.
- The sharp pitch fall in the initial rhythmic structure of a sentence with completed intonation is not perceived.
- The even movement of the pitch tone on the nucleus and post-nuclear syllable of a syntagma is not identified.
- The neutral position on the altitude scale of the non-emphasized pre-tact in the initial part of a sentence is substituted by a higher position.

The phonetic peculiarities of the Russian-German interference were discussed in [21].

4   Conclusion

The experiment has shown that the greatest number of doubts and errors is caused by the peculiarities which make the language in question different from the subjects native language or from other languages that they know. Therefore, to prepare them for the perceptual identification experiment, it is advisable to familiarize them with those peculiarities beforehand and to have them practice, so that they would be able to discern and approximately identify at least to a certain extent, say, e.g., diphthongs in English.

For that, special tests should be developed in the languages under analysis, using the available data on the substitution, insertion or omission of speech units (from sounds and syllables to phrases and fragments of text.) After completing this task and practicing for a while, the listeners should be tested on the set material: several listening sessions should be held. If it is necessary, participants may practise, listening to recorded utterances pronounced with different speech tempo. For convenience, they should be provided with tables of main phonetic peculiarities of the language under analysis, and of variants of coding (to standardize their records).

On the basis of our experiment, it is clear that the native-language background of listeners has a great influence on results of phonologic, syllabic, prosodic and rhythmic perceptual decoding of unfamiliar spoken language flow. There are different kinds of insertion, metathesis, prothesis, substitution, false target, lapse of target etc., according to phonologic and prosodic rules of the listeners native language. As a result, it would be necessary to devise special methods for training experts of forensic phonetics especially for auditory perception.

The results of our experiments seem to be relevant for forensic speaker identification concerning auditory analysis of speech material in foreign languages, and first of all for creation of foreign language line ups.

Acknowledgments. This investigation was supported by the Russian Foundation of Fundamental Researches. Project No. 14-06-00363 (2014-2015).

References

1. French, P.: An Overview of Forensic Phonetics with Particular Reference to Speaker Identification. Forensic Linguistics 1(2), 169–181 (1994)
2. French, P.: Caller on the Line: An Illustrated Introduction to the Work of a Forensic Speech Scientist. Medico-Legal Journal 75(3), 83–96 (2007)
3. Goggin, J.P., Thompson, C.P., Strube, G., Simental, L.R.: The Role of Language Familiarity in Voice Identification. Memory and Cognition 19, 448–458 (1991)
4. Hollien, H.: The Acoustics of Crime: The New Science of Forensic Phonetics. Plenum Press, New York (1990)
5. Kster, O., Schiller, N.O.: Different Influences of the Native-Language of a Listener on Speaker Recognition. Forensic Linguistics. The International Journal of Speech, Language and the Law 4, 18–28 (1997)
6. Kster, O., Schiller, N.O., Knzel, H.J.: The Influence of Native-Language Background on Speaker Recognition. In: 13th International Congress of Phonetic Sciences, 3, pp. 306–309. KTH and Stockholm University, Stockholm (1995)
7. Kolly, M.-J., Dellwo, V.: How do Listeners Perceive the Origin of a Foreign Accent? Travaux Neuchtelois de Linguistique 59, 127–148 (2013)
8. Kolly, M.-J., Dellwo, V.: Cues to Linguistic Origin: The Contribution of Speech Temporal Information to Foreign Accent Recognition. Journal of Phonetics 42, 12–23 (2014)
9. Laubstein, A.S.: Problems of Voice Line Ups: Forensic Linguistics. The International Journal of Speech, Language and the Law 4(2), 262–279 (1997)
10. Leemann, A., Siebenhaar, B.: Perception of Dialectal Prosody. In: Interspeech 2008, pp. 524–527. Brisbane (2008)

11. Munro, M.J., Derwing, T.M., Burgess, C.S.: Detection of Non Native Speaker Status from Content-Masked Speech. Speech Communication 52, 626–637 (2010)
12. Neuhauser, S.: Foreign Accent Imitation and Variation of VOT and Voicing in Plosives. In: 15th International Congress of Phonetic Sciences (ICPhS), pp. 1462–1465. Barcelona (2003)
13. Park, H.: Detecting Foreign Accent in Monosyllables: The Role of L1 Phonotactics. Journal of Phonetics 41, 78–87 (2013)
14. Potapov, V.V.: Der Sprachrhythmus im Russischen und Deutschen. Phonetica Francofortensia 7, 99–123 (1999)
15. Potapov, V.V.: Dynamik und Statik des Sprachlichen Rhythmus. Bhlau Verlag, Kln, Weimar, Wien (2001)
16. Potapova, R.K.: Prosodic Features of Standard Russian Connected Speech. Phonetica Francofortensia 5, 67–91 (1991)
17. Potapova, R.K.: Zur Vergleichenden Analyse der Phonetischen Besonderheiten des Deutschen und Russischen. Phonetica Francofortensia 6, 105–151 (1993)
18. Potapova, R.K., Lindner, G.: Osobennosti Nemetskogo Proiznosheniya. Vysshaya shkola, Moskva (1991)
19. Potapova, R.K., Potapov, V.V.: Auditory Perception of Speech by Non-Native Speakers. In: International Workshop Speech and Computer (SPECOM 2001), pp. 205–214. Moscow (2001)
20. Potapova, R.K., Potapov, V.V.: Yazyk, Rech, Lichnost. Yazyki slavyanskoy kultury, Moskva (2006)
21. Potapova, R.K., Potapov, V.V.: Kommunikative Sprechttigkeit: Russland und Deutschland im Vergleich. Bhlau Verlag, Kln, Weimar, Wien (2011)
22. Potapova, R., Potapov, V.: Auditory and Visual Recognition of Emotional Behaviour of Foreign Language Subjects (by Native and Non-native Speakers). In: Železný, M., Habernal, I., Ronzhin, A. (eds.) SPECOM 2013. LNCS (LNAI), vol. 8113, pp. 62–69. Springer, Heidelberg (2013)
23. Schiller, N.O., Kster, O.: Evaluation of a Foreign Speaker in Forensic Phonetics: A Report. Forensic Linguistics 3(1), 176–185 (1996)
24. Schiller, N.O., Kster, O., Duckworth, M.: The Effect of Removing Linguistic Information upon Identifying Speakers of a Foreign Language. Forensic Linguistics 4(1), 1–17 (1997)

Automatic Alignment of Phonetic Transcriptions for Russian

Daniil Kocharov

Department of Phonetics, Saint-Petersburg State University
Universitetskaya Emb., 11, 199034, Saint-Petersburg, Russia
kocharov@phonetics.pu.ru
http://www.phonetics.pu.ru

Abstract. This paper presents automatic alignment of Russian phonetic pronunciations using the information about phonetic nature of
speech sounds in the aligned transcription sequences. This approach has
been tested on 24 hours of speech data and has shown significant improvement in alignment errors has been obtained in comparison with
commonly used Levenstein algorithm: the numbers of error has been
reduced from 1.1 % to 0.27 %.

Keywords: automatic alignment, phonetic transcription, Russian.

1 Introductions

The goal of the work described in this paper is to align effectively two sequences
of phoneme labels (phonetic transcriptions) that describe the same speech signal.
There are two main use cases for aligning phonetic transcriptions and measuring
distance between. The first one is a research of how various people read or speak
the same text, e.g. dialectic [1] and sociolinguistic [2] studies. The other one is
the alignment of speech transcriptions produced by different transcribers, e.g. in
automatic speech recognition systems [3] or while annotating speech corpora [4].

The current work has been done as a part of a research on speaker individual characteristics. The aim has been to register and quantitatively measure the
deviation of various native speakers of Russian from Standart Russian pronunciation. To make a correct comparison of individual pronunciations these pronunciation has to be well aligned. The nature of phonemes, relations between them,
the behaviour of phonemes in fluent speech under different conditions should be
considered to perform a perfect alignment of phoneme sequences.

Automatic transcriptions aligners, that used knowledge of phoneme relations,
have been done for many languages, including Basque [5], Dutch [6], English [3],
Norwegian [1], Spanish [2]. Such an aligner that has been developed for Russian
is presented in the paper. It is based on the usage of sets of phonemes that could
substitute each other, be inserted into speech or not pronounced in continuous
speech.

Section 2 describes the basic ideas of the presented aligner. Section 3 presents
the phoneme set that has been considered in the aligner. The achieved results
are shown in section 4.

A. Ronzhin et al. (Eds.): SPECOM 2014, LNAI 8773, pp. 123–128, 2014.

2   Transcription Alignment

There are different ways of aligning transcriptions, but using dynamic programming is the most common approach, including Levenstein algorithm [7] and Hirschberg's algorithm [8]. The basic setup is that a cost of any substitution, deletion or insertion is '1', and cost of match is '0'. These algorithms do not distinguish the substitution of similar sounds from substitution of very different sounds and do not take into account that ellision or epenthesis of some sounds is highly probable.

There have been efforts to measure phonetic difference more precisely assuming that a cost of substitution of one phoneme by another should depend on phonetic distance between these phonemes.

Consider a phoneme to be represented as a vector of articulatory features, than the phonetic distance between two phonemes is a sum of absolute differences between feature values of the phonemes [6]. The phonetic distance may be dependent on pointwise mutual information, the number of times phonemes corresponded to each other in aligned transcriptions [9]. In [3] the better results were obtained calculating phonetic distance on the basis of misrecognitions of phones by ASR phone-decoder in comparison with using phonemes perceptual similarity and phonological similarity.

The proposed approach of improving phonetic transcription alignment is based on the idea to define sets of phonemes that are highly probable to substitute each other. The substitution cost for phonemes within a set should be less than substitution cost for phonemes from different sets. This cost reduction is equal for all the sets and for this work is equal to 0.1. Thus, the substitution of phonemes within a set cost 0.9, and the substitution of phonemes across sets cost 1. The cost of probable phoneme deletions and insertions is also reduced to 0.9.

The next section presents all applied phoneme sets.

3   Frequent Phonetic Changes in Russian

The information about phonetic changes in Russian speech may be found in [10] [11]. There are context-dependent and context-independent phonetic changes, elisions or epenthesis in Russian speech. The majority of these speech events are context-dependent and happen due to assimilation (e.g. eventual elision of /f/ in a phoneme sequence /f s/, when labialized /s/ is pronounced instead of /f s/ or consonant devoicing in prepausal position). An example of relatively context-independent phonetic change in Russian is a realization of /y/ instead of /a/ in a post-tonic syllables.

All phonetic changes are treated as context-independent within this work for a purpose of simplicity.

Vowel allophones behave in different manner depending on whether they are stressed or not. In this cases, vowel symbol contained indication of the sounds position regarding stress. Thus, '0' is used for a stressed vowel (e.g. /a0/ is a stressed /a/), '1' – for an unstressed vowel in a pretonic syllable (e.g. /a1/ is a pre-stressed /a/), '4' – an unstressed one in a post-tonic syllable (e.g. /a4/ is a post-stressed /a/).

In terms of phonetic distance calculation the change is a phoneme substitution, the elision is a phoneme deletion and the epenthesis is a phoneme insertion.

3.1   Phoneme Sets Defining Substitutions

Proposed phoneme sets may intersect, i.e. a phoneme/allophone may be found in different sets. For example, allphones of /a/ appear in both sets of back vowels and front vowels, as they could be pronaunced in a front manner or back manner depending on speaker individual preferences and a context. Sets of phonemes and allophones that are highly probable to substitute each other:

- allophones of phoneme /a/: {a0, a1, a4}
- allophones of phoneme /e/: {e0, e1, e4}
- allophones of phoneme /i/: {i0, i1, i4}
- allophones of phoneme /o/: {o0, o1, o4}
- allophones of phoneme /u/: {u0, u1, u4}
- allophones of phoneme /y/: {y0, y1, y4}
- front unstressed vowels: {a1, a4, e4, e1, i4, i1, y1, y4}
- back unstressed vowels: {a1, a4, o1, o4, u1, u4}
- /j/ and allophones of /i/: {j, i1, i4}
- labial consonants and unstressed rounded vowels: {v, v', o1, o4, u1, u4}
- sibilants: {s, s', š, š':, z, z', ž}
- unvoiced stops and affricates: {t, t', t͡s, t͡š'}
- voiced stops and affricates: {d, d', d͡z, d͡ž'}

Note, that d͡z is used to denote voiced allophone of t͡s, and d͡ž' is used to denote voiced allophone of t͡š'.

There is also a number of phonetic processes in Russian speech which affect almost all Russian consonants. They are listed below with a couple of examples:

- consonant voicing, i.e. /t/ –>/d/ or /s/ –>/z/
- consonant devoicing, i.e. /d/ –>/t/ or /z/ –>/s/
- consonant palatalization, i.e. /t/ –>/t'/ or /s/ –>/s'/
- consonant depalatalization, i.e. /t'/ –>/t/ or /s'/ –>/s/
- affricate and stop spiratization, i.e. /t͡s/ –>/s/

3.2   Phoneme Elision

The elision of /j/ in intervocal position is so often in fluent speech that this type of phoneme deletion was the first phonetic change taken into account to improve transcription alignment. The eventual and context dependent elision of /h/, /h'/, /f/ and /f'/ prior to sibilants was not used otherwise there is need to consider a transformation of phoneme sequences and not single phonemes in transcription.

Table 1 shows an effect of taking into account phoneme sets and a possibility of /j/ elision.

Table 1. Alignment of rule-based and acoustic transcriptions using and not using phoneme classes for a word /b r a1 s a0 j i4 t/ pronounced with a lot of elisions as /b r s e0 t/

Alignment method	Alignment
Rule-based transcription	b r a1 s a0 j i4 t
Alignment not using phoneme sets	b r - s - - e0 t
Alignment using phoneme sets	b r - s e0 - - t

3.3   Phoneme Epenthesis

The only epenthesis taken into account is an epenthesis of a vowel inserted in between plosives and sonants acoustically similar to /e/ or /y/. That means a possible insertion of an element of set {e1, e4, y1, y4}. Table 1 shows an effect of taking into account possibility of phoneme epenthesis.

Table 2. Alignment of rule-based and acoustic transcriptions using and not using phoneme classes for a word /b r a1 s a0 j i4 t/ pronounced with epenthetic vowel /y1/ and elision of /a1/ as /b y1 r s a0 j i4 t/

Alignment method	Alignment
Rule-based transcription	b - r a1 s a0 j i4 t
Alignment not using phoneme sets	b - y1 r s a0 j i4 t
Alignment using phoneme sets	b y1 r - s a0 j i4 t

4   Experimental Results

4.1   Material

There are two Russian speech corpora annotated with several phonetic transcription tiers. The first one is COrpus of Russian Professonally REad Speech [4], which has manual acoustically-based and automatic rule-based text-to-phonemes phonetic transcriptions for 24 hours of speech data. The other one was created within INTAS 00-915 project [12], [13] and has manual acoustical and perceptional phonetic transcriptions and automatic rule-based text-to-phonemes one for 1 hour of speech data. The first one was selected as an experimental material as it contains much more data.

The experiments were carried out on the annotated part of the Corpus of Professionally Read Speech [4], which consists of recordings of read speech made from 8 professional speakers of Standard Russian. The annotated part of the corpus contains about 24 hours of speech with more than 1 million of speech sounds pronounced. There are two pronunciation tiers. The first one was produced automatically by grapheme-to-phoneme transcriber following orthoepic rules of Russian. The second one was produced manually by expect phoneticians during perceptual and acoustic analysis. These transcriptions were automatically aligned with each other and the alignement was manually corrected.

4.2   Results

Two transcripts were automatically aligned within the reported experiments. While the orthoepic transcription was used as a reference transcription, the manually-produced one was used as a hypothesis transcription. The existing alignment available with the corpus was used a "gold standard". Overall different ways of aligning these transcriptions with each other were evaluated.

The simplest way of taking into account acoustic nature of speech sounds is to divide them into two large phoneme sets: consonants and vowels. A more complex way is consider all the sets described in section 3.

Table 3 presents the comparison the alignment efficiency when the information about phonetic changes was not used and when it was used either in a simple or a complex way. Levenstein distance gives an efficiency of almost 99 %. But if we consider speech data with more than 20 hours of speech this leads us to more than 10 000 mistakes.

Vowels and consonants separation already brings an improvement and reduces the error rate by 29 %, see 2nd row. The use of all the phonetic information reduces the erro rate by another 46 %.

Table 3. Comparison of overall alignment efficiency using different setups

Alignment method	Error rate (%)	Total number of errors
Levenstein dist.	1.11	11 899
Levenstein dist. + V \C separation	0.78	8 496
Levenstein dist. + all phonet. classes	0.27	2 905

5   Conclusions

The further improvement is to clarify phoneme sets. The next refinement step is to use information on phonetic changes according to their context-dependency. The further improvement would be to differenciate a cost for different phonetic events according to their probability.

The results of this work is to be used in the development of automatic segmentation of Russian speech into suprasegmental speech units for accurate alignment of automatically produced phonetic sequences along a speech signal considering that many speech sounds could be mispronounced, elised or inserted in continuous speech.

Acknowledgment. The author acknowledges Russian Scientific Foundation for a research grant 14-18-01352 "Automatic segmentation of speech signal into suprasegmental speech units".

References

1. Heeringa, W.J.: Measuring Dialect Pronunciation Differences Using Levenshtein Distance. PhD Thesis, Rijksuniv., Groningen (2004)
2. Valls, E., Wieling, M., Nerbonne, J.: Linguistic Advergence and Divergence in Northwestern Catalan: A Dialectometric Investigation of Dialect Leveling and Border Effects. LLC: Journal of Digital Scholarship in the Humanities 28(1), 119–146 (2013)
3. Álvarez, A., Arzelus, H., Ruiz, P.: Long Audio Alignment for Automatic Subtitling Using Different Phone-Relatedness Measures. In: Proc. of the 2014 IEEE International Conference on Acoustic, Speech and Signal Processing (ICASSP), pp. 6321–6325 (2014)
4. Skrelin, P., Volskaya, N., Kocharov, D., Evgrafova, K., Glotova, O., Evdokimova, V.: CORPRES - Corpus of Russian Professionally Read Speech. In: Sojka, P., Horák, A., Kopeček, I., Pala, K. (eds.) TSD 2010. LNCS (LNAI), vol. 6231, pp. 392–399. Springer, Heidelberg (2010)
5. Bordel, G., Nieto, S., Penagarikano, M., Rodríguez-Fuentes, L.J., Varona, A.: A Simple and Efcient Method to Align Very Long Speech Signals to Acoustically Imperfect Transcriptions. In: 13th Annual Conference of the International Speech Communication Association (2012)
6. Elffers, B., Van Bael, C., Strik, H.: ADAPT: Algorithm for Dynamic Alignment of Phonetic Transcriptions. Internal report, Department of Language and Speech, Radboud University Nijmegen, the Netherlands. Electronically (2005), http://lands.let.ru.nl/literature/elffers.2005.1.pdf
7. Levenstein, V.: Binary codes capable of correcting deletions, insertions and reversals. Doklady Akademii Nauk SSSR 163, 845–848 (1965) (in Russ.)
8. Hirschberg, D.S.: A Linear Space Algorithm for Computing Maximal Common Subsequence. Communications of the ACM 18(6), 341–343 (1975)
9. Wieling, M., Nerbonne, E.M., Nerbonne, J.: Inducing a Measure of Phonetic Similarity from Pronunciation Variation. Journal of Phonetics 40, 307–314 (2012)
10. Bondarko, L.V.: Phonetics of contemporary Russian language. St. Petersburg (1988) (in Russ.)
11. Phonetics of spontaneous speech. Svetozarova N. D. (ed). Leningrad (1988) (in Russ.)
12. Bondarko, L.V., Volskaya, N.B., Tananiko, S.O., Vasilieva, L.A.: Phonetic Propeties of Russian Spontaneous Speech. In: 15th International Congress of Phonetic Studies (2003)
13. De Silva, V., Iivonen, A., Bondarko, L.V., Pols, L.C.W.: Common and Language Dependent Phonetic Differencies between Read and Spontaneous Speech in Russian, Finnish and Dutch. In: 15th International Congress of Phonetic Studies (2003)

Automatic Post-Editing Method Using Translation Knowledge Based on Intuitive Common Parts Continuum for Statistical Machine Translation

Hiroshi Echizen'ya[1], Kenji Araki[2], Yuzu Uchida[1], and Eduard Hovy[3]

[1] Hokkai-Gakuen University,
1-1, South-26, West-11, Chuo-ku, Sapporo, 064-0926 Japan
{echi@lst,yuzu@eli}.hokkai-s-u.ac.jp
http://www.lst.hokkai-s-u.ac.jp/~echi/eng-index.html
[2] Hokkaido University,
North-14, West-9, Kita-ku, Sapporo 060-0814 Japan
araki@ist.hokudai.ac.jp
[3] Carnegie Mellon University,
5000 Forbes Avenue, Pittsburgh, PA 15213 USA
hovy@cmu.edu

Abstract. We propose a new post-editing method for statistical machine translation. The method acquires translation rules automatically as translation knowledge from a parallel corpus without depending on linguistic tools. The translation rules, which are acquired based on **I**ntuitive **C**ommon **P**arts **C**ontinuum (ICPC), can deal with the correspondence of the global structure of a source sentence and that of a target sentence without requiring linguistic tools. Moreover, it generates better translation results by application of translation rules to translation results obtained through statistical machine translation. The experimentally obtained results underscore the effectiveness of applying the translation rules for statistical machine translation.

Keywords: Linguistic knowledge, learning method, machine translation, parallel corpus

1 Introduction

For statistical machine translation (SMT), various methods have been proposed. The salient advantage of SMT is that it can process various languages using only a parallel corpus[1,2,3,4]. However, it is difficult for SMT to address the global structure of a sentence because it is based only on the correspondence of local parts, which have adjacent words between the source sentence and the target sentence. To overcome this shortcoming, in SMT, linguistic tools are used in most cases (*i.e.*, POS tagger, parser)[5,6,7]. Those tools are effective for correct analysis of the global structure of a sentence, but it is difficult to translate

A. Ronzhin et al. (Eds.): SPECOM 2014, LNAI 8773, pp. 129–136, 2014.
© Springer International Publishing Switzerland 2014

various languages because few languages have those linguistic tools. Moreover, in previous works of post-editing for MT, various linguistic tools (*i.e.*, a dictionary, parser) have been used[8][9].

Therefore, we propose a new post-editing method for SMT. Our method acquires translation rules as translation knowledge, which can process the global structure of sentence solely from a parallel corpus without the linguistic tools. The translation rules are acquired by recursively determining the common parts between two parallel sentences using determination processes of **I**ntuitive **C**ommon **P**arts **C**ontinuum (ICPC)[10][11]. The parallel sentence represents a pair of a source sentence and target sentence. Moreover, ICPC-based method applies the acquired translation rules to the translation results obtained by SMT. Results show that ICPC-based method, which uses only a parallel corpus, can generate better translation results particularly addressing the global structure of a sentence. Experimentally obtained results using automatic evaluation metrics (*i.e.*, BLEU[12], NIST[13] and APAC[14]) show that the scores produced using ICPC-based method were superior to those obtained using SMT. These results demonstrate the effectiveness of ICPC-based post-editing method.

2   Proposed Method

2.1   Outline

Figure 1 presents the outline of our method. Our method automatically performs post-editing of the translation results obtained using **P**hrase-**B**ased Statistical **M**achine **T**ranslation (PBMT)[3][4]. The PBMT generates the translation model using a parallel corpus. Then it translates the source sentences in the evaluation data. However, in global correspondence between the source sentence and the target sentence, those translation results are insufficient.

Our method acquires translation rules automatically as translation knowledge from a parallel corpus using the determination process of **I**ntuitive **C**ommon **P**arts **C**ontinuum (ICPC). Moreover, the conclusive translation results are generated by combining the translation results obtained using PBMT with the acquired translation rules for the source sentences in the evaluation data. The ICPC-based method is effective at addressing global correspondence between the source sentence and the target sentence using the translation rules.

2.2   Acquisition of Translation Rules Based on ICPC

The translation rules are acquired using common parts between two parallel sentences by the determination process of ICPC. Figure 2 depicts an example of acquisition of translation rule in English-to-Japanese parallel sentences. First, ICPC-based method selects two parallel sentences from the parallel corpus for learning. In Fig. 2, two parallel sentences "(Do you have any liquor or cigarettes ? ; *o sake ka tabako wo o mochi desu ka*[1] *?*)" and "(Do you have any fruits or

---

[1] Italic indicates the Japanese pronunciation.

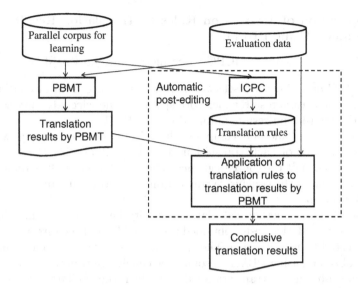

Fig. 1. Outline of our method.

vegetables ? ; *kudamono ka yasai wo o mochi desu ka ?*)" are selected from the parallel corpus. The ICPC-based method determines "Do you have any", "or" and "?" as the common parts of the two English sentences, and "*ka*" and "*wo o mochi desu ka ?*" as the common parts between two Japanese sentences. The different parts are replaced with the variable "*@0*". Consequently, "(Do you have any @0 or @1 ? ; *@0 ka @1 wo o mochi desu ka ?*)" is acquired as the translation rule. This translation rule corresponds to translation knowledge, which indicates the global structure in two parallel sentences. Moreover, it indicates the correspondence between the global structure of the source sentence "Do you have any ... or ... ?" and that of the target sentence "*... ka ... wo o mochi desu ka ?*".

---

(1) Selection of two parallel sentences

<u>Do you have any</u> liquor <u>or</u> cigarettes <u>?</u> ; *o sake <u>ka</u> tabako <u>wo o mochi desu ka ?</u>*

<u>Do you have any</u> fruits <u>or</u> vegetables <u>?</u> ; *kudamono <u>ka</u> yasai <u>wo o mochi desu ka ?</u>*

(2) Extraction of common part

Common parts: (Do you have any @0 or @1 ? ; *@0 ka @1 wo o mochi desu ka ?*)

Fig. 2. Example of translation rule acquisition.

2.3   Application of Translation Rules to Translation Results Obtained Using PBMT

Details of processes using the ICPC-based method are presented below.

(1) The ICPC-based method selects one source sentence from evaluation data and one translation result, which corresponds to the selected source sentence, from the translation results obtained using PBMT.
(2) The ICPC-based method compares the selected source sentence with the source sentence of each translation rule. Then it obtains the translation rules which can fit the source sentence. The translation result obtained using PBMT becomes the conclusive translation result when it cannot obtain any translation rules.
(3) The ICPC-based method calculates similarity based on word-matching between the translation result obtained using PBMT and the target sentence of the selected translation rule. The similarity is less than 1.0. The translation result obtained using PBMT becomes the conclusive translation result when it cannot obtain any translation rule for which the similarity is equal to or greater than threshold 0.4.
(4) The ICPC-based method determines the part, which corresponds to the variable in the target sentence of the translation rule, from the translation result. Moreover, it generates the definitive translation result replacing the variable in the target sentence of the translation rule with the corresponding part in the translation result obtained using PBMT.

Figure 3 depicts an example of generation of the conclusive translation result applying a translation rule. First, ICPC-based method selects "Where is the bus stop for the city center ?" as one source sentence from the evaluation data and "*shinai busu no noriba wa doko kara demasu ka ?*" as the corresponding translation result from the translation results obtained using PBMT. This translation result is the broken Japanese sentence because it corresponds to "Where does the bus stop for the city center leave?" in English. Next, ICPC-based method compares "Where is the bus stop for the city center ?" with "Where is @0 ?", which is the source sentence of the translation rule "(Where is @0 ? ; *@0 wa doko desu ka ?*)". This translation rule can be fit to the source sentence "Where is the bus stop for the city center ?" because "Where is" and "?", which are all parts except variable "@0", are included in the source sentence.

In between the translation result of PBMT "*shinai basu no noriba wa doko kara demasu ka ?*" and the target sentence of the translation rule "*@0 wa doko desu ka ?*", the similarity is 0.4 because the word number of the translation result is 10. Also, the word number of the matching-words is 4. Therefore, the translation rule "(Where is @0 ? ; *@0 wa doko desu ka ?*)" is used as the effective translation rule for generation of the conclusive translation result. The target sentence of translation rule "*@0 wa doko desu ka ?*" possesses the global structure of the correct sentence "*shinai busu no noriba wa doko desu ka ?*".

The ICPC-based method determines the part in the translation result which corresponds to the variable "*@0*" in the target sentence of the translation rule. In

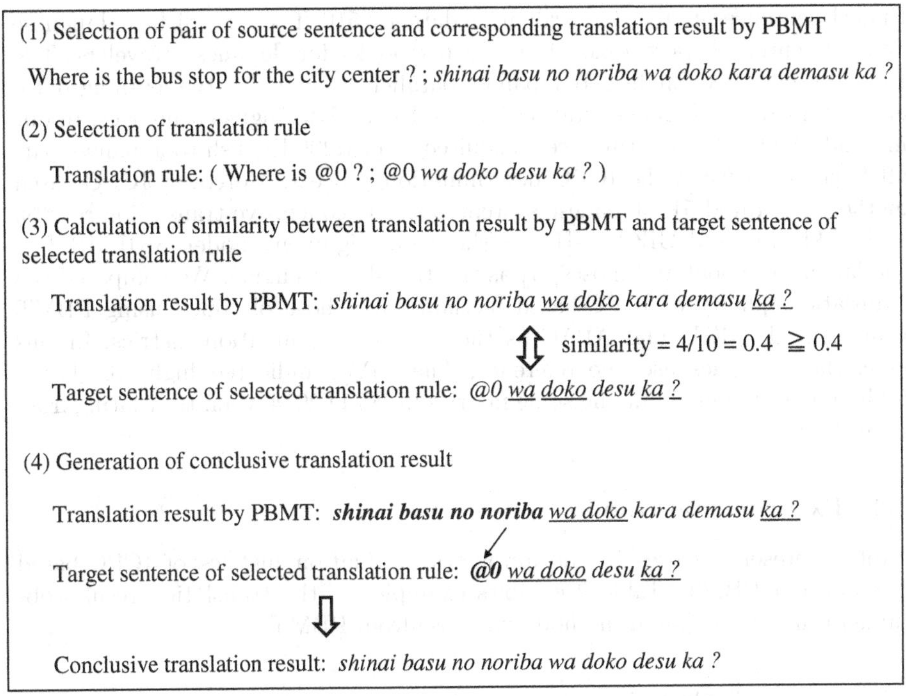

---

(1) Selection of pair of source sentence and corresponding translation result by PBMT

Where is the bus stop for the city center ? ; *shinai basu no noriba wa doko kara demasu ka ?*

(2) Selection of translation rule

Translation rule: (Where is @0 ? ; @0 *wa doko desu ka ?*)

(3) Calculation of similarity between translation result by PBMT and target sentence of selected translation rule

Translation result by PBMT: *shinai basu no noriba <u>wa doko</u> kara demasu <u>ka ?</u>*

$\updownarrow$ similarity = 4/10 = 0.4 $\geqq$ 0.4

Target sentence of selected translation rule: *@0 <u>wa doko</u> desu <u>ka ?</u>*

(4) Generation of conclusive translation result

Translation result by PBMT: **shinai basu no noriba** <u>wa doko</u> *kara demasu <u>ka ?</u>*

Target sentence of selected translation rule: **@0** <u>wa doko</u> *desu <u>ka ?</u>*

$\Downarrow$

Conclusive translation result: *shinai basu no noriba wa doko desu ka ?*

Fig. 3. Example of generation of the conclusive translation result applying a translation rule.

between the translation result *"shinai basu no noriba wa doko kara demasu ka ?"* and the target sentence of the translation rule *"@0 wa doko desu ka ?"*, *"shinai basu no noriba"* is determined as the part which corresponds to the variable *"@0"* by the order of appearance of the common parts and different parts. The variable *"@0"* in the target sentence of the translation rule is replaced with *"shinai basu no noriba"*. Therefore, *"shinai basu no noriba wa doko desu ka ?"* is obtained as the correct translation result.

The translation rules, which are acquired using the determination process of ICPC, can deal with the global structure of sentence. Namely, they are useful as a framework for both the source sentences and the target sentences. As a result, ICPC-based method can generate these high-quality translation results obtained using only the parallel corpus with no linguistic tools.

3   Experiments

3.1   Experimental Procedure

We used English-to-Japanese travel conversation as the parallel corpus. The number of English-to-Japanese parallel sentences for learning is 1,200. The

English sentences used as the evaluation data are 510. These English-to-Japanese parallel sentences were taken from 10 textbooks for Japanese travelers. The PBMT used 1,200 English-to-Japanese parallel sentences as the learning data, and obtained 510 Japanese translation results for 510 English sentences. In our method, the translation rules were acquired from 1,200 English-to-Japanese parallel sentences using the ICPC determination process. Moreover, ICPC-based method generated 510 Japanese sentences as the conclusive translation results. In PBMT, we used GIZA++[15] as the word alignment model, SRILM[16] as the language model and moses[17] as the translation engine. We compared the translation quality of ICPC-based method with those obtained using PBMT using BLEU, NIST, and APAC as the automatic evaluation metrics. In this case, these metrics use one reference. The APAC indicated high correlation with human judgment among some metrics in WMT2014 when translating from English[14].

3.2   Experimental Results

Table 1 presents scores in the automatic evaluation metrics of ICPC-based method and PBMT. Table 2 exhibits examples of the translation results obtained using ICPC-based method and those from PBMT.

Table 1. Scores for the automatic evaluation metrics.

method	BLEU	NIST	APAC
PBMT	0.0646	1.3832	0.2539
ICPC-based method	0.0635	1.3908	0.2546

Table 2. Examples of translation results.

source sentence	translation result	
	PBMT	ICPC-based method
Is this Mr. Brown ?	*kore wa* Mr. Brown *ka ?*	*kore wa* Mr. Brown *desu ka ?*
Is this Ms. Brown ?	*kore wa* Ms. Brown *ka ?*	*kore wa* Ms. Brown *desu ka ?*
May I speak in English ?	*o namae de* English *mo ii desu ka ?*	*o namae de* English *te mo ii desu ka ?*

3.3   Discussion

Table 1 shows that the scores of NIST and APAC in ICPC-based method are higher than those in PBMT. The BLEU score in the ICPC-based method is lower than that only in PBMT. The reason is that BLEU might be insufficient in two languages for which the structure of source sentence is grammatically different from that of the target sentence[18].

In Table 2, the translation results of PBMT alone are insufficient in the source sentences "Is this Mr. Brown ?" and "Is this Ms. Brown ?" because *"desu"* is not included in the Japanese translation results. The Japanese word "*desu*" is an extremely important word in this translation result. It corresponds to "is" in English. The translation results of ICPC-based method "*kore wa* Mr. Brown *desu ka ?*" and "*kore wa* Ms. Brown *desu ka ?*" are almost correct. However, "*kore wa*", which corresponds to "this" in English, should be removed from Japanese sentences in telephone conversation scenarios.

Moreover, regarding the source sentence "May I speak in English ?", both the translation result only of PBMT and ICPC-based method are insufficient because "*o namae de* English" is broken as Japanese. However, the translation result of ICPC-based method "*o namae de* English *te mo ii desu ka ?*" is better than that of PBMT "*o namae de* English *mo ii desu ka ?*" because "*te*" is included in the translation result of the ICPC-based method: "*te mo ii desu ka ?*" corresponds to "May I" in English. The ICPC-based method can generate the translation result "*o namae de* English *te mo ii desu ka ?*" using the translation rule "(May I @0 ? ; @0 te mo ii desu ka ?)". This translation rule is useful as a frame for the source sentence "May I speak in English ?". Therefore, ICPC-based method produced better translation results "*o namae de* English *te mo ii desu ka ?*" using the translation rule "(May I @0 ? ; @0 te mo ii desu ka ?)", which can accommodate the global structure of sentence.

The translation results that were improved using the translation rules were 17 among all 510 translation results. The number of the effective translation rules acquired by the determination process of ICPC was insufficient, although about 2,000 translation rules were acquired. The ICPC-based method must acquire the translation rules efficiently from a parallel corpus. For example, it is effective to use the statistical information when acquiring effective translation rules. The scores of the evaluation metrics improve by increasing the effective translation rules in ICPC-based method.

4 Conclusion

As described herein, we propose a new post-editing method that uses translation rules acquired by the ICPC determination process. The ICPC-based method can process the global structure of sentences using the acquired translation rules only from a parallel corpus with no linguistic tools. Therefore, ICPC-based method is effective for the various languages. Future studies are expected to improve ICPC-based method to acquire more translation rules using statistical information, and to perform the evaluation results using the various languages.

References

1. Brown, P.F., Cocke, J., Pietra, S.A.D., Pietra, V.J.D., Jelinek, F., Lafferty, J.D., Mercer, R.L., Roosin, P.S.: A Statistical Approach to Machine Translation. Computational Linguistics 16(2), 79–85 (1990)
2. Brown, P.F., Pietra, V.J.D., Pietra, S.A.D., Mercer, R.L.: The Mathematics of Statistical Machine Translation: Parameter Estimation. Computational Linguistics 19(2), 263–311 (1993)

3. Koehn, P., Och, F.J., Marcu, D.: Statistical Phrase-based Translation. In: Proc. of the 2003 Conference of the North American Chapter of the Association for Computational Linguistics on Human Language Technology, pp. 48–54 (2003)
4. Chiang, D.: A Hierarchical Phrase-based Model for Statistical Machine Translation. In: Proc. of the 43rd Annual Meeting on Association for Computational Linguistics, pp. 263–270 (2005)
5. McDonald, R., Crammer, K., Pereira, F.: Online Large-Margin Training of Dependency Parsers. In: Proc. of the 43rd Annual Meeting on Association for Computational Linguistics, pp. 91–98 (2005)
6. Chiang, D., Marton, Y., Resnik, P.: Online Large-Margin Training of Syntactic and Structural Translation Features. In: Proc. of the Conference on Empirical Methods in Natural Language Processing, pp. 224–233 (2008)
7. Cherry, C., Moore, R.C., Quirk, C.: On Hierarchical Re-ordering and Permutation Parsing for Phrase-based Decoding. In: Proc. of the Seventh Workshop on Statistical Machine Translation, pp. 200–209 (2012)
8. Dugast, L., Senellart, J., Koehn, P.: Statistical Post-Editing on SYSTRAN's Rule-Based Translation System. In: Proc. of the Second Workshop on Statistical Machine Translation, pp. 220–223 (2007)
9. Plitt, M., Masselot, F.: A Productivity Test of Statistical Machine Translation Post-Editing in a Typical Localisation Context. The Prague Bulletin of Mathematical Linguistics 93, 7–16 (2010)
10. Echizen-ya, H., Araki, K.: Automatic Evaluation of Machine Translation based on Recursive Acquisition of an Intuitive Common Parts Continuum. In: Proc. of the Eleventh Machine Translation Summit, pp. 151–158 (2007)
11. Echizen'ya, H., Araki, K., Hovy, E.: Optimization for Efficient Determination of Chunk in Automatic Evaluation for Machine Translation. In: Proc. of the 1st International Workshop on Optimization Techniques for Human Language Technology (OPTHLT 2012) / COLING 2012, pp. 17–30 (2012)
12. Papineni, K., Roukos, S., Ward, T., Zhu, W.-J.: BLEU: A Method for Automatic Evaluation of Machine Translation. In: Proc. of the 40th Annual Meeting of the Association for Computational Linguistics, pp. 311–318 (2002)
13. Doddington, G.: Automatic Evaluation of Machine Translation Quality Using N-gram Co-Occurrence Statistics. In: Proc. of the second International Conference on Human Language Technology Research, pp. 138–145 (2002)
14. Echizen'ya, H., Araki, K., Hovy, E.: Application of Prize based on Sentence Length in Chunk-based Automatic Evaluation of Machine Translation. In: Proc. of the Ninth Workshop on Statistical Machine Translation, pp. 381–386 (2014)
15. Och, F.J., Ney, H.: A Systematic Comparison of Various Statistical Alignment Models. Computational Linguistics 29(1), 19–51 (2003)
16. Stolcke, A.: SRILM – An Extensible Language Modeling Toolkit. In: Proc. of the International Conference on Spoken Language Processing, pp. 901–904 (2002)
17. Koehn, P., Hoang, H., Birch, A., Callison-Burch, C., Federico, M., Bertoldi, N., Cowan, B., Shen, W., Moran, C., Zens, R., Dyer, C., Bojar, O., Constantin, A., Herbst, E.: Moses: Open Source Toolkit for Statistical Machine Translation. In: Proc. of the 45th Annual Meeting of the ACL on Interactive Poster and Demonstration Sessions, pp. 177–180 (2007)
18. Isozaki, H., Sudoh, K., Tsukada, H., Duh, K.: Head Finalization: A Simple Reordering Rule for SOV Languages. In: Proc. of the Joint Fifth Workshop on Statistical Machine Translation and MetricsMATR, pp. 244–251 (2010)

Automatic Stop List Generation for Clustering Recognition Results of Call Center Recordings

Svetlana Popova[1,2], Tatiana Krivosheeva[3], and Maxim Korenevsky[3]

[1] Saint-Petersburg State University, Saint-Petersburg, Russia
[2] Scrol, Saint-Petersburg, Russia
`svp@list.ru`
[3] STC-innovations Ltd., Saint-Petersburg, Russia
{`krivosheeva,korenevsky`}`@speechpro.com`

Abstract. The paper deals with the problem of automatic stop list generation for processing recognition results of call center recordings, in particular for the purpose of clustering. We propose and test a supervised domain dependent method of automatic stop list generation. The method is based on finding words whose removal increases the dissimilarity between documents in different clusters, and decreases dissimilarity between documents within the same cluster. This approach is shown to be efficient for clustering recognition results of recordings with different quality, both on datasets that contain the same topics as the training dataset, and on datasets containing other topics.

Keywords: clustering, stop words, stop list generation, ASR.

1 Introduction

This paper deals with the problem of clustering recognition results of call center recordings in Russian. Solving this task is necessary in speech analytics, in order to find groups of specific calls, as well as thematically similar calls. Clustering of recognition results involves classifying recordings into groups of thematically close recordings. The resulting clusters can be used to produce annotations or to discover specific features of the topics of each cluster. Solving these tasks is important for structuring and visualizing speech information.

This paper deals with one aspect of improving clustering quality, which is the automatic generation of domain dependent stop lists. Using stop lists makes it possible to remove words that have a negative effect on clustering quality. We propose and test a method for automatic generation of this list. The principle behind it is that removing stop words should result in an increase in average dissimilarity between texts from different clusters and a decrease in dissimilarity between texts from the same cluster.

2 Motivation and State of the Art

Stop words are defined as words that do not carry any important information. Stop lists can be constructed based on frequency statistics in large text corpora

A. Ronzhin et al. (Eds.): SPECOM 2014, LNAI 8773, pp. 137–144, 2014.

[1]. The principle is that the more documents contain a word, the less useful it is for distinguishing documents. This principle does not always work, since words occurring in many documents can have high context significance [2]. Using stop words improves computational efficiency of algorithms and the quality of their work [3]. Importantly, stop lists are domain dependent, that is, they are ill suited for use outside the field for which they were developed. This problem is dealt with in [2] for the task of integrating different web resources.

In [4] we used a simple method of stop list generation for the task of key phrase extraction. It was based on searching through the dataset vocabulary and choosing words which improved the quality of key phrase extraction when added to the stop list. The stop list was built on the training dataset, and was used for extracting key phrases from the test dataset. In [5] we used a stoplist that was constructed by an expert by means of analyzing the frequency list of the dataset and parts of the data. The use of that stoplist significantly improved clustering quality. However, an expert is not always on hand for making specialized stop lists. For this reason we need automatic approaches to stop list generation that can replace expert work. Solving this task is the goal of our research described in this paper.

3   Experimental Data

The dataset consists of spontaneous speech recordings (8kHz sample rate) recorded in different analogue and digital telephone channels. The recordings were provided by Speech Technology Center Ltd and contain customer telephone calls to several large Russian contact centers. All test recordings have manual text transcripts.

We used both manual transcripts of the recordings and recognition results with different recognition accuracy. The transcripts and recognition results were manually classified by experts into the most frequent call topics. Three datasets were constructed. The first two datasets comprise different documents classified into the same five topics. One of these datasets, which we will further refer to as TRAIN, was used for automatically generating a stop list, while the other, which we will refer to as TEST, was used for testing the changes in clustering quality before and after using the expanded stop list. The description of the TRAIN and TEST datasets is presented in Table 1.

In order to demonstrate that the generated stop list can be useful for clustering recognition results of the given type of calls but does not depend on the call topic, we made a third test dataset comprising clusters on other topics. We will refer to it as TEST_NEXT. In contrast to the former two datasets, which contain documents on relatively distinct (dissimilar) topics, the latter dataset contains documents on comparatively similar topics: issues of wages and unemployment in various professions (medicine, education, etc). Each of the three datasets was available in three versions: manual transcripts with ideal quality (TRAIN_100, TEST_100), recognition results with $45-55\%$ accuracy (TRAIN_55, TEST_55), and recognition results with $65-80\%$ accuracy (TRAIN_80, TEST_80). For receiving results with low recognition accuracy we specially used non-target

Table 1. The description of the datasets: topics and $|D|$ - the number of documents

Dataset	Topic 1, $|D|$	Topic 2, $|D|$	Topic 3, $|D|$	Topic 4, $|D|$	Topic 5, $|D|$
TRAIN	Municipal issues, 44	Military service issues, 24	Political issues, 28	Family & maternity issues, 55	Transport issues, 35
TEST	Municipal issues, 128	Military service issues, 39	Political issues, 61	Family & maternity issues, 75	Transport issues, 58
TEST-NEXT	Medical worker's salary issues, 49	Teachers' salary issues, 20	Jobs & Un-emploiment issues, 53		

language model (LM). We used the speaker-independent continous speech recognition system for Russian developed by Speech Technology Center Ltd [6][7], which is based on a CD-DNN-HMM acoustic model [8]. The recognition results were obtained: 1) *using a general (non-target) LM* trained on a text database of news articles (3-gram model, 300k word vocabulary, 5 mln n-grams) - recognition accuracy for parts of the test database with different quality varies from 45 to 55%; 2) *using an interpolation of a general news LM with a thematic language model* trained on a set of text transcripts of customer calls to the contact center (70MB of training data, the training and test datasets did not overlap) - recognition accuracy on the test dataset under these conditions reached $65-80\%$.

4   Special Requirements for Stop Words in Call Center Dialog Transcripts

It should be noted that all our datasets contain unilateral phone calls, that is, the recording contains a monologue of the caller who is recounting his or her opinion or problem. Importantly, the actual problem or the core of the message is described by only a small fraction of words in the monologue, while its substantial part consists of the callers introducing themselves, saying where they come from, greetings, goodbyes, thanks and a large number of common conversational expressions. The words that are not included in the topical part of the call are often very similar and used in different texts independent of their topic, so they can be considered noise. This leads us to the task of improving clustering quality by purging recognition results of noise words characteristic for such calls. We formulate this task as the task of automatically expanding the stop list. It should be noted that for this task, as well as for many others [2], the method of extracting stop words based on maximum frequency is not very effective. The reason for this is probably that this type of data is characterized by a relatively small set of words that define the call topic and that can be found in call transcripts in very small numbers. Removing such words from the text has a negative effect. For instance, words important for topic detection, such as "ZhKH 'municipality', detej 'children"' turn out to be more frequent than such noise words as esche 'still', takie 'such'... We need to find a more sophisticated method of stop list generation.

5   Quality Evaluation

Our criterion for evaluating the quality of the generated stop list was the result of clustering the test dataset with and without the stop list. The greater the improvement in clustering quality provided by using the stop list, the more successful the stop list is considered to be.

The clustering algorithm we use is k-means [9]. We used a vector model for representing documents. The feature space was defined using the dataset vocabulary. The weight of the $i-th$ feature in the $j-th$ document was estimated using $tf - idf$. We did not use the whole dataset vocabulary for document representation; instead, we used only words whose document frequency exceeded the value of the df parameter. The reason for deleting rare words from the vocabulary was to remove incorrectly recognized words and words specific for certain callers but not for the call topic.

In order to evaluate the clustering quality, the k-means algorithm was run 100 times. We used the average estimate of all results, as well as the best and the worst result. The implementation of the k-means algorithm we used was provided by the Weka library (http://www.cs.waikato.ac.nz/ml/weka/). The parameters for seeds initialization were numbers from 0 to 99. The number of centroids was the same as the number of topics in the gold standard for the dataset (the result of manual topic labeling). Dissimilarity (documents similarity for k-means) was estimated using $dist(j,k) = 1 - cos(j,k)$, $0 <= dist <= 1$. Small values of $dist$ mean that the documents represented by the vectors are similar, values close to 1 imply a strong dissimilarity between the documents.

For evaluating clustering quality we used a measure comparing the result of automatic clustering to the result of manual clustering [10] [11]: F-measure, we will sign it as F:

$$F = \sum_i \frac{|G_i|}{|D|} \max_j F_{ij}, \tag{1}$$

where: $F_{ij} = \frac{2 \cdot P_{ij} \cdot R_{ij}}{P_{ij} + R_{ij}}$, $P_{ij} = \frac{|G_i \bigcap C_j|}{|G_i|}$, $R_{ij} = \frac{|G_i \bigcap C_j|}{|C_j|}$,
$G = \{G_i\}_{i=1,\dots,n}$ - is an obtained set of clusters, $|D|$ - the number of documents, $C = \{C_j\}_{j=1,\dots,n}$ - is set of classes, defined by experts.

6   Stop List Generation

The stop list was generated from the TRAIN_100 dataset (TRAIN_80, TRAIN_55 for datasets with the corresponding recognition quality) which was manually labeled by an expert. Let V be the TRAIN dataset vocabulary. For each word vi in V we tested a special condition described below. If the condition was met, the word was added to the stop list S. The resulting list was then used for clustering the datasets TEST and TEST_NEXT.

The Method of Stop List Generation. The proposed approach is based on the principle of silhouette coefficient [12], witch combines two characteristics: characteristic that shows how well the i-th element correlates with its own cluster and characterizes the degree of dissimilarity of the i-th object to the objects of the other clusters. The average value of the coefficient for all objects in the dataset shows how well the objects are clustered: whether similar documents ended up in different clusters or differing documents in the same cluster. This coefficient was successfully used (for clustering short texts) as a function whose optimal value obtained for the clustering result means that the clustering decision is also optimal [13]. For stop word extraction we used the principles that lie behind this coefficient: 1) we need to select stop words that will lead to an increase in the average dissimilarity between the texts in the dataset and the texts in the other clusters, 2) deleting the stop words must reduce the average dissimilarity between texts within the same cluster. Based on these principles, we chose a number of conditions that a stopword must meet. However, in contrast to the silhouette coefficient, we did not combine these two principles into one weight characteristic. Instead, we generated stopwords based on the first principle and on the second principle separately, and then combined the resulting stoplists.

Condition Variants. We defined a number of conditions for stop word extraction. For each condition, a separate stop list was generated. Each resulting stop list was used for clustering. Let us define the following conditions and terms: **p_max condition** - adding a word to the stop list must increase the dissimilarity between documents from different clusters; **k_min condition** - adding a word to the stop list must decrease average value of the dissimilarity between documents within the same cluster; **k_min&p_max condition** - adding a word to the stop list, if it satisfies the condition k_min or the condition k_max. We used a combination of two stop lists (k_min and p_max) instead of combining the weight characteristics into one, because otherwise only a very small number of stopwords is extracted.

7   Results and Discussions

Table 2 shows the results of k-means if no stop list was used for the TEST and TEST_NEXT datasets. We use the following notation: *df* - only words with document frequency in the dataset higher than *df* were used for representing documents and defining the feature space.

The F-score is higher in the case of TEST_NEXT set compared to TEST set. We suppose that the reason for this is that even though all documents in the TEST_NEXT set are on the same topic, the classes found within this topic contain keywords that are more specific than those in the classes in the TEST set. This is indirectly demonstrated by the fact that recognition quality influences clustering quality for TEST_NEXT more than it does for TEST. We argue that it is caused by deteriorated recognition of keywords, which has a greater impact on the dataset where they are more prominent.

Table 3 shows the clusterting results for the TEST datasets with stop lists using. We use the following notation: *df* - only words with document frequency

Table 2. F-measure of clustering without using stoplists

df	2			4			6			8		
	avg	min	max	avg	min	max	avg	min	max	avg	min	max
TEST_100	0.36	0.30	0.46	0.37	0.32	0.48	0.38	0.31	0.51	0.37	0.32	0.46
TEST_80	0.35	0.28	0.45	0.36	0.28	0.46	0.36	0.29	0.47	0.36	0.29	0.48
TEST_55	0.35	0.29	0.43	0.35	0.29	0.47	0.35	0.30	0.43	0.35	0.29	0.42
TEST_NEXT_100	0.47	0.36	0.65	0.50	0.38	0.71	0.48	0.35	0.67	0.48	0.36	0.67
TEST_NEXT_80	0.44	0.35	0.59	0.45	0.34	0.59	0.46	0.36	0.59	0.45	0.36	0.59
TEST_NEXT_55	0.43	0.34	0.57	0.45	0.36	0.57	0.46	0.36	0.61	0.45	0.37	0.57

in the dataset higher than df were used for representing documents and defining the feature space; p_max, k-min, p_max&k_min are used to signify the cases of using stoplists generated according to the corresponding conditions (Sections 6).

Table 3. F-measure of clustering the TEST datasets using stoplists generated according to the different conditions (see Section 6)

df	2			4			6			8		
TEST_100	avg	min	max	avg	min	max	avg	min	max	avg	min	max
p_max	0.36	0.30	0.49	0.39	0.31	0.52	0.40	0.33	0.52	0.41	0.34	0.55
k-min	0.38	0.30	0.49	0.39	0.32	0.49	0.39	0.32	0.47	0.38	0.31	0.49
p_max&k_min	**0.44**	0.33	0.60	**0.44**	0.33	**0.61**	0.43	0.32	0.57	**0.44**	**0.36**	0.55
TEST_80	avg	min	max	avg	min	max	avg	min	max	avg	min	max
p_max	0.36	0.29	0.47	0.37	0.29	0.47	0.39	0.32	0.51	0.39	0.33	0.51
k-min	0.37	0.29	0.48	0.37	0.28	0.47	0.37	0.28	0.48	0.37	0.29	0.46
p_max&k_min	**0.43**	**0.33**	**0.57**	0.42	0.32	0.51	0.40	0.32	0.53	0.40	0.31	0.55
TEST_55	avg	min	max	avg	min	max	avg	min	max	avg	min	max
p_max	0.35	0.30	0.43	0.36	0.31	0.45	0.35	0.30	0.45	0.36	0.29	0.49
k-min	0.36	0.29	0.49	0.36	0.29	0.48	0.36	0.30	0.45	0.36	0.30	0.42
p_max&k_min	0.39	0.31	0.48	**0.40**	**0.33**	**0.51**	0.39	0.32	0.51	0.37	0.31	0.47

Table 4 present the results for TEST_NEXT datasets. The analysis of the results shows that using automatically constructed stop lists improves clustering results (both on average and for the best and the worst results), especially when the two stop lists obtained using p_max and k_min are combined.

For TEST_NEXT (in contrast to TEST), if words with frequency df=6 (df=8) or lower are removed from the lexicon, using only the p_max criterion works better than using a combination of p_max and k_min. The TEST_NEXT dataset is smaller than TEST, and the df of words in TEST_NEXT is lower than in TEST. Deleting words with such frequencies from TEST_NEXT results in few words remaining in the dataset (fewer than for TEST), while the k_min criterion

Table 4. F-measure of clustering the TEST_NEXT datasets using stoplists generated according to the different conditions (see Section 6)

df	2			4			6			8		
TEST_NEXT_100	avg	min	max	avg	min	max	avg	min	max	avg	min	max
p_max	0.52	0.42	0.68	0.57	0.42	0.73	**0.57**	0.41	**0.75**	0.56	0.39	0.72
k-min	0.48	0.38	0.64	0.47	0.37	0.62	0.44	0.37	0.61	0.43	0.35	0.59
p_max&k_min	0.54	0.42	0.70	0.54	0.43	0.67	0.52	0.44	0.68	0.50	**0.47**	0.64
TEST_NEXT_80	avg	min	max	avg	min	max	avg	min	max	avg	min	max
p_max	0.48	0.38	0.60	0.51	0.42	0.62	**0.55**	0.44	**0.70**	**0.55**	0.45	**0.72**
k-min	0.43	0.36	0.57	0.43	0.35	0.55	0.42	0.34	0.52	0.42	0.33	0.52
p_max&k_min	0.53	0.43	0.69	**0.55**	0.45	0.70	0.54	**0.46**	0.65	0.51	0.44	0.64
TEST_NEXT_55	avg	min	max	avg	min	max	avg	min	max	avg	min	max
p_max	0.47	0.38	0.60	0.51	0.40	0.68	0.54	0.39	0.74	0.55	0.43	0.73
k-min	0.44	0.35	0.57	0.44	0.35	0.53	0.43	0.36	0.57	0.43	0.35	0.55
p_max&k_min	0.53	0.43	**0.69**	**0.57**	0.48	0.68	0.55	0.48	0.65	0.54	**0.52**	0.62

selects a more stopwords than p_max. The negative influence of the combination of p_max and k_min compared to p_max is caused by the decrease in lexicon size, combined with the fact that deleting some of the words selected by k_min as stopwords reduces the dissimilitary between clusters.

Table 5 shows the clustering result for the case when the stop list consisted of top words with the highest frequency. We use the following notation: t is the number of the most frequent words included in the stoplist. The results in Table 5 show that the method of choosing high-frequency vocabulary words as a stop list is inferior to generating a stop list using conditions.

Table 5. F-measure of clustering the TEST_100 and TEST_NEXT_100 datasets using stoplists consisted of all words with frequency higher than t

t	10			30			50			70		
	avg	min	max	avg	min	max	avg	min	max	avg	min	max
TEST_100	0.36	0.30	0.47	0.35	0.28	0.47	0.35	0.29	0.44	0.34	0.28	0.44
TEST_NEXT_100	0.47	0.37	0.64	0.47	0.38	0.61	0.46	0.36	0.63	0.45	0.36	0.60

8   Conclusions

This paper proposes a supervised domain dependent method for automatically generating stop lists. The method is based on finding words whose removal increases the dissimilarity between documents of different clusters and decreases the dissimilarity between documents within the same cluster. The proposed approach was tested for clustering recognition results of telephone calls and was shown to be efficient for recognition results with different quality, both on datasets containing the same call topics as the training set, and on datasets with different topics.

Acknowledgements. The work was financially supported by the Ministry of Education and Science of Russian Federation. Contract 14.579.21.0008, ID RFM EFI57914X0008

References

1. Zipf, K.: Selective Studies and the Principle of Relative Frequency in Language. MIT Press, Cambridge (1932)
2. Dragut, E., Fang, F., Sistla, P., Yu, C., Meng, W.: Stop Word and Related Problems in Web Interface Integration. In: 35th International Conference on Very Large Data Bases (VLDB 2009), Lyon, France, pp. 349–360 (2009)
3. Yang, Y.: Noise Reduction in a Statistical Approach to Text Categorization (pdf). In: Proc of the SIGIR 1995, pp. 256–263 (1995)
4. Popova, S., Kovriguina, L., Mouromtsev, D., Khodyrev, I.: Stop-words in keyphrase extraction problem. In: Open Innovations Association (FRUCT), pp. 131–121 (2013)
5. Popova, S., Khodyrev, I., Ponomareva, I., Krivosheeva, T.: Automatic speech recognition texts clustering. In: Sojka, P. (ed.) TSD 2014. LNCS (LNAI), vol. 8655, pp. 489–498. Springer, Heidelberg (2014)
6. Korenevsky, M., Bulusheva, A., Levin, K.: Unknown Words Modeling in Training and Using Language Models for Russian LVCSR System. In: Proc. of the SPECOM 2014, Kazan, Russia (2011)
7. Tomashenko, N.A., Khokhlov, Y.Y.: Fast Algorithm for Automatic Alignment of Speech and Imperfect Text Data. In: Železný, M., Habernal, I., Ronzhin, A. (eds.) SPECOM 2013. LNCS (LNAI), vol. 8113, pp. 146–153. Springer, Heidelberg (2013)
8. Schwarz, P.: Phoneme recognition based on long temporal context, Doctoral thesis, Brno, Brno University of Technology, Faculty of Information Technology (2008)
9. MacQueen, J.B.: Some Methods for classification and Analysis of Multivariate Observations. In: Proc. of 5th Berkeley Symposium on Mathematical Statistics and Probability 1, pp. 281–297. University of California Press, Berkeley (1967)
10. Meyer zu Eissen, S., Stein, B.: Analysis of Clustering Algorithms for Web-based Search. In: Karagiannis, D., Reimer, U. (eds.) PAKM 2002. LNCS (LNAI), vol. 2569, pp. 168–178. Springer, Heidelberg (2002)
11. Stein, B., Meyer zu Eissen, S., Wilbrock, F.: On Cluster Validity and the Information Need of Users. In: Hanza, M.H. (ed.) 3rd IASTED Int. Conference on Artificial Intelligence and Applications (AIA 2003), Benalmadena, Spain, pp. 216–221. ACTA Press, IASTED (2003) ISBN 0-88986-390-3
12. Rousseeuw, P.J.: Silhouettes: A Graphical Aid to the Interpretation and Validation of Cluster Analysis. Computational and Applied Mathematics 20, 53–65 (1987)
13. Cagnina, L., Errecalde, M., Ingaramo, D., Rosso, P.: A discrete particle swarm optimizer for clustering short text corpora. In: BIOMA 2008, pp. 93–103 (2008)

Blur Estimation Methods for System of Audiovisual Monitoring of Meeting Participants

Irina Vatamaniuk[1], Andrey Ronzhin[2,3], and Alexander Ronzhin[3]

[1] SUAI, 67, Bolshaya Morskaia, St. Petersburg, 199000, Russia
[2] ITMO University, 49 Kronverkskiy av., St. Petersburg, 197101, Russia
[3] SPIIRAS, 39, 14th line, St. Petersburg, 199178, Russia
{vatamaniuk,ronzhin,ronzhinal}@iias.spb.su

Abstract. The problem of analysis and development of mathematical methods and software for estimation of blur and other quality metrics of digital images is considered. The classification of modern methods of blur estimation used for real-time systems is presented. During experiments several methods of image part segmentation were applied for enhancement of the processing speed and reliability of image quality assessment. The proposed method of preliminary extraction of face area on the image and estimation of its blur was successfully used for elimination of distorted images at the automatic registration of participants in the intelligent meeting room.

Keywords: Digital image processing, image quality estimation, image blur, face segmentation and recognition.

1 Introduction

Nowadays, the automatic monitoring systems are widely used in various fields of human activity. The development of technologies for the automated processing of audiovisual and other types of data is required at a constant growth of volumes of recorded data. The sufficient part of these data is related to photo and video recording. The procedure of automatic image processing usually includes preliminary processing (elimination of unsatisfactory quality images, light normalization, noise clearing, etc.), features extraction, object segmentation, and pattern recognition. Often it is necessary to select some images of high quality corresponding to requirements of a particular technical task from an image database. For an operator such work is not difficult, however, if the amount of a data is large, especially at the stage of preliminary processing is advisable to automate the process of image quality evaluating and filtering of the frames with no reliable data.

The main causes of image distortions that lead to sharpness degradation are: 1) limited resolution of recording equipment; 2) defocusing; 3) the movement of the camera relative to the capturing object, etc. A mathematical model of captured image $s(x, y)$ can be presented as:

A. Ronzhin et al. (Eds.): SPECOM 2014, LNAI 8773, pp. 145–152, 2014.

$$s(x,y) = h(x,y) * u(x,y) + n(x,y) =$$
$$= \iint\limits_{(v,v)} h(x - v, y - v)u(v,v)dvdv + n(x,y),$$

where $u(x, y)$ is brightness function of an image, $h(x, y)$ is two-dimensional impulse response (point spread function, PSF) of linear distorting system, $n(x, y)$ is two-dimensional additive noise, * denotes the two-dimensional convolution. Thereby, value of the brightness function $u(v, v)$ of the original image in the point (v, v) is smudged in accordance with PSF $h(x, y)$ and distorted by additive noise.

Image sharpness is characterized by reproduction of small parts and determined by resolution of the forming system. At the defocusing a point is reproduced in the shape of a spot (blur circle), and two closely spaced points on the original image are merged into one observable point. The size of the blur circle depends on the focal length of the lens as well as the distances from the lens to the object and to the plane of the formed image. Discrete image will be sharp (focused), if the blur circle diameter does not exceed the sampling of the observed image. Otherwise, the linear distortion becomes visible. Thus, image blur can be estimated by focus estimation. In addition, a comprehensive quality assessment also helps to reveal a blurred image.

Further the methods capable for determination of the low quality of unfocused images will be discussed. In Section 3 four blur estimation methods, which can be used in real-time applications will be described. In Section 4 several methods of selection of the area of interest in image will be presented. The results of experiments of blur estimation methods applied for the photographs of participants in the intelligent meeting room and used in the audiovisual monitoring system will be shown in Section 5.

2   Approaches to Image Blur Determination

There are different ways of classification of blur estimation methods. An image can be blurred globally or locally. Either camera shake or out of focus may cause globally blurred image, they can be verified by the PSF. The PSF describes the response of an image to a point source or a point object. After calculating the PSF of an image, the globally blurred image can be classified into camera shake or out of focus. Simultaneously the locally blurred image can be classified into two aspects: depth of field and moving object. The blurred regions can be found by segmentation method, and the PSF estimation on the blurred region can sort out the image with depth of field or moving object [1].

Also the methods of blur estimation can be divided in two major categories [2, 3]: reference-based estimation and blind estimation. For the reference-based estimation, information from the original undistorted image is needed together with its corresponding blur image for the deduction of the blur metric while for the blind estimation, no information is needed at all from the original image. Reference-based estimation can be subdivided into two types – full-reference and reduced-reference estimations. Full-reference estimation requires the availability of the whole original image while reduced-reference estimation only uses some extracted features or information from the original image [2].

There is another classification of image blurriness evaluation methods, where the following six groups of methods are proposed based on [4]:

1) evaluation of gradient (GRA), where the gradient (first derivative) of the image indicates sharp brightness changes at the edges of the objects presented in the image;

2) estimation of Laplacian (LAP), where the Laplacian (second derivative) of the image determines amount of sharp edges in the image;

3) wavelet transform (WAV), where changes of the coefficients of discrete wavelet transform is used to describe the frequency and spatial areas of the image;

4) statistical characteristics of the image (STA), estimate the blurriness as a deviation from the normal distribution, which is usually appeared on distorted images;

5) discrete cosine transform (DCT), which estimates image focus in the frequency domain;

6) complex assessment (MIS).

These types of methods have different complexity and time processing, so the optimum method of image processing is selected depending on the subject area and dedicated computing resources and time.

3   Real-Time Methods of Blur Estimation

Here four methods from several categories listed above that have shown the best results during the evaluation of blurred images and could be used in real-time applications are considered.

Method Tenengrad (GRA1) described in [5] belongs to the category GRA. It is based on estimation of the mean squared gradient (MSG) of pixel brightness of grayscale image. The approximate brightness gradient vector at each pixel is calculated by convolution of horizontal and vertical Sobel masks with the original image:

$$G_x(x,y) = \begin{bmatrix} +1 & 0 & -1 \\ +2 & 0 & -2 \\ +1 & 0 & -1 \end{bmatrix} * A(x,y), \ G_y(x,y) = \begin{bmatrix} +1 & +2 & +1 \\ 0 & 0 & 0 \\ -1 & -2 & -1 \end{bmatrix} * A(x,y),$$

where $A(x, y)$ is the original image; G_x, G_y are Sobel masks; $*$ is two-dimensional convolution operation. The approximate value of the MSG G_{TENG} is calculated by the following formula:

$$G_{TENG} = \sum (G_x(x,y)^2 + G_y(x,y)^2).$$

Increasing of the MSG indicates presence of sharp brightness transitions in the image, and hence, higher edge sharpness. The method gives the best results in a small area of the image, where contrasting transitions exist.

In [6] the method based on measuring local contrast is described. It belongs to the category MIS, so we denote it MIS1. The local contrast is calculated as the ratio of the intensity of each pixel of the grayscale image and the mean gray level in the neighborhood of this pixel.

$$R(x,y) = \begin{cases} \dfrac{\mu(x,y)}{I(x,y)}, I(x,y) \le \mu(x,y) \\ \dfrac{I(x,y)}{\mu(x,y)}, I(x,y) > \mu(x,y) \end{cases},$$

where $I(x, y)$ is the intensity of the current pixel; $\mu(x, y)$ is its neighborhood. The neighborhood size $\mu(x, y)$ centered at the point (x, y) is determined heuristically. The image blur is the sum of values $R(x, y)$ throughout the image or the selected area.

Next, let us to consider another method of category MIS, a method for measuring the blurriness by the image curvature [6], we denote it MIS2. The grayscale image matrix of pixel brightness is represented as a three-dimensional surface. The coordinates of each point of this surface are the two coordinates of each pixel and the value of its brightness. The surface curvature corresponds to transitions between pixels and is approximated by the following function:

$$f(x,y) = ax + by + cx^2 + dy^2.$$

The image is focused if the curvature value is high. The coefficients a, b, c, d are approximately calculated by the method of least squares by convolution of the original image and the matrices M_1, M_2:

$$M_1 = \frac{1}{6}\begin{pmatrix} -1 & 0 & 1 \\ -1 & 0 & 1 \\ -1 & 0 & 1 \end{pmatrix}, \quad M_2 = \frac{1}{5}\begin{pmatrix} 1 & 0 & 1 \\ 1 & 0 & 1 \\ 1 & 0 & 1 \end{pmatrix},$$

$$a = M_1 * I, \quad b = M_1' * I,$$

$$c = \frac{3}{2}M_2 * I - M_2' * I, \quad d = \frac{3}{2}M_2' * I - M_2 * I,$$

where M_1', M_2' are the transposed matrices M_1, M_2. I is the original image. The sum of absolute values of the coefficients a, b, c, d reveals the image blurriness:

$$G_c = |a| + |b| + |c| + |d|.$$

The method is not suitable for homogeneous images with smooth brightness transitions (such as a cloudless sky), because in this case three-dimensional surface curvature varies slightly and cannot serve as an adequate measure of the blurriness.

Another perspective method is NIQE (No-Reference Image Quality Assessment) based on a statistical study of natural images [3]. The natural images are images that are not artificially generated and not distorted by artificial noises, e.g. images obtained using photography, screen capture of video and so on. In natural monochrome images the matrix of normalized coefficients of pixel brightness tends to a normal distribution. Any noise, including blurring, leads to a deviation from the normal distribution. The idea of the method consists in comparing two multivariate Gaussian models of features: calculated for the test image and constructed on the basis of a pre-arranged set of images.

To calculate the features for building the model, the brightness coefficients of image pixels are normalized by subtracting the local mean of the original coefficient matrix of grayscale image brightness and then dividing by the standard deviation:

$$\hat{I}(i,j) = \frac{I(i,j) - \mu(i,j)}{\sigma(i,j) + 1},$$

where $i \in \{1,2...M\}$, $j \in \{1,2...N\}$ are spatial indexes, M, N are the image height and width, $\mu(i,j)$ is the expected value and $\sigma(i,j)$ is the variance.

This normalization can significantly reduce the dependence between the brightness coefficients of the neighboring pixels, leading them to a form, suitable for the construction of a multivariate Gaussian model. Since the entire image sharpness is often limited by the depth of field of the camera, so the image is split into patches of $P \times P$ pixels and then the local sharpness of each patch is estimated. The sharpest patches are selected for further analysis. Local sharpness is calculated by summing the dispersion $\sigma(i,j)$ over the patch. The local area sharpness of the patches is estimated relatively to a threshold, which is selected heuristically. The selected areas passed the sharpness threshold are described by the asymmetric generalized normal distribution:

$$f(x; \gamma, \beta_l, \beta_r) = \begin{cases} \dfrac{\gamma}{(\beta_l + \beta_r)\Gamma\left(\frac{1}{\gamma}\right)} exp\left(-\left(\frac{-x}{\beta_l}\right)^\gamma\right), \forall x < 0 \\[3mm] \dfrac{\gamma}{(\beta_l + \beta_r)\Gamma\left(\frac{1}{\gamma}\right)} exp\left(-\left(\frac{x}{\beta_r}\right)^\gamma\right), \forall x \geq 0 \end{cases},$$

where $\Gamma(\cdot)$ is the gamma function, γ is a parameter that controls the shape of the distribution curve, β_l, β_r are parameters that control the spread on the left and the right side respectively. The coefficients γ, β_l, β_r can be effectively evaluated using the method of moments. The multivariate Gaussian model is compared with another multivariate Gaussian model trained on a set of various images with known quality:

$$f_X(x_1, ..., x_k) = \frac{1}{(2\pi)^{\frac{k}{2}}|\Sigma|^{\frac{1}{2}}} exp\left(-\frac{1}{2}(x - v)^T \Sigma^{-1}(x - v)\right),$$

where $(x_1,...,x_k)$ is a set of calculated features, v and Σ are mean and covariance matrix of multivariate Gaussian model respectively, which are calculated by the method of maximum likelihood. The image quality coefficient is calculated by the formula:

$$D(v_1, v_2, \Sigma_1, \Sigma_2) = \sqrt{\left((v_1 - v_2)^T \left(\frac{\Sigma_1 + \Sigma_2}{2}\right)^{-1} (v_1 - v_2)\right)},$$

where v_1, v_2 are mean vectors of template multivariate Gaussian model and of the model constructed for the test images respectively, Σ_1, Σ_2 - covariance matrices of these models. The coefficient D indicates the difference between the models. When its value is smaller, the distribution of the test image is closer to the normal distribution; otherwise the image contains a noise, which can be a blur too.

4 Approaches to Selection of Areas of Interest in Image

The selection of an area for blur assessment depends on subject domain, in which image processing is implemented. This area may be either a whole image or the contoured object or the area, in which the object is located. For example, in the research of images with people it is advisable to choose for analysis mainly those areas, where their appearance is the most expectable.

The selection of area of interest can increase the robustness of quality assessment, because distorted areas, which are located out of the region of interest, are not analyzed. Also the speed of image processing significantly increases by reducing the amount of processing data. In our case, during solving the problem of automatic registration of participants in the intelligent meeting room the areas, which contain person faces, are most important in the image [7, 8]. The examples of the segmentation of areas of interest in the image are shown in Table 1.

Table 1. The examples of selection of interest areas on photos of the meeting room participants

Description of the selected area	Example of segmentation
The whole image is analyzed without preliminary face detection	
The selected face area is analyzed, the size of which is not less than 200x200 pixels	
The selected face area bounded by the size of 200x200 pixels is analyzed	

The captured face database was received by video monitoring system based on detection of occupied sits by analysis of zone of chairs and AdaBoosted cascade classifier for face detection [9, 10]. These three types of regions in the image were used to compare the performance of the four methods of blur estimation described above.

5 Experiments

In the experiments the participant photo database compiled during events in the intelligent meeting room was analyzed. The participant images were captured by the camera model AXIS 215 of the audiovisual monitoring system in the intelligent meeting room [11, 12]. The resolution of the obtained photographs is 640x480 pixels.

During the experiments three segmentation types of the image part were applied: the whole image, the face area and the face area of 200x200 pixels. The annotated database consisted of 50 sharp and 50 blurred photos. The blurriness coefficients of blurred photos were used to calculate the threshold value for each evaluation method.

Then, each blur estimation method was applied for the set of sharp images and the percentage of photos with blur coefficient exceeded the threshold was estimated. The accuracy of every method is determined as a number of the sharp photos passed the threshold. The experimental results with accuracy and processing time estimates are presented in Table 2.

Table 2. The experiment results

Blur esti-mation method	Processing accuracy, %			Processing time, ms		
	Whole image	Face area	200x200 pixels	Whole image	Face area	200x200 pixels
GRA1	4	22	26	13.81	5.23	4.81
MIS1	0	0	30	12.80	5.81	4.86
MIS2	2	34	30	10.42	7.70	7.30
STA1	10	54	94	31.65	38.08	35.08

As seen from Table 2, the best results for most of the methods are revealed by the small segment found on the selected face region. Naturally, the processing speed is improved by decreasing of analyzed area size. Furthermore, the accuracy of blur detection also increases while the analyzed region is decreasing. For example, the blur evaluation method based on the local contrast assessment does not work on large areas, however, shows an acceptable result for the area of 200x200 pixels. The most accurate method of the above is STA1, but it is also the most time-consuming.

The proposed procedure of prior search of faces area in the frame and evaluating its blurring based on the STA1 method of statistical analysis of the coefficients of pixel brightness allowed us to determine 94% of undistorted frames received during the automatic registration of the participants in the intelligent meeting room. Implementation of the development procedure is perspective in other information and telecommunication applications [13, 14, 15].

6   Conclusion

The blur evaluation is a necessary step in the processing systems working with large input stream of visual information. Preliminary assessment allows a system to exclude images with poor quality carrying no useful information from the further analysis, thus saving the processing memory and speed of automatic vision systems. The image blurriness caused by unsatisfactory shooting conditions occurs owing to the wrong focusing or unexpected movement of the subject. Image blur value can be estimated by various methods, particularly by evaluation of the brightness gradient of image, the ratio of the brightness values of pixels on a certain region, the statistical analysis of the brightness coefficients of pixels.

The discussed methods quantify the magnitude of blurring, which is one of the criteria of image quality. These methods are convenient to use in the modeling and processing of different visual information. Preliminary extraction of face area in the image and its blurriness estimation were successfully applied for elimination of distorted photos in the system of automatic registration of participants in the intelligent meeting room.

Acknowledgments. This work was partially financially supported by Government of the Russian Federation, Grant 074-U01 and RFBR (grant 13-08-0741-a).

References

1. Krasil'nikov, N. N.: Principles of Image Processing Based on Taking into Account their Semantic Structure. Information Control Systems 1(32), 2–6 (2008) (in Russ.)
2. Serir, A., Beghdadi, A., Kerouh, F.: No-reference blur image quality measure based on multiplicative multiresolution decomposition. Journal of Visual Communication and Image Representation 24, 911–925 (2013)
3. Mittal, A., Soundarajan, R., Bovik, A.C.: Making a 'Completely Blind' Image Quality Analyzer. IEEE Signal Processing Letters 20(3), 209–212 (2013)
4. Pertuz, S., Puig, D., Garcia, M.A.: Analysis of Focus Measure Operators for Shape-from-focus. Pattern Recognition 46(5), 1415–1432 (2013)
5. Lorenzo-Navarro, J., Déniz, O., Santana, M.C., Guerra, C.: Comparison of Focus Measures in Face Detection Environments. In: Proc. of ICINCO-RA 2, pp. 418–423. INSTICC Press (2007)
6. Helmli, F., Scherer, S.: Adaptive Shape from Focus with an Error Estimation in Light Microscopy. In: Proceedings of International Symposium on Image and Signal Processing and Analysis, pp. 188–193 (2001)
7. Ronzhin, A.L., Budkov, V.Y., Karpov, A.A.: Multichannel System of Audio-Visual Support of Remote Mobile Participant at E-Meeting. In: Balandin, S., Dunaytsev, R., Koucheryavy, Y. (eds.) ruSMART 2010. LNCS, vol. 6294, pp. 62–71. Springer, Heidelberg (2010)
8. Yusupov, R.M., Ronzhin, A.L.: From Smart Devices to Smart Space. Herald of the Russian Academy of Sciences. MAIK Nauka 80(1), 63–68 (2010)
9. Schiele, B., Schiele, J.L.: Object recognition using multidimensional receptive field histograms. In: Buxton, B., Cipolla, R. (eds.) ECCV 1996. LNCS, vol. 1064, pp. 610–619. Springer, Heidelberg (1996)
10. Viola, P., Jones, M., Snow, D.: Detecting pedestrians using patterns of motion and appearance. In: Proc. of IEEE ICCV, pp. 734–741 (2003)
11. Ronzhin, A.L., Budkov, V.Y.: Multimodal Interaction with Intelligent Meeting Room Facilities from Inside and Outside. In: Balandin, S., Moltchanov, D., Koucheryavy, Y. (eds.) NEW2AN/ruSMART 2009. LNCS, vol. 5764, pp. 77–88. Springer, Heidelberg (2009)
12. Ronzhin, A., Budkov, V.: Speaker Turn Detection Based on Multimodal Situation Analysis. In: Železný, M., Habernal, I., Ronzhin, A. (eds.) SPECOM 2013. LNCS (LNAI), vol. 8113, pp. 302–309. Springer, Heidelberg (2013)
13. Saveliev, A.I.: Optimization algorithms distribution streams of multimedia data between server and client in videoconferencing application. SPIIRAS Proceedings 31, 61–79 (2013)
14. Kryuchkov, B.I., Karpov, A.A., Usov, V.M.: Promising Approaches for the Use of Service Robots in the Domain of Manned Space Exploration. SPIIRAS Proceedings 32, 125–151 (2014)
15. Basov, O.O., Saitov, I.A.: Basic channels of interpersonal communication and their projection on the infocommunications systems. SPIIRAS Proceedings 30, 122–140 (2013)

Controlling the Uncertainty Area in the Real Time LVCSR Application

Nickolay Merkin[1], Ivan Medennikov[2,3],
Alexei Romanenko[2], and Alexander Zatvornitskiy[1]

[1] Speech Technology Center, Saint-Petersburg, Russia
www.speechpro.com
[2] ITMO University, Saint-Petersburg, Russia
www.ifmo.ru
[3] SPb State University, Saint-Petersburg, Russia
www.spbu.ru
merkin@speechpro.com,
ipmsbor@yandex.ru,
183460@niuitmo.ru,
zatvornitskiy@speechpro.com

Abstract. We propose an approach to improving the usability of an automatic speech recognition system in real time. We introduce the concept of an "uncertainty area" (UA): a time span within which the current recognition result may vary. By fixing the length of the UA we make it possible to start editing the recognized text without waiting for the phrase to end. We control the length of the UA by regularly pruning hypotheses using additional criteria. The approach was implemented in the software-hardware system for closed captioning of Russian live TV broadcasts.

Keywords: Automated closed captioning, ASR, respeaking technology, real-time editing of ASR results, live broadcasting.

1   Introduction

Speech recognition in real time is always a compromise between quality (word error rate), throughput (real time factor) and delay.

The more delay is allowed, the higher the quality. In the ideal case, the decoder processes the whole recording from beginning to end. This is possible in batch processing or in a dialogue (IVR applications, where phrases are short). However, some applications require a predictable rate of the output of speech recognition results. For example, in case of automated generation of closed captions [1] the vocal flow is continuous, and even artificially inserted punctuation [2] does not divide it into phrases short enough to provide an acceptable rate of displaying closed captions.

This motivated us to develop a mechanism for producing consistent and noncontradictory intermediate results of speech recognition.

A. Ronzhin et al. (Eds.): SPECOM 2014, LNAI 8773, pp. 153–160, 2014.

The simplest implementation of live output in time-synchronous Viterbi decoders, namely periodically displaying the word trace of the best hypothesis, is not suitable for many applications. The reason is that the best hypothesis at the next instant may differ from the current one by several words. Usually the difference is 1-2 words, but sometimes it may be many more. This varies unpredictably during the process.

This fact made us pay attention not only to the "width" of the decoder hypotheses (i.e. the number of different hypotheses), but also to their "depth" (i.e. the length of word traces).

The idea to explore the word network in depth is taken from the algorithm of Viterbi convolutional decoding [3], with a core difference: we have already scored hypotheses using WFST [4].

2   Uncertainty Area

2.1   Definition

Every instant the decoder tracks a network of word hypotheses, the variants of an unfinished phrase. The live result of recognition is the best-scored hypothesis, which is in fact a bunch of hypotheses with a common beginning that we will refer to as the head:

<common head of the phrase> + { <varied continuations> }

At different times, different hypotheses may be in the lead. The common head grows in the course of time, because the decoder prunes weak hypotheses (using beam and quantity limitations). The time span from the end of the common head to the current instant is referred to as the **uncertainty area** (UA).

If we tell the decoder to display only the definitely recognized common head, it may seem that the decoder sometimes slows down. If we tell the decoder to display the whole hypothesis, the variable continuation will flicker.

Apart from the "**True UA**" (TUA), there is also an "**Observable UA**" (OUA).

TUA covers the time span where all hypotheses branch. The word network before TUA is degenerated into a single line.

Some weak hypotheses may survive for a very long time, never getting the top score and not being pruned either. OUA is the time span where top-scored variants change their continuations, which we will refer to as tails. (Fig. 1)

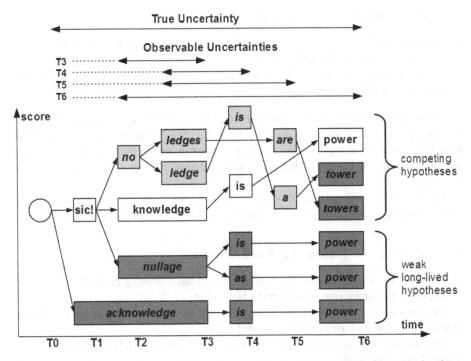

Fig. 1. Uncertainty areas in a word hypotheses network. White and light-gray blocks show observable hypotheses that compete to be the live output; dark-gray blocks show weak hypotheses that are unlikely to ever rise to the top.

Our pilot experiments showed that the OUA is 1.0s and 1.2 words on average, but can reach 20 seconds and 8 words.

That is, the main issue is not the average delay but rare significant outliers. To eliminate these outliers we forcibly freeze the common beginning of the phrase.

2.2   Approaches to Fixing Lasting Uncertainty

Freezing the beginning of the phrase can be done after the decoder (AD), by post-processing its live outputs. To do this, we need to remember the previous output, freeze its head and use it to overwrite the current output. This approach is easy to implement, but the result of merging can be inconsistent. Moreover, the decoder does redundant work tracking hypotheses that branch before the freezing point.

To avoid this, we developed an algorithm for freezing the network within the decoder (WD). It is described in the section "Algorithm for Freezing the Word Network".

In both AD and WD approaches, we take the current result and calculate the distance from its end by a given duration (in seconds) and a given length (in words). Then we freeze the word chain behind this point and, in the latter case, prune all hypotheses that do not begin with this word chain.

We implement two modes of freezing:

- **strict mode**, where neither duration nor length can exceed the given boundaries (OR-condition in the algorithm below)
- **relaxed mode**, where either duration or length can exceed the boundaries, but not both of them (AND-condition)

The strict mode may decrease quality in the WD approach because of more aggressive pruning. If the boundaries are too tight, it virtually degenerates our language model from n-gram to 1-gram. This is due to pauses in speech that simply push words out of the duration limit, making the decoder derive all hypotheses from the last recognized word.

The relaxed mode can be treated as yet another criterion for pruning weak hypotheses (by search beam width, by number, and now by their branching point).

2.3   Algorithm for Freezing the Word Network

The word network consists of nodes, each of which has following properties:

T(node) – the timestamp of the word's beginning

P(node) – the previous word node (in the N-best case each node may have multiple predecessors, but we look at the best-scored one)

Path(node) – the sequence of predecessors, i.e. Path(n) = [n,P(n),P(P(n)), ..., R] where R is the root node.

All hypotheses start from the R node for which T(R)=0, W(R)="", Path(R)={R}

Let us define the function L(node1,node2) as the length in words between the node1 and its predecessor node2, i.e. L(n,n) = 0, L(n,P(n))=1, L(n,P(P(n)))=2, etc. The function is undefined for L(n,m) if m $\notin$ Path(n).

The decoder deals with the set of nodes corresponding to the endings of actual hypotheses, let us call it ENDS.

The whole hypothesis can be picked up by back-tracking Path(node).

The algorithm of pruning consists of four steps.

First, we define the crossing line with the given parameters: MaxDuration and MaxLength. If either parameter is unlimited, we assume it to be $+\infty$.

Second, we take the top scored hypothesis TopScoredNode and backtrack it up to the node K which is the word that crosses the line.

Third, we find out which nodes of ENDS are descendants of the node K. In other words, we backtrack every hypothesis until it crosses the line or reaches K.

Finally, we prune all nodes of ENDS that are not descendants of K. The garbage collector automatically drops the corresponding inner nodes.

Thus, only the K node stays on the crossing line, and the decoder will deal with its descendants only.

```
# "Exceeds" checks if the node has crossed the line
def Exceeds(end, node) :
  return (
      T(node) <= MaxDuration-Now
    and/or     # depending on relaxed/strict mode
      L(end, node) >= MaxLength
  )

# "Backtrack" stops at the crossing line
# or at the key node
def Backtrack(end, key) :
  for node in Path(end) :
    if node == key or Exceeds(end,node) :
      return node
  # if reached the root
  return R

# "IsDescendant" checks if the given end node
# descends from the key
def IsDescendant(end, key) :
  # stopped exactly on the key
  return Backtrack(end,key) == key

# let us find the key node
K = Backtrack(TopScoredNode, R)

# let us find its descendants
DESCENDANTS = {
    end
    for end in ENDS
    if IsDescendant(end, K)
  }

# finally, prune other nodes
# and go on with the rest
Prune(ENDS-DESCENTANTS)
ENDS = DESCENDANTS
```

Algorithm 1. Algorithm for freezing the word network. The condition "and/or" in the code above depends on the relaxed/strict mode.

Backtracking all ENDS is preferred to traversing the tree of descendants of K, because traversing would require variable-size lists of successors of each node (this is expensive and redundant for other purposes).

3   Experiments

In order to test the algorithm, we performed a set of experiments.

We use the speaker dependent continuous speech recognition system for Russian developed by Speech Technology Center Inc. This system is based on principles described in [5,6,7,8,9].

The system was trained on 32 hours of speech of the target speaker (16kHz sample rate). The training database was recorded during real closed caption respeaking process to avoid mismatches between speech styles. The system uses a speaker dependent CD-DNN-HMM [10] acoustic model (SD AM) based on a DNN with 6 hidden layers with 1000 neurons in each and 3500 neurons in the output softmax layer, which correspond to the decision tree tied states of a previously trained tandem model. The DNN input is a context vector of MFCC features taken from 31 consecutive recording frames (the sizes of the left and right contexts equal 15). The basic tandem model was trained on LC-RC features [11].

The general trigram language model (LM), which contains 300k words and 5 million n-gramms, was trained on a 6GB text corpus of news articles. We used Good-Turing smoothing (cutoff=1 for all orders of n-gramms). In the process of ASR tuning we performed fast adaptation of the general news language model to language models for specific topics (using interpolation with optimal coefficient selection).

The test set contained 66 minutes of sports TV comment (biathlon) after respeaking by a professional respeaker.

We request intermediate decoding results (and then freeze hypotheses) each 500 ms.

First, we measure the distribution of OUA (how many times specific variable tails appear). (See Table 1).

Note that we measure the observable UA but control the true UA.

Table 1. Length and duration of OUA without freezing

OUA length (words)	Times occured	% of total times		Duration (seconds)		
		including empty OUA	excluding empty OUA	min	max	avg
0 (empty)	5421	65.80%		0.00	0.00	0.00
1	2635	31.99%	93.54%	0.50	6.45	0.90
2	133	1.61%	4.72%	0.67	7.57	1.39
3	30	0.36%	1.06%	0.92	2.38	1.41
4	13	0.16%	0.46%	1.02	2.86	1.81
5	3	0.04%	0.11%	2.07	2.85	2.47
6	3	0.04%	0.11%	2.45	4.99	3.39

As we can see, sometimes the decoder had to change the last 5-6 words, and many times it had to change the last 2 words after 7.5 seconds delay.

Then we introduce the boundaries. (See Table 2 and Table 3).

The similarity between strict and relaxed modes can be explained by the stable rate of the respeaker's speech, without unnecessary pauses. The experiment shows that the loss of accuracy is 1.49% at most with minor changes of the RT factor.

Table 2. Accuracy loss, from baseline (92.4%) in **relaxed** WD mode

duration: length:	unlimited	1.0s	1.5s	2.0s
unlimited	0.00%	-0.59%	-0.31%	-0.21%
2	-1.43%	-0.36%	-0.21%	-0.17%
3	-0.38%	-0.11%	-0.17%	-0.09%
4	-0.27%	-0.17%	-0.17%	-0.09%

Table 3. Accuracy loss, from baseline (92.4%) in **strict** WD mode

duration: length:	unlimited	1.0s	1.5s	2.0s
unlimited	0.00%	-0.40%	-0.21%	-1.43%
2	-1.49%	-1.43%	-1.43%	-1.43%
3	-0.38%	-0.69%	-0.42%	-0.46%
4	-0.27%	-0.50%	-0.31%	-0.34%

4   Conclusion

We propose the idea of UA (uncertainty area) to describe the changing recognition result in the course of working with speech recognition in real time. The changes in the recognition result mean that it is necessary to wait for an unknown time until the result stabilizes, which produces a delay and is uncomfortable for the person reading the recognized text (for instance, a closed captioning editor).

By controlling the UA (freezing the beginning of the phrase) we make the behavior of the ends of phrases predictable, decreasing the risk of flickering of recognized text.

We demonstrate that freezing the beginning of the phrase leads only to a small decrease in quality, while it is an additional way of pruning weak hypotheses. This enables further research in increasing decoder speed.

Acknowledgements. This work was partially financially supported by the Ministry of Education and Science of the Russian Federation, Contract 14.575.21.0033, and by the Government of the Russian Federation, Grant 074-U01

References

1. Evans, M.J.: Speech Recognition in Assisted and Live Subtitling for Television. R&D White Paper WHP 065, BBC Research & Development (2003)
2. Pražák, A., Loose, Z., Trmal, J., Psutka, V.J., Psutka, J.: Novel Approach to Live Captioning Through Re-speaking: Tailoring Speech Recognition to Re-speaker's Needs. In: Proc. of the INTERSPEECH, Portland, USA, September 9-13 (2012)
3. Viterbi, A.J.: Convolutional codes and their performance in communication systems. IEEE Transactions on Communication Technology 19(5), 751–772 (1971)
4. Mohri, M., Pereira, F., Riley, M.: Weighted Finite-State Transducers in Speech Recognition. Computer Speech and Language 16(1), 69–88 (2002)
5. Chernykh, G., Korenevsky, M., Levin, K., Ponomareva, I., Tomashenko, N.: Cross-Validation State Control in Acoustic Model Training of Automatic Speech Recognition System. Scientific and Technical Journal Priborostroenie 57(2), 23–28 (2014)
6. Yurkov, P., Korenevsky, M., Levin, K.: An Improvement of robustness to speech loudness change for an ASR system based on LC-RC features. In: Proc. of the SPECOM, Kazan, Russia, September 27-30, pp. 62–66 (2011)
7. Prisyach, T., Khokhlov, Y.: Class acoustic models in automatic speech recognition. In: Proc. of the SPECOM, Kazan, Russia, September 27-30, pp. 67–72 (2011)
8. Korenevsky, M., Bulusheva, A., Levin, K.: Unknown Words Modeling in Training and Using Language Models for Russian LVCSR System. In: Proc. of the SPECOM, Kazan, Russia, pp. 144–150 (2011)
9. Tomashenko, N., Khokhlov, Y.: Fast Algorithm for Automatic Alignment of Speech and Imperfect Text Data. In: Proc. SPECOM, Plzen, Czech Republic, September 1-5, pp. 146–153 (2013)
10. Dahl, G.E., Yu, D., Deng, L., Acero, A.: Context-Dependent Pre-Trained Deep Neural Networks for Large-Vocabulary Speech Recognition. IEEE Transactions on Audio, Speech, and Language Processing 20(1), 30–42 (2012)
11. Schwarz, P.: Phoneme recognition based on long temporal context (PhD thesis). Faculty of Information Technology BUT, Brno (2008)

Convolutional Neural Network for Refinement of Speaker Adaptation Transformation

Zbyněk Zajíc, Jan Zelinka, Jan Vaněk, and Luděk Müller

University of West Bohemia in Pilsen, Faculty of Applied Sciences,
New Technologies for the Information Society,
Univerzitní 22, 306 14 Pilsen, Czech Republic
{zzajic,zelinka,vanekyj, muller}@ntis.zcu.cz

Abstract. The aim of this work is to propose a refinement of the shift-MLLR (shift Maximum Likelihood Linear Regression) adaptation of an acoustics model in the case of limited amount of adaptation data, which can lead to ill-conditioned transformations matrices. We try to suppress the influence of badly estimated transformation parameters utilizing the Artificial Neural Network (ANN), especially Convolutional Neural Network (CNN) with bottleneck layer on the end. The badly estimated shift-MLLR transformation is propagated through an ANN (suitably trained beforehand), and the output of the net is used as the new refined transformation. To train the ANN the well and the badly conditioned shift-MLLR transformations are used as outputs and inputs of ANN, respectively.

Keywords: ASR, Adaptation, shift-MLLR, ANN, CNN, bottleneck.

1 Introduction

A speaker adaptation of an acoustic model in the task of the Automatic Speech Recognition (ASR) is a standard approach how to improve the performance of the speech recognition. The most used adaptation techniques are methods based on a linear transformation, where the number of free parameters to be estimated significantly decreases via clustering of similar parameters in comparison with other adaptation methods. However, the number of free parameters of the transformation is still high to be estimated properly when dealing with extremely small data sets.

Various solutions to avoid this problem have been proposed, e.g. lowering the number of free parameters by using diagonal or block diagonal transformation matrices [1] or finding transformation matrices as a linear combination of basis matrices [2]. Another solution is performing a proper initialization of transformation matrices [3], [4]. In this work we try to incorporate an Artificial Neural Network (ANN) in order to refine the poor estimates of the shift-MLLR transformation. The adaptation approach is described in Section 2.

Our idea is based on the principle of information reduction. The ill-conditioned adaptation matrix estimated on a dataset containing a small amount of adaptation data is propagated through a bottleneck neural network (a special type of ANN used for dimensionality reduction, see the Section 3), hence it is transformed in a non-linear fashion in order to map it to a robust estimate (reduce the influence of bad estimates of parameters). This approach was introduced in work [5]. In this paper, a deep neural network

A. Ronzhin et al. (Eds.): SPECOM 2014, LNAI 8773, pp. 161–168, 2014.

was used for improvement of our firs idea. Convolutional Neural Network (CNN) [6] is one of the deep ANNs with a special training process to handle the huge amount of training parameters (more in the Section 4).

To train the ANN, first, shift-MLLR transformations are estimated on sufficiently large variable datasets, and subsequently these transformations are used as inputs and outputs of the ANN. Tests and their results are given in Section 5, they are performed on SpeechDat-East Corpus.

2 Adaptation Based on Linear Transformation

These adaptation techniques adjust the Speaker Independent (SI) model so that the probability of adaptation data would be maximized. Let the SI model be represented by a Hidden Markov Model (HMM) with output probabilities described by Gaussian Mixture Models (GMMs) with mean μ_{jm}, covariance matrix C_{jm} and weight ω_{jm} of each mixture component $m = 1, \ldots, M$, and of each state $j = 1, \ldots, J$ of HMM. The mth mixture component's posterior of the jth state of the HMM given an acoustics feature vector o_t is

$$\gamma_{jm}(t) = \frac{\omega_{jm}p(o_t|jm)}{\sum_{m=1}^{M} \omega_{jm}p(o_t|jm)}. \tag{1}$$

One of the most popular adaptation techniques in cases of small amount of adaptation data are methods based on Linear Transformations (LT), e.g. the Maximum Likelihood Linear Regression (MLLR) [1], which transform the mean of output probabilities of HMM μ_{jm} by an affine transformation

$$\bar{\mu}_{jm} = A_{(n)}\mu_{jm} + b_{(n)}, \tag{2}$$

where $W_{(n)} = [A_{(n)}, b_{(n)}]$ is the transformation matrix composed from the matrix $A_{(n)}$ and the bias $b_{(n)}$, and $\bar{\mu}_{jm}$ is the adapted mean. The advantage of MLLR is that it can adapt more HMM components at once (in this work only means are adapted) using the same transformation matrix. For this purpose similar model components are clustered into clusters $K_n, n = 1, \ldots, N$, hence the number of parameters to be estimated decreases. Denoting d the dimension of acoustics features, the number of free parameters for adaptation is $D = N \times (d^2 + d)$. The clusters can be obtained using a regression tree [8]. It is a binary tree where the root (first) node contains all the means of all the GMM mixture components contained in the HMM. The splitting of nodes is based upon the euclidean distance of GMM means belonging to a given node – two new child nodes are formed so that the distance of centroids computed from GMM means in these nodes is maximized. Once the tree is constructed and adaptation data are available, an occupation of each node $v_k = \sum_{t=1}^{T} \sum_m \gamma_{jm}(t)$ of the tree is computed. The index m ranges over all the indexes of GMM means contained in the node k, and T is the number of feature vectors used for the adaptation. A threshold θ_{th} has to be specified, the transformation matrix W is computed only for the deepest nodes for which the condition $v_k > \theta_{th}$ still holds. Thus, means in such a node will be transformed by the same transformation matrix, for detail see [8]. Note that the number of clusters N depends on the amount of given adaptation data and on the value of the threshold θ_{th}. If θ_{th} is high and only a low amount of adaptation data is available than only one (global) transformation will be used (same transformation matrix for all the GMM means). Hence, N determines the depth of the regression tree and it is the upper bound on the number of clusters that could be acquired if enough data would be available.

Another popular method based on linear transformations is called shift-MLLR [9], where only the bias vector $b_{(n)}$ is utilized (the matrix $A_{(n)}$ is assumed to be the identity matrix)

$$\bar{\mu}_{jm} = \mu_{jm} + b_{(n)}. \tag{3}$$

Thus, the number of free parameters further significantly decreases ($D = N \cdot d$). To estimate the bias $b_{(n)}$ Maximum Likelihood (ML) criterion is used. The auxiliary function, which is maximized has the form

$$Q(\lambda, \bar{\lambda}) = -\frac{1}{2} \sum_{t=1}^{T} \sum_{jm \in K_n} \gamma_{jm}(t)(\log |C_{jm}| + \tag{4}$$
$$+ (o(t) - \bar{\mu}_{jm})^T C_{jm}^{-1}(o(t) - \bar{\mu}_{jm})).$$

The bias $b_{(n)}$ is then given by

$$b_{(n)} = S \sum_{t=1}^{T} \sum_{jm \in K_n} \gamma_{jm}(t)[C_{jm}^{-1}(o(t) - \mu_{jm})], \tag{5}$$

where

$$S = (\sum_{t=1}^{T} \sum_{jm \in K_n} \gamma_{jm}(t)C_{jm}^{-1})^{-1}. \tag{6}$$

In the case, where the number of clusters N is set using a regression tree [8], it is possible to choose a smaller threshold θ_{th} for the shift-MLLR than for the MLLR adaptation. The reason is that the number of free parameters for the shift-MLLR is much lower since the matrix A has not to be estimated.

3 Information Reduction via ANN

Bottleneck ANN is frequently used in order to reduce the dimensionality of feature vectors [10]. The bottleneck strategy consists in distributing the D dimensional input data through a hidden layer with number of neurons smaller than the dimension. However, the number of neurons in the output layer is same as the dimension of input vectors, for details see Figure 1.

The training of bottleneck ANN is supervised, the output for each input is supplied by a teacher. The task of the hidden layer with B neurons is to reduce the dimension of the input space to a smaller dimension B, while requesting the best possible match with the output vector. The principle of the bottleneck can be divided into two parts: compression and decompression of information. and it is usually trained on same input and output. The ANN is then used for the task of data compression. In the task of speech recognition, the bottlenecks were presented e.g. in the work [12] or [13].

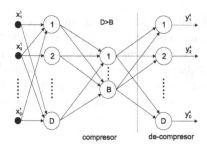

Fig. 1. Bottleneck ANN

4   CNN

Deep neural network CNN is very useful in the task of traffic sign classification [7], where convolutional filters (repeating sets of ANN parameters - neural weights) were used for decomposition of the input image. The entire image is covered by one filter-bank. Many filterbanks was used there, eg. hundreds. A response of these filterbanks was used for the representation of the traffic sign in the input image. This idea is useful for our problem too: we try to find suitable information from our input - the adaptation matrix. The CNN consists of two types of alternating layers, convolutional and max-pooling. On the end of CNN, the full-connected subnet is usually attached. The proposed topology of our net consists of CNN and the bottleneck on the end, see 2.

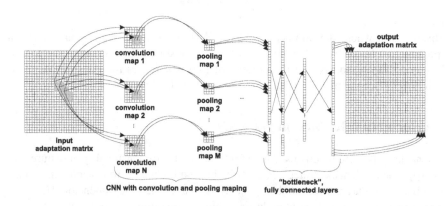

Fig. 2. Convolutional ANN

The input matrices are processed by the convolutional layer with **N** filters (convolutional map). Next polling layer (pooling map) decreases the complexity of the input. The pairs of these two layers are repeating with different number of filters **N**. Through these layers the input adaptation matrices are decomposed into the response of the convolutional filters. The output information is processed by a full-connected subnet (the bottleneck in our case) into the desired output (adaptation matrices without the badly estimated information).

A problem of the deep neural networks lies in the computational complexity. Huge amount of training parameters demand a proportionate amount of training data and the training process is very time-consuming. The topology of the convolutional network is suitable for reduction of the number of training parameters, the weights of each convolutional filers in one filterbank have the same values. The realization of the training process on Graphical Processor Unit (GPU) decreases the training time to an acceptable level.

4.1 Refinement of Adaptation

Our goal is not to find the low-dimensional representation of the input data (this is the case of the dimensionality reduction task), but to filter out the useless and inaccurate information contained in the adaptation matrices. An estimation of the adaptation matrices with small amount of adaptation data (the insufficient information for the estimation of all free adaptation parameters) can lead to the improperly adjusted adaptation parameters. These parameters contained wrong information for speaker adaptation and it can cause the poor recognition rates.

The input to the ANN is a vector, not a matrix. Hence in order to cope with matrices (e.g. with MLLR transformation matrix $W = [A, b]$) a vector $w = vec(W)$ has to be formed. The operator vec concatenates the rows of the matrix so that a high dimensional vector – supervector – is formed. Unfortunately, since the matrix W has to be decomposed to a vector, treated like a vector and again reassembled to a matrix, the properties of the linear space generated by the matrix W can be spoiled in a large extent and the matrix multiplication $A_{(n)}\mu_{jm} + b_{(n)}$ in (2) can lead to poor recognition.

The same problem is solved in method [2], where the new adaptation matrix is constructed as a linear combination of some basis matrices $w_e = vec(W_e)$, but the final matrix W_{out} is found using the ML criterion.

To avoid this problem, we turn to the shift-MLLR, where only bias vectors b have to be processed. These are then used as the input to the ANN.

4.2 ANN for Shift-MLLR

The proposed approach of the shift-MLLR refinement has the following steps:

- **Format of data:** $w_s = [b_{s(1)}^T, \ldots, b_{s(N)}^T]^T$ is the sth speaker's input vector – all the transformation vectors $b_{s(n)}, n = 1, \ldots, N$ from all clusters K_n are concatenated into one supervector. The number of clusters N is fixed. Dimension of the supervector is $D = N \cdot d$.
- **Training**: Input supervectors w_s^{train} from the training dataset are estimated for each speaker s utilizing MLLR-shift adaptation using only one sentence from this given speaker (to simulate the limited adaptation data case). Output supervectors $w_s^{train-out}$ (the information from the teacher - supervised training) are composed from transformations estimated on all available training data from speaker s. Finally, pairs $(w_s^{train}, w_s^{train-out}), s = 1, \ldots, S$ are continuously introduced

one-by-one to the ANN in order to train ANN parameters. Hence, a non-linear transformation is trained, the ANN learns the relation between ill- and well-conditioned estimates of the shift-MLLR biases. The ANN should remove the inconsistency between input and output.

– **Testing**: After a speaker model was adapted, the supervector w^{test} is constructed. This supervector w^{test} is distributed through the bottleneck ANN so that the output supervector $w^{test-out}$ is obtained. The output supervector $w^{test-out} = [b_{(1)}^{test-out}, \ldots, b_{(N)}^{test-out}]$ (refined transformation) is than decomposed and utilized to adapt the speaker independent model (the previous adaptation is left out).

5   Experiments

5.1   SpeechDat-East (SD-E) Corpus

For experiment purposes we used the Czech part of the SpeechDat-East corpus (see [15]). In order to extract the features Mel-frequency cepstral coefficients (MFCCs) were utilized, 11 dimensional feature vectors were extracted each 10 ms utilizing a 32 ms hamming window, Cepstral Mean Normalization (CMN) was applied, and Δ, Δ^2 coefficients were added.

A 3-state HMM based on triphones with 2105 tied-states in total and 8-components GMM with diagonal covariances in each of the states was trained on 700 speakers with 50 sentences for each speaker (cca 4 sec. on a sentence).

To test the systems performance, different 200 speakers from SD-E were used with 50 sentences for each speaker. However, a maximum of 12 sentences was used for the adaptation. A language model based on trigrams was used for the recognition process. The vocabulary consisted of 7000 words.

5.2   Setup

In our experiments we used the unsupervised shift-MLLR adaptation with 64 transformations $b_{(n)}, n = 1, \ldots, 64$ depending on classes in the regression tree and MLLR adaptation with only one global transformation. The bottleneck ANN was trained with IRPROP training algorithm [14] and ANN with 3 layers was used. For the global and shift-MLLR adaptation with 64 transformations the number of neurons in each layer of ANN was 33, 10, 33 and 2112, 100, 2112, respectively. The topology of ANN can be seen in Figure 1, the sigmoid activation function was utilized in hidden layers and the linear function was used in the output layer. The bottleneck ANN was trained with IRPROP algorithm, the topology of our proposed CNN consist of different layers, see Figure 2. We used only one pair of convolutional-pooling layers with 5 filterbanks with the sigmoid activation function. Final subnet was similar to the bottleneck described above.

In the training of ANN we utilized 700 speakers (used in the training phase of HMM) from the SD-E corpus. Input vectors – shift-MLLR biases – used in the training phase of ANN were estimated on one and two adaptation sentences from all the 700 speakers to prepare for cases of small amount of adaptation data. Next, for each speaker 20 input vectors were collected based on different sentences. Each output vector (shift-MLLR bias) was estimated on all available data from one speaker (cca 50 sentences). Note that the same output vector was assigned to all the 20 input vectors of one speaker. The task of ANN is to find the relation between poorly and well estimated transformations.

In the testing phase, first, the shift-MLLR adaptation was performed. The supervector was formed and propagated through ANN. The output vector was decomposed to the individual biases – refined transformation. Finally, the acoustic SI model was adapted by the refined transformation.

5.3 Results

The proposed method using CNN was tested on varying number of adaptation sentences. The Accuracy (Acc) in % of ASR using the shift-MLLR adaptation with a global transformation and with 64 transformations (denoted as shift-MLLR-global and shift-MLLR-64, respectively), and results of the refined shift-MLLR adaptation utilizing CNN (denoted as shift-MLLR-CNN) are shown in Table 1. The accuracy of SI model is 68.75%. Note that we chose a global transformation for MLLR, because of an insufficient amount of the adaptation data.

Table 1. The results (Acc)[%] of speech recognition utilizing unadapted SI model, MLLR adaptation, shift-MLLR adaptation, and refined shift-MLLR-CNN adaptation for different number of adaptation sentences

No. Sentence	MLLR -global	shiftMLLR -64	shiftMLLR- CNN
1	14.04	69.84	70.11
2	56.36	70.56	70.77
3	66.74	70.79	70.89
4	69.58	70.94	70.71
5	70.23	71.16	70.59
6	70.74	71.31	70.03
8	72.30	71.76	70.79
10	72.30	72.14	70.95

As we expected ordinary MLLR with only a global transformation matrix $W = [A, b]$ completely failed in the case of small amount of adaptation data (1-4 sentences, which is approx. 4-16s of speech without reference transcription). On the other hand the shift-MLLR approach with only a bias vector used as a transformation seems to be a good choice for the adaptation with a few adaptation data. For all different amounts of adaptation data the performance of the recognition system is not spoiled, as was the case for MLLR adaptation. The proposed approach – shift-MLLR refined by CNN (shift-MLLR-CNN) – improves the accuracy for small amounts of adaptation data (1-4 sentences) in comparison to shift-MLLR, however no additional improvement is acquired when more adaptation data are available. The reason is that ANN was tuned for cases with small amounts of adaptation data (1-2 sentences).

6 Conclusions

Presented experiments proved the increase of the accuracy of the speech recognition utilizing MLLR based adaptation, especially the involvement of the shift-MLLR refined by CNN in the task of extremely small data sets. The CNN with bottleneck obviously suppresses the influence of the ill-conditioned parameters of the adaptation. In future work we would like to extend proposed methods based on cNN also to MLLR with full transformation matrix.

Acknowledgments. This research was supported by the Ministry of Culture Czech Republic, project No.DF12P01OVV022.

References

1. Gales, M.J.F.: Maximum likelihood linear transformations for HMM-based speech recognition. Computer Speech and Language 12, 75–98 (1997)
2. Povey, D., Yao, K.: A Basis Representation of Constrained MLLR Transforms for Robust Adaptation. Computer Speech & Language 26, 35–51 (2012)
3. Li, Y., Erdogan, H., Gao, T., Marcheret, E.: Incremental on-line feature space MLLR adaptation for telephony speech recognition. In: 7th International Conference on Spoken Language Processing, pp. 1417–1420 (2002)
4. Zajíc, Z., Machlica, L., Müller, L.: Initialization of fMLLR with Sufficient Statistics from Similar Speakers. In: Habernal, I., Matoušek, V. (eds.) TSD 2011. LNCS, vol. 6836, pp. 187–194. Springer, Heidelberg (2011)
5. Zajíc, Z., Machlica, L., Müller, L.: Bottleneck ANN: Dealing with small amount of data in shift-MLLR adaptation. In: Proc. of the IEEE 11th ICSP, pp. 507–510 (2012)
6. LeCun, Y., Bengio, Y.: Convolutional networks for images, speech, and time-series. In: Arbib, M.A. (ed.) The Handbook of Brain Theory and Neural Networks. MIT Press (1995)
7. Ciresan, D., Meier, U., Masci, J., Schmidhuber, J.: A Committee of Neural Networks for Traffic Sign Classification. In: Proc. of the IJCNN, pp. 1918–1921 (2011)
8. Gales, M.J.F.: The Generation and use of Regression class Trees for MLLR Adaptation, Techreport Cambridge University Engineering Department (1996)
9. Giuliani, D., Brugnara, F.: Acoustic model adaptation with multiple supervisions, TC-STAR Workshop on Speech-to-Speech Translation, pp. 151–154 (2006)
10. Parviainen, E.: Dimension Reduction for Regression with Bottleneck Neural Networks. In: Fyfe, C., Tino, P., Charles, D., Garcia-Osorio, C., Yin, H. (eds.) IDEAL 2010. LNCS, vol. 6283, pp. 37–44. Springer, Heidelberg (2010)
11. Bishop, C.M.: Neural Networks for Pattern Recognition. Oxford University Press, USA (1996)
12. Grézl, F., Karafiát, M., Burget, L.: Investigation into bottle-neck features for meeting speech recognition. In: Interspeech, vol. 9, pp. 2947–2950 (2009)
13. Zelinka, J., Trmal, J., Müller, L.: Low-dimensional Space Transforms of Posteriors in Speech Recognition. In: Interspeech, vol. 10, pp. 1193–1196 (2010)
14. Igel, C., Hsken, M.: Improving the Rprop Learning Algorithm. In: Second International Symposium on Neural Computation, pp. 115–121 (2000)
15. Pollak, P., et al.: SpeechDat(E) - Eastern European Telephone Speech Databases, In: XLDB - Very Large Telephone Speech Databases, ELRA (2000)

Corpus-Based Regiolect Studies: Kazan Region

Kamil Galiullin, Azaliya Gizatullina, Elena Gorobets,
Guzel Karimullina, Rezeda Karimullina, and Denis Martyanov

Kazan Federal University, Russia
{Kamil.Galiullin,Azaliya.Gizatullina,Elena.Gorobets,
Guzel.Karimullina,Rezeda.Karimullina,Denis.Martyanov}@kpfu.ru

Abstract. Our paper aims to regard the specificity of building and usage of e-corpora created in Kazan (Volga region) Federal University: dictionary and textual corpus "Kazan region: the language of Russian documents (16th to 17th centuries), e-corpus of Russian dialects in Kazan region (19th to 21st centuries), e-corpus of Russian texts connected with Kazan region / the Republic of Tatarstan (20th to 21st centuries). The article describes the informational potential of e-references containing and reflecting the significant data connected with general and specific characteristics of Kazan regiolect (the territory variant of Russian language used in Kazan region, which is well-known as a region of interlingual contacts).

Keywords: Electronic language reference, Internet-linguography, informational potential, Kazan region, regiolect, language contacts.

1 Introduction

Modern linguistics needs a significant expansion of source base. It is obviously necessary to supplement a wide range of various sources with new linguistic materials in order to provide its scientific analysis.

This expansion is realized with the help of different information technologies, creation of linguistic databases and corpora – both general and specific.

Electronic language references (ELR) give an opportunity to conduct the extended search, selection and processing of included materials in comparison with traditional (paper) sources.

Russian and foreign researchers point to different advantages of ELR: a) serviceability, easy adaptation to users' queries; b) frequent access to information (even if the quantities of information are large); c) exact query execution; d) multiple choice of entries, possibility of search by different parameters; e) extended support in actual status; f) removed restrictions to the volume of information.

Nowadays there is a new form of language references application; ELR begin to function not only as a result of research accumulating the received data, not only as a source of information for further analysis, but also as a means of organization, holding, search and transformation of data as well as an effective instrument of research [1; 6; 12].

A. Ronzhin et al. (Eds.): SPECOM 2014, LNAI 8773, pp. 169–175, 2014.
© Springer International Publishing Switzerland 2014

The department of applied linguistics (professors, associate professors, assistants and students) and the programmers of Kazan Federal University realize the project aimed to creation of electronic corpora and funds containing and describing textual and vocabulary data from Russian and Tatar languages (see [2; 3]).

The research aimed to development of electronic collections (corpora) is conducted with a support of different foundations and programs:

1) Federal target grant «The Russian Language» (the project «Computer linguographic fund of the Russian Language»)

2) Federal target scientific-technical program «Researches and developments of priority trends in science and technique" (2002 – 2006)

3) Analytic departmental target program "The development of high school scientific potential" (2009 – 2010)

4) Russian Humanitarian Scientific Foundation projects: "Computer support of Russian lexicography (18th century)", "Computer corpus of the Tatar Language: lexicographical subcorpus", "Large corpus of the Russian language of the 18th century", "Comprehensive corpus of Russian written monument of Kazan region (16th to 17th centuries): textual and lexicographical subcorpora", "Comprehensive reference corpus of the Russian language dictionaries (18th to the 1st half of 19th century)"

5) Thematic plan of research work granted by the Ministry of Education and Science (Russian Federation), project "Linguistic Internet bases: creation and usage (№ 8.2001.2011), Republic target program "The Russian language in Tatarstan".

Several e-corpora are registered in the Federal Service for Intellectual Property. They are prize-winners of All-Russian and International exhibitions as well as they are awarded the national certificates of quality in the nomination "The best information project".

2   Baseline Features of Corpora

Our paper describes the features and informational potential of electronic corpora which accumulate and register different data connected with Kazan regiolect (a territorial variant of Russian language used and being used in Kazan region):

1) corpus of dictionaries and texts "Kazan region: the language of Russian documents (16th to 17th centuries)"

2) electronic collection of Russian dialects registered in Kazan region (19th to 21th centuries)

3) electronic corpus of Russian texts connected with Kazan region / Tatarstan (20th to 21th centuries).

The collections contain following sources: a) connected by their origin or by their content with Kazan region which traditionally includes the territory of contemporary Republic of Tatarstan as well as some parts of adjoining republics (Chuvash Republic and Republic of Mari El); b) reflecting different periods and times from the 16th century to nowadays.

The main characteristic of this region is its polyethnic and polylingual status. It is a territory of long and active Russian-Turkic (Republic of Tatarstan, Chuvash

Republic), Russian-Finno-Ugric (Republic of Mari El), Turkic-Finno-Ugric language contacts. That's why the presence of a large quantity of borrowings from foreign languages is one of the most significant features of Kazan regiolect of Russian language. So, it is certainly necessary to pay close attention on the analysis of regional language contacts.

The software of corpora gives the opportunity to make search queries containing: a) the queried unit b) the part of any component of the unit(s) with the indication of position and quantity of symbols or any other characteristics if necessary. Besides, it is necessary to mention one more important advantage of ELR: a user can define the parameters of processing and delivering; in particular, he or she can define the volume of the corpus where the search will be conducted (one source, any group of sources or all of them).

Besides, using ELR one can receive a wide range of quantitative data which helps to compare and characterize different language materials [8].

2.1 "Kazan Region: The Language of Russian Documents (16th to 17th Centuries)": Corpus of Dictionaries and Texts

The corpus of Russian documents of Kazan region of the 16th – 17th centuries doesn't have any alternatives in contemporary Russian regional studies. It helps to register entirely and to describe the textual materials of all written sources connected with the region (nearly 900 records containing about 1 100 000 word usages). The Internet version of the corpus is located on the web portal of Kazan Federal University (the web-site of Kazan linguographic collection: http://www.klf.kpfu.ru/kazan/). As the analysis shows, this complex of dictionaries and texts contains the comprehensive data important for historical linguistics – both general and regional.

The comparative analysis involving the information from general and regional as well as dialect dictionaries helps to reveal regional (dialect) and interdialect units in Kazan documents.

The written monuments of Kazan region contain several unites which appeared because of the influence of Eastern languages, mainly of Tatar, i.e. *абыз* 'a scribe' (compare *абыз* 'Muslim priest' in the Dictionary of Russian language of the 18th century); compare Tatar *абыз* 'a scribe, a clerk in holy orders' (in the 15th – 18th centuries); *маазин* 'muezzin, a minister in a mosque'; compare Tatar *мәзин* 'muezzin', *мизгить* 'mosque'; compare Old Turkic *mäzgit* 'mosque' etc.

Analyzed sources also include the additional materials which enrich the information of contemporary historical and linguistic research and dictionaries. The comparison of this data with the data from historical dictionaries of Russian language – particularly with "The Dictionary of the Russian Language of the 11th – 17th centuries" [9] (indexed here as D17) – helped to reveal:

1) the units with no registration in D17.

These units form rather large group in the written monuments of Kazan region; for instance, the quantity of such lexemes in analyzed documents only of the first part of 17th century is more than 100. The lexemes of this group represent different significant parts of speech.

2) the units dated more precisely due to the information of Kazan documents.

This group is also extensive; for example, the quantity of such units in the documents of only the first part of the 17th century is more than 150. The chronology of some units is defined more precisely on the base of its usage as a proper noun (for example, the names of persons and other groups); in such cases the abbreviation PN is usually used after the dating.

In order to optimize the comparative analysis of the corpus data involving the information from historical language sources the scientific group of Kazan Federal University is creating the composite corpus of historical dictionaries of Russian language [4] (at the moment it includes the e-glossaries of 36 dictionaries).

Besides, the corpus of Kazan texts referring to the following – the 18th – century is being worked out.

2.2   Electronic Collection of Russian Dialects Registered in Kazan Region (19th to 21st Centuries)

The corpus sources are: 1) linguographical collections (it is necessary to mention specially "The Dictionary of Russian dialects of the interfluve of Volga and Sviyaga" prepared by M.F.Moiseenko [7] as well as the consolidated version of "The Dictionary of Russian Folk Dialects" [11], b) dialect materials written in the 19th – 21st centuries, c) various publications describing the dialect speech on the territory of Kazan region; d) some archive materials of Kazan and St. Petersburg.

This collection including textual and vocabulary materials (in general more than 1200 000 word usages) is the basis of subcorpora, one of which contains so called «Kazan words» (KW) – the lexical units registered in the dialect speech of our region.

KW subcorpus is a platform which helped to create the cumulative index of KW with a glossary containing the systemized description of KW. Besides lexemes (with variants), it includes also a) grammar characteristics, b) the meaning presented in region dialects, c) precise address.

The analysis shows that the cumulative corpus of KW provides us with materials for analysis of functional specificity of Russian dialects on the territory of Kazan region, its features and its interaction with other languages.

KW can be classified by the sphere of their usage: interregional and regional dialect units. The significant part of words which are being used in Kazan region is registered in other regions of Russia as well. From the point of view of regional linguistic studies the most interesting words are the units registered only in our region; see, for instance, the nouns *здынка, зины, зобец, издыхалка* etc.; the verbs *заскуртать, затальянить, испрашиться, исстояться, истомиться, кевилить, килажничать, коноботиться, кочутать, кубиться* etc.; the adjectives *захердяшный, зверий, калончаковый (калончаковый товар), крупущий* etc. There are some cases in which only one meaning of the word is specifically "Kazan": *зорянка* (the 5th meaning), *зрятина* (the 1st), *избойна* (the 1st), *изгарь* (the 3rd), *ищаулить* (the 2nd), *кадра* (the 1st) etc.

KW contain a significant group of words, Turkic (Tatar) by their origin as a result of the interaction mentioned above (the dialects of Kazan region and Tatar language);

i.e. *абдрага'н, айда', алы'рить, апа'йка, аптра'ть, ахма'к, бастри'к / бастри'г / ба'стрик, баурса'к, бля'зик, бутка', джиги'н, зила'н, зила'нт, ка'рда / карда', кошта'н, лагу'н, ная'н* etc.

The examination of materials connected with the loan words helped to reveal the absent lexical units in some dictionaries – for instance, a number of dialect turkisms are not included into the dictionary of E.N.Shipova [10]: *аптрать, аслам, ахмак, балчужник, бодран, джигин, карда, карга, куштыль* etc.

There are some cases when dictionary entries of contemporary language references contain wrong or not full information; i.e. several dictionary entries [10] don't include the indications of word usage in Kazan region (*карга, кацап* etc.), while the geographical description of the word gives possibilities to make its history and etymology more precise. For instance, the information about the word *баурсак* allows to refer this lexeme to words, Tatar by their origin.

Besides, sometimes different types of KW variants are absent in lexicographic sources and linguistic researches; i.e. E.N.Shipova's dictionary [10] doesn't include a number of phonetic and orthographic variants of turkisms registered in Kazan dialects.

At present time the data from new sources is being included into the corpus; besides, the additional information about the described units is being incorporated into the e-collection.

2.3 Electronic Corpus of Russian Texts Connected with Kazan Region / Tatarstan (20th to 21st Centuries)

This corpus consists of different texts: works of art (including translations), mass media, regional studies, recordings of oral speech etc. (more than 2,4 millions of word usages).

Our corpus includes several subcorpora, among them we would like to mention especially 1) the subcorpus "The dictionary of the language of Kazan"; 2) the subcorpus of Tatar (Eastern) borrowings registered in different texts of our region.

Tatarisms (words borrowed from the Tatar language) take a significant place in the language of regional texts. They refer to a wide range of thematic groups (more than 40): habitations, buildings, food, drinks, clothes, shoes, head-dresses, art, religion, the names of persons etc. (*баурсак, губадия, катык, перемяч, чак-чак; джилян, калфак, каляпуш, читек; баит, дастан, кубыз, сурнай; медресе, минарет, мулла, намаз, ураза; абый, апа, бабай, малай* etc.). Tatarisms can be divided into two groups: properly Tatar (Turkic) by their origin and borrowed by Turkic languages from other eastern languages (Arabic, Persian, Mongol, Chinese, Indian).

It is very important to compare the data from our corpus with materials from other regions of Turkic-Russian contacts (Republic of Bashkortostan, Kazakhstan, Uzbekistan, Turkmenistan, Kyrgyzstan, Azerbaijan etc.). In order to provide the comparative research of linguistic data and to reveal the regional and interregional borrowings the subcorpus containing Turkisms of other regions is being worked out at present time.

Besides, our department creates the corpus-based dictionary of Tatar borrowings in Russian texts.

3   Conclusion

As our research shows, electronic language references created in Kazan University give a user a rich material for research in the sphere of Kazan regiolect from the 16th to the 21st century.

The usage of electronic language collections helps to replenish the source base not only in the sphere of regional linguistics. In particular, the corpus data are used in different researches of Russian language and in various lexicographical (linguographical) projects, including academic, such as The Dictionary of the Russian language (11th to 17th centuries) (The Institute for Russian Language, Russian Academy of Sciences), "The Dictionary of the Russian language (18th century)" (The Institute for Linguistic Studies, Russian Academy of Sciences), "The Dictionary of everyday Russian language of the 16th – 18th centuries: Moskovskaya Rus'" (Saint Petersburg State University) etc.

We continue to work out the corpora; in particular, we enrich the sphere of materials described in dictionaries. It increases the informational potential of ELR and widens the search options.

The tendencies in modern lexicography (linguography) and the informational potential of language references are the evidence of the fact that the most perspective type of a reference is its Internet version [5].

The possibilities of ELR to increase its informational potential are defined by their connection with different corpora (subcorpora) containing similar, comparable or additional data. It is really actual to provide such connection with other corpora and collections created or being created by different scientific groups.

References

1. Dictionaries. An International Encyclopedia of Lexicography. Supplementary Volume: Recent Developments with Focus on Electronic and Computational Lexicography. De Gruyter Mouton, Berlin (2013)
2. Galiullin, K., Gorobets, E., Karimullina, G., Karimullina, R., Gizatullina, A., Martyanov, D.: Kompleksnye slovarno-tekstovye internet-korpusy (na materiale russkogo i tatarskogo yazykov). In: Proceedings of the SPECOM 2011: The 14th International Conference Speech and Computer, Kazan, Russia, September 27-30, pp. 447–449 (2011) (in Russian)
3. Galiullin, K., Gorobets, E., Karimullina, G., Karimullina, R.: Computational Corpus of Tatar Proverbs and Sayings: Electronic Database of Paremias. In: Phraseology in Multilingual Society, pp. 350–362. Cambridge Scholars Publishing, Newcastle upon Tyne (2014)
4. Galiullin, K.R.: Svodnyj internet-fond istoricheskikh slovarej russkogo yazyka. In: Slovo i Tekst v Kul'turnom Soznanii Ehpokhi. Part 10, pp. 7–11. Legiya, Vologda (2012) (in Russian)
5. Galiullin, K.: Internet-lingvografiya: russkiye tekstoopisyvayuschiye slovari. In: Problemy Istorii, Filologii, Kul'tury. 2(24), pp. 635–639. Analit, Magnitogorsk (2009) (in Russian)
6. Kompyuternaya lingvografiya. Izdatel'stvo Kazanskogo universiteta, Kazan (1995) (in Russian)
7. Moiseenko, M.F.: Slovar' russkikh govorov Volzhsko-Sviyazhskogo mezhdurech'ya. Izdatel'stvo Kazanskogo universiteta, Kazan (2002) (in Russian)

8. Quantitative Linguistik: Ein internationales Handbuch. Walter de Gruyter, Berlin (2005)
9. D17 – Slovar' russkogo yazyka XI – XVII vv. Vol. 1-29. Nauka, Moskva (1975-2011) (in Russian)
10. Shipova, E.N.: Slovar' tyurkizmov v russkom yazyke. Nauka, lma-ta (1976) (in Russian)
11. SRNG – Slovar' russkikh narodnykh govorov. vol. 1-45. Nauka, Leningrad; Sankt-Peterburg (1965– 2013) (in Russian)
12. Zholobov, O.: The corpus of the Old Russian copies of the Paraenesis of Ephraem Syrus: BAN 31.7.2. Russian Linguistics 35(3), 361–380 (2011)

Crowdsourcing Interactive Technology
for Natural-Technical Objects Integrated Monitoring

Andrejs Romanovs[1], Boris V. Sokolov[1,2,3], Arnis Lektauers[1],
Semyon Potryasaev[2], and Viacheslav Shkodyrev[4]

[1] Riga Technical University, Kalku Street 1, LV-1658 Riga, Latvia
[2] St. Petersburg Institute for Informatics and Automation of Russian Academy of Sciences,
14 Linia V.o., 39, SPIIRAS, St. Petersburg, 199178, Russia
[3] University ITMO St. Petersburg, 199101, Russia
[4] St.Petersburg State Technical University (SPbSPU), Grazhdansly prosp., 28
St.Petersburg, 195220, Russia
{andrejs.romanovs,arnis.lektauers}@rtu.lv,
sokol@iias.spb.su, {semp,shkodyrev}@mail.ru

Abstract. This article discusses the possibility of combining modern social interactive technologies and the process of ground-space monitoring of natural and technical objects, as well as improving the efficiency and social importance of this process, by involving public representatives to the dissemination and use of the monitoring data. Specific information-analytical monitoring system is proposed in the paper. This system is based on suggested technology of remote sensing data as well as data of other sources with social information integration in the current context.

Keywords: Social interactive technologies, crowdsourcing, ground space monitoring, natural-technological objects, intelligent technological platform.

1 Introduction

The monitoring information regarding incidents and disasters is received typically from different data sources (e.g. biometric systems, aerospace systems, etc.), and, therefore, it is heterogeneous by nature (e.g. electrical signals, graphical, audio, video information, text, etc.). Thus, since modern natural-technological objects (hydroelectricity dams, large industrial plants, thermoelectric plants) are very complex and multifunctional ones, their monitoring should be performed in conditions of large-scale heterogeneous data sets. Currently, the monitoring and control of natural and technological systems are still not fully automated.

Developed within the project INFROM "Integrated Intelligent Platform for Monitoring the Cross-Border Natural-Technological Systems" technology [1] involves the creation of an intellectual platform for the processing and use of the results of both ground-and space monitoring. Project provides the development of a common information space to monitor natural and technical objects states, providing for the government and the public topical environmental information for use in education,

A. Ronzhin et al. (Eds.): SPECOM 2014, LNAI 8773, pp. 176–183, 2014.

science, business, case management, and will also provide additional independent source of operational information on natural and technological hazards processes.

Another important result is to attract people to the development of innovative technologies and the active use of space activities. Developed intellectual platform will also help to reduce the risk and minimize the impact of natural or technological disasters by helping the timely notification of the population in the case of the disaster and its prognosis. To achieve this, it is proposed to use modern social technologies (crowdsourcing) that have been widely spread in many areas of the economy.

2   Crowdsourcing as a Modern Social Technology

Recently conducted by a well-known Gartner Inc. company studies have shown the need for entrepreneurs, willing to win the competition in the market, choosing the new business models (instruments and processes), which primarily will be based on social networks and media [2]. One of the such tools is the crowdsourcing, which is a conceptual part of the Human Computing, which can take various forms (Participatory Sensing, Urban Sensing, Citizen Sensing), in accordance with the scale of involvement of the people, tasks, they are addressed to design, and incentives that are designed to facilitate their participation.

The term "Crowdsourcing" is derived from the words crowd and outsourcing; this is a process requiring people, who are not organized in any other system, to perform a specific job. The creator of the term Jeff Howe considered crowdsourcing as a new social phenomenon that is beginning to emerge in certain areas [3], as a phenomenon of bringing people together for the solution of the problem without any reimbursement, and the consequences of such groups/associations for business, solving similar tasks professionally. The method consists in the fact that the task is offered to an unlimited number of people, regardless of their professional status or age. Participants of a crowdsourcing project form the society that chooses by discussing the most successful solution of the given problem. For businesses, this method is an inexhaustible resource for finding solutions to solve their own problems and issues, a powerful tool that allows to adjust the cost-effectively development, including the development of the most customer-oriented products.

Currently a number of social tools are ranked as a crowdsourcing; researchers from "Crowdsourcingresults" [4] proposed a comprehensive classification of modern methods of crowdsourcing.

Crowdsourcing can be applied not only to monitor the status of the selected object or area, but also at the same time, increase the awareness of people about the behaviour of the monitoring object. The motivation for engaging the public in monitoring is two-fold [5]. On the one hand, the system of crowdsourcing can complement modern assessment methods to achieve a high degree of spatial-temporal granularity at lower costs. On the other hand, the active involvement of citizens in the processes of decision-making control and increases their self-awareness and sense of responsibility.

There is huge number of available free-ware and paid methods of information protection from unauthorized access by unwanted individuals [6].

3   Integration of Traditional and Social Data

Mobile phones increasingly become multi-sensor devices, accumulating large volumes of data related to our daily lives. These trends obviously raise the potential of collaboratively analyzing sensor and social data in mobile cloud computing [7].

In the same time, there exists a growing fleet of various robotic sensors (e.g., robotic fishes) coupled with the emergence of new and affordable monitoring technology that increases exponentially the amount of data collected from the world's geo-spheres. This puts decision-makers and researchers who work with these data in a completely fresh situation.

The two popular data types, social and sensor data, are in fact mutually compensatory in various data processing and analysis. Participatory / citizen sensing [8-9], for instance, enables to collect people sensed data via social network services (e.g., Twitter, Waze, Ushahidi) over the areas where physical sensors are unavailable. Simultaneously, sensor data (Figure 1) is capable of offering precise context information, leading to effective analysis of social data. Obviously, the potential of blending social and sensor data is high; nevertheless, they are typically processed separately, and the potential has not been investigated sufficiently. Therefore, there is an urgent need for fusing various types of data available from various data sources.

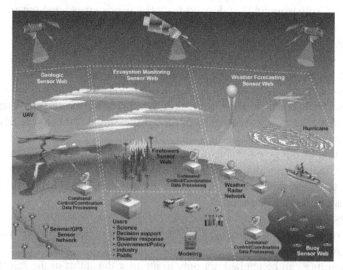

Fig. 1. Various sensor data sources [11] arranged in a Sensor Web [9]

Data fusion is the process of combing information from a number of different sources to provide a robust and complete description of an environment or process of interest [10]. Automated data fusion processes allow essential measurements and information to be combined to provide knowledge of sufficient richness and integrity that decisions may be formulated and executed autonomously.

The existing projects and platforms for data collection and processing, e.g., GOOS [12], Marinexplore [13], Social.Water [14], show that the bottleneck of the data market is not in collecting the data, but in the processing the data. Most available data is disconnected, often archived, and sometimes never used again [13].

4   Crowdsourcing Model for the Integrated Intelligent Platform of Monitoring the Cross-Border Natural-Technical Objects

Existing space-ground monitoring information processing platform can be without significant cost supplemented with an application that processes the data of social sensors. At a minimum, this social application could consist of two components: a mobile application and server public knowledge base.

Mobile applications are for free downloaded and installed on smartphones, to turn them into mobile monitoring systems social sensors. Smartphones collects information from various sensors (microphone, GPS, descriptive or qualifying user-typed information), and in real time sends to the public knowledge base servers.

Public knowledge base (called also Web-based Community Memory) can be defined as a resource of information and communication technologies that enable the public to record and archive information relating to the management of common property [15]. Thus, it is part of the software that operates on a central Web server, collects and processes all data received from mobile social sensors, supports a website that allows users to search, analyse and visualize data.

4.1   System Architecture

The objective of the proposed crowdsourcing-supported software platform is to allow blending the heterogeneous social and sensor data for integrated analysis, extracting and modeling environment-dependent information from social and sensor data streams. The general system architecture consists of four coupled layers: external data sources; high-performance computing layer; storage layer; presentation/service layer.

4.2   Modelling Scenarios

The developed application has a wide range of use, mainly in the form of two scenarios. First scenario: Citizen-led initiatives. Because of the low barrier, in terms of both cost and complexity, concerned individuals can use the platform. The participants can be self-organized citizens with varying levels of organizational involvement: ranging from total strangers that happen to live in the same area; over loosely organized groups of neighbors facing a shared problem; to well-organized previously existing activism groups. The motivation for such initiatives can be diverse: from curiosity about one's daily environment to the gathering of evidence on concrete local issues.

Second scenario: Authority-led initiatives. Social application can be used by the authorities and public institutions – usually at the municipal or regional level – to collect data on the behavior of natural and technological objects in their territory. These data can be used to support decision-making and policy-making in areas such as health and urban planning, environmental protection and mobility. When used alongside an existing monitoring system a participatory sensing platform could make up for missing data, help to estimate error margins of simulation models, add semantics (e.g. identification of pollution sources), etc.

In the most effective way, social application can be used to control and rapid dissemination of information on natural disasters, major accidents, etc. The prototype of the social application, developed under the supervision of the RTU and SPIIRAS researchers J. Petuhova and S.A. Potryasaev, allow to effectively implementing both of the above-described scenarios by the example of the Daugavpils City (Republic of Latvia).

Specific information-analytical system was developed to perform modeling of flood spreading process for its operational forecasting. The main duty cycle of the system consists of input data gathering stage, input data preprocessing stage, execution of modeling process, output data interpretation and dissemination of information (Fig. 2).

The system has possibility to work autonomously, gathering information from sensors, providing hydrological data automatically, and performing duty cycle regularly. In this case, we may encounter different technological errors: inaccuracy of hydrological model coefficients, errors in the input data, imprecise sensors. All this leads to significant reduction of flood forecast accuracy.

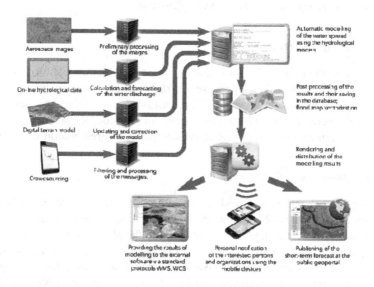

Fig. 2. Main duty cycle of the information-analytical system

Such systems usually have feedback. However, in some cases physical sensors are unavailable. Thus, along with sensors crowdsourcing technology was used. First aim of involving citizens in the process was to validate forecasted inundation areas. The second one was to validate existing physical sensor precision.

The developed information-analytical system can be used by any interested person. The only requirement is the presence of smartphone or tablet PC connected to the Internet. The system implementation based on open source products thereby substantially increasing number of users as compared to expensive commercial platforms. Moreover, easy to use application allows involving various categories of citizens, without requiring them to have special knowledge in the field of geoinformation technologies.

Thus, with web-application provided by researchers, everyone has constant access to the latest flood forecast results (Fig. 3). If someone notices distinction in earlier forecasted flood area and real flooded area, it is possible to take picture of this point and if necessary give a short description. Usually this description has text form. So users have to type messages on theirs smartphones. In case of normal situation this type of input is suitable, but in case of emergency situation sometimes it is easier to send short voice message to the system.

During spring flood in April 2013 in Daugavpils the crowdsourcing information was used for: hydrological model calibration (Manning's coefficient variation depending on the actual water distribution); digital terrain model correction (e.g. lowering level for hills that are in fact vegetation areas); physical sensors output validation (it was found that one of the water level sensors gave erroneous values).

Examples of voice messages that would help in the hydrological model calibration were: "Water level have just reached Nometnu street" or "we were standing knee-deep in the water".

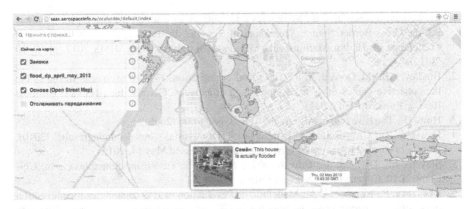

Fig. 3. User interface of web application

The aforementioned tasks were performed manually by operator or developers. However, new prototype develops nowadays. It is assumed that users could provide more structured information to use it automatically in model calibration processes. One of directions of development is to ensure the possibility of recognition of voice messages and allocation of semantic information [16]. Next stage of development is a synthesis of the voice message for users with personalized information about the required actions in an emergency situation, e.g. direction of evacuation, meeting point.

5   Conclusions

On the basis of research results presented in this paper it can be marked the importance and effectiveness of integration of remote sensing data, as well as data of other sources with social information in the context of the monitoring of natural-technological systems by focusing on the issues of changing ecosystems, geo systems, climate and providing services for sustainable economy, healthy environment and better human life. Moreover results of our investigation can be used during structure-functional synthesis multi-model interfaces in modern integrated monitoring systems [17].

Acknowledgments. The research described in this paper is partially supported by the Russian Science Foundation (grants 14-11-0048, 14-21-00135), the Russian Foundation for Basic Research (grants 13-07-00279, 13-08-01250, 13-07-12120, 13-07-00279, 12-06-00276, 12-07-00302, 13-08-00702, grant 074-U01 is supported by Government of Russian Federation), project "5-100-2020" (arrangement 6.1.1 is supported by NRU St. Petersburg SPU), Department of nanotechnologies and information technologies of the RAS (project 2.11), by ESTLATRUS projects 1.2./ELRI-121/2011/13 «Baltic ICT Platform».

References

1. Merkuryev, Y., Sokolov, B., Merkuryeva, G.: Integrated Intelligent Platform for Monitoring the Cross-Border Natural-Technological Systems. In: Proc. of the 14th International Conference on Harbor Maritime and Multimodal Logistics M&S, HMS 2012, pp. 7–10 (2012)
2. Bradley, A.J., McDonald, M.P.: The social organization: How to use social media to tap the collective genius of your customers and employees. Gartner, Inc., Harvard Business Review Press, Boston (2011)
3. Howe, J.: The Rise of Crowdsourcing. Wired, Iss. 14.06 (2006)
4. Dawson, R.: Crowdsourcing Landscape – Discussion. Crowdsourcingresults (2010), http://crowdsourcingresults.com/ (accessed May 14, 2013)
5. Stevens, M., D'Hondt, E.: Crowdsourcing of Pollution Data using Smartphones. In: UbiComp 2010, Copenhagen, Denmark (2010)
6. Dorogovs, P., Romanovs, A.: Modelling and evaluation of IDS capabilities for prevention of possible information security breaches in a Web-based application. In: Proc. of the 14th International Conference on Harbor Maritime and Multimodal Logistics M&S, HMS 2012, pp. 165–170 (2012)
7. Yerva, S.R., Jeung, H., Aberer, K.: Cloud based Social and Sensor Data Fusion. In: 15th International Conference on Information Fusion (2012)
8. Boulos, M.N.K., Resch, B., Crowley, D., Breslin, J., Sohn, G., Burtner, R., Pike, W., Jezierski, E., Chuang, K.-Y.S.: Crowdsourcing, citizen sensing and sensor web technologies for public and environmental health surveillance and crisis management: trends, OGC standards and application examples. International Journal of Health Geographics 10(1), 67 (2011)

9. Fraternali, P., Castelletti, A., Soncini-Sessa, R., Ruiz, C.V., Rizzoli, A.E.: Putting humans in the loop: Social computing for Water Resources Management. Environmental Modelling & Software 37, 68–77 (2012)
10. Durrant-Whyte, H., Henderson, T.C.: Multisensor Data Fusion. In: Sicilliano, B., Oussama, K. (eds.) Springer Hand-book of Robotics, Springer, Heidelberg (2008)
11. NASA, Report from the Earth Science Technology Office (ESTO) Advanced Information Systems Technology (AIST) Sensor Web Technology Meeting (2008)
12. GOOS, The Global Ocean Observing System (2013), http://www.ioc-goos.org (accessed July 5, 2013)
13. Marinexplore: Cutting Ocean Data Processing Time Fivefold. Marine Technology Reporter, no. 11/12, pp. 30–35 (2012)
14. Fienen, M.N., Lowry, C.S.: Social. Water—A crowdsourcing tool for environmental data acquisition. Computers & Geosciences 49, 164–169 (2012)
15. Steels, L., Tisseli, E.: Social Tagging in Community Memories. In: Social Information Processing – Papers from the 2008 AAAI Spring Symposium, March 26-28, pp. 98–103. Stanford University (2008)
16. Ronzhin, A.L., Budkov, V.Y., Karpov, A.A.: Multichannel system of audio-visual support of remote mobile participant at e-meeting. In: Balandin, S., Dunaytsev, R., Koucheryavy, Y. (eds.) ruSMART 2010. LNCS, vol. 6294, pp. 62–71. Springer, Heidelberg (2010)
17. Yusupov, R.M., Ronzhin, A.L.: From smart devices to smart space. Herald of the Russian Academy of Sciences 80(1), 63–68 (2010)

Dramatic Piece Reader and It's Evaluation by the Blind and Sighted Assessors

Milan Rusko, Marián Trnka, Sakhia Darjaa, and Marian Ritomský

Institute of Informatics of the Slovak Academy of Sciences, Bratislava, Slovakia
{milan.rusko,marian.trnka,utrrsach,marian.ritomsky}@savba.sk

Abstract. This work builds on the work presented in [1]. It recalls the concept and realization of the intelligent audio-book reader for the visually handicapped. The system is capable of presenting different characters. The first version mimics the way how a puppeteer portrays different characters, i.e. only one voice talent was used for recording the speech databases in this concept and all the modifications were made using speech synthesis methods. The expressive speech databases are used to adapt the neutral voice to different levels of vocal effort. The architecture of the dramatic piece reader is explained and objective tests of the synthesizers are briefly discussed. The subjective evaluation was done by two groups of evaluators – one consisting of the blind and the second one of the sighted users.

Keywords: Audio-book, speech synthesis, acceptance by the visually impaired.

1 Introduction

Reading a book by an actor is time consuming and costly. The authors of this paper would like to make much more books available – via reading by advanced expressive speech synthesis system. Text-to-speech (TTS) uses speech synthesizer to read out the given text. The main advantages of eBooks with TTS over performed audio books is the availability, ease of access and new titles becoming available much quicker. [2]

Several authors have checked the possibilities of expressive speech synthesis for storytelling (e.g. [3] [4]). So did the authors in this study, but their aim was to design a system capable of creating a unique voice for each character.

The problem with synthesized speech is that it has smaller variability than the natural speech and it becomes tedious after a short while. The authors have presented a new concept of semi-automatic synthetic audio-books generation, a concept that was called DRAPER - the virtual dramatic piece reader. [1] The idea is that the synthetic or virtual reader should not only read the text of the dramatic piece, but that it should change its voice according to the character being depicted. This concept stems from the former research on the presentation of the personality of the dramatic characters by puppeteers [5]. Deriving all the synthetic voices from the original voice of one voice-talent has an advantage to fulfill the requirement of consistency of chosen voices for audio-book reading, that: " ... the voice for each character has to not only be

A. Ronzhin et al. (Eds.): SPECOM 2014, LNAI 8773, pp. 184–191, 2014.

distinctive and appropriate for the character in isolation, but it must also make sense in an ensemble of various characters." [6].

2   Speech Synthesizers

The modern speech synthesis system development is dependent on speech databases that serve as a source of synthesis units or a source of data needed to train the models. In the current work we use some of our earlier results, such as neutral speech database [7] and unit-selection synthesizer [8]. On the other hand the expressive databases and expressive HMM voices belong to the most recent results of our research [9].

2.1   Speech Databases

The set of speech databases containing the voice of our voice talent consists of:

1. Neutral database (Level 0) – 2000 sentences
2. Expressive speech database with higher levels of voice effort
   a. Base level (Level 1) – 300 sentences
   b. Increased level (Level 2) -300 sentences
   c. Highly increased level (Level 3) - 300 sentences
3. Expressive speech database with lower levels of vocal effort
   a. Base level (Level -1) - 150 sentences
   b. decreased level (Level -2) 150 sentences
   c. Highly decreased level (Level -3) 150 sentences
4. Whispered speech database - 150 sentences

The Neutral database, VoiceDat-SK, serves for creating the neutral voice with good coverage of synthesis elements. The method of development of smaller expressive databases that serve for adaptation to voices with higher and lower expressive load (limited to the dimension of emphasis and insistence) was published in [10]. One of the features that are known to be correlated with the level of arousal and vocal effort is the average F0. Figure 1 shows the histograms of F0 for our three databases with one reference-neutral and two increased levels of vocal effort.

Histograms of F0 for the expressive databases with one reference-neutral and two lower levels of arousal are presented in Figure 2. A Gaussian approximation is added to each of the histograms. In the databases with increasing expressive load the second and third levels of expressivity are clearly distinguishable from the base (reference) level 1. In addition to the neutral voice it is therefore possible to train two more significantly different expressive voices - one with higher and the second one with very high emphasis and insistence.

In the databases with decreasing expressive load it was very hard for the speaker to make the second and third levels distinguishable one from another. The differences in vocal intensity and timbre were small and the average F0 was nearly the same for these two databases (level -2 and -3 of expressive load – soothing and very soothing speech). This was probably due to a physiological limit - the lowest frequency of oscillation of the glottal chords. We therefore decided to train only one voice with low expressive load. This reminds us of the set of modes examined by Zhang and Hansen from the point of view of vocal effort in their work on classification of speech modes [11] (i.e.: whispered, soft, neutral, loud and shouted in Zhang's description).

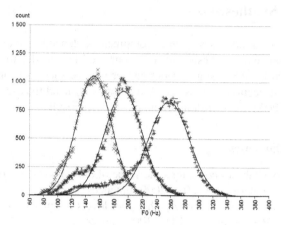

Fig. 1. Histograms of F0 for the databases with increasing vocal effort (from left: Level 1, 2, 3)

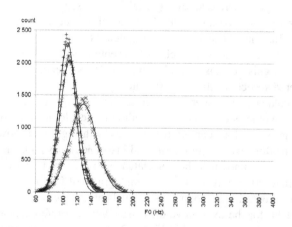

Fig. 2. F0 histograms - databases with decreasing vocal effort (from left: Level -3, -2, -1)

A special database of whispered voice has the same set of 150 phonetically rich sentences as was used in the preceding expressive databases. As it turned out this volume was sufficient to achieve a good quality of synthesized whisper by direct training the HMM voice on this database, without using the neutral voice and adaptation. This is probably due to the absence of voiced parts, which are critical in HMM synthesis because of the problems with pitch tracking. In contrast to voiced parts of the other HMM voices the vocoder buzz is nearly unobservable in the synthesized whisper.

2.2 Synthesizer Voices

The authors have several types of synthesizers available derived from the voice of the same voice talent [12]. Two of the used synthesis methods provide sufficient quality for the audio-books reading – the Unit-selection [13] and Statistical-parametric synthesis [14].

Kempelen 2.0 unit-selection synthesizer utilizes the Neutral database with a CART [15] [16] prosody model consisting of F0 model and segmental lengths model. It offers possibilities to change average F0, to linearly change average speech rate and to change the depth of application of the prosody model.

Only neutral voice Unit-selection is available in the actual version of DRAPER as the volume of expressive databases is too small to create good quality expressive Unit-selection voices from them.

Other voices are based on Statistical-parametric speech synthesis [14]. The neutral voice created in the HTS [17] system and adopted to six other voices using smaller expressive databases.

2.3 Voices with Different Levels of Vocal Effort, Objective Tests

The original authors' intent was to record voices at different levels of Arousal. As the Valence dimension was not addressed, the resulting databases can be considered as databases containing speech with different levels of vocal effort.

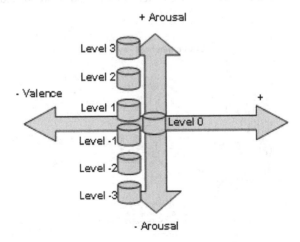

Fig. 3. Schematic diagram of the position of the databases in the two-dimensional emotion space

A comprehensive analysis of the acoustic, phonetic and prosodic features of the databases is far beyond the scope of this article. In addition to F0 histograms (see section 2.1) we therefore present for illustration only one of the characteristics - the long-term average spectrum (LTAS) differences with respect to the Neutral database LTAS. Figure 4 shows graphs of LTAS spectra of individual "expressive" databases, from which the LTAS spectrum of neutral database was always subtracted. Therefore the areas of biggest difference among databases show spectral areas that are mostly influenced by the change of vocal effort level.

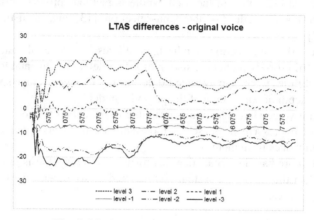

Fig. 4. LTAS differences – original voice

Figure 5 shows the same characteristics measured on the speech databases consisting utterances synthesized by the synthesizers adapted by the above mentioned databases. In this case the LTAS of the Neutral voice is subtracted. It can be seen, that the position of the spectral areas of biggest difference (around 1700 Hz and 3000 Hz) are well preserved.

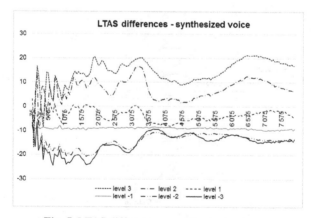

Fig. 5. LTAS differences – synthesized voice

3   DRAPER Architecture

The software system for reading texts of dramatic works of art called "Dramatic Piece Reader - DRAPER" makes use of the set of synthesizers with different expressive load and with wide possibilities to change the characteristics of voices. The schematic diagram of DRAPER is shown in Figure 6.

The Operator assigns and tunes the voice to the characters and the system generates the sound file – the whole piece read by synthetic voices.

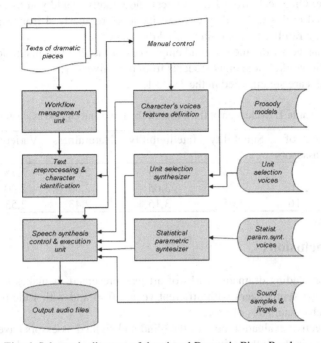

Fig. 6. Schematic diagram of the virtual Dramatic Piece Reader

4   Subjective Evaluation

For the purposes of the objective evaluation the DRAPER was used to generate the audio book from the text transcription of the puppet piece Don Jouan, originally played by a traditional folk puppeteer Bohuslav Anderle [19]. The resulting sound file was sent to the Slovak Union of the blind and visually impaired and to the Slovak Library for the Blind in Levoča, as well as to the Technical University of Košice. The following questions were asked:

Blind/Sighted: Is the assessor blind - Yes or No.

Suitability: Do you find this type of speech synthesis suitable for making big number of literary works available for blind and partially sighted – at least until classic recordings will be done by actors . Similar to Mean Opinion Score (MOS) rating the scale was 1 to 5, where 5 represents an excellent solution and 1 means totally inappropriate.

Intelligibility: Asses on the scale 1 to 5 intelligibility of voice and words. (5 means perfect, 1 means non- acceptable).

Naturalness: On the scale from 1 to 5 assess the naturalness of the voices, their similarity to human speech.

Variety: On a scale from 1 to 5 assess the presented variety of possibilities to express different characters.

Own use: On a scale from 1 to 5 indicate how likely would you listen to the audio books created in this way if they were available. (5 regularly, 4 from time to time 3 I am not sure, 2 rarely , 1 - I definitely would not listen).

We got answers from the six blind employees of the first two institutions, and from two scientific workers and eight students from the university.

The results are summarized in the Table 1.

Table 1. Evaluation of the DRAPER by blind and sighted evaluators

	No. of assesors	Suitability	Intelligibility	Naturalness	Variety	Own use
Blind	6	2,75	3,25	2,50	2,75	1,50
Sighted	10	3,30	3,05	2,35	2,30	1,40
Average	16	3,05	3,15	2,43	2,53	1,45

5   Conclusions

Software for reading dramatic works of art was presented. It makes use of a set of various speech synthesizers with different vocal effort and with wide possibilities to change the characteristics of voices.

The subjective evaluation both of the blind and sighted assessors have shown relatively high ratings for the suitability of the concept for generating dramatized audio books, as well as for the intelligibility. The weaker quality of the used freely available vocoder probably influenced the evaluation negatively.

Both groups are much more skeptical about their own regular use of such a system. Although most of the blind use some kind of synthesizer in their tools, they are not ready to listen to the literature read by speech synthesizer.

The choice of the piece was probably also not ideal for the first contact with "synthesized drama", as it contained too much very short sentences and one of the characters (Gašparko (~ Slovak Mr. Punch)) has a lisp, which lowers the intelligibility.

Several blind evaluators have commented that there is still no high quality speech synthesizer in Slovak available on the market for their everyday use with their screen-readers and that this is of higher importance for the blind.

Acknowledgements. This publication is the result of the project implementation: Technology research for the management of business processes in heterogeneous distributed systems in real time with the support of multimodal communication, ITMS 26240220064 supported by the Research & Development Operational Program funded by the ERDF. All the voices based on the statistical parametric synthesis used in this work utilize the HMM-based Speech Synthesis System (HTS) [19].

References

1. Rusko, M., Trnka, M., Darjaa, S., Hamar, J.: The dramatic piece reader for the blind and visually impaired. In: Proceedings of the 4th Workshop SLPAT, Grenoble, pp. 83–91 (2013), http://www.slpat.org/slpat2013/W13/W13-39.pdf
2. http://www.rnib.org.uk/livingwithsightloss/reading/how/ebooks/accessibility/Pages/text-to-speech.aspx (accessed on March 19, 2013)
3. Raimundo, G., Cabral, J., Melo, C., de Oliveira, L.C., Paiva, A.C.R., Trancoso, I.: Telling Stories with a Synthetic Character: Understanding Inter-modalities Relations. In: Esposito, A., Faundez-Zanuy, M., Keller, E., Marinaro, M. (eds.) COST Action 2102. LNCS (LNAI), vol. 4775, pp. 310–323. Springer, Heidelberg (2007)
4. Buurman, H.A.: Virtual Storytelling: Emotions for the narrator, Master's thesis, University of Twente (2007)
5. Rusko, M., Hamar, J.: Character Identity Expression in Vocal Performance of Traditional Puppeteers. In: Sojka, P., Kopeček, I., Pala, K. (eds.) TSD 2006. LNCS (LNAI), vol. 4188, pp. 509–516. Springer, Heidelberg (2006)
6. Greene, E., Mishra, T., Haffner, P., Conkie, A.: Predicting Character-Appropriate Voices for a TTS-based Storyteller System. In: INTERSPEECH 2012 (2012)
7. Rusko, M., Trnka, M., Daržágín, S., Cerňak, M.: Slovak Speech Database for Experiments and Application Building in Unit-Selection Speech Synthesis. In: Sojka, P., Kopeček, I., Pala, K. (eds.) TSD 2004. LNCS (LNAI), vol. 3206, pp. 457–464. Springer, Heidelberg (2004)
8. Darjaa, S., Trnka, M.: Corpus Based Synthesis in Slovak with Simplified Unit Cost and Concatenation Cost Computation. In: Proceedings of the 33rd International Acoustical Conference - EAA Symposium ACOUSTICS, High Tatras, Štrbské Pleso, Slovakia, pp. 316–319 (2006) ISBN 80-228-1673-6
9. Darjaa, S., Trnka, M., Cerňak, M., Rusko, M., Sabo, R., Hluchý, L.: HMM speech synthesizer in Slovak. In: GCCP 2011, Bratislava, pp. 212–221 (2011)
10. Rusko, M., Darjaa, S., Trnka, M., Cerňak, M.: Expressive speech synthesis database for emergent messages and warnings generation in critical situations. In: Workshop LRPS 2012 at LREC 2012 Proceedings, Istambul, pp. 50–53 (2012)
11. Zhang, C., Hansen, J.H.L.: Analysis and classification of speech mode: whispered through shouted. In: Interspeech 2007, Antwerp, Belgium, pp. 2289–2292 (2007)
12. Rusko, M., Trnka, M., Daržágín, S.: Three Generations of Speech Synthesis Systems in Slovakia. In: Proceedings of XI International Conference Speech and Computer, SPECOM 2006, Saint-Petersburg, Russia, pp. 297–302 (2006)
13. Hunt, A.J., Black, A.W.: Unit selection in a concatenative speech synthesis system using a large speech database, ICASSP-96. In: ICASSP 1996. Conference Proceedings, pp. 373–376 (1996)
14. Zen, H., Tokuda, K., Black, A.W.: Statistical parametric speech synthesis. Speech Communication 51(11), 1039–1064 (2009)
15. Breiman, Friedman, Stone, Ohlsen: Classification and Regression Trees. Chapman Hall, New York (1984)
16. Trnka, M., Darjaa, S., Kováč, R.: Modelling acoustic parameters of prosody in Slovak using Classification and Regression Trees. In: Proceedings HLT Conference, Poznań, Poland, pp. 231–235 (2007) ISBN 978-83-7177-407-2
17. http://hts.sp.nitech.ac.jp (accessed on December 13, 2012)
18. Hamar, J.: Hry ľudových bábkárov Anderlovcov z Radvane. Slovenské centrum pre tradičnú kultúru, Bratislava, pp. 61–88 (2010)
19. Zen, H., Nose, T., Yamagishi, J., Sako, S., Masuko, T., Black, A.W., Tokuda, K.: The HMM-based speech synthesis system version 2.0. In: Proc. of ISCA SSW6 (2007)

Estimating Stochasticity of Acoustic Signals

Sergei Aleinik[1,2] and Oleg Kudashev[2]

[1] Speech Technology Center, Krasutskogo-4, St. Petersburg, 196084, Russia
[2] ITMO University, 49 Kronverkskiy pr., St. Petersburg, 197101, Russia
{aleinik,kudashev}@speechpro.com

Abstract. In this paper, known methods for estimating the stochasticity of acoustic signals are compared, along with a new method based on adaptive signal filtration. Statistical simulation shows that the described method has better characteristics (lower variance and bias) than the other stochasticity measures. The parameters of the method, and their influence on performance, are investigated. Practical implementations for using the method are considered.

Keywords: Stochasticity, spectral entropy, linear prediction, event detection.

1 Introduction

Spectral flatness (SF) and Spectral entropy (SE) as well as Zero crossing rate (ZCR) are widely used and useful measures in acoustic signal processing [1-7]. For example, in [1], [2] SE is claimed to be a useful feature in speech recognition. In [3] SF is used for acoustic source separation. In [4], [5] ZCR is used as a parameter for voiced/unvoiced sound separation and language classification. A comparison of SF and SE is presented in [6]. In general, these values are claimed to be the characteristics of a single physical parameter of a signal – its stochasticity, e.g. in [7] is noted, that: "Spectral Flatness Measure is a method for quantifying the amount of randomness (or "stochasticity") that is present in a signal." In fact, if the signal is harmonic or a constant value (i.e. not stochastic), its estimated SF and SE are equal to zero. On the other hand, if the signal is white noise, SF and SE fluctuate near some high value (near 1 in a normalized case). In [8] it was introduced another approach, and used an adaptive linear predictor (ALP) [9] to evaluate signal stochasticity. In the present study, we propose a new stochasticity coefficient that is also based on ALP, but results in better performance than the aforementioned values.

2 Measuring Stochasticity

Addressing an important question, "Chaos or Stochasticity" [10], [11] is beyond the scope of the present paper. According to [11], [12], we assume here that: "Stochasticity means Randomness" and "Randomness implies a lack of Predictability". Following this definition, we assume that white noise (unpredictable process) is a "totally" stochastic process with stochasticity equal to 1 in theory. In contrast, constant value or

A. Ronzhin et al. (Eds.): SPECOM 2014, LNAI 8773, pp. 192–199, 2014.

harmonical signals (predictable processes) are deterministic signals with stochasticity equal to 0. Pink noise (as a partially predictable process) has stochasticity between 0 and 1. This lets us suggest that SE, SF and ZCR do not quite give us the values we want to measure. Indeed, SE and SF are values that characterize the degree to which the spectrum is narrowband. Of course, harmonical signal produces narrowband spectrum and white noise produces wideband spectrum. However the estimated power spectrum (needed for SE and SF calculation) of white noise fluctuates quite strongly, which leads to a high bias (to the lower side) of SE and SF. On the other hand, a sequence of rectangular pulses (not a stochastic signal) has a set of harmonics in the power spectrum, which leads to an inadequate increase of SE. Another problem arises with ZCR. Let x_i, $i = 0, N-1$, is a zero-mean sampled signal. It is clear that the mean value of ZCR (calculated using (1) in [4]) is equal to 0.5 if x_i is white noise, and:

$$ZCR = \begin{cases} 0, & \text{if } x_i = c \ \ (\text{i.e. constant}) \\ 1, & \text{if } x_i = +c, -c, +c, \ldots = (-1)^i c, \ \forall i = 0,1,\ldots \end{cases} \tag{1}$$

However signal: $x_i = (-1)^i c$ is not a stochastic, but a deterministic signal. So, the phrase [4]: "zero crossing rates are low for voiced part and high for unvoiced part of speech" is correct, but the reason is that unvoiced parts of speech usually contain more high-frequency components, but not "because of its random nature" [5].

3   Basic Approach

In [8] the following coefficient of signal stochasticity has been introduced:

$$S_{pow} = <\xi^2>/<x^2> = \sum_i \xi_i^2 / \sum_i x_i^2 , \tag{2}$$

where '$<>$' is the averaging symbol, x_i is the input signal, ξ_i is the output error signal of ALP [9] and the subscript "pow" refers to the way the metric S is computed, i.e in (2) using estimated powers. Indeed, in [9] it is shown that, after ALP has converged: if x_i is a deterministic process, then $\xi_i = 0$; if x_i is white noise, then $<\xi^2> \approx <x^2>$. So we have $S_{pow}=0$ and $E(S_{pow})=1$ in the first and the second cases, respectively (here $E(\cdot)$ is mathematical expectation). It easy to show [8] that S_{pow} characterizes the unpredictability of the signal and if x_i can be represented as a sum of its deterministic x_i^d and stochastic x_i^s components, then:

$$E(S_{pow}) = P_s/P = P_s/(P_s + P_d), \tag{3}$$

where P is the total power of the signal, P_d and P_s are powers of the deterministic and stochastic components of the signal, respectively. Moreover, closer inspection of (2) shows that S_{pow} is the inverse value of the known value called "prediction gain." This value is widely used in linear predictive coding (LPC) [13]. Thus, it is possible to calculate stochasticity without using ALP, but by using, for example, Levinson-Durbin recursion, evaluating the prediction gain and then calculating:

$$S_{lpc} = 1/\ prediction\ gain. \tag{4}$$

4   Proposed Stochasticity Coefficient

We note here that ALP generally has two outputs: output of an error signal ξ_i and output of a predicted signal y_i [9]. After ALP has converged, the ideal case results in only a stochastic component as the error signal output and only a deterministic component as the predicted signal output. Hence, by analogy with (2) and using predicted signal y_i we define the following coefficient:

$$S_d = <y^2>/<x^2> = \sum_i y_i^2 / \sum_i x_i^2 . \tag{5}$$

It is clear that (5) leads to:

$$E(S_d) = P_d/(P_s + P_d) , \tag{6}$$

so $E(S_d) = 1$ when x_i is deterministic, and $E(S_d) = 0$ when x_i is a stochastic process. Comparing (3) and (6) we get: $E(S_d) + E(S_{pow}) = 1$, hence:

$$E(S_{pow}) = 1 - E(S_d) . \tag{7}$$

Equation (7) shows that ALP lets us evaluate signal stochasticity in two ways: via S_{pow} and via $1 - S_d$. At the same time, it is known that one of the basic properties of ALP is that the correlation between the error signal ξ_i and the predicted signal y_i is small [9]. Accordingly, it can be assumed that the arithmetical mean:

$$S = 0.5(S_{pow} + (1 - S_d)) \tag{8}$$

has a lower variance than each of the components. Using (2), (5), (8), and the equation for the error signal: $\xi_i = x_i - y_i$ from [9], we obtain the new coefficient:

$$S_{cor} = \frac{1}{2}\left(1 + \frac{\sum_i \xi_i^2}{\sum_i x_i^2} - \frac{\sum_i y_i^2}{\sum_i x_i^2}\right) = \frac{1}{2}\left(1 + \frac{\sum_i (x_i - y_i)^2 - \sum_i y_i^2}{\sum_i x_i^2}\right) = 1 - \frac{\sum_i x_i\, y_i}{\sum_i x_i^2} \tag{9}$$

Eq. (9) shows that S_{cor} (as well as S_{pow}) does not depend on signal power. It is also clear that S_{cor} theoretically changes from 0 to 1 and characterizes the unpredictability of the input signal by ALP. In fact, the value $\sum_i x_i\, y_i$ in (9) is an estimated cross-correlation coefficient of the input and the predicted signals. This coefficient is close to zero when the input signal is a high stochastic signal (e.g. white noise) and, in this case, S_{cor} is close to 1. When x_i is totally deterministic, y_i is equal to x_i (after the adaptation has converged), so $S_{cor} = 0$. In real life, of course, estimated values of S_{pow} and S_{cor} can sometimes be more than 1 due to fluctuations.

5   Experiments and Results

5.1   Distributions and Mean Values

We investigated the behavior of four coefficients: SE, S_{lpc}, S_{pow} and S_{cor} for different types of signals and noises. For all simulations there were fixed main parameters: frame length K=512 samples; number of LPC and ALP coefficients M =16; number of trials to estimate distributions and mean values=106. We also note here that we used normalized SE [8]:

$$SE = -1/\log_2(N)\sum_{i=0}^{N-1} S_i \log_2(S_i) \tag{10}$$

where N is the number of power spectrum samples; S_i is the amplitude of i-th spectrum sample, normalized so that: $\sum_{i=0}^{N-1} S_i = 1$. Spectra were calculated using a rectangular window, without overlapping and accumulation. Levinson-Durbin recursion [14] was used to calculate S_{lpc} (4). The finite-impulse response ALP [9], with the Normalized Least-Mean Squares (NLMS) algorithm (step size or adaptation constant $\mu = 0.1$, regularization constant $\delta = 1$) [15], was used. Fig.1 shows the estimated distributions of coefficients for white and pink noises. The upper graph of Fig.1 (A) demonstrates that there are notable biases and variances in the estimated coefficients (although white noise stochasticity must be theoretically equal to 1). The maximum downward shift is in SE. This is clear because SE=1 only when $S_i = const$ for all $i = 0, N - 1$ which is unreachable in the real world, where every sample of the estimated power spectrum fluctuates notably. S_{lpc} also shifted downward. On the other hand, S_{pow} is shifted upward. In our opinion this is due to an incomplete adaptation process. The proposed coefficient S_{cor} has the lowest bias and fluctuates near the theoretical value of 1. Fig.1, B and C, shows distributions when input signal is pink noise, created using one-pole lowpass filter [16]:

$$y_i = \alpha y_{i-1} + (1-\alpha)x_i \tag{11}$$

where: y_i and x_i are samples of pink and white noise at time i, $0 \leq \alpha < 1$ is the filter parameter. It is known that the closer α is to 1, the more predictable (i.e. more deterministic) is y_i. Therefore, in Fig. 1 there are results for high-stochastic

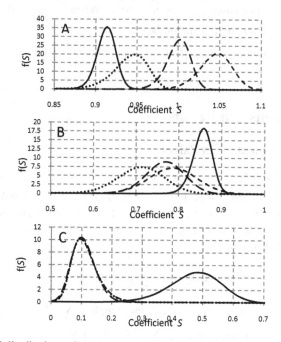

Fig. 1. Estimated distributions of stochasticity coefficients for: A – white noise; B – pink noise $\alpha = 0.5$; C – pink noise $\alpha = 0.95$. Solid, dotted, dashed and long dashed curves are SE, S_{lpc}, S_{pow} and S_{cor}, respectively.

process ($\alpha = 0$, A), a middle-stochastic process ($\alpha = 0.5$, B), and a low-stochastic process ($\alpha = 0.95$, C). We can see that the densities of all the coefficients move downward when α moves from 0 to 0.95. In the low-stochastic process (C), we see that all coefficients, except SE, have almost identical distributions and SE has maximum variance. Also the "sensitivity" of the coefficients (to changes in α) is different.

5.2   Stability

Despite its poor performance, SE has two important advantages: SE has a single parameter (frame length) and SE is always stable. S_{lpc} has two parameters: frame length, and number of LPC coefficients. S_{pow} and S_{cor} have four parameters: frame length, number of ALP coefficients, step size $\mu > 0$ and regularization constant $\delta \geq 0$. Frame length is trivial: the higher the frame length, the smaller the variance of all the coefficients. The constant δ also has little effect on S_{pow} and S_{cor} (unless δ is extremely high or low); $\delta = 1$ is suitable for most situations. The most critical parameter of S_{pow} and S_{cor} is μ. Theoretical bounds for the stability of the NLMS algorithm are: $0 < \mu < 2$ [17]. So $\mu \geq 2$ causes the unstability of ALP and, correspondingly, dramatically increases S_{pow} and S_{cor} variance. If μ is too small ALP cannot converge at the end of a frame, which also leads to an increase in variance. A comparison of standard deviation for S_{pow} and S_{cor} as a function of μ is shown in Fig. 2.

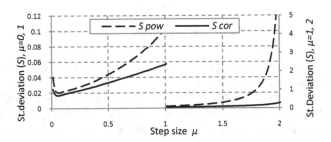

Fig. 2. Estimated standard deviation of S_{cor} and S_{pow} when step size μ increases

To improve the readability interval $(0, 2]$ divided into two parts: $(0, 1)$ and $[1, 2]$ (different scales on left and right vertical axes, respectively). It is seen that for all μ the standard deviation of S_{cor} is less than it is for S_{pow}. We suggest that S_{cor} has the best stability and the interval $0.05 < \mu < 0.2$ is acceptable for most situations.

6   Practical Suggestions and Results

In practice, S_{cor} can be used for sounds classification, short clicks sound detection, determining voiced/unvoiced speech fragments, etc. Also S_{cor} can be used as a detector of short changes in signal stochasticity i.e. as a short event detector. When computing S_{pow} and S_{cor} it is useful to do the following preprocessing before ALP:

- Remove the constant component of a signal.
- Add a fixed constant bias (50...500) to avoid small noise influence (avoid coefficient increase).

Also for sample-by-sample processing it is useful to substitute summation in (9) with lowpass filtering. Figs. 3-4 present the results of processing real acoustic signals. We used the following parameters: sample-by-sample processing; the number of ALP coefficients M=128; the constant bias: 100; one-pole lowpass filter (11) instead of a sum in (9), filter parameter α is calculated using 50 ms equivalent window length [18]. The example of a well-known phrase from the TIMIT data base: "She had your dark suit in greasy wash water all year", and the corresponding S_{cor} are shown

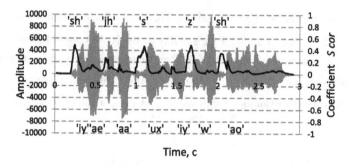

Fig. 3. Speech signal (grey) and its S_{cor} (black)

in Fig. 3. It is evident that the proposed coefficient is high on sibilant and fricative consonants and low on voiced sounds.

Fig. 4 shows the results of processing data taken from the NOISEX-92 [19]: factory noise (factory1.wav). In this experiment we used a one-pole high-pass filter [16] to remove a constant component of S_{cor} with the aim to emphasize the stochasticity changes. The cut-off frequency of the filter was 10 Hz.

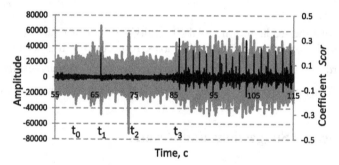

Fig. 4. Factory-1 noise (grey) and the corresponding S_{cor} (black)

Visible low-power bursts (at the time t_0 and t_2) do not affect the S_{cor}. On the other hand, short high-frequency bursts of sound (t_1 – presumably a door clap) are detected quite well. Also easy to see (after t_3) are the periodic bursts of stochasticity caused by the sound of some running machine.

7   Conclusions

This paper has presented a simple method for calculating signal stochasticity, a method that has some benefits over traditional stochasticity measures: low bias and variance, as well as good stability. The presented method has proven to be useful in acoustic signal processing systems (for example, in speaker identification systems such as described in [20]). The method can be used as a robust discriminator of voiced/unvoiced sounds, a detector of fricative consonant sounds, as well as an event detector that is robust to signal power.

Acknowledgments. This work was partially financially supported by the Government of the Russian Federation, Grant 074-U01.

References

1. Misra, H., Ikbal, S., Sivadas, S., Bourlard, H.: Multi-resolution Spectral Entropy Feature for Robust ASR. In: Proc. ICASSP, vol. 1, pp. 253–256 (2005)
2. Toh, A.M., Togneri, R., Nordholm, S.: Spectral entropy as speech features for speech recognition. In: Proc. PEECS, pp. 22–25 (2005)
3. Bardeli, R.: Source Separation Using the Spectral Flatness Measure. In: Proc. Machine Listening in Multisource Environments, pp. 80–85 (2011)
4. Bachu, R.G., Kopparthi, S., Adapa, B., Barkana, B.D.: Separation of Voiced and Unvoiced Using Zero Crossing Rate and Energy of the Speech Signal. In: Proc. American Society for Engineering Education, pp. 1–7 (2008)
5. Khan, A.U., Bhaiya, L.P., Banchhor, S.K.: Hindi Speaking Person Identification Using Zero Crossing Rate. Int. J. of Soft Computing and Engineering 2(3), 101–104 (2012)
6. Madhu, N.: Note on Measures for Spectral Flatness. Electronics Letters 23, 1195–1196 (2009)
7. Dubnov, S.: Non-gaussian source-filter and independent components generalizations of spectral flatness measure. In: Proc. of the 4th International Conference on Independent Components Analysis, pp. 143–148 (2003)
8. Aleinik, S.: Time series determinancy evaluation. Radiotekhnika 9, 16–22 (1999)
9. Widrow, B., Lehr, M., Beaufays, F., Wan, E., Bileillo, M.: Learning algorithms for adaptive processing and control. In: IEEE International Conference on Neural Networks, vol. 1, pp. 1–8 (1993)
10. Puente, C.E., Obregón, N., Sivakumar, B.: Chaos and stochasticity in deterministically generated multifractal measures. Fractals 10(1), 91–102 (2002)
11. Sivakumar, B.: Is a Chaotic Multi-Fractal Approach for Rainfall Possible? Hydrological Processes 15(6), 943–955 (2001)
12. http://encyclopedia.thefreedictionary.com/stochasticity
13. Heim, A., Sorger, U., Hug, F.: Doppler-variant modeling of the vocal tract. In: Proc. ICASSP-2008, pp. 4197–4200 (2008)
14. Corneliu, M., Costinescu, B.: Implementing the Levinson-Durbin Algorithm on the SC140. Freescale Semiconductor (AN2197), Rev. 1, 1 (2005)
15. Bitzer, J., Brandt, M.: Speech Enhancement by Adaptive Noise Cancellation: Problems, Algorithms and Limits. In: Proc. AES–39, pp. 106–113 (2010)
16. Orfanidis, S.J.: Introduction to Signal Processing, http://www.ece.rutgers.edu/~orfanidi/intro2sp/orfanidis-i2sp.pdf
17. Haykin, S.: Adaptive Filter Theory. Englewood Cliffs, Prentice-Hall (1996)
18. Ignatov, P., Stolbov, M., Aleinik, S.: Semi-Automated Technique for Noisy Recording Enhancement Using an Independent Reference Recording. In: Proc. 46th International Conference of the Audio Engineering Society, pp. 57–64 (2012)
19. Varga, A., Steeneken, H.J.M.: Assessment for automatic speech recognition II: NOISEX-92: a database and an experiment to study the effect of additive noise on speech recognition systems. Speech Communication 12(3), 247–251 (1993)
20. Kozlov, A., Kudashev, O., Matveev, Y., Pekhovsky, T., Simonchik, K., Shulipa, A.: SVID speaker recognition system for NIST SRE 2012. In: Železný, M., Habernal, I., Ronzhin, A. (eds.) SPECOM 2013. LNCS, vol. 8113, pp. 278–285. Springer, Heidelberg (2013)

Exploiting Non-negative Matrix Factorization with Linear Constraints in Noise-Robust Speaker Identification

Nikolay Lyubimov[1], Marina Nastasenko[2], Mikhail Kotov[2],
and Danila Doroshin[2]

[1] Moscow State University,
[2] STEL Computer Systems, Moscow, Russia
http://cs.msu.ru,
http://www.stel.ru

Abstract. This paper exploits non-negative matrix factorization (NMF)-based method for speech enhancement within speaker identification framework. The proposed algorithm considers speech atoms in deterministic way as a sum of harmonically-related sinusoids in spectral domain. This approach allows us to estimate specific signal structure of vowel signal in the presence of noise in order to make an efficient noise reduction using only noise exemplars. The experiments of the present research in application to the speaker identification are conducted on the computational hearing in multisource environments (CHiME) dataset. The obtained results demonstrate the effectiveness of the preprocessing enhancement, and outperforming the general NMF-based speech enhancer. Further studies show the channel compensation effect of the proposed method leads to performance comparable to the common mismatch reduction methods such as feature warping.

Keywords: speech enhancement, speaker identification, non-negative matrix factorization.

1 Introduction

Noise reduction and speech enhancement is a long lasting task in audio signal processing. The wide range of speech processing applications require denoising of the input speech data. In presented paper we are focused to a specific task of speaker identification.

There are many and different approaches for denosing the speech signals depending on the nature of the noise: stationary and non-stationary. For stationary noise reduction there are known statistical approaches based on spectral subtraction, or using minimum mean squared error (MMSE) criteria [16].

The problem appears more challenging when the noise is non-stationary which always accompanies the task of speaker identification within telephone channel with all containing noises respectfully. Several successful attempts in building noise-robust speaker and speech recognition systems have been recently made

A. Ronzhin et al. (Eds.): SPECOM 2014, LNAI 8773, pp. 200–208, 2014.

in the works of [1,2,3]. The non-negative factorization of input spectrogram is a common way in those studies.

This paper presents a regularized version of the general non-negative matrix factorization (NMF) algorithm, originally proposed by Lee and Seung [4]. In previous work [12] we have demonstrated the advance of the method in application to the speech enhancement task. Present research is focused on the demonstration of the usefulness of proposed denoising scheme considering speaker identification task.

The key idea of the approach is that clean speech signal can be sparsely represented by a speech dictionary, which is not necessary remains true for non-stationary noise. Similarly, non-stationary noise can also be sparsely represented by a noise dictionary, whether speech cannot. There could be highlighted that the dictionary doesn't comprise any specific speech model in general NMF approach, e.g. [8,9]. This leads to the fact that there exist speech atoms containing a lot of noise data that further harms filtering stage.

The proposed NMF algorithm based on the modelling speech atoms in deterministic way as a sum of harmonically-related sinusoids in spectral domain. This way it allows to estimate specific signal structure of vowel signal in the presence of noise and making efficient noise reduction using only noise exemplars. Applying the modification of NMF to the speech data we test the efficiency of the noise reduction in correspondence to the speaker identification performance

2 Speech Enhancement Using Non-negative Matrix Factorization

Non-negative matrix factorization (NMF)-based methods have shown to be effective tool in various audio source separation tasks [6,5], particularly for single-channel speech enhancement in the presence of non-stationary noise [7][8,9]. These methods rely on the assumption that magnitudes of speech and noise signals in spectro-temporal domain are additive, and speech and noise components could be estimated via matrix factorization techniques. When some isolated noise audio data is available for training, the corresponding noise component is extracted before, and then removed from factorized noisy input spectrogram to obtain denoised signal. This section discusses the NMF-based speech enhancement process in details, and introduces the ancillary model for speech component.

2.1 Non-negative Matrix Factorization

By given audio magnitude spectrogram $Y \in \mathbb{R}^{n \times T}$ with T columns representing short-time magnitude spectrum of size n, NMF attempts to build factorized representation $Y = DX$. Matrix $D \in \mathbb{R}^{n \times m}$, called *dictionary*, contains the typical spectral profiles d_j pasted in columns (also called *atoms*). Matrix $X \in \mathbb{R}^{m \times T}$ possess the weights with which atoms are summed up each time frame $t = 1 \ldots T$. Sometimes these weights are required to be sparse, by imposing l_1-norm constraints on optimization task (see e.g.[1,2]):

$$D_{KL}(Y\|DX) + \lambda\|X\|_1 \to \min_{D,X} \qquad (1)$$

The estimation error is controlled by Kullback-Leibler divergence $D_{KL}(Y\|DX) = \sum_{i,j} Y_{ij} \log \frac{Y_{ij}}{(DX)_{ij}} - Y_{ij} + (DX)_{ij}$. $\lambda \geq 0$ is sparsity parameter. The optimization task is performed using alternative least squares algorithm (ALS) or by using multiplicative updates [10]. The initialization of both algorithms is assumed to be random.

2.2   Speech Enhancement

According to [8] NMF-based speech enhancement consists of two major steps. First, the noise dictionary D_n is trained over noise-only spectrograms using (1). Typically there is no any sparsity requirements imposed on weights, so λ in this case. Then the matrix D_n is concatenated with random matrix D_s which represents speech atoms hypothesis. NMF runs on the target noisy signal, fixing the columns of D_n unchanging during optimization procedure. Naturally speech atoms are more sparse, so the corresponding λ parameter is set to be positive.

Finally it gives D_s with speech spectral profiles, and X_s and X_n with weights of speech and noise atoms respectively. The estimated parameters are used to obtain filtering matrix W as

$$W = \frac{D_s X_s}{D_s X_s + D_n X_n} \qquad (2)$$

where division is element-wise. The output denoised signal is made by applying this filtering matrix to each bin in complex spectrogram, followed by taking inverse transform using overlap-and-add method.

This approach has lack that dictionary D_s doesn't follow any specific speech model. This leads to the fact that some speech atoms d_j contain a lot of noise data, that harmfully affects filtering stage (2).

2.3   Sinusoidal and Noise Atoms

This section introduces the specific speech and noise model used to form corresponding atoms. Unlike [5] this model has deterministic nature, so that it gives the explicit atom's representation rather than relying on bayesian prior probabilistic constraints.

The basic of vowel sound production at specific time frame t assumes harmonically-related sinusoids with some fundamental frequency falling into specific interval $\overline{\omega}_{\min} \leq \overline{\omega}_t \leq \overline{\omega}_{\max}$. In magnitude domain it is roughly expressed as summing spectra of individual harmonics, scaled by their corresponding amplitudes. Therefore it is possible to use the following representation of speech atoms inside NMF: $d_j = \Psi_j a_j, j = 1, 2, \ldots m$. In the other words, for the low rank matrices Ψ_j the dictionary atoms are constrained to lie in a linear subspace. This fact gives the name of the presented method as *non-negative matrix factorization with linear constraints* (LC-NMF).

The columns of matrices $\Psi_j \in \mathbb{R}^{n \times p}$ are magnitudes of window-shaped sinusoids, related to some fundamental frequency $\overline{w}_j$ by multiplicative factor. The spectral envelope shape of vowel sound is presented in vector of harmonic amplitudes $a_j \in \mathbb{R}^p$. This vectors should be estimated from target spectrogram. The number of atoms m equals to the number of hypothesized fundamental frequencies L multiplied by the number of different envelope shapes k per each fundamental frequency. The parameter p controls the maximum number of harmonics in each atom d_j, and it depends on fundamental frequency in order to avoid sinusoids with frequency higher than Nyquist.

Since there is no information about fundamental frequency presented in actual frame, it is possible to retrieve it implicitly by inducing sparsity constraints on atom's activations. As stated before, it has to be done in common way applying l_1-regularization on matrix X in NMF optimization task (1). It is also preferred that extracted envelope shapes are smooth functions of harmonic frequency for speech signals. In order to avoid drastic changes of a_j values additional constraints are needed to imply on these vectors. We have used l_2-regularization while keeping l_1-norm to be constant. That results into that each vector a_j tends to have more identical values. The final NMF optimization task is stated as follows:

$$\begin{cases} D_{KL}(Y\|DX) + \lambda\|X\|_1 + \alpha\sum_j \|a_j\|_2^2 \to \min \\ d_j = \Psi_j a_j, \ \|a_j\|_1 = 1 \qquad j = 1,2,\ldots m \end{cases} \tag{3}$$

As in previous work [12], the iterative multiplicative updates optimization procedure is used until convergence:

$$a_j \longleftarrow \tilde{a}_j \cdot \frac{\mathbb{1}_j \tilde{a}_j^T \Psi_j^T \mathbb{1}\overline{x}_j^T + \Psi_j^T \frac{Y}{DX}\overline{x}_j^T + \alpha\mathbb{1}_j \tilde{a}_j^T \tilde{a}_j}{\Psi_j^T \mathbb{1}\overline{x}_j^T + \mathbb{1}_j \tilde{a}_j^T \Psi_j^T \frac{Y}{DX}\overline{x}_j^T + \alpha\tilde{a}_j}$$

$$X \longleftarrow X \cdot \frac{D^T \frac{Y}{DX}}{(D^T \mathbb{1} + \lambda)} \tag{4}$$

where $\tilde{a}_j$ denotes l_1-normalized coefficients $\tilde{a}_j = a_j/\|a_j\|_1$.

It should be mentioned that noise atoms are represented in the same manner as speech atoms, besides the fact that corresponding matrices Ψ_j consist of noise spectral profiles instead of harmonics. These spectral profiles are preliminary extracted from noise-only signals. This is done by taking unconstrained NMF on target noise spectrograms, and then pooling together all atoms from estimated dictionary matrix. By summing columns of noise dictionary it possible to control variabilities of estimated noise spectrum rather than using noise atoms with fixed spectral profiles.

The overall speech enhancement process with proposed method is depicted on figure 1. It is also available as MATLAB scripts at https://github.com/lubimovnik/NMFdenoiser.

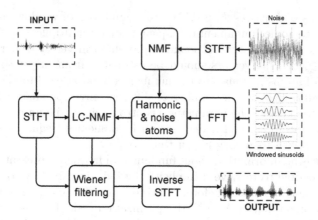

Fig. 1. Schematic diagram of proposed speech enhancement using NMF with linear constraints (LC-NMF) on speech and noise atoms

3   Experiments

3.1   Database Description

All experiments were conducted on the PASCAL computational hearing in multisource environments (CHiME) speech separation and recognition challenge dataset[13]. This dataset simulates reverberant and noisy conditions using the data consisted of 34000 utterances of six word length each, collected from 34 speakers. The 16 kHz stereo signals were converted to mono by averaging two channels. The train set consists of 17000 utterances, convolved with real room impulse response to simulate reverberant environment. The test set constructed by adding various noise signals to utterances at different SNR levels: 9dB, 6dB, 3dB, 0dB, -3dB, -6dB. Each SNR condition includes 600 utterances. There are also two auxiliary sets available for development purposes: the 6 hours of noise background data, and the development set with clean and noisy signals at SNR levels likewise in test set.

3.2   Experimental Protocol

The training set is used to train speaker models, which then evaluated on each part of test set independently. The speaker recognition error rate is measured by $\sum_{utt} Err(utt)/N$, where $Err(utt)$ is equal 1 for misclassified utterance, otherwise 0, and N is a total number of utterances. The development set is used for estimate parameter α based on signal-to-noise ratio as described bellow.

3.3   Baseline System

The baseline system is similar to those proposed in paper [1]. All systems comprise GMM-UBM as speaker modeling process [14]. The features used in all experiments are 13 dimensions of MFCC including log-energy 0-th coefficient, extracted from 25ms frame each 10ms, normalized by with cepstral mean normalization and concatenated with delta and acceleration coefficients. The universal background model (UBM) is build on the pooled train set with approximately 9,5 hours of reverberated speech, using the method proposed by [11]. Each speaker model is obtained via maximum a posteriori (MAP) adaptation of UBM towards target speaker data using the same method as described in [14].

3.4 Speech Enhancement

Speech enhancement is preliminary applied to every speech signal in train and test sets. The α parameter that affects on extraction of true harmonic atoms is estimated on development set set by measuring mean relative signal-to-noise ratio ($mrSNR$), that is just ordinary SNR measure averaged over all corresponding clean and noisy utterance files, for each SNR level:

$$mrSNR = \left\langle 20 \log_{10} \frac{\|clean - noisy\|_2}{\|clean - denoised\|_2} \right\rangle$$

The resulted curves are depicted on figure 2. From this experimental result, it is shown that the higher values of α play more important role when SNR decreases, since harmonic-like prior structure of a magnitude spectrum is more appropriate to recovering signal in very noisy conditions. However, for cleaner signals, by imposing this type of regularization constraint, the denoised signal gets more distortion due to unnatural flat envelope shapes appeared in speech atoms. In the later experiments the value $\alpha = 0.2T$ is fixed, that seems to be a reasonable choice to handle this trade-off.

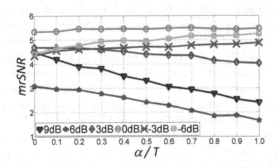

Fig. 2. The mean relative signal-to-noise ratio w.r.t. envelope smoothness controlled by alpha parameter in (3)

32 noise atoms were extracted using NMF on each noisy file from background dataset. It gives 2688 atoms in total, which were linearly combined with different weights to produce 16 noise atoms of the form $d = \Psi a$.

Initial harmonic atoms were constructed by splitting hypothesized fundamental frequency interval $[80, 600]Hz$ on equally spaced segments of 10 Hz length, and taking 4 different amplitude vectors a for each fundamental frequency, so that 212 speech atoms were used in total. Though it is also possible to estimate from target signal, the maximum possible harmonics per atom have been set to $p = 30$, in order to avoid atoms with low fundamental frequency become noise-like. Sparsity parameter was set to $\lambda_s = .2$ for speech weights, and $\lambda_n = 0$ for noise weights according to [9].

3.5   Results and Discussion

The table 1 shows the identification error rate for different methods and SNR conditions on CHiME test set. As could be seen, by applying NMF method without any dictionary priors [8,9] doesn't improve the results comparing with baseline system without initial denoising step. The reason might be due to a lot of speech presented in noise backgrounds, that prevents to properly modeling the target speaker speech in NMF enhancement step. This also explains the accuracy falling for LC-NMF at negative SNRs: the modeling process can not distinguish harmonic spectrum of background children voices, music and female speakers which interfering with harmonic spectrum of target speaker itself. It is also observed manually on some audio files, where the speaker voice was erroneously attenuated in opposite to the background speech. However, it seems that for positive SNR harmonic linear constraints the inner modeling process becomes more adaptive to the target speech, and the error significantly reduces.

The surprisingly good result obtained by applying log MMSE method led to the suggestion that speech enhancement method could be considered as data equalization which decreases the mismatch between train and test data set. To check this, the non-linear warped version of MFCC features [15] is also exploited. Since this type of transformation was namely designed to reduce the effect of mismatch, the obtained comparatively good results reaffirm that suggestion. From this point of view NMF-based methods aren't the best candidates to make such equalizations due to locality of speech processing. So it explains the performance advance of log MMSE in low SNR conditions. However, by combining the proposed LC-NMF and MMSE by chain, the results improve further, showing that better results could be reached by properly investigating not only intrinsic short-time speech model, but also statistical properties of background noise. The same conclusion could be made by observing the results of LC-NMF followed by warped feature extraction, which gives slightly improved result at lowest SNR. The degradation of LC-NMF performance compare with no enhanced warped signals at high SNRs could be also explained as disability to properly modeling unvoiced sounds.

The future work should be addressed to found issues: incorporating long-term / statistical properties of speech backgrounds into NMF framework, building the model of speech atom which describes unvoiced sounds as well, and also investigating more deeply the observed effect of mismatch compensation.

Table 1. The speaker identification error rate obtained on CHiME database test set. The speaker modeling system is GMM-UBM with MAP adaptation [14]. 3 different speech enhancement methods are exploited as preprocessing step: *NMF* [8,9], proposed NMF with linear constraints (*LC-NMF*) and log *MMSE* [16]. The *Warping*-based [15] system is included to demonstrate the effect of mismatch between training and test conditions.

method	9dB	6dB	3dB	0dB	-3dB	-6dB
no enhancement	0.13	0.22	0.33	0.48	0.58	0.65
NMF	0.13	0.21	0.33	0.51	0.62	0.69
LC-NMF	0.06	0.10	0.19	0.37	0.50	0.58
MMSE	0.08	0.11	0.19	0.33	0.45	0.55
Warping	0.05	0.10	0.17	**0.31**	**0.41**	0.54
LC-NMF+MMSE	**0.05**	**0.09**	**0.16**	0.34	0.47	0.55
LC-NMF+Warping	0.07	0.11	0.18	0.34	0.44	**0.53**

4 Conclusions

In this paper the advanced method of speech enhancement is presented. This method relies on deterministic harmonic model of spectral atoms in more general NMF-based spectrogram decomposition algorithm. The proposed method is tested within the speaker identification task on CHiME dataset. Though the obtained results are far from the best [1,2], they still show the importance of speech enhancement as audio preprocessing step, especially when there is a strong conditions mismatch between train and test data sets. Despite the promising performance gains with respect to dealing with non-enhanced signals, more deep experimentation is needed to properly tune the parameters of proposed method so that it will become valuable for speaker identification/verification task.

References

1. Saeidi, R., Hurmalainen, A., Virtanen, T., van Leeuwen, D.A.: Exemplar-based Sparse Representation and Sparse Discrimination for Noise Robust Speaker Identification. In: Proc. Odyssey: The Speaker and Language Recognition Workshop, Singapore (2012)
2. Hurmalainen, A., Saeidi, R., Virtanen, T.: Group Sparsity for Speaker Identity Discrimination in Factorisation-based Speech Recognition. In: Proc. of the Interspeech (2012)
3. Wu, Q., Liu, J., Sun, J., Cichoki, A.: Shift-invariant Features with Multiple Factors for Robust Text-independent Speaker Identifcation, J. of Computational Information Systems 8(21), 8937–8944 (2012)
4. Lee, D.D., Seung, H.S.: Learning the parts of objects by non-negative matrix factorization. Nature 401(6755), 788–791 (1999)
5. Bertin, N., Badeau, R., Vincent, E.: Fast bayesian nmf algorithms enforcing harmonicity and temporal continuity in polyphonic music transcription. In: IEEE Workshop on App. of Signal Proc. to Audio and Acoustics, pp. 29–32 (2009)

6. Virtanen, T.: Monaural Sound Source Separation by Nonnegative Matrix Factorization With Temporal Continuity and Sparseness Criteria. IEEE Trans. on Audio, Speech and Language Processing 15(3) (2007)
7. Schmidt, M.N., Olsson, R.K.: Single-Channel Speech Separation using Sparse Non-Negative Matrix Factorization. In: Proc. of Interspeech, pp. 2614–2617 (2006)
8. Schmidt, M.N., Larsen, J., Hsiao, F.-T.: Wind Noise Reduction using Non-Negative Sparse Coding. In: IEEE Workshop on Machine Learning for Signal Proc., pp. 431–436 (2007)
9. Cauchi, B., Goetze, S., Doclo, S.: Reduction of non-stationary noise for a robotic living assistant using sparse non-negative matrix factorization. In: Proc. of the 1st Workshop on Speech and Multimodal Interaction in Assistive Environments, pp. 28–33 (2012)
10. Berry, M.W., et al.: Algorithms and applications for approximate nonnegative matrix factorization 52(1), 155–173 (2007)
11. Doroshin, D., Tkachenko, M., Lubimov, N., Kotov, M.: Application of l_1 Estimation of Gaussian Mixture Model Parameters for Language Identification. In: Železný, M., Habernal, I., Ronzhin, A., et al. (eds.) SPECOM 2013. LNCS, vol. 8113, pp. 41–45. Springer, Heidelberg (2013)
12. Lyubimov, N., Kotov, M.: Non-negative Matrix Factorization with Linear Constraints for Single-Channel Speech Enhancement. In: Proc. of Interspeech (2013)
13. Christensen, H., Barker, J., Ma, N., Green, P.: The CHiME corpus: a resource and a challenge for computational hearing in multisource environments. In: Proc. Interspeech, pp. 1918–1921 (2010)
14. Reynolds, D.A., Quatieri, T.F., Dunn, R.B.: Speaker Verification Using Adapted Gaussian Mixture Models. Digital Signal Processing 10(1–3), 19–41 (2000)
15. Pelecanos, J., Sridharan, S.: Feature Warping for Robust Speaker Verification. In: Proc. Odyssey: the speaker recognition workshop, Crete (2001)
16. Ephraim, Y., Malah, D.: Speech enhancement using a minimum mean-square error log-spectral amplitude estimator. IEEE Trans. on Acoustic, Speech and Signal Proc. 33(2), 443–445 (1985)

Extraction of Features for Lip-reading Using Autoencoders

Karel Paleček

The Institute of Information Technology and Electronics,
Technical University of Liberec, Studentská 2/1402, 46117 Liberec, Czech Republic
karel.palecek@tul.cz

Abstract. We study the incorporation of facial depth data in the task of isolated word visual speech recognition. We propose novel features based on unsupervised training of a single layer autoencoder. The features are extracted from both video and depth channels obtained by Microsoft Kinect device. We perform all experiments on our database of 54 speakers, each uttering 50 words. We compare our autoencoder features to traditional methods such as DCT or PCA. The features are further processed by simplified variant of hierarchical linear discriminant analysis in order to capture the speech dynamics. The classification is performed using a multi-stream Hidden Markov Model for various combinations of audio, video, and depth channels. We also evaluate visual features in the join audio-video isolated word recognition in noisy environments. English

Keywords: Autoencoder, Hidden Markov Model, Kinect, Lip-reading.

1 Introduction

Automatic visual speech recognition, or lip-reading, has been an active research area for over two decades now. Many studies conducted over the time demonstrated an improved accuracy when incorporating visual information over audio-only speech recognition) [1], [2], [3], especially in noisy environments.

Existing lip-reading methods may be broadly classified into two main groups: methods solely exploiting appearance-based features and methods modeling shape as well. For the appearance-based methods, visual features are extracted from a region of interest (ROI), usually a rectangular area centered around the speaker's mouth. Some of the most commonly used features are Discrete Cosine Transformation (DCT) and Principal Component Analysis (PCA) [4]. For the second class of algorithms, shape can be represented using e.g. a set of several facial landmarks and then modeled by multivariate distributions. Examples of such methods include e.g. Active Appearance Model (AAM) [4], [5]. While the combined shape and appearance methods usually perform better, they require stable and reliable landmark detection, which is a non-trivial task. In this work, we extract the visual features from the ROI, not modeling the shape of the speaker's lips.

Most of the research has been focused on extracting visual cues from the frontal image of the speaker's face, therefore not modeling 3D properties of the

A. Ronzhin et al. (Eds.): SPECOM 2014, LNAI 8773, pp. 209–216, 2014.

ROI. There have been studies where the authors recorded speakers by multiple cameras and then performed lip-reading using 3D information reconstructed by stereo-vision algorithms [6], [7]. However, due to sensitivity to lighting conditions, hardware requirements, and computational complexity, these methods remain rather scarcely used in the context of visual speech recognition. In the recent years, few affordable devices such as Asus Xtion, Creative Senz3D or Microsoft Kinect have become popular for 3D reconstruction. These devices are able to reconstruct depth information using structured light and depth from focus techniques. One of the pioneering efforts in lip-reading with incorporating facial depth data from Kinect was [8], where the authors applied 2D DCT to both video and depth streams, and combined the modalities via multi-stream hidden Markov model. In [9], patch trajectories were extracted from video and depth, and used in a random forest manifold alignment algorithm for lipreading.

Recently, a class of methods known as deep learning has gained an increased attention in the computer vision and speech recognition communities. Deep learning algorithms are most commonly used as an unsupervised pre-training procedure that automatically extracts useful information from the data for deep neural network classification. This is done in a greedy layer-wise manner by fitting e.g. Restricted Boltzmann Machine (RBM) or an autoencoder for each layer. For an overview, see [10]. In [11] and [12], authors used deep neural networks, pre-trained on several concatenated PCA-reduced frames using RBM, for visual speech parametrization and achieved better results than using hand-engineered features.

In our work, we propose a single layer only autoencoder as a feature extraction method for visual speech recognition, and use it to extract features from both video and depth streams. In contrast to [11] and [12], we apply the autoencoder directly on the image and not on concatenated feature vectors. Instead, similarly to [8], we incorporate speech dynamics on higher-level features and classify using a multi-stream Hidden Markov Model. In the experiments on our database recorded by Kinect, we demonstrate the improved performance of the autoencoder features over DCT and PCA in the task of isolated word recognition with incorporated facial depth data.

2   Feature Extraction

An autoencoder [10], also called an autoassociator, is a type of neural network that learns a distributed representation of the input. In consists of two parts: an encoder that converts the input into activations of its hidden units, and decoder that reconstructs the input from the encoder's internal representation. The input vector $x \in \mathbb{R}^n$ is encoded by m hidden units as

$$h(x) = f(Wx + b) \tag{1}$$

where W is $m \times n$ matrix of weights of each unit, b is a $m \times 1$ bias vector, and $f(\cdot)$ is an element-wise activation function. If $m < n$ and f is linear, it can be shown that the learned representation $h(x) \in \mathbb{R}^m$ lies in the subspace of eigenspace of the input data. In order to find more interesting features that are better suited for classification, we use the sigmoid activation, i.e. $f(z) = \sigma(z) = \frac{1}{1+\exp(-z)}$. The input is then reconstructed by the decoder as

$$y = f\left(W'h(x) + c\right) \tag{2}$$

where W' is $n \times m$ matrix of decoder's connection weights and c is a $n \times 1$ bias vector. In our work, we consider autoencoder with tied weights, i.e. where $W' = W^\top$. The aim of the autoencoder is to learn W, b, and c such that a reconstruction error $L(x, y)$ is minimized. Since we deal with real-valued data, we define the reconstruction error as

$$L(x, y) = \|y - x\|^2 + \alpha \sum_{ij} w_{ij}^2 \tag{3}$$

The regularization term in (3) prevents overfitting by keeping the weights w_{ij} of the matrix W small. From the probabilistic perspective this corresponds to imposing a Gaussian prior on the weights w_{ij}.

In order to limit the number of images for which each neuron is active (i.e. its output value is close to 1), we apply additional L_1 regularization penalty on the input to the sigmoid function. The complete objective function of our autoencoder therefore takes the form

$$J(W, b, c) = \frac{1}{|X|} \sum_{x \in X} \|y - x\|^2 + \alpha \sum_{ij} w_{ij}^2 + \beta \sum_{x \in X} \sum_{j=1}^{m} |w_i^\top x| \tag{4}$$

where $w_i^\top$ is the i-th row of the matrix W. We find the optimal W, b, and c by minimizing (4) with respect to using the Limited memory Broyden-Fletcher-Goldfarb-Shanno (L-BFGS) algorithm. The weights of each unit are initialized to small uniformly distributed random values inversely proportional to the total number of its connections. The bias vectors b and c are initialized to zeros. After the optimal W, b, and c has been found, the hidden representation (1) is used as a visual speech parametrization vector.

Since optimization of the objective function (4) is a computationally expensive task, tuning the hyper-parameters α and β using exhaustive grid search techniques is not feasible, because the number of experiments would be too large. Therefore, in order to find the optimal values for α and β, we employ Bayesian optimization strategy with the expected improvement acquisition function [18]. Bayesian optimization is a general method for minimization of an unknown function. It utilizes Monte-Carlo techniques to select each evaluation point in the parameter space. In our case, the objective function is defined as the word error rate (WER) that is achieved by classifying the features learned by the autoencoder. The classification is performed using a whole-word Hidden Markov Model (HMM) on the full cross validated database. Examples of features learned by our autoencoder (AE) are shown in Fig. 1. Note that some AE features fail to converge.

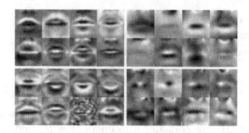

Fig. 1. Examples of learned features. Top row: PCA features, bottom row: AE. Left: video, right: depth channel.

3 Visual Front-End

Region of interest extraction and data preprocessing consists of several stages in our work. In the first stage, position of the speakers face is approximately estimated using Viola-Jones detector (VJ) [13], a well known method based on computationally inexpensive Haar-like features that are combined into a strong classifier using boosting technique.

In the second stage, location and shape of speakers lips, chin and mouth are refined using Explicit Shape Regression algorithm (ESR) [14]. Similarly to traditional face alignment methods such as Active Appearance Model (AAM), ESR models shape of an object by set of N landmarks, but instead of modeling complex distributions of the shape variance, it predicts optimal joint landmark configuration discriminatively based on the current estimate. However, since there is no objective function to be minimized during the face alignment stage, the predicted facial shape is slightly different in each frame, causing random noise in the position of the landmarks. In order to extract the region of interest (ROI) in a more stable way, we therefore average the fitting results over three neighboring frames in time.

In our work, the region of interest (ROI) is defined as square region covering the mouth and its closest surroundings. The scale invariance is achieved by defining the ROI on the unit-normalized mean facial shape obtained by aligning and then averaging all shapes in the training database. For each frame, the mean facial shape is aligned to the detected shape by Euclidean transformation such that the mean square error is minimized. The size of the ROI is fixed to 32×32 pixels because of efficiency reasons of the auto-encoder fitting procedure.

4 Data Preparation

For experimenting with visual speech features incorporating depth information we recorded an audio-visual database containing both isolated word and continuous speech utterances. Our database contains 54 speakers (23 female and 31 male), each uttering 50 isolated words in Czech language. The database also contains 583 manually annotated images of all speakers in various poses, expressions and face occlusions, which constitute a training dataset for the ESR detector. The database was recorded in an office environment using Microsoft Kinect sensor and Genius lavalier microphone.

Because of uncertainty of the stereo vision reconstruction in Kinect, there exist points in space, for which the depth is ambiguous and cannot be inferred without further assumptions about the observed scene. In such cases (e.g. inside of an opened mouth or around the nose), the Kinect device returns zero values. In order not to have skewed results, we therefore reconstruct all missing values in the depth maps by using nearest neighbor interpolation. We then remove the mean and clamp the depth values to the range $[-30, 30]$ in order to remove occasional large spikes manifesting when the background is partially visible.

For both video and depth streams, the average pixel value of the whole utterance is subtracted from each ROI to partially remove differences in light conditions between sequences recorded in different time. ROI images are also whitened to remove correlations between adjacent pixels. For the audio, we down-sample the original 44.1 kHz signal to 16 kHz before parametrization by MFCC.

5   Experiments

In order to reduce the effect of overfitting, we employ the cross validation strategy in all our experiments. The database of 54 speakers is split in a 43 : 11 ratio in 5 different combinations[1]. We trained the ESR detector and all visual features separately for each training/testing split. All of the reported results are the average word recognition accuracies achieved over the five different splits. We used the Spearmint [18] library for Bayesian optimization and HTK toolkit [15] as implementation of Hidden Markov Models.

We compare the autoencoder (AE) features with features extracted using 2D DCT and PCA. The DCT coefficients are sorted according to their average energy achieved on the training set. The features are evaluated in three settings: static, static+delta (Δ), and dynamic linear discriminant analysis (LDA) [1]. In case of static and delta features, we exhaustively search for the optimal number of DCT and PCA features by maximizing the classification score. For DCT and PCA the respective optimal dimensions were 22 and 28 for video, and 16 and 14 for depth. The number of AE features is fixed to 144. In case of LDA, we reduce feature vector of each frame to 33 coefficients, concatenate $(2K + 1)$ neighboring frames into a single hyper-vector, and then reduce its dimension using LDA. We set $K = 5$ as an empirically found optimum between performance and complexity (LDA-K5). We use phonemes as class labels for the LDA. As a final step we perform feature mean subtraction for each utterance, in order to increase robustness against between-speaker variation of the visual features.

Table 1 presents achieved recognition accuracies of the considered features. The recognition was performed using a whole word 14 state HMM. As can be seen, AE features outperform both DCT and PCA in all three settings. However, the difference is smaller for LDA case. This is probably caused by violating the assumption of shared covariance matrices between all phoneme classes. In

---

[1] One testing group contains only 10 speakers.

Table 1. Word accuracy [%] for visual features individually

	Video			Depth		
	Static	Δ	LDA-K5	Static	Δ	LDA-K5
DCT	63.5	71.5	76.6	56.5	59.3	71.2
PCA	59.0	68.4	77.3	63.1	68.3	72.0
AE	67.7	75.4	78.2	64.0	68.3	75.4

order to improve the results of dynamic LDA, we therefore selected subset of the AE features according to their variance and then whitened the reduced features before frame concatenation. Note that for DCT and PCA only basic dimension reduction is needed. The recognition accuracies and the optimal vector dimensions also suggest that the depth stream contain less useful information than video. However, as we shall see next, the information contained in the depth stream is to some extent complementary.

Table 2. Word accuracy [%] for combinations of video and depth features

	LDA-K5		LDA-K5
DCT-DCT	81.6	AE-DCT	84.3
DCT-PCA	81.0	AE-PCA	85.0
AE-AE	85.9	DCT-AE	83.8

Table 2 shows results achieved for selected feature combinations. The features were combined by a multi-stream HMM using 0.6 : 0.4 weight ratio (video:depth). As can be seen, the recognition accuracy was improved when incorporating both modalities via multi-stream HMM as compared to single-source models. This holds for all pairs of features, suggesting that the depth-based features are complementary to video-based features. Similarly to previous experiment, the best result was achieved when the features were extracted by autoencoder from both video and depth streams. The absolute increase of accuracy for AE when incorporating depth was 7.7 %, which corresponds to 35 % relative improvement of word error rate (WER).

We also evaluate the AE features with incorporated depth information in simulated noisy environment. Since our database was recorded in a relatively quiet environment, babble noise from the NOISEX [16] database was added to the clean audio artificially using various signal-to-noise ratios (SNR). For audio and video feature fusion, the weight ratio was set to 0.5:0.5. When combining all three modalities the weights were 0.5:0.3:0.2 for audio, video, and depth, respectively. We also compare the achieved results with Multi-band Spectral Subtraction algorithm [17], a popular method for audio enhancement. The results are presented in Fig. 2. The graph again confirms the benefit when incorporating depth data in the lip-reading task. As one can expect, the improvement of audio-visual fusion as compared to audio-only recognition is highest for low SNR.

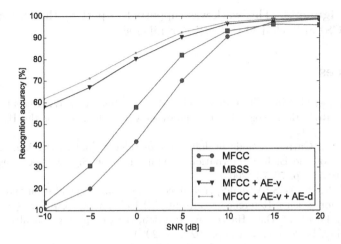

Fig. 2. Recognition accuracy in a noisy audio environment

The resulting scores are critically dependent on the individual stream weights, i.e. the results could be further improved by changing the weights dynamically depending on the SNR. Because of the spectral distortion, the MBSS algorithm is also beneficial especially for low SNRs.

6 Conclusions

We have evaluated the benefit of incorporating visual and depth information in the task of isolated word recognition. Based on the experiments we can conclude that the information contained in the depth data displays complementary character to the information captured by the video channel as confirmed by the 35 % relative WER reduction. In order to extract features from both video and depth streams, we have proposed to use a single layer autoencoder. We have shown an improvement of our autoencoder features over traditional techniques such as DCT and PCA for both video and depth channels. Compared to DCT, our AE features achieved 4–8 % higher absolute accuracy, depending on the data source and inclusion of speech dynamics. A disadvantage of our autoencoder features is higher dimensionality and additional required processing.

So far, the video and depth autoencoder features were evaluated only in the task of isolated word recognition. Our conclusions should also be confirmed in continuous speech recognition with phoneme-based models. The results achieved by autoencoder features could be potentially improved by utilizing deep learning algorithms for both video and depth streams. Also, the deep neural network could be utilized in other ways, e.g. as a feature fusion method or speech dynamics enhancement instead of LDA.

Acknowledgments. This work was supported in part by the Student Grant Scheme (SGS) at Technical University of Liberec.

References

1. Potamianos, G., Neti, C., Gravier, G., Garg, A., Senior, A.W.: Recent Advances in the Automatic Recognition of Audiovisual Speech. Proc. of the IEEE 91(9), 1306–1326 (2003)
2. Goecke, R.: Current Trends in Joint Audio-Video Signal Processing: A Review. In: Proc. of the Eighth International Symposium on Signal Processing and Its Applications, pp. 70–73 (2005)
3. Liew, A.W.Ch., W.S.: Visual Speech Recognition: Lip Segmentation and Mapping. Information Science Reference – Imprint. IGI Publishing, New York (2009)
4. Lan, Y., Theobald, B.J., Harvey, R., Bowden, R.: Comparing Visual Features for Lipreading. In: Proc. AVSP, pp. 102–106 (2009)
5. Paleček, K., Chaloupka, J.: Audio-visual Speech Recognition in Noisy Audio Environments. In: 36th International Conference on Telecommunications and Signal Processing (TSP), pp. 484–487 (2013)
6. Goecke, R., Millar, J.B., Zelinovsky, A., Ribes, R.J.: Stereo Vision Lip-Tracking for Audio-Video Speech Processing. In: Proceedings of the 2001 IEEE International Conference on Acoustics, Speech, Signal Processing (2001)
7. Císař, P., Krňoul, Z., Železný, M.: 3D Lip-Tracking for Audio-Visual Speech Recognition in Real Applications. In: Proc. INTERSPEECH (2004)
8. Galatas, G., Potamianos, G., Makedon, F.: Audio-visual Speech Recognition Incorporating Facial Depth Information Captured by the Kinect. In: Proc. EUSIPCO, pp. 2714–2717 (2012)
9. Pei, Y., Kim, T.-K., Zha, H.: Unsupervised Random Forest Manifold Alignment for Lipreading. In: Proc. ICCV, pp. 129–136 (2013)
10. Bengio, Y.: Learning Deep Architectures for AI. Foundations and Trends in Machine Learning 2(1), 1–127 (2009)
11. Ngiam, J., Khosla, A., Kim, M., Nam, J., Lee, H., Ng, A.Y.: Multimodal Deep Learning. In: Proc. ICML, pp. 689–696 (2011)
12. Huang, J., Kingsbury, B.: Audio-visual Deep Learning for Noise Robust Speech Recognition. In: Proc. ICASSP, pp. 7596–7599 (2013)
13. Viola, P.A., Jones, M.J.: Robust Real-Time Face Detection. International Journal of Computer Vision 57, 137–154 (2004)
14. Cao, X., Wei, Y., Wen, F., Sun, J.: Face Alignment by Explicit Shape Regression. In: Proc. CVPR, pp. 2887–2894 (2012)
15. Steve, Y., Odel, J., Ollason, D., Valtchev, V., Woodland, P.: The HTK Book, version 2.1. Cambridge University, United Kingdom (1997)
16. Varga, A.P., Steeneken, H.J.M., Tomlinson, M., Jones, D.: The NOISEX-92 Study on the Effect of Additive Noise on Automatic Speech Recognition. Technical Report, DRA Speech Research Unit (1992)
17. Kamath, S., Loizou, P.: A Multi-band Spectral Subtraction Method for Enhancing Speech Corrupted by Colored Noise. In: Proc. ICASSP, pp. IV-4164 (2002)
18. Snoek, J., Larochelle, H., Adams, R.P.: Practical Bayesian Optimization of Machine Learning Algorithms. Advances in Neural Information Processing Systems 25, 2951–2959 (2012)

F0 Declination Patterns in Russian

Daniil Kocharov, Pavel Skrelin, and Nina Volskaya

Department of Phonetics, Saint-Petersburg State University
Universitetskaya Emb., 11, 199034, Saint-Petersburg, Russia
kocharov,skrelin,volni@phonetics.pu.ru
http://www.phonetics.pu.ru

Abstract. This paper deals with F0 declination in Russian. The study was conducted using statistical data derived from the Corpus of Professionally Read Speech to determine F0 declination patterns, to describe several aspects of declination line such as top-line F0 variations due to the type of utterances having different intonation contours, to confirm or reject the steepness-duration dependency found for other languages.

The results confirm the relationship between F0 slope and the utterance length for Russian. At the same time they reveal strong dependency of the slope on the intonation pattern of the utterance: thus complete final declaratives have steeper slope than non-final units, interrogatives with rising nuclear tone display no declination in the pre-nuclear part, the results also show individual strategies in pre-planning declination slope of the intonational phrase.

Keywords: phonetics, prosody, declination, Russian.

1 Introduction

Declination, defined as the tendency for fundamental frequency to glide gradually down in the course of an utterance [1, p. 77] [2], has been studied in many aspects and for many languages and it is considered to be a universal [3] [4]. It is said to characterize sentences spoken in isolation, reading aloud, and less so spontaneously produced speech [5] [6] [7], its pattern and slope may vary with style and sentence length [8] [9] [10] [11]. For Swedish [12], for example, a difference was defined in degree of declination between the two speaking styles: read-aloud speech was reported to have steeper slope and a more apparent time-dependency than spontaneous speech. Similar results were reported for some other languages. On the other hand, the variability in data is so large, that there are growing doubts about universality of declination [5] [13].

Data on declination in Russian is limited [14] [15] [16], since studies were based on small amount of material or were obtained using mostly laboratory speech.

Despite numerous studies of this phenomenon the courses of declination still remain a matter of dispute. If we assumed that declination was systematically determined by dropping sub-glottal pressure, we could easily model pitch patterns for all intonation types in a particular language, but the intonation models

A. Ronzhin et al. (Eds.): SPECOM 2014, LNAI 8773, pp. 217–226, 2014.

for speech synthesis, using a uniform declination for all utterances of the same length and sentence type proved to be too simple [17]. With so many influencing factors involved, the situation seems to be more complicated: in Russian, for example, we also observe an effect of sentence type on declination pattern.

2   Method

2.1   Material

For the present study, we analyzed recordings of read speech made from 8 professional (4 male and 4 female) speakers of Standard Russian. The material was For the present study, we analyzed recordings of the Corpus of Professionally Read Speech [18], which contains read speech made from 8 professional (4 male and 4 female) speakers of Standard Russian. The speech material is segmented, phonetically transcribed, manually prosodically annotated. We concentrated on two prosodic constituents: the widely used and accepted intonational phrase [19] and the prosodic word (other terms for it are "metrical group", "rhythmic group", "accent group", "phonological phrase" etc.). We use the term "a prosodic word" (PW) in its traditional sense for a content word and its clitics, which include all items that in a particular intonation unit, a phrase or an utterance, lose their lexical stress and thus form one rhythmic unit with a "properly" stressed word. In Russian many function (form) words may be unstressed or weakly stressed but deaccented, so a PW is the only one which is both stressed and carries a pitch accent.

Intonation units which we selected from the CORPRES to use as our material differ in size and intonation pattern, i.e., intonational phrases from 3 to 7 PWs, representing different types of utterances: final complete declarative statements, non-final incomplete statements, and general questions. These types of utterances have different (polar) intonation contours (IC): falling for complete final statements (IC01), rising for non-final units (IC11) and questions (IC07) [20]. The total amount of the material analyzed per speaker is presented in Table 1.

Table 1. The number of intonation units per speaker per contour

Intonation	Speakers							
contour	M1	M2	M3	M4	F1	F2	F3	F4
IC 01	931	611	1251	782	971	626	667	1326
IC 11	697	795	878	334	1003	721	632	749
IC 07	41	17	66	36	64	21	21	81
Total	1669	1423	2195	1152	2038	1368	1320	2156

Figs 1–3 illustrate typical F0 tracks (st) of a broad focus declarative (IC01), a non-final intonational phrase (IC11) and a general question (IC07), containing 5-7 PWs.

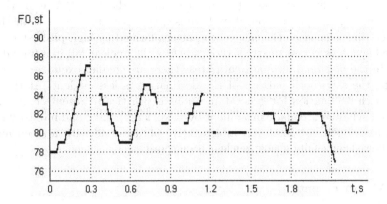

Fig. 1. The gradual declination of pitch over an intonational phrase of the final declarative containing 5 prosodic words. IC 01.

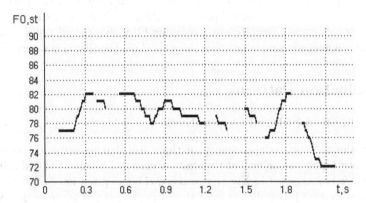

Fig. 2. F0 declination in a non-final intonational phrase containing 5 prosodic words. IC11.

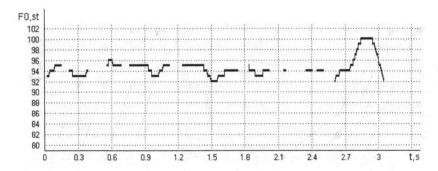

Fig. 3. The sustained pitch level in the pre-nuclear part in a general question containing 7 prosodic words. IC 07.

As it is evident from Figs. 1, 2 in declaratives the first PW is marked by maximum F0, the pitch level of each subsequent accent is lower than that of the preceding one. Note the saw-tooth pattern formed by high-pitched accented stressed syllables versus unstressed ones before the nuclear fall in a final declarative. In the non-final intonational phrase there are smaller excursions on pitch accents, the saw-tooth pattern of the declination is less evident. At the same time, pitch declination for general questions is practically absent (Fig. 3). The accented syllables are made prominent by vowel lengthening and intensity rather than pitch. Both non-final and interrogative phrases end with a steep nuclear rise followed by a falling post-nuclear tone ("tail").

2.2   Measurements

Top-line declination was calculated using F0 data (in semitones) for each successive pitch accent in the intonational phrase as the difference (in semitones) of the F0 maximum of the accented vowel and the F0 maximum of the accented vowel of the first PW in the intonational phrase. Scaling of pitch accents for various intonation contours was calculated by averaging F0 values for all the intonational phrases of a corresponding type (final, non-final declarative and interrogative).

3   Declination Patterns

3.1   Declination in Final Declaratives

All intonational units independently of their size demonstrate F0 declination from the beginning to the end of the unit. A classical image of the 'disciplined' F0 downdrift is presented in Fig. 4 (speaker M1): the pitch level of all the PWs is strictly scaled and distributed over the intonational phrase is such a way as to 'hit' the final pitch level of − 6 semitones.

Similar data is found for a female speaker F4 (Fig. 5).

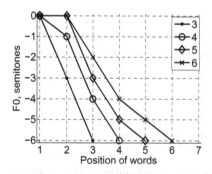 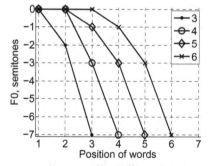

Fig. 4. Scaling of pitch accents in final declaratives. Speaker M1.

Fig. 5. Scaling of pitch accents in final declaratives. Speaker F4.

The end F0 values of intonational phrases spoken by these speakers show practically no variation. It is also evident from the F0 trend that the slope of the declination decreases with growing number of PWs.

Some speakers demonstrate a different strategy, sustaining the pitch level of the first 2 initial PWs and slightly varying the pitch level of the end of the intonational phrase (Figs. 6, 7).

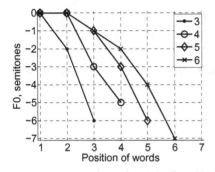 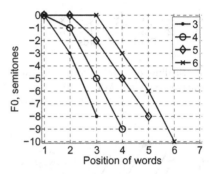

Fig. 6. Scaling of pitch accents in final declaratives. Speaker F1.

Fig. 7. Scaling of pitch accents in final declaratives. Speaker M4.

Pitch range adjustment within the intonational phrase demonstrates individual strategies to the downstepping of pitch accents in the units containing more than 5 words. As we know from previous studies [17, p. 139], such an adjustment can take the form of breaking the declination line and raising slightly the pitch level of the subsequent PW (variously termed "reset", "special rise", "accidental rise") to cope with the pitch range of the whole intonational phrase. For two subjects (M3 and F3) having a relatively narrow pitch range it took the form of sustaining the pitch level of the first 2–4 PWs before resuming F0 downstepping (Figs. 8, 9). Fig. 10 allows us to compare scaling of the pitch level of successive pitch accents with the increasing number of PWs for the speaker M3: actually, for all the intonational phrases, except those containing 3 PWs, the declination proper begins with the last but two PWs.

For some speakers the increased size of the intonational phrase triggers lowering of the pitch level of the final pitch accent, at the same time the declination slope of the first 3–4 pitch accents is nil (see, for example, Figs. 8, 9)

3.2   Declination in Non-Final Intonational Phrases

As we can conclude from the data, for non-final intonational phrases declination line is less steep, though it also demonstrates dependency on the length of the intonational phrase – for all speakers it increases with the number of the PWs, but does not exceed 4 semitones (Figs. 11–13).

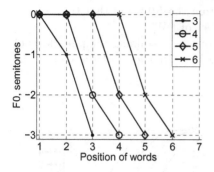

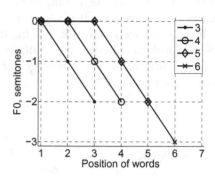

Fig. 8. Scaling of pitch accents in final declaratives. Speaker M3.

Fig. 9. Scaling of pitch accents in final declaratives. Speaker F3.

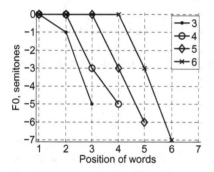

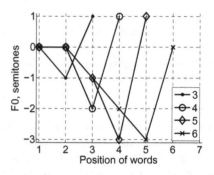

Fig. 10. Scaling of pitch accents in final declaratives. Speaker M2.

Fig. 11. Scaling of pitch accents in non-final intonational phrases. Speaker M1.

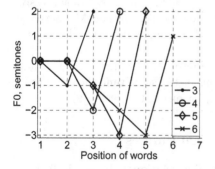

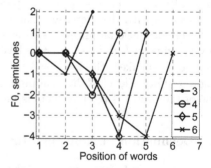

Fig. 12. Scaling of pitch accents in non-final intonational phrases. Speaker F4.

Fig. 13. Scaling of pitch accents in non-final intonational phrases. Speaker M4.

For some speakers the F0 declination takes the form of lowering the last pitch accent before the rising nucleus and does not exceed 1–2 semitones. It is evident from the F0 trend, but in fact it is not perceived (Figs. 14–17).

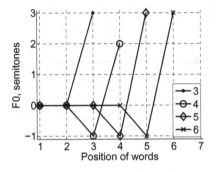

Fig. 14. Scaling of pitch accents in non-final intonational phrases. Speaker M2.

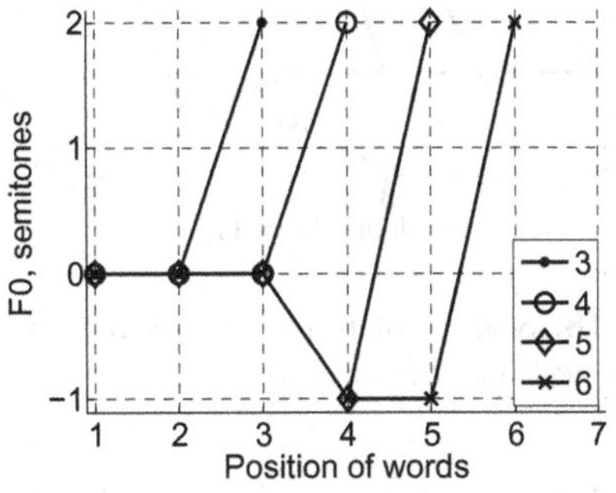

Fig. 15. Scaling of pitch accents in non-final intonational phrases. Speaker M3.

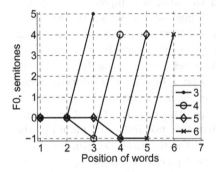

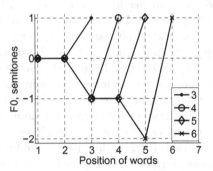

Fig. 16. Scaling of pitch accents in non-final intonational phrases. Speaker F2.

Fig. 17. Scaling of pitch accents in non-final intonational phrases. Speaker F3.

3.3 Declination in General Questions

We present data on general questions having maximum 4 PWs, since normally questions are pretty short. Example given on Fig.3 is an exception rather than the rule.

F0 trend in Russian general questions shows that declination is under control of the speaker and that pre-planning of the whole contour does take place, for in this type of utterance there is no F0 declination regardless of the length of the intonational phrase (Figs. 18–19).

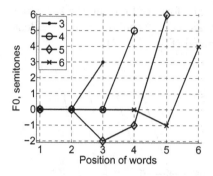 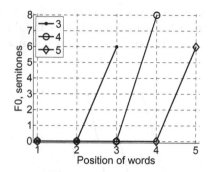

Fig. 18. Scaling of pitch accents in general questions. Speaker M1.

Fig. 19. Scaling of pitch accents in general questions. Speaker F1.

4   Discussion and Conclusion

The results of the study based on the statistical analysis of large data of the corpus of professionally read Russian speech confirm the tendency for F0 to decline to the end of final declaratives in Russian. At the same time our approach to calculating declination (using F0 values of accented vowels) revealed various strategies a speaker follows to fulfill the task of completing the downstepping trend within the intonational unit: "classical", in which the length of the intonational phrase "sets" the end frequency level for the speaker (constant slope); "proportional", within a fixed range: when pitch accents are almost regularly spaced out and the pitch level of each successive accent is defined by the length of the intonational unit in prosodic words; "obligatory" (induced), when downstepping involves the last three pitch accents in the intonational phrase.

The relationship between F0 slope and the utterance length – the shorter the utterance the steeper the slope – confirm the possibility of planning the declination. Pitch scaling is also the function of the utterance length. Ideally, it implies decreased tonal space between subsequent pitch accents to cope with the tonal space of the intonation phrase or utterance, thus confirming the existence of the look-ahead strategy of the speaker [19]. At the same time, there is clear evidence of the individual strategies in scaling pitch level of successive accents particularly in intonational phrases containing more than 5 words: for speakers with narrow individual range the pitch level at the beginning of the intonational phrase is sustained until the last two pitch accents before the nucleus when downstepping of the pitch accents is resumed to reach the pre-planned F0 target end level. For other speakers increased length of the intonational phrase results in lowering the pitch level of the final accent. Thus pitch range adjustment also depends on the length of the intonational unit, but it may take various forms depending on the speaker's individual preferences.

The actual placement of this adjustment within the intonational phrase seems to be governed by many factors: apart from the intention of the speaker to cover the tonal span and reach the preplanned F0 "bottom" level, there are also semantic – resetting at prominent words [21] [22], syntactic – resetting at prosodic boundaries [23], and pragmatic reasons [17, p. 148].

On the basis of the results of the present investigation based on large data of the corpus of professionally read speech it is possible to draw the conclusion that presence or absence of declination is used in Russian to distinguish sentence types – declarative versus interrogative, and different rate of declination alone may contribute to the contrast between non-final declaratives which end with a continuation rise and interrogative sentences proper.

Similar data was reported for Danish [24] – the use of different rates of declination for different sentence types; non-final statements in Danish are characterised by a more gradual declination. Moreover, declination is claimed to be absent from Danish questions (see also data for Dutch in [25]), which means that "not only to declination reset, but also to declination, a communicative function can be attributed" [17, p. 148].

It is worth mentioning here, that the use of different rates of declination as opposed to local pitch movements to distinguish sentence types was found to be a typological parameter differentiating between Danish and Dutch [26].

We may also conclude, following [3, p. 57] that "the natural tendency for F0 to decline has been integrated into the linguistic code, in the form of controlling or entirely suppressing the F0 decline".

Acknowledgments. The authors acknowledge Saint-Petersburg State University for a research grant 31.0.145.2010.

References

1. Pike, K.L.: The Intonation of American English. University of Michigan Press, Ann Arbor (1945)
2. Cohen, A., Collier, R., Hart, J.'t.: Perceptual Analysis of Intonation Patterns. In: 5th International Congress on Acoustics, Paper A16 (1965)
3. Vaissière, J.: Language-Independent Prosodic Features. In: Cutler, A., Ladd, D.R. (eds.) Prosody: Models and Measurements, vol. 14, pp. 53–66. Springer, Heidelberg (1983)
4. Hirst, D., Di Christo, A.: Intonation Systems: A Survey of Twenty Languages. Cambridge University Press, Cambridge (1998)
5. Umeda, N.: F0 Declination is Situation Dependent. Journal of Phonetics 10, 279–290 (1982)
6. Lieberman, P., Katz, W., Jongman, A., Zimmerman, R., Miller, M.: Measures of the Sentence Intonation of Read and Spontaneous Speech in American English. Journal of the Acoustical Society of America 77(2), 649–657 (1985)
7. Anderson, S.W., Cooper, W.E.: Fundamental Frequency Patterns During Spontaneous Picture Description. Journal of the Acoustical Society of America 79(4), 1172–1174 (1986)
8. Pierrehumbert, J.: The Perception of Fundamental Frequency Declination. Journal of the Acoustical Society of America 66(2), 363–369 (1979)
9. Thorsen, N.: Intonation Contours and Stress Group Patterns in Declarative Sentences of Varying Length in ASC Danish. Nordic Prosody 2, 75–90 (1981)

10. Ladd, R.D.: Declination "Reset" and the Hierarchical Organization of Utterances. Journal of the Acoustical Society of America 84(1), 530–544 (1988)
11. Shih, C.: Declination in Mandarin, In Intonation: Theory, Models and Applications. In: ESCA workshop, pp. 293–296. Athens (1997)
12. Swerts, M., Strangert, E., Heldner, M.: F0 Declination in Read-Aloud and Spontaneous Speech. In: ICSLP-1996, pp. 1501–1504. Philadelphia (1996)
13. Ladd, R.D.: Declination: a Review and Some Hypotheses. Phonology Yearbook 1, 53–74 (1984)
14. Svetozarova, N.D.: The Inner Structure of Intonation Contours in Russian. In: Fant, G., Tathham, M.A.A. (eds.) Automotic Analysis and Perception of Speech. Academic, London (1975)
15. Ode, C.: Russian Intonation: a Perceptual Description. Rodopi, Amsterdam (1989)
16. Volskaya, N.: Declination in intonation modeling for speech synthesis. In: Zmogus Kalbos Erdveje, pp. 194–199. Kaunas (2000) (in Russian)
17. Hart, J.'t., Collier, R., Cohen, A.: A Perceptual Study of Intonation. Cambridge University Press, Cambridge (1990)
18. Skrelin, P., Volskaya, N., Kocharov, D., Evgrafova, K., Glotova, O., Evdokimova, V.: CORPRES - Corpus of Russian Professionally Read Speech. In: Sojka, P., Horák, A., Kopeček, I., Pala, K. (eds.) TSD 2010. LNCS, vol. 6231, pp. 392–399. Springer, Heidelberg (2010)
19. Levelt, W.: Speaking: from Intention to Articulation. Cambridge University Press, Cambridge (1989)
20. Volskaya, N., Skrelin, P.: Prosodic Model for Russian. In: Proceedings of Nordic Prosody X, pp. 249–260. Peter Lager, Frankfurt am Main (2009)
21. O'Connor, J.D., Arnold, G.F.: Intonation of Colloquial English, 2nd edn. Longman, London (1973)
22. Volskaya, N., Vorobyova, S.: Declination reset as a means for providing prominence. In: 4th International Workshop Analysis of Russian Speech. St. Petersburg (2012) (in Russian)
23. De Pijper, J.R., Sanderman, A.A.: On the Perceptual Strength of Prosodic Boundaries and Its Relation to Suprasegmental Cues. Journal of the Acoustical Society of America 96, 2037–2047 (1994)
24. Thorsen, N.: A Study of the Perception of Ssentence Intonation – Evidence from Danish. Journal of the Acoustical Society of America 67, 1014–1030 (1980)
25. Van Heuven, V.J., Haan, J.: Phonetic Correlates of Statement versus Question in Dutch. In: Botinis, A. (ed.) Intonation: Analysis, Modelling and Technology, pp. 119–143. Kluwer Academic Publishers (2000)
26. Gooskens, C., Van Heuven, V.J.: Declination in Dutch and Danish: Global versus Local Pitch Movements in the Perceptual Characterisation of Sentence Types. In: The International Congress of Phonetic Scences, vol. 2, pp. 374–377, Stockholm (1995)

Filled Pauses and Lengthenings Detection Based on the Acoustic Features for the Spontaneous Russian Speech

Vasilisa Verkhodanova[1] and Vladimir Shapranov[2]

[1] SPIIRAS, 39, 14th line, 199178, St. Petersburg, Russia
[2] Betria Systems, Inc, 50, Building 11, Ligovskii Prospekt, St. Petersburg, Russia
verkhodanova@iias.spb.su, equidamoid@gmail.com

Abstract. The spontaneous speech processing has a number of problems. Among them there are speech disfluencies. Although most of them are easily treated by speakers and usually do not cause any difficulties for understanding, for Automatic Speech Recognition (ASR) systems their appearance lead to many recognition mistakes. Our paper deals with the most frequent of them (filled pauses and sound lengthenings) basing on the analysis of their acoustical parameters. The method based on the autocorrelation function was used to detect voiced hesitation phenomena and a method of band-filtering was used to detect unvoiced hesitation phenomena. For the experiments on filled pauses and lengthenings detection an especially collected corpus of spontaneous Russian map-task and appointment-task dialogs was used. The accuracy of voiced filled pauses and lengthening detection was 80%. And accuracy of detection of unvoiced fricative lengthening was 66%.

Keywords: speech disfluencies, filled pauses, lengthenings, hesitation, speech corpus, spontaneous speech processing, speech recognition.

1 Introduction

There are a number of factors such as speech variation and different kinds of speech disfluencies that has a bad influence on automatic speech processing [1, 2]. Mainly such phenomena are characteristic to a spontaneous speech. Speech disfluencies are any of various breaks or irregularities that occur within the flow of otherwise fluent speech. These are filled pauses, sound lengthenings, self-repairs, etc. The occurrence of these phenomena may be caused by exterior influence as well as by failures during speech act planning [3]. Hesitations are breaks in phonation that are often filled with certain sounds. Filled pauses are those hesitations that are filled with certain sounds. The nature of sound lengthenings is also hesitational. Such phenomena are semantic lacunas and their appearance means that speaker needs an additional time to formulate the next piece of utterance [4]. In oral communication filled pauses and lengthenings may play a valuable role such as helping a speaker to hold a conversational turn or to express the speaker's thinking process of formulating the upcoming utterance fragment.

A. Ronzhin et al. (Eds.): SPECOM 2014, LNAI 8773, pp. 227–234, 2014.

These phenomena are an obstacle for processing of spontaneous speech as well as its transcriptions, because speech recognition systems are usually trained on the structured data without speech disfluencies, this decreases speech recognition accuracy and leads to inaccurate transcriptions [5, 6]. Nowadays there are two main types of methods of dealing with speech disfluencies: methods that process them by means of only acoustic parameters analysis, such as fundamental frequency transition and spectral envelope deformation [7] and methods that process them by means of combined language and acoustic modeling [8].

There are lots of works devoted to speech disfluencies modeling within the systems of automatic speech recognition [9, 10]. Also there are approaches that deal with speech disfluencies at the stage of signal preprocessing [11], as well as speech disfluencies removal using speech transcriptions [10, 12].

In [13] authors describe a method for automatic detection of filled pauses. This method detects filled pauses and word lengthening on the basis of two acoustical features: small F0 transition and small spectral envelope deformation, which are estimated by identifying the most predominant harmonic structure in the input. The method has been implemented and tested on a Japanese spontaneous speech corpus consisting of 100 utterances by five men and five women (10 utterances per subject). Each utterance contained at least one filled pause. Experimental results for a Japanese spoken dialogue corpus showed that the real-time filled-pause-detection system yielded a recall rate of 84.9% and a precision rate of 91.5%.

In [14] authors focus on the identification of disfluent sequences and their distinct structural regions, based on acoustic and prosodic features. For the experiments a speech corpus of university lectures in European Portuguese "Lectra" with a relatively high percentage of disfluencies (7.6%) was used. The corpus contains records from seven 1-semester courses, where most of the classes are 60-90 minutes long, and consists of spontaneous speech mostly, and its current version contains about 32h of manual orthographic transcripts. Several machine learning methods have been applied, and the best results were achieved using Classification and Regression Trees (CART). The set of features which were most informative for cross-region identification encompasses word duration ratios, word confidence score, silent ratios, pitch, and energy slopes. The performance achieved for detecting words inside of disfluent sequences was about 91% precision and 37% recall, when filled pauses and fragments were used as a feature. Presented results confirm that knowledge about filled pauses and fragments has a strong impact on the performance. Without it, the performance decayed to 66% precision and 20% recall.

There are number of publications aimed to raise speech disfluencies recognition quality by means of additional knowledge sources such as different language models. In [8] three types of speech disfluencies are considered: repetition, revisions (content replacement), restarts (or false starts). A part of Switchboard-I as well as its transcription (human transcriptions and ASR output) was taken for research. Normalized word and pause duration, pitch, jitter (undesirable phase and/or random frequency deviation of the transmitted signal), spectral tilt, and the ratio of the time, in which the vocal folds are open to the total length of the glottal cycle, were taken as the prosodic features. Also three types of language models were used: (1) hidden-event word-based language model that describes joint appearance of the key words and speech disfluencies in spontaneous speech; (2) hidden-event POS-based language model that uses statistics on part-of-speech (POS) to capture syntactically generalized patterns, such as the tendency to repeat prepositions; (3) repetition pattern language model for detection of repetitions.

For the application of disfluencies detecting methods based on language modeling a large corpus of transcriptions is needed while for rule-based approaches there is no need for such corpus. Also rule-based approaches have an advantage of not relying on lexical information from a speech recognizer. For this research we decided further to test the effectiveness of rule-based approach for detecting filled pauses and lengthenings in Russian spontaneous speech.

This paper is organized as follows: in Section 2 the methodology for corpus recording and the collected corpus description are given. Section 3 is devoted to description of the method of filled pauses and lengthenings detection. In Section 4 the experimental results of hesitations and sound lengthenings are presented.

2 Corpus of Russian Spontaneous Speech

Usually corpora with Rich Transcription [12] are used for studying the speech disfluencies of different kind. Czech Broadcast Conversation MDE Transcripts [15] is an example of such corpus. It consists of transcripts with metadata of the files in Czech Broadcast Conversation Speech Corpus [16], and its annotation contains such phenomena as background noises, filled pauses, laugh, smacks, etc [17].

For our purposes a corpus of spontaneous Russian speech was collected based on the task methodology: map-tasks and appointment-task [18]. Thus, the recorded speech is informal and unrehearsed, and it is also the result of direct dialogue communication, what makes it spontaneous [19].

For example, in Edinburgh and Glasgow the HCRC corpus was collected, which consists only of map-task dialogs [20], and half of the another corpus, corpus of German speech Kiel, consists of appointment tasks [21].

Map task dialogs in the collected corpus represent a description of a route from start to finish, basing on the maps. Pair of participants had a map which had various landmarks drawn on it with one of them having a map with a route. And the task was to describe the route to the other participant, who had to draw this route onto his/her own map. After fulfilling this task participants switched their roles and dialogue continued. Several pairs of maps of varied difficulty were created, the criterion of difficulty being the number of unmatched landmarks. For dialogs based on appointment task, a pair of participants tried to find a common free time for: a) telephone talk (at least 15 minutes), b) meeting (1 hour) based on their individual schedules. Participants could not see maps or schedules of each other. Due to maps and schedules structure they had to ask questions, interrupt and discuss the route or possible free time. This resulted in speech disfluencies and artifacts appearance.

The recorded corpus consists of 18 dialogs from 1.5 to 5 minutes. Recording was performed in the sound isolated room by means of two tablets PCs Samsung Galaxy

Tab 2 with Smart Voice Recorder. Sample rate was 16 kHz, bit rate - 256 Kbit/s. All the recordings were made in St. Petersburg in the end of 2012 - beginning of 2013. Participants were students: 6 women speakers and 6 men speakers from 17 to 23 years old with technical and humanitarian specialization. Corpus was manually annotated in the Wave Assistant [22] on two levels: those disfluencies and artifacts that were characteristic for one speaker were marked on the first level, those that were characteristic for the other speaker - on the second level. During annotation 1042 phenomena such as filled pauses (for example pauses filled with [ə] and [ɐ] sounds), artifacts (as laugh, breath), self-repairs and false-starts as well as word-fillers were marked.

Sighs and loud breath, filled pauses [ə] and [m], self-repairs and lengthening of sound /i/ appeared equally often in the speech of all 12 speakers. In the speech of 11 speakers also lengthening of /a/ and filled pause [ɐ] were common. And almost everyone used such fillers as /vot/ ("there") and /nu/ ("well").

Due to the fact that certain disfluencies are communicatively significant and hardly can be distinguished from normal speech, on this stage of research we have confined ourselves to the most frequent elements of in speech disfluencies: filled pauses and sound lengthenings.

3   Method of Filled Pauses and Lengthenings Detection

The basic idea of our method is to find acoustical features of filled pauses and sound lengthenings in speech signals by using spectrum analysis. Our method assumes that filled pauses and lengthenings contain a continuous voiced sound of an unvaried phoneme; due to this the neighboring instantaneous spectra are similar. For these phenomena such characteristics as unvaried value of pitch and duration of about 150-200ms are peculiar. This duration value is a reliable threshold for perception of speech pauses, because it is close to the value of mean syllable duration [23].

This paper logically follows from [18]. The method for voiced hesitational phenomena detection is based on the algorithm described in [24]. In the following, we describe the main procedure of our method (Figure 1).

The main idea of voiced hesitational phenomena detection algorithm is to find continuous segments in the signal where formants position remains the same. The "formant spectrum" for every moment T_n, where $T_n = d_t\, n$ was calculated basing on the algorithm described in [24]. The value of d_t is constrained by the duration of sound transitions and also by the needed temporal resolution.

Window length for autocorrelation procedure was 128 samples or 8 ms. The consequential spectra were compared by means of the K, that is the formants stability coefficient:

$$K = \frac{\sum_k A_k B_k}{(\sum_k A_k^2)(\sum_k B_k^2)} \,, \tag{1}$$

where A_k and B_k are neighboring formant spectra.

The coefficient K reflects the constancy of formants position. The value of K is close to 1 when the formants position does not change. The function of K is presented in the Figure 2. There are intervals in the function K where its value exceeds the experimentally set threshold value (0.79). The boundaries of the intervals are then checked whether there are occlusive consonants. And if these consonants are word's beginning/end the interval length is increased by the consonant duration. Intervals shorter than 0.16 sec are ignored. All the rest are then compared to the markup.

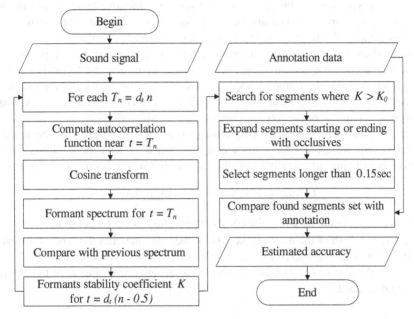

Fig. 1. Scheme of the method of voiced hesitational phenomena detection

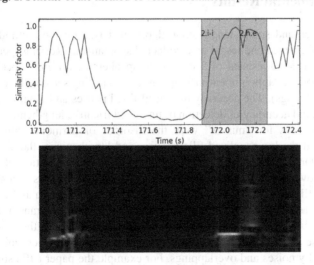

Fig. 2. The diagram of similarity function K (above), with the gray background indicating mark in the annotation, and the resampled spectrogram (below) of the same signal part for filled pause /e/

The method described above does not perform well on the lengthenings of unvoiced fricatives. Due to the small amount of these elements (about only 1% of all annotated phenomena), almost all of them being sibilants lengthenings, we relied on the fact that they are characterized by wide bands of certain frequencies ("fricative factors"). The situation of such bands for each unvoiced fricative sound is independent from the speaker. At this stage to detect unvoiced fricative lengthenings the following temporal series were computed: the ratios of the mean value of instantaneous spectrum samples in the band to the mean value of samples of the spectrum. Those intervals, where the series value exceeds a certain constant (more than 3), presumably contain the sound in question [23]. For fricatives separation the following actions were performed. For the found intervals values of "fricative factors" were examined by turns to detect among them those intervals that are corresponding to consonant lengthenings. The rest of the found elements were considered as breath.

The detected filled pause and lengthening events were compared to the markup. For each event we looked for a mark that overlapped it, with the common part of these intervals being sufficiently large (the value of 0.4 was defined experimentally):

$$L_{Ev \cup Mark} > 0.4 min(L_{Ev}, L_{Mark}), \tag{2}$$

where $L_{Ev \cup Mark}$ is the length of the common part, L_{Ev} is the length of the event, and L_{Mark} is the length of the mark. If the type of the mark matches the type of the event then the event was considered as match, otherwise it was considered as a false positive. All marks that were not matched during the events processing were treated as a false negative result.

4   Experimental Results

The filled pauses and sound lengthening algorithm based on the method described above was implemented and tested on a collected spontaneous Russian speech corpus. The development set consisted of 3 dialogs (4 speakers of different specialization): two map-task and one appointment-task dialogue. The testing set was the other part of the corpus (15 dialogs). The accuracy of voiced filled pauses and lengthenings detection was 80%. And accuracy of detection of unvoiced fricative lengthenings was 66%.

The main reasons for "misses" were the disorder of harmonic components in hoarse voice and the laryngealized filled pauses and lengthenings: the algorithm has found parts of laryngealized filled pauses and lengthening the duration of which was not enough to overcome the threshold for correctly found elements. Another reason for misses was filled pauses consisting of two different sounds, such as /ae/. In such a case algorithm detected two lengthenings /a/ and /e/ ignoring the transition part, and both these lengthenings appeared to be too short to overcome the threshold. On the other hand, false alarms were mainly caused by lengthenings that were missing in the annotation and by noises and overlappings. For example the paper riffle sometimes is very similar to lengthening of a /s/ consonant and can be detected incorrectly.

5   Conclusions

This paper presents the method of filled pauses and sound lengthening detection by using the analysis based on the autocorrelation function. The experiments were based on the corpus of spontaneous Russian speech that was especially collected and manually annotated taking into account speech disfluencies and artifacts. The criterion of matching with the annotation marks was used as estimation of algorithm work. The accuracy achieved for the voiced filled pauses and lengthenings detection was 80%. And the accuracy of the unvoiced fricative lengthening detection was 66%.

Further experiments are planned to be focused on more precise physical boundaries detection, on dealing with laryngealized sounds as well as on performing similar experiments with other Russian speech corpora within the other domain. Another stage of investigation will be devoted to context of filled pauses and lengthenings. This would help to detect more precisely their physical boundaries, which are of different nature, such possible sounds as glottal stops in the beginning of filled pauses, transition parts between two sounds, etc. We also are going to apply our method to Russian speech recognition at the stage of signal preprocessing. Future work will also include an integration of the method with speech dialogue systems to make full use of filled pauses communicative functions in the various domains [25].

Acknowledgements. This research is supported by the Committee on Science and Higher Education of the Administration of St. Petersburg.

References

1. Karpov, A., Markov, K., Kipyatkova, I., Vazhenina, D., Ronzhin, A.: Large vocabulary Russian speech recognition using syntactico-statistical language modeling. Speech Communication 56, 213–228 (2014)
2. Kipyatkova, I.S.: Software complex for recognition and processing of Russian conversational speech. Information-control systems 53, 53–59 (2011) (in Rus)
3. Podlesskaya, V.I., Kibrik, A.A.: Speech disfluencies and their reflection in discourse transcription. In: Proc. of VII International Conference on Cognitive Modelling in Linguistics, pp. 194–204 (2004)
4. Clark, H.H., Fox Tree, J.E.: Using uh and um in spontaneous speaking. Cognition 84, 73–111 (2002)
5. Verkhodanova, V.O., Karpov, A.A.: Speech disfluencies modeling in the automatic speech recognition systems The Bulletin of University of Tomsk 363, 10–15 (2012) (in Rus.)
6. Kipyatkova, I., Karpov, A., Verkhodanova, V., Zelezny, M.: Analysis of Long-distance Word Dependencies and Pronunciation Variability at Conversational Russian Speech Recognition. In: Proc. of Federated Conference on Computer Science and Information Systems, pp. 719–725 (2012)
7. Veiga, A., Candeias, S., Lopes, C., Perdigao, F.: Characterization of hesitations using acoustic models. In: Proc. of 17th International Congress of Phonetic Sciences, pp. 2054–2057 (2011)

8. Liu, Y., Shriberg, E., Stolcke, A., et al.: Enriching Speech Recognition with Automatic Detection of Sentence Boundaries and Disfluencies. IEEE Transactions on Audio, Speech and Language Processing 1(5), 1526–1540 (2006)
9. Verkhodanova, V.O.: Algorithms and Software for Automatic Detection of Speech Disfluencies in an Audio Signal. SPIIRAS Proceedings 31, 43–60 (2013)
10. Lease, M., Johnson, M., Charniak, E.: Recognizing disfluencies in conversational speech. IEEE Transactions on Audio, Speech and Language Processing 14(5), 1566–1573 (2006)
11. Kaushik, M., Trinkle, M., Hashemi-Sakhtsari, A.: Automatic Detection and Removal of Disfluencies from Spontaneous Speech. In: Proc. of 13th Australasian International Conference on Speech Science and Technology, pp. 98–101 (2010)
12. Liu, Y.: Structural Event Detection for Rich Transcription of Speech. PhD thesis, Purdue University and ICSI, Berkeley (2004)
13. Masataka, G., Katunobu, I., Satoru, H.: A Real-time Filled Pause Detection System for Spontaneous Speech Recognition. In: Proc. of 6th European Conference on Speech Communication and Technology, pp. 227–230 (1999)
14. Medeiros, R.B., Moniz, G.S., Batista, M.M., Trancoso, I., Nunes, L.: Disfluency Detection Based on Prosodic Features for University Lectures. In: Proc. of 14th Annual Conference of the International Speech Communication Association, pp. 2629–2633 (2013)
15. Corpus "Czech Broadcast Conversation MDE Transcripts", LDC., http://www.ldc.upenn.edu/Catalog/CatalogEntry.jsp?catalogId=LDC2009T20 (accessed January 5, 2014)
16. Corpus "Czech Broadcast Conversation Speech", LDC., http://www.ldc.upenn.edu/Catalog/CatalogEntry.jsp?catalogId=LDC2009S02 (accessed January 5, 2014)
17. Kolar, J., Svec, J., Strassel, S., et al.: Czech Spontaneous Speech Corpus with Structural Metadata. In: Proc. of 9th European Conference on Speech Communication and Technology, pp. 1165–1168 (2005)
18. Verkhodanova, V., Shapranov, V.: Automatic detection of speech disfluencies in the spontaneous russian speech. In: Železný, M., Habernal, I., Ronzhin, A. (eds.) SPECOM 2013. LNCS (LNAI), vol. 8113, pp. 70–77. Springer, Heidelberg (2013)
19. Zemskaya, E.A.: Russian spoken speech: linguistic analysis and the problems of learning, Moscow (1979) (in Rus.)
20. Anderson, A., Bader, M., Bard, E., Boyle, E., Doherty, G.M., Garrod, S., Isard, S., Kowtko, J., McAllister, J., Miller, J., Sotillo, C., Thompson, H.S., Weinert, R.: The HCRC Map Task Corpus. Language and Speech 34, 351–366 (1991)
21. Kohler, K.J.: Labelled data bank of spoken standard German: the Kiel corpus of read/spontaneous speech. In: Kohler, K.J. (ed.) Proc. of 4th International Conference on Spoken Language, vol. 3, pp. 1938–1941 (1996)
22. Wave Assistant, the speech analyzer program by Speech Technology Center, http://www.phonetics.pu.ru/wa/WA_S.EXE (accessed October 6, 2013)
23. Krivnova, O.F., Chadrin, I.S.: Pausing in the Natural and Synthesized Speech. In: Proc. of Conference on Theory and Practice of Speech Investigations (1999) (in Rus)
24. Nelson, D.: Correlation based speech formant recovery. In: Proc. of IEEE International Conference on Acoustics, Speech, and Signal Processing, ICASSP 1997, vol. 3, pp. 1643–1646 (1997)
25. Meshcheryakov, R.M., Kostyuchenko, E., Yu, B.L.N., Choinzonov, E.L.: Structure and database of software for speech quality and intelligibility assessment in the process of rehabilitation after surgery in the treatment of cancers of the oral cavity and oropharynx, maxillofacial area. SPIIRAS Proceedings 32, 116–124 (2014)

First Experiments with Relevant Documents Selection for Blind Relevance Feedback in Spoken Document Retrieval

Lucie Skorkovská

University of West Bohemia, Faculty of Applied Sciences
New Technologies for the Information Society
Univerzitní 22, 306 14 Plzeň, Czech Republic
{lskorkov}@ntis.zcu.cz

Abstract. This paper presents our first experiments aimed at the automatic selection of the relevant documents for the blind relevance feedback method in speech information retrieval. Usually the relevant documents are selected only by simply determining the first N documents to be relevant. We consider this approach to be insufficient and we would try in this paper to outline the possibilities of the dynamical selection of the relevant documents for each query depending on the content of the retrieved documents instead of just blindly defining the number of the relevant documents to be used for the blind relevance feedback in advance. We have performed initial experiments with the application of the score normalization techniques used in the speaker identification task, which was successfully used in the multi-label classification task for finding the "correct" topics of a newspaper article in the output of a generative classifier. The experiments have shown promising results, therefore they will be used to define the possibilities of the subsequent research in this area.

Keywords: query expansion, blind relevance feedback, spoken document retrieval, score normalization.

1 Introduction

The field of information retrieval (IR) has received a significant attention in the past years, mainly because of the development of World Wide Web and the rapidly increasing number of documents available in electronic form. Recently the Internet has been looked upon as an universal information media, more than the text information source it becomes the multimedia information source. Especially since large audio-visual databases are available on-line, the research in the field of information retrieval extends to the retrieval of speech content.

Experiments performed on the speech retrieval collections containing conversational speech [11][2][7] suggest that classic information retrieval methods alone are not sufficient enough for successful speech retrieval, especially when the collections contain speech data in other languages than English. The biggest issue here is that the query words are often not found in the documents from the collection. One cause of this problem is the high word error rate of the automatic speech recognition (ASR) causing the

A. Ronzhin et al. (Eds.): SPECOM 2014, LNAI 8773, pp. 235–242, 2014.

query words to be misrecognized. This problem can be dealt with through the use of ASR lattices for IR. The second cause is that the query words was actually not spoken in the recordings and thus are not contained in the documents. To deal with this issue the query expansion techniques are often used.

One of the possible query expansion methods often used in the IR field is the relevance feedback method. The idea is to take the information from the relevant documents retrieved in the first run of the search and use it to enhance the query with some new terms for the second run of the retrieval. The selection of the relevant documents can be done either by the user of the system or automatically without the human interaction - the method is then usually called the blind relevance feedback. The automatic selection is usually handled only by selecting the first N retrieved documents, which are considered to be relevant.

In this paper we will present the first experiments aimed at the better automatic selection of the relevant documents for the blind relevance feedback method. Our idea is to apply the score normalization techniques used in the speaker identification/verification task [12][14], which was successfully used in the multi-label classification task for finding the threshold between the "correct" and "incorrect" topics of a newspaper article in the output of a generative classifier [13], to dynamically select the relevant documents for each query depending on the content of the retrieved documents instead of just experimentally defining the number of the relevant documents to be used for the blind relevance feedback in advance.

2   Query Likelihood Model

Language modeling approach [8] was used as the information retrieval method for the experiments, specifically the query likelihood model with an linear interpolation of the unigram language model of the document with an unigram language model of the whole collection. The idea of this method is to create a language model M_d from each document d and then for each query q to find the model which most likely generated the query, that means to rank the documents according to the probability $P(d|q)$. The Bayes rule is used:

$$P(d|q) = P(q|d)P(d)/P(q), \tag{1}$$

where $P(q)$ is the same for all documents and the prior document probability $P(d)$ is uniform across all documents, so we can ignore both. We have left the probability of the query been generated by a document model $P(q|M_d)$, which can be estimated using the maximum likelihood estimate (MLE):

$$\hat{P}(q|M_d) = \prod_{t \in q} \frac{tf_{t,d}}{L_d}, \tag{2}$$

where $tf_{t,d}$ is the frequency of the term t in d and L_d is the total number of tokens in d. To deal with the sparse data for the generation of the M_d we have used the mixture model between the document-specific multinomial distribution and the multinomial distribution of the whole collection M_c with interpolation parameter λ. So the final equation for ranking the documents according to the query is:

$$P(d|q) \propto \prod_{t \in q} (\lambda P(t|M_d) + (1 - \lambda)P(t|M_c)). \tag{3}$$

The retrieval performance of this IR model can differ for various levels of interpolation, therefore the λ parameter was set according to the experiments presented in [5] to the best results yielding value - $\lambda = 0.1$.

3 Query Expansion - Blind Relevance Feedback

Query expansion techniques based on the blind relevance feedback (BRF) has been shown to improve the results of the information retrieval. The idea behind the blind relevance feedback is that amongst the top retrieved documents most of them are relevant to the query and the information contained in them can be used to enhance the query for acquiring better retrieval results.

First, the initial retrieval run is performed, documents are ranked according to the query likelihood computed by (3). Then the top N documents are selected as relevant and the top k terms (according to some importance weight L_t, for example *tf-idf*) from them is extracted and used to enhance the query. The second retrieval run is then performed with the expanded query.

Since we are using the language modeling approach to the information retrieval, for the terms selection we have used the importance weight defined in [8]:

$$L_t = \sum_{d \in R} \log \frac{P(t|M_d)}{P(t|M_c)}, \tag{4}$$

where R is the set of relevant documents.

In the standard approach to the blind relevance feedback the number of documents and terms is defined experimentally in advance the same for all queries. In our experiments we would like to find the number of relevant documents for each query automatically by selecting the "true" relevant documents for each query to dynamically define the number of top retrieved documents to be used in BRF.

4 Score Normalization for Relevant Documents Selection

The score normalization methods from the open-set text-independent speaker identification (OSTI-SI) problem were successfully used in the task of the multi-label classification to select the relevant topics for each newspaper article [13] in the output of a generative classifier. This is the same problem as in the information retrieval task, where as the result only the ranked list of documents with their likelihoods is returned. Usually the idea is, that the user of the retrieval system will look though the top N documents and therefore the specific selection of which document is relevant and which not is not needed. On the contrary when the blind relevance feedback is used, the selection of the true relevant documents can be very useful.

This problem is quite similar to the OSTI-SI problem. Similarly as in the speaker identification, the relevant documents selection in the retrieval results can be described as a twofold problem: First, the speaker model best matching the utterance has to be found and secondly it has to be decided, if the utterance has really been produced by this best-matching model or by some other speaker outside the set. The difficulty in this task is that the speakers are not obliged to provide the same utterance that was the system trained on.

The relevant documents selection can be described in the same way: First, we need to retrieve the documents which have the best likelihood scores for the query and second, we have to choose only the relevant documents which really generated the query. The only difference is that we try to find more than one relevant document. The normalization methods from OSTI-SI can be used in the same way, but have to be applied to all documents likelihoods.

4.1   Score Normalization Methods

After the initial retrieval run, we have the ranked list of documents with their likelihoods computed by (3). We have to find the threshold for the selection of the relevant documents. A score normalization methods have been used to tackle the problem of the compensation for the distortions in the utterances in the second phase of the open-set text-independent speaker identification problem [12]. In the IR task, the likelihood score of a document is dependent on the content of the query, therefore the beforehand set number of relevant documents is not suitable.

A frequently used form to represent the normalization process [12] can be modified for the IR task:

$$L(A) = \log P(d_R|q) - \log P(d_I|q), \tag{5}$$

where $P(d_R|q)$ is the score given by the relevant document and $P(d_I|q)$ is the score given by the irrelevant document. Since the normalization score $\log P(d_I|q)$ of an irrelevant document is not known, it has to be approximated.

World Model Normalization. The unknown model d_I can be approximated by the collection model M_c which was created as a language model from all documents in the retrieval collection. This technique was inspired by the World Model normalization [10]. The normalization score of a model d_I is defined as:

$$\log P(d_I|q) = \log P(M_c|q). \tag{6}$$

Even when we have the likelihood scores normalized, we still have to set the threshold for verifying the relevance of each document in the list. Based on the experiments presented in [13] we have selected only the documents which are better scoring than the collection model and we have defined the threshold as 60% of the normalized score of the best scoring document. The documents which achieved better normalized score are selected as relevant. The threshold selected in this way was experimentally proven to be robust, the change in the range of percents does not influence the result.

5   Experiments

In this section the experiments with the score normalization method are presented. All experiments were performed on the spoken document retrieval collection.

5.1 Information Retrieval Collection

Our experiments were performed on the spoken document retrieval collection that was used in the Czech task of the Cross-Language Speech Retrieval track organized within the CLEF 2007 evaluation campaign [2]. This collection contains automatically transcribed spontaneous interviews (segmented by sliding a fixed-size window over the transcribed text into 22 581 "documents") and two sets of TREC-like topics - 29 training and 42 evaluation topics. Each topic consists of 3 fields - <title> (T), <desc> (D) and <narr> (N) (an example of a topic can be seen on Figure 1). Both topic sets

```
<top>
<num>1166
<title>Chasidismus
<desc>Chasidové a jejich nezlomná víra
<narr>Relevantní materiál by měl vypovídat o Chasidismu
v období před holokaustem, v průběhu holokaustu a po
něm. Informace o chasidských dynastiích a založených a
zničených geografických lokalitách.
</top>
```

Fig. 1. Example of a topic (query) from Czech task of the CLEF 2007 evaluation campaign

were used for our first experiments and the queries were created from all terms from the fields T, D and N since is has been shown to achieve better results than when only T and D fields are used [3]. Stop words were omitted from all sets of query terms. All the terms were also lemmatized, since lemmatization was shown to improve the effectiveness of information retrieval in highly inflected languages (as is the Czech language) [1][9][3]. For the lemmatization an automatically trained lemmatizer described in [4][5] was used.

5.2 Evaluation Metrics

The mean Generalized Average Precision (mGAP) measure that was used in the CLEF 2007 Czech task was used as an evaluation measure. The measure (described in detail in [6]) is designed for the evaluation of the retrieval performance on the conversational speech data, where the topic shifts in the conversation are not separated as documents. The mGAP measure is based on the evaluation of the precision of finding the correct beginning of the relevant part of the data.

5.3 Results

This section shows the results for our first experiment with score normalization methods. For the standard blind relevance feedback we have chosen the settings used for BRF in the paper dealing with the experiments on this collection [3] - take first 20 documents as relevant and extract 5 terms with the best score for the query enhancement.

On the training topic set the experiments with the selection of another number of top retrieved documents to be chosen as relevant for standard BRF was also performed.

As can be seen from the Table 1, for the training topic set the results for the BRF with the score normalization method used are better than with the standard BRF with the predefined number of documents. For the evaluation topic set the results with the standard BRF are even slightly worse than without BRF, but with the score normalization used, the results are better than without BRF. It can be also seen that the results

Table 1. IR results (mGAP score) for no blind relevance feedback, with standard BRF and BRF with score normalization (SN). 5 terms were used to enhance each query in all cases.

query set / method # of documents	no BRF -	standard BRF 10	standard BRF 20	standard BRF 30	BRF with SN SN
train TDN	0.0392	0.0436	0.0432	0.0438	**0.0442**
eval TDN	0.0255	-	0.0245	-	**0.0272**

for the standard BRF are almost the same for different number of documents. This is caused by the fact that for each query different number of documents is relevant. For one query the result for BRF with 10 documents was better than with 30 documents, for another one the other way around. The dynamic number of relevant documents chosen by the score normalization method deals with this problem.

6   Future Work

Since this were only our first experiments on this subject, there is a lot of future work which can be done. We plan to try different methods for the score normalization from the area of speaker identification task. The score normalization methods can also be tested with another IR method, for example the Vector Space method, where the Rocchio's relevance feedback can be used. We would like to use the score normalization method to dynamically find also the number of irrelevant documents used in Rocchio's relevance feedback formula. We would also like to try the query expansion with the different collection and use the terms extracted from the relevant documents from that collection (selected with the use of score normalization) to enhance the query.

The number of terms to be selected for query expansion was chosen the same as used in [3]. We have performed experiments on the training query set for the BRF with score normalization with different number k of terms to be selected, the results can be seen in Table 2. It can be seen that the number of terms significantly affects the retrieval results. The experiments on how to select this number automatically will also be the subject of our future research.

7   Conclusions

This article has shown the first experiments with the use of score normalization method for selection of the relevant documents for the blind relevance feedback in speech information retrieval. The result are showing that with the score normalization better retrieval

Table 2. IR results (mGAP score) for BRF with score normalization for different number k of terms selected

query set / # of terms k	5	10	20
train TDN	0.0442	0.0480	0.0501

results can be achieved than with the standard blind relevance feedback with the number of relevant documents set beforehand. We have also confirmed that the blind relevance feedback in any form is very useful in the speech information retrieval.

The retrieval results are for each query the best with different number of documents used (because the number of truly relevant documents is different for each query). In the standard BRF the number of relevant documents is set the same for all the queries, therefore the mean results for the set of queries can not be the best which can be achieved. The use of score normalization methods for the automatic dynamic selection of relevant documents for each query independently solves this problem.

Acknowledgments. The work has been supported by the Ministry of Education, Youth and Sports of the Czech Republic project No. LM2010013 and by the grant of the University of West Bohemia, project No. SGS-2013-032.

References

1. Ircing, P., Müller, L.: Benefit of Proper Language Processing for Czech Speech Retrieval in the CL-SR Task at CLEF 2006. In: Peters, C., Clough, P., Gey, F.C., Karlgren, J., Magnini, B., Oard, D.W., de Rijke, M., Stempfhuber, M. (eds.) CLEF 2006. LNCS, vol. 4730, pp. 759–765. Springer, Heidelberg (2007)
2. Ircing, P., Pecina, P., Oard, D.W., Wang, J., White, R.W., Hoidekr, J.: Information Retrieval Test Collection for Searching Spontaneous Czech Speech. In: Matoušek, V., Mautner, P. (eds.) TSD 2007. LNCS (LNAI), vol. 4629, pp. 439–446. Springer, Heidelberg (2007)
3. Ircing, P., Psutka, J., Vavruška, J.: What Can and Cannot Be Found in Czech Spontaneous Speech Using Document-Oriented IR Methods – UWB at CLEF 2007 CL-SR Track, pp. 712–718. Springer, Heidelberg (2008),
   http://portal.acm.org/citation.cfm?id=1428850.1428952
4. Kanis, J., Müller, L.: Automatic lemmatizer construction with focus on OOV words lemmatization. In: Matoušek, V., Mautner, P., Pavelka, T. (eds.) TSD 2005. LNCS (LNAI), vol. 3658, pp. 132–139. Springer, Heidelberg (2005)
5. Kanis, J., Skorkovská, L.: Comparison of different lemmatization approaches through the means of information retrieval performance. In: Sojka, P., Horák, A., Kopeček, I., Pala, K. (eds.) TSD 2010. LNCS, vol. 6231, pp. 93–100. Springer, Heidelberg (2010)
6. Liu, B., Oard, D.W.: One-sided measures for evaluating ranked retrieval effectiveness with spontaneous conversational speech. In: Proceedings of the 29th Annual International ACM SIGIR Conference on Research and Development in Information Retrieval, SIGIR 2006, pp. 673–674. ACM, New (2006),
   http://doi.acm.org/10.1145/1148170.1148311
7. Mamou, J., Carmel, D., Hoory, R.: Spoken document retrieval from call-center conversations. In: Proceedings of the 29th Annual International ACM SIGIR Conference on Research and Development in Information Retrieval, SIGIR 2006, pp. 51–58. ACM, New York (2006),
   http://doi.acm.org/10.1145/1148170.1148183

8. Ponte, J.M., Croft, W.B.: A language modeling approach to information retrieval. In: SIGIR 1998: Proceedings of the 21st Annual International ACM SIGIR Conference on Research and Development in Information Retrieval, pp. 275–281. ACM, New York (1998)

9. Psutka, J., Švec, J., Psutka, J.V., Vaněk, J., Pražák, A., Šmídl, L., Ircing, P.: System for fast lexical and phonetic spoken term detection in a czech cultural heritage archive. EURASIP J. Audio, Speech and Music Processing (2011)

10. Reynolds, D.A., Quatieri, T.F., Dunn, R.B.: Speaker verification using adapted gaussian mixture models. In: Digital Signal Processing (2000)

11. Saraclar, M., Sproat, R.: Lattice-based search for spoken utterance retrieval. In: Proceedings of HLT-NAACL 2004. pp. 129–136 (2004)

12. Sivakumaran, P., Fortuna, J., Ariyaeeinia, M.: A.: Score normalisation applied to open-set, text-independent speaker identification. In: Proceedings of Eurospeech 2003. pp. 2669–2672. Geneva (2003)

13. Skorkovská, L.: Dynamic threshold selection method for multi-label newspaper topic identification. In: Habernal, I. (ed.) TSD 2013. LNCS, vol. 8082, pp. 209–216. Springer, Heidelberg (2013)

14. Zajíc, Z., Machlica, L., Padrta, A., Vaněk, J., Radová, V.: An expert system in speaker verification task. In: Proceedings of Interspeech, vol. 9, pp. 355–358. International Speech Communication Association, Brisbane (2008)

How Speech Technologies Can Help People with Disabilities

Vlado Delić[1], Milan Sečujski[1], Nataša Vujnović Sedlar[1,2],
Dragiša Mišković[1,2], Robert Mak[1,2], and Milana Bojanić[1]

[1] Faculty of Technical Sciences, University of Novi Sad, Serbia
vlado.delic@uns.ac.rs
[2] "AlfaNum - Speech Technologies", Novi Sad, Serbia
dragisa.miskovic@alfanum.co.rs

Abstract. Neither eyes nor arms are necessary in human-machine speech communication. Both human and machine just speak and/or listen, or machine does it instead of people. Therefore, speech communication can help people who cannot use their eyes or arms. Apart from both the visually impaired and physically disabled, speech technology can also help to the speech impaired and the hearing impaired, as well as to the elderly people. This paper is a review how speech technologies can be useful for different kind of persons with disabilities.

Keywords: Persons with disabilities, assistive technologies, aids based on speech technologies: text-to-speech synthesis, speech and speaker recognition.

1 Introduction

Speech technologies can help most people with disabilities to overcome their handicap to some extent, giving practical contribution to their equality and inclusion into the society and everyday life [1]. On one side there are the visually impaired, who cannot see any written text, but can listen to speech synthesized from a given text - Text-to-Speech (TTS) conversion. On another side there are the hearing impaired, who cannot listen to speech, but could receive it if it is converted to text, which has been made possible by the development of Automatic Speech Recognition (ASR). Moreover, TTS can help the speech impaired, who can write any text that will be converted to audible speech, while ASR can understand voice commands and help most people to manage home appliances in a smart home – it is particularly useful for the physically disabled: the paraplegic, the dystrophic, people with cerebral palsy, etc. Speech technologies (ASR and TTS) can be adapted to a person depending on his/her kind of disability – it is an open and challenging area of research [2]. Speech technologies included in dialogue systems together with language technologies and cognition aspects of speech communication can help people who cannot use conventional types of communication using either speech or text. For example, people with autism are usually able to choose the sequence of images in order to express their thoughts, questions or commands. The sequence of images has to be converted to corresponding

A. Ronzhin et al. (Eds.): SPECOM 2014, LNAI 8773, pp. 243–250, 2014.

text (which is not an easy task) and then to audible synthesized speech. This is an example of augmentative alternative communication (AAC) [3].

A more detailed classification of people with disabilities, their needs and preferences, as well as the possibilities to overcome their handicaps based on speech technologies are presented in the paper. The case study for Serbian is described based on the experience in the development of applications and aids, assistive technologies and ICT services for people with disabilities, based on speech technologies in Serbian, although the experience can be useful for applications in any other language for which speech technologies have been developed. Section 2 is devoted to the visually impaired, as well as aids and some ICT services developed for them in Serbia, including both completely blind and partially visually impaired persons, as well as persons with disorders such as dyslexia. The needs and solutions for the speech impaired are described in the Section 3, including the experience with different kinds of temporary or permanent speech disorders from profound hearing loss and/or loss of speech, which could be either congenital or acquired. Section 4 is devoted to the people who prefer to issue voice commands to the devices in their environment (e.g. home appliances), which is most useful for the physically disabled. Aids and ICT services based on speech technologies for the hearing impaired are presented in the Section 5. In Section 6, some AAC applications suitable for autistic people are presented.

2   Aids for the Visually Impaired Based on TTS

Regardless of whether someone's sight impairment is partial or total, such a person can have huge benefits from the development of text-to-speech (TTS) technology. The visually impaired can access or manipulate any text from the screen of their computers, phones, or other assistive devices – by listening to the synthesized speech. TTS as an aid for visually impaired computer users provides an important contribution to their equality in education, information access and privacy in communication, allowing them to perform tasks and apply for jobs that would otherwise have been inaccessible to them. There are about 2,000 visually impaired computer users all over the former Yugoslavia and most of them use *anReader* [4, 5], as their aid of choice. It has consequently been recognized as an aid for the visually impaired by the Institute for Health Insurance of the Republic of Serbia (RZZO).

Several ICT services have been developed based on *anReader,* including: (i) *Audio library for the visually impaired,* (ii) Voice portal *Contact* for the visually impaired, (iii) Speech enabled web sites.

Audio library for the visually impaired was initially developed as an aid for the education of visually impaired children, as an alternative to both Braille books and audio-books that are usually more expensive, require a lot of time for preparation, and also a large amount of storage space. The audio library based on TTS offers the access to a significantly greater number of books and magazines, both from local servers and over the Internet. The audio library is a client-server system containing a large amount of books and texts from different sources stored at the server side, accessible by a large number of users over the Internet. More technical details related to the *Audio library for the visually impaired* can be found in [6]. The latest version of the library is multilingual, taking full advantage from the fact that *anReader* has been developed for the Serbian, Croatian and Macedonian languages, and that, on the other hand, speech synthesis integrated into MS Windows can be used for reading books in English. A similar ongoing project is the *Audio library for the disabled*, aimed at enabling the people with different kinds of disabilities to access to the library's collection over the Internet. From one side, the interface to different persons with disabilities is multimodal (speech, touch, gaze) and support special keyboards, mice, screens activated by gaze. On the other side, the interface to digital libraries is designed based on the BISIS system and it has been recently implemented [7].

The voice portal *Contact* represents an interactive voice response (IVR) application that enables the visually impaired and the elderly to read news from four well known Serbian news sites [8]. The portal can be accessed via the Internet or by phone. Telephone access is enabled through an intelligent network (0700 number), so that each user from Serbia is charged the standard price of a local telephone call. Besides news updated from national news websites, there are links to books and magazines in electronic form that can be downloaded and read out through speech synthesis. As such, the portal serves as an excellent starting point from which the visually impaired would enter the world of modern technologies.

For many Internet users it is much more convenient to listen to natural sounding speech instead of having to read the text on a web page. The eyes and arms are free for other jobs while someone is listening to e.g. news from a web site [9, 10]. Listening to the news is a particularly useful option for smart phones due to their small screens. For people with disabilities this is sometimes the only possibility to access web pages. In order to make the visually impaired less dependent on screen readers, web pages have been made more accessible from any of the widely used web browsers by using the specialized server-side TTS software.

Apart from the visually impaired, persons with dyslexia can also have benefits from using TTS. The reading ability of the dyslexic can be impaired with regard to both accuracy and reading speed, which also affects their ability to completely understand a written text. The aforementioned problems of the disabled affect their independence in both work and personal life. This is particularly disastrous for children and young people as developing individuals, but can also significantly reduce the quality of life of the elderly. TTS can help the dyslexic people to acquire information from text more efficiently.

TTS can also be very useful as an educational tool for general population. It gives the possibility to convert lessons or other textual material into audio files and make it accessible to everyone. Therefore, anyone can learn (using their mobile phones or MP3 players) even when they otherwise could not (on the road, during some physical activity, etc.).

3   Aids for the Speech Impaired Based on TTS

Speech communication is one of the most important forms of human interaction and people without speech are in a significantly inferior position when it comes to socialization and everyday communication with others, regardless of whether their condition is congenital or acquired (e.g. due to laryngectomy).

Speech disorders may be related to intellectual disabilities, but they are more often consequences of hearing loss, neurological disorders, physical impairments or surgery. An efficient alternative to using devices that vibrate vocal folds and thus enable mute persons to speak is text-to-speech (TTS) software, which allows mute or otherwise speaking disabled persons to convert typed text into intelligible and natural sounding speech using a smart phone or a similar portable device. Most of the speech impaired persons can write down what they would want to say, and the device will produce the sound for them as a speech generating device based on TTS.

TTS applications for smart phones are available as aids for the speech impaired for many languages, e.g. [11], and one is under development for Serbian, called "The power of speech", is initially intended for the people who have undergone laryngectomy.

4   Aids for the Physically Disabled Based on ASR

Even a small vocabulary ASR is sufficient for the recognition of spoken commands, e.g. in a smart home of a person with physical disability, who can lock the door, turn the light on or off, change a TV program, or make a telephone call, using speech commands from his/her bed or wheelchair. Of course, a large vocabulary ASR and high-quality TTS enable the development of more complex dialogue systems which can recognize different speakers living in the same house and adapt the dialogue to the interlocutor and to his/her speech disorder and even to his/her emotional state [12].

For the persons unable to move unaided or unable to use their hands, but able to issue voice commands, an environment such as a speech-enabled smart home would be most beneficial, as it would allow them to control devices such as lights or home appliances in a much more convenient way. Speech commands should be issued through a microphone near the speaker or through a mobile device such as a smart phone, while some smart homes are equipped with microphone arrays that can locate the speaker and, to some extent, cancel the noise coming from other directions.

The physically disabled like the paraplegic, the dystrophic, as well as those with multiple sclerosis or infantile cerebral palsy are often unable to read, but are usually able to issue speech commands and to listen to information in the form of speech. However, some of them have speech disorders and if their speech is not comprehensible, ASR system has to be adapted to each of them personally.

Apart from the physically disabled, the principal beneficiaries of speech-enabled smart homes include the elderly, but also all people who prefer giving voice commands to using their hands.

5   Aids for the Hearing Impaired Based on ASR

The most useful ASR systems for the disabled are large vocabulary continuous speech recognition (LVCSR) systems. Such systems are very complex and they still have not been developed for a majority of languages including Serbian, but they can be expected to appear quite soon [13]. LVCSR systems are of particular importance to the hearing impaired since they allow speech transcription, i.e. automatic conversion of speech into text.

As the hearing impaired have problems in following TV programs that are not subtitled, LVCSR systems can be used for automatic subtitling, and this option can be used via digital TV broadcasting which supports several versions of the same TV program e.g. suitable for different kinds of people with disabilities. Apart from subtitling for the hearing impaired, digital TV can provide a program with an audio description for the visually impaired etc. This possibility has been available for some time in some of the more developed countries, and the development of such a service for Serbian is to be expected [14].

Figure 1. shows an overview of the categories of the disabled who could benefit from the progress in the development of speech technologies for their languages.

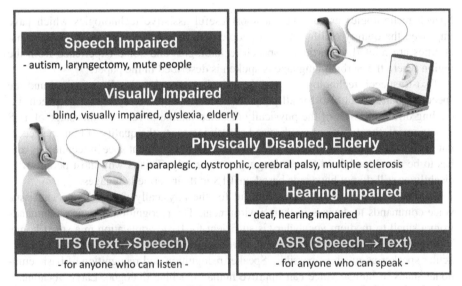

Fig. 1. People with disabilities as beneficiaries of speech technologies as assistive technologies

6   Aids for the People with Autism

Speech technologies are useful for people with disabilities that use either speech or text in communication. Speech technologies can also be useful for the people with various forms of autism or intellectual disability. They can select a sequence of given images instead of textual content, the system has to interpret the sequence of images, convert it to text and subsequently to speech. This is a problem whose solution goes beyond basic speech technologies and relies on natural language processing (NLP) much more heavily, [2], [15].

People with autism or intellectual disability often use augmentative alternative communication (AAC), which is a term describing any communication method used to supplement or replace speech or writing for those with impairments in the production or comprehension of spoken or written language. There is a wide range of speech-related AAC applications, from simple AAC for giving simple answers such as yes/no to an advanced AAC allowing the construction of spoken utterances from sequences of selected images. However, as was the case with basic speech technologies until recently, the most sophisticated systems are currently available only for a small number of languages with very large speaker bases [16].

Nowadays the assistive technologies for disabled and retired are usually based on multimodal approach. Apart from analysis and synthesis of speech, such interfaces use gaze, gestures, handwriting and other natural modalities [17, 18, 19].

7   Conclusion

Speech technologies are among the most useful assistive technologies which have improved the quality of life for most people with disabilities. Different kinds of disabilities are related to particular speech technologies and some experience from the region where the Serbian language is spoken is described in the paper.

Text-to-speech technology is useful particularly for the visually impaired and the speech impaired, but also for all people who can to listen to synthesized speech, including different kinds of the physically disabled unable to read. At this stage of TTS development, the quality of synthesized speech is near to the quality of human speech, but not for all languages. TTS is a heavily language dependent speech technology and has to be developed for different languages separately. This is why most people with disabilities still do not have aids based on TTS in their native languages.

Automatic speech recognition is useful for the physically disabled who can issue voice commands to devices in their environment. The recognition of voice commands from a small to medium vocabulary is sufficient for basic application in a smart home. Various speech disorders can represent a problem, and ASR has to be adapted to a particular speaker as much as possible. Speaker recognition and recognition of basic emotional states in human voice can improve human-machine dialogue. Large vocabulary continuous ASR enables speech to text conversion, which is most useful for the hearing impaired. Unfortunately, LVCASR has been developed for just a few languages and it is still not available for most of the hearing impaired persons all over the world.

Finally, aids for people with disabilities that are unable to use either speech or text have to be developed based on alternative communication methods, which are based not only on speech technologies but are also much more heavily dependent on natural language processing (NLP) and cognitive aspects of communication.

Acknowledgments. The presented study was sponsored by the Ministry of Education and Science of the Republic of Serbia under the Research grant TR32035, and by the Secretariat for Science and Technological Development of Vojvodina under the project Audio Library for the Disabled. The responsibility for the content of this paper lies with the authors.

References

1. Delić, V., Sečujski, M., Bojanić, M., Knežević, D., Vujnović Sedlar, N., Mak, R.: Aids for the Disabled Based on Speech Technologies - Case Study for the Serbian Language. In: 11th Int. Conf. ETAI, pp. E2-1.1-4, Ohrid, Macedonia (2013)
2. Delić, V., Sečujski, M., Jakovljević, N., Gnjatović, M., Stanković, I.: Challenges of Natural Language Communication with Machines. Chapter VIII in Challenges for the Future – Industrial Engineering. In: Zelenovic, D., Katalinic, B. (eds.) Published by Faculty of Technical Sciences (Novi Sad, Serbia), DAAAM International (Vienna, Austria) and Fraunhofer IAO (Stuttgart, Germany), pp. 153–169 (2013)
3. Beukelman, D., Mirenda, P.: Augmentative and Alternative Communication. Management of severe communication disorders in children and adults. Paul H. Brookes Publishing Co., Baltimore (1998)
4. Secujski, M., Obradovic, R., Pekar, D., Jovanov, L., Delic, V.: AlfaNum system for speech synthesis in serbian language. In: Sojka, P., Kopeček, I., Pala, K. (eds.) TSD 2002. LNCS (LNAI), vol. 2448, pp. 237–244. Springer, Heidelberg (2002)
5. Delić, V., Vujnović Sedlar, N., Sečujski, M.: Speech-Enabled Computers as a Tool for Serbian-Speaking Blind Persons. In: 5th IEEE Int. Conf. EUROCON, pp. 1662-1665, Belgrade, Serbia (2005)
6. Mišković, D., Vujnović Sedlar, N., Sečujski, M., Delić, V.: Audio Library for the visually impaired – ABSS 2.0. In: 6th Conference of Digital Signal and Image Processing - DOGS, pp. 67-70, Serbia (2006)
7. Tešendić, D., Boberić Krstićev, D., Milosavljević, B.: Linking Visually Impaired People to Libraries. In: 3rd Int. Conf. on Information Society Technology, ICIST, Kopaonik, Serbia, pp. 212–217 (2013)
8. Delić, V.: A Review of R&D of Speech Technologies in Serbian and their Applications in Western Balkan Countries. In: 12th International Conference "Speech and Computer", a Keynote Lecture at SPECOM, Moscow, Russia pp. 64–83 (2007)
9. Radio-televizija Srbije, http://www.rts.rs/
10. Pekar, D., Mišković, D., Knežević, D., Vujnović Sedlar, N., Sečujski, D.V.: Applications of Speech Technologies in Western Balkan Countries. In: Shabtai, N. (ed.), Advances in Speech Recognition, SCIYO, Croatia, pp. 105–122 (2010)
11. Tóth, B., Nagy, P., Németh, G.: New Features in the VoxAid Communication Aid for Speech Impaired People. In: Miesenberger, K., Karshmer, A., Penaz, P., Zagler, W. (eds.) ICCHP 2012, Part II. LNCS, vol. 7383, pp. 295–302. Springer, Heidelberg (2012)
12. Delić, V., Gnjatović, M., Jakovljević, N., Popović, B., Jokić, I., Bojanić, M.: User-awareness and adaptation in conversational agents. Facta Universitatis, Series: Electronics and Energetics 27(3) (2014) (in press)
13. Jakovljević, N., Mišković, D., Janev, M., Pekar, D.: A Decoder for Large Vocabulary Speech Recognition. In: 18th International Conference on Systems, Signals and Image Processing - IWSSIP, Sarajevo, Bosnia and Herzegovina, pp. 287–290 (2011)
14. Delić, V., Sečujski, M., Jakovljević, N., Pekar, D., Mišković, D., Popović, B., Ostrogonac, S., Bojanić, M., Knežević, D.: Speech and Language Resources within Speech Recognition and Synthesis Systems for Serbian and Kindred South Slavic Languages. In: Železný, M., Habernal, I., Ronzhin, A. (eds.) SPECOM 2013. LNCS, vol. 8113, pp. 319–326. Springer, Heidelberg (2013)
15. Gnjatović, M., Delić, V.: Cognitively-inspired representational approach to meaning in machine dialogue. In: Knowledge-Based Systems (2014)
doi: 10.1016/j.knosys.2014.05.001

16. Bourlard, H., Dines, J., Magimai-Doss, M., Garner, P.N., Imseng, D., Motlicek, P., Liang, H., Saheer, L., Valente, F.: Current trends in multilingual speech processing. Sādhanā, Invited paper for special issue on the topic of Speech Communication and Signal Processing 36(5), 885–915 (2011)
17. Kindiroglu, A., Yalcın, H., Aran, O., Hruz, M., Campr, P., Akarun, L., Karpov, A.: Automatic Recognition of Fingerspelling Gestures in Multiple Languages for a Communication Interface for the Disabled. Pattern Recognition and Image Analysis 22(4), 527–536 (2012)
18. Argyropoulos, S., Moustakas, K., Karpov, A., Aran, O., Tzovaras, D., Tsakiris, T., Varni, G., Kwon, B.: A Multimodal Framework for the Communication of the Disabled. Journal on Multimodal User Interfaces 2(2), 105–116 (2008)
19. Karpov, A., Krnoul, Z., Zelezny, M., Ronzhin, A.: Multimodal Synthesizer for Russian and Czech Sign Languages and Audio-Visual Speech. In: Stephanidis, C., Antona, M. (eds.) UAHCI 2013, Part I. LNCS, vol. 8009, pp. 520–529. Springer, Heidelberg (2013)

HTK-Based Recognition of Whispered Speech

Jovan Galić[1,2], Slobodan T. Jovičić[1,3], Đorđe Grozdić[1,3], and Branko Marković[4]

[1] School of Electrical Engineering,
University of Belgrade, Telecommunications Department, Belgrade, Serbia
jgalic@etfbl.net
[2] Faculty of Electrical Engineering, University of Banja Luka,
Department of Electronics and Telecommunications, Banja Luka, Bosnia and Herzegovina
[3] Life Activities Advancement Center, Laboratory for Psychoacoustics and Speech Perception,
Belgrade, Serbia
jovicic@etf.rs, djordjegrozdic@gmail.com
[4] Čačak Technical College, Computing and Information Technology Department,
Čačak, Serbia
brankomarko@yahoo.com

Abstract. This paper presents results on whispered speech recognition of isolated words with Whi-Spe database, in speaker dependent mode. Word recognition rate is calculated for all speakers, four train/test scenarios, three values of mixture components, with modeling of context independent monophones, context dependent triphones and whole words. As a feature vector, Mel Frequency Cepstral Coefficients was used. The HTK, toolkit for building Hidden Markov Models, was used to implement isolated word recognizer. The best obtained results in match scenarios showed nearly equal recognition rate of 99.86% in normal speech recognition, and 99.90% in whispered speech recognition. Specifically, in mismatch scenarios, the best achieved recognition rate was 64.80% for training on part of normally phonated speech and testing on whispered speech and, in the opposite case, with training on whispered speech, the normal speech recognition was 74.88%.

Keywords: speech recognition, whispered speech database, HTK, speech signal processing.

1   Introduction

Whispered speech, as a specific way of verbal communication, is often used in everyday life. It is used for quite and private communication, especially by mobile phones [1]. Also, besides conscious production of whisper, whispering may occur due to health problems which appear after rhinitis and laryngitis [2]. The whisper has a lot of specific characteristics. Due to the absence of the glottal vibrations, whispering lacks the fundamental frequency of the voice and much prosodic information. In addition, whispered speech has a significantly lower energy as compared to the normal speech [2], and the slope of the spectrum is much flatter than in the normal speech [3]. The formant frequencies for whispered phonation were found to be higher

A. Ronzhin et al. (Eds.): SPECOM 2014, LNAI 8773, pp. 251–258, 2014.

than for the normal voice [4, 5]. Therefore, automatic recognition of whispered speech is much more difficult than of normal speech. The speaker ID performance significantly degrade with a change in vocal effort ranging from whisper through shouted, where whispered speech had the most serious loss in performance [3]. However, it is interesting that this type of speech communication, in spite of increased efforts in perception, performs perfectly understandable [6]. There are different approaches, techniques and methods of speech recognition. These techniques are usually based on algorithms of the HMM (Hidden Markov Model), the DTW (Dynamic Time Warping), the ANN (Artificial Neural Network) and their hybrid solutions [7]. This paper presents results on investigation of recognition of isolated words from Whi-Spe database [8], using a software toolkit HTK (Hidden Markov Model Toolkit). The HTK is a portable toolkit for building and manipulating hidden Markov models that was originally developed at the Machine Intelligence Laboratory of the Cambridge University Engineering Department [9]. The reminder of this paper is organized as follows. In Section 2 description of database Whi-Spe is presented. In Section 3 we describe HTK tools used in experiments. The experimental results, as well as its discussion, are given in Section 4, while concluding remarks and further directions are stated in Section 5.

2   Whi-Spe Database

The Whi-Spe database is designed to contain two parts: the first one contains speech patterns of a whispered speech, while the second one contains speech patterns of the normal speech. All patterns were collected from the five female and five male speakers. During the session of recording, each speaker read fifty isolated words of Serbian language. The words were divided in three sub-corpora: basic colors (6 words), numbers (14 words) and phonetically balanced words (30 words). Balanced words were taken from the Serbian emotional speech database GEES [10], which satisfies the basic linguistic criteria of Serbian language (phonemes distribution, syllable composition, accentual structure, consonant clusters). Sessions were repeated ten times, with a pause of a few days between recordings. Finally, the database collection grew to 10.000 utterances, half in the whispered speech and half in the normal speech. The speakers with ages between twenty and thirty were Serbian native volunteers from Čačak Technical College. Each of them had good articulation in speech and whisper production as well as correct hearing.

The speech was digitized by using the sampling frequency of 22.050 Hz, with 16 bits per sample, and stored in the form of Windows PCM (Pulse-Code Modulation) wave files. More details about the database could be found in [8]. In this experiment, all utterances from database were used.

3   Description of HTK Tools in Experiment

The HTK system is widely used platform for training HMM models. In this work, all experiments were conducted on the latest version, 3.4.1 [11]. HTK tools are designed to run with a traditional command line style interface. The toolkit was ported to Windows 7, and all experiments were done under this operating system. For obtaining a MFCC (Mel Frequency Cepstral Coefficients) feature vector, Hamming window with preemphasis coefficient of 0.97 was used. The window size was set to 24 ms, and frame shift to 8 ms. Also, cepstral coefficient C_0, delta and acceleration coefficients were appended and cepstral mean subtraction was performed. These auxiliary features and modification techniques significantly improves recognition rate [12]. Number of filterbank channels was set to 26, and number of output cepstral coefficients per frame was set to 12. In filterbank analysis, power was used instead of magnitude (default) and normalization of energy was not included.

The model topology is a continuous density HMM and Gaussian mixtures are with diagonal covariance matrices. There were 5 states in total, 3 of which are emitting. As an acoustic modeling units, we used context independent (CI) monophones, context dependent (CD) triphones and whole word (WW) models. Triphones were not tied. The WW models consisted of the same number of states as their CI and CD counterparts and followed the same transition matrix structure that is strictly left-right, with no skip. Phonetic transcription was done manually. Stops and affricates are labeled as pairs of semi-phones that consist of occlusion and explosion parts. Phoneme /ə/ (schwa) is marked separately when phoneme /r/ is found in the consonant environment [13]. The model of silence is added at the start and the end of every utterance. Initial model parameters were estimated using the flat-start method [12], since training data is not time labeled. The number of training cycles in embedded re-estimation is restricted to 5 and the variance floor for Gaussian probability density functions was set to 1%. To reduce the computation time, pruning threshold of 250 with increment of 150 and limit of 1.000 was used in training. After creating triphones, additional two cycles of re-estimation were done. In the training phase, Viterbi decoding algorithm was applied to determine an optimum state sequence (a forced alignment). At last, in the testing phase the Viterbi algorithm was applied to determine the most likely model that best matched each test utterance.

Our goal was to compare the performance of different acoustic models and number of mixture components in four train/test scenarios:

1. Normal/Normal (Nor/Nor) - the system is trained on normally phonated speech and tested on the speech of same mode;
2. Normal/Whisper (Nor/Whi) - the system is trained on normally phonated speech and tested against whispered speech;
3. Whisper/Normal (Whi/Nor) - the system is trained on whispered speech and tested against normally phonated speech;
4. Whisper/Whisper (Whi/Whi) - the system is trained on whispered speech and tested on the speech of same mode.

4   Results and Discussion

In match scenarios, 80% utterances were in the part for training, while the other 20% was in the part for testing. The test set was rotated, in deterministic manner, which gave 4 additional tests. Recognition rate is calculated as mean value of 5 tests. In mismatch scenarios, all utterances of one mode were in the part for training, while in testing part were all utterances of the other mode of speech. Afterwards, results are statistically evaluated by computing mean and standard deviation (square root of un-biased estimator of variance). The results are presented in Tables 1-3 for modeling monophones, triphones and whole words, respectively. For better clarity, results are summarized and depicted in Fig. 1 (match scenarios) and Fig. 2 (mismatch scenarios). For the sake of better comparison of different models in match scenarios, important part of chart (recognition rate over 90%) in Fig. 1 is depicted.

Table 1. Mean value and standard deviation (in %) of word recognition rate for monophone models with different number of mixtures and various scenario

Mixtures/	1 mixture		4 mixtures		16 mixtures	
Scenario	μ	σ	μ	σ	μ	σ
Nor/Nor	97.66	0.98	99.52	0.33	99.66	0.28
Nor/Whi	64.80	12.82	58.56	16.00	57.16	15.33
Whi/Nor	74.68	8.41	74.88	11.28	73.90	11.12
Whi/Whi	95.20	2.22	98.66	0.71	98.52	0.69

Table 2. Mean value and standard deviation (in %) of word recognition rate for triphone models with different number of mixtures and various scenario

Mixtures/	1 mixture		4 mixtures		16 mixtures	
Scenario	μ	σ	μ	σ	μ	σ
Nor/Nor	99.86	0.13	99.52	0.36	77.96	8.55
Nor/Whi	28.32	11.69	15.54	7.64	7.22	4.13
Whi/Nor	64.94	14.26	41.60	15.05	16.24	6.83
Whi/Whi	99.90	0.14	98.56	1.08	46.06	10.87

Table 3. Mean value and standard deviation (in %) of word recognition rate for whole word models with different number of mixtures and various scenario

Mixtures/	1 mixture		4 mixtures		16 mixtures	
Scenario	μ	σ	μ	σ	μ	σ
Nor/Nor	99.26	0.67	99.66	0.43	99.76	0.31
Nor/Whi	36.24	8.44	36.06	9.94	26.54	9.94
Whi/Nor	48.36	10.90	51.86	14.07	46.66	14.28
Whi/Whi	96.34	2.47	98.34	1.00	98.52	0.82

As it can be seen from Fig. 1, in match scenarios, the best results (recognition almost 100%) are obtained with CD models with one mixture. However, very high sensitivity of CD models to increased number of mixtures is observed, since these untied models are much more specialized and there might not had been enough realizations for training. For tied CD models, increased number of mixtures did not result in performance degradation [12]. The best results obtained with CI models and

WW models are over 99.5% for normal speech and over 98.5% for whispered speech. Increasing number of Gausssians to 4 causes stabilization of recognition rate, for both models, as depicted in Fig. 1.

All models have poor recognition of whispered speech (1-3%), compared to normal speech, with the exception of triphone modeling with one mixture. As well, higher speaker dependance is observed for whispered speech (higher standard deviation), in comparison with normal speech, for each model.

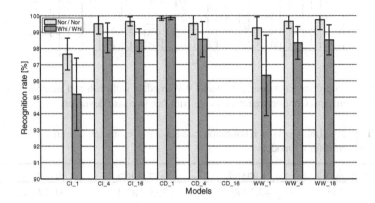

Fig. 1. Word recognition rates for CI, CD and WW models with different number of mixtures in match scenarios. Confidence intervals are with one standard deviation.

The mismatch train/test scenarios, namely Nor/Whi and Whi/Nor, show significantly lower recognition scores. From results in Fig. 2, one can see that in mismatch scenarios, CI models were the most robust. The maximum performance in Nor/Whi scenario is achieved with one mixture, scoring recognition rate of 64.80%. In the opposite case, the highest recognition rate of 74.88% in Whi/Nor scenario is obtained with four mixtures. So, difference between scores of word recognition in Whi/Nor and Nor/Whi scenarios is around 10%. It is interesting that almost same difference is achieved with neural network-based recognition [14] with same feature vector. This phenomenon was also spotted in [1], and it was explained with fact that the most of whisper features exist in normal speech, which is not in the opposite case. The increase of number of mixture components caused slightly lower recognition scores in Nor/Whi scenario, while in the scenario Whi/Nor significant influence on performance is not observed.

The CD and WW models give much poorer recognition scores, compared to CI models, for each number of mixture components.

As it can be seen from Table 1, there is a very high difference of recognition rate among different speakers in adverse conditions. For CI models with one mixture, in Nor/Whi scenario standard deviation was 12.82%. Because of the number of speakers is not so high, beside mean and standard deviation, range of recognition scores are shown in Table 4. The best recognition rate was 85.4%, while the worst was 47.2%. On the other hand, in Whi/Nor scenario extreme recognition scores were 56.8% and 87.2%. Further research will try to give the cause for this phenomenon.

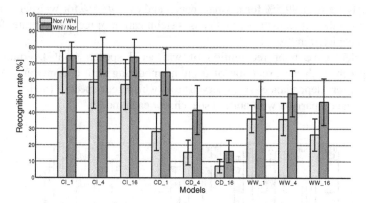

Fig. 2. Word recognition rates for CI, CD and WW models with different number of mixtures in mismatch scenarios. Confidence intervals are with one standard deviation.

Table 4. The range (min/max) of recognition rate (in %) in mismatch conditions with different number of mixtures for CI models

Mixtures/Scenario	1 mixture	4 mixtures	16 mixtures
Nor/Whi	47.2 / 85.4	33.8 / 81.4	31.4 / 78.2
Whi/Nor	56.8 / 87.2	48.2 / 88.2	47.4 / 86.6

In [15], it was determined that SNR (Signal to Noise Ratio) of tested whispered speech has significant impact on performance of neutral trained speaker identification system. Degradation of performance is concentrated for a certain number of speakers, while other shown consistent performance to that seen in neutral speech. Same study used MFCC-GMM based system employing 28 female subject database.

5   Conclusion and Further Directions

Whispered speech, as an alternative speech production mode, is commonly employed for communication. Because of its specifics and major differences compared to normal speech, whisper is problematic in application of ASR systems, which are primarily trained to recognize normal speech.

An isolated words speech recognition based on software toolkit HTK, in speaker dependant fashion, provide high enough recognition rates in same conditions during training and testing phase. The context dependent phonemes word modeling with single Gaussian mixture outperformed the context independent and whole word modeling, with the average recognition rate over 99.9%.

Since the speaker dependant whisper data is often not available during training, performance of recognizer in mismatch conditions are also evaluated. The results in mismatch scenarios are much more interesting from the viewpoint of applications in ASR systems. As expected, in mismatched conditions there were significant performance drop for all models. However, the CI models were more robust, compared to untied CD and WW models. Maximum achieved recognition scores in Nor/Whi and Whi/Nor scenarios were 64.80% and 74.88%, respectively. Based on obtained results, a high dependence of recognition rate among different speakers was observed.

Further research would include feature vectors other than MFCC. Preliminary investigation has shown that a speech parameterization with PLP (Perceptual Linear Prediction) feature vector is more robust, with noticeable improvement in recognition in Nor/Whi scenario. The experiments with neural networks and same database had shown superiority of TECC (Teager Energy Cepstral Coefficients) over MFCC, so there is optimistic expectation that similar results could be obtained with HMM based speaker dependant recognizer. A frontend enhancement might include breath noise removing filter for performance improvement, as well.

A combined whisper and normal utterances in training part is expected to give better performance compared to completely mismatch conditions, but it is interesting to examine if performance could reach the separately trained conditions.

Also, the future research should include comparative analysis of word recognition efficiency using different algorithms such as DTW, HMM and ANN, using the same feature set.

Acknowledgements. The research was supported by NORBOTECH (NORway-BOsnia TECHnology Transfer) project for Programme in Higher Education, Research and Development by Norwegian Ministry of Foreign Affairs, and the projects OI-178027 and TR-32032 of Ministry of Science and Technological Development of the Republic of Serbia.

References

1. Ito, T., Takeda, K., Itakura, F.: Analysis and Recognition of Whispered speech. Speech Communication 45, 139–152 (2005)
2. Zhang, C., Hansen, J.H.L.: Analysis and classification of Speech Mode: Whisper through Shouted. In: Interspeech 2007, Antwerp, Belgium, pp. 2289–2292 (2007)
3. Jovičić, S.T., Šarić, Z.M.: Acoustic analysis of consonants in whispered speech. Journal of Voice 22(3), 263–274 (2008)
4. Jovičić, S.T.: Formant feature differences between whispered and voiced sustained vowels. ACUSTICA - Acta Acoustica 84(4), 739–743 (1998)
5. Swerdlin, Y., Smith, J., Wolfe, J.: The effect of whisper and creak vocal mechanisms on vocal tract resonances. Journal of Acoustical Society of America 127(4), 2590–2598 (2010)
6. Grozdić, Đ.T., Marković, B., Galić, J., Jovičić, S.T.: Application of Neural Networks in Whispered Speech Recognition. Telfor Journal 5(2), 103-106 (2013)
7. Holms, J., Holms, W.: Speech synthesis and recognition. Taylor & Francis, London (2001)
8. Marković, B., Jovičić, S.T., Galić, J., Grozdić, D.: Whispered speech database: Design, processing and application. In: Habernal, I. (ed.) TSD 2013. LNCS, vol. 8082, pp. 591–598. Springer, Heidelberg (2013)

9. Young, S., Evermann, G., Hain, T., Kershaw, D., Moore, G., Odell, J., Ollason, D., Povey, D., Valtchev, V., Woodland, P.: The HTK Book V.3.2.1. Cambridge University Engineering Department (2002)
10. Jovičić, S.T., Kašić, Z., Đorđević, M., Rajković, M.: Serbian emotional speech database: design, processing and evaluation. In: SPECOM-2004, St. Petersburg, Russia, pp. 77–81 (2004)
11. The Hidden Markov Model Toolkit, http://htk.eng.cam.ac.uk/
12. Kacur, J., Rozinaj, G.: Practical Issues of Building Robust HMM Models Using HTK and SPHINX Systems. In: Mihelic, F., Zibert, J. (eds.) Speech Recognition, Technologies and Applications. I-Tech, pp. 171–192 (2008)
13. Sovilj-Nikić, S., Delić, V., Sovilj-Nikić, I., Marković, M.: Tree-based Phone Duration Modeling of the Serbian Language. Electronics and Electrical Engineering (Elektronika ir Elektrotechnika) 20(3), 77–82 (2014)
14. Grozdić, Đ.T., Marković, B., Galić, J., Jovičić, S.T., Furundžić: Neural-Network Based Recognition of Whispered Speech. In: Speech and Language-2013, Belgrade, Serbia, pp. 223–229 (2013)
15. Fan, X., Hansen, J.H.L.: Speaker identification within whispered speech audio stream. IEEE Transactions on Audio, Speech and Language Processing 19(5), 1408–1421 (2011)

Human Resources Management in Conditions of Operators' Psychophysiological State Changes

Oleg Basov, Angelina Basova, and Maksim Nosov

Academy of Federal Agency of protection of Russian Federation, Orel, Russia
{oobasov,line_30,nosovm}@mail.ru

Abstract. Improving the efficiency of human resources management of science intensive production is an actual scientific and technical challenge. Decision based on improving the scientific and methodological apparatus determining operators' psycho-physiological state by information from multimodal workstation's input interface and mechanisms for the dynamic allocation development of their functions in the case of departure of psychophysiological state from the normal state is offered in the paper.

Keywords: interaction channel, multimodal interface, automated workstation, jitter.

1 Introduction

By the early XXI century, together with significant results in the automation of technological processes and production scope, new approaches to the use infocommunication technologies and the creation of favorable information environment of the enterprise based on knowledge are appeared [1-3]. Intellectual resources or intellectual capital – knowledge, skills and individuals' work experience and intangible assets (patents, databases, software, trademarks, etc.) – are forcibly used in order to maximize profits and other economic and technical results. Intellectual resources' key role in the production of high technology products defines a high proportion of the costs of research and development work in the production cost. It includes flexible automated manufacturing cells, lines of machine tools with numerical control, robotics, automated transport devices, information, telecommunications, aerospace and nuclear technology, technologies and products of electronics and optoelectronics, technologies and products, medical technology and biotechnology.

Development of Science Intensive Production (SIP) in the whole world is characterized by more extensive use of CALS-technologies. However, existing manufacturing information systems support the Product Data Management (PDM) and Enterprise Resources Planning (ERP) and do not provide intellectual control, especially human, resources management.

Human intellectual resources are considered in this paper in the immediate manifestation of employee competencies (operator), amplified by means of an intelligent automation processes based on human-machine systems (automated workstations).

A. Ronzhin et al. (Eds.): SPECOM 2014, LNAI 8773, pp. 259–267, 2014.

Successful execution of their professional duties, maintaining the operators' health and as a consequence, increase the effectiveness of human resources SIP management can be achieved by improving the scientific and methodological apparatus determining psychophysiological state of operators on information from multimodal workstation's input interface and the development of mechanisms of dynamic allocation of their functions in the case of deviations from the normal psychophysiological state.

2   Criterion of Efficiency of Human Resources Management

In the new economy context a promising approach to the intellectual, especially human resources management, SIP resources is the automation of human resource management from Skills-Based management positions [4], implementing the idea of science intensive project in the form of a complex of interrelated activities. The execution of each work is to implement one or more production and technological functions (PTF). To execute PTF operator or with his participation is necessary that a person should have the appropriate knowledge, skills and abilities. Automation under Skills-Based Management is based on two types of models [5].

Model representing the required employee's competencies levels $\overline{R}_j = (R_{j1}, R_{j2}, ... R_{jk}, ..., R_{jK})$ that are necessary to execute the functions of the j-th technological process is called normative profile j-th PTF $(j = \overline{1...N})$. Profile PTF is formed with the help of expert way by designing technological process and is included in its operating certificate. To get $(R_{j1}, R_{j2}, ... R_{jk}, ..., R_{jK})$ expert reviews on the scale [6] are used (Table 1). Set of estimations $\overline{P}_i = (P_{i1}, P_{i2}, ..., P_{ik}, ..., P_{iK})$, where P_{ik} – the actual level of the i-th operator on the k-th competence named qualification profile (competences profile) i-th operator $(i = \overline{1...M})$. Methods of evaluation $(P_{i1}, P_{i2}, ..., P_{ik}, ..., P_{iK})$ are represented in [6].

Table 1. Assessment of skills and abilities

Level of competence	The score
Skills / abilities are absent	0
Common superficial ideas	1
Initial level of exploration t	2
The average level with the dynamics of growth	3
Full ownership	4
Deep exploration, level expert	5

PTF matrix $[R]_{N \times K}$ production unit and $[P]_{M \times K}$ qualification profiles of employees form the basis of fixing the problem of optimal functions for operators:

$$E = \sum_{i=1}^{M} f_i \sum_{j=1}^{N} e_{ij} x_{ij} \to \max, \tag{1}$$

under the condition that a sufficient number of operators for each function are reserved

$$\sum_{i=1}^{M} x_{ij} = 1 \tag{2}$$

and restrictions on the operators' load

$$\sum_{j=1}^{N} x_{ij} Q_j \le q_i, \tag{3}$$

where $0 \le f_i \le 1$ – assessment of psychophysiological state i-th operator ($f_i = 1$ corresponds to the operative rest); $0 \le x_{ij} \le 1$ – share of j-th function $\left(j = \overline{1...N}\right)$ performed by i – executor; $\left(i = \overline{1...M}\right)$; $e_{ij} = w_j \sum_{k=1}^{K} \left(\min\left(P_{ik}, R_{jk}\right)\right) \Big/ \sum_{k'=1}^{K} R_{jk'}$ – efficiency fixing i-th operator for the j-th function; w_j – a significance j-th function; Q_j – labour intensity (man-hours) performing the j-th functions; q_i – human resource (man-hours) i-th operator.

3   Algorithms of Signal Identification of Multimodal Interface of Automated Workstation

To solve the problem (1) is necessary to identify the most frequently used operators' communication channels (communications) and hardware of automated workstations. Analysis showed that it is necessary to take the multimodal interfaces into account based on:

1. the traditional keyboard input and "mouse" manipulator (further - the "mouse"), as the main means of text channel interaction, providing direct execution PTF using PC automated workstations;
2. the speech signal as a mean of transmitting information over the corresponding channel present in the interaction (communication) operators with each other.

Using a variety of information from the text and speech channels of hardware communication can improve the accuracy of determining the psychophysiological state automated workstation operator, executing various PTF, compared with unimodal (eg, only keyboard input) interaction interfaces. A characteristic feature of multimodal interfaces is a common approach to formalize and study the interaction of the hardware channel signals and automated workstations operator, allowing based on the same mathematical software to assess psychophysiological state of a person.

As a unique behavioral characteristic of the study of interaction channels, determining operator' psychophysiological state, in this paper the degree of arrhythmia (aperiodicity) is proposed that is described the pitch-jitter of the speech signal, duration jitter and period jitter pressing buttons on the keyboard, and the duration jitter and the period jitter pressing the left "mouse" button (LMB), and also jitter signal its movements. Thus, under a quasi-periodic jitter signal refers to the change of its period, estimated by subtracting from each value of the sequence of the period of his closest (previous) values:

$$Jitter_i = T_i - T_{i-1}, \tag{4}$$

where T_i – the value of the period, calculated on the i-th fragment signal.

For forming investigated jitters according to (4), algorithms for estimating the values T_i of the speech signal [7–10], and text channels of multimodal workstation's input interface are developed.

To determine when pressing the keyboard and a "mouse", a program of determining the parameters of text modalities [11], fixing an array $[A\_k]_{i \times 3}$ ($i = 1,2,...$ – key pressed position number): key code, key condition (1 – pressed, 0 – released) and a reading moment (computer time) is developed. To convert it to the desired values of duration pressing buttons on the keyboard $t_{PRESS\ i} \in t\_n$, period pressing buttons on the keyboard $T_{PRESS\ i} \in T\_n$, duration pressing LMB $t_{PRESS.LMB\ i} \in t\_n\_1$ and period pressing LMB $T_{PRESS.LMB\ i} \in T\_n\_1$ the corresponding algorithm is developed.

Also, the program [11] fixes as an array $[A\_m]_{i \times 3}$: the moment of reading the "mouse" cursor position and its relative position $C.X$ horizontally and $C.Y$ vertically. The principle of forming the signal of its moving is based on its measuring the duration of rise and fall times of the output signal of the "mouse" by comparing its output voltage $U_M = \sqrt{C.X^2 + C.Y^2}$ with two threshold levels U_1 and U_2. Output pulse duration $t_k = (U_1 - U_2)/V_k$ is inversely proportional to the rate of change rise and fall of the output signal of the "mouse" and characterizes the "frequency" of the movement of the manipulator (operator's hand). On the basis of the above principle an array $[A\_m]_{i \times 3}$ is transformed into an array of values "the mouse's movement period" $T_{MOUSE\ i} \in t\_T\_m$.

Periodic sequences' received arrays of values of keyboard and LMB pressing and moving the "mouse" are used to determine their jitter (4).

Calculation of its values for speech signals of 17 people (duration 54 minutes) and keyboard signals and the "mouse", registered on 26 human subjects (duration 183 minutes) were in different psychophysiological states has allowed to obtain their distribution experimentally. Psychophysiological state is artificially changed by physical and psychological stress [12]. Assessing the degree of closeness the theoretical distributions to the empirical ones by Kolmogorov allowed to take on a critical significance level $\alpha = 0,01$ of the hypothesis the normality of the distribution of these quantities. Statistical analysis's results of these values separately for each human subject pointed to their nonparametric nature and the need for further analysis.

4   Separation of Jitter Signals of Multimodal Workstation's Input Interface and Its Components Evaluation

According to the proposed method [13] total jitter (TJ) available text signals and/or speech interaction channels are formed

$$TJ = \left[Jitter^{PITCH}, Jitter^{tPRESS}, Jitter^{TPRESS}, Jitter^{tPRESS.LMB}, Jitter^{TPRESS.LMB}, Jitter^{TMOUSE} \right]. \quad (5)$$

Further, out of the total jitter $TJ^{tPRESS} = Jitter^{tPRESS}$ and $TJ^{TPRESS} = Jitter^{TPRESS}$ components *DDJ* are eliminated by well-known methods, depending on the data – intersymbol interference *(ISI)* and distortion coefficient *(DCD)* impulse sequence filling. To solve this problem (interpolation of unknown jitter values on the nearest known ones) existing separation methods of periodic jitter *(PJ)* and random jitter *(RJ)* relevant algorithm are proposed [5].

Dependences of the obtained frequency of periodic components of *PJ* from time have exacting nature of task due to the influence of the intonation pattern of spoken phrases and typical vibrations of the vocal cords (for PJ^{PITCH}); parasitic modulation of the keyboard ("mouse") harmonics of the supply voltage (for PJ^{tPRESS}, PJ^{TPRESS}, $PJ^{tPRESS.LMB}$, $PJ^{TPRESS.LMB}$) and the backward motion of the "mouse" on reaching borders of the workspace (screen) (for PJ^{TMOUSE}). Therefore, to determine the psychophysiological state in the current investigation it is proposed to use only random jitter signals components of multimodal workstation's input interface.

In consequence of experimental studies was founded that random jitter RJ^{PITCH}, RJ^{tPRESS}, RJ^{TPRESS}, $RJ^{tPRESS.LMB}$, $RJ^{TPRESS.LMB}$, RJ^{TMOUSE} by the critical significance level $\alpha = 0,01$ has a normal distribution and characteristic that depends on the operator' psychophysiological state, is part of frames (fragments) of the analyzed signal, in which the absolute value of the random jitter exceeds a threshold value Thr_{RJ} (is defined experimentally for each jitter):

$$Over_{RJ} = 100(\{RJ : |RJ| > Thr_{RJ}\})/R \quad [\%], \quad (6)$$

where R – the number of frames in which accidental random jitter RJ is determined.

The analysis of dependencies of the average $Over_{RJ}$ from the duration of the time window of analysis shows a monotonic increase in the number of frames for which $RJ > Thr_{RJ}$, for all the considered signals. At that, the least steep has a curve characterizing the normal state (curve 1), the steep' growth is observed with the transition from it into the fatigue state (curve 2) and to a greater extent – into the emotional stress state (curve 3). The degree of steep change $Over_{RJ}$ is different for different accidental random jitters.

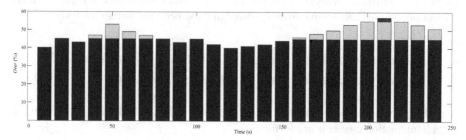

Fig. 1. Evaluation $Over_{RJ^{T_{MOUSE}}}$ moving average for operator, remaining in the normal state

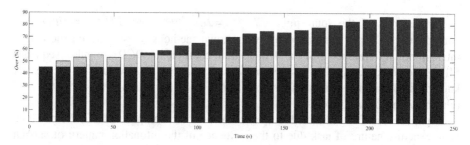

Fig. 2. Evaluation $Over_{RJ^{T_{MOUSE}}}$ moving average for operator, remaining in the emotional stress state

The evaluation results by moving average (for example $RJ^{T_{MOUSE}}$) for two operators remaining in the operative rest states (Fig. 1) and emotional stress state (Fig. 2), testify the capacity to generate estimates of the characteristics of the operator's psychophysiological states:

$$Over_{RJ} = \left[Over_{RJ^{PITCH}}, Over_{RJ^{tPRESS}}, Over_{RJ^{TPRESS}} \right.$$
$$\left. Over_{RJ^{tPRESS.LMB}}, Over_{RJ^{TPRESS.LMB}}, Over_{RJ^{T_{MOUSE}}} \right] \tag{7}$$

5   Consolidation of Information about Operators' Psychophysiological States

On the basis of the proposed analysis for combining the characteristics $Over_{RJ}$ the generalized Harrington's desirability function is suggested to use:

$$f_i = \sqrt[s]{d_1 \cdot d_2 \cdot \ldots \cdot d_s}, \tag{8}$$

where s – number of features available for analysis; $d_t = \exp[-\exp(-y_t)]$ – Harrington's logistic function, also called "desirability curve" (Fig. 3).

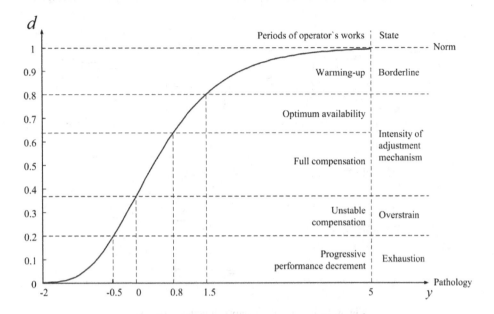

Fig. 3. Harrington's logistic function

Values of these characteristics $Over_{RJ}$ are distributed at a scale appropriated to their requirements, in the interval of the effective values of the scale of private parameters y:

$$y_t = \left(Over_{RJ\,t} - Over_{RJ\,t}^{MAX}\right)/\left(Over_{RJ\,t}^{MAX} - Over_{RJ\,t}^{MIN}\right), \tag{9}$$

where $Over_{RJ\,t}$ – property value in the original scale; $Over_{RJ\,t}^{MAX}$ and $Over_{RJ\,t}^{MIN}$ – upper and lower area boundaries of "satisfactory" in the initial scale, which can be calculated for each of the operators in accordance with the following recommendations: lower boundary is equal to the value of an average arithmetic quantity, and the top boundary is equal to the mean square of the average arithmetic quantity and its mean square deviation.

6   Evaluation of the Effectiveness of Human Resources

Generated estimates f_i (8) allow us to combine local solutions for the analysis of (7) according to the operators' psychophysiological states and on the basis of the task (1) dynamically allocate their PTF.

Example of estimation changing three operators' PPS working only: using the "mouse" – f_1, keyboard – f_5 and in mode communicative interaction – f_7 (at optimum working capacity even seven operators) is shown in the upper graph (Fig. 4).

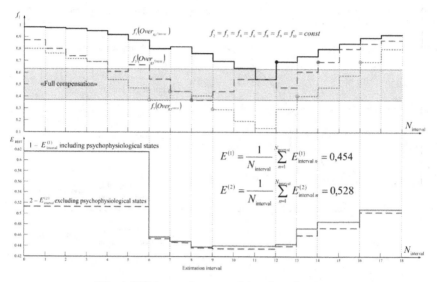

Fig. 4. Efficiency of operators' functions fixation

Efficiency of optimization operators' functions fixation is determined by the graph excess 1, corresponding values of performance indicator (1) taking into account operators' PFS f_i at intervals estimates $Over_{RJ}$, above the curve 2, calculated excluding PPS. The effectiveness of the PTF distribution between operators during the shift (18 intervals rated PPS) in this example is increased by 7.4% [14].

7   Conclusion

On the basis of the submitted data it can be said that the dynamic allocation of PTF is based on the developed criterion (1) in the conditions of the psychophysiological state task performers changes is adequate to human management resource and effective at 7,4% compared with existing solutions.

References

1. Brooking, E.: Intellectual Capital, p. 288. St. Petersburg, Piter (2001)
2. Gluhov, V.V., et al.: Knowledge Economy, p. 528. St. Peter (2003)
3. Kleiner, G.: Knowledge about Knowledge Management. Voprosy Economiki 1, 151–155 (2004)

4. Skills Management. Reasonable Expectations, Strategic Considerations and Success Factors. SkillView Technologies, Inc. (2001), access http://www.skillview.com/library.html
5. Ankudinov, I.G.: Automation of Management and Comprehensive Utilization of Human Resources and Structural Knowledge-Intensive Industries (industry): Ph.D. dissertation., p. 298. St. Petersburg (2009)
6. Eremenko, V.T., Sazonov, M.A., Fomin, S.I., Petrov, V.A.: Simulation of the formation of an expert group on over-the subject. Information Systems and Technologies 3, 23–31 (2012)
7. Nosov, M.V., Basov, O.O., Shalaginov, V.A.: Study Jitter Characteristics of the Pitch Period of the Speech Signals. SPIIRAS Proceedings 1(32), 27–44 (2014)
8. Li, D.: Time series analysis of jitter in sustained vowels. In: ICPhS XVII, Hong Kong, August 17-21, pp. 603–606 (2011)
9. Schoentgen, J., Guchteneere, R.D.: Time series analysis of jitter. Journal of Phonetics 23(1-2), 189–201 (1994)
10. Silva, D.G., Oliveira, L.C., Andrea, M.: Jitter Estimation Algorithms for Detection of Pathological Voices. EURASIP Journal on Advances in Signal Processing. Hindawi Publishing Corporation, 1–9 (2009)
11. Basov, O.O., Nosov, M.V., Nikitin, V.V., Gulyaykin, D.A.: Textual Modalities Parameters Determination Program / Certificate of state registration of the computer № 2014613478.
12. Makarenko, N.V., Pukhov, B.A., Kol'chenko, N.V.: Fundamentals of professional psychophysiological selection. Kiev Sciences, 244 (1987)
13. Nosov, M.V.: Jitter Separation Technique for Signals of Different Channels of Technical Equipment Interaction and Automated Workstation's Operator. Information Systems and Technologies 3(83), 20–23 (2014)
14. Nosov, M.V., Basov, O.O.: Criterion of Efficiency of Human Resources Management. In: Collected materials VII-International Youth Scientific Conference GFR MTUCI "INFOCOM 2014", pp. 64–65.

Impact of Emotional Speech to Automatic Speaker Recognition - Experiments on GEES Speech Database

Ivan Jokić[1], Stevan Jokić[1,2], Vlado Delić[1], and Zoran Perić[3]

[1] Faculty of Technical Sciences, University of Novi Sad, Serbia
[2] DunavNET Ltd., Novi Sad, Serbia
[3] Faculty of Electronic Engineering, University of Niš, Serbia
{ibahjokih,stevan.jokic}@gmail.com, vlado.delic@uns.ac.rs
zoran.peric@elfak.ni.ac.rs

Abstract. In this paper an automatic speaker recognizer is tested on a speech database with emotional speech. The automatic speaker recognizer is based on mel-frequency cepstral coefficients as features of a speaker and covariance matrices as speaker models. The speaker models are trained on one sentence of neutral speech for each speaker. Other sentences from the same speech database are used for testing, including both neutral and four emotional states: happiness, fear, sadness, and anger. The aim of research is to investigate the impact of acted emotional speech to accuracy of automatic speaker recognition.

Keywords: Automatic speaker recognition, mel-frequency cepstral coefficients, Gaussian distribution, covariance matrix, GEES speech database, emotional speech.

1 Introduction

Automatic speaker recognition aims at recognizing of person identity from his/her speech. Generally, the recognition accuracy depends on similarity between training and test conditions. Differences between training and test conditions can be a consequence of either environment conditions (e.g. impact of the noise) or speaker's manner of pronunciation including speaker emotional state. Speech is a complex signal produced as a result of several transformations which occur at different levels: semantic, linguistic, articulatory, and acoustic [1], [2]. The influence of these transformations on speech production depends on emotional state of a speaker. Also, they reflect in both prosody and spectral content of speech signal. Therefore Mel-Frequency Cepstral Coefficients (MFCCs) are one of commonly used features for automatic speaker recognition [3].

Determination of MFCCs is based on observation of short-time speech frames of about 25 ms, mutually shifted by about 10 ms. Vectors of MFCCs are calculated for speech frames. Thus, each of speech recordings (e.g. sentences) is characterised by a lot of these feature vectors. From the statistical point of view, the multitude of feature vectors estimated for each speech signal can be described by corresponding probability

A. Ronzhin et al. (Eds.): SPECOM 2014, LNAI 8773, pp. 268–275, 2014.

density function. Gaussian multidimensional distributions are commonly used for speaker modelling [4].

Unavoidable intra-speaker variability of voice is the main cause of speaker mis-recognition. In an ideal case, the speaker model would be constant, i.e. non-time variable. However, short-time speaker features, as well as MFCCs, are variable from frame to frame of speech analyzed and this variability should be mapped in the models of speakers. So, one of solutions is to chose the smaller number of dimensions which are more suitable for the given space of speaker features. Principal Component Analysis (PCA) [5] is one of transformation algorithms which can be used to determine more compact dimensions inside the origin MFCC feature space. By the other way, it is possible to apply some kind of the features weighting in order to reduce the intra-speaker variability of speaker models - one example is given in [6]. The intra-speaker model variability is unavoidable even when training and test speech are pronounced by neutral speech. It is expected that this variability will be much higher when the training and test speech are pronounced in different emotional states and therefore it is necessary to apply some methods to compensate the impact of emotions in speech [7] or by some way to provide referent models of speakers also in other emotional states [8], [9]. All these conclusions and results have motivated us to investigate which emotions can cause the most impact to the accuracy of automatic speaker recognition when training was done on the neutral speech and tested on the emotional speech. A speech database of "Speech Expressions of Emotions and Attitudes" was available for our experiments. The automatic speaker recognizer and experiment preparation are described in the Section 2. The experimental results are presented and evaluated in the Section 3, while some conclusions are drawn in the Section 4 including the directions for the future work.

2 Experiment Preparation

Automatic speaker recognizer used in experiments is based on MFCCs as speaker features and multidimensional Gaussian distributions as model of speakers.

2.1 Determination of MFCCs

Before of MFCCs calculation, given speech is windowed by Hanning window functions in duration of 23 ms, mutually shifted by 8.33 ms. Each frame of speech signal is presented by 18-dimensional MFCC feature vector by using of equality [10]:

$$c_n = \sum_{k=1}^{20} \log(E_k) \cdot \cos\left[n \cdot \left(k - \frac{1}{2}\right)\right], \qquad n = 1,2,...,18, \tag{1}$$

where E_k is the energy inside k^{th} auditory critical band and n is the ordinal number of the MFCC calculated. As is evident in (1) the twenty auditory critical bands were used. Auditory critical bands are of exponential form, based on the lower part of exponential function, width of 300 mel and mutually shifted by 150 mel [6].

2.2   Models and Decision Making

Modeling of speakers was based on the assumption that feature vectors are distributed in accordance with Gaussian multidimensional distribution. Since the shape of this distribution depends on the covariance matrix of observed data set, modeling was done by appropriate covariance matrix determined by equality:

$$\Sigma = \frac{1}{n-1} \cdot (X - \mu) \cdot (X - \mu)^T , \qquad (2)$$

where n is the number of feature vectors modeled, X is the matrix which contains of n feature vectors modeled and μ is the vector of mean values of data matrix X.

The test speech file is modeled by appropriate covariance matrix. The automatic speaker recognition was conducted on the closed set of speakers. Model of each of speakers in the database was compared to model of the test speech file, and the identity of the most similar model was recognized for given test speech file. The measure of difference between the model of the test speech and the model's of the ith speaker is defined by:

$$m(i, test) = \frac{1}{18^2} \cdot \sum_{i=1}^{18} \sum_{j=1}^{18} \left| \Sigma_i (i, j) - \Sigma_{test} (i, j) \right| , \qquad (3)$$

where Σ_i and Σ_{test} are covariance matrices for modeling of the ith speaker and the test speech. The observed test speech belongs to the ith speaker if:

$$m(i, test) < m(j, test), \qquad \forall j \in \{1, 2, ..., N\} \setminus \{i\}, \qquad (4)$$

where N is the number of speakers in the speech database.

2.3   Speech Database

Recordings from the GEES (Serbian abbreviation for "*Govorna Ekspresija Emocija i Stavova*", in English "Speech Expression of Emotions and Attitudes") speech database [11] were used in experiments. This speech database contains the recordings of six speakers, three female and three male, whose initials are: BM, MM, MV, OK, SK, and SZ. The speech database contains utterances of these six speakers in both neutral emotional state and acted four emotional states: happiness, sadness, fear and anger. The recordings of each emotional state of these six speakers were classified by its textual content in four groups signed as:

- "long" – 30 long sentences,
- "short" – 30 short sentences,
- "words" – 32 isolated words,
- "text" – one passage with 79 words in size.

3   Results and Discussion

The experiments in this paper are conducted in order to estimate the impact of basic emotions on automatic speaker recognition when training is performed on neutral speech. In real applications an automatic speaker recognizer often deals with utterances which represent one sentence. Therefore in this paper such tests were performed. The training model for each speaker is based on one sentence uttered in neutral emotional state. For each test, one of spoken sentences of each speaker is chosen, in either neutral or one of four emotional states, but with different textual content, since the GEES speech database contains each sentence pronounced by all six speakers in both neutral and all four emotional states. Since the GEES speech database contains speech recordings signed as "long" whose duration is about 3 to 5 seconds, just these recordings of sentences are chosen as appropriate for the training and testing.

Table 1. Differences (eq. (3)) between models of test speech in **neutral** emotional state and models of speakers trained on neutral emotion speech (accuracy=6/6)

Test file: neutral speech	Models of speakers (trained on **neutral** speech)					
	BM	MM	MV	OK	SK	SZ
BM	1st **0.682**	1.242	1.237	2nd **1.096**	1.333	1.313
MM	1.233	1st **0.453**	0.802	0.816	2nd **0.772**	0.986
MV	1.261	2nd **0.729**	1st **0.571**	0.856	0.746	0.851
OK	0.954	2nd **0.762**	0.964	1st **0.522**	0.960	0.867
SK	1.331	2nd **0.687**	0.849	0.855	1st **0.583**	0.915
SZ	1.110	0.863	0.939	2nd **0.740**	0.951	1st **0.609**

The results of recognition on the speech recordings in neutral emotional state are given in Table 1 and show accuracy of 100% which is in accordance with previous experiments on other speech databases and experiments in real applications. Also it is evident a significant distinction between the differences (Eq. (3)) to the most similar speaker model (1st) and differences to the first next similar speaker model (2nd). This is not the case when test speech is pronounced in some of four emotional states. Then the differences between distances (1st - 2nd) in Tables 2 to 5 are much smaller. The automatic speaker recognizer does not favor any particular speaker in tests based on emotional speech. Average measures of distinctions in Table 6 also show this result.

Based upon differences between models of the test speech files and models of the speakers, it is evident that when the test recordings were in neutral emotional state the differences between test models and the nearest speaker's model had the smallest values. In tests on emotional speech the distinctions to the most similar speaker model often have the values higher than 1. This is the case even if the speaker is correctly recognized.

Table 2. Differences (eq. (3)) between models of test speech in **happiness** emotional state and models of speakers trained on neutral emotion speech (accuracy=4/6)

Test file: speech in **happiness**	Models of speakers (trained on **neutral** speech)					
	BM	MM	MV	OK	SK	SZ
BM	1st **1.593**	1.797	2nd **1.725**	1.862	1.914	1.789
MM	1.396	2nd **1.039**	1st **1.016**	1.162	1.114	1.172
MV	1.077	1.073	1st **0.909**	2nd **1.031**	1.222	1.053
OK	2nd **1.203**	1.433	1.438	1st **1.202**	1.576	1.459
SK	1.095	2nd **0.822**	0.886	1st **0.813**	0.887	0.950
SZ	2.114	2.105	2nd **1.979**	2.046	2.070	1st **1.930**

The voice can be described by three basic spectral properties: fundamental frequency, loudness and timbre. Additionally, the speech can be characterized also by prosody features such as speaking rate. The change in speaker's emotional state, changes the previously mentioned speech properties and his/her speech is colored by the characteristics of given emotional state in more or less different way. The timbre of emotional speech has significant differences in comparison to neutral speech. Since covariance matrices determined for vectors of MFCCs are modeling the timbre, therefore the models of emotional test speech are not close to any model of speakers.

As is evident from the results in Tables 2, 3, 4 and 5, the accuracy of automatic speaker recognition heavily depends on the speaker emotional state. The happiness emotional state has shown the smallest impact to recognition accuracy in experiments. Contrary, in sadness emotional state, only test speech file of the speaker with initials MM is correctly recognized. That is because both the speaking rate and the voice fundamental frequency are much smaller in the sadness.

Table 3. Differences (eq. (3)) between models of test speech in **sadness** emotional state and models of speakers trained on neutral emotion speech (accuracy=1/6)

Test file: speech in **sadness**	Models of speakers (trained on **neutral** speech)					
	BM	MM	MV	OK	SK	SZ
BM	1.192	2nd **1.134**	1.188	1st **0.945**	1.213	1.184
MM	1.230	1st **0.704**	1.001	2nd **0.731**	0.931	0.996
MV	1.172	1st **0.670**	0.812	2nd **0.752**	0.830	0.887
OK	1.123	1st **0.680**	0.928	2nd **0.688**	0.833	0.857
SK	1.213	1st **0.649**	0.823	2nd **0.703**	0.773	0.873
SZ	1.249	2nd **0.782**	0.942	1st **0.722**	0.846	0.806

The obtained results show that sadness causes the most impact on the accuracy of automatic speaker recognition when training was done on the neutral speech.

Table 4. Differences (eq. (3)) between models of test speech in **fear** emotional state and models of speakers trained on neutral emotion speech (accuracy=2/6)

Test file: speech in **fear**	Models of speakers (trained on **neutral** speech)					
	BM	MM	MV	OK	SK	SZ
BM	2.198	1st **2.082**	2nd **2.107**	2.220	2.266	2.122
MM	1.455	1st **1.052**	2nd **1.082**	1.131	1.126	1.187
MV	1.212	1st **0.780**	2nd **0.825**	0.858	0.941	0.944
OK	1.108	2nd **0.963**	1.143	1st **0.838**	1.190	1.154
SK	1.182	1st **0.629**	0.831	2nd **0.669**	0.724	0.937
SZ	1.280	1.208	2nd **1.146**	1st **1.088**	1.320	1.168

Table 5. Differences (eq. (3)) between models of test speech in **anger** emotional state and models of speakers trained on neutral emotion speech (accuracy=2/6)

Test file: speech in **anger**	Models of speakers (trained on **neutral** speech)					
	BM	MM	MV	OK	SK	SZ
BM	1st **1.583**	1.837	2nd **1.740**	1.831	1.927	1.770
MM	1.242	1st **0.656**	2nd **0.830**	0.864	0.834	0.911
MV	1.252	1st **0.968**	2nd **0.985**	1.001	1.058	1.047
OK	1st **1.136**	1.540	1.497	2nd **1.393**	1.729	1.419
SK	1.572	1.304	1st **1.215**	1.302	2nd **1.284**	1.306
SZ	1st **1.270**	1.357	1.414	2nd **1.293**	1.544	1.313

Table 6. The average measure of **differences** (eq. (3)) to the most similar speaker (1st), m_{min}, and the average **distinction** between differences to the second most similar speaker model and the first most similar speaker model (1st - 2nd), $d_{1,min}$, in dependency on the emotional state

neutral		happiness		sadness		fear		anger	
m_{min}	$d_{1,min}$	m_{min}	$d_{1,min}$	m_{min}	$d_{1,min}$	m_{min}	$d_{1,min}$	m_{min}	$d_{1,min}$
0.570	0.228	1.244	0.056	0.728	0.070	1.078	0.054	1.138	0.116

The impact of emotions in voice to accuracy of automatic speaker recognition can be significant. If an automatic speaker recognizer is trained on neutral speech, the presence of the emotions in test speech impacts to the misrecognition. The recognition rate reduction and resulted confusion matrices draw to the conclusion that it is necessary to have separate speaker models in variable emotional states in order to get a reliable automatic speaker recognition. In real applications, such as automatic speaker recognition in some kind of robotic system, it should be interplayed in cooperation with other recognition systems including face recognition, and provide constant training process. On that way the system for automatic speaker recognition will be able to form different models of the same speaker for different emotional states. The existence of such models, in mobile phone for example, could help in generation of some warnings addressed to the speaker in dependence of speaker's emotional state. Mobile phone equipped by software which enables him to be a part of a telemedical system [12], together with incorporated automatic speaker recognition algorithm can detect variability in emotional states of the user. As is evident from the obtained results, in most cases the measure of differences between model of test speech file in some emotional state and referent model in neutral emotional state have significant values, often higher than 0.7. So if the threshold value be for example 0.8 or 0.9 it can be sure that if difference between test speech file and reference model is higher than threshold value, than speaker is in deeper emotional state and the telemedical system can generate some message for alerting of speaker.

4   Conclusion

This paper presents the first study on automatic speaker recognition on a Serbian GEES speech database containing speech expressions of emotions and attitudes. The GESS speech database is available to other researchers who want to investigate robustness of their automatic speaker recognition systems depending on basic emotional states: happiness, fear, sadness, and anger.

The training in this paper is based on neutral speech, while the testing is conducted on both neutral and emotional speech - in the four basic emotional states. The results have shown strong impact of acted emotions to the accuracy of tested automatic speaker recognition system, and proved the concept to develop separate models for speaker recognition and apply them after emotion recognition.

In the future work we will try to make separate models for different emotions for each speaker, and compare the confusion matrices obtained in this paper. Apart from detailed analysis of the impact of particular emotional states to the accuracy of automatic speaker recognition, it would be interesting to compare robustness of different speaker recognition systems.

Acknowledgements. The presented study is performed as part of the project "Development of dialogue systems for Serbian and other South Slavic languages" (TR32035), funded by the Ministry of Education, Science and Technological development of the Republic of Serbia.

References

1. Campbell Jr., J.P.: Speaker recognition: a tutorial. Speaker recognition: a tutorial. Proceedings of the IEEE 85(9), 1437–1462 (1997)
2. Delić, V., Sečujski, M., Jakovljević, N.: Action model of human-machine speech communication. In: Proceedings of the 16th Telecommunications forum TELFOR 2008, Serbia, Belgrade, pp. 680–683 (2008) (*in Sebian*)
3. Kinnunen, T., Li, H.: An overview of text-independent speaker recognition: From features to supervectors. Speech Communication 52, 12–40 (2010)

4. Bimbot, F., Bonastre, J.-F., Fredouille, C., Gravier, G., Magrin-Chagnolleau, I.,, M.S., Merlin, T., Ortega-Garcia, J., Petrovska-Delacrétaz, D., Reynolds, D.A.: A Tutorial on Text-Independent Speaker Verification. EURASIP Journal on Applied Signal Processing 4, 430–451 (2004)
5. Jokić, I., Jokić, S., Perić, Z., Gnjatović, M., Delić, V.: Influence of the Number of Principal Components used to the Automatic Speaker Recognition Accuracy. Electronics and Electrical Engineering 7(123), 83–86 (2012)
6. Jokić, I., Jokić, S., Delić, V., Perić, Z.: Towards a Small Intra-Speaker Variability Models. In: 18th International Conference ELECTRONICS 2014, Palanga, Lithuania, 16th-18th June 2014, Electronics and Electrical Engineering, Kaunas, vol. 20(6), pp. 100–103 (2014)
7. Raja, G.S., Dandapat, S.: Speaker recognition under stressed condition. International Journal of Speech Technology 13(3), 141–161 (2010)
8. Devi, J.S., Srinivas, Y., Nandyala, S.P.: Automatic Speech Emotion and Speaker Recognition based on Hybrid GMM and FFBNN. International Journal on Computational Sciences & Applications (IJCSA) 4(1), 35–42 (2014)
9. Wu, W., Zheng, T.F., Xu, M.-X., Bao, H.-J.: Study on Speaker Verification on Emotional Speech. In: INTERSPEECH 2006 – ICSLP, Pittsburgh, Pennsylvania, September 17-21, pp. 2102–2105 (2006)
10. Wildermoth, B.R.: Text-Independent Speaker Recognition Using Source Based Features. M. Phil. Thesis, Griffith University, Brisbane, Australia (2001)
11. Jovičić, S.T., Kašić, Z.: Đorđević, M., Rajković M.: Serbian emotional speech database: design, processing and evaluation. In: Proc. of the SPECOM 2004: 9th Conference Speech and Computer, St. Petersburg, Russia, pp. 77–81 (2004)
12. Jokić, S., Krčo, S., Sakač, D., Jokić, I., Delić, V.: Autonomic telemedical application for Android based mobile devices. In: Proc. of the 11th Symposium of Neural Network Applications in Electrical Engineering, NEUREL 2012, Beograd, Srbija, pp. 231–234 (2012)

Improving Speech Synthesis Quality for Voices Created from an Audiobook Database

Pavel Chistikov[1,2], Dmitriy Zakharov[2] and Andrey Talanov[2]

[1] National Research University of Information Technologies, Mechanics and Optics
49 Kronverkskiy pr., Saint-Petersburg, Russia, 197101
chistikov@speechpro.com
http://en.ifmo.ru
[2] Speech Technology Center Ltd.
4 Krasutskogo st., Saint-Petersburg, Russia, 196084
zakharov-d,andre@speechpro.com
http://speechpro.com

Abstract. This paper describes an approach to improving synthesized speech quality for voices created by using an audiobook database. The data consist of a large amount of read speech by one speaker, which we matched with the corresponding book texts. The main problems with such a database are the following. First, the recordings were made at different times under different acoustic conditions, and the speaker reads the text with a variety of intonations and accents, which leads to very high voice parameter variability. Second, automatic techniques for sound file labeling make more errors due to the large variability of the database, especially as there can be mismatches between the text and the corresponding sound files. These problems dramatically affect speech synthesis quality, so a robust method for solving them is vital for voices created using audiobooks. The approach described in the paper is based on statistical models of voice parameters and special algorithms of speech element concatenation and modification. Listening tests show that it strongly improves synthesized speech quality.

Keywords: speech synthesis, database quality control, hidden Markov models, Unit Selection, speech modification.

1 Introduction

At the present time the main requirements for synthesized speech are quality and pleasantness of the voice. But good quality comes at a price: we need a large (up to 10 hours) speech database labeled with high accuracy [1]. Its preparation takes up most of the time and financial resources spent on creating a new voice.

To reduce the price of a TTS voice, a new voice can be made using an audiobook or a similar database. Despite the obvious opportunities for reducing time and financial expenses, there are some problems with this method. Such a database usually consists of recordings that were made at different times under different acoustic conditions, which leads to high voice parameter variability.

A. Ronzhin et al. (Eds.): SPECOM 2014, LNAI 8773, pp. 276–283, 2014.

This effect is intensified by specific reading styles: the speaker often uses different accents for different roles in dialogues, imitates the characters' emotions, etc. Additionally, automatic techniques for sound file labeling make more errors due to the large variability of the database, especially as there can be mismatches between the text and the corresponding sound files [2]. All of these problems dramatically affect speech synthesis quality.

In this paper we propose an approach to improving speech quality for voices created by using audiobooks. The method is based on a hybrid TTS system [3], where the speaker parameters are modeled based on HMM models [4] and the speech is produced using the Unit Selection algorithm [5], but with the following improvements. First, the database is preprocessed to remove speech elements with characteristics that are not typical for the speaker. In our case these are the speech zones where the timbre, original intonation or pitch was changed for the purpose of representing a character. Also, recordings with high background noise and with various sound artifacts, like snaps, are removed. Second, special algorithms for speech element concatenation and modification are implemented in order to improve the resulting quality under the conditions of database labeling errors. Such complex techniques strongly improve the quality of synthesized speech for voices created by using an audiobook database, which is confirmed by expert listening tests that were performed for voices created using the Blizzard Challenge 2013 English audiobook database [6].

This paper is organized as follows: the proposed system is presented in Section 2, which describes the database preprocessing procedure and speech element modification and concatenation algorithms; experimental results illustrating the system's performance are included in Section 3; conclusions and future developments are presented in Section 4.

2   The Proposed System

Structurally, the text-to-speech system consists of two parts: the training part and the synthesis part (Figure 1).

The main purpose of the training part is to create an appropriate speech database containing speech elements that are suitable for the TTS system (without noise and with a pronunciation style typical for the speaker) and to build an appropriate voice model that summarizes parameters of all speech elements in the speech database. To perform this we need a source audiobook (or similar) database comprising more than 20 hours of speech, where each sound file has a corresponding label file containing information about its speech elements [2]. First of all, linguistic and acoustic features [3,8] are calculated for the audiobook database. Then, voice model building is performed. The model is a set of HMMs that generalize sound element parameters (MFCC, pitch, energy and duration). After that the source audiobook database is filtered to remove all speech elements that contain deviant fragments. Finally, based on the new speech database, feature extraction and voice model building are preformed in order to obtain a model that will be used in the speech synthesis process to

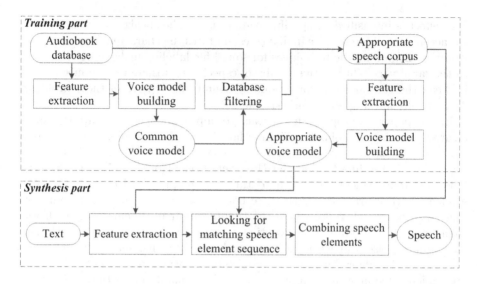

Fig. 1. Diagram illustrating the basic steps conducted by the TTS system

emulate speaker parameters for an arbitrary utterance. A detailed description of voice model building and database filtering is presented in Section 2.1.

Speech synthesis is performed based on the voice model and the speech database prepared at the previous step. The TTS system input is raw text without any manual preprocessing. Based on the input text, the target speech element sequence is formed, and linguistic and acoustic features are calculated based on the model. The type and structure of features are the same as those used in the training part. After that the most appropriate speech element sequence is selected from the database based on the predicted acoustic features using the Unit Selection algorithm [1]. Then the selected speech elements are smoothed and concatenated with each other to produce synthesized speech. These two steps are very important, especially if there are errors in speech database labeling and possible variations in the acoustic environment of speech elements in the database. So it is vital to implement special methods that, on the one hand, can ensure appropriate intonation and rhythm of the synthesized utterance (in terms of the modeled parameters) and, on the other hand, provides smooth synthesized speech. These methods are described in Sections 2.2 and 2.3 respectively.

2.1 Database Preprocessing

As noted above, the main steps of the training part are voice model building, which generalizes the speech element parameters, and audiobook database filtration in order to create an appropriate speech database. The second step, as well as the generation of target speech element parameters, is based on the voice model. Both of these steps are detailed in the next corresponding subsections.

Voice model building starts with feature set extraction for every sound file [7], where each member of the set represents a 25ms fragment of the speech signal and contains a sequences of MFCC vectors [9], pitch and energy values. Then linguistic and prosodic features are calculated [3,8]. At the next step, HMM prototypes for each speech element in the database are created. Each HMM corresponds to a no-skip 5-state left-to-right model. Each output observation vector $\mathbf{o}^i$ for the i-th frame consists of 5 streams $\mathbf{o}^i = \left(\mathbf{o}_1^{iT}, \mathbf{o}_2^{iT}, \mathbf{o}_3^{iT}, \mathbf{o}_4^{iT}, \mathbf{o}_5^{iT} \right)$, where the streams are vectors composed by MFCCs, their delta and delta-delta components, by F0s, by F0 delta components, by F0 delta-delta components and by energies, their delta and delta-delta components respectively. For each k-th HMM the durations of the 5 states are regarded as a vector $\mathbf{d}^k = \left(d_1^k, ..., d_5^k \right)$, where d_n^k represents the duration of the n-th state. Furthermore, each duration vector is modeled by a 5-dimensional single-mixture Gaussian distribution. The output probabilities of the state duration vectors are thus re-estimated by Baum-Welch iterations in the same way as the output probabilities of the speech parameters [9]. At the end of the voice model building, a tree-based clustering method is applied to the HMM states of MFCC, F0 and energy values and their delta and delta-delta as well as to the state duration models. Eventually we have the voice model, which is then used to perform audiobook database filtration as well as to generate voice parameters for a synthesized utterance even for speech elements absent in the database.

The main purpose of the database filtering step is to remove speech elements that have negative influence on the resulting speech quality. These are elements that were recorded in bad acoustic conditions (with high background noise or various sound artifacts, for example, snaps) or with timbre, intonation or rhythm that are not typical for the speaker. Speech element filtering is performed in the following way. First, for each speech element in the database its acoustic parameters are predicted based on the general voice model. These parameters are represented by the vectors of MFCC $\mathbf{M}_p^m$, pitch $\mathbf{M}_p^p$, energy $\mathbf{M}_p^e$ and the value of duration M_p^d with their corresponding variance estimations of MFCC $\mathbf{V}^m$, pitch $\mathbf{V}^p$, energy $\mathbf{V}^e$ and duration V^d, where N is the number of HMM states in the model (N equals 5 in our work). Then the same parameters are determined based on the element's sound: $\mathbf{M}_r^m$, pitch $\mathbf{M}_r^p$, energy $\mathbf{M}_r^e$ and the value of duration M_r^d. After that, the goodness criterion G for each allophone is calculated by the Equation (1).

$$
G = \frac{\left(M_p^d - M_r^d \right)^2}{V^d} + \frac{1}{KN} \sum_{k=1}^{K} \sqrt{ \sum_{i=1}^{N} \frac{\left(M_{p_{i,k}}^m - M_{r_{i,k}}^m \right)^2}{V_{i,k}^m} } +
$$

$$
+ \frac{1}{N} \left(\sqrt{ \sum_{i=1}^{N} \frac{\left(M_{p_i}^p - M_{r_i}^p \right)^2}{V_i^p} } + \sqrt{ \sum_{i=1}^{N} \frac{\left(M_{p_i}^e - M_{r_i}^e \right)^2}{V_i^e} } \right), \tag{1}
$$

where K is the number of MFCC coefficients in the vector.

Finally, the speech elements are ranged by the value of G, and bad ones are removed so as to achieve the database volume of approximately 8-10 hours. This step makes it possible to prepare a speech database with quality sufficient for synthesizing natural speech, assuming that in general the audiobooks were recorded under good and relatively uniform acoustic conditions.

2.2   Speech Element Modification

When the most appropriate speech element sequence is selected, the F0 and duration parameters are adjusted according to the predicted ones. This step is needed to ensure proper intonation of the synthesized sentence. In our system we use the LP model [9] to get the prediction of the residual, modify it by TD-PSOLA [9], and eventually use the obtained modified prediction of the residual to recover the source signal with a new pitch. To implement this method, pitch periods in the sound files must be labeled with high accuracy, which is usually not the case when files are labeled automatically. To avoid negative effects of speech modification, such incorrectly labeled periods are determined and only the vector of correct periods $\mathbf{p}'$ is obtained using the Equation (2).

$$p_i' = \begin{cases} p_i, & D \leqslant 0.2 \\ 2W_i(\mathbf{p}') - W_{i-1}(\mathbf{p}'), & D > 0.2 \end{cases}, \tag{2}$$

where $D = \dfrac{|W_i(\mathbf{p}') - p_i|}{\min(W_i(\mathbf{p}'), p_i)}$, $W_i(\mathbf{p}) = \dfrac{p_{i-1} + p_{i-2} + \cdots + p_{i-n}}{n}$, p_i is the i-th period of the speech element and n is the simple moving average filter size. The initial period p_k is selected by the equation: $k = \underset{i=\{n...N\}}{\arg\min} \left(\sum_{j=i-n}^{i} |W_i - p_j| \right)$, where N is the size of $\mathbf{p}$.

If the number of incorrectly labeled periods is more than half the total number of periods in the speech element, the duration and pitch parameters are modified in the following way. Rhythm is changed by using the WSOLA algorithm [10]. This approach is similar to LP-PSOLA but periods are determined in real-time based on cross-correlation (3) and average magnitude difference (4) metrics.

$$C_C = \frac{\sum_{i=0}^{N-1} x_i y_i}{\sum_{i=0}^{N-1} x_i^2}, \tag{3}$$

$$C_A = \sum_{i=0}^{N-1} |x_i - y_i|, \tag{4}$$

where N is the size of the compared fragments, x_i and y_i are the corresponding values of the compared fragments. Pitch is modified by using TD-PSOLA applied to the LP residual, where pitch period boundaries are determined by the epoch detection technique [11]. Applying these methods strongly improves the robustness of duration and pitch modification if pitch period labeling errors are present in the database.

2.3   Speech Element Concatenation

The last step, after the most appropriate speech elements have been selected and have been adjusted to reliable intonation parameters, is speech element concatenation. The problem is the mismatch of spectrum and pitch components at speech element boundaries. We perform speech element boundary correction in order to minimize spectrum distortions in the positions of concatenation. The process is illustrated in Figure 2. For example, at the previous step diphones a1_a2 and a2_a3 were selected as the most appropriate. The position B is the original boundary of diphones in the corresponding source files. This position is compared with two others, A and C, which are obtained by shifting B by the offset Δ that is usually two or three F0 periods.

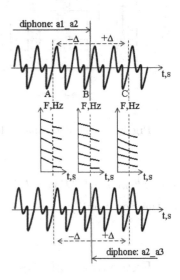

Fig. 2. Boundary correction

The optimal speech element boundary P_{opt} position is calculated by the Equation (5):

$$P_{opt} = \underset{P=\{A,B,C\}}{\arg\min}\; L_2(P), \qquad (5)$$

where $L_2(P) = \sqrt{\sum_{i=1}^{M}\left(C_{Li}(P) - C_{Ri}(P)\right)^2}$, $C_{Li}(P)$ is the i-th MFCC coefficient of the left diphone boundary P, $C_{Ri}(P)$ is the i-th MFCC coefficient of the right diphone boundary P, the number of MFCC coefficients M is set as 12.

The main idea of pitch smoothing at speech element boundaries is, on the one hand, to avoid F0 envelope discontinuities and, on the other hand, to preserve local F0 fluctuations, so as to make synthesized speech less static and as a result more natural. Let us assume that $\mathbf{p}_L = \{p_{L_1}, p_{L_2}, \ldots, p_{L_N}\}$ are the N boundary pitch points of the left speech element and $\mathbf{p}_R = \{p_{R_1}, p_{R_2}, \ldots, p_{R_M}\}$ are the M boundary pitch points of the right speech element (these boundaries are determined as described in Subsection 2.2). They form the mutual pitch envelope $\mathbf{p} = \{p_{L_1}, p_{L_2}, \ldots, p_{L_N}, p_{R_1}, p_{R_2}, \ldots, p_{R_M}\}$ that must be smoothed. The resulting pitch envelope $\mathbf{p}' = \{p'_1, p'_2, \ldots, p'_{N+M}\}$ can be calculated as detailed below.

First of all the pitch envelope $\mathbf{p}$ is represented as the superposition of its filtered part $\mathbf{p}_m$ and fluctuation part $\mathbf{p}_f$, where $p_{m_i} = \alpha p_i + (1 - \alpha)p_{m_{i-1}}$, $\mathbf{p}_f = \mathbf{p} - \mathbf{p}_m$, $0 < \alpha < 1$. Then $\mathbf{p}_m$ is smoothed based on the Bezier curve as calculated in the Equation (6):

$$p'_{m_i} = \sum_{j=1}^{N+M}\left(\frac{i-1}{N+M-1}\right)p_{m_j} b_{j-1, N+M-1}, \qquad (6)$$

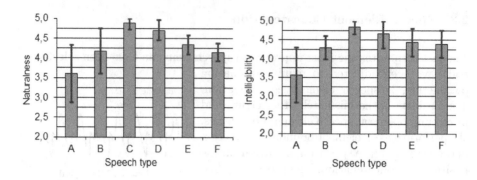

Fig. 3. Speech naturalness (left) and intelligibility (right) evaluation results

where $b_{i,n}(t) = C_i^n\, t^i\, (1-t)^{n-1}$, $\quad C_i^n = \dfrac{n!}{i!(n-i)!}$. The result $\mathbf{p}'$ is calculated by the Equation(7):

$$\mathbf{p}' = \mathbf{p}'_m + \mathbf{p}_f. \tag{7}$$

3   Experimental Results

This section describes the results of a Mean Opinion Score evaluation procedure which was performed to evaluate the proposed system and to compare it with others under the same conditions. The assessment procedure consists of two different parts: speech naturalness and speech intelligibility evaluation, which are presented in Figure 3 (left and right diagrams, respectively). The evaluated systems are the following: A is the baseline TTS system which was improved upon in our work; B is the proposed system; C is natural speech; D is the best TTS system of the Blizzard Challenge 2013 competition; E and F are the second and the third top systems of the competition respectively. As we can note from the results, applying the proposed approach strongly improves synthesized speech quality. Worse performance in comparison to the best Blizzard Challenge 2013 system can be explained as follows. First, we did not use all the 300 hours of the audiobook database that were available; due to time and computational resource limitations, only 70 hours of data were taken as our source database. Second, the database was labeled fully automatically. Third, no manual tuning of the TTS system and error correction was performed. It is expected that minimal human adjustment of the system will improve the performance and bring the quality closer to the best system.

4   Conclusions

In this paper we presented an approach to improving TTS quality for voices created by using an audiobook database. Our aim was to solve two problems that dramatically affect speech synthesis quality. First, the recordings were made under different acoustic conditions, with a variety of intonations and accents, which leads to high voice parameter variability. Second, automatic techniques for sound file labeling make more errors due to the large variability of the database and possible text mismatches. Experiments and subjective expert evaluation made using the Blizzard Challenge 2013 database show that the proposed approach strongly improves synthesized speech quality and reduces requirements for the acoustic quality of database and the accuracy of database labeling.

Acknowledgments. This work was partially financially supported by the Government of the Russian Federation, Grant 074-U01.

References

1. Black, A., Hunt, A.: Unit Selection in a Concatenative Speech Synthesis Using a Large Speech Database. In: Proc. of the ICASSP 1996, Atlanta, Georgia, May 7–10, vol. 1, pp. 373–376 (1996)
2. Prodan, A., Chistikov, P., Talanov, A.: Voice building system for hybrid Russian TTS system "VitalVoice". In: Proc. of the Dialogue-2010 International Conference, Bekasovo, Russia, May 26–30, vol. 9(16), pp. 394–399 (2010)
3. Chistikov, P., Korolkov, E., Talanov, A.: Combining HMM and Unit Selection technologies to increase naturalness of synthesized speech. Computational Linguistics and Intellectual Technologies 2, 12(19), 607–615 (2013)
4. Yamagishi, J., Zen, H., Toda, T., Tokuda, K.: Speaker independent HMM-based speech synthesis system - hts-2007 system for the blizzard challenge 2007. Paper presented at the Blizzard Challenge 2007, Bonn, Germany (2007)
5. Breuer, S., Bergmann, S., Dragon R., Möller, S.: Set-up of a Unit-Selection Synthesis with a Prominent Voice. Paper Presented at the 5th International Conference on Language Resources and Evaluation, Genoa, Italy (2006)
6. King, S., Karaiskos, V.: The Blizzard Challenge 2013. Paper Presented at the Blizzard Challenge 2013 Workshop, Barcelona, Spain (2013)
7. Chistikov, P., Talanov, A.: High Quality Speech Synthesis Using a Small Dataset. In: Proc. of the SLTU-2014 International Conference, St. Petersburg, Russia, May 14–16, pp. 105–111 (2014)
8. Chistikov, P., Khomitsevich, O.: Improving prosodic break detection in a russian TTS system. In: Železný, M., Habernal, I., Ronzhin, A. (eds.) SPECOM 2013. LNCS, vol. 8113, pp. 181–188. Springer, Heidelberg (2013)
9. Zen, H., Tokuda, K., Masuko, T., Kobayashi, T.: Hidden semi-Markov model based speech synthesis. In: Proc. of the 8th International Conference on Spoken Language Processing, Jeju Island, South Korea, October 4–8, pp. 1393–1396 (2004)
10. Grofit, S., Lavner, Y.: Time-Scale Modification of Audio Signals Using Enhanced WSOLA With Managment of Transients. IEEE Transaction on audio, speech, and language processing 16(1), 106–115 (2008)
11. Pratosh, A., Ananthapadmanabha, T., Ramakrishnan, A.: Epoch Extraction Based on Integrated Linear Prediction Residual Using. IEEE Transaction on audio, speech, and language processing 21(12), 2471–2480 (2013)

«INFANT.MAVS» - Multimedia Model for Infants Cognitive and Emotional Development Study

Elena Lyakso[1], Aleksei Grigorev[1], Anna Kurazova[1], and Elena Ogorodnikova[2]

[1] St. Petersburg State University, St. Petersburg, Russia
lyakso@gmail.com
[2] Pavlov Institute Physiology, RAS, St. Petersburg, Russia
elena-ogo@mail.ru

Abstract. A model of multimodal sensory environment «INFANT.MAVS» is elaborated. It comprises two bases of stimuli of different perceptual complexity: 1) simple stimuli (visual, audible, tactile and graphic) and 2) a set of complex stimuli synthesized as combinations of simple ones. The software includes a database management component and the database itself. The management component is created with Microsoft Visual Basic v.6.0 and is designed to run on operating systems of Windows. The model test results showed that stimuli evoked children's responses in the form of focused attention, vocalizations, smiles and simulation activity; in adults they evoked positive emotions. These data allow us to conclude that the model "INFANT.MAVS" complies with the objectives it was intended for.

Keywords: Software, multimedia model, infants, children, early cognitive development, emotional development.

1   Introduction

Studies of multimodal human-computer interaction are in the center of rapt attention among researchers [1, 2]. An audiovisual speech synthesis model "talking head" was created on Russian material. It included synchronization of speech and visual speech modalities [3]. An information system for training audio and verbal functions in children with hearing and speech disturbances was developed and introduced into clinical (rehabilitation of patients after cochlear implantation) and correctional practice [4]. There are very few such systems for young children, teaching and creating conditions of sensory-cognitive interaction with the outside world. More widely used are children's social networks, designed for primary school children. Their main feature is the predominant focus on the 'edutainment' of a small user through game and parental control over the child's activities on the network.

Commercial software "Audio nurse - Video nurse" is frequently used to help parents and caregivers. This is a special device that can help adults watch their child ("Video nurse") and/or hear the baby's voice anywhere in the apartment ("Audio nurse"). Another system implemented in practice is «Why Cry Baby Analyzer HC-WHYCRY» [5]. It shows parents and caregivers what is happening with their baby.

A. Ronzhin et al. (Eds.): SPECOM 2014, LNAI 8773, pp. 284–291, 2014.

After an approximately 20 second analysis of the baby's crying power, frequency and crying intervals, the unit lights up the corresponding illustrated face diagram on the front. There are five categories: hungry, bored, annoyed, sleepy and stressed. A chart offers advice to help comfort and calm the baby based on the category. The system is designed to help parents. It should not be used as a medical device. These devices are more auxiliary than training.

Our data about the features of vocal-speech interaction in "mother-child" dyads with normally developing infants and infants having neurological disorders, proverbial orphans [6, 7, 8] – are the fund for constructing the model "Virtual mother" [9] intended for orphans and children with disabilities. The training computer program allows a child to stimulate vocalizations activity in the first 6 months of life; which results in quality complication of vocalizations in the second half-year: expanding the repertoire of sounds, appearance syllabic structures, providing a transition to the subsequent step of speech development - emergence of the first words. However, there is no special software to create adequate conditions for the development of sensory-motor, emotional and cognitive abilities of infants.

The purpose of this project was to create a model of multimedia sensory environment with interactive elements for infants and young children and develop of software to work with the model.

The model is designed to prevent and remove negative effects of sensory deprivation and to normalize communicative and psychophysiological state of infants under prolonged lack of contact with mother and limitations of social interactions.

The tasks of the study: 1) selection of stimuli of different modalities and creating a database of stimuli, differentiated by the degree of complexity; 2) software development framework; 3) testing the program to determine the effect caused by the presentation of different modality stimuli from the created database.

2   Methods

2.1   Stimuli Selection and Organization

A model of a multimedia sensory environment "INFANT.MAVS" including basic stimuli of different perceptual complexity and software to work with them is elaborated.

The base consists of two parts - simple stimuli (BSS) and complex stimuli (BCS) (fig. 1).

2.1.1 The Base of Simple Stimuli

The base of simple (1380 files, 1.47 Gb) stimuli contains directory video (915 files, 732.3 Mb), audio (401 files 533.4 Mb), tactile (64 files, 229.6 Mb) stimuli.

Section "Visual stimuli" contains two subsections video and graphics. The subsection "Graphics" includes black-white and color images. Catalog "black -white image" includes faces, face-like stimuli with all the elements (eyes, nose, mouth, hair), and face-like stimuli with three or two elements presented in different combinations.

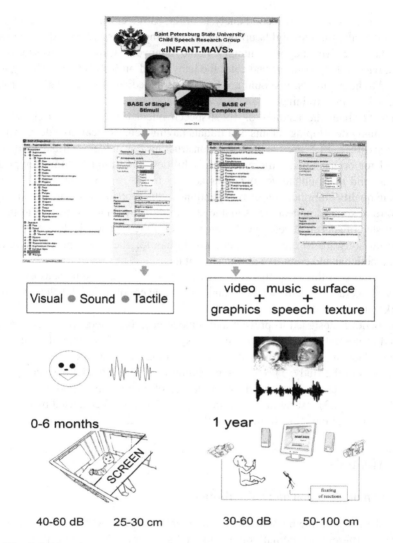

Fig. 1. Schematic model and conditions for its uses in testing infants and children

This subsection includes lines of different thickness and orientation (vertical, horizontal, inclined); lattices; patterns - simple and complex (consisting of a set of simple patterns); geometric figures - simple, two-dimensional and three-dimensional; images of animals and toys. In the "Color image" catalog includes photographs and drawings of people, animals, birds, toys, plants, geometric shapes, household items and everyday scenes. It presents cartoons and illustrations of fairy tales.

Section "Sound stimuli" contain subsections of music and speech. The music subsection includes songs and musical tunes, "mothers songs" and lullabies, nature sounds; physiological and life sounds; acoustic stimuli. Subsection 'speech' comprises 'comfortable' infant's vocalizations; samples of "mother's" and "father's" speech soothing, attracting infant's attention and stimulating vocal imitation; nursery rhymes and poems.

Section "Tactile stimuli" - includes photographs of surfaces and textures.

Stimulus is used to refer to letter writing, corresponding to the type of the stimulus, followed by division into subtypes according to the partition used in the listing of stimuli. Stimulus modality: a - audio, v - video, g - graphics; Audio stimuli: sp - speech: ms - maternal speech: (c - soothing, at - attracting attention, i - sounds to stimulate imitation, r - poetry).

2.1.2. The Base of Complex Stimuli

The base of the complex includes stimulus complexes of different modalities (177 complex stimuli, 15 - compounds) synthesized by the use of simple stimuli, and provide the basis for creating audio and /or video track.

Visuals can be represented as a sequence of videos, static images and animations of specified duration. Compound stimuli are synthesized on the basis of complex stimuli. Sound and speech stimuli are presented in the format - *.WAV, music - *.MP3, video - *.MPG. The organization of the complex stimuli base implies storage of ready-made combinations of stimuli and the ability to create new combinations of stimuli by the user.

The model contains a dynamic system of sensory stimulation, the corresponding change depending on the age of the child and competencies of an additional section for adult users. Section "Stimulus for infants from 0 to 6 months" includes subsections - faces, black-white images (audio-graphic and video), lullabies (picture change with appropriate musical accompaniment).

Section "Stimuli for 6-12 months old infants," contains all simple stimuli of different modalities in various combinations. Special section "Stimuli for user" includes the subsection "for adult users" assigned for relaxation, fatigue relief and create a positive attitude in the caregivers and parents.

3   Software

Software to work with stimuli was created. It allows users to do the following: 1) input and storage of stimulus material in the directories; 2) selection of the stimuli, depending on the problem (for the activation of the filter); 3) viewing and listening to the stimulus material; 4) creating a complex stimulus based on a compound of simple stimuli.

This software includes a component database operation and the database per se. Database stimulus material is divided into two large relatively independent parts (with the possibility of interacting with each other). One part of database is the database of simple stimuli. It serves for the orderly storage and retrieval of media data that are the basis for designing complex (composite) stimulus. The second part is the database of complex stimuli. They are a combination of media materials, that are formed by user requirement in a certain order and in a specify method. The management component of the program is developed in Microsoft Visual Basic v 6. 0 and is designed to run under the operating systems of MS Windows (9x, NT, ME, 2000, XP, Vista, 7). Outer shells are used: Microsoft Visual Basic Run-time (integrated in the installation package), video and audio codec installed on the user's operating system, allowing to work with the following compression standards: video - MPEG (2,4), AVC, H.265, for the sound - MP3 (MPEG-1 Layer I, II, III), AAC, WMA. The program interface is graphical.

The main window of the program allows the user to access the database of interest. On the left is the category tree, right at the top - the control panel with 1) the playback button, 2) button to go to the main menu, 3) button to save the changes and filter settings. Category tree provides efficient navigation all over the database. The software allows you to edit the category via the context menu, and by 'dragging'. Context menu is used to open a window for editing stimuli. The created model "INFANT.MAVS" is a software product that is ready to be installed on personal computers.

4   Result

The model "INFANT.MAVS" was tested on the 22 children (from 1.5 months to 7 years), growing at home and normally developing. Informed consent for the study was approved by the Ethics Committee of St. Petersburg State University (№ 02-36, 1.16.2014).

4.1   Testing Procedure

Children were presented the «INFANT. MAVS» stimuli in a computer screen. Infants of 0-6 months were lying in bed, the monitor was placed in front of the baby's face approximately at 25 cm; 6 - 12 months infants were sitting on the mother's lap in front of the monitor; 1-7 years old children were located in front of the monitor without an adult. The child's behavior during testing was recorded on two video cameras: one of them fixed the child's reactions and the stimuli presented on the monitor, the second one was focused only on the child. Adult subjects viewed the stimuli presented with multimedia. Prior to starting the test adults reported in the questionnaire on their state and mood and after watching - on the sensations they had.

Stimulus material presented to children was combined into three groups: stimuli with images, i.e. "parent speech" (stim-1); lullabies from different images (stim-2), tales and fairy tales (stim-3). The total duration of stimulus presentation for children aged 0-6 months was 1-2 min; for children 6-12 of months - 2-5 min; 1-3 years - 2-7 min; 4-7 years - 2-10 min. Adults were presented two tests of combined stimuli "Flowers and Herbs" (5min 17s) and "Mood" (3m 40s). Video analysis was performed using Pinnacle Video Studio. A statistical analysis was made in «SPSS v. 20» using the Mann-Whitney test.

4.2 Child's Reactions

The following types of the child's responses were selected: 1. Look at the monitor; 2. Look away from the monitor; 3. Smile; 4. Crying sounds of discomfort and/or the appropriate facial expressions; 5. Comfortable vocalizations; 6. Movement toward the screen; 7. Turning away from the screen (distracted); 8. Falling asleep or yawning.

The most common reactions in children of all age groups were the direction of gaze towards the monitor, movement toward the screen, comfortable vocalization and smile (fig. 2).

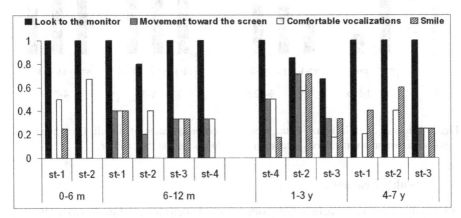

Fig. 2. Child's reactions to stimulus presentation. On a horizontal axis – stimulus; on a vertical axis – the frequency of children's reactions.

In the first six months olds infants, presentation of black and white images with faces of children and adults (no sound) caused a smile. Comfortable vocalizations were recorded in response to nursery rhymes combined with "mother's speech."

Second half-year infants voiced upon presentation of stimuli containing video with "mother's speech» and tales or stories with music. Movement to the side of the screen, waving or clapping hands, rising to their feet and bouncing is registered. Lullabies caused infants' decreased motor activity, closing their eyes and yawning. Upon presentation of audio sequences, children turned to the sound source, smiling and vocalize.

One to three years old children are demonstrating a greater range of diverse reactions. On music stimuli, all the children registered dance moves (3-5 min), color pictures of animals - pronouncing sounds, imitating animal sounds. Children from an older age group (4-7 years) imitated the sounds of animals; singing; listening to lullabies they yawned and closed their eyes.

Children above one year of age, for all the stimuli presented, looked at the monitor longer, than children of the first year of life. Significant differences were found in the time for the stimulus-1 fixation in children 1-3 years old ($p < 0.01$) and 4-7 years ($p < 0.01$) compared to 6-12 months old infants; between 0-6 months old infants and 6-12 months old infants ($p < 0.05$). On lullabies with different images (stimuli-2) differences between infants of the first and second half-year of life ($p < 0.05$), between the infants of the second half of life and 1-3 year old children (p <0.01) and children aged 4-7 years (p <0.01) were obtained too. Duration of the sight fixation on the monitor when viewing stimuli-3 was significantly longer in children aged 1-3 years and 4-7 years, than infants of the second half-year of life (p <0.01) (fig. 3).

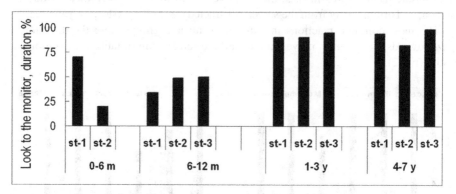

Fig. 3. Duration of child's gaze at the monitor upon presentation of stimuli. On a horizontal axis – stimulus; on a vertical axis – duration of of child's gaze at the monitor.

4.3   Adult's Reactions

Adult subjects were 84 people (73 women and 11 men) aged 19 to 84 years, divided into four groups: group 1: mean age 19.5 ± 0.5 years, (n = 22); group 2: age 29.9 ± 0.7 years (n = 25); group 3: age 30.1 ± 10 years (n = 30); group 4: age 75 ± 8.3 years, (n = 7). Adults of all groups show positive emotions evoked by the two tests; the third group of informers described more complex state, where alongside with positive emotions, negative ones appear. For the older age group, brief positive answers are most typical.

5   Discussion and Conclusion

Model test results showed that formed base of stimuli is consistent with the purposes for which it was created. In children, stimuli evoked responses in the form of focused attention, response vocalizations, smiles, simulation activity. It seems to be a very important opportunity to cause a variety of reactions in children not interacting with adults, but on the stimuli. That allows us to create not just a rich sensory environment for a child, but also to receive an adequate response to it. Early stimulation is a prerequisite for further normal cognitive development and social adaptation of children. For example, we know that a child's ability to mimic and vocal imitation is a prerequisite for the development of communication skills [10]. In accordance with these data, the model is supposed to be of use in research of early psychophysiological and emotional development of children in native family and in orphanage.

Important area supported by the model is associated with the original set of stimuli "For adult users" intended for parents and caregivers. Testing conducted on adult subjects showed that the stimuli presented caused positive feelings of rest, relaxation and the sense of beauty. We believe that the use of this part of the model will help to avoid or reduce the risk of professional 'burnout' among the personnel of nursery and medical institutions [11], and will be useful for mothers with unstable emotional condition [12], or depression.

Acknowledgements. This research is supported by the Russian Fund for Humanities (projects №11-06-12019в, № 13-06-0041a).

References

1. Karpov, A., Kipyatkova, I., Ronzhin, A.: Very Large Vacabulary ASR for Spoken Russian with Syntactic and Morpheme Analysis. In: Proc. 12th International Conference INTERSPEECH -2011, ISCA Association, Florence, Italy, pp. 3161–3164 (2011)
2. Ronzhin, A., Karpov, A.: Russian Voice Interface. Pattern Recognition and Image Analysis 17(2), 321–336 (2007)
3. Ronzhin, A., Budkov, V.: Speaker turn detection based on multimodal situation analysis. In: Železný, M., Habernal, I., Ronzhin, A. (eds.) SPECOM 2013. LNCS, vol. 8113, pp. 302–309. Springer, Heidelberg (2013)
4. Ogorodnikova, E.A., Koroleva, I.V., Lublinskaja, V.V., Pak, S.P., Stoljarova, E.I., Baljakova, A.A.: Computer in rehabilitation of patients with cochlear implants. In: Proc. of 13th International Conf., SPECOM 2009. SPb: SPIIRAS, pp. 483–486 (2009)
5. Why Cry Baby Analyzer HC-WHYCRY http://www.harriscomm.com/catalog/product_info.php?products_id=18239 (2014)
6. Lyakso, E., Frolova, O.: Russian Vowels System Acoustic Features Development in Ontogenesis. In: Proc. 8th International Conference INTERSPEECH -2007, ISCA Association Interspeech 2007, Antwerp, Belgium, pp. 2309–2313 (2007)
7. Lyakso, E., Novikova, I., Petrikova, N., Chelibanova, O.: Development of language acquisition during the child's first year. In: Proceeding IX Session of the Russian Acoustic Society "Speech Technology Today" M.: GEOS, pp.100-103 (1999)
8. Lyakso, E.: Development of vocal imitation during the first year of infants' age. Thesis for the joint conference of the X international congress for the study of child language and the symposium on research in child language disorders. Madison, US., pp.138–139 (2003)
9. Lyakso, E., Kurazhova, A., Gajkova, J., Frolova, O., Ostrouhov, A., Soloviev, A.: B.E., Grigoriev, A., Losik, G., Erchak, H.: Model "Virtual Mother" for Orphans' Speech Development. In: Proc. of 13th International Conference «Speech and Computer» SPECOM - 2009. SPb. Russia. pp. 295–299 (2009)
10. Poon, K.K., Watson, L.R., Baranek, G.T., Poe, M.D.: To what extent do joint attention, imitation, and object play behaviors in infancy predict later communication and intellectual functioning in ASD? Journal of Autism and Developmental Disorders 42(6), 1064–1074 (2012)
11. Kenworthy, J., Fay, S., Frame, M., Petree, R.: A meta-analytic review of the relationship between emotional dissonance and emotional exhaustion. J. of Applied Social Psychology 44(2), 94–105 (2014)
12. Azak, S., Raeder, S.: Trajectories of parenting behavior and maternal depression. Infant Behavior and Development 36, 391–402 (2013)

Influence of Agent Behaviour
on Human-Virtual Agent Body Interaction

Igor Stanković[1], Branislav Popović[2], and Florian Focone[3]

[1] UEB, Lab-STICC, ENIB, France
stankovic@enib.fr
[2] Faculty of Technical Sciences, University of Novi Sad, Serbia
bpopovic@uns.ac.rs
[3] LIMSI-CNRS, Orsay, France
focone@limsi.fr

Abstract. This paper describes influence of different types of agent's behaviour in a social human-virtual agent gesture interaction experiment. The interaction was described to participants as a game with the goal of imitating the agent's slow upper-body movements, and where new subtle movements can be proposed by both the participant and the agent. As we are interested only in body movements, simple virtual agent was built and displayed at a local exhibition, and we asked visitors one by one to play the game. During the interaction, the agent's behaviour varied from subject to subject, and we observed their responses. Interesting observations have been drawn from the experiment and it seems that only a small variation in the agent's behaviour and synchronization can lead to a significantly different feel of the game in the participants.

Keywords: Human-virtual agent interaction, gestural body interaction, behaviour experiment.

1   Introduction

Human-Computer Interaction (HCI) combines efforts from different areas of study, such as computer science, cognitive science, psychology, sociology, medicine, etc. Most HCI applications choose verbal language as the principal communication tool, as it is one of the most natural forms of human-human interaction. However, in realistic settings, average word recognition error rates are 20-30% (they go up to 50% for non-native speakers [1]). In an uncontrolled environment, speech recognition accuracy may degrade dramatically to an extent that the system becomes unusable [2]. Forcing users to follow a predefined grammar or interaction scenario is too restrictive and therefore impractical. Gesture is another important modality of HCI. Gestures can be easily recognized and included in more natural human-computer interfaces [3]. Different approaches have already been developed in order to classify, characterise and represent gestures [4].

One of recently most investigated sub-fields of HCI is human-virtual agent interaction. Several studies [5] have demonstrated that humans prefer to interact with the virtual agent in the same way as they do with the real humans.

A. Ronzhin et al. (Eds.): SPECOM 2014, LNAI 8773, pp. 292–299, 2014.

In other words, humans expect virtual agent to behave "naturally", and the goal of researchers is to better define this term. For example, a study by [6] suggested that a combination of facial and postural expressions helps the user to derive a better perception of the agent's emotional state, and therefore to form a better level of commitment. Emotional feedback, expressed through facial expressions, is one of the cues that helps agents build a better rapport with humans. However, back-channels are considered the most accessible example of the real-time responsiveness that underpins many successful interpersonal interactions. For instance, expressive feedback, such as a nod or an "a-ha" (which literally means "I am listening, tell me more"), given at the right moment, heightens the degree of convergence. One of these back-channels is synchrony, considered as an important parameter in the feeling of interaction [7], and investigated in this work. In this paper, we examine the usage of upper-body movements in HCI and the influence of the agent's behaviour to participant's responses.

We propose a simple gestural upper-body interaction setup that allows variations in the synchrony between a human and a virtual agent. Such study gives us an insight on how important the interaction synchrony is and how it influences participants' behaviour and emotional state when interacting with a virtual agent. Additionally, this pilot experiment can help us conclude what principles are necessary to implement into virtual characters, and it could establish recommendations for the future evaluation of "feeling" of interaction.

Section 2 presents the setup/game, and the technical description of the virtual agent is given in Section 3. The slight variations in the agent's behaviour/responses are explained in Section 4, while Section 5 offers our observations and a conclusion of the experiment. Some future work is presented in the final Section 6.

2   Game

As the focus of the experiment is more on the feeling of the game and not the game itself, we ensured that it is easy to comprehend and simple to play. Participants were explained not to employ legs, hence interacting with the upper-body. As an introduction to the game, they were been told that the goal is that the user and the agent imitate each other's movements, but also propose some new, slow, and subtle movements from time to time. Each participant was alone in the room during the experiment, allowing them to express freely and interact as long as they want.

This kind of body interaction exercise is often utilized by theatre groups actors to build a filling of connection with an other actor. The exercise suits our needs perfectly, as we wanted to examine how small changes in the agent's behaviour, as one of the "actors" in the game, will influence the users' responses.

3   Agent

For this game we utilized the INGREDIBLE project's framework [8]. It is composed of five modules, each with a specific task. At the start of the framework is a motion capture system (Kinect) that captures users' skeleton. Because noise can occur in the this system, received skeletons are slightly filtered using a simple average filter, and sent forward to the virtual agent.

In several studies, authors concluded that the avatar's appearance does not affect the interaction. In [9] they compute arousal to see impact of virtual character proximity on participant. The avatar, represented by a cylinder or a woman-like character, approaches the participants alone or in a group of four avatars. The results show that both proximity and number of avatar approaching are positively correlated with arousal increasing, but no effects of the type of avatar (cylinder or woman) was found. On our case, due to the artistic nature of the exhibition, one of Joan Miró's colourful paintings was utilized as a background, and a minimalistic devil-like 3D virtual avatar (see Fig. 1), similar to the character in the original painting, was employed to represent our agent for the purpose of the game. Participants were asked to stay at a specific point in front of the motion capture system and they were been explained the game. When the introduction to the game is done and the user is detected by the motion capture system, the character in the painting disappears, the 3D agent is displayed instead, and the interaction starts.

Fig. 1. Scene installation at the exhibition: Once the user is detected by the system, the avatar "jumps out" of the image, leaving the white space behind, and the interaction begins

The participants could stop the game at any point, and the length of interactions provided us with additional information of the users' feel of the game - the more engaging the game was, the longer they played. Also, we observed other behaviour cues (e.g. talking, emotion expression, facial grimaces) in the participants during the interaction.

4   Agent's Behaviour

The same game rules were given to all, but the agent's behaviour differed between the participants, and was randomly chosen by our program from one of the six predefined behaviours (see Table 1).

Table 1. Properties of the scenarios used in the experiment

	ACTION	DELAY
Behaviour 1	imitate	0.0 s
Behaviour 2	imitate	0.5 s
Behaviour 3	imitate	2.0 s
Behaviour 4	imitate	variable
Behaviour 5	imitate + propose	0.5 s
Behaviour 6	propose	-

As shown in [10], there is a correlation between movement synchrony and the consideration of something as entity (entitativity). In their experiment, stick figures waving in synchrony were found to be rated higher on entitativity than stick figures waving in different rhythms. Our study was partially driven by this observation, and in the first four types of agent's behaviour/responses in our experiment, the agent is strictly copying user's movements through the Kinect system. However, to test different interaction experiences, the agent has a different delay over user. For example, in Behaviour 3 the agent copies user with a two-second delay; similarly, Behaviour 1 does not have any delay and Behaviour 2 has a half-a-second delay, which during tests prior to the experiment seemed as a human-like response time. The idea is that even if the agent is strictly copying the user's movements, certain delay could affect the interaction and the user's responses. To test this idea even further, in Behaviour 4 we employed a variable delay - all through the interaction the delay will automatically change by a small random value that may cause the agent to respond differently at different times during the interaction - at one point it could seem very "sleepy" and then more "focused" on the interaction. This could change the users' feeling of the agent and the game, and the idea was put to test.

In Behaviour 5 the agent is both imitating and proposing. It is named "Wizard of Oz", as in this case the agent can be additionally controlled by a keyboard. The base of the agent's movements is still strict copying of the user (with a half-a-second delay), but by utilizing eight keyboard keys (see Table 2) we were able to slightly manipulate the agent's hands. These changes were very subtle, but strong enough for participants to fill them and interpret them as if the agent is proposing a new movement/direction. The hands were simply controlled by adding or subtracting a small value to the X- and/or Y-axes (depending on a pushed key) to skeletons received by the motion capture system. For this purpose, a member of our team was placed behind the screen to control the agent.

Table 2. Keys used to control the agent's hands during Behaviour 5

movements	**UP**	**DOWN**	**LEFT**	**RIGHT**
left hand	w	s	a	d
right hand	i	k	j	l

In the final Behaviour 6 the agent was controlled from a pre-recorded file, thus "proposing" new movements all the time without copying or taking into account any of the user's movements. It was interesting to see whether participants will, for instance, be easily bored due to the lack of any real interaction and response from the agent. As presented in our observations (see Section 5), analysing only the interaction lengths during Behaviour 5 and 6 answers this question.

5   Observation and Conclusion

As expected, Behaviour 6, in which the agent was controlled by a pre-recorded motion capture file and did not take into account any movements of the user, very quickly led to boredom in the participants. Just after a few seconds participants were able to notice that they do not have any influence on the agent's behaviour. This conclusion was usually followed with expressed disappointment through facial expressions, gesture movements (rapid waving as an attempt to influence the agent, attract his attention, and/or disturb his movement/behaviour patterns), and by talking out loud and concluding the obvious - the agent is not following.

Behaviour 5 was much more satisfactory for the participants - they expressed happiness when they realized the agent is imitating their body movements. Additionally, when Wizard of Oz proposed new agent's movements through keyboard, the users usually expressed facial expressions of happiness and laughed. This type of agent's behaviour is very human-like and it seems to please people the most, and the interaction lasted longer than under the other five behaviour scenarios.

Finally, even though Behaviour 1-4 are very similar, some interesting differences were noticed. Surprisingly, no significant difference in game experience is noticed between employing a half a second (Behaviour 2), two seconds (Behaviour 3), and variable delay (Behaviour 4), except that one might seemed more "lazy" than the other. But there is a big difference in feeling of the game in absence and presence of a delay (Behaviour 1 versus Behaviour 2-4). All these four types or the agent's response were strict mirroring/copying of the users' movements, but it seems that even a small delay added to that mirroring (no matter how long the delay is) creates a more natural feeling of the agent's actions. This proves our assumption that synchrony alone, disregarding the other cues, is an important part of any interaction. For example, with no delay added, the users very quickly concluded that their movements are just being copied. Those interactions were again followed by disappointment and were usually very short. On the other hand, when employing a delay, the agent was more natural and human-like, according to the users.

It is surprising that a trivial technical difference–delay–made such a strong sensation in the participants. This might mean that humans do not examine gestures and body movements in as complex way as we previously thought. Also, it is more appealing if the virtual agent is acting more human-like. Copying the movements with a normal "brain-processing" time and proposing new ones from time to time is what we expect from other human beings, and as soon as the users got these kind of responses from the agent, the "feeling" of the interaction increases (usually followed by a big smile and laughter), which led to a longer interaction. However, further tests need to be performed to conclude what characterizes human-like gesture and body movements, what kind of behaviour triggers different emotions in users, what else users expect from an agent, etc. Also, as concluded in [11], it is important to compute some subjective parameters (i.e. likeability and embarrassment) when studying human-agent interaction.

In this pilot behaviour experiment we addressed body interaction, which represents only a small portion in the field of human-virtual agent interaction, but some interesting observations were drawn on how people expect virtual agents to move. If synchrony proved as such an important part of body communication, we assume that it has the similar effects on other cues of interaction. As a part of our future research, we plan to develop more user-aware agent with conversational abilities. The importance of speech in humans was clear even in this simple experiment - even though the participant were told to employ only body for interaction, they could not resist the urge to express their feeling through speech (i.e. "Yes, it's following me!", "It's not working"), especially when the interaction was under a strong emotional state such as satisfaction or disappointment.

6   Future Work

In the current pilot version of our system, in order to test human reactions to the agent, the agent's behaviour was randomly chosen from one of the six pre-defined behaviours, either by strictly copying user's movements, or by controlling the agent using a pre-recorded motion capture file or partially from a keyboard. Our next step would be to develop a more user-aware and adaptive conversational agent, capable to dynamically adapt its behaviour according to the user and his emotional state. This requires the integration and synergy between the present modules, and the modules for emotion, speech and user recognition, as well as the dialogue management module.

Emotion recognition cues could be obtained from classification of changes of the user's behaviour from prosodic and linguistic cues [12], cues from facial expressions [13], body movements, etc. Our current research on acoustic information-based emotion recognition was supported by the GEES corpus of emotional and attitude-expressive speech [14]. The corpus contains recordings of acted speech-based emotional expressions, spoken by six drama students, divided into 32 isolated words, 30 short semantically neutral sentences, 30 long semantically neutral sentences and one passage with 79 words for a single emotional state. The utterances are labelled by four primary emotional states, i.e., happiness, anger, fear, and sadness, and two attitude expressions, i.e. commands and threats, using neutral speech as referent. This emotion recognition system could be integrated into the game to make it broader.

Low-level prosodic and spectral features, high-level features and language information contained within the acoustic, linguistic and language models, could be efficiently combined and used for speech, speaker and emotion recognition, e.g. [15] and [16]. Speech recognition systems are heavily language dependent. Speech corpora have to be appropriately produced and annotated, in terms of vocabulary size, number of speakers and linguistic content [17]. Context-awareness is one of the fundamental requirements for advanced conversational agents. In [18], the authors propose the strategy developed in order to deal with miscommunication in human-machine interaction (i.e. the recovery strategy) and detect miscommunication (i.e. detecting changes of the user's behaviour).

Currently, the speech recognition module and the dialogue management module are fully implemented and integrated with the natural language processing modules. Emotion recognition and speaker recognition modules are implemented at a prototype level.

Acknowledgements. This research work has been funded by the ANR IN-GREDIBLE project: ANR-12-CORD-001 (http://www.ingredible.fr), and supported by the Ministry of Education, Science and Technological Development of the Republic of Serbia, as a part of the research project TR 32035.

References

1. Bohus, D., Rudnicky, A.: Sorry, I Didn't Catch That! An Investigation of Non-Understanding Errors and Recovery Strategies. In: Recent Trends in Discourse and Dialogue, 39th edn., pp. 123–154. Springer, Heidelberg (2008)
2. Lee, C.H.: Fundamentals and Technical Challenges in Automatic Speech Recognition. In: SPECOM 2007, Moscow, Russia, pp. 25–44 (2007)
3. Xiao, Y., Yuan, J., Thalmann, D.: Human-virtual Human Interaction by Upper-body Gesture Understanding. In: 19th ACM Symposium on Virtual Reality Software and Technology, New York, USA, pp. 133–142 (2013)
4. Ruffieux, S., Lalanne, D., Khaled, O.A., Mugellini, E.: Developer-Oriented Visual Model for Upper-Body Gesture Characterization. In: Kurosu, M. (ed.) HCII/HCI 2013, Part V. LNCS, vol. 8008, pp. 186–195. Springer, Heidelberg (2013)
5. Gratch, J., Wang, N., Okhmatovskaia, A., Lamothe, F., Morales, M., van der Werf, R.J., Morency, L.-P.: Can Virtual Humans Be More Engaging Than Real Ones? In: Jacko, J.A. (ed.) HCI 2007. LNCS, vol. 4552, pp. 286–297. Springer, Heidelberg (2007)

6. Clavel, C., Plessier, J., Martin, J.-C., Ach, L., Morel, B.: Combining facial and postural expressions of emotions in a virtual character. In: Ruttkay, Z., Kipp, M., Nijholt, A., Vilhjálmsson, H.H. (eds.) IVA 2009. LNCS, vol. 5773, pp. 287–300. Springer, Heidelberg (2009)
7. Poppe, R., Truong, K.P., Heylen, D.: Backchannels: Quantity, type and timing matters. In: Vilhjálmsson, H.H., Kopp, S., Marsella, S., Thórisson, K.R. (eds.) IVA 2011. LNCS, vol. 6895, pp. 228–239. Springer, Heidelberg (2011)
8. Stanković, I., De Loor, P., Demulier, V., Nédélec, A., Bevacqua, E.: The INGRED-IBLE database: A First Step Toward Dynamic Coupling in Human-Virtual Agent Body Interaction. In: Aylett, R., et al. (eds.) IVA 2013. LNCS, vol. 8108, pp. 430–431. Springer, Heidelberg (2013)
9. Llobera, J., Spanlang, B., Ruffini, G., Slater, M.: Proxemics with Multiple Dynamic Characters in an Immersive Virtual Environment. ACM Trans. Appl. Perce. 8(1), 3:1–3:12 (2010)
10. Lakens, D.: Movement Synchrony and Perceived Entitativity. J. Exp. Soc. Psychol. 46(5), 701–708 (2010)
11. Bailenson, J.N., Swinth, K., Hoyt, C., Persky, S., Dimov, A., Blascovich, J.: The Independent and Interactive Effects of Embodied-Agent Appearance and Behavior on Self-Report, Cognitive, and Behavioral Markers of Copresence in Immersive Virtual Environments. Presence-Teleop. Virt. 14(4), 379–393 (2005)
12. Popović, B., Stanković, I., Ostrogonac, S.: Temporal Discrete Cosine Transform for Speech Emotion Recognition. In: 4th IEEE International Conference on Cognitive Infocommunications (CogInfoCom 2013), Budapest, Hungary, pp. 87–90 (2013)
13. Popović, B., Ostrogonac, S., Delić, V., Janev, M., Stanković, I.: Deep Architectures for Automatic Emotion Recognition Based on Lip Shape. In: 12th International Scientific Professional Symposium INFOTEH-JAHORINA, Jahorina, Bosnia and Herzegovina, pp. 939–943 (2013)
14. Jovičić, S.T., Kašić, Z.: Serbian Emotional Speech Database: Design, Processing and Evaluation. In: 9th International Conference on Speech and Computer (SPECOM 2004),, pp. 77–81 (2004)
15. Schuller, B., Rigoll, G., Lang, M.: Speech Emotion Recognition Combining Acoustic Features and Linguistic Information in a Hybrid Support Vector Machine-Belief Network Architecture. In: Acoustics, Speech, and Signal Processing (ICASSP 2004), pp. I-577–I-580 (2004)
16. Kinnunen, T., Haizhou, L.: An Overview of Text-Independent Speaker Recognition: From Features to Supervectors. Speech Commun. 52(1), 12–40 (2010)
17. Delić, V., Sečujski, M., Jakovljević, N., Pekar, D., Mišković, D., Popović, B., Ostrogonac, S., Bojanić, M., Knežević, D.: Speech and language resources within speech recognition and synthesis systems for serbian and kindred south slavic languages. In: Železný, M., Habernal, I., Ronzhin, A. (eds.) SPECOM 2013. LNCS, vol. 8113, pp. 319–326. Springer, Heidelberg (2013)
18. Gnjatović, M., Bojanić, M., Popović, B., Delić, V.: An Adaptive Recovery Strategy for Handling Miscommunication in Human-Machine Interaction. In: 18th Telecommunications Forum (TELFOR 2004), Belgrade, Serbia, pp.1121–1124 (2010)

Modeling of Process Dynamics by Sequence of Homogenous Semantic Networks on the Base of Text Corpus Sequence Analysis

Alexander A. Kharlamov[1], Tatyana V. Yermolenko[2], and Andrey A. Zhonin[3]

[1] Institute of Higher Nervous Activity and Neurophysiology, Russian Academy of Science,
Moscow, Russia
kharlamov@analyst.ru
[2] Institute of Artificial Intelligence Problems, Donetsk, Ukraine
etv@iai.dn.ua
[3] Microsystems, Ltd, Moscow, Russia
neurofish@yandex.ru

Abstract. The paper describes an approach to modeling of process dynamics based on the technology of automatic semantic analysis of textual information. During processing of text an associative network is generated, the key concepts of which, including lexical markers of the analyzed process, are ranked by their semantic weight. Defined by the marker status on the "good-bad" scale, this weight provides the marker value for characterization of the process state. It is changes in the normalized characteristic of the process combined for all markers from time sample to time sample that characterize the process trend.

Keywords: automatic text processing, associative (homogeneous semantic) network, modeling of process dynamics, lexical markers.

1 Introduction

A huge amount of personal data, including textual information shared by users is monitored not only by security services, friends or casual acquaintances; potential or existing clients are surveilled by banks and microfinance institutions that seek to evaluate borrowers' creditworthiness. The purpose of the surveillance is to search and analyze messages on a particular subject [1].

In addition to social networks, information for analysis can be obtained from bloggers, as the number of their followers is comparable to the media audience, and finally, from the media themselves.

With tools for automatic detection of emotional and evaluative text characteristics, one can study samples of bloggers' texts in significant amount. Knowing the subject or other characteristics of the texts studied, one can determine which blogosphere segments are associated with expression of positive or negative estimations and emotions. Analyzing emotional characteristics of a sequence (yesterday, today and tomorrow) of text samples from social networks, it is possible to reveal the dynamics of the social development process (improvement, deterioration, stability).

Detection of author's emotive lexis and emotional evaluation of objects in a document is the primary object of the text polarity analysis, or Sentiment analysis, which is

A. Ronzhin et al. (Eds.): SPECOM 2014, LNAI 8773, pp. 300–307, 2014.

a developing computer-related field of linguistics. Emotional evaluation expressed in a text is also called polarity, or sentiment of a text [2].

Most methods of emotional estimation existing today are based on the use of the dictionary of emotive words [3,4]. In dictionary methods every word has some weight that characterizes its emotional colouring.

Statistical methods of identification of such terms include methods of text analysis implemented on the basis of neural network algorithms. One of the proven methods of statistical analysis of the semantics of a whole text is a method based on formalism of artificial neural networks with neural-like elements with temporal summation of signals used to generate the statistical portrait of the text [5,6]. This approach provides high speed of analysis and does not depend on language or subject area.

During the analysis of the text an index is automatically extracted as a network of basic concepts and their relations with weight characteristics. The semantic portrait of the text includes not just a list of keywords, but a network of concepts - many interconnected key words or collocations. Each concept in the network has some weight, which reflects the importance of this concept in the text. The relation between the concepts also has some weight. Using these relations allows one to weigh the text concepts more accurately. Next, lexical markers are analyzed that are included in the semantic portrait of the text.

A text as a complete idea (sentiment) of an author describes a situation. Therefore, the correct semantic analysis of the text reveals key concepts of the text and their ranks (semantic weights) in this text. If there are some texts that describe the dynamics of a situation (one text describes yesterday, the second one – today, and the third one – tomorrow), then the analysis of each of these texts reveals ranks of key concepts and states of the situation for the yesterday-today-tomorrow range. Thus, the associative (homogeneous semantic) network obtained by analyzing the text that describes the state of the situation at the current time, includes key concepts in the text and their interrelations and their (key concepts and their relations') weight characteristics (ranks) supplemented by the same networks obtained in previous and subsequent time points and presents the model of the situation dynamics. Combining of similar concepts in such a sequence of networks (along the time axis) with horizontal relations supplemented by the ranks of these concepts at the appropriate time points, shows the dynamics of their involvement in the situation. In this the closest assiociants of the key concepts (concepts that are separated from analyzed concept by one relation) allow to interpret the dynamics of key concepts (influence of the concomitants).

The sequence of such semantic networks describing text samples sequential in time with their (networks, and therefore texts) combined numerical characteristics, is a model of the process in its dynamics. At the same time in each network only that part is filtered, which contains lexical and psycholinguistic markers characterizing the simulated process (and their closest associants). The combined numerical values of the markers' weights defined by their status on the "good-bad" scale characterize the current state of the process. And in the networks' sequence the dynamics of semantic rankings for relevant concepts can be observed, which simulates the dynamics of the social process: improvement, deterioration, stability.

2   Modeling the Process Dynamics Based on Analysis of the Text Samples Sequence

The proposed quantitative analysis of the processes' dynamics rests upon two basic approaches.

To analyze the process, the automatic formation of the text semantic network (text corpus) is used [6], containing information on the process. In this case lexical and psycholinguistic markers derived from the text apart from other key concepts and characterizing the process, are automatically ranked according to their importance in the text. The combined rank of these markers determines the process state (good-neutral-bad).

The sequential time samples of the text corpora are studied, with their semantic networks (and the markers' ranking), which allows to determine the process dynamics as a change of the combined rank of the markers characterizing the process, from sample to sample.

Consider these two approaches in more detail.

2.1   Formation of an Associative (Homogeneous Semantic) Network of a Text

The analysis of the words statistics and their relations in a text allows to reconstruct the internal structure of this text and thus form a description of the semantics of the text subject area.

The homogenous semantic (associative) network is formed from words' stems or their word collocations present in the text, as well as on the basis of information about their joint (pairwise) occurrence in semantic fragments of the text (for example in sentences).

In this case the morphologic processing is performed using a previously prepared morphological dictionary (the dictionary of inflectional morphemes) $\{B_i\}_1$. As a result, a dictionary $\{B_i\}_2$ is formed – the dictionary of stems (and collocations).

At the stage of formation of the frequency portrait of the text, p_i frequencies are identified for occurrences of B_{i2} stems of the key concepts and their combinations, as well as p_{ij} frequencies for their pairwise occurrence in the sentences of the text. And thus the dictionary $\{B_i\}_3$ of word pairs is formed.

Further, the occurrence frequencies are renormalized in semantic weights. As a result of the iterative renormalization procedure the greatest weights are assigned to the key concepts associated with the greatest number of other concepts with great weight, that is, those concepts which are the core of the semantic structure of the text.

$$w_i(t+1) = \left(\sum_{\substack{i \\ i \neq j}} w_i(t)w_{ij} \right) \sigma(\bar{E}), \tag{1}$$

where $w_i(0) = p_i$; $w_{ij} = p_{ij}/p_j$ and $\sigma(\bar{E}) = 1/(1 + e^{-k\bar{E}})$ – the function of normalization of energies of all the vertices of the network $\bar{E}$ to the average value, wherein

p_i is the frequency of the ith word occurrence in the text, p_{ij} is the frequency of co-occurrence of the ith and jth words in the text fragments.

The result is a so-called associative (homogeneous semantic) network N as a set of asymmetric pairs of concepts $< c_i c_j >$ where c_i and c_j are key concepts related to each other through the associativity relation (co-occurrence in a text fragment):

$$N \cong \{< c_i c_j >\}. \tag{2}$$

Otherwise, the semantic network can be represented as a set of stars $< c_i < c_j >>$ where $< c_j >$ is a set of closest associants of the key concept c_i:

$$N \cong \{z_i\} = \{< c_i < c_j >>\}. \tag{3}$$

2.2   Determination of the Process Dynamics

The resulting network is a semantic (structural) portrait of a text (text corpora). If the text or the texts corpora describe some structure (scientific development, subject area, sociological situation), then the semantic network thus formed is a semantic slice of this structure at the time of writing of the text.

The semantic network built on a text written later and describing the same structure may be different from the first one, since it represents the text relevant to the state of the process described at a later time point than the previous one. The network may contain the same key concepts but may not contain some of them that were "withdrawn" from the structure described, and may include other concepts that appeared during this time in the structure described in this text. And, most importantly, weight characteristics of the concepts contained in the network may differ from weight characteristics in the first network.

If we take texts of the next time sample, construct another network and combine it with the previous two ones, then we will have a picture of the structure (scientific development, subject area, sociological situation) unfolding in time. And this can be done any number of times. Such a model of the process dynamics is illustrative and convenient to study (the network is presented as a static semantic slice of the analyzed structure, an object convenient for time navigation by virtue of associative links between the key concepts), and has numerical characteristics, which makes it convenient for the analytical study of the processes and, consequently, convenient for automatic analysis.

The sequence of similarly-named stars belonging to different semantic time samples – semantic networks, is an elementary processes π:

$$\pi = z_i(t_1) \Rightarrow z_i(t_2) \Rightarrow z_i(t_3) \Rightarrow ..., \tag{4}$$

where $z_i(t_k)$ is a specific star at time t_k. The weight of the key concept at the current time that determines its rank in the semantic network is $w_i(t_k)$.

The associant events c_j of the main concept of the star ci are its semantic characteristics, and allow to interpret its content at each step of the process.

To study a specific process in its dynamics, we select key concepts of the semantic network, which lexical and psycholinguistic markers of this process, and observe the development dynamics for quantitative characteristics of these concepts. Like other key concepts, these concepts may appear at some times, appear sequentially at different time samples and, finally, disappear. Their numerical characteristics may also vary from time sample to time sample.

We eliminate all the key concepts of all networks other than those mentioned markers. In this case the remainder of the text dynamics model becomes a model of the dynamics of the studied process. Moreover, the numerical characteristics of the remaining key concepts of the network characterize the state of the process at the current time, and their change from time sample to time sample characterize the dynamics of the process in time.

3   Information Model of Estimation of the Process Trend Based on the Homogenous Semantic (Associative) Network

The information model includes the following:

- a module for searching relevant input information (texts from public (open) sources);
- a module for extraction of the common semantic network from the prepared texts (a module of formation of the semantic network of the text corpus);
- a module for estimation of the analyzed process trend.

The search module for texts relevant for processing runs over specified text sources meeting the set requirements. In particular, a region is specified, for which the study is supposed, as well as a time period $\Delta T_l = (t_{lend} t_{lbeg}), l = 1..L$, which is taken as the 1st time sample (one of Ls), and lexical and psycholinguistic markers M, describing the subject of the process studied. The later are set by an expert, characterize strictly their own process, and finally determine the quality of the analysis. On the other hand the information model is not dependent on the subject area. It represents anything.

The search of texts for each marker $M_k, k = 1..K$ is performed separately by specified search parameter (place and time). The obtained texts are processed separately with formation of a semantic network N for each text solely for the purpose of ranking them in the corpus of texts in terms of the relevance of the search results by this very marker. To do this, in each text the semantic weight $r_i = w_i$ is calculated for the specified marker. It defines the relevance of the text to this marker.

Next, for each marker texts are selected whose rank for that marker is above a given threshold $r_j \geq h_{selection}$. These texts, with an aggregate of all the markers, constitute the text corpus to be used for processing in the next step.

The module of formation of the semantic network N for the text corpus includes several procedures. The initial texts undergo preprocessing and the procedure of the frequency analysis provides the frequency portrait of the text in the form of the primary associative network. Both vertices of the network and their relationships have numerical characteristics – the frequency (p_i for the vertices and p_{ij} for their relationships) of occurrence in the analyzed text.

The renormalization procedure iteratively recalculates the frequency characteristics of the network vertices (the key concepts of the text) in semantic weights w_i and w_{ij}.

In this case, the lexical and psycholinguistic markers of the analyzed process M_k selected by the expert filter the semantic network $N = \{< c_i < c_j >>\}$. All its vertices are removed except the concept-markers c_i, as well as the closest assiociants of the markers, the vertices of the semantic network (the concepts) that are separated from the concept-markers by one step $< c_j >$ that are their semantic features.

Each marker in each time sample has its semantic weight $w_i = 0..100$ obtained from the previous stage, which becomes a rank of this marker M_i for this time sample l.

The module of dynamics detection determines the numerical characteristics of the markers by their summation for a particular time sample of texts, and reveals the dynamics of changes in the generalized characteristics of the process from time sample to time sample.

For all markers the value P_i is calculated – the product of the marker status (on the "good-bad" scale), for example, $S_i \in (-2, -1, 0, 1, 2)$ and its rank:

$$\Pi_i = S_i * r_i \tag{5}$$

The products P_i for each marker M_i are summarized over all the markers:

$$\Pi = \sum \Pi_i \tag{6}$$

Thus, the total value of $P(l)$ of the time sample l is obtained for the process being evaluated.

4   Example of Information Modeling of the Process Trend Estimation

As an example, a model is presented that evaluates the process trend based on texts with the subject of internal policy of the Russian Federation from the news portal newsru.com in the light of relationships between the governments and the society. The model includes the following:

- texts from public sources related to the same topic and various time samples;
- semantic networks built for text corpora for each sample;
- estimation of social tension based on the features of lexical and psycholinguistic markers.

The objective of process estimation modeling is building of a model for estimation of social tension based on the example of the abovementioned texts on the subject of internal policy of the Russian Federation.

The list of markers selected by the expert includes: "conflict" (status -2), "consensus" (status 1), "consent" (status 2), "conflict-free" (status 2). The status reflects the degree of relationship between the government and the society; the higher the status - the greater the consent. The rank reflects the contribution of each marker's weight in the final integral estimation of the social tension process.

The thematic terms of the process are "government", "society".

The time samples are: September and October 2013.

Selected texts: 22 news texts for September 2013 and 17 news texts for October 2013. Not all texts have all the selected markers.

Next, all the texts for each sample are combined into a single text and processed by the automatic analysis module. The processing provides a final semantic network containing markers, for which their semantic weights (ranks) were calculated (Table 1).

Finally, numerical characteristics of the process are identified by summing-up and weighting of all the markers of the specific time sample, and by revealing the dynamics of changes in the generalized characteristics of the process from sample to sample.

Table 1. Process trend estimation

Marker	Status	Rank 09.2013	Contribution 09.2013	Rank 10.2013	Contribution 10.2013
conflict	-2	65	-130	79	-158
consensus	1	72	72	98	98
consent	2	54	108	93	186
conflict-free	2	83	166	52	104
Total:			216		230

The total values are integral estimations of the social tension process on the given subject for the specified time sample. However it is not feasible to consider integral estimates in isolation from the dynamics of their change, since the sum of statuses for markers under consideration is not in balance and almost certainly has a deviation either way, which results in a random deviation of the integral estimation. The composition of the markers is the same for various time samples, and therefore the difference of the integral estimates between samples is not subject to this effect – random components of the contribution are mutually eliminated.

The standard (RMS) deviation of the integral estimation calculated by the bootstrap method (formation of a random subsample) is 8.7. The estimation of the dynamics made on this sample with the given distribution, and with this standard deviation is credible.

The difference of integral estimates is an estimation of the social tension process. The indicator of the model quality is a stable estimation regarding adding or removing markers similar to markers of this type. This means that models with a larger number of markers being evaluated are preferred, and more texts of the same subject should be analyzed. It is possible to "calibrate" the model in order to calculate the average deviation of the integral estimation if the model is stable (recognized expertly). To do this, a time sample shall be taken for the "0" (zero number) and the integral estimation in this sample shall be further deducted from integral estimates of other time samples. Anyway, it is necessary to bear in mind that this example is of a purely technical nature and is presented for demonstration of the algorithm operation.

Evaluation of the model: this model has an unbalanced contribution of a set of considered markers (the total contribution of the markers is +3, the average +0.75), and on the sample of news texts on relationships between the society and the government (defined by keywords "government" and "society") demonstrates positive polarity of the process of social tension from the time sample "September 2013" to the time sample "October 2013".

5 Conclusion

The described approach to modeling the processes' dynamics is based on the proven technology of automatic semantic analysis of textual information. During processing of texts an associative network is formed, the key concepts of which (including lexical and psycholinguistic markers of the analyzed process) are ranked by their semantic weights. Multiplied by the marker status on the "good-bad" scale, this weight determines the contribution of the marker in the characterization of the process state. Changes in the combined characteristic of the process from time sample to time sample characterize the process trend. The above example does not show the quality of the processing, but only illustrates the operating principle of the estimation mechanism. For experts, the proposed approach is a tool for process modeling, the adjustment of which to some criteria, some real process allows to achieve some adequacy in modeling.

Acknowledgments. The works was performed within the research "Study of the mechanism of associative links in human verbal and cogitative activity using the method of neural network modeling in the analysis of textual information" (with financial support from the Russian Foundation for Basic Research, grant 14-06-00363).

References

1. Kontorovich, S.D., Litvinov, S.V., Nosko, V.I.: Metodika monitoringa i modelirovaniya struktury politicheski aktivnogo segmenta sotsial'nykh setey [Electronic resource]. Inzhenerny vestnik Dona, 4 (2011) (in Russia), http://ivdon.ru/magazine/archive/4yn2011642/2/1428
2. Rozin, M.D., Svechkarev, V.P., Kontorovich S.D., Litvinov S.V., Nosko V.I.: Issledovanie sotsial'nykh setey kak ploschadki sotsial'noy kommunikatsii runeta, ispol'zuemoy v tselyakh predvybornoy agitatsii. Inzhenerny vestnik Dona, 1 (2011) (in Russia), http://ivdon.ru/magazine/archive/n1y2011/397
3. Denecke, K.: Using SentiWordNet for multilingual sentiment analysis. Denecke Kerstin. In: IEEE 24th International Conference on Data Engineering Workshop. pp. 507–512 (2008)
4. Thelwall, M., Buckley, K., Paltoglou, G., Cai, D., Kappas, A.: Sentiment strength detection in short informal text. JASIST, 2544–2558 (2010)
5. Kharlamov, A.A., Raevskiy, V.V.: Perestroyka modeli mira, formiruemoy na materiale analiza tekstovoy informatsii s ispol' zovaniem iskusstvennykh neyronnykh setey, v usloviyakh dinamiki vneshney sredy. Rechevye tekhnologii 3, 27–35 (2008) (In Russ.)
6. Kharlamov, A.A., Yermolenko, T.V.: Semanticheskie seti kak formal'naya osnova resheniya problem integratsii intellektual'nykh system. Formalizm avtomaticheskogo formirovaniya semanticheskoy seti s pomoschyu preobrazovaniya v mnogomernoe prostranstvo. In: Proc. of the OSTIS 2011, pp. 87–96 (2011) (In Russ.)

New Method of Speech Signals Adaptive Features Construction Based on the Wavelet-like Transform and Support Vector Machines

Alexander Soroka, Pavel Kovalets, and Igor Kheidorov

Belarusian State University,
Department of Radiophysics and Digital Media Technologies
Minsk, Belarus
soroka.a.m@gmail.com, feanor-pk@yandex.by, igorhmm@mail.ru

Abstract. In this paper it is proposed the original method of adaptive feature vector construction for speech signals based on wavelet transform and support vector machines (SVM). For wavelet basic function generation it was proposed to use genetic algorithm and SVM based classification accuracy as the objective function. It was shown that the usage of the generated in such a way wavelet functions lets to improve speech signals classification accuracy. In particular the accuracy improvement is 1% to 5% in comparison with mel-frequency cepstral coefficients.

Keywords: Speech recognition, feature extraction, wavelet transformation, support vector machine, genetic algorithm.

1 Introduction

The choice of feature vector is one of the most important stages for audio signal recognition task. There is a number of different feature estimation algorithms, feature vectors based on mel-frequence cofficients (MFCC), linear predicition coefficients(LPC), energy-based, etc [7] and wavelet-transforms [8] are widely used for audio signal description.

In a series of papers it was shown that it is possible to significantly improve recognition performance by optimizing and adaptation of signal description parameters for the certain classification task [14], [10]. One of the best way to optimize audio feature description is the usage of genetic algorithm [4], [14], [6]

Another possible approach in order to improve the audio description is to use a combination of different audio characters but this leads to significant growth of feature vector dimension and it becomes too sparse as the result, that impairs the accuracy of the ensuring statistical analysis and recognition [3]. To solve the problem mentioned above it is a good idea to decrease the dimension of feature space based on the assumption that a number of parameters have low information significance [11], [9], [5], [15], [12]

Unfortunately such approach has several drawbacks:

- some significant information for following analysis can be lost during the feature vector reduction procedure;

A. Ronzhin et al. (Eds.): SPECOM 2014, LNAI 8773, pp. 308–314, 2014.

– feature vectors can be distributed with considerable cluster overlapping for the same audio signals which requires usage of complex nonlinear classifiers.

In order to overcome these drawbacks we have proposed the new approach to feature vector construction based on wavelet-like transform with adaptive basic function built using genetic algorithm. Unlike other described methods we do not optimize separate parameters of wavelet but basic wavelet function form is optimized directly. The proposed method let to achieve the feature vector which is optimal from the classification viewpoint, in such case it is possible to improve the recognition accuracy and simplify the classifier, ideally the linear one.

2 Adaptive Wavelet Function Construction Method Based on Genetic Algorithm and Support Vector Machines

Wavelet transform is an integral transform [8], defined by the function of two variables:

$$W(\alpha, \tau) = \int_{-\infty}^{+\infty} \frac{s(t)}{\sqrt{\alpha}} w\left(\frac{t-\tau}{\alpha}\right) dx \tag{1}$$

where $s(t)$ - signal to be analyzed, $w(t)$ - base wavelet function, α - scale, τ - time shift.

This function has to satisfy the following condition [8]:

$$\int_{-\infty}^{+\infty} \psi(t) dt = 0 \tag{2}$$

Let us assume that the base wavelet function w_p exists that is described by the set of parameters p and allows to localize significant coefficients of the wavelet transform in such a way that provides the best separation of the given classes in the feature space.

Linear classifier based on the support vector machines is used to evaluate the distribution of the vectors in the feature space [13]. This method allows to build optimal separating hyperplane $\langle b, x \rangle - b_0 = 0$ in case of binary classification by maximizing the distance between the separating hyperplane and boundaries of the classes, where x - point on the hyperplane, b - the normal vector to the hyperplane, b_0 - the offset of the hyperplane from the origin along the normal vector b. Decision rule for this classifier is described by the following expression:

$$a(x) = sign\left(\langle b, x \rangle - b_0\right) \tag{3}$$

Then the set of feature description vectors $X = \{x_i | i = 1...N\}$ of speech signals which belong to two different classes is built with the help of wavelet transform. The exact classification of these vectors $c(x) = \{-1, 1\}$ is known. Decision rule (3) is built using k-fold crossvalidation. The X set is divided into K disjoint subsets: $X_i | X_i \bigcup X_i ... \bigcup X_k; X_i \bigcap X_j = \emptyset; i = 1...K; j = 1...K; i \neq \jmath$ and each subset X_i contains n_k feature vectors. The set of classifiers $\{a_k(x) | k = 1...K\}$ is then trained using the set of feature vectors $X^l = X \backslash X_k$. Average classification accuracy of the set of classifiers is used as an objective function:

$$f = \frac{1}{K} \sum_{k=1}^{K} \frac{1}{n_k} \sum_{x \in X_k} \frac{|a_k((x)) + c((x))|}{2} \tag{4}$$

Vector $p = (p_1, p_2 \ldots p_n)$, $p_i \in R$ should be found that describes the wavelet transform $W(\alpha, \tau)$ such that $f \rightarrow max$ to construct the required adaptive wavelet function.

Numerical optimization methods are used for the construction of the base wavelet function, adapted to the classification of the studied acoustic signals. Genetic algorithm [2] is chosen as an optimization method as it has a number of significant advantages, the most important of which are:

- possibility of finding a global extremum of the objective function;
- conditional optimization;
- convergence speed;
- algorithm parallelization that allows to significantly reduce calculation time with the help of modern parallel data processing systems.

The genetic algorithm operates with vector p mediately through sequence of code symbols $q = (q_1, q_2 \ldots q_n)$, which is accepted to be called a chromosome in the theory of evolutionary optimization methods. Vector of parameters p is unambiguously defined by the chromosome q, while:

1. Each parameter $p_i, i \in 1 \ldots N$ is described by the corresponding gene $q_i, i \in 1 \ldots N$;
2. Each gene $q_i, i \in 1 \ldots N$ consists of M alleles, selected from a finite set. The finite set $\{0, 1\}$ is used for the convenience of the genetic algorithm implementation.

To construct the adaptive function w_p of the wavelet transform the time representation of the required functions is defined by a parametrical curve, namely Akima spline [1]. This choice of a parametrical curve is caused firstly by the fact that the resultant curve passes through all sample points. Secondly by resistance of the Akima spline to local overshoots this spline practically has no curve oscillations near overshoot points, as distinct from cubic splines [1]. This property of the Akima spline is quite significant as any additional oscillations worsen the localization of the wavelet function in the frequency domain. The spline is defined by a set of base points ordinates $p(n) = \{p_i, i = 1 \ldots N\}$ where p_i value is coded by q_i gene, and $p_i \in [-1, 1]$.

To comply with the condition (5) let us build the Akima spline $s_p(x)$ and normalize the acquired set of parameters:

$$\widetilde{p_i} = p_i - \frac{1}{N} \int_0^{+N} s_p(x) \, dx, \tag{5}$$

where N - the size of vector p The required wavelet function is built as Akima spline [1] using the set of parameters $\widetilde{p_i}$.

As the genome consists of the finite number of alleles, the values are coded with some accuracy ϵ accordingly. In this case the maximum number of values which can be coded by gene, is described by following expression: $K_{max} = \frac{max(p_i) - min(p_i)}{\epsilon}$ the minimum number of alleles in a gene, necessary for coding all values, makes: $L(q_i) = \lceil log_2(K_{max}) \rceil$

Operations of mutation and crossover in this case are trivial because any combination of alleles is valid. The elitism strategy is used as an individuals selecting algorithm to generate next population. It provides higher convergence speed when solving the problem of base wavelet function optimization in comparison with the pure methods of roulette wheel or tournament selections [2].

The flowchart of the developed method for the adaptive wavelet function construction with the use of genetic algorithm is shown on the (1). The solution of the optimiza-

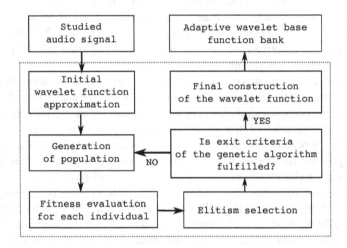

Fig. 1. The general scheme of the adaptive wavelet function construction with the use of genetic algorithm

tion problem formulated above is the vector of parameters p, describing the adaptive wavelet function. This function localizes significant wavelet coefficients in the desired strip of scales. This in turn allows to increase distinctive ability of the features.

One of the advantages of the constructed adaptive wavelet function is the fact that it considers dynamics of a signal throughout all its length. At each scale the wavelet function depending on all signal is constructed and it respectively comprise information about all changes in a studied signal. Delta coefficients are traditionally used for the accounting of acoustic signal's dynamic characteristics at a stage of features description creation in classic methods of the primary analysis. They allow to consider only local changes of a signal, in difference from proposed adaptive wavelet function.

3 Experimentation

3.1 Dataset Description

All experimentations were performed on the Russian speech corpus. Dataset contains 750 Russian records in lossless flac 16bit 44.1kHz mono format. There were 25 male and 50 female speakers. The majority part of speakers were 18-23 years old and there were also 11 speakers in age 30 upto 50 years. The training set consisted of multiple realizations of phonemes, 5000 realizations per phoneme at least. The test set - 1000 realizations per phoneme at least.

3.2 Experimental Results

Base wavelet functions, adapted for the analysis of various classes of phonemes, were constructed using the proposed algorithm. For the construction of an adaptive wavelet function the method described in this paper was used. The number of optimized parameters p_i was $N = 256$, the population size 25000, $K_{max} = 2000$, $L(q_i) = 11$. All calculations were conducted on an MPI cluster consisted of 50 nodes, on each node four Dual Core AMD Opteron 875 HE processors were used, 2.2 GHz and 1024 kB cache. Average adaptive function search time was 170 hours for the problem of phoneme recognition from two phonemes.

The comparative testing was conducted for various features with various dimensions d for the estimation of the distinctive ability of the adaptive feature vectors (AFV), constructed using the proposed algorithm. The linear support vector machine classifier was used to avoid the influence of non-linear classification effects on the classification accuracy. The SVM penalty parameter C for each classification task was found with the help of the grid search. The feature descriptions, constructed using the wavelet transform and Haar wavelet function $d = 13$, Morlet $d = 13$, adaptive features constructed using the proposed algorithm ($d_1 = 13$, $d_2 = 26$), features constructed using MFCC $d = 13$, delta-MFCC $d = 26$ (13 MFCC + 13 delta coefficients), delta-delta-MFCC $d = 39$ (13 MFCC, 13 delta coefficients, 13 delta-delta coefficients) were chosen for comparison. The results of linear binary classification for the phonemes of different types (vowel, resonant, noise-like) are presented in the table (1). In the table (2) results of linear binary classification using various feature dimensions are shown. Here the notation $ph - ph_1, ph_2 \ldots ph_N$ means the solution of the classification problem of the ph phoneme from the set of phonemes $ph_1, ph_2 \ldots ph_N$. According to the results presented in the tables (1, 2) the usage of the proposed algorithm of feature vectors construction allows to improve the classification accuracy of acoustically similar phonemes in general by 3%. The comparison of average classification accuracy of vowel and consonant phonemes, achieved with the help of the proposed features construction algorithm and with the help of MFCC, is proposed in table (1). It can be seen that there is no significant difference between the usage of the proposed algorithm and MFCC for vowel phonemes. But for consonant phonemes the proposed algorithm allows to achieve 3,3% more classification accuracy in the average. This is particularly notable in case of classification of such acoustically similar phonemes as [m],[n] (increase by 5,2%). This result is significantly important as consonant phonemes form the semantic basis of the speech message [7]. Also it should be noted that the proposed algorithm allows to use the feature description of 1.5 times smaller dimension to achieve the approximately equal accuracy of classification compared to MFCC.

Table 1. Various phoneme classes classification accuracy,%

	Haar-13	Morlet-13	AFV-13	MFCC-13
a-a,o	84,6	88,0	**91,5**	**91,5**
a-vowels	73,4	77,1	**90,0**	89,9
a-all phonemes	72,1	75,8	84,0	**85,2**
n-n,m	59,8	62,0	**74,8**	67,8
n-all phonemes	54,8	60,2	**72,3**	66,3
z-z,zh,sh,s	70,1	74,8	**78,6**	75,2
z-all phonemes	69,9	73,2	**77,4**	74,9

Table 2. Various feature dimensions classification accuracy,%

	AFV-26	MFCC-26	MFCC-39
a-a,o	**94,2**	90,8	91,0
a-vowels	**93,0**	87,4	87,3
a-all phonemes	**87,0**	80,4	80,4
n-n,m	**75,0**	69,8	68,5
n-all phonemes	**71,4**	66,9	65,8
z-z,zh,sh,s	**82,2**	78,4	79,9
z-all phonemes	**79,1**	76,3	77,1

Table 3. Average phoneme classification accuracy,%

	AFV-13	MFCC-13
Vowel	88,2	88,1
Consonant	**76,9**	73,7

Table 4. Timit evaluation,%

	AFV-13	MFCC-13
f - v	**91,2**	88,1
s - z	**83,1**	79,2

3.3   Timit Evaluation

To be able to compare the results of classification with other feature extraction methods we began to study the characteristics of the proposed algorithm on the TIMIT speech corpus. Currently we have received results for only few number of consonant phonemes, but those results are consistent with the results for Russian speech corpus in general:

4   Conclusion

The method for generating the adaptive wavelet function for the construction of speech signals feature vector using the genetic algorithm and support vector machines was proposed in this article. It was shown that using the base wavelet functions generated by the proposed algorithm to construct feature description allows to achieve the steady increase of the classification accuracy. In particular, the improvement of accuracy compared to mel-frequency cepstral coefficients varies from 1% to 5% for various phonemes. Also it was shown that the generated adaptive wavelet function contains information regarding the dynamic processes of the given signal. As a consequence, the dimension of the feature description decreases 1.5 times without the loss of the classification accuracy.

References

1. Akima, H.: A new method of interpolation and smooth curve fitting based on local procedures. Journal of the ACM 17(4), 589–602 (1970)
2. Back, T.: Evolution algorithms in theory and practice. Oxford University Press, Oxford (1996)
3. Bellman, R.E.: Adaptive Control Processes A Guided Tour. Princeton University Press, Princeton (1961)
4. Goldberg, D.E.: Genetic Algorithms in Search, Optimization and Machine Learning, 1st edn. Addison-Wesley Longman Publishing Co., Amsterdam (1989)
5. Huang, C.-L., Wang, C.-j.: A ga-based feature selection and parameters optimization for support vector machines. Expert Systems with Applications (31), 231–240 (2006)
6. Huang, L.-x., Evangelista, G., Zhang, X.-y.: Adaptive bands filter bank optimized by genetic algorithm for robust speech recognition system. Journal of Central South University of Technology 18, 1595–1601 (2011)
7. Huang, X., Acero, A., Hon, H.W.: Spoken Language Processing: A Guide to Theory, Algorithm, and System Development. Prentice Hall PTR (2001)
8. Mallat, S.: A Wavelet Tour of Signal Processing: The Sparse Way. Academic Press (2008)
9. Mkinen, T., Kiranyaz, S., Raitoharju, J., Gabbouj, M.: An evolutionary feature synthesis approach for content-based audio retrieval. EURASIP Journal on Audio, Speech, and Music Processing 2012 (2012)
10. Murthy, D. A.S., Holla, N.: Robust speech recognition system designed by combining empirical mode decomposition and a genetic algorithm. International Journal of Engineering Research & Technology (IJERT) 2, 2056–2068 (2013)
11. Schuller, B., Reiter, S., Rigoll, G.: Evolutionary feature generation in speech emotion recognition. In: 2006 IEEE International Conference on Multimedia and Expo., pp. 5–8 (2006)
12. Srinivasan, V., Ramalingam, V., Sellam, V.: Classification of normal and pathological voice using ga and svm. International Journal of Computer Applications 60(3) (2012)
13. Vapnik, V.: The Nature of Statistical Learning Theory. Springer (2000)
14. Vignolo, L.D., Rufiner, H.L., Milone, D.H., Goddard, J.C.: Evolutionary splines for cepstral filterbank optimization in phoneme classification. EURASIP Journal on Advances in Signal Processing 2011 (2011)
15. Zhuo, L., Zheng, J., Wang, F., Li, X., Ai, B., Qian, J.: A genetic algorithm based wrapper feature selection method for classification of hyperspectral images using support vector machine. In: SPIE, vol. 7147 (2008)

On a Hybrid NN/HMM Speech Recognition System with a RNN-Based Language Model

Daniel Soutner, Jan Zelinka, and Luděk Müller

University of West Bohemia, Faculty of Applied Sciences
New Technologies for the Information Society
Univerzitní 22, 306 14 Plzeň, Czech Republic
dsoutner,zelinka,muller@ntis.zcu.cz

Abstract. In this paper, we present a new NN/HMM speech recognition system with a NN-base acoustic model and RNN-based language model. The employed neural-network-based acoustic model computes posteriors for states of context-dependent acoustic units. A recurrent neural network with the maximum entropy extension was used as a language model. This hybrid NN/HMM system was compared with our previous hybrid NN/HMM system equipped with a standard n-gram language model. In our experiments, we also compared it to a standard GMM/HMM system. The system performance was evaluated on the British English speech corpus and compared with some previous work.

Keywords: hidden Markov model, neural networks, acoustic modelling, language modelling, automatic speech recognition.

1 Introduction

We present a combination of a neural network (NN) based acoustic models and a recurrent neural network (RNN) based language model in this paper. A motivation for this combination is to replace all possible parts of recognition system with a part on which neural networks could be applied. We suppose that applying NN, as a widespread used machine learning application, could lead to a speech recognition system which is much more accurate than a system designed in a standard way. A lot of current experiments with either speech processing or image processing showed that this approach is significantly beneficial.

According to modern speech recognition methods a NN-based acoustic model has context-dependent units (i.e. triphones). We described this acoustic model, adaptation techniques and some other issues in [1]. Similar approach in the same corpus is shown in [2]. Our results were compared with the results in that paper. We believe, that we chose a more straightforward approach which – as we anticipate – allows to make a much more robust model.

RNN have attracted much attention in the last years among the other language models caused by their better performance and their ability to learn on a corpus which is smaller than conventional n-gram models. When RNNs are trained in a combination with maximum entropy features, they provide very positive results [3]. In this paper,

A. Ronzhin et al. (Eds.): SPECOM 2014, LNAI 8773, pp. 315–321, 2014.

we want to show that combination this RNN-based language model with a NN-based acoustic model can be beneficial as well. A cooperation of these two models is shown in Figure 1.

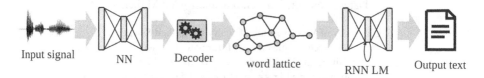

Input signal   NN   Decoder   word lattice   RNN LM   Output text

Fig. 1. The scheme of our NN-based system

The next section describes our NN-based acoustic model. Our language model is described in the third section. Experiments and its results are in the fourth section. Last section concludes this paper.

2   Neural-Network-Based Acoustic Model

The described NN-based acoustic model is basically an estimator of a posterior probability $P(s|x)$ where s is a state (leaf) of an HMM and x is a feature vector. Phonetic units were modelled as three state units. The states for context-dependent units (triphones) were determined during the training of the baseline GMM/HMM system and they were used as they were, without any modification [4]. The long temporal spectral patterns parameterization technique [5,6] was used in our hybrid NN/HMM systems to create a sequence of feature vectors.

As a baseline, we use a standard GMM-based acoustic model which has 2547 states. A NN input has 506 elements. Our NN has one hidden layer with 3000 neurons and an output layer with 2547 outputs. Thus, the NN-base acoustic model has circa 9.2M parameters.

The usual logistic sigmoid function plays role of the activation function in each hidden neuron and the usual softmax function is the activation function in the output layer. The cross-entropy error function (XENT), which is commonly used together with the softmax, was in our experiment used also as the optimality criterion. The NN weights and biases were initialized randomly before the training process. For training the neural network, the gradient descent based algorithm iRPROP [7] was used. At first, the NN was trained on a small subset of the complete training set until the overtraining phenomenon was detected. After that, the training algorithm continued with the complete training set. From our experiments, this approach accelerates noticeably the convergence speed of the training process.

In a speech recognition system a probability density $p(x|s)$ is required. For this probability holds

$$p(x|s) = \frac{P(s|x) \cdot p(x)}{P(s)}, \tag{1}$$

where x is a feature vector, s is a state of the HMM and $p(x)$ can be certainly ignored. Our previously reported experiments suggest that straightforward conversion of posterior probabilities $P(s|x)$ to the conditional probabilities $p(x|s)$ according to the equation (1) is beneficial in case of context-independent units (i.e. monophones). But in case of context-dependent units this approach could be damaging. Especially when $P(s)$ is estimated as a relative frequency of occurrence.

In the case of context-dependent units, the use of the probability densities $p(x|s)$ leads to lower word error rate compared to the case, when the probabilities $P(s|x)$ were used, although the first case is theoretically correct. This give us the right to try to modify the a prior probabilities $P(s)$. A one possible way how to "rectify" the estimates of the prior probabilities is to increase the prior probabilities of the low-occurrence states. When the occurrence of a state is low, the application of the equation (1) increases the influence of the numerical inaccuracies of this state posterior estimate. Due to the extreme computational complexity, finding a prior probabilities that yield the lowest word error rate seems impossible by means of standard optimization methods (including even the evolutionary computing). Therefore, in our experiments, we have optimized only the prior probabilities of states representing the silence because they are the most frequent states and thus they might have considerably distorted posterior estimates. Furthermore, we suppose that a prior probabilities of all three silence states are equal to simplify the optimization process. We decided to circumvent this problem by thresholding the values of the prior probabilities.

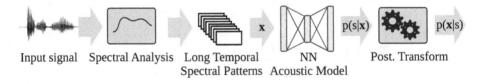

Input signal   Spectral Analysis   Long Temporal   NN   Post. Transform
                                     Spectral Patterns   Acoustic Model

Fig. 2. Schematic diagram of posteriors estimation in hybrid NN/HMM system

Figure 2 shows the complete NN-based acoustic model. We used a proprietary software for NN training which is capable of exploiting the available GPU devices. The software can use either the iRPROP of the L-BFGS training algorithm. In experiments presented in this paper, only the iRPROP training algorithm was used due to faster convergence. To function correctly, the iRPROP needs to operate on the global gradient. Because of the memory constraints, we computed the global gradient in small batches. The partial gradients (or per-batch gradients) were then summed together to obtain the global gradient. To detect the occurrence of the overtraining phenomenon, the early stopping technique was used. During the training process, LVCSR performed a speech recognition using an actual NN, word error rate for the set si_dt5a (see Section 4) was monitored and the training was terminated as soon as the error rate measured on the set si_dt5a started to increase.

3   Recurrent-Neural-Network-Based Language Model

In standard back-off n-gram language models words are represented in a discrete space – in the vocabulary. This prevents better interpolation of the probabilities of unseen n-grams because a change in this word space can result in an arbitrary change of the n-gram probability. The basic architecture of neural network model was proposed by Y. Bengio in [8]. The main idea is to understand a word not as a separate entity with no specific relation to other words, but to see words as points in a finite dimensional (separable) metric space.

In essence, a word indices are converted into a continuous representations and after that a probability estimator operating in this space is employed. More suitable generalization to unknown n-grams can be expected if the probability density of a word representation is replaced by a smooth continuous function. Probability estimation and interpolation in a metric space is mathematically well grounded and powerful and efficient algorithms could perform interpolations even with only a limited amount of a training material.

The recurrent neural networks were successfully introduced to the field of language modelling by Mikolov [9]. The basic scheme of neural-network-based language model is shown in Figure 3.

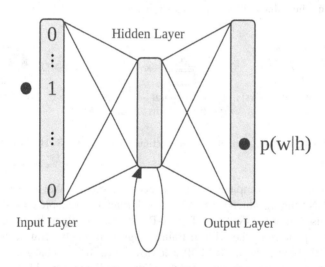

Fig. 3. Neural-network-based language model architecture

RNN-based language model works on these principals:

– The input vector is a word encoded as 1-of-N coding (i.e. a zero vector which has the same length as the used vocabulary length with 1 on the position of the input word).
– During the training process, the output vector is also in 1-of-N coding.

- A standard softmax function is used in the output layer to produce normalized probabilities.
- The XENT is used as a criterion for gradient descent.

The language model was trained with The RNNLM Toolkit[1]. This toolkit allows to train a model together with maximum entropy (ME) features [3]. The training data for the model was the text from the corpus WSJ0 [10]. The vocabulary was truncated to the same set of 4989 words which are contained in vocabulary originally contained in WSJCAM0 language model (denoted as tcb05cnp-small). The trained models were moreover interpolated (the linear interpolation was used) with Kneser-Ney 5-gram. The width of hidden layer was changed from 200 to 700, the number of 4-gram maximum entropy features from 1M to 4M. Finally, the best model was chosen on the development data (the set si_dt5a in our experiments), the best results we achieved for the model with 600 hidden neurons and 3M of 4-gram ME features.

4   Experiments and Results

The acoustic model of the baseline GMM/HMM was trained using the HTK software. Our proprietary real-time decoder was employed in our experiments. The decoder is of production quality and it is used in a wide variety of research projects as well as real-world commercial applications. Present-day applications of the decoder include commercial dictation software, automatic subtitling system, dialogue system and systems for searching in archives [11] [12].

The word error rate (WER) is in the scope of this paper defined as $WER = \left(\frac{D+S+I}{N}\right) \cdot 100\%$, where the symbol D denotes the number of deletions, the symbol S denotes the number of substitutions, the symbol I denotes the number of insertions and the symbol N denotes the total number of words.

Our intention was to compare the performance of the presented system with the previously reported by [2]. Therefore, the system performance was evaluated on the British English speech corpus WSJCAM0 [13] in our experiments. There are 7861 utterances (i.e. approximately 15 hours of speech) in the training set. Phonetic alphabet consists of 43 monophones (including silence). The experiments were performed on the development sets si_dt5a and si_dt5b. The set si_dt5a was used to find the optimal word insertion penalty, to find the optimal language model weight and to find the optimal a prior probabilities. The set si_dt5b was used as a strictly evaluation set. Except the experiment with RNN-based language model the decoder used a trigram language model (denoted as "trigram" in Table 1). All the obtained results are gathered in Table 1.

The first row of Table 1 contains the results for the standard context-dependent GMM/HMM ($ID = 1$). The MFCC parameters together with the Δ and $\Delta\Delta$ coefficients were used as feature vectors. Each GMM had 26 mixtures. In the paper [2], similar results for another GMM/HMM are published. These results are in the penultimate row in Table 1 ($ID = 5$).

In the second experiment the context-dependent NN with no speaker adaptation technique are investigated ($ID = 2$). These results show the benefit NN-based acoustic

---

[1] http://rnnlm.org/

Table 1. WERs of hybrid decoders. The results from the aforesaid paper [2] are in the penultimate and the last row

ID	Acoustic Model	Language Model	WER (si_dt5a)	WER (si_dt5b)
1	GMM (5.2M)	trigram	8.91%	10.21%
2	NN (9.2M)	trigram	6.16%	7.15%
3	NN (9.2M)	RNN-ME	5.48%	6.18%
4	NN (9.2M)	RMM-ME mix	5.17%	5.79%
5	GMM [2] (5.8M)	trigram	10.06%	10.87%
6	NN [2] (7.2M)	trigram	6.08%	7.29%

model and establish the baseline for RNN-based language model as well. In the paper [2], the lowest word error rate achieved for the set si_dt5a was $WER = 6.08\%$ and the corresponding result for the set si_dt5b was $WER = 7.29\%$ ($ID = 6$). These results were obtained using so called "bottleneck tandem" approach.

Our last experiment was performed to evaluate the influence of RNN-ME language model ($ID = 3$). The perplexity decreases from 91 (3-gram model) to 77 (RNN-ME model) measured on set si_dt5a. As usual, we used a two-pass process in recognition for implementing RNN-ME model and rescored n-best list in the second pass. In our case was n-best list with $n = 1000$, which was sufficient for our task. Again, the set si_dt5a was used to find the best RNN parameters, the optimal word insertion penalty and the optimal language model weight. The set si_dt5b was used as a strictly evaluation set. The word error rate achieved for the set si_dt5a was $WER = 5.48\%$ and the corresponding result for the set si_dt5b was $WER = 6.18\%$ ($ID = 3$). If we employ a mix of RNN-ME models, they performs even a bit better with $WER = 5.17\%$ for the set si_dt5a and the corresponding result for the set si_dt5b was $WER = 5.79\%$ ($ID = 4$).

The combination of NN-based acoustic model and NN-based language model gives the lowest WER. Because the used sets are relatively small, we performed statistical tests of significance to verify the strength of the influence on the WER of the individual approaches[2]. The mix of RNN-ME models ($ID = 4$) performs significantly better than trigram language model ($ID = 2$) and NN acoustic model ($ID = 2$) performs significantly better than GMM model ($ID = 1$). Both were measured at the significant level 0.05 for the set si_dt5b.

5   Conclusion and Future Work

The combination of NN-based acoustic model and RNN-based language model is presented in this paper. It was widely reported that NN-based acoustical model is beneficial for speech recognition. Our experiments give some evidences that NN-based acoustic model is beneficial with classical trigram language models and even more beneficial in a combination with the RNN-based language model.

---

[2] Speech Recognition Scoring Toolkit (SCTK) Version 2.4.0 was employed. See http://www.itl.nist.gov/iad/mig/tools/

However, the system described in this paper must be called as partially NN-based because uses parameterization which is not NN-based. In the future work, we will replace the parameterization, as the remaining block of speech recognition system, also with a NN and design a complete NN-based system. We have already done some such experiments with context-independent units.

Acknowledgements. This research was supported by the Ministry of Culture Czech Republic, project No.DF12P01OVV022.

References

1. Zelinka, J., Trmal, J., Müller, L.: On context-dependent neural networks and speaker adaptation. In: Proceedings 2012 IEEE 11th International Conference on Signal Processing (2012)
2. Wang, G., Sim, K.C.: Sequential classification criteria for nns in automatic speech recognition. In: INTERSPEECH, pp. 441–444 (2011)
3. Mikolov, T.: Statistical Language Models Based On Neural Networs. Ph. D. Thesis (2012)
4. Young, S.J., Evermann, G., Gales, M.J.F., Hain, T., Kershaw, D., Moore, G., Odell, J., Ollason, D., Povey, D., Valtchev, V., Woodland, P.C.: The HTK Book, version 3.4. Cambridge University Engineering Department, Cambridge (2006)
5. Grézl, F.: TRAP-Based Probabilistic Features for Automatic Speech Recognition. PhD thesis (2007)
6. Trmal, J.: Spatio-temporal structure of feature vectors in neural network adaptation. PhD thesis (2012)
7. Riedmiller, M., Braun, H.: A direct adaptive method for faster backpropagation learning: the rprop algorithm. In: IEEE International Conference on Neural Networks, 1993, vol. 1, pp. 586–591 (1993)
8. Bengio, Y., Ducharme, R., Vincent, P., Janvin, C.: A neural probabilistic language model. J. Mach. Learn. Res. 3(3), 1137–1155 (2003)
9. Mikolov, T., Kombrink, S., Burget, L., Cernocky, J.H., Sanjeev, K.: Extensions of recurrent neural network language model. In: IEEE International Conference on Acoustics, Speech and Signal Processing (ICASSP), vol. 5531, p. 5528 (2011)
10. Garofalo, J., et al.: CSR-I (WSJ0) Complete. Linguistic Data Consortium, Philadelphia (2007)
11. Psutka, J., Švec, J., Psutka, J.V., Vaněk, J., Pražák, A., Šmídl, L.: Fast phonetic/Lexical searching in the archives of the czech holocaust testimonies: Advancing towards the MALACH project visions. In: Sojka, P., Horák, A., Kopeček, I., Pala, K. (eds.) TSD 2010. LNCS, vol. 6231, pp. 385–391. Springer, Heidelberg (2010)
12. Pražák, A., Psutka, J.V., Psutka, J., Loose, Z.: Towards live subtitling of tv ice-hockey commentary. In: Cabello, E., Virvou, M., Obaidat, M.S., Ji, H., Nicopolitidis, P., Vergados, D.D. (eds.) SIGMAP, pp. 151–155. SciTePress (2013)
13. Robinson, T., Fransen, J., Pye, D., Foote, J., Renals, S.: Wsjcam0: A british english speech corpus for large vocabulary continuous speech recognition. In: IEEE Proc. ICASSP 1995, pp. 81–84 (1995)

On Principles of Annotated Databases of the Semantic Field "Aggression"

Rodmonga Potapova and Liliya Komalova

Moscow State Linguistic University, Institution for Applied and Mathematical Linguistics,
Moscow, Russia
{RKPotapova,GenuinePR}@yandex.ru

Abstract. The article describes main principles of elaboration of annotated databases of the semantic field "aggression" and describes Russian and English Digital Mass Media Full-Text Databases containing verbal representatives of the concept "aggression"©. Each database consists of 120 manually annotated text units. The annotation covers lexical, semantic and pragmatic levels. Special metrics and local dictionary of the semantic field "aggression" accompany each text. The databases can be implemented in scientific research on Speechology, computer-aided Internet monitoring systems teaching, in educative process, for further elaboration of searching systems based on the semantic field "aggression".

Keywords: Corpus linguistics, verbal aggression, annotated database, semantic field "aggression", digital mass media.

1 Introduction

Digital mass media texts as usual serve for building public opinion and aim at modeling recipient's point of view on real facts. Positive and negative emotions on pages stimulate similar emotions and modalities of a recipient. That's why it's of great importance to monitor this sector and elaborate special automatic Internet monitoring systems based on different thematic databases of emotionally colored texts.

In the framework of the survey of the semantic field "aggression" we focus on means and mechanisms of motivation and realization of negative emotions and modalities, including those provoked mediate texts of digital Internet mass media. Linguistic analysis of modern publications in European languages (English, Spanish, Russian languages) confirms that nowadays semantic field "aggression" in mass media texts is widening and the perception criticality threshold is reducing. However, accessibility of digital texts and modern programming means allow monitoring Internet textual content and revealing texts provoking aggression, extremism and separatism.

In this context elaboration of special thematic verbal databases and knowledge bases which can be implemented in Internet filter systems becomes perspective way to cluster language and speech texts' tendencies of modern digital Internet mass media along with the possibility of assessment of their effecting potential to different forms of aggressive behaviour.

A. Ronzhin et al. (Eds.): SPECOM 2014, LNAI 8773, pp. 322–328, 2014.

2   Method and Procedure

Necessary request for the first phase of database constructing is to provide a scientific research resulting in the list of characteristics describing how concept "aggression" is functioning on pages of digital Internet mass media. The next phase is material selection which must be homogeneous: it must contain topics with approx equal number of text units each, representing particular time period. The list of sources determines attitude of the editors and therefore directives and stereotype concepts translated to the audience.

Once the material is collected it must be correctly described. Description gives understanding of social context in which the corpus was made. It's significant socio-cultural index, especially for users of other lingua-cultures. It also gives clue to the next phase – annotation.

Our Russian and English Digital Mass Media Full-Text Databases© have identical annotation form and contain verbal representatives of the concept "aggression". Each of them was gathered from authentic sources: articles from digital analogues of newspapers, scripts of TV-news programmes, messages of news agencies, web-site news kits (time period: 2011-2013). Results of the survey and principles used for marking words related to state of aggression are discussed in [2,3]. Each unit of both databases consists of the text and its annotation:

I. Date-line of the text:

1. Headline,
2. Name of the source,
3. Date of publication,
4. Name of the author,
5. Web-site address;

II. Linguistic passport of the text:

6. Main topic of the text (choose one of the following: geopolitical conflicts, political conflicts, military operations, criminal behaviour, personal violence, family violence, aggressive economics, hearings, extremist acts, racism, inter-confessional dissention, xenophobia, call to violence and discrimination),

7. Genre (choose one of the following: brief article, report, article, leaflet, commentary, satirical article, interview, essay),

8. Pragmatic component (choose one of the following: informing, analysis, polemics, interpretation, announcement, agitation, propaganda, criticism);

III. Each text has special metrics showing:

9. Total amount of notional and non-notional words in the text,
10. Number of graphemes without blanks,
11. Annotation also includes local dictionary of the semantic field "aggression" (a list of words from the text which belongs to the semantic field "aggression") which consists of corresponding words from a particular text. All these words are marked in the text.
12. Density of words from the semantic field "aggression". Table 1 and table 2 give examples of annotated text units.

Each database consists of 120 manually annotated text units selected out of 4000 articles sample from 29 Russian and 43 English sources (table 3). To analyze texts we use content-analysis algorithm supplemented by method described in [5,6] and recom-

Table 1. An example of annotated text unit in Russian Digital Mass Media Full-Text Database

Название текста	Президент Сирии ужесточил наказание за похищения и убийства людей
Название источника	Информационный Интернет-портал РИА-Новости
Дата публикации текста	02 апреля 2013 года
Автор текста	Денис Малков
Ссылка на источник	http://ria.ru/arab_sy/20130402/930583218.html
Тема текста	Основной тематической составляющей данного текста является похищение. Об этом свидетельствует абсолютная доминирующая позиция следующих слов и словосочетаний «похищения», «похитил», «похититель», «смерть похищенного», «массовые похищения» в составе семантического поля «агрессия» для данного текста.
Жанр текста	Заметка
Прагматическая составляющая текста	Информирование
Количество слов	151
Количество знаков (графем) без пробелов	969
Слова, относящиеся к семантическому полю «агрессия»	Ужесточение наказания, похищение людей, похитить человека, приговорить, пожизненные каторжные работы, причинения вреда здоровью, изнасилование, смерть, похищенный, похититель, казнить, наказание, сроки заключения, массовые похищения людей, повстанцы, криминальные группировки, похищенный, вооруженный конфликт, оппозиция, погибнуть, противостоять организованным действиям, вооруженный, боевик, наемник
Плотность СПА	25,16%
Исходный текст	

Президент Сирии Башар Асад подписал указ об ужесточении наказания за похищение людей, сообщает во вторник пресс-служба главы государства.

"Каждый, кто похитил человека, будет приговорен к пожизненным каторжным работам, а в случае причинения вреда здоровью, в случае изнасилования или смерти похищенного, похититель будет казнен — говорится в указе сирийского президента.

Ранее наказание в зависимости от последствий предусматривало различные сроки заключения.

Массовые похищения людей в Сирии отмечаются на территориях, контролируемых повстанцами, суммы выкупа, которые криминальные группировки требуют от близких и родственников похищенных, разнятся от нескольких тысяч до нескольких миллионов долларов.

Вооруженный конфликт в Сирии между властями и оппозицией продолжается с марта 2011 года. По данным ООН, за это время в стране погибли около 70 тысяч человек. Сирийские власти заявляют, что противостоят организованным действиям хорошо вооруженных и обученных местных боевиков и наемников из-за рубежа.

Table 2. An example of annotated text unit in English Digital Mass Media Full-Text Database

Headline	When violence hits a nerve
Name of the source	The Washington Post
Date of publication	06.02.2013
The author of the text	Esther J. Cepeda
Web-site address	http://www.jsonline.com/news/opinion/when-violence-hits-a-nerve-2b8lpp9-190094521.html
Main topic of the text	Critics of people's attitude toward violence in case of a girl murder
Genre	Critic article
Pragmatic component	Analysis
Total amount of notional and non-notional words	672
A number of graphemes without blanks	3123
Local dictionary of the semantic field "aggression"	Violence, hit a nerve, dangerous, corrupt, racially divided, murder, outrage, unspeakable, violence, victim, death, strike a chord, hit a nerve, to die, woe, victim, rough, die, frighten, clout, power, quell, violence, gun down, tough, murder, homicide, interminable, murder, spree, violence, homicide, victim, troops, kill, Afghanistan, tragedy, post-mortem, victim, gun, violence, kill, gunman, die, gunman, shoot, heartbreak, victim, tragedy, ugly, violence, brushes with the law, gang affiliations, hurt, shoot , die, bad, horror, shooting, rallying cry, prevent horror, violence, rip apart, struggling, ache, disadvantaged, at-risk, victim, senseless, violence, fall short, gun-related, violence, bad, harm, tragic, harm
Density of words from the semantic field "aggression" in the text	11%
Full text	

Chicago - To a lifelong resident of one of America's most dangerous, corrupt and racially divided cities, the murder of Hadiya Pendleton has brought to light what really drives coverage – and outrage – of unspeakable violence: a virtuous victim.

Did a 15-year-old's death really strike a chord nationally because she had, a week before, been to our nation's capital performing at the inauguration festivities? No, that wasn't it – nor did her story hit a nerve because of where she died.

The typical woe of victims in the rough parts of town is that their stories don't get reported in as much detail as those who die in a nicer parts – the neighborhoods that, when people are frightened, have the clout to make those in power listen to their demands that something to be done to quell the violence.

But Pendleton was gunned down in a tough neighborhood – one about a mile from the Chicago home of Barack Obama, a president who has yet to acknowledge publicly that his hometown has gotten an international reputation for being a "Murder City". The city recorded 550 homicides between January 2012 and the end of last month, so many that most of them have just become footnotes to Chicago's interminable murder spree.

Obama's South Side neighbors have pleaded with the president to come back and call for national action on inner-city violence. Yet their pleas have been ignored ever since last summer, when the city reached the milestone of having had more homicide victims through the first six months of the year than the number of U.S. troopskilled in Afghanistan in the same time period.

Also notable in the tale of this most recent child tragedy is that the teenager didn't rocket to post-mortem attention because of the perennial complaint that victims of gun violence are only acknowledged when large numbers of them are killed by a single gunman. Pendleton was the only child to die after a gunman shot into a crowd of 12 students.

Now, you could make the argument that the national heartbreak was due to the same reason that seems to sort some victims of tragedy into the media spotlight, while leaving others in anonymity: beauty. As one Chicago newspaper put it: "City's ugly violence now has a pretty face".

But that's only partially right. The rest of it is that Pendleton was as close to being as innocent as you can get.

Media accounts tell of a girl who had no brushes with the law or gang affiliations and was an honor-roll student attending a selective-enrollment college prep school. She was an athlete and a majorette in the school's marching band, and a girl with dreams of a profession after getting in and making it through an elite university.

In short, she was the kind of bright child any one of us would be proud to parent or mentor, and it hurts to think of her getting shot in the back and dying in the middle of the street.

These are not bad impulses. They're quite human, and they're the ones credited with turning the horror of the Newtown, Conn., school shootings into a rallying cry that mustered the political courage to look for measures that would prevent such a horror from ever happening again.

Unfortunately, those instincts won't get us far enough in stemming the violence that rips struggling communities apart every day.

Until our hearts start aching for every disadvantagedat-risk child who becomes a victim to senseless violence – whether perfectly virtuous or not – our aspirations for safe communities will be sure to fall short.

Far too many of us have become too accepting of the steady stream of gun-related violence that happens in "bad neighborhoods", "somewhere else" or only to "bad people". It's time to start believing that a harm to the least of us is every bit as tragic as a harm to the rest of us.

---

mendations given in [4]. Density of words from the semantic field "aggression" was calculated with the open license programme "Textus Pro 1.0" [1].

3 Conclusions

Russian and English Digital Mass Media Full-Text Databases can be implemented as:

- wordforms databases of the semantic field "aggression" for computer-aided Internet monitoring systems teaching to reveal potential provocative/conflictive messages in official digital Internet mass media sources and also to determine places of geopolitical "hot spots" in the world;
- wordforms databases for thematic frequency dictionary elaboration in Russian and English;

Table 3. Russian and English digital Internet-sources

Russian sources	British English sources	American English sources
	Digital versions of newspapers	
aif.ru gazeta.ru izvestia.ru kp.ru mk.ru mn.ru novayagazeta.ru rg.ru tambov.mk.ru utro.ru	belfasttelegraph.co.uk cambridge-news.co.uk express.co.uk dailymail.co.uk edp24.co.uk ellesmereportpioneer.co.uk nwemail.co.uk socialistworker.co.uk icbirmingham.icnetwork.co.uk prestoncitizen.co.uk guardian-series.co.uk guardian.co.uk yorkpress.co.uk voice-online.co.uk theweek.co.uk walesonline.co.uk	chicagotribune.com ctpost.com dailyherald.com democratandchronicle.com freep.com examiner.com lasvegassun.com latimes.com jsonline.com nypost.com newsok.com post-gazette.com politicshome.com theadvocate.com bostonglobe.com economist.com mcall.com nytimes.com thelede.blogs.nytimes.com nytsyn.com observer.theguardian.com seattletimes.com tbo.com washingtonpost.com
Russian sources	British English sources	American English sources
	News agencies	
regnum.ru ria.ru top.rbc.ru itar-tass.com	–	ap.org reuters.com
	Internet-portals	
komionline.ru lenta.ru newsru.com online812.ru rbcdaily.ru ridus.ru news.mail.ru news.rambler.ru memo.ru	–	news4theworld.com 7.politicalbetting.com
	Broadcasting company news-lines	
echo.msk.ru rus.ruvr.ru vesti.ru ntv.ru	ru.euronews.com bbc.co.uk	–

- wordforms databases for elaboration of searching systems based on the semantic field "aggression";
- texts databases for scientific research on Speechology to carry out a morphological and syntactical analysis with aim to reveal the text structure which can provoke a recipient's state of aggression;
- texts databases in educative process within training disciplines as "Linguaconflic-tology", "Linguacriminalistic text expertise", "Fundamental and Applied Speechology", "Sociolinguistics";
- texts databases in complex survey of language and speech characteristics of broadcasting and production of aggressive behaviour through digital Internet mass media texts.

4 Prospects of Investigation

Further investigation can be related with elaboration of inner searching system trained to filter Internet-content.

Acknowledgments. The survey is being carried out with the support of Russian Science Foundation (RSF) in the framework of the project No.14-18-01059 at Moscow State Linguistic University (scientific head of the project – R.K. Potapova).

References

1. Kaplunov, D.A.: Textus Pro 1.0, http://www.blog-kaplunoff.ru/programmy-dlya-kopirajterov.html
2. Potapova, R.K., Komalova, L.R.: Lingvokognitivnoe Issledovanie Sostoyaniya, "Agressiya" v Mezhyazykovoj i Mezhkul'turnoj Kommunikatsii: Pis'mennyj Tekst. In: Semioticheskaya Geterogennost' Yazykovoj Kommunikatsii: Teoriya i Praktika. Chast' II, vol. 15(675), pp. 164–173. MGLU, Moscow (2013)
3. Potapova, R., Komalova, L.: Lingua-Cognitive Survey of the Semantic Field "Aggression" in Multicultural Communication: Typed Text. In: Železný, M., Habernal, I., Ronzhin, A. (eds.) SPECOM 2013. LNCS, vol. 8113, pp. 227–232. Springer, Heidelberg (2013)
4. Potapova, R., Potapov, V.: Auditory and visual recognition of emotional behaviour of foreign language subjects (by native and non-native speakers). In: Železný, M., Habernal, I., Ronzhin, A. (eds.) SPECOM 2013. LNCS, vol. 8113, pp. 62–69. Springer, Heidelberg (2013)
5. Potapova, R.K., Potapov, V.V.: Semanticheskoe Pole "Narkotiki": Diskurs kak Obekt Prikladnoj Lingvistiki. URSS, Moscow (2004)
6. Potapova, R.K., Potapov, V.V.: Yazyk, Rech, Lichnost. Yazyki Slavyanskoj Kultury, Moscow (2006)

On the Possibility of the Skype Channel Speaker Identification (on the Basis of Acoustic Parameters)

Rodmonga Potapova, Arkadij Sobakin, and Aleksej Maslov

Moscow State Linguistic University, Moscow, Russia
RKPotapova@yandex.ru

Abstract. The paper presents the research method proposed for speaker identification by speech signals in the Skype system based on the use of speech pulse conversion (SPC). Speech signals recorded in an acoustic studio (anechoic chamber), and the same speech signals transmitted via the IP-telephony Skype channel were studied. The goal of the research was to identify individual features of the speaker's vocal source (phonations) depending on the speech signal transmission channel in order to ascertain the possibility of speaker identification by speech characteristics in information systems.

Keywords: speech pulse conversion, speech signals, IP-telephony Skype channel, speaker identification.

1 Introduction

Speaker recognition by their voice and speech, ways and means of solving this problem become more and more relevant aspects of the problem of identifying persons acting in a destructive manner, calling for destabilization of state foundations, terrorism, regime change, etc. (see e.g. [11]). It should be emphasized that the development of new information and communication technologies and, in particular, of the Internet has made its "contribution" to the social component of interpersonal interaction.

Currently, on the Internet the voice communication based on Skype is widely used along with written speech [1]. The speaker identification, diarization and other speech processing methods is often implemented for automation of the telecommunication services in order to reduce the amount of transmitted data during communication [25,17,19,4].

In this regard, a new danger of using this tool for destructive purposes arises. It is likely that the use of masking techniques (e.g. makeup, false beards, mustaches, etc.) can change the visual image of the speaker via Skype. However, we can assume that certain parameters of the speaker speech signal, despite the impact of the transmission channel, carry "traces" of the individual voice and speech of the speaker, involved in the act of verbal communication, and it may relate primarily to the fine structure of the speech signal (see e.g. [16,6]).

R.K. Potapova in her investigation showed [8,9,10] that the process of verbal communication is a complicated and not fully studied phenomenon. One approach to research this phenomenon is the procedure of its simplifying, highlighting its most important characteristics and functional relations. The optimal approach to the study of

A. Ronzhin et al. (Eds.): SPECOM 2014, LNAI 8773, pp. 329–336, 2014.

verbal communication is creation of a functional model of the speech communication process, including blocks of speech production and perception.

The speech production process can be represented in the form of two components:
- formation of neuronal control commands by phonation and articulation organs;
- direct generation of sound effects by phonation and articulation organs, correlated with the fundamental frequency and the language segmental structure.

The recipient's organs of hearing register wave motion in air pressure, and the higher parts of the brain performs further data processing. All these levels of verbal communication are difficult for direct observation and recording of their operational characteristics, which creates additional difficulties in this phenomenon research.

R.K.Potapova, V.V.Potapov, V.G.Mikhajlov showed in their investigations that in a number of speech study fields [9,10,12,13] only the speech signal is available for measurements. In the sequel this signal is used as the basic source of information about the processes of speech production and perception, their parameters and characteristics.

Based on the study of the spatial distribution of sound pressure in the vocal tract, G.Fant summarized the obtained results [2] and suggested a one-dimensional model of speech production that is suitable for the development of parametric speech synthesis and analysis mathematical methods. According to this model, speech is considered as sound sources filtered by a linear system of the vocal tract. This model is a linear analogue of a two-port network with lumped parameters, which has a power voltage source at its input port. The transfer function of the quadrupole describes resonance properties of the vocal tract [2, pp.39-58].

The voltage source mimics the work of vocal cords in voiced segments of speech and (or) the stochastic excitation function for noise-like segments. Based on the linear model of speech production a speech pulse conversion method (SPC) was developed, which allows to study the characteristics of the vocal cords functioning by the speech signal. A.N.Sobakin in his pitch pulse shape investigations proposed to analyze this phenomenon on the basis of the speech pulse conversion method (SPC) [20,21,22], which allows to determine the analog of a pitch pulse by sound vibrations without the use of additional channels for measuring the acoustic characteristics of speech vibrations. The SPC method proved its efficiency in the study of the vocal cords vibrations in speech signals recorded in an acoustic studio.

2   Methods

This report considers the problem of the applicability of this method in the study of the transformed IP-telephony signals as the most common means of communication on the Internet.

As an example of a synthetic transmission of voice messages in the Internet space the Skype program was selected. The choice of a system like Skype is determined by wide coverage of Internet users, and it can be applied to the field of the speaker identification for special purposes (e.g. to identify authorship of utterances). The main problems associated with the use of SPC in the study of the voice source and possible speaker identification from the obtained data are the follows.

1. Check the operation of the SPC method in speech signals recorded with Skype.

2. Carry out a comparative analysis of the obtained data with the results of the same speech signals recorded in an acoustic studio (anechoic chamber).

3. Determine the presence or absence of the individual characteristics of the speakers' voice sources, dependent from specificity of the transmission over Skype.

The necessity for the SPC method testing is explained by encoding, transmission and voice messages synthesis in the Skype system that are kept secret. Every company that develops a system for analysis and synthesis of speech (not merely), in the present conditions has a software product as the final result. This allows not to disclose methods and algorithms for speech converting during its initial description, the methods of encoding and transmission over the communication channel, as well as methods for synthesizing voice messages. In this study of the greatest interest are methods of the pitch pulse shape reconstruction (simulation). At the same time both methods of the pitch pulses synthesis and characteristics of the voice source used in the voice excitation synthesis of the vocal tract remain unknown.

In speech researches four main types of the speech vibrations source are considered [18, pp.31-37]:

1. voice (tone) excitation;

2. noise (turbulent) excitation;

3. mixed excitation;

4. pulse excitation (explosion).

There are also aspirated sounds and sounds with air flow modulation when there is a narrowing in the glottis, but no cord vibrations.

Speech sounds are divided into vowels (only voice excitation source), voiceless consonants (turbulent excitation source), voiced consonants (mixed excitation source) and explosives. Type of the excitation source is one of the sound features and its distinguishing characteristic. The most informative of these sources is the voice excitation source of the vocal tract [7,12,13]. Vibrations of the vocal cords during the speech sound production contain individual characteristics of the speaker, and are captured by the listener during the perception of the auditory image. The larynx individual characteristics are most remarkable at the production of vowel sounds.

Vowel sounds of speech are found among other various speech sounds and, in particular, can be produced in an isolated (stationary) version. In this case only the voice excitation source functions.

The main characteristics of the voice source are the following:

1. the intensity level - time envelope of the speech signal;

2. the period of vocal cords vibrations (pitch period), or the inverse value of this period - fundamental frequency;

3. pitch pulse shape, defined by the microstructure of the vocal cords vibrations during the production of speech vowel sounds.

The first two features of the voice source (intensity level and fundamental frequency), along with formant characteristics are used in many speaker identification systems [15] and much of the information about the speaker's voice timbre is not considered in this approach. This situation has a negative impact on the quality of the speaker identification procedure.

Thus, it seems appropriate to use information about the pitch pulse shape or its analogue for speaker identification. The problem of determining the pitch pulse shape by the voice signal is rather complex and it has no effective solution so far. Sobakin previously showed that there is one of the possible approaches to its solution is described in [23].

The pitch pulse shape in the model representation is sometimes described by the pulse maximum position, the maximum magnitude (amplitude), the tilt of the initial and final portions of the pulse [3]. It is generally accepted that the maximum excitation of the vocal tract is defined as a slope of the throat pulse at the time of closing of the vocal cords. However, more detailed studies of voice source functioning shows that the approximation of the pitch pulse by straight lines and its extremes does not take the longitudinal and transverse vibrations of the vocal cords in account.

According to the work [24], in the interval of closing of the vocal cords, airflow is reduced to zero not immediately, but gradually. This is because the vocal cords are not located in parallel in the inverse process. Sometimes in the closure interval a small pulsation is observed.[4]

3   Results and Discussion

In this study speech pulse conversion (SPC) is used for identification of individual characteristics of the vocal cords by the speech signal.

Speech-to-pulse conversion, synchronized with the vibrations of the vocal cords, allows to explore the form of produced pulses by methods of mathematical statistics. It is proposed to make normalization of the produced pulses by their centers, and implement addition of normalized pulses. These procedures allow to obtain a statistically significant "image" of the resulting sequence of pulses in the form of a fuzzy set, preserving individual characteristics of the speaker's voice source functioning.

The hardware and software complex used for audio recording in the acoustic studio during the study, consisted of the following elements:

1. Hardware
1.1. Laptop Toshiba Qosmio G30-211-RU
1.2. Sound card Creative Professional E-MU 1616m PCMCIA
1.3. Measuring amplifier Bruel & Kjaer, type 2610
1.4. Microphone Shure SM48, quality class 1
1.5. Announcer booth AUDIOSTOP-1
2. Software
2.1. Operating system Microsoft Windows XP
2.2. Program for recording and researching of speech signals "ZSignalWorkshop" [26].
2.3. Virtual mixing console Creative (comes with a sound card, specified in § 1.2).

In order to monitor and control the quality of produced records professional grade quality headphones Beyerdynamic DT 770 PRO were used additionally, as well as software and hardware complex Computerized Speech Lab (CSL), model 4500, and software package Sony Sound Forge 9.0.

In the present study the hypothesis was tested of the possibility to determine individual characteristics of the pitch pulse by the voice signal using SPC for two types of voice signals recording:

1. signals recorded in the acoustic studio and put through a telephone channel bandpass filter (signals not distorted in the transmission system of the communication channel);

2. signals of the first type put through the Skype phone system. Vowel sounds were processed by a computer program implemented in the numerical computing environment MATLAB 7.6.0.324 by A. Maslov [14].

In the first stage the signals of the first type without distortion of the communication channel were studied. The segment of the speech signal (Fig.1) selected by the researcher is divided into vectors (one-dimensional arrays) of type x (j), ..., x (j + N + p-1), where Nis vectors lengths, p – an order of the autocorrelation matrix. The parameters are set by the researcher.

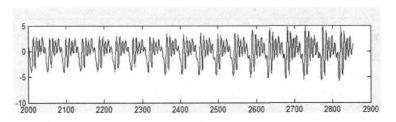

Fig. 1. [a] sound oscillogram, female speaker

An autocorrelation matrix is built on a set of vectors. The determinant of each built matrix is calculated with the change of the current time parameter n. In some cases, for smoothing of singled-out pulses the root of a determinant of the autocorrelation matrix order was used. A sequence of the calculated determinants forms the pulse function, which represents the model of the vocal cords functioning (Fig.2).

The resulting quasi-periodic sequence of pulses is fully consistent, at least visually, with the work of the voice source: pulses correspond to an increase of the amplitude of vibrations in the voice pitch period. It must be exactly so in our model of speech production at the time of disclosure of the vocal cords: subglottic pressure energy coming

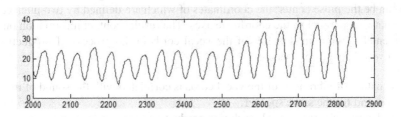

Fig. 2. Sequence of pulses

to the vocal tract (the linear dissipative system), increases the amplitude of the signal at the output of the system.

The following statistical analysis of obtained pulses is aimed at statistically meaningful evaluation of a pitch pulse form ("image"). Such processing of the resulting pulse sequence is associated with the solution of several complex tasks:

1. selection of pulses themselves;
2. normalization of the pulses by amplitude;
3. statistical evaluation of the pulse shape.

In the pulse sequence extrema (maxima and minima, respectively) were determined, which allowed to single out isolated pulses. The values of the sequence which do not exceed a threshold were reset to zero.

In this work, the threshold was taken equal to 1/100 of a single pulse maximum or time envelope maximum calculated for several (typically 3-5) adjacent pulses. The example of the pulse isolation method is shown in Fig.3.

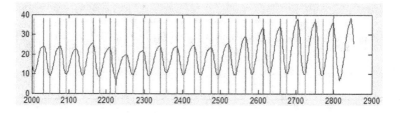

Fig. 3. Singled out maximums and minimums

In this case the isolated pulse was defined as a part of the function change in the segment from a minimum to the nearest minimum. This example shows that the thus obtained pulses will vary in amplitude and duration. Therefore, simple overlapping of these pulses is incorrect and in this case such a procedure does not allow to single out statistically significant pitch pulse shape.

4   Conclusion

In this paper we propose to use integral characteristics of the recovered pulse, depending on the configuration of the entire pulse as a whole. Such an integral characteristic of the pulse can be the pulse center, the coordinates of which are defined by two intersecting areas relatively parallel to the coordinate axes. The results contain information on two fundamentally important features of the vocal cords in the process of production of isolated vowel sounds of speech:

- The nature of vibrations of the vocal cords is correlated with the sound of the spoken sound for the same speaker;
- Vocal cords of various speakers during production of identical sounds function differently and have definite individual characteristics.

We recall that in this paper we discuss the applicability of speech pulse conversion in studies of speech signals, converted in IP-telephony systems, as the most common means of communication of the Internet.

As it was previously indicated, the popular Skype program was chosen as an example of synthetic voice communication system in the Internet space, i.e. e signals of the second type were considered that were put through the Skype system, and comprised additional noise and distortion inherent in this voice message transmission system.

In the present study, the recovery methods (simulation) of the pitch pulse shape in Skype are of greatest interest. At the same time methods of synthesis of pulses and characteristics of the voice source used in the synthesis of voice excitation of the vocal tract remain unknown. Efficiency of the method was tested on the material obtained from six speakers. In a stationary mode, each speaker uttered six Russian vowels «a» [a], «э» [ɛ], «и» [i], «o» [o], «y» [u], «ы» [ɨ].

Vowels were recorded in an acoustic room (anechoic chamber) using a broadband microphone. The recorded vowels were put through voice messages transmission system Skype and recorded again. The recording quality of initial and transformed vowels in both cases was high (time sampling frequency was more than 40 kHz; amplitude sampling was 16 bits/sample). The recorded signals of vowels were filtered by a band-pass filter with a bandwidth of 300 Hz to 3400 Hz with attenuation of approximately 60 dB at the ends of the frequency range from 0 Hz to 4000 Hz, corresponding to the frequency range of the telephone channel. Then the signal was decimated 1:5 that approximately corresponds to the time sampling frequency of 8 kHz [5].

The preliminary answer to the question stated in this study should be considered positive. The SPC method can be applied to the signals in the Skype system in the studies of individual voice source characteristics, for male and female voices.

At this stage the results allow to conclude the following:

1. The SPC method works well on speech signals (vowel sounds), recorded at the receiving end of the IP - telephony system Skype.

2. The comparative analysis of the pulse characteristics of the vowels obtained in the system Skype, and the results of the same speech signals recorded in the acoustic studio (anechoic chamber) showed that the average "images" of the pulses differ from each other for the same speaker, i.e. intraspeaker variability takes place.

3. The singled-out pulse sequences and statistically significant "images" of pitch pulses in the system Skype, describing the work of the voice source, are different in forms for different vowels of the same speaker (intraspeaker variability) and, more importantly, significantly differ from each other for different speakers (interspeaker variability), which can be used as a basis for speaker identification.

Acknowledgments. The survey is being carried out with the support of Russian Science Foundation (RSF) in the framework of the project No.14-18-01059 at Moscow State Linguistic University (scientific head of the project – R.K. Potapova).

References

1. Cicco, L., Mascolo, S., Palmisano, V.: Skype Video Congestion Control: An Experimental Investigation of Computer Networks. 55, 558–571 (2011)

2. Fant, G.: Akusticheskaja teorija recheobrazovanija. Nauka, Moscow (1968)
3. Fant, G.: Speech Production: Glottal Source and Excitation Analysis. Quart Progr. and Status. Rept. Speech Transmiss. Lab. 1, 85–107 (1979)
4. Farnsworth, D.W.: High Speed Motion Pictures of the Human Vocal Cords. Bell Teleph. Lab.: Record 18 (1940)
5. Kotel'nikov, V.A.: O Propusknoj Sposobnosti Efira i Provoloki v Elektrosvjazi Vsesojuznyj Energeticheskij komitet. In: Materialy k I Vsesojuznomu Sezdu po Voprosam Tehnicheskoj Rekonstrukcii Dela Svjazi i Razvitija Slabotochnoj Promyshlennosti (1933)
6. McLaren, M., et al.: Improving Speaker Identification Robustness to Highly Channel-Degraded Speech through Multiple System Fusion. In: ICASSP 2013 (2013)
7. Ondrachkova, J.: Glottographical Research in Sound Groups. In: Modeli Vosprijatija Rechi: Mezhdunarodnyj Psihologicheskij Kongress, pp. 90-94. Leningrad, Moscow (1966)
8. Potapova, R.K.: Novye Informacionnye Tehnologii i Lingvistika. LIBROKOM (2012)
9. Potapova, R.K.: Rech': Kommunikacija, Informacija, Kibernetika. Librokom (2010)
10. Potapova, R.K.: Rechevoe Upravlenie Robotom: Lingvistika i Sovremennye Avtomatizirovannye Sistemy. Komkniga, Moscow (2012)
11. Potapova, R., Komalova, L.: Lingua-cognitive survey of the semantic field "Aggression" in multicultural communication: Typed text. In: Železný, M., Habernal, I., Ronzhin, A. (eds.) SPECOM 2013. LNCS, vol. 8113, pp. 227–232. Springer, Heidelberg (2013)
12. Potapova, R.K., Mihajlov, V.G.: Osnovy Rechevoj Akustiki. IPK MGLU "Rema" (2012)
13. Potapova, R.K., Potapov, V.V.: Rechevaja Kommunikacija: Ot Zvuka k Vyskazyvaniju. JaSK, Moscow (2012)
14. Potapova, R.K., Sobakin, A.N., Maslov, A.V.: Vozmozhnost' Identifikacii Govorjashhego po Golosu v Sisteme Internet-Telefonii Skype. Vestnik Moskovskogo Gosudarstvennogo Lingvisticheskogo Universiteta 673, 177–188 (2013)
15. Ramishvili, G.S.: Avtomaticheskoe Opoznavanie Govorjashhego po Golosu. Radio i Svjaz', Moscow (1981)
16. Riedhammer, K., Bocklet, T., Nöth, E.: Compensation of Extrinsic Variability in Speaker Verification Systems on Simulated Skype and HF Channel Data. In: ICASSP (2011)
17. Ronzhin, A., Budkov, V.: Speaker turn detection based on multimodal situation analysis. In: Železný, M., Habernal, I., Ronzhin, A. (eds.) SPECOM 2013. LNCS, vol. 8113, pp. 302–309. Springer, Heidelberg (2013)
18. Sapozhkov, M.A.: Rechevoj Signal v Kibernetike i Svjazi. Svjaz'izdat, Moscow (1963)
19. Saveliev, A.I.: Optimization Algorithms Distribution Streams of Multimedia Data between Server and Client in Videoconferencing Application. In: SPIIRAS Proc., vol. 31, pp. 61–79 (2013)
20. Sobakin, A.N.: Artikuljacionnye Parametry Rechi i Matematicheskie Metody ih Issledovanija. In: Vestnik MGLU. IPK MGLU "Rema", Moscow (2006)
21. Sobakin, A.N.: Ob Opredelenii Formantnyh Parametrov Golosovogo Trakta po Rechevomu Signalu s Pomoshh'ju JeVM. Akusticheskij Zhurnal AN SSSR 1, 106–114 (1972)
22. Sobakin, A.N.: Osnovnoj Ton Rechi i Metod ego Issledovanija. In: IX Sessija RAO: Sovremennye Rechevye Tehnologii, pp. 47–50. GEOS, Moscow (1999)
23. Sobakin, A.N.: Vydelenie Impul'sov Osnovnogo Tona po Rechevomu Signalu. In: XXII Sessija RAO: Sovremennye Rechevye Tehnologii, pp. 48–52. GEOS, Moscow (2010)
24. Sundberg, J., Gauffin, J.: Logopedics Wave-Form and Status Rept. Speech Transmiss. Lab. 2-3, 35–50 (1978)
25. Volfin, I., Cohen, I.: Dominant Speaker Identification for Multipoint Videoconferencing. Computer Speech and Language 27, 895–910 (2013)
26. Zhenilo, V.R.: ZSignalWorkshop. Jelektronnyj resurs "Masterskaja signalov" (2012) http://zhenilo.narod.ru/main/index.htm

Parametrc Representation of Kazakh Gestural Speech

Saule Kudubayeva and Gulmira Yermagambetova

Department of Informatics, Kostanay State University
named after A. Baytursynov, Kostanay, Kazakhstan
{saule.kudubayeva,ngan7322}@gmail.com

Abstract. The article presents results of recent experiments on recognition of gestural speech in Kazakh language. It provides overview of the process of collection and pre-processing of the gestural speech base as well as the parametric representation of the Kazakh gestural speech. Application prototype can be used as a foundational block for the recognition of gestural speech and pictures in Kazakh language.

Keywords: sign language, speech and image recognition, recognition dictionary, visual signs.

1 Introduction

Speech technologies for sign languages (including Kazakh) and their peculiarities have not gathered enough attention in the world science, therefore development of such technologies is somewhat delayed [1]. Same sources claim that Kazakh language can be considered an endangered language, and it requires special attention from linguists and application developers. There are practically no qualitatively and reliably acting systems of automatic recognition of the Kazakh sounding as well as gestural speech. Besides existing technical-economic difficulties the development of the Kazakh speech technologies is first of all influenced by the difficulties of the Kazakh language and speech causing difficulties in the process of the automatic processing: rules of word formation, presence of seven cases in the formation of nouns, variability of the Kazakh language and speech because of the presence of several dialects.

The presence of a gestural speech base (database) is necessary for teaching people modern system of gestural speech recognition based on the probability models and methods of processing. However, such visual gestural speech base that would be suitable for training automatic recognition systems has not yet been created.

2 The Problem of Kazakh Gestural Speech Recognition.

The recognition problem reduces to classification of a set of data on the basis of many data classes. Markov hidden model can be considered as classifier. Besides Markov hidden models on recognition other classifiers such as method of support vectors can be used. The essence of the method is in the fact that data are presented in multidimensional space and classified with the help of hyper planes. Both methods in the considered studies show fairly high recognition accuracy. The reason for approach to gesture

A. Ronzhin et al. (Eds.): SPECOM 2014, LNAI 8773, pp. 337–344, 2014.

recognition using the method of support vectors is in the necessity to represent a gesture as a set of main characteristics, which in future will be subjected to comparison and classification. Division of data into intersecting segments and frames is done before. Then characteristics are extracted from each of the frames, and on their basis the meanings vector defining gesture is formed. After that gesture classification the method of support vectors is used.

The problem of gestural speech recognition is characterized by many parameters; first of all, it is the characteristic of the gestural speech transmission path, recognition dictionary volume, gestures variability. Word boundaries in the flow of gestural speech can be defined only in the process of recognition (decoding signs) by the selection of optimal sequence of gestures, which is best concordant with the input flow of gestures according to mathematical models [2].

For performing studies on the Kazakh gestural speech recognition there appeared the necessity to create a nontrivial dictionary of the Kazakh gestural speech containing dactylic alphabet presented on Fig. 1, some hundreds of thousands of video files with words of different topics, including numerical, geographical, consumer information and other topics. Work on the creation of multimedia database of the Kazakh gestural speech accompanied by the sounding speech were carried out separately. Both information flows (audio and visual) are captured by a single device (for example, by digital video camera). This way it's possible that acoustic part will contain data of unsatisfactory quality. That is why to obtain the best quality of data recording independent capture of video flow from the digital video camera and audio flow from a professional microphone is used. It is better to use high-speed video camera (providing capture of full video frames in VGA resolution with progressive scan having a frame rate of 200 Hz).

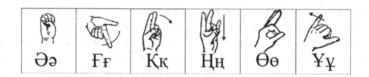

Fig. 1. Dactylic alphabet of the Kazakh sign language

3 Experiments with Parametric Representation of Gestural Speech.

Two different systems of signs were used and investigated as visual signs describing position of human hands:

1. Pixel visual signs applying analysis of the main components (Principal Component Analysis - PCA) of visual area of breast and hands of a person using sign language with automatic detection of this area of interest. This type of visual signs are provided in one of the first versions of OpenCV AVSR computer vision library [3].

2. Geometrical visual signs applying analysis of picture colour differentiation and describing geometrical form of human hands: fingers width, palm size, clenched fingers visibility.

With both of these methods initial processing of video frames obtained from video camera (with optical picture resolution of 720x576 pixels, progressive scan and frame rate of 25 Hz) is done the same way in accordance with the scheme presented on Fig. 2. On each video frame we search for breast and hands area with the help of classifier by the Adaptive Boosting method based on the Viola-Jones algorithm [4] which is implemented and previously trained on the pictures of faces and facial organs of different people using OpenCV library [5].

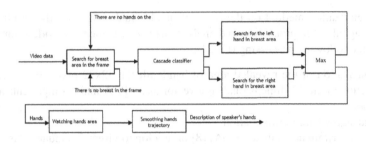

Fig. 2. Functional scheme of searching for hands area of the speaker using sign language on video frames

The essence of our method in relation to the problem of identification/detection of graphical objects on pictures is in combination of simple classifiers/recognizers of certain signs of an object to create an integral multi-level classifier (simple classifiers group). First of all, such classifier is trained on the basis of many available samples/models of required objects (area of breast, hands, lips, if the speaker pronounces sounds, etc.), which are positive samples and on the basis of the selection among negative samples there are normalized pictures, which do not contain this object. In this case every following simple classifier is trained in a selection of samples of the required object, which have been incorrectly classified by previous classifiers (for example, pictures of hands on knees, while standing, having mittens on the hands or while holding objects, etc.). Then, a classifier training process is used to identify the required object on the arbitrary picture. If video frame has a high resolution, then classified is consecutively used to find the object with the picture fragment, which is moved across the frame with different scaling factors of the picture to find the necessary object of different size [6]. Cascade classifier is implemented via a decision tree containing simple classifiers, each of which is consecutively used with the graphical area of interest. It makes only one decision out of the linear combination of intermediate results about the presence of the object in the frame (within a probability set of a required object) [7]. On Fig. 3 there are examples of video frames from our gestural speech base with areas of breast (oval) and hands (rectangle) of the speaking sign language interpreter, which have been revealed automatically using our method.

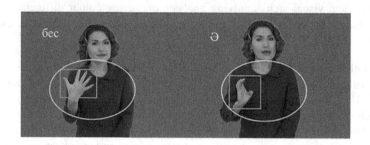

Fig. 3. Examples taken from video files representing gestural speech

Parameterization method on the basis of pixel visual signs uses the results of the previous signal video processing and analyses hands movements on video frames performing the following processing (Fig. 4):

- normalization of the revealed area of hands till the 32x32 pixels picture and the reflection in the 32-dimensional sign vector using PCA main components analysis method
- visual sign vector normalization
- linear discriminant analysis (LDA) [8] in relation to visems' standard classes.

Such processing transforms the sequence of video frames in chains of 10-dimensional sign vectors with the rate of 100 Hz.

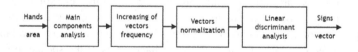

Fig. 4. Functional scheme of pixel visual signs calculation method for the sequence of video frames

The basis for the pixel signs calculation method is made by the method of PCA main components analysis, which is used to compress information without significant losses of information [7].For every graphical area of interest the main components (several tens) are calculated, all other components encode only small differences between the signal and noise and cannot be taken into consideration. In the parameterization method used search for hands in the frame is being performed, and after the successful hands detection the corresponding rectangular area of the picture is normalized till the 32x32 pixels size, after that color pixels are reduced to the gradation of grey and normalized picture is subjected to analysis of PCA main components to calculate 32-dimensional vector of signs. PCA projection is calculated beforehand out of a large amount of training pictures containing hands area of a person who uses gestures while speaking [9].

Linear Discriminant Analysis (LDA) is also used in the presentation of parameterization method [8]. Its task is to find projection into space in which the difference between various classes of objects will be maximal. This requirement is formulated as obtaining maximally compact clusters corresponding to different classes as far remote as possible. With the help of LDA method it is possible to get the lower-dimensional subspace in which clusters of visems models are nominally intersecting. This method of visual signs calculation is provided in software OpenCV computer vision library [3] and is used in this study.

The second studied type of parameterization implements geometric visual signs which allow us to describe the shape of hands of the speaker in sign language [10]. The color of the object of interest (human hand) on the picture is an effective sign of distinction and classification of objects on the picture. The skin color of different people takes a small limited subdomain of the color space, even when considering the skin colors of different races. In this case the main difference is in brightness, not in the color shade and this allows to make a conclusion about the proximity in skin color shade of different people and use characteristic color of the skin as a sign for the detection of faces and hands on pictures.

In this method pre-processing of pictures is in search for human body on the picture with the help of AdaBoost method with cascade classifiers, after that areas of interest containing only skin colour are found and these areas are kept as bitmap graphics pictures. In parametric files average values of the color of speaker's hands skin and in graphical files – areas of breast and hands are also kept. Then every video file from the multimedia database is processed individually searching for the vertical body's position. Inside the found area we perform a search for the position of breast and hands. Hands region size is calculated being based on the distance between shoulders on the picture. For every frame the centre of shoulders and hands is calculated and this information is used to find moving hands. This allows us to define, for example, the face size on the picture as well as head's rotation angle. During the eyes detection on the picture it is also necessary to check, whether eyes are closed or not; if eyes are closed, detection on the picture does not happen and the required values from the previous frame are taken. For every processed file parameters file with the description containing information about the center of breast, its rotation and size is created. Using this information picturing hands area can be reconstructed for every video frame during processing.

Another researched type of parameterization implements geometric visual signs which are also based on the description of a hand/hands form and position (visibility) of fingers. For that it is necessary to define on the picture contours of fingers and palm for each frame. To obtain binary description of the form of hands we used the method based on the final processing of the color information [9]. Hands search happens only in the found breast area, in this case every pixel is represented by three paths in accordance with RGB format (R – red, G – green, B – blue). We used chromatic colors, which is why consecutive transformation of all the colors in accordance with the formula (normalization) happens:

$$G_{ch} = \frac{G}{R + G + B}. \tag{1}$$

Chromatic colors are used to avoid the influence of changing the angle of hands illuminance. The border for the hands position is adaptively determined by automatic clustering. Clustering algorithm subdivides all the pixels into two clusters with calculation of mathematical expectation and dispersion. Adaptive border is calculated in the following way:

$$t = m_L + (\frac{(m_S - m_L)}{n_S + n_L} * n_1),$$ (2)

where
m_L mathematical expectation of hands brightness
m_S mathematical expectation of brightness of clothes colour on breast
n_L number of hands points
n_S number of skin points (pixels).

We used a well known clustering algorithm which is quite demanding in terms of computer resources. Therefore borders are only calculated for the first frame and kept its value further. When the border is used to get the binary image (mask), we obtain the result shown on Fig. 5(a). This object quite well corresponds to the outer contours of the hand, but not always. The problem is related to the difficulty of detecting bent fingers and dark places inside the folded palms. During further processing the main calculations are connected with searching for the internal surface of the palm inside the picture restricted by external contours. Algorithm uses a line connecting centers of the palms with fingers. Then we search for local minimums - these minimums represent internal borders of the bent fingers of the hand on this line. Having the value of brightness of the internal border it is possible to determine the limit of brightness for the internal surface of the hand. The final form of the hand's picture obtained as binary image is shown on Fig. 5(d).

However, on this picture there is quite a lot of noise, so it is necessary to reconstruct the whole form of the hand, for this purpose an active model of hands is used: the model consists of 32 points and is run by PCA parameters. This model can be changed to describe any possible configuration of hand's form. To "attach" this model to the real pictures of hands a training set of 150 pictures of breast and hands area was selected for 8 different sign language interpreters. Internal and external contours were marked by an expert on every training picture, and then 16 points for every contour were selected. Points of internal hands contour are normalized in accordance with the size (width) of external hands contours, and then these points are centered by the line connecting angles of the external hands contour. The given binary image localizes 32 points from the model as it is shown on Fig. 5(e). Then the model is smoothed and reconstructed by the picture of hands form shown on Fig. 5(f). Additional problem is when after the border's usage we have several scattered objects on the binary image, if we just choose the biggest object it is possible to lose some parts of hands as it is shown on Fig. 5(b). Thus, hands model from the previous frame is used to determine which parts correspond to the graphical object of interest, and which of them relate to the background as it is shown on Fig. 5(c).

The first part of the parameters vector is calculated directly from the detected contour of the hand. 5 signs to describe absolute size of the hand (the length and width of the

Fig. 5. The process of hands video processing: a) picture with the border; b) the biggest continuous binary object; c) reconstruction of the whole binary object; d) area inside the palm; e) finding control points by the model; f) reconstructed hand's form

palm, its thickness, the length of the thumb, the length of the forefinger) were chosen. These parameters have been chosen because they are easily normalized. Final signs vector contains a number of visual parameters [10], describing geometrical form of the hands while using sign language in speech.

While designing speech automatic recognition system working in the real time scale with using cameras (on-line mode), it is often required to find a compromise between the accuracy of recognition and speed of processing. Setting up some parameters for gesture recognition can improve the accuracy of recognition, but reduce the processing speed.

The results of recognition of continuous gestural Kazakh speech for the dictionary of small volume in one module system with existing noise conditions gave large uncertainties. The advantage of asynchronous CCMM in the system of audiovisual speech recognition is explained by its possibility to process non-transient temporary mismatch of acoustic and visual units in the flow of speech. The system of recognition on the basis of synchronous multithreaded hidden Markov's models of the first order implies using different scales to set information fullness of speech modalities under the conditions of recognizer's functioning, but current state of every flow in the model should be synchronous.

4   Conclusion

Simultaneous use of speech and visual interface in Kazakh language, verbal human-machine communication is a promising concept. We hope it would be especially helpful to those having hearing and speech problems.

– As a result of our analytical review we can conclude that there were no scientific investigations in the sphere of recognition of the Kazakh gestural speech with the application of complex analysis and combination of audio and video information about speech.
– Database of the visual gestural Kazakh speech (multimedia speech base) KazA-VSpeechCorpus consisting of synchronized audio and video dactylic alphabet, set of numbers and figures, texts and phrases of the gestural Kazakh speech was firstly created and filed for registration. Multimedia recordings of the continuous speech of 8 sign language interpreters were collected and processed (each of them has pronounced 300 prepared phrases, 50 texts, proverbs and other types of information). Segmentation of audio and video data into phrases and words was done.

– Development of automatic system of visual recognition of Kazakh gestural speech is in process. Experimental findings have shown that the accuracy of recognition of words of continuous gestural speech by video information currently reaches 67%.

References

1. Besacier, L., Barnard, E., Karpov, A., Schultz, T.: Automatic speech recognition for under-resourced languages: A survey. Speech Communication 56, 85–100 (2014)
2. Kindiroglu, A., Yalcın, H., Aran, O., Hruz, M., Campr, P., Akarun, L., Karpov, A.: Automatic Recognition of Fingerspelling Gestures in Multiple Languages for a Communication Interface for the Disabled. Pattern Recognition and Image Analysis 22(4), 527–536 (2012)
3. Open Source Computer Vision Library (OpenCV), http://sourceforge.net/projects/opencvlibrary
4. Castrillyn, M., Deniz, O., Hernandez, D., Lorenzo, J.: Comparison of Face and Facial Feature Detectors based on the Viola-Jones General Object Detection Framework. Machine Vision and Applications 22(3), 481–494 (2011)
5. Bradsky, G., Kaehler, A.: Learning OpenCV. O'Reilly Publisher (2008)
6. Karpov, A.: Computer analysis and synthesis of Russian sign language. Voprosy Jazykoznanija 6, 41–53 (2011)
7. Neti, C., Potamianos, G., Luettin, J.: Audio-visual speech recognition. In: Final Workshop 2000 Report, Center for Language and Speech Processing. The Johns Hopkins University, Baltimore (2000)
8. Yu, H., Yang, J.: Direct LDA algorithm for high-dimensional data with application to face recognition. Pattern Recognition 34(10), 2067–2070 (2001)
9. Liang, L., Liu, X., Zhao, Y., Pi, X., Nefian, A.: Speaker independent audio-visual continuous speech recognition. In: Proc. International Conference on Multimedia and Expo ICME 2002, Lausanne, Switzerland (2002)
10. Devyatkov, V., Alfimcev, A.: Raspoznovanie manipulyativnich jestov. Herald of the Bauman Moscow state technical university. Priborostroenie 68(3), 56–75 (2007)

Personified Voice Interaction Software in Billing Systems

Daria A. Suranova[1,2] and Roman V. Meshcheryakov[2]

[1] AGU, 61, Lenina pr., Barnaul, Russia
[2] TUSUR, 40, Lenina pr., Tomsk, Russia
`daria@suranova.ru, mrv@keva.tusur.ru`

Abstract. Applying voice possibilities in modern speech billing systems can significantly reduce the operators' time and costs and in some cases improve the accuracy of the initial data. For example, the software will evaluate the possibility of applying the technology of synthesis and speech recognition for billing systems. It considers individual user's features. Experiments illustrate examples of voice technology effective implementation.

Keywords: Billing system, speech interface, communication, human-computer interaction.

1 Introduction and Descriptions Review

Due to the omnipresence of computers in various spheres of social life, there is a need in simple and direct way of human-computer interaction[1]. Currently, usability is a top priority, and to achieve this goal we have got not only graphics, but also voice, sensitive, tactile solutions. Despite the opportunities, many software products are limited only to the use of the graphical method of communication, especially when it comes into interaction with a personal computer. In complex computing systems, much attention is paid to the accuracy of calculations, but not to the process of user interaction. Nevertheless, well-designed interface, including verbal interaction between the man and the computer, can significantly reduce time spent by operators and in some cases improve the accuracy of the initial data. In billing systems the operator and the computer center are connected by means of applications containing forms for data entry, screen and printed report forms and tools for payment operations execution. Working with user application takes place in simplex mode, without feedback, it is unnatural and may become a cause of errors.

The volume of input and output data is usually large, so interactions can be improved and adapted to the more conventional way of human communication via speech. This will not only improve the quality of the operators work, but also may become a tool for disables people [2].

Voice solutions for different spheres can exist for English language. For example, applications for mobile devices (Siri), the system of "smart home" single solutions , such as Watson program (IBM), which has an extensive knowledge base mainly in medicine, and is used to receive counseling when a doctor has trouble in drawing conclusions. In addition, the latest operating systems contain embedded synthesis and speech recognition to speech commands and text listening.

A. Ronzhin et al. (Eds.): SPECOM 2014, LNAI 8773, pp. 345–352, 2014.

In June 2013 the company i-Free (St. Petersburg) released a mobile 3D- assistant in Russian for Android - application "Sobesednica". The product has a good quality of Russian speech recognition and is partially paid (synthesis). It lets you dial, know the weather, open the site, set the alarm. "Center of Speech Technology" has developed solutions for the communal sector with the use of speech technology: service of reminding about the debt, taking statements from subscribers. These solutions are used to improve communication with external clients. Also, many search systems provide voice input in addition to the existing data entry using the mouse and the keyboard.

Voice solutions for billing systems are often designed for subscribers. As an example there exist applications to collect evidence on the counter by the phone, programs reminding of debts in services, programs serving to obtain information via a call to the certain number, payment services through pronouncing the contract number, and others. However, voice solutions are not used to organize the work of billing systems operators.

2   Interaction Software in Billing Systems

To implement programmatic interaction we used multimodal interfaces [3]. Concept modality determines the number of ways (flows) of input / output information. As part of this work verbal and graphical modality were used. The choice depended on the modality of work settings and user preferences. When using natural language information is presented as a set of phrases that have some syntax constructions. Set of words allowed in the composition of such constructions makes up a system dictionary. In an early stage a billing system dictionary was limited to a set of words and phrases, based on the most frequently used functions. Later it will be limited by the sphere of billing systems and based on the workflow vocabulary.

The most frequently used forms of data entry, search, and the shape of the sampling data on certain conditions in a report were chosen for initial implementation. Possible scenarios of interactive voice response based on this reference model were designed for each of these modes of thought and interaction. Additional mapping of input voice phrases on the screen was provided in order to improve security and correct data entry and validation. Spoken phrases were analyzed, and if errors were clarified by users. A set of reference phrases has been developed for each mode of operation, include support words. Support words which help to understand user's goals can be necessarily or variably present in a phrase. Consider the phrase used when entering the readings in the billing system "Account 1234 type hot initial 7 finish 8". The key words here are "account", "initial", "finish". When choosing a structure for each user he/ she was enquired how he would ask another person to do something. This approach stems from the fact that in the process the man communicates with the computer as an equal. Phrases were provided for variations in the words pronunciation and sets of synonyms that users sometimes replaced by the reference support words in phrases. Phrases for filling out the form may be the following: "Account 1234 cold start 5 final 7" or "Account 1234 hot difference 3." A form filled out in this manner is represented in the figure.

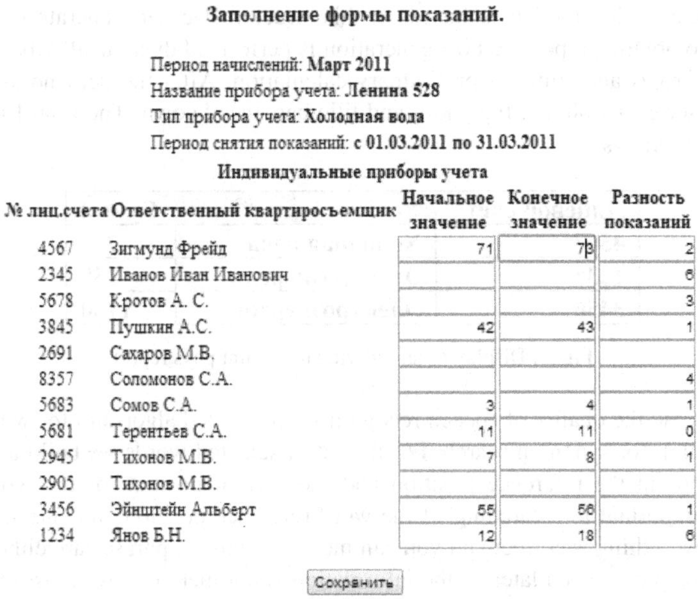

Заполнение формы показаний.

Период начислений: **Март 2011**
Название прибора учета: **Ленина 528**
Тип прибора учета: **Холодная вода**
Период снятия показаний: **с 01.03.2011 по 31.03.2011**

Индивидуальные приборы учета

№ лиц.счета	Ответственный квартиросъемщик	Начальное значение	Конечное значение	Разность показаний
4567	Зигмунд Фрейд	71	73	2
2345	Иванов Иван Иванович			6
5678	Кротов А. С.			3
3845	Пушкин А.С.	42	43	1
2691	Сахаров М.В.			
8357	Соломонов С.А.			4
5683	Сомов С.А.	3	4	1
5681	Терентьев С.А.	11	11	0
2945	Тихонов М.В.	7	8	1
2905	Тихонов М.В.			
3456	Эйнштейн Альберт	55	56	1
1234	Янов Б.Н.	12	18	6

Сохранить

Fig. 1. Input readings form

Instruments for account search by number or by address are frequently used. If a user wants to find the account number "1234" he says "Find account 1234" or "Get account 1234". If a user wants to find an account by address he says "Find by address city Barnaul street Popova house 19 flat 13". The system translates this command to the sequence of actions and the form looks like the following figure.

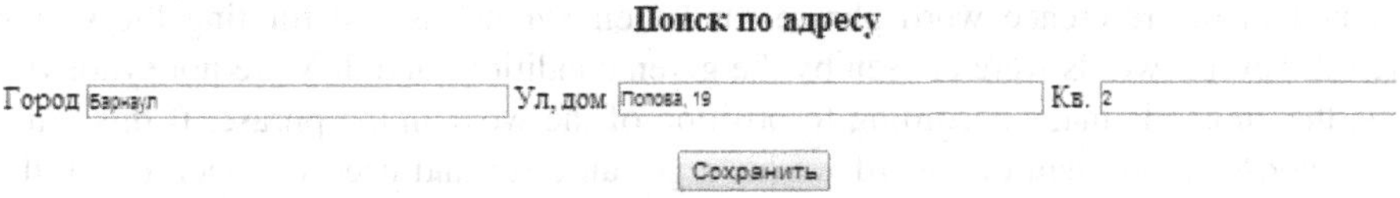

Поиск по адресу

| Город | Барнаул | Ул, дом | Попова, 19 | Кв. | 2 |

Сохранить

Fig. 2. Searching address form

Another option is creating reports. Shaping the report, the user usually knows what he wants to get and in what form. For example, getting data on the services accrual phrase may be the following: "select report accrual address Barnaul street Popova house 19 month January front account and service."

In addition to sampling and data storage we used a special indexed consolidated table of data for several sections (personal account, house, service, type the amount, period, etc.). Queries generated by user phrases shall have the simplest structure and highest productivity [4]. OLAP was used for this technology. It involves storing data in a table as a number and a set of attributes defined for this number. For each attribute, there must be a directory with the appropriate name, and if the attribute "House" is defined as a field «Id_House», then the system must have a directory of houses called «House». Then, based on this structure we can generate queries, for example to obtain a report. Report generation is performed dynamically, based on the number of rows and columns preliminary calculation. After the demand assignment data type for each column, the width and title becomes known. The final form of the report is as follows.

Лицевой счет	Услуга	Сумма
4567	Холодная вода	200
1234	Электроэнергия	150
3456	Электроэнергия	1180

Fig. 3. Display of an individual account pays report

To increase the quality of speech recognition we created algorithm for word search and algorithm for synonym search. For the set of selected words we build a synonym list. A word in the reference position and the current position of the word in the phrase is important for searching. If the word reference position and current position coincide everything is correct and you can move on. Missed phrases are either optional or will be pronounced later. If the information is not met later, we must request the data from the user. If we find the word before the algorithm location it means that there was data correction (the user made a mistake and corrected it) and we should take only the latest data. After parsing phrases, check for missing values takes place and their clarification if necessary. Then we compare words with directories. Finding synonyms may not sometimes be enough. Some words have the same or similar spelling but different meanings. We used the concept of "similarity measure" for these words and implemented all this by means of word search algorithm using Levenshtein distance and considering getting into the subject area. Word search algorithm is called in if the synonyms search algorithm fails. Selecting the minimum value is made with account of the reference word phrases and their synonyms and limiting the search area. If several words were chosen by the given conditions and they are not synonymous, the choice is made according to position of the word in the phrase. If this criterion chooses more than one word we have got an error and need to check up on the result.

During the development process Google Voice was used as a speech recognition module service [5]. This module was chosen by virtue of the following experiments confirmed advantages: acceptable quality of Russian speech recognition; no need to train the system (the base for training is formed on the basis of a large number of Internet users); high recognition rate due to the use of resources; ease of implementation in web-form. For speech synthesis we used synth module from Microsoft. These modules are selected on the ground of experiments as most comfortable in listening and having minimal number of errors in the utterance.

Program complex was developed to estimate the possibility of introducing voice communication methods to the billing system [6]. This complex includes the most frequently used program modes. The dialog programs interaction is characterized of the ability to switch between graphic and voice mode of interaction in the process, as well as taking into account individual user settings. The main parts of the complex are the dialog module and interaction analysis results module. In the dialog module the user selects settings to build a dialogue and implementation modalities of interaction using speech synthesis and recognition modules, as well as graphical tools. Dialogue scripts are described in the corresponding data structures. The choice of a script is determined by the initial settings and the user's current actions. Users can switch between the input methods by means of voice commands or using a keyboard and mouse in work process.

Analysis module parses and analyzes user phrases, creates a structure and checks errors. This module uses the computing proximity measure of words algorithm. It considers the structure of words in phrases and limitation of billing systems domain. In case of uncertain situations the information is checked with the user.

The configuration module selects the domain, user settings, the mode of interaction - verbal or graphical input and output data and other settings. Generation output data module determines the format and the display mode of the interaction result. It can be a form with data, a layout form, or the result of command execution.

3 Setting and Evaluation Results of Applying Modules Experiments

To estimate the result of adaptive voice interaction we make some experiments. For experiments we used test modules, available to the public on the Internet. In assessing the recognition module words from the domain billing systems were used. Test modules are available to the public on the Internet. Words from the domain billing systems were used in estimating the recognition module. They were made for the billing system data used to calculate the pay of communal services in Barnaul. A group of users from 25 to 60 years old were chosen to participate in the experiment. All of them had experience in billing system before. Difference in people's voice characteristics was an important selection criterion. Experiments conditions met conventional setting - silence, a room without customers.

3.1 Selecting Recognition Module Experiment

For billing systems dictionary analysis for four modules of speech recognition was performed and compared in several stages: recognition of a single word, a set of words and phrases (Fig. 4). The experiment was made for one speaker who had experience in billing systems. The vertical noted the number (percentage) of correctly recognized words or phrases. The number of experiments for each module for each parameter comprised up to 280 pronunciations for each element. Based on the figure, we can conclude that the recognition module M1 (Google Voice) showed the best quality of individual words and phrases recognition for billing systems.

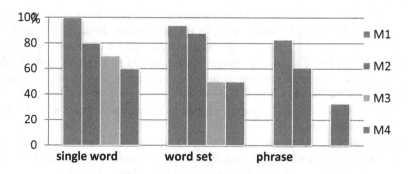

Fig. 4. Comparison result of speech recognition modules

3.2 Selecting Synthesis Module Experiment

For billing system dictionary we compared quality for synthesis modules C1, C2, C3 for the correct intonation (O1), acceleration / deceleration speech playback (O2), the bias stress (O3), skipping sound / presence of extraneous sounds (O4), unnecessary pause / no delay (O5). Set of individual words and sentences was formed on the basis of words dealing with billing systems sphere and considering GOST 16600-72: Voice transmission through radiotelephone paths [7] and GOST 50840-95: Voice transmission through communication paths. Quality, legibility and recognition assessment methods were used from [8]. Errors were evaluated on the following principle: if at least one person words or sentences noted negative feelings while listening, the module for a given parameter was given negative evaluation [9]. The aim of the experiment was to choose the modules that can be used with some restrictions in the billing system. Since the choice of the synthesis module does not affect the system as a whole, a small number of sentences and words was chosen. Despite the fact that C3 showed the best results based on the testing results in comparison to C1 and C2, observations showed C2 to be more pleasant to listen to than C3. C3 voice had a metallic tone and sounded less natural. C2 is Acapela TTS (female) for Windows, C3 is Digalo (male).

3.3 Search Speed in Voice and Graphics Mode Estimation Experiment

The experiment was aimed at evaluating the advantages of time, which can be obtained by using voice data input. On the basis of overall statistics analysis and counting acts done by users in April 2013, most users were concluded to work with personal accounts. Searching personal account operation was selected for the experiment. For this operation we can compare working time with graphical and speech interfaces. The purpose of this experiment was to evaluate the advantages, which can be obtained by using the voice data input. To gain an advantage of time interaction it is necessary to choose the most often used mode, or the mode with long execution time. D1- D6 are different modes of each of the search methods: D1, D3, D5 - search by number, D1, D3, D5 - search by address. The results are shown in Table 1 time of using the context based search is given in parentheses. In some cases the speech mode showed a three-fold time advantage. 20 experiments were performed for each type of action.

Table 1. Average time for account search in seconds

Way of interaction	D1	D2	D3	D4	D5	D6
Graphics	18	42	9	20	7	15
Voice	7	6 (14)	5	6 (14)	7	6 (14)

As seen from the table, the account search takes from 7 to 42 seconds on an average, depending on the mode and the type of the search. Thus, it can be arguable that voice search of the personal account can speed up this operation.

3.4   Estimating the Improvement by Applying Algorithms Experiment

The aim of the experiments is to determine the effectiveness of synonyms search algorithms and word search when applied to a set of sentences containing errors. High percentage of errors can lead to customers negative reactions and refuse to work with the system. We estimated the effect of algorithm on the basis of phrases conversion. Experiments were conducted for a sample of erroneous phrases from 3.1. Algorithm was applied to each phrase, the correct phrase resulted in converted, transformed or incorrect transformed or original incorrect phrase. The results are shown in table.

Table 2. The result of a search algorithm for word

Phrase type	Transformed		Original
	correct	incorrect	incorrect
Amount, %	68	4	28

Thus, the algorithm allows word search to achieve a result in 68% of cases of errors, improving the recognition result is the average from 75% to 92%.

Algorithm evaluation is not primarily concerned with the quality of speech recognition but with users' features and habits in the use of words and phrases. Consider the example of the algorithm operation in terms of account search phrases. Personal account reference search phrase line is as follows: "Find personal 1234". Several utterance variations of the phrase are allowed. Their structure is shown in table 3. The given data was collected on the basis of user phrases statistics in October 2013. The number of sentences totaled to1327. Based on the data in Table 3 it can be concluded that about 70% of the account search is successful. In other situations, clarification dialogue with the user takes place and the result is obtained. Phrases "Account 1234" and "Find 1234" were précised and we succeeded in 62% of cases.

Table 3. Results of applying the synonyms search algorithm

Phrase structure	Amount, %	Is success?	Reason
Find personal 1234	34,8	Yes	standard
Find account 1234	15,2	Yes	replaced by synonym
Finding account 1234	9,1	Yes	replaced by synonym
Find account 1234	11,7	Yes	replaced by synonym
Personal 1234	10,6	No	pass the word
Find 1234	13	No	pass the word
Other	5,6	No	incorrect structure

4   Conclusion

Developed algorithms and software can be used to improve the human-computer interaction in billing systems. By the example of Barnaul billing system used in personal accounts, houses, organizations searching we obtained sevenfold speed advantage. In case when some simple reports were drawn speed advantage comprised 15-20%. The number of errors on the example of the search of personal accounts has slightly changed (2-3%) due to the fact that many accounts even mistakenly entered exist in the system. In total, the effect of the introduction equaled to about 15-20%. In future we plan to develop functionality by adding the possibility of dialogue, including more complex interaction scenarios.

References

1. Potapova, R.K.: Secrets of modern Centaur. Speech interaction "human-machine". URSS (2003)
2. Bondarenko, V.P., Meshcheryakov, R.V.: Dialogue as a basis for constructing speech systems. Cybernetics and Systems Analysis 2, 30–41 (2008)
3. Ronzhin, A., Budkov, V.: Speaker Turn Detection Based on Multimodal Situation. In: Železný, M., Habernal, I., Ronzhin, A. (eds.) SPECOM 2013. LNCS, vol. 8113, pp. 302–309. Springer, Heidelberg (2013)
4. Suranova, D.A.: Stand structure for the study of human-machine interface in natural language. News of Altai State University 1-2(77), 114–117 (2013)
5. Lobanov, B.M., Zhitko, V.A.: Application of cloudy internet technologies in speech recognition. Informatica 4 (2012)
6. Suranova, D.A.: Using natural language for queries in billing systems. TUSUR reports 1(25), part 2, 216–219 (2012)
7. Standard GOST 16600-72. Voice over paths radiotelephone. Requirements for speech articulation and methods of measurement. Reissued. Instead of GOST 16600-71; Introduced. 27.09.72. Moscow: Publishing Standards (1973)
8. Standard GOST 50840-95 Voice over paths of communication. Methods for assessing the quality, legibility and recognition 01.01.1997. Moscow: Publishing Standards (1995)
9. Meshcheriakov, R.V., Ponizov, A.G.: Quality assessment of hearing based on mobile computing devices. SPIIRAS Proceedings 18, 93–107 (2011)

Phrase-Final Lengthening in Russian: Pre-boundary or Pre-pausal?

Tatiana Kachkovskaia

Department of Phonetics, Saint Petersburg State University, Russia
www.spbu.ru
tania.kachkovskaya@gmail.com

Abstract. It has been shown for many languages that words are lengthened in phrase-final position. However, it is not quite clear whether this lengthening is caused more by the presence of a boundary or by the presence of a pause. The present paper aims to answer this question by analysing the duration of stressed and post-stressed vowels in words occurring at the beginning/middle vs. end of intonational phrase, and with vs. without a following pause. In addition, the present study attempts to explain how lengthening is distributed among the the final word's segments, especially in cases when the boundary is not marked by a pause.

Keywords: phrase-final lengthening, pre-boundary lengthening, pre-pausal lengthening, segment duration.

1 Introduction

In papers on the subject several terms are used to describe the phenomenon of segmental lengthening at the end of prosodic units. The most common are phrase-final lengthening, pre-boundary (pre-juncture) lengthening and pre-pausal lengthening. While the former two can be considered synonyms, the latter differs in the way that it excludes the situations when the boundary is not marked by a pause. Most authors do not distinguish between these two types of lengthening. However, it is clear that the lengthening effect is higher in the presence of a pause [1] [7].

Previous studies for Russian [2] [3] also show that segmental duration values are low for words in intonational-phrase-final position with no pause following, as opposed to those with a pause.

Another study [6] for Russian shows that in non-final phrases (i. e. intonational phrases, but not utterances) the degree of final lengthening is very small and there is often no pause, since the boundary is marked primarily by changes in melody.

There are, therefore, at least two questions to be asked:

1. Is *pre-pausal* lengthening caused only by the presence of a pause or also by the phrase-final position?
2. Are final segments lengthened at the end of an intonational phrase if the boundary is *not* marked by a pause?

Therefore, the present paper does not deal with utterance-final lengthening: the prosodic units analysed here are intonational phrases (IP).

A. Ronzhin et al. (Eds.): SPECOM 2014, LNAI 8773, pp. 353–359, 2014.

It has been shown that in Russian final lengthening affects not only the final rhyme, but also the stressed vowel [2] [6] if the final syllable is unstressed. The results presented in [4] showed that final unstressed vowels are lengthened more in open syllables than if followed by a consonant. These are the reasons why in the present study we are analysing three types of vowels:

– stressed vowels in IP-final accentual phrases ending in -cVcv or cVcvc (as /o/ in /ˈvdomʲi/ ("at home") or /a/ in /dvʲiˈnatsitʲ/ ("twelve"));
– post-stressed vowels in IP-final accentual phrases ending in -cVcv (as /i/ in /ˈvdomʲi/ ("at home"));
– post-stressed vowels in IP-final accentual phrases ending in -cVcvc (as /ɨ/ in /dvʲiˈna t͡sitʲ/ ("twelve")).

The CV-patterns ("c" stands for "consonant", "v" for "unstressed vowel", and "V" for "stressed vowel") are chosen based on frequency data.

2 Experiment Design

2.1 Material

The present study is based on the Corpus of Professionally Read Speech (CORPRES) [5] for Russian. The corpus is manually segmented and contains phonetic and prosodic annotation, which enables to measure segmental characteristics in different prosodic contexts. For the present analysis 4 of the 8 speakers, 2 male (A and M) and 2 female (C and K), were chosen since they had recorded more material than others (4–5 hours for each speaker).

2.2 Method

To answer the questions formulated in the Introduction, it is reasonable to analyse segmental duration values in words occurring in four positions.

1. IP-initail/medial with a pause (e. g. /gaˈtova [pause] prʲiˈtʲi naˈpomaɕ:/ ("is ready [pause] to help"));
2. IP-final with a pause (e. g. /uˈdarʲil jiˈvo nʲiˈtrʲi ˈraza [pause]/ ("kicked him not three times [pause] [, but ... times]"));
3. IP-initail/medial with no pause (e. g. /ˈʂtobɨ ˈnʲebɨla ˈputanʲit͡sɨ/ "to avoid confusion");
4. IP-final with no pause (e. g. /nʲet nʲiɕiˈvo taˈkova/ "there is nothing like that [which...]").

If the duration values are greater for position 2 compared to position 1, then prepausal lengthening is caused not only by the presence of a pause, but also by the position of the word within the intonational phrase. This comparison will give us an answer to question 1 formulated in the Introduction.

If the duration values for position 4 are greater than those for position 3, then preboundary lengthening can be observed even when the boundary is not marked by a pause. This comparison will give us an answer to question 2.

Additionally, by comparing data for positions 1 and 3, we will find out whether segments are lengthened in non-phrase-final words followed by a pause. A comparison of duration values for positions 2 and 4 can confirm or reject the statement that the degree of final lengthening is greater when the boundary is marked by a pause.

To eliminate the influence of pitch movement type on vowel duration, we are observing only words *not* bearing nuclear stress.

In order to calculate the duration values for the stressed and post-stressed vowels in words (accentual phrases) ending in -cVcvc and -cVcv (see Introduction), a Python script was written which processed the annotation files of the corpus.

Despite the large size of the corpus, it appeared impossible to analyse different types of vowels separately, since the restrictions on the CV-pattern and the position of the word within the IP reduced the sample sizes drastically. In order to be able to compare duration values for different types of vowels it was reasonable to calculate *normalized* duration values. Here the formula given in [7, formula (4)] was used, which allowed us to compensate for the average duration of the segment, its standard deviation, and tempo:

$$\tilde{d}(i) = \frac{d(i) - \alpha \mu_p}{\alpha \sigma_p}$$

where $\tilde{d}(i)$ is the normalized duration of segment i, $d(i)$ is its absolute duration, α is the tempo coefficient, and μ_p and σ_p are the mean and standard deviation of the duration of the corresponding phone p.

The tempo coefficient (α) was calculated using formula provided in [7, formula (6)]:

$$\alpha = \frac{1}{N} \sum_{i=1}^{N} \frac{d_i}{\mu_{p_i}}$$

where d_i is the duration of segment i, and μ_{p_i} is the mean duration of the corresponding phone.

To estimate the influence of word position and presence of a pause on vowel duration, statistical analysis was carried out using R. For normally distributed data Welch's t-test was used; for non-normally distributed data (according to Shapiro-Wilks test) Wilcoxon-Mann-Whitney test was used instead.

3 Results

3.1 Stressed Vowels in Penultimate Syllables

The mean and median values for normalized duration of stressed vowels in words ending in -cVcv and -cVcvc are given in Table 1 and Table 2 respectively.

Statistical analysis has shown that the duration values of stressed vowels in penultimate syllables are higher in phrase-final words followed by a pause compared to phrase-initial/medial words also followed by a pause. The difference is statistically significant for all 4 speakers for pattern -cVcvc, and for 3 of 4 speakers for pattern -cVcv (for the remaining speaker the sample size is too small).

Table 1. Mean and median normalized duration values and sample sizes (N) for stressed vowels in words ending in -cVcv, for 4 types of position

| | | IP-initial/medial | | | | IP-final | | | |
| | | speaker | | | | speaker | | | |
		A	C	K	M	A	C	K	M
pause	mean	-0.28	0.31	0.08	-0.97	0.17	0.34	0.55	0.29
	median	-0.39	0.32	0.28	-0.93	0.08	0.38	0.51	0.05
	N	25	4	11	9	46	30	41	30
no pause	mean	-0.51	-0.38	-0.43	-0.48	-0.27	0.19	0.05	0.07
	median	-0.56	-0.42	-0.52	-0.51	0.04	0.2	0.05	0.07
	N	1456	1727	1502	1745	15	20	34	43

A similar difference can be observed for final and initial/medial words not followed by a pause, although this difference is weaker in statistical terms: significance holds true for all 4 speakers in words ending in -cVcv, but for only 1 speaker in words ending in -cVcvc.

There seems to be no influence of a following pause on the duration of stressed vowels in phrase-initial/medial words for pattern -cVcvc. For words ending in -cVcv there are statistically significant differences between duration values for 3 of 4 speakers, but the direction of the difference is not consistent between the speakers.

Finally, there seems to be a tendency for more IP-final lengthening in the presence of a pause: the difference is statistically significant for 1 of 4 speakers for pattern -cVcv, and for for 2 of 4 speakers for pattern -cVcvc.

Table 2. Mean and median normalized duration values and sample sizes (N) for stressed vowels in words ending in -cVcvc, for 4 types of position

| | | IP-initial/medial | | | | IP-final | | | |
| | | speaker | | | | speaker | | | |
		A	C	K	M	A	C	K	M
pause	mean	-0.46	-0.51	-0.62	-0.88	0.27	0.08	0.36	0.27
	median	-0.4	-0.53	-0.8	-0.79	0.18	0.25	0.32	0.36
	N	16	6	11	10	21	15	18	14
no pause	mean	-0.58	-0.49	-0.64	-0.54	-0.55	-0.16	-0.18	-0.25
	median	-0.61	-0.49	-0.62	-0.52	-0.58	-0.21	-0.24	-0.24
	N	705	869	724	794	6	8	17	21

4   Post-stressed Vowels in Final Open Syllables

Table 3 provides mean and median values for normalized duration of unstressed vowels in words ending in -cVcv. Since these vowels immediately precede the boundary, we expected them to show most differences between boundary types.

Surprisingly, in words followed by a pause the duration values are *lower* in phrase-final than in phrase-inital/medial position; statistical significance is observed for 2 of 4

Table 3. Mean and median normalized duration values and sample sizes (N) for post-stressed vowels in words ending in -cVcv, for 4 types of position

| | | IP-initial/medial | | | | IP-final | | | |
| | | speaker | | | | speaker | | | |
		A	C	K	M	A	C	K	M
pause	mean	1.24	1.74	0.23	2.11	0.35	0.99	0.12	0.34
	median	0.97	1.84	-0.23	1.7	0.14	1.01	0.16	0.07
	N	25	4	11	9	46	30	41	30
no pause	mean	-0.1	-0.15	-0.06	-0.02	0.36	-0.15	0	0.11
	median	-0.16	-0.22	-0.09	0.1	0.11	-0.27	-0.03	-0.07
	N	1456	1727	1502	1745	15	20	34	43

speakers. An auditory analysis of the data showed that all speakers but speaker K sometimes make prolongations of word-final vowels before a pause, with normalized duration values above 3. However, excluding these cases from the analysis does not change the whole picture, showing statistical significance for the same two speakers (A and M).

Another interesting result is as follows: statistically, in the absence of a pause there is no difference in the duration of absolute final post-stressed vowels between phrase-initial/medial and phrase-final words. That is, absolute final vowels are *not* lengthened phrase-finally if there is no following pause.

For words in IP-initial/medial position the presence of a following pause shows more lengthening of absolute-final unstressed vowels; the difference is statistically significant for 3 of 4 speakers.

The influence of pause on phrase-final lengthening is not confirmed by statistical analysis, showing a significant difference for only 1 of 4 speakers.

5   Post-stressed Vowels in Final Closed Syllables

Table 4 provides mean and median values for normalized duration of unstressed vowels in words ending in -cVcvc.

Table 4. Mean and median normalized duration values and sample sizes (N) for post-stressed vowels in words ending in -cVcvc, for 4 types of position

| | | IP-initial/medial | | | | IP-final | | | |
| | | speaker | | | | speaker | | | |
		A	C	K	M	A	C	K	M
pause	mean	-0.09	-0.14	0.14	-0.08	-0.16	-0.05	-0.32	-0.39
	median	0.02	-0.16	0.18	-0.33	-0.2	-0.1	-0.26	-0.72
	N	16	6	11	10	21	15	18	14
no pause	mean	-0.37	-0.31	-0.13	-0.28	-0.37	-0.36	-0.2	-0.16
	median	-0.4	-0.33	-0.35	-0.36	-0.38	-0.42	-0.28	-0.25
	N	705	869	724	794	6	8	17	21

Just looking at the values given in Table 4 is enough to notice that here the position of the word has no influence on vowel duration. Not surprisingly, statistical analysis confirms this claim, revealing only one statistically significant difference (for vowels in IP-initial/medial words followed vs. not followed by a pause, speaker A). Moreover, there is no difference between *any* of the positions observed in this study (e. g. positions 2 and 3 as listed in the section "Methods").

This leads to a conclusion that post-stressed vowels in ultimate closed syllables are *not lengthened* in IP-final position. As shown above, in this case the lengthening affects the stressed vowel of the word; it probably affects the final consonant as well, but this is beyond the scope of the present study.

6   Conclusions

It is now possible to answer the questions formulated in the Introduction.

1. Is *pre-pausal* lengthening caused only by the presence of a pause or also by the phrase-final position?
   - In words followed by a pause, **stressed vowels in penultimate syllables** are longer in IP-final position than in IP-initial/medial position. Therefore, here the lengthening is caused not only by the presence of a pause, but also by the position of the word within the phrase.
   - For **post-stressed vowels in final open syllables** the opposite is observed: absolute final vowels are much longer in *non*-phrase final position before a pause than in phrase-final position before a pause. Thus, before a pause phrase-final position yields less lengthening than phrase-initial/medial position.
   - **Post-stressed vowels in final closed syllables** do not show any lengthening in either of the cases. Neither the position within the phrase, nor the presence of a pause affects vowel duration.
2. Are final segments lengthened at the end of an intonational phrase if the boundary is *not* marked by a pause?
   - The answer is "yes" for **stressed vowels in penultimate syllables**.
   - The answer is "no" for **post-stressed vowels in final open and closed syllables**.

In addition, the following observations have been made:

- In words occurring in IP-final position, stressed vowels in penultimate syllables tend to be lengthened more when the boundary is marked by a pause.
- In words occurring in IP-initial/medial position, post-stressed vowels in final open syllables are lengthened more if there is a pause following.

Acknowledgments. The research was supported by St. Petersburg State University (grant 31.0.145.2010).

References

1. Chow, I.: Quantitative analysis of preboundary lengthening in Cantonese. In: Proceedings of the Speech Prosody 2008 Conference, pp. 543–546 (2008)
2. Kachkovskaia, T., Volskaya, N., Skrelin, P.: Final Lengthening in Russian: a Corpus-based Study. In: Proc. of the Interspeech-2013, pp. 1438–1442 (2013)
3. Kachkovskaia, T., Volskaya, N.: Phrase-Final Segment Lengthening in Russian: Preliminary Results of a Corpus-Based Study. In: Železný, M., Habernal, I., Ronzhin, A. (eds.) SPECOM 2013. LNCS, vol. 8113, pp. 257–263. Springer, Heidelberg (2013)
4. Kachkovskaia, T.V.: Temporal Aspects of Intonational Phrasing. SPIIRAS Proceedings 1(32), 68–82 (2014) (Evidence from Russian) (in Russian)
5. Skrelin, P., Volskaya, N., Kocharov, D., Evgrafova, K., Glotova, O., Evdokimova, V.: A fully annotated corpus of Russian speech. In: Proc. of the 7th Conference on International Language Resources and Evaluation, pp. 109–112 (2010)
6. Volskaya, N., Stepanova, S.: On the temporal component of intonational phrasing. In: Proceedings of SPECOM 2004, pp. 641–644 (2004)
7. Wightman, C.W., Shattuck-Hufnagel, S., Ostendorf, M., Price, P.J.: Segmental durations in the vicinity of prosodic phrase boundaries. The Journal of the Acoustical Society of America 91(3), 1707–1717 (1992)

Proportional-Integral-Derivative Control of Automatic Speech Recognition Speed

Alexander Zatvornitsky[1], Aleksei Romanenko[2], and Maxim Korenevsky[1]

[1] Speech Technology Center, Saint-Petersburg, Russia
[2] ITMO University, Saint-Petersburg, Russia
{zatvornitskiy,korenevsky,khitrov}@speechpro.com
183460@niuitmo.ru

Abstract. We propose a technique for regulating LVCSR decoding speed based on a proportional-integral-derivative (PID) model that is widely used in automatic control theory. Our experiments show that such a controller can maintain a given decoding speed level despite computer performance fluctuations, difficult acoustic conditions, or speech material that is out of the scope of the language model, without notable deterioration in overall recognition quality.

Keywords: Speech recognition, decoding, pruning, recognition time control, PID controller.

1   Introduction

Nowadays, LVCSR can be used in many different ways, and there can often be special speed requirements. For example, a call to a contact center should be processed within a certain period of time regardless of the workload of the hardware that performs the recognition. Audio stream indexing should work in real time, otherwise the accumulated delay may cause the entire system to break down. Mobile device performance varies depending on the energy-saving mode, but it is preferable for the user to get results at a predictable rate.

Adjustment of recognition speed is a well-known problem. For example, [1] showed that limiting the number of hypotheses is not only a very simple method but also a very effective one. In [2], algorithm is proposed, which fades the word end pruning over a large part of the search network. In [3,4] an integral autotuning controller changes the number of active hypotheses by manipulating the beam width. Compared with histogram pruning, it reduces pruning cost and eliminates an additional pass through the hypothesis set. [5] uses confidence measures to calculate the optimal beam width on each frame. [6,7] choose the method of reducing GMM computations. [8] describes speeding up recognition on mobile devices by switching to DNN, exploiting integer arithmetics, choosing the suitable number of context-dependent models, using batch computations and frame-skipping.

These methods shorten recognition time by reducing the most time-consuming calculations. However, they are not intended for managing recognition speed directly. There are some situations where it may cause difficulties for real-time systems.

A. Ronzhin et al. (Eds.): SPECOM 2014, LNAI 8773, pp. 360–367, 2014.

Firstly, performance of a server or a mobile system may vary significantly. Other problems are recognition of speech that substantially differs from acoustic model training samples (mismatching acoustic conditions), and situations when the language model describes the speech poorly (i.e. out-of-domain utterances). In such cases the acoustic and/or language models may discriminate hypotheses badly and that can cause recognition speed to decrease.

In our experience, developers of real-time recognition systems usually use the following approaches to this problem. One is to obtain a reserve of time by using a tighter beam, a smaller number of hypotheses, etc. Another one is to implement simple heuristics (i.e. switching to "emergency" settings in case of slowdowns, or changing the beam proportionally to the degree of the slowdown). We are not aware of publications that estimate the quality of such heuristics, and our experiments show that they work well only under a narrow range of conditions.

In this paper we propose a new algorithm for recognition speed regulation. It is based on one of the most well-researched models of automatic control theory, a proportional-integral-derivative (PID) controller [9]. It is widely used in many areas that require precise control: robotics, operating power stations, temperature regulation, etc.

The algorithm aims to ensure good recognition quality if the available system resources and the resolving capability of the models are sufficient, as well as smoothly restrict processing time in other situations. Compared with [3,4], the proposed algorithm controls recognition time instead of the number of hypotheses. The algorithm can also provide faster reaction to disturbances, compared with the purely integral controller in [3,4].

2   Decoding and Automatic Control

We are dealing with the problem of time-synchronous recognition based on Hidden Markov Models. It can be solved by the Viterbi algorithm, which is often expressed in the form of the token passing algorithm [10,11]. To speed it up, the number of tokens on each frame is being limited artificially. The two most common methods are beam pruning and histogram pruning. Beam pruning removes tokens with a probability less than $\max(p_r)/K_{beam}$. Histogram pruning is an efficient method for approximate finding the best H_{max} tokens using a histogram sorting.

In terms of automatic control theory, the decoder is the object under control and recognition is the process to be controlled. As a process variable (PV) – the current status of the process under control – we use the current recognition time, measured in realtime factors (RTF). The desired value of the process variable is called a setpoint (SP). The control system adjusts the manipulated variable (MV) to reach and maintain the setpoint. In this paper we deal with a closed-loop control system. Closed-loop controller is based on negative feedback. It permanently monitors the PV, calculates the error $E(t) = SP(t) - PV(t)$, and uses the MV to eliminate it. The error can be caused by changing the SP, by internal dynamics of the process (e.g., characteristics of the speech), or by external disturbances (e.g., performance fluctuations).

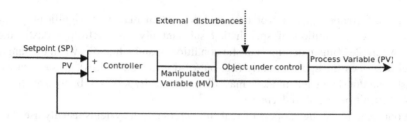

Fig. 1. Block diagram for the closed-loop system

A PID controller is one of the most widely used controller types that do not require a mathematical model of the system. It takes into account the current error, its rate of change, and the history of the process. The output of the PID controller is:

$$MV(\tau) = K_p E(\tau) + K_I \int_0^\tau E(\tau)dt + K_d \frac{d}{dt}E(\tau) \tag{1}$$

where K_p, K_I, K_d are proportional, integral and derivative gains respectively.

The proportional term produces an output which is inversely proportional to the current error value. But with only the proportional term, the setpoint usually cannot be achieved. The integral term is proportional to the duration and magnitude of the error. This term allows the system to reach the setpoint. If the system does not suffer external disturbances and has no internal dynamics, then after a while the process value is stabilized at the setpoint, the signal from the proportional term will be zero, and the output will be fully formed by the integral term. However, if the integral component is configured incorrectly, that can lead to self-sustained oscillations. The derivative term is proportional to the slope of the error over time and derivative gain. Derivative action predicts system behavior and thus improves settling time and the stability of the system. When using the differential part it is important to avoid problems caused by high-frequency random noise.

Below is a discrete implementation of the equation (1):

$$MV(t_i) = K_p E(t_i) + K_I \Delta t \sum_{j=0}^i E(t_j) + K_d \frac{E(t_i)-E(t_{i-1})}{\Delta t} \tag{2}$$

A recurrent expression for optimizing the calculations can be obtained by discretizing the derivative from (1):

$$MV(t_i) = MV(t_{i-1}) + K_p[E(t_i) - E(t_{i-1})] + K_I \Delta t E(t_i) + \tag{3}$$

$$+K_d \frac{E(t_i) - 2E(t_{i-1}) + E(t_{i-2})}{\Delta t}$$

The quality of the PID controlling greatly depends on the values of its parameters. Poor settings may cause self-excited oscillations, or make it impossible to reach the setpoint. There is a lot of literature on methods of tuning PID-controllers, both empirical and theoretically well-founded. There are also software packages and devices for automatic configuration [12]. We use one of the simplest tuning procedures, the Ziegler–Nichols method. It usually requires some manual tuning, for example, using the table in [9] which contains an analysis of the influence of the parameters on rise time, overshoot, settling time, steady-state error and the stability of the process.

3   The Experimental Setup

For testing purposes we used our WFST-decoder created similarly to [11,13,16]. Graphs were produced by a tool which was created according to [14,15], the only significant difference being the application of the Kleene closure to the generated automaton[16] – this feature improves the quality of the regulated recognition.

The maximum number of hypotheses (H_{max}) was chosen as a control variable. The controller output was not limited from above but it was limited by the minimal acceptable value for H_{max} as H_{low} (we found that it slightly improves the recognition). In order to tune the controller, we built a simple model of the process as follows. We performed recognition after removing the limitation on the number of hypotheses ($H_{max} = \infty$) and measured the free number of hypotheses $H_{free} = \{h_{f,t}\}_{t=0..T-1}$ and processing time $RTF_{free} = \{rtf_{f,t}\}_{t=0..T-1}$ for each frame (T – number of frames). In this mode, the number of hypotheses was constrained only by the search beam K_{beam}.

This way we obtained a model of the dependence of frame recognition time RTF_{mod} on the number of hypotheses in the form of

$$RTF_{mod}(h) = a_1 h + a_2 \qquad (4)$$

using linear regression. With the limitation on H_{max} on frame t, we have

$$RTF_{mod}(t, H_{max}) = a_1 \min(h_{f,t}, H_{max}) + a_2 \qquad (5)$$

This model reflects real workload sufficiently well, despite its simplicity.

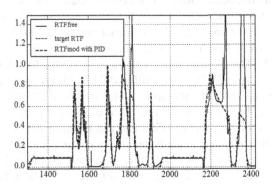

Fig. 2. An example of "free" time of recognition and a model under PID-controller, target RTF=0.2

Then the controller was tuned. It is difficult to tune the controller on (5), since H_{free} fluctuations are strong during speech processing. So during the first phase we set $h_{f,t} = \infty \forall t \in 0..T-1$, which means that we actually tuned the controller according to the model $a_1 H_{max} + a_2$, where $H_{max}(t) = MV(t)$ is a limitation made by the controller on the frame t. After that, it was manually tuned considering real H_{free} (normally a slight increase of K_I is enough). To prevent controller's reaction to short performance outliers, we set $K_p = 0$. After this tuning the controller was applied to the decoder without any additional tuning. In Figure 2 we give an example of "free" time of recognition and a model under PID-controller. Evidently the controller deals carefully with slowdowns which sometimes arise, cutting off the hills only if the slowdowns are accumulated.

4   Experiments

The goal of the first experiment is to make sure that the controller can maintain the target RTF despite the slowdowns caused by out-of-domain speech and/or acoustic conditions mismatch.   The experiment was performed using a tandem AM which is a combination of the LCRC ANNs [17] and standard gaussian mixture triphone models. The GMMs contain 4000 decision-tree-tied GMM states, with 15 gaussians per state on average. A special RASTA-like filter is used to increase the noise robustness of the features [18]. Acoustic models are trained on TV broadcast data produced by automatic segmentation and filtering of 3500 hours of data with imperfect transcripts [19]. A 3-gram language model contains 300K words and 7,3M n-grams. The LM is trained on an internet news corpus which contains 855M words.

The test set contains 2.4 hours of TV broadcast recordings. Additional signal and speech processing (word confidence filtering, language identification, music and voice activity detection) was turned off during speech recognition.

While studio speech (e.g. news, talk-shows, etc) is recognized with about 75% accuracy, there are problems with speed and quality of recognition on spontaneous speech in noisy environments. Often it is speech cocktail from the synchronous translation and muted foreign speech, or speech against a musical background. In what follows, we refer to recordings taken in such environments as "difficult".

We tune the speed of decoding of studio recordings using H_{max} to achieve the target time 0.45 RTF. This is achieved when $H_{max} = 50000$ (we will call this value "optimistic H_{max}"), Acc=73.21%. But "difficult" recordings with the optimistic setting of H_{max} were recognized with Acc=47.44% in 0.66 RTF, which is much worse than the target time. In a real-time system, exceeding the time boundaries for a long time may cause overflow of input buffers and can result in skipping of fragments of the sound. Therefore, we need to guarantee the target time on "difficult" recordings. We tune the H_{max} to achieve the target time (we will call this value "safe H_{max}"). So on "difficult" records, the safe $H_{max} = 5500$, Acc=45.71% in 0.45 RTF. Unfortunately, safe settings deliver worse performance on studio records – Acc=71.67%. We want to avoid this.

Model (4) of this system takes the form $RTF_{mod}(h) = 10^{-6}h + 0.0028186$. After tuning the controller, we have $K_p = 1200, K_I = 60000, K_d = 0, H_{low} = 1000$. The results of the experiments are presented in Table 1.

Table 1. Accuracy and recognition time of recognition with target time t=0.45 RTF

Base/Settings	"optimistic" $H_{max} = 50000$	"safe" $H_{max} = 5000$	Controlled ASR
Studio recordings	73.21% t=0.45 rtf	71.67% t=0.35 rtf	73.13% t=0.44 rtf
„difficult" recordings	47.44% t=0.66 rtf	45.71% t=0.45 rtf	46.66% t=0.45 rtf
Δ of accuracy, gained from control of studio recordings compared to "safe" $H_{max} = +1.46\%$ (with time = target time 0.45 rtf)			
Δ of accuracy, gained from control of "difficult" recordings compared to "safe" $H_{max} = +0.95\%$ (with time = target time 0.45 rtf)			

As we can see, the time of controlled recognition of "difficult" records is not higher than target time – just as with the safe H_{max}. So the real-time system with controlled recognition can safely process any volume of "difficult" speech. At the same time, the accuracy on studio recordings is almost equal to the accuracy in the optimistic case. We even have an increase in accuracy from controlling the recognition of the "difficult" recordings compared to the safe H_{max} (although such an increase can be achieved not for any combination of test set and acoustic model).

The results of the second experiment are presented in Figure 3. The experiment was designed to test the controller's ability to deal with fluctuations in computer performance. It was performed on call-center conversation data. In the beginning of a conversation, the user can ask a question in free form. The LVCSR system recognizes it and gives the answer automatically, or, if that is not possible, connects the user to an operator. The system processes about 1.3 million calls a month in one of the largest outsourcing call centers in Europe. We studied the possibility of increasing the recognizer stability in case of an overload (for example, due to failure of one of the servers). To do this, we measured the dependency of the recognition time on the number of parallel recognition channels; to make the experiments more restrictive they were performed not on servers, but on commodity hardware (Intel Core i5,4 cores).

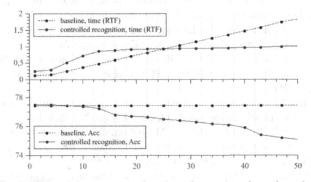

Fig. 3. RTF and Accuracy as a function of operation channel number

The acoustic model used for this setting was a DNN (5 hidden layers of 1000 neurons each; inputs were standard 13xMFCC spliced from 31 frames; output softmax layer had 1523 neurons, corresponding to the states of triphone models tied by the decision tree). A trigram class language model with 1.5M n-grams of 10K words was trained on transcripts of requests to the call-center. The test set was 1K calls (about 1.35 hrs). The parameters of the regulator were =500; =25000; =0; =1000. The model (4) of this system has the form $RTF_{mod}(h) = 3.79 * 10^{-7}h + 4.97 * 10^{-4}$.

As we can see in Figure 3, controlled recognition on 50 channels works with about the same speed as on 15 channels, with accuracy slowly degrading from 77.49% (1 channel) to 76.4%(28 channels) and 75.1% (50 channels).

5   Conclusion

We describe an implementation of the PID controller for recognition time.

Although using beam width as a manipulated variable may yield slightly higher speed, using limit on maximum number of hypothesis for this purpose provides more predictable behavior of the system and memory consumption for hypothesis storage. This feature was more important for our applications.

In our experience, the procedure of tuning the controller proved to be relatively simple and does not require high precision.

Our experiments show that the proposed algorithm can successfully deal with performance degradation of the computer under high load, and with speech segments that are difficult for recognition.

Acknowledgements. This work was partially financially supported by the Government of the Russian Federation, Grant 074-U01.

References

1. Steinbiss, V., Tran, B.-H., Ney, H.: Improvements in Beam Search. In: Proc. of the ICSLP, Yokohama, Japan, September 18-22, pp. 2143–2146 (1994)
2. Nolden, D., Schluter, R., Ney, H.: Extended search space pruning in LVCSR. In: Proc. of the ICASSP, Kyoto, Japan, March 25-30, pp. 4429–4432 (2012)
3. Hamme, H., Aellen, F.: An Adaptive-Beam Pruning Technique for Continuous Speech Recognition. In: Proc. of the ICSLP, Philadelphia, Pennsylvania, October 3-6, pp. 2083–2086 (1996)
4. Zhang, D., Du, L.: Dynamic Beam Pruning Strategy Using Adaptive Control. In: Proc. of the INTERSPEECH, Jeju Island, Korea, October 4-8, pp. 285–288 (2004)
5. Fabian, T., Lieb, R., Ruske, G., Thomae, M.: A Confidence-Guided Dynamic Pruning Approach-Utilization of Confidence Measurement in Speech Recognition. In: Proc. of the INTERSPEECH, Lisbon, Portugal, September 4-8, pp. 585–588 (2005)
6. Chan, A., Mosur, R., Rudnicky, A., Sherwani, J.: Four-layer Categorization Scheme of Fast GMM Computation Techniques in Large Vocabulary Continuous Speech Recognition Systems. In: Proc. of the ICSLP, Jeju Island, Korea, October 4-8, pp. 689–692 (2004)

7. Dixon, P., Oonishi, T., Furui, S.: Harnessing graphics processors for the fast computation of acoustic likelihoods in speech recognition. Computer Speech & Language 23(4), 510–526 (2009)
8. Lei, X., Senior, A., Gruenstein, A., Sorensen, J.: Accurate and Compact Large Vocabulary Speech Recognition on Mobile Devices. In: Proc. of the INTERSPEECH, Lyon, France, August 25-29, pp. 662–665 (2013)
9. Ang, K., Chong, G., Li, Y.: PID control system analysis, design, and technology. IEEE Transactions on Control Systems Technology 13(4), 559–576 (2005)
10. Young, S., Russell, N., Thornton, J.: Token Passing: a Conceptual Model for Connected Speech Recognition Systems. CUED Technical Report F INFENG/TR38. Cambridge University, Cambridge (1989)
11. Saon, G., Povey, D., Zweig, G.: Anatomy of an extremely fast LVCSR decoder. In: Proc. of the INTERSPEECH, Lisbon, Portugal, September 4-8, pp. 549–552 (2005)
12. Li, Y., Ang, K., Chong, G.: Patents, software and hardware for PID control: an overview and analysis of the current art. IEEE Control Systems Magazine 26(1), 42–54 (2006)
13. Dixon, P., Caseiro, D., Oonishi, T., Furui, S.: The Titech large vocabulary WFST speech recognition system. In: Proc. of the ASRU, Kyoto, Japan, December 9-13, pp. 443–448 (2007)
14. Novak, J., Minematsu, N., Hirose, K.: Open Source WFST Tools for LVCSR Cascade Development. In: Proc. of the FSMNLP, Bois, France, July 12-16, pp. 65–73 (2011)
15. Allauzen, C., Mohri, M., Riley, M., Roark, B.: A Generalized Construction of Integrated Speech Recognition Transducers. In: Proc. of the ICASSP, Montreal, Canada, May 17-21, vol. 1, pp. 761–764 (2004)
16. Mohri, M., Pereira, F., Riley, M.: Weighted Finite-State Transducers in Speech Recognition. Computer Speech and Language 16(1), 69–88 (2002)
17. Schwarz, P.: Phoneme recognition based on long temporal context (PhD thesis). Faculty of Information Technology BUT, Brno (2008)
18. Yurkov, P., Korenevsky, M., Levin, K.: An Improvement of robustness to speech loudness change for an ASR system based on LC-RC features. In: Proc. of the SPECOM, Kazan, Russia, September 27-30, pp. 62–66 (2011)
19. Tomashenko, N.A., Khokhlov, Y.Y.: Fast Algorithm for Automatic Alignment of Speech and Imperfect Text Data. In: Železný, M., Habernal, I., Ronzhin, A. (eds.) SPECOM 2013. LNCS, vol. 8113, pp. 146–153. Springer, Heidelberg (2013)

Quality Assessment of HMM-Based Speech Synthesis Using Acoustical Vowel Analysis

Marvin Coto-Jiménez[1,2], John Goddard-Close[2],
and Fabiola M. Martínez-Licona[2]

[1] Universidad de Costa Rica, Electrical Engineering School
San José, Costa Rica
marvin.coto@ucr.ac.cr

[2] Universidad Autónoma Metropolitana, Electrical Engineering Department
Mexico City, México
{jgc,fmml}@xanum.uam.mx

Abstract. The synthetic speech produced from a Hidden Markov Model (HMM)-based system is often reported as sounding muffled when it is compared to natural speech. There are several reasons for this effect: some precise and fine characteristics of the natural speech are removed, minimized or hidden in the modeling phase of the HMM system; the resulting speech parameter trajectories become over smoothed versions of the speech waveforms. This means that each synthetic voice constructed from an HMM-based system must be tested for its speech quality. Usually, costly subjective testing is required and it is interesting to find objective alternatives. This paper considers nine acoustic parameters, related to jitter and shimmer, and considers their statistical significance as objective measurements of synthetic speech quality.

Keywords: HMM, speech synthesis, jitter, shimmer.

1 Introduction

Subjective measures involving human subjects are currently the most accurate indicators of the quality of synthetic speech [1]. There are several kinds of information that a human processes when listening to synthetic speech, from phonetic to prosodic and semantic. All this information is related to the voice quality which is perceived by a listener. Even though it is desirable to have subjective tests of things such as the intelligibility or naturalness in the evaluation of synthetic speech, subjective tests are time consuming and expensive.

There have been various studies evaluating objective speech quality measures as predictors of things such as speech intelligibility, e.g. [2]. The possibility of predicting subjective evaluations using objective measures are of interest since they might replace the former, thus saving time and lowering costs, especially in cases where many synthetic voices require evaluation. In this paper, we consider the use of several acoustic features, related to shimmer and jitter measurements, as indicators of speech naturalness produced by HMM-based speech synthesis. Some of these acoustic features have been used to analyze stress in human

A. Ronzhin et al. (Eds.): SPECOM 2014, LNAI 8773, pp. 368–375, 2014.

speech [3], as well as various pathologies [4] [5], including vowel analysis [6] to mention a few.

The rest of this paper is organized as follows. Section 2 presents the HMM-based speech synthesis. Section 3 describes the Spanish speech database, the synthetic voices constructed using HMM-based synthesis, and introduces the methods of analysis of jitter and shimmer for vowels. Section 4 describes the results, which are then discussed in Section 5. Concluding remarks and future work are presented in Section 6.

2   HMM-Based Speech Synthesis

HMM-based speech synthesis uses Hidden Markov Models in order to generate the vocoder parameters used to produce synthetic speech [7]. HMM are usually trained with parameters extracted from natural speech, producing synthetic voices similar to those of the original human speaker. In the training process, linguistic and prosodic contexts are also taken into consideration, and with a large training set this can aid in producing better sounding speech. Due to its statistical nature, HMM-based speech synthesis has many advantages over other approaches. However, the averaging that occurs in the HMM training often results in less natural sounding speech [8].

Three kind of models are simultaneously trained in order to generate speech parameters which are used to generate the synthetic speech waveform: $f0$, spectral parameters (the most popular representation being mfcc) and duration models. Training conditions and natural speech data both have an impact on the speech quality obtained, for example, the amount of the recorded voice data available [9] and the contextual factors [10], which are related to the phonetic and prosodic context of each phoneme.

Synthesized speech produced using this HMM technique has been reported as sounding muffled compared with natural speech, because the generated speech parameter trajectories are often oversmoothed [11] [12]. This means that detailed characteristics of the speech parameters are removed in the modeling part, so the models' output is unable to reproduce them.

3   Methods

In this section we shall describe the data employed for training the synthetic speech models, the four synthetic voices produced by the HMM-speech synthesis system used in our experiments and obtained varying the training conditions for each one, the precise jitter and shimmer measurements used, and finally the subjective assessment performed.

3.1   Data

A mexican professional actor recorded a set of 184 Mexican Spanish utterances: these included isolated words as well as affirmative and interrogative sentences as shown in Table 1.

Table 1. Spanish Corpus Contents

Identifier	Corpus contents
1-100	Affirmative
101-134	Interrogative
135-150	Paragraphs
151-160	Digits
161-184	Isolated words

The selection of the words, sentences and paragraphs were the same as that of [13]. The records were carried out in a professional studio where all the technical aspects and the recording conditions were completely controlled. Of particular interest to us for the objective feature measurements are the five Spanish vowels: /a/, /e/, /i/, /o/, /u/.

3.2 Synthetic Voices

The HMM-system was adapted from HTS-CMU-US-ARCTIC demo in [16]. An analysis of the pitch range was made with Praat, so that a correct $f0$ range could be defined in three of the cases, and the same contextual factors were used for each phoneme in training, in order to set the phonetic and prosodic features. One additional voice was trained using a subset of 50 of the utterances in the database. These 50 utterances were those which had coincidences for the phonemes and their context (the two previous and the two following phonemes) to the phrases that were going to be synthetized. The four synthetic voices were trained using the following conditions:

- Normal Training: The voice obtained from normal training using the complete set of utterances.
- Wide $f0$ Range: Similar to Normal, but defining a very wide range for the $f0$ (40 to 800 Hz), in order to evaluate how this parameter affects the synthetized voice.
- Duplicated Data: The 184 utterances of data were duplicated without any additional changes in the conditions used in Normal, and the voice trained using them (368 utterances) as a whole set.
- Reduced Data: Trained using the 50 best related phonetical context utterances from the whole set.

3.3 Acoustic Features

The acoustic features used in this analysis are similar to those extracted in [15], and are related to jitter and shimmer measurements applied to Spanish vowels. Jitter is a measure of period-to-period fluctuations in the fundamental frequency. In general it is calculated between consecutive periods of voiced speech, and is defined as shown in Table 2 with some related acoustic features. Shimmer is a

Table 2. Jitter related parameters. P_i is the period of the ith cycle in ms, and n the number of periods in the sample

Parameter	Definition
Jitter radio (local)	$jitt = 1000 \left(\frac{1}{n-1} \sum_{i=1}^{n-1} P_i - P_{i+1} \right) / \left(\frac{1}{n} \sum_{i=1}^{n} P_i \right)$
Jitter (local, absolute)	$jittla = \left(\sum_{i=2}^{n} |P_i - P_{i-1}| \right) / (N - 1)$
Relative average perturbation rap (rap)	$rap = \left(\frac{1}{n-2} \sum_{i=2}^{n-1} | \frac{P_{i-1} + P_i + P_{i+1}}{3} - P_i| \right) / \left(\frac{1}{n} \sum_{i=1}^{n} P_i \right)$
Five-point period perturbation $ppq5$ quotient (ppq5)	$ppq5 = \dfrac{\frac{1}{n-4} \sum_{i=3}^{n-2} \left| \left(\frac{\sum_{j=-2}^{2} P_{i+j}}{3} \right) - P_i \right|}{\frac{1}{n} \sum_{i=1}^{n} P_i}$
ddp (Difference of differences of periods)	$\left(\frac{\sum_{i=2}^{N-1} |P_{i+1} - P_i - (P_i - P_{i-1})|}{N-1} \right) / \left(\frac{\sum_{i=1}^{n} P_i}{n} \right)$

measure of the period-to-period variability of the amplitude value, and is defined as shown in Table 3 with some related features. These five acoustic features related to jitter, and four related to shimmer were extracted from the speech signals of the synthetic voices using Praat [14].

Table 3. Shimmer related parameters. A_i is the amplitude of the ith cycle in ms, and n the number of periods of the sample.

Parameter	Definition
Local shimmer	$shimm = \left(\frac{1}{n-1} \sum_{i=1}^{n-1} |A_i - A_{i-1}| \right) / \left(\frac{1}{n} \sum_{i=1}^{n} A_i \right)$
apq3 (three point amplitude $apq3$ perturbation)	$apq3 = \left(\frac{1}{n-1} \sum_{i=2}^{n-1} | \frac{A_{i-1} + A_i + A_{i+1}}{3} - A_i| \right) / \left(\frac{1}{n} \sum_{i=1}^{n} A_i \right)$
apq5 (five point amplitude per-turbation quotient)	$apq5 = \left(\frac{1}{n-4} \sum_{i=3}^{n-2} | \frac{\sum_{j=-2}^{2} A_{i+j}}{3} - A_i| \right) / \left(\frac{1}{n} \sum_{i=1}^{n} A_i \right)$
apq11 (eleven point amplitude $apq11$ perturbation quotient)	$apq11 = \left(\frac{1}{n-10} \sum_{i=6}^{n-5} | \frac{\sum_{j=-5}^{5} A_{i+j}}{11} - A_i| \right) / \left(\frac{1}{n} \sum_{i=1}^{n} A_i \right)$

3.4 Subjective Assessment

A Mean Opinion Score (MOS) test of synthetic speech naturalness was applied to 5 randomly selected utterances from the 100 synthetized for each synthetic voice. The test was carried out using 20 volunteers, who replied to each utterance giving a value from the scale: 5 (completely natural) to 1 (completely unnatural).

In order to evalute the acoustic features in their relation to this subjective MOS test, 100 utterances were produced using each of the synthetic voices. The utterances were related to giving the time of day, and consist of phrases with 5 to 7 words.

4   Results

100 utterances were produced using each of the synthesized voices, and 5 utterances were chosen randomly from each. A MOS test was applied to these 5 utterances using 20 volunteers. We use these subjective evaluations as a reference to compare the possibly significant differences between the acoustic parameters of the synthesized voices. Table 4 shows the results of the MOS test of the naturalness of the four synthetic voices obtained from the data. For the four synthetic voices considered, we calculated the 9 acoustic features for each of the Spanish vowels in the whole set of utterances. Table 5 shows the total number of vowels that were obtained from the 100 utterances analyzed.

Table 4. MOS test results

Voice	MOS-Naturalness
Wide $f0$ range	3.10
Normal Training	2.96
Reduced Data	2.74
Duplicated Data	2.68

Table 5. Number of vowels analyzed in each synthetic voice

Vowel	Quantity
/a/	185
/e/	256
/i/	129
/o/	223
/u/	17

In order to decide if the differences of the nine parameters were statistically significant, we conducted a Friedman test, with a significance level of $\alpha = 0.05$. Friedman's test was carried out for each of the five Spanish vowels and the four training conditions, and a Post-hoc test was used to decide which groups were significantly different from each other. Statistically significant differences were detected for all the synthesized voices for each vowel, with the exception of vowel /u/, which appeared only 17 times in the synthetized utterances. The test shows bigger differences between the nine acoustic parameters of the synthesized voices

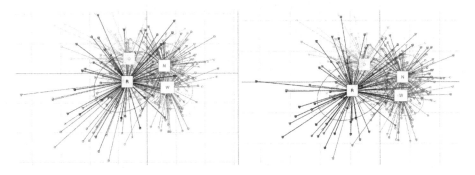

Fig. 1. PCA map onto two components of the nine acoustic features for the vowel /a/ (left) and /o/(right) for the four synthetic voices. N: Normal training, D: Duplicated data, R:Reduced data, W:Wide $f0$ range.

with the highest and lowest MOS naturalness score (p-value less than 2×10^{-16} in all cases).

Principal Component Analysis (PCA), was applied to each vowel in order to visually corroborate the differences determined by the statistical test. Figure 1 shows a mapping of the 9-dimensional acoustic feature space to a 2-dimensional space, using PCA. All the vowels show a similar behavior to the /a/ in their projection onto 2-dimensional space.

5 Discussion

The MOS test results indicate that the synthetic voices corresponding to Normal Training and Wide f0 Range were considered as similar in the subjective perception of their naturalness. These voices received higher scores, whilst the Reduced and Duplicated data voices were considered as similar and received lower scores. The Friedman test shows statistically significant differences between all the voices, with a higher degree of difference for the voices with highest and lowest MOS naturalness score.

The PCA analysis helps to visually illustrate these dissimilarities upon dimensionality reduction. For the data used, the vowels' behavior were very similar to that of the vowel /a/ projected into 2-dimensional space. The Principal Component Axes separate the synthetic voices with higher MOS-naturalness scores from the voices with low MOS-naturalness scores.

If we consider the Normal Training and Wide f0 Range voices as one cluster and the Reduced and Duplicated data voices as the other one, then we can see that the Principal Components split the data into two major groups as shown in Figure 2 for vowel /a/. Although the projected data is spread into all the quadrants of the principal components plane, it suggests that there are some trends that lead to identify the similarity among the voices.

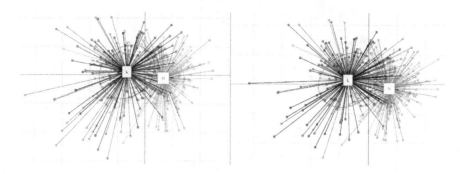

Fig. 2. PCA map onto two components of the nine acoustic features for the vowel /a/ (left) and /o/(right) for the four synthetic voices in two groups. H: High naturalness, L:Low naturalness.

6   Conclusions

In this paper we have trained four synthesized voices using HMM-based speech synthesis by varying their training conditions. A MOS test was applied to subjectively gauge the synthetic speech naturalness for each of the synthetic voices. Nine acoustic parameters, related to jitter and shimmer, were used to obtain objective measurements from all of the five Spanish vowels appearing in our corpus, using Praat.

The aim was to see if these acoustic parameters could predict the result of the subjective MOS test. To this end, a Friedman test was conducted to decide if statistically significative differences could be found from the measurements of the nine parameter on each of the vowels for each of the four synthetic voices. It was found that the test showed differences in all of the cases.

PCA was applied to the 9-dimensional acoustic parameter space and the projections of the vowels onto a 2-dimensional space was obtained. This lower dimensional visualization illustrated the relationship between the different levels of naturalness and the acoustic features.

These results may lead to establishing the employment of jitter and shimmer as a useful objective alternative to determining synthetic speech quality instead of more costly subjective evaluations. Procedures for clustering voices with similar quality may be possible using this parameters, but further research into suitable parameters is required.

It is necessary to repeat the experiments using other voices, ideally with larger speech databases and perhaps different languages, to confirm the conclusions obtained in this paper.

Acknowledgments. This work was supported by the SEP and CONACyT under the Program SEP-CONACyT, CB-2012-01, No.182432, in Mexico, as well as the University of Costa Rica in Costa Rica. We also want to thank ELRA for supplying the original Emotional speech synthesis database.

References

1. Valentini-Botinhao, C., Yamagishi, Y., King, S.: Evaluation of objective measures for intelligibility prediction of HMM-based synthetic speech in noise. In: IEEE International Conference on Acoustics, Speech and Signal Processing, pp. 5112–5115 (2011)
2. Taal, C.H., Hendriks, R.C., Heusdens, R., Jensen, J., Kjems, U.: An evaluation of objective quality measures for speech intelligibility prediction. In: INTERSPEECH, pp. 1947–1950 (2009)
3. Martínez-Licona, F.M., Goddard, J., Martínez-Licona, A.E., Coto-Jiménez, M.: Assessing Stress in Mexican Spanish from Emotion Speech Signals. In: Proc. 8th International Workshop on Models and Analysis of Vocal Emissions for Biomedical Applications, MAVEBA, pp. 239–242 (2013)
4. Falcone, M., Yadav, N., Poellabauer, C., Flynn, P.: Using isolated vowel sounds for classification of Mild Traumatic Brain Injury. In: IEEE International Conference on Acoustics, Speech and Signal Processing, pp. 7577–7581 (2013)
5. Wertzner, H., Schreiber, S., Amaro, L.: Analysis of fundamental frequency, jitter, shimmer and vocal intensity in children with phonological disorders. Revista Brasileira de Otorrinolaringologia 71, 582–588 (2005)
6. Brockmann, M., Drinnan, M.J., Storck, C., Carding, P.N.: Reliable jitter and shimmer measurements in voice clinics: the relevance of vowel, gender, vocal intensity, and fundamental frequency effects in a typical clinical task. Journal of Voice 25(1), 44–53 (2011)
7. Zen, H., Tokuda, K., Black, A.W.: Statistical parametric speech synthesis. Speech Communication 51(11), 1039–1064 (2009)
8. Yamagishi, J., Zen, H., Wu, Y.J., Toda, T., Tokuda, K.: The HTS-2008 system: Yet another evaluation of the speaker-adaptive HMM-based speech synthesis system in the 2008 Blizzard Challenge (2008)
9. Hanzlíček, Z.: Czech HMM-based speech synthesis. Text, Speech and Dialogue, pp. 291–298. Springer, Heidelberg (2010)
10. Cernak, M., Motlicek, P., Garner, P.N.: On the (Un) importance of the contextual factors in HMM-based speech synthesis and coding. In: IEEE International Conference on Acoustics, Speech and Signal Processing, pp. 8140–8143 (2013)
11. Tokuda, K., Nankaku, Y., Zen, H., Yamagishi, J., Oura, K.: Speech synthesis based on hidden Markov models. Proceedings of the IEEE 101, 1234–1252 (2013)
12. Black, A., Zen, H., Tokuda, K.: Statistical parametric speech synthesis. In: IEEE International Conference on Acoustics, Speech and Signal Processing, pp. IV-1229–IV-1232 (2007)
13. ELRA catalogue: Emotional speech synthesis database, http://catalog.elra.info
14. Praat: doing phonetics by computer, http://www.praat.org
15. Goddard, J., Schlotthauer, G., Torres, M.E., Rufiner, H.L.: Dimensionality reduction for visualization of normal and pathological speech data. Biomedical Signal Processing and Control 4(3), 194–201 (2009)
16. HTS Voice Demos, http://hts.sp.nitech.ac.jp/?VoiceDemos

Quality Improvements of Zero-Concatenation-Cost Chain Based Unit Selection

Jiří Kala and Jindřich Matoušek

Dept. of Cybernetics, Faculty of Applied Sciences,
University of West Bohemia, Czech Rep.
jkala,jmatouse@kky.zcu.cz

Abstract. In our previous work, we introduced a zero-concatenation-cost (ZCC) chain based framework of unit-selection speech synthesis. This framework proved to be very fast as it reduced the computational load of a unit-selection system up to hundreds of time. Since the ZCC chain based algorithm principally prefers to select longer segments of speech, an increased number of audible artifacts were expected to occur at concatenation points of longer ZCC chains. Indeed, listening tests revealed a number of artifacts present in synthetic speech; however, the artifacts occurred in a similar extent in synthetic speech produced by both ZCC chain based and standard Viterbi search algorithms. In this paper, we focus on the sources of the artifacts and we propose improvements of the synthetic speech quality within the ZCC algorithm. The quality and computational demands of the improved ZCC algorithm are compared to the unit-selection algorithm based on the standard Viterbi search.

Keywords: speech synthesis, unit selection, Viterbi algorithm, zero-concatenation-cost chain, duration, F0.

1 Introduction

Despite the increasing popularity of HMM based and hybrid speech synthesis methods, the unit selection concatenative method still remains a very popular approach to speech synthesis. It is a mature method popular in many real life applications in which the ability of unit selection to deliver a highly natural synthetic speech is required and acknowledged by end users. However, to achieve such high-quality output, the unit-selection systems utilize very large speech corpora (general text-to-speech systems often include up to tens of hours of speech) that aim to cover as many phonetic and prosodic contexts as possible. As a result, the corpora contain a very large number of candidates of each speech unit (typically diphones, context-dependent phones or other phone-like units), and the selection of the best candidates from the many which are available is computationally very demanding.

A. Ronzhin et al. (Eds.): SPECOM 2014, LNAI 8773, pp. 376–385, 2014.

In our previous work [8] we proposed a novel scheme of unit-selection speech synthesis as an alternative to caching [1, 3], preselection [2, 4, 6, 10], or pruning techniques [12, 16, 18]. The main goal was to speed up the unit selection process and, at the same time, to maintain the quality of synthesized speech. Text-to-speech (TTS) systems utilizing such a unit-selection scheme could be employed in computationally less powerful devices like smartphones and tablets, or in server solutions in which many parallel requests must be synthesized in real time. The proposed scheme is based on zero-concatenation-cost (ZCC) chains, sequences of unit candidates immediately neighboring in source speech corpus utterances. The motivation is clear—such candidates concatenate perfectly, and, unless they violate a "target specification", they can be preferred during unit selection with no need to compute the concatenation cost, resulting in a selection of longer (*non-uniform*) units.

The proposed ZCC framework [8] proved to be very fast—in the experiments with two voice databases [11] it was approx. 500 times faster than the standard Viterbi search algorithm [8] and approx. 50 times faster than a Viterbi search with a pruning scheme initially proposed by Sakai et al. [16] and further elaborated on by Tihelka et al. [18]. According to listening tests, the quality of synthetic speech was not deteriorated [8]. However, the listening tests revealed that synthetic speech produced both by the proposed ZCC and by the standard unit-selection algorithms contained some artifacts, mainly caused by discontinuities in fundamental frequency (F0) and duration patterns.

In this paper we focus on the analysis of the artifacts perceived in synthetic speech and mainly on the elimination of the artifacts within the ZCC unit-selection scheme by avoiding to concatenate ZCC chains or single candidates with different F0 and temporal tendencies. The impact of the artifact elimination on the quality of synthetic speech and on the unit-selection speed-up is evaluated.

2 Zero-Cost-Concatenation Chain Based Viterbi Algorithm

The zero-cost concatenation (ZCC) chain based algorithm (hereinafter ZCCVIT) is basically similar to the standard Viterbi search algorithm (VITBASE) used in unit-selection based speech synthesis [7]. ZCCVIT also utilizes two cost functions—the *target cost* $C^t(t_k, u_k)$, which describes how well or poorly a unit candidate u_k meets target specification t_k (i.e. phonetic and prosodic contexts of neighboring units, various positional aspects in the utterance, etc.), and the *concatenation cost* $C^c(u_k, u_{k+1})$, which expresses how well or poorly two potentially joinable unit candidates u_k and u_{k+1} join together (mainly with respect to spectral continuity). The resulting cost function $C(t_1^K, u_1^K)$ then combines both cost functions and expresses the total (cumulative) cost of a sequence of K candidates

$$C(t_1^K, u_1^K) = \sum_{k=1}^{K} C^t(t_k, u_k) + \sum_{k=1}^{K-1} C^c(u_k, u_{k+1}). \tag{1}$$

The difference between ZCCVIT and VITBASE is that, instead of single unit candidates, ZCCVIT to a large extent tries to utilize ZCC chains as the nodes of the search network. The ZCC chain is defined as a sequence of at least two speech segments (unit candidates) that immediately neighbored in a source speech corpus. The advantage of ZCC chains is that the concatenation cost C^c is zero for all unit candidates within a ZCC chain and it needs not be computed explicitly. Thus, the cumulative cost of a ZCC chain can be computed, simplifying the Eq. (1), as a sum of target costs C^t

$$
\mathrm{zcc}C(t_m^M, u_m^M) = \sum_{k=m}^{M} C^t(t_k, u_k) \tag{2}
$$

where m is a starting position and M an ending position of a ZCC chain within a whole synthesized utterance. Hence, ZCCVIT aims to minimize the total cumulative cost C by preferring to select ZCC chains. As a result, less C^c computations are required, and subsequently the process of unit selection is sped up.

The procedure of searching for the optimal path through the network of K units with each unit u_k having $N(k)$ candidates (i.e. the selection of optimal sequence of candidates $u_k(i)$, $k = 1 \ldots K$ and $i = 1 \ldots N(k)$, for a given utterance) using the ZCCVIT algorithm is outlined in Fig. 1.A and could be described as follows:

1: For each candidate $u_k(i)$ compute the target cost $C^t(u_k(i))$.
2: Identify all ZCC chains in the network, supplement them with all their sub-chains, and store them to a ZCC set Z.
3: Sort ZCC chains in Z according to their starting positions in the network.
4: Set $C^{\mathrm{best}} = \infty$ {defines minimum cumulative cost computed so far through the whole network}.
5: Set $P^{\mathrm{best}} = \emptyset$ {defines the best path found so far}.
6: **for** z in Z **do**
7:    **if** no ZCC chain precedes ZCC chain z **then**
8:       **if** distance of z from the beginning of the network is L^b at the most **then**
9:          Search for the path of single candidates from the beginning of the network to the start of z (ZCC1, ZCC3, ZCC4, ZCC8), see Fig. 1.B. Store the resulting path (could be empty as for ZCC3 and ZCC8) and its cumulative cost, and associate these with z.
10:      **else**
11:         Remove z from Z and do not process this chain any more (ZCC6).
12:      **end if**
13:   **else**
14:      Find the closest ZCC chain(s) that precede z (their distance from z is the same and minimal). Search for paths between these preceding ZCC chains and z (see Fig. 1.C).
15:      The best preceding ZCC chain is the one with the minimum cumulative cost. Store the path and its cumulative cost to this ZCC chain, and associate these with z.
16:   **end if**
17:   **if** the distance of z from the end of the network is L^e at the maximum **then**

18:    Search for the path from the end of z to the end of the network (ZCC2) as shown in Fig. 1.D. The path could be empty as for ZCC5, ZCC7, ZCC10.

19:    Backtrack the network from z to the beginning of the network and together with the path found in Step 18 create the full path P^{full} through the whole network. Set C^{full} to be the cumulative cost of the created full path P^{full}.

20:    **if** $C^{full} < C^{best}$ **then**

21:        $C^{best} = C^{full}$

22:        $P^{best} = P^{full}$

23:    **end if**

24:    **end if**

25: **end for**

26: The optimal path through the network of all candidates (i.e. the optimal sequence of candidates for the given utterance) is stored in P^{best}.

The supplement of the sub-chains in Step 2 of the algorithm made the ZCC chain framework more flexible as the number of points to concatenate ZCC chains increased. This prevented the algorithm from selecting ZCC chains at the expense of any higher values of target costs C^t. On the other hand, with the higher number of ZCC chains the computational load significantly increased too. To reduce the computational load, ZCC chains were pruned by setting a maximum allowable target cost C^t (see [8] for more details).

To search for a path of single candidates between non followup ZCC chains in Step 14 (shown in Fig. 1.C), and at the beginning (Step 9, Fig. 1.B) or at the end (Step 18, Fig. 1.D) of the network the

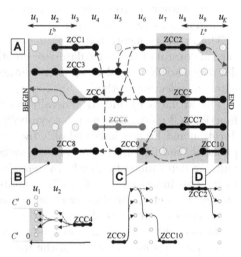

Fig. 1. Scheme of the ZCCVIT algorithm

bounded-depth best-first search algorithm was found to be very effective [8].

Since the strategy is to select ZCC chains as much as possible, the best preceding ZCC chain in Step 14 is selected only from the closest ZCC chains. In Fig. 1.A, ZCC2 can be concatenated only with ZCC3 or ZCC4 and not with ZCC1 or ZCC8.

3 Synthetic Speech Artifacts Description

Since the ZCCVIT algorithm principally prefers to select longer segments of speech (ZCC chains), an increased number of audible artifacts were expected to occur especially at concatenation points of longer ZCC chains. Indeed, the listening tests revealed a number of artifacts present in synthetic speech [8].

However, the artifacts of a very similar kind occurred in a similar extent in synthetic speech of both ZCCVIT and VITBASE methods. The following kinds of artifacts typical for a concatenative method were observed:

a) **Voice talent based artifacts.** This kind of artifact is caused by various types of voice and/or pronunciation failures (like a mispronunciation, mixing of different speaking styles, wrong intonation, etc.) of the voice talent during the recording of source utterances.

b) **Speech segmentation errors.** These errors are a consequence of an imperfect automatic phonetic segmentation of source recordings and they often result in a concatenation of inappropriate parts of speech signals.

c) **Duration mismatch.** In this case the optimal sequence of unit candidates includes a segment whose duration is significantly different from the duration expected for the given phonetic context at that particular position.

d) **F0 discontinuities.** This kind of artifact corresponds to discontinuities in F0 contour at concatenation points. Such discontinuities are assessed by listeners as very disturbing.

The artifacts mentioned in a) and b) can essentially be avoided only by a careful control of the voice database creation process. Using an erroneous voice database, artifacts tend to occur in synthetic speech without regard to a particular unit-selection method.

The artifacts c) and d) generally result from the imperfection of the cost functions C^t a C^c. Since we use a symbolic prosody model [19] in which both the duration and F0 are described only by a set of symbolic (positional, contextual, phonetic, and linguistic) features, the values of duration and F0 contour of each unit are determined implicitly by selecting their optimal candidates according to the cost functions C^t a C^c. Given many parameters involved in the selection process, the actual duration or F0 value could be "sacrificed" to meet some other parameters, resulting in discontinuities of temporal and/or F0 patterns. These artifacts could be avoided, or at least reduced by proposing various "smoothing" techniques and modifications of the unit-selection algorithm. Two of them will be described in the next section.

4   Synthetic Speech Improvements

4.1   Duration Control

This modification of the unit-selection algorithm is aimed at the elimination of artifacts caused by units with an inappropriate duration. The inappropriate duration of a unit at a given position in an utterance is revealed by comparing its duration to a duration predicted by an explicit duration model. To do that, CART (Classification and Regression Tree) based duration model [13] as implemented by Romportl and Kala [14] was employed. This approach to duration control can be used in any unit-selection framework.

The training data consisted of phone instances (unit candidates) from all utterances of a given speech corpus used to build the voice database. Each phone instance was tagged by 172 linguistic and phonetic features which described its

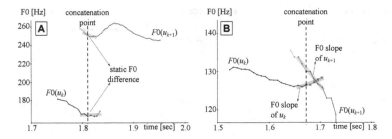

Fig. 2. Examples of F0 artifacts caused by static (A) and dynamic (B) differences around a concatenation point

context (up to 2 phones to the left and to the right), a category of the phone according to a place of articulation (i.e short/long vowels, plosives, vocalic diphthongs, nasals, affricates, fricatives, glides, liquids, vibrants), manner of articulation (glottals, rounded/unrounded vowels and diphthongs, bilabial, labiodental, postalveolar, alveodental, palatals, velars), and a position of the phone within the prosodic structure of the utterance [15]. An independent regression tree for each phone was trained using the EST tool *wagon* [17]. The resulting trees with the duration statistics of each phone were then supplemented to the voice database (see Fig. 3.A.1).

At the runtime, the synthesis scheme was modified to preselect unit candidates according to the CART-based duration model before the process of the selection of the optimal unit candidates starts. For each unit u_k (a diphone in our case, assume the diphone labeled $p1$-$p2$ consists of the parts of phones $p1$ and $p2$) at the position k in the synthesized utterance, its duration $\hat{d}_k$ is estimated by traversing the regression trees corresponding to phones $p1$ and $p2$. The resulting leaf of the tree p_j denotes the mean $\mu_k^{p_j}$ and standard deviation $\sigma_k^{p_j}$ of all phone p_j instances assigned to it. Subsequently, the diphone candidates u_k coming from phones p_j with duration $d_k^{p_j}$ are pruned by eliminating those whose duration $d_k^{p_j}$ does not meet the following criterion

$$\mu_k^{p_j} - 2\sigma_k^{p_j} < d_k^{p_j} < \mu_k^{p_j} + 2\sigma_k^{p_j}, \quad j = 1, 2. \tag{3}$$

The process is illustrated in Fig. 3.B. In the case of the ZCCVIT algorithm described in Sec. 2, the pruning can be done in Step 1, and only the candidates u_k which meet the criterion (3) are used for further processing.

4.2   F0 Control

The avoid the artifacts caused by discontinuities in F0 contours, an *F0 continuity* criterion was proposed and implemented in Steps 9 and 14 of the ZCCVIT algorithm.

The first experiments were based on constraining the local F0 difference between two neighboring candidates u_k, u_{k+1} at a concatenation point (hereinafter *static F0* difference, see Fig. 2.A). The F0 values at the beginning, $F0_{k+1}^b$, and

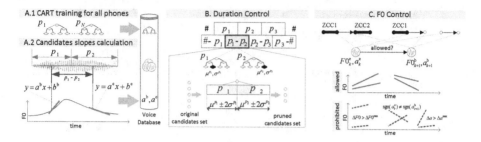

Fig. 3. Artifact elimination scheme within the modified ZCC algorithm ZCCVIT^{mod}

at the end, $F0_k^e$, of the candidates were pre-calculated from pitch marks detected in electroglottograph (EGG) signals [9]. The F0 continuity criterion was defined as

$$\left| F0_k^e - F0_{k+1}^b \right| \leq \Delta F0^{\max}, \tag{4}$$

i.e. the concatenation of candidates u_k and u_{k+1} is not permitted when the F0 difference exceeds a given range $\Delta F0^{\max}$ (in hertz). The corresponding concatenation cost C^c is not computed, speeding up the selection process. A similar technique was introduced by Conkie and Syrdal [5]; however, instead of using F0 at unit boundaries, they used a mean $F0$ value per a candidate and aimed at a speed-up of the unit-selection algorithm, not at an improvement of synthetic speech quality.

To find an optimal $\Delta F0^{\max}$, a set of utterances containing F0-based artifacts was collected. The utterances were then synthesized by the modified ZCCVIT algorithm, and the value of parameter $\Delta F0^{\max}$ was gradually decreased until the artifacts were audible. We found that many artifacts still remained even when an extremely low $\Delta F0^{\max} = 5$ Hz was applied. An analysis of these artifacts showed the importance of *F0 dynamics*—if F0 trends between the concatenated candidates differed too much, the concatenation was perceived as very disturbing (see Fig. 2.B).

To minimize computational demands, we decided to approximate the F0 dynamics around a concatenation point between unit candidates u_k and u_{k+1} by lines

$$y_{F0}^e(u_k) = a_k^e x + b_k^e \tag{5}$$
$$y_{F0}^b(u_{k+1}) = a_{k+1}^b x + b_{k+1}^b \tag{6}$$

where a_k^e and a_{k+1}^b represent the *F0 slope* at the end of candidate u_k and at the beginning of candidate u_{k+1}. Coefficients b_k^e and b_{k+1}^b are approximated values of F0 at the concatenation point. As the difference $\left| b_k^e - b_{k+1}^b \right|$ corresponds to the static F0 difference in relation (4), the corresponding values of $F0_k^e$ and $F0_{k+1}^b$, already present in a voice database, were used to express the static difference as defined in relation (4). The slopes a_k^e and a_{k+1}^b were estimated from pitch-marks around the concatenation point using linear regression. Thus, each unit candidate u_k in a voice database was supplemented with two dynamic features describing F0 trends at the beginning a_k^b and at the end a_k^e of the candidate (see Fig. 3.A.2).

Subsequently, the F0 continuity criterion defined by relation (4) was extended to take the difference in F0 slopes around a concatenation point into account

$$\text{sgn}\,[a_k^e] = \text{sgn}[a_{k+1}^b] \tag{7}$$

$$\left| a_k^e - a_{k+1}^b \right| \leq \Delta a^{\max} \tag{8}$$

where relation (7) requires the slopes of both F0 lines, a_k^e and a_{k+1}^b to have the same direction. Then, relation (8) allows the F0 slopes to differ by a maximum of $\Delta a^{\max}$. The F0 continuity criterion is illustrated in Fig. 3.C. After a series of experiments we set the maximum permissible static difference $\Delta F0^{\max} = 20$ Hz and the maximum permissible difference $\Delta a^{\max} = \tan 30°$.

5   Improvements Evaluation

To evaluate the modifications of the ZCCVIT algorithm, two Czech voices from the ARTIC unit-selection TTS system [18], male and female, were used. Unit inventories of both voices are of similar size (≈ 18 hours of news-style speech), as the same text prompts were utilized to record the speech corpus of each voice [11]. Twenty randomly selected news-style utterances with the average length being 39 units / 7 words (not included in the source speech corpus) were synthesized by the standard VITBASE, baseline ZCCVIT described in Sec. 2, and the ZCC algorithm with the modifications described in Sec. 4 (hereinafter denoted as ZCCVIT^{mod}). Both the quality of synthetic speech and computational demands were evaluated.

Pairwise preference listening tests were carried out to compare the overall quality of speech synthesized by the three different versions of the Viterbi algorithm. Twelve listeners (both TTS experts and inexperienced listeners) took part in the tests. Each pair of synthetic utterances A and B were compared on a 3-point scale (A is better than B, A sounds same as B, A is worse than B). As shown in Table 1, listeners preferred ZCCVIT^{mod} over ZCCVIT and they evaluated it even better than the reference VITBASE algorithm.

Table 1. Listening test results

Voice	Compared algorithms		Preference rating [%]		
	A	B	A=B	A >B	A <B
Male	ZCCVIT	VITBASE	87.50	5.42	7.08
	ZCCVIT^{mod}	VITBASE	46.67	38.67	14.67
Female	ZCCVIT	VITBASE	80.81	9.09	10.10
	ZCCVIT^{mod}	VITBASE	45.38	30.77	23.85

Since concatenation cost computations were found to cover approx. 90% of all synthesis-time computations in the VITBASE algorithm [8], the *speed-up rate*

$S = \frac{1}{n} \sum_{j=1}^{n} \frac{\text{base}N^c(j)}{N^c(j)}$ was used to measure how much the algorithm in question (with $N^c(j)$ being the number of computations of C^c when synthesizing j-th testing utterance; $n = 20$) is faster than the reference VITBASE (with $_{\text{base}}N^c(j)$ being the number of C^c computations). As shown in Table 2, the elimination of temporal artifacts and F0 discontinuities in ZCCVIT^{mod} resulted also in another small speed-up of the unit selection algorithm.

Table 2. Comparison of computational demands in terms of speed-up rate S

Voice	VITBASE	ZCCVIT	ZCCVIT^{mod}
Male	1.00	556.54	616.11
Female	1.00	438.30	458.57

6   Conclusions

As we found that synthetic speech produced by both the standard unit-selection algorithm and its alternative which uses zero-concatenation-cost (ZCC) chains to speed up the selection process contained artifacts related to discontinuities in F0 and temporal patterns, we proposed techniques to eliminate these artifacts. The techniques were incorporated into the ZCC algorithm aiming at avoiding a concatenation of ZCC chains (or single unit candidates) with different F0 and temporal tendencies. According to listening tests the modified ZCC algorithm was judged better than the original ZCC algorithm and even better than the standard Viterbi-search unit-selection algorithm. In addition, the computational load of the modified ZCC algorithm was slightly reduced as well. The results both in quality improvements and in the computational complexity reduction were consistent across the male and female voice in question.

Acknowledgements. Support for this work was provided by the Technology Agency TA CR, project No. TA01030476, and by the University of West Bohemia, project No. SGS-2013-032.

References

1. Beutnagel, M., Mohri, M., Riley, M.: Rapid unit selection from a large speech corpus for concatenative speech synthesis. In: Proc. EUROSPEECH, Budapest, Hungary, pp. 607–610 (1999)
2. Blouin, C., Bagshaw, P.C., Rosec, O.: A method of unit pre-selection for speech synthesis based on acoustic clustering and decision trees. In: Proc. ICASSP, Hong Kong, vol. 1, pp. 692–695 (2003)
3. Čepko, J., Talafová, R., Vrabec, J.: Indexing join costs for faster unit selection synthesis. In: Proc. Internat. Conf. Systems, Signals Image Processing (IWSSIP), Bratislava, Slovak Republic, pp. 503–506 (2008)

4. Conkie, A., Beutnagel, M., Syrdal, A.K., Brown, P.: Preselection of candidate units in a unit selection-based text-to-speech synthesis system. In: Proc. ICSLP, Beijing, China, vol. 3, pp. 314–317 (2000)

5. Conkie, A., Syrdal, A.K.: Using F0 to constrain the unit selection Viterbi network. In: Proc. ICASSP, Prague, Czech Republic, pp. 5376–5379 (2011)

6. Hamza, W., Donovan, R.: Data-driven segment preselection in the IBM trainable speech synthesis system. In: Proc. INTERSPEECH, Denver, USA, pp. 2609–2612 (2002)

7. Hunt, A.J., Black, A.W.: Unit selection in concatenative speech synhesis system using a large speech database. In: Proc. ICASSP, Atlanta, USA, pp. 373–376 (1996)

8. Kala, J., Matoušek, J.: Very fast unit selection using Viterbi search with zero-concatenation-cost chains. In: Proc. ICASSP, Florence, Italy (2014)

9. Legát, M., Matoušek, J., Tihelka, D.: On the detection of pitch marks using a robust multi-phase algorithm. Speech Commun. 53(4), 552–566 (2011)

10. Ling, Z.H., Hu, Y., Shuang, Z.W., Wang, R.H.: Decision tree based unit preselection in Mandarin Chinese synthesis. In: Proc. ISCSLP, Taipei, Taiwan (2002)

11. Matoušek, J., Romportl, J.: On building phonetically and prosodically rich speech corpus for text-to-speech synthesis. In: Proc. 2nd IASTED Internat. Conf. on Computational Intelligence, San Francisco, USA, pp. 442–447 (2006)

12. Nishizawa, N., Kawai, H.: Unit database pruning based on the cost degradation criterion for concatenative speech synthesis. In: Proc. ICASSP, Las Vegas, USA, pp. 3969–3972 (2008)

13. Riley, M.: Tree-based modeling for speech synthesis. In: Bailly, G., Benoit, C., Sawallis, T. (eds.) Talking Machines: Theories, Models and Designs, pp. 265–273. Elsevier, Amsterdam (1992)

14. Romportl, J., Kala, J.: Prosody modelling in czech text-to-speech synthesis. In: Proceedings of the 6th ISCA Workshop on Speech Synthesis, pp. 200–205. Rheinische Friedrich-Wilhelms-Universität Bonn, Bonn (2007)

15. Romportl, J., Matoušek, J., Tihelka, D.: Advanced prosody modelling. In: Sojka, P., Kopeček, I., Pala, K. (eds.) TSD 2004. LNCS (LNAI), vol. 3206, pp. 441–447. Springer, Heidelberg (2004)

16. Sakai, S., Kawahara, T., Nakamura, S.: Admissible stopping in Viterbi beam search for unit selection in concatenative speech synthesis. In: Proc. ICASSP, Las Vegas, USA, pp. 4613–4616 (2008)

17. Taylor, P., Caley, R., Black, A., King, S.: Edinburgh speech tools library: System documentation (1999), http://www.cstr.ed.ac.uk/projects/speech_tools/manual-1.2.0/

18. Tihelka, D., Kala, J., Matoušek, J.: Enhancements of Viterbi search for fast unit selection synthesis. In: Proc. INTERSPEECH, Makuhari, Japan, pp. 174–177 (2010)

19. Tihelka, D., Matoušek, J.: Unit selection and its relation to symbolic prosody: a new approach. In: Proc. INTERSPEECH, Pittsburgh, USA, pp. 2042–2045 (2006)

Robust Multi-Band ASR Using Deep Neural Nets and Spectro-temporal Features

György Kovács, László Tóth, and Tamás Grósz

MTA-SzTE Research Group on Artificial Intelligence,
Tisza Lajos krt. 103, 6720 Szeged, Hungary
gykovacs,tothl,groszt@inf.u-szeged.hu

Abstract. Spectro-temporal feature extraction and multi-band processing were both designed to make the speech recognizers more robust. Although they have been used for a long time now, very few attempts have
been made to combine them. This is why here we integrate two spectro-
temporal feature extraction methods into a multi-band framework. We
assess the performance of our spectro-temporal feature sets both individually (as a baseline) and in combination with multi-band processing in
phone recognition tasks on clean and noise contaminated versions of the
TIMIT dataset. Our results show that multi-band processing clearly outperforms the baseline feature recombination method in every case tested.
This improved performance can also be further enhanced by using the
recently introduced technology of deep neural nets (DNNs).

Keywords: TIMIT, deep neural net, multi-band processing, spectro-
temporal features, robust speech recognition.

1 Introduction

While current speech recognizers yield reasonable accuracy scores in controlled
conditions, they still fall short in more realistic situations like spontaneous speech
and/or speech with noise. Several methods have been proposed to remedy these
shortcomings. In this paper, we combine two of them, namely multi-band recognition and localized spectro-temporal processing. In multi-band recognition the
input is decomposed into spectral bands, a partial recognition is performed over
these bands, then the local scores are combined to produce a final recognition
result [1,2,3,4,5]. Early papers on this method applied standard techniques like
perceptual linear prediction (PLP) to extract features from the spectral bands
[2,3,4]. However, feature extraction methods that are specially tailored for processing spectral bands may produce a more optimal feature set. One such method
is spectro-temporal processing, where features are extracted from local spectro-
temporal patches using (among others) 2D DCT [6] and Gabor filters [7].

One can reasonably expect both of these methods to be more robust against
noise compared to the standard methods that process the whole spectrum in one
go. In fact, in earlier experiments both 2D DCT and Gabor filters produced more
noise-robust features than conventional, full-band representations like MFCC [8].
In spite of this, we found only a few and quite recent papers that try to combine

A. Ronzhin et al. (Eds.): SPECOM 2014, LNAI 8773, pp. 386–393, 2014.

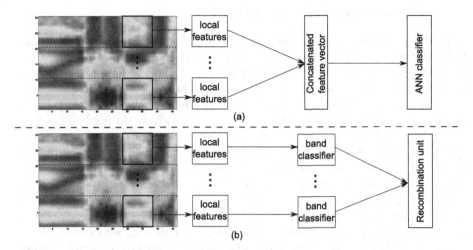

Fig. 1. Schematic diagrams of the baseline system that applies feature recombination (a) and a multi-band recognition system (b)

these feature extraction methods with the multi-band approach [9,10]. For this reason, here we will examine the effects of combining multi-band processing with spectro-temporal (2D DCT and Gabor filter based) features.

The multi-band approach has mostly been studied in combination with artificial neural net (ANN)-based speech recognition techniques, using the HMM/ANN hybrid technology [1,2,4,9]. A difficult question is how to combine the results from the various bands. One solution is to train another neural net that combines the band-based probability estimates into one overall estimate. Here we apply this method, but using DNNs [11]. To the best of our knowledge, this is the first attempt at applying DNNs within a multi-band speech recognition framework.

We will evaluate the various models on the TIMIT phone recognition task [17]. The robustness of the models will be tested by adding various types of artificial noise and realistic noise to the input signals using different signal-to-noise ratios.

2 Multi-band Speech Recognition

Figure 1 shows the schematic diagram of spectro-temporal (a), and multi-band (b) speech-recognition. In both methods, a set of acoustic features are extracted separately from each band. The difference is that while in standard spectro-temporal processing the features are concatenated and classified together (hence this approach is sometimes referred to as 'feature recombination' [12]), in multi-band processing these features go into different classifiers, the outputs of which are combined into one score by the recombination unit. The multi-band processing scheme provides a lot of options as regards the band-level classifier, the level of recombination, and the recombination method used. Below we will describe our choices, along with the feature extraction methods we applied to get a good performance.

2.1   Localized Spectro-temporal Features

In localized spectro-temporal processing, we apply transforms like 2D DCT and Gabor filters on spectro-temporally localized patches of the spectrogram of the input signal [8]. This is quite different from the conventional approaches where each acoustic feature relies on the whole spectral range. These techniques, however, have many parameters (such as the exact filter coefficients, the position and overlap of the patches on the spectrogram) which would need to be optimized. To avoid this, we used preexisting spectro-temporal feature sets – more specifically a 2D DCT and a Gabor feature set we introduced earlier [8]. In that paper, we decomposed the spectrum into six 9 mel-band wide frequency bands with an overlap of roughly 55%. For comparison purposes, here, we applied the exact same parameters, but instead of using the original feature recombination approach (illustrated in Fig. 1 (a)), we applied the multi-band approach (Fig. 1 (b)), and used our earlier results as the baseline. This way, we will be able to see how well the multi-band approach performed compared to the simple feature recombination approach.

2.2   Processing and Recombination of the Bands

In the multi-band model, we first process each spectral band using separate classifiers. Most authors apply ANNs for this task, and we will also do so here. These ANNs give phone posterior estimates for each band, which have to be recombined (which we will perform at the frame level). Numerous methods exist for this step, ranging from simple fixed linear and non-linear combinations (via ANNs) to sophisticated methods that try to dynamically assess the reliability of the bands [1,3,9,13,14,15,16]. As this paper was partially inspired by the recent renaissance in ANN-based recognition (especially with DNNs [11]), we opted to use ANNs as recombination units as well. It is also often argued that the recombination of bands should be non-linear [1], which is in accord with the findings of Hermansky et al., who found that ANN-based merging consistently outperformed linear combination schemes in different experimental configurations [2,9]. The ANNs we apply here and in the processing of separate spectral bands range from standard neural nets with one hidden layer to DNNs which use the pre-training algorithm introduced by Hinton et al. [11]. To the best of our knowledge, the spectro-temporal features we use here have not yet been thoroughly investigated in the multi-band framework, or when combined with DNNs.

3   Experimental Settings

3.1   Speech Database

All the experiments reported here were conducted on the TIMIT [17] corpus, following the standard train-test partitioning of having 3696 train and 192 test sentences. The phonetic labels here were fused into 39 categories. To create a phone recognizer, we used a HMM/ANN hybrid model (where the frame-level phone posterior estimates of the neural net were combined by an HMM, got by modifying the Hidden Markov Model toolkit [18]) and a simple bigram language model.

3.2 Noise

Here, we expected an increased noise robustness to be the biggest gain in multi-band processing. To learn whether this was actually the case, the models trained on clean data were also tested on noise contaminated test sets of TIMIT. For these tests, we created a bandlimited noise sample by filtering white noise with a bandpass filter, with a passband between 3000 and 5000 Hz. It was shown earlier that multi-band ASR is quite robust in the case of bandlimited noise [19]. To demonstrate that this also holds true for other types of noise, we took noise samples from the NOISEX-92 database [20]. The first sample was pink noise (another type of artificial noise), which has the highest energy at 0Hz and tails off at higher frequencies. The second sample was babble noise, which simulates the effect of people talking in the background. The third type of noise was Volvo noise, to simulate conversations taking place in a moving car. And the fourth and last noise type was 'factory-1' noise, to simulate the effect of a nearby production line on ASR rates. We added the noise by applying the FaNT tool [21] with the proper signal to noise ratio (20db and 10 dB, respectively).

3.3 Time-Frequency Processing

We chose the log-mel scaled spectrogram as the initial time-frequency representation of the speech signal. We computed the spectrogram using 4000 samples (25 ms) per frame at 160 sample (10 ms) hops, and applied a 1024-point FFT on the frames. Next, the spectrograms were transformed to a log mel-scale with 26 channels, and each sentence was normalized so as to give a zero mean and unit variance. Then, a copy of the lowest four channels were mirrored in order to avoid artificially down-weighting low frequency bins of the spectrogram.

To get a frame-level representation, each Gabor or 2D DCT filter was evaluated on each patch of the spectrogram (the patches had a length of 9 frames, and a height of 9 channels, with a step size of 4 channels in frequency). These features were associated with the centre position of the patch, giving a set of features for each frame. Next, to make use of available temporal information, the Δ and $\Delta\Delta$ features were added. Then, in the multi-band processing framework the resulting features were grouped into 6 vectors, based on the frequency band they had been derived from.

3.4 Neural Net Classifier

In our experiments we applied four different neural net architectures. Their only common features were their hidden layers using sigmoid neurons, and their output layer consisting of 39 softmax units. In the first net (FC) we sought to

Table 1. Phone recognition accuracy scores got on the clean core test set of TIMIT, and the number of free parameters (in millions) for the different settings

Settings	2D DCT	Gabor	No. of ANN parameters
FC	73.15%	73.22%	~ 6
MB small	73.93%	74.55%	~ 6
MB big	75.30%	75.21%	~16
MB deep	**76.53%**	**77.19%**	~17

evaluate the performance of the feature recombination approach. This neural net consisted of one hidden layer of 4000 neurons, using 9 neighbouring frames during training. The second net (MB small) applied the multi-band approach, and to ensure comparability (by means of parameter count) with the feature recombination method, it had the following parameters: the neural nets trained on the individual frequency bands had one hidden layer of 1000 neurons, while the recombination neural net had one hidden layer of 4000 neurons, and both used 5 neighbouring frames. In the next model (MB big), both nets were replaced by larger neural nets that used 9 neighbouring frames and had hidden layers of 4000 neurons. For the last configuration (MB deep), the nets that processed the bands were replaced by a DNN consisting of three hidden layers of 1000 neurons. This deep net was trained using the pre-training algorithm of Hinton et al. [11] As for the recombination unit, a net with two hidden layers of 1000 neurons was applied. Again, both nets used 9 neighbouring frames.

The neural nets were trained with random initial weights, using standard backpropagation on the randomly selected 90% of the training data in semi-batch mode, while the remaining 10% was used as the validation set. In each case where the neural net outputs were also used as inputs for some other net, the training was carried out ten times, and the average performance was reported. We viewed the difference between two results as significant if the p value resulting from a two-tailed Student's t-test with unequal variance was smaller than 0.05.

4   Results and Discussion

4.1   Experiments on TIMIT With Clean Speech

Although we expected to get the biggest gains from multi-band processing under noisy conditions, we still found it useful to present results on clean speech as well. One reason for this was that Morris et al. in the 2000s found this method had a detrimental effect on the speech recognition performance for clean speech [15].

Table 1 lists the phone recognition accuracy scores we got on the clean test set. We notice that for both feature sets, the first multi-band setting (MB small) already significantly outperforms the feature recombination (FC) approach, and then with each new setting we get a better recognition accuracy than with the one before. And as we anticipated, for both feature sets, the DNN provided the best recognition accuracy scores (giving an overall 12.62% and 14.83% relative

Table 2. Phone recognition accuracy scores got with 2D DCT and Gabor features on the core test set of TIMIT, artificially contaminated with bandlimited noise and pink noise

Feature set	Settings	Bandlimited		Pink	
		20db	10db	20db	10db
2D DCT	FC	63.96%	52.02%	55.73%	34.84%
	MB small	65.55%	58.79%	58.03%	37.50%
	MB big	67.13%	60.34%	**59.89%**	**38.39%**
	MB deep	**69.32%**	**62.79%**	59.78%	36.45%
Gabor	FC	63.59%	50.87%	55.74%	34.24%
	MB small	66.89%	59.53%	60.13%	39.90%
	MB big	68.25%	61.02%	60.69%	**40.46%**
	MB deep	**70.43%**	**64.07%**	**62.00%**	38.54%

error rate reduction in the case of 2D DCT and Gabor filters, respectively). It is also interesting here that for the FC setting the recognition accuracy scores for the 2D DCT and Gabor features do not differ much; but this was not the case for most multi-band settings, where the scores we got with the Gabor filters were significantly better than the ones we got with the 2D DCT features.

As we thought that switching from full-band to multi-band recognition would be beneficial for the case of speech recognition with noise, we also decided to test our models on speech signals contaminated with noise. We report these experiments below, first describing the case where we contaminated the test set with various types of artificial noise (Section 4.2), then we described the case where the noise samples came from real-life situations (Section 4.3).

4.2   Experiments on TIMIT with Artificial Noise

The accuracy scores we got when we added artificial noise to the test set are listed in Table 2. As can be seen, our simplest multi-band model (MB small) already outperforms the feature concatenation (FC) approach for each type of noise. And as we anticipated, the multi-band has the biggest gain for bandlimited noise with a small (10db) signal to noise ratio (a relative error reduction of 14.09% with 2D DCT, and 17.62% with Gabor features). Also, the relative error reduction is bigger in each case here than it was for clean speech. It can also be seen that in most cases the DNN yielded the best scores. Moreover, just like the case of clean speech, in the full-band approach we can see comparable phone recognition accuracy scores for the 2D DCT and the Gabor features (with 2D DCT features being better in most cases); and for the multi-band settings the Gabor features consistently provided better phone recognition accuracy scores.

4.3   Experiments on TIMIT with Real Environmental Noise

Apart from testing the multi-band approach on clean speech and speech signals contaminated with artificial noise, we wanted to evaluate its performance on

Table 3. Phone recognition accuracy scores got with 2D DCT and Gabor features on the core test set of TIMIT, artificially contaminated with Babble, Car and Factory noise samples

Feature set	Settings	Babble		Car		Factory	
		20db	10db	20db	10db	20db	10db
2D DCT	FC	62.89%	46.54%	70.86%	67.79%	59.73%	41.18%
	MB small	64.37%	49.26%	71.74%	68.42%	61.45%	43.16%
	MB big	65.99%	50.87%	73.43%	70.17%	62.76%	45.02%
	MB deep	**68.12%**	**51.62%**	**75.40%**	**73.17%**	**64.68%**	**45.50%**
Gabor	FC	63.21%	47.03%	70.47%	67.13%	59.62%	40.22%
	MB small	65.23%	50.31%	72.46%	69.30%	62.81%	44.29%
	MB big	66.18%	51.34%	73.60%	70.51%	63.87%	45.41%
	MB deep	**68.93%**	**53.34%**	**76.06%**	**74.20%**	**66.18%**	**46.83%**

speech with real-environmental noise types as well. First, because these are the types of noise that typically arise in real life applications; and, second, Hagen et al. earlier reported the failure of multi-band systems when acting on situations with real-environmental noise [15].

The accuracy scores we got on the TIMIT core test set contaminated with real-environmental noise are summarized in Table 3. As can be seen, similar to the previous cases, even the worst performing multi-band setting (MB small) significantly outperforms the feature recombination (FC) approach. It can also be seen that for real-environmental noise, the DNNs provide the best accuracy scores in every case. And again, while in the feature recombination (FC) approach Gabor filter-based recognition results in some cases are slightly poorer than the 2D DCT-based results, they take the lead in the multi-band case, where we consistently got better accuracy scores for them, than those for 2D DCT.

5   Conclusions and Future Work

In this paper we showed – by evaluating 2D DCT and Gabor filters on the TIMIT phone recognition task – that both yield better results in a multi-band framework than they do in the case of simple feature recombination. We also found that this improved performance could be further enhanced by using DNNs and a pre-training method. Next, we showed that different filter sets might be optimal in the feature recombination approach and in the multi-band approach. For this reason, in the future we plan to explore the possibility of training the filter sets themselves based on their performance on different frequency bands, similar to the way we trained the filter sets in our study [8] by introducing a special layer of neurons to the ANN that simulate the behaviour of spectro-temporal filters.

Acknowledgments. This publication is supported by the European Union and co-funded by the European Social Fund. Project title: Telemedicine-focused research activities in the fields of mathematics, informatics and medical sciences. Project number: TÁMOP-4.2.2.A-11/1/KONV-2012-0073.

References

1. Bourlard, H., Dupont, S.: A New ASR Approach Based on Independent Processing and Recombination of Partial Frequency Bands. In: ICSLP, pp. 426–429 (1996)
2. Hermansky, H., Timbrewala, S., Pavel, M.: Towards ASR On Partially Corrupted Speech. In: ICSLP, pp. 464–465 (1996)
3. Hagen, A., Morris, A., Bourlard, H.: Subband-Based Speech Recognition in Noisy Conditions The Full Combination Approach. Research Report, IDIAP (1998)
4. Janin, A., Ellis, D., Morgan, N.: Multi-Stream Speech Recognition: Ready for Prime Time? In: Eurospeech 1999, pp. 591–594 (1999)
5. Cerisara, C., Fohr, D.: Multi-band Automatic Speech Recognition. Computer Speech and Language 15, 151–174 (2001)
6. Kovács, G., Tóth, L.: Phone Recognition Experiments with 2D DCT Spectro-temporal Features. In: SACI 2011, pp. 143–146 (2011)
7. Kleinschmidt, M., Gelbart, D.: Improving Word Accuracy with Gabor Feature Extraction. In: ICSLP, pp. 25–28 (2002)
8. Kovács, G., Tóth, L.: The Joint Optimization of Spectro-temporal Features and Neural Net Classifiers. In: TSD 2013, pp. 552–559 (2013)
9. Mesgarani, N., Thomas, S., Hermansky, H.: A multistream multiresolution framework for phoneme recognition. In: INTERSPEECH, pp. 318–321 (2010)
10. Zhao, S.Y., Ravuri, S.V., Morgan, N.: Multi-stream to many-stream: using spectro-temporal features for ASR. In: INTERSPEECH, pp. 2951–2954 (2009)
11. Hinton, G., et al.: Deep Neural Networks for Acoustic Modeling in Speech Recognition. IEEE Signal Processing Magazine 29, 82–97 (2012)
12. Okawa, S., Bocchieri, E., Potamianos, A.: Multi-band Speech Recognition in Noisy Environments. In: ICASSP, pp. 641–644 (1998)
13. Hagen, A., Morris, A., Bourlard, H.: From Multi-Band Full Combination to Multi-Stream Full Combination Processing in Robust ASR. ISCA ASR2000 Tutorial and Research Workshop (2000)
14. Hagen, A., Bourlard, H., Morris, A.: Adaptive ML-Weighting in Multi-Band Recombination of Gaussian Mixture ASR. In: ICASSP, pp. 257–260 (2001)
15. Morris, A., Hagen, A., Glotin, H., Bourlard, H.: Multi-stream adaptive evidence combination for noise robust ASR. Speech Communication 34, 25–40 (2001)
16. Hagen, A., Neto, J.P.: Multi-stream Processing Using Context-independent and Context-dependent Hybrid Systems. In: ICASSP, pp. 277–280 (2003)
17. Lamel, L.F., Kassel, R., Seneff, S.: Speech database development: Design and analysis of the acoustic-phonetic corpus. In: DARPA Speech Recognition Workshop, pp. 100–109 (1986)
18. Young, S.J., et al.: The HTK book version 3.4. Cambridge University Press, Cambridge (2006)
19. Hagen, A., Morris, A., Bourlard, H.: From Multi-Band Full Combination to Multi-Stream Full Combination Processing in Robust ASR. In: ISCA ASR2000 Tutorial and Research Workshop (2000)
20. Varga, A., Steeneken, H.: Assessment for automatic speech recognition: II. NOISEX-92: A database and an experiment to study the effect of additive noise on speech recognition systems. Speech Communication 12, 247–251 (1993)
21. Hirsch, H.-G.: FaNT: Filtering and Noise-Adding Tool Retrieved March 22 (2010), http://dnt.kr.hs-niederrhein.de/download.html

Semantic Entity Detection in the Spoken Air Traffic Control Data

Jan Švec and Luboš Šmídl

University of West Bohemia, Faculty of Applied Sciences, Department of Cybernetics
Univerzitní 22, 306 14 Plzeň, Czech Republic
{honzas,smidl}@kky.zcu.cz

Abstract. The paper deals with the semantic entity detection (SED) in the ASR lattices obtained by recognizing the air traffic control dialogs. The presented method is intended for the use in an automatic training tool for air traffic controllers. The semantic entities are modeled using the expert-defined context-free grammars. We use a novel approach which allows processing of uncertain input in the form of weighted finite state transducer. The method was experimentally evaluated on the real data. We also compare two methods for utilization of the knowledge about the dialog environment in the SED process. The results show that the SED with the knowledge about target semantic entities improves the equal error rate from 24.7% to 17.1% in comparison to generic SED.

Keywords: spoken language understanding, semantic entity detection.

1 Introduction

The development of spoken dialog systems requires to incorporate a lot of task- and situation-dependent knowledge. This requirement is very important in a spoken language understanding (SLU) module of a dialog system. Although the statistical-based SLU modules are able to automatically derive the lexical realisations of various annotated semantic entities without the need of aligned data [4], the learning process strongly depends on the variability of the data. The automatic inference of lexical realisations is unreliable when the number of possible lexical realisations for a given semantic entity is high and comparable to the number of training examples [6].

For many tasks the expert knowledge of the target domain is available. The use of such additional information during SLU ensures good generalisation with a positive effect on the prediction performance. In the simplest case, the expert knowledge can be expressed in the form of a list of possible lexical realisations of a given semantic entity. This kind of representation is relatively simple but can lead to some parsing problems such as ambiguity. The list representation also cannot be easily generalized (e.g. the list of all possible representations of time).

Common requirement on the SLU is the ability to process uncertain speech recognition output and also the ability to generate uncertain output [3]. The uncertainty of automatic speech recognizers (ASR) is encoded in a word lattice

A. Ronzhin et al. (Eds.): SPECOM 2014, LNAI 8773, pp. 394–401, 2014.

or a word confusion network. The use of additional information included in ASR lattices can significantly improve the SLU performance [5,13] in comparison with an one-best ASR output.

In this work we focused on the SLU of air traffic control communication data. This kind of communication has very rigid standardized form and therefore some parts of the utterances can be fromally described by a human expert. To incorporate this knowledge into an SLU module we use our method described in [12] which has the advantage of parsing uncertain ASR output and the ability to generate multiple output hypotheses with posterior probabilities assigned.

2   Motivation

In this paper we present an extension of our method presented in [12]. This method allows to incorporate the expert knowledge into a SLU module and at the same time process the uncertain speech recognizer output (in the form of ASR lattice) and produce the uncertain SLU output. The SLU works in a similar way as the named-entity detection – we extract the semantic entities with the specific type and semantic interpretation and with the posterior probability assigned. Therefore we call this process the semantic entity detection (SED).

The following sections deal with the development of an SLU module for a new task which is the Air Traffic Control (ATC) domain. This domain is appropriate for the SED algorithm because many of the task-dependent semantic entities can be defined and formally described by an expert in the ATC domain. The developed SLU module will be used in a spoken dialog system which will simulate the dialog with a real aircraft pilot during the training process of air traffic controllers. The dialog system will be coupled with the simulated environment including simulated aircrafts, runways, navigation points etc. Therefore there is a strong need for a method which allows us to dynamically change the SED process and continuously adapt the SLU module to the simulated environment. In this paper we propose a method which use the generic (not adapted to a current environment state) speech recognizer and generic models for semantic entities. The hypotheses not consistent with the state of the simulated environment are pruned from the SLU output.

Generally, the pruning of the possible SLU hypotheses leads to an improved SLU performance. This paper introduces an algorithm for such an adaptation in real-time and without the need for any ASR and SLU parameters adaptation.

3   Algorithm Description

In this section we will briefly summarize the semantic entity detection algorithm [12]. From the point of view of the SED algorithm, the semantic entity (SE) is virtually a named entity with assigned semantic interpretation. Each SE consists of a type (e.g. the time, date, name) and semantic tags used to describe the SE meaning. Semantic tags are also used to convert the lexical realisation of SE into a "computer readable" representation of the SE. In this approach each SE type is represented by the separate context-free grammar (CFG). The structure of many SE types is fixed. Therefore the CFGs can be defined by an expert in the given domain or they can be generated automatically from the domain database.

In almost every modern speech recognizer the ASR lattices are a by-product of the Viterbi decoding. Converting the raw ASR lattices into the form of weighted finite state transducer (WFST) usually requires some preprocessing. Alternative solution is to use a WFST-based decoder and generate the WFST lattices directly [9]. In this paper we use the lattice preprocessing method adapted from [2]; for the description of WFST operations see [8]:

1. Start with the lattice defined over the tropical semiring.
2. If the transition represents a non-speech event, change the label to ϵ.
3. Apply ϵ-removal algorithm.
4. Prune the lattice using threshold t_p.
5. Change the semiring of the lattice to the logarithmic semiring.
6. Apply weight-pushing algorithm which ensures that the sum of all transition probabilities from any given state is one.
7. Determinize the lattice, the result of determinization is the *optimized lattice*.

The optimized lattices are normalized so that the sum of weights of all paths is one according to the probabilistic semiring. In addition these lattices are deterministic. Although the determinization complexity is generally exponential, the pruning performed in step 4 can ensure reasonable processing times for sentences with lengths which are common in spoken dialog systems.

Each type of semantic entity z has a corresponding CFG G_z. The grammars used to describe semantic entities in this work are non-recursive and therefore they can be converted into finite state transducers T_z without the need for an approximation. The grammars are designed in this way: the input side of transducer T_z represents terminal symbols of CFG G_z and the output side provides the interpretation of the corresponding path in T_z.

To illustrate it, consider a sequence of words *ten past three*. Let's suppose that this sequence represents the time information and we use the transducer T_{time} created from the corresponding grammar G_{time}. Thereafter the output semantic interpretation can be *time:10:p:3* and the corresponding machine representation *3:10 pm*. The process of generating the semantic interpretation is implemented by using the transducer composition algorithm. This approach has the advantage that it can be easily extended to the case where the input is the ASR lattice. There is also an optimized implementation of WFST composition [1]. At the same time, it has some disadvantages: (1) we need to model all possible symbol sequences including meaningless words, (2) there could be ambiguities in the semantic entity assignment, (3) the given part of the utterance could have assigned multiple semantic representations, which is caused by the uncertain ASR hypotheses.

The solution of these problems was suggested in [12]. The issue (1) was solved by applying the approach of a *factor automaton* [7]. The factor automaton of a WFST represents a set of all paths and subpaths of the WFST. Therefore the subpaths containing meaningless words (i.e. words which are not among the terminal symbols of any G_z) are silently ignored and only the subpaths which can bear the meaning (according to the set of G_z) are processed.

The issues (2) and (3) are solved by using the *heuristics of maximum unambiguous coverage*. From the set of all possible assignments of semantic entities the heuristics uses the subset where each transition in the lattice has assigned at most one semantic entity and the number of transitions with semantic entities assigned is maximized. This leads to an optimization process which can be modelled as an integer linear programming (ILP) [12]. The solution of the ILP is the set $\mathcal{F}^*$ of unambiguous semantic entities which occur in the ASR lattice.

4   Dialog Domain Description

We used the ILP-based SED algorithm in an SLU module designed for understanding the air traffic control communication. The goal of the dialog system is to improve the training process of air traffic controllers (ATCs) by automating the simulation of air traffic and bringing more realistic responses from simulated aircrafts by using customized text-to-speech system which simulates the noisy channel. Virtually the dialog system simulates the pilot of an aircraft. In current simulation environments the pilots are simulated by humans (pseudo-pilots). The dialog system should automatize this process and eliminate the pseudo-pilots' effort from the training process (to some degree).

The dialog system should understand the command or clearance from an air traffic controller undergoing the training and then (in the simulation environment) perform the specific action (e.g. change the heading of an aircraft after passing some navigation point). The communication between the pilot and the controller is standardized and contains a number of explicit confirmations (readbacks). From the semantic point of view the utterances contain a large number of semantic entities such as flight levels, speed and heading changes etc.

We collected a corpus containing communication between real pilots and ATCs [11]. The audio data – especially from the pilots – are very noisy due to the use of analog push-to-talk radiotelephony. The corpus was transcribed and the acoustic and language models for speech recognition were trained. The training data consisted of 216k utterances (221 hours of data), the metaparameters of an ASR were tuned on the development data consisting of 1422 utterances (1.38 hours) and all experiments were performed on the test data (1877 utterances and 2.2 hours). We used standard HMM-based speech recognizer. The triphone acoustic model has 1k states with 16 Gaussian mixtures per state and 3-state left-to-right structure. We used PLP parameterization with Δ and $\Delta\Delta$ coefficients (39 features per frame). The acoustic signal was sampled at 8kHz and 16 bits per sample. The language model was trained as a standard 3-gram model from the annotated training data. The recognition vocabulary consisted of 10.3k words. To recognize the data we used a real-time ASR decoder described in [10]. The accuracy of an ASR was 83.9% and the corresponding oracle accuracy of ASR lattices was 89.9%. To prune the lattice we used $t_p = 3$.

5   Semantic Entities

To implement the SLU module for the ATC domain we had to express the expert knowledge in the form of CFGs. In cooperation with experts in the ATC communication we developed the grammars for the following types of semantic entities: call-sign (shortened as CS, name of an aircraft operating agency and one to four digits or letters), flight level (FL, indicated by the words *flight level* or *level* and three digits), heading (HE, word *heading* and three digits), speed (SP, word *speed* and three digits), frequency (FR, three digits, optional decimal point and three digits), runway number (RWY, word *runway* and two digits) and navigation point (PO, consists of list of known navigation points pronounced as a single word). Although the set of all SE types is rich the corresponding CFGs are simple and can be derived from the rules for ATC communication.

To create the reference annotation of semantic entities we used the algorithm described in Section 3 which was applied to the reference transcription created by human annotators. In this paper we evaluate just the influence of the ASR errors on the SED performance. We do not evaluate the CFG coverage. If some SE type is not covered by the CFG, the modification of the CFG is straightforward and can be performed by a human expert. The statistics of SE types computed from the test data are shown in Tab. 1. We can see that the call-sign is the most frequent semantic entity. This is because each utterance in ATC domain should contain the designator of the aircraft which is the subject of the command or clearance. This semantic entity is also the entity with the largest variability; the test data contains 308 different call-signs.

6   Experiments

In the first part of our work we focused on the evaluation of the SED algorithm on English data which come from a real environment. In the second part we performed experiments with incorporating the knowledge about the dialog context and situation into the SED algorithm.

Semantic entity detection in the ATC data. For evaluation of the presented algorithm we used the area under the ROC curve (AUC) on the interval from 0 to 1 false alarm per utterance [12]. In addition we also evaluated the equal error rate (EER). It represents a point on the ROC curve where $EER = 1 - DR = FPR$. Here DR stands for the detection rate (ratio of correctly detected SEs) and FPR is the false positive rate (average number of falsely detected SEs per one utterance).

First of all we evaluated the performance for every SE type without considering other SE types. The results are summarized in Tab. 1. The common trend is that the performance of SED from the ASR lattices is significantly better than from the single top ASR hypothesis (1-best). The comparison of SED performance for all SE types together is shown in Tab. 2 (rows *1-best* and *lattice*). These results prove that the method of [12] is usable also for English data (the original method was validated on Czech data).

Table 1. SE statistics and detection performance (AUC metric in %) by SE type. $n(z)$ denotes the number of occurrences of a given SE type in the test data and $|z|$ the number of distinct values.

SE type z	$n(z)$	$|z|$	1-best AUC	lattice AUC
CS	1424	308	59.5	70.7
FL	476	32	87.4	94.0
HE	43	18	74.4	86.0
SP	41	14	97.4	97.5
FR	322	50	83.2	88.3
RWY	158	3	92.9	93.0
PO	320	70	77.0	85.4

Table 2. SE detection performance (1-best stands for the SED from the best ASR hypothesis, limited SEs are based on the results obtained from the ASR lattices)

	AUC[%]	EER[%]
1-best	63.5	30.6
lattice	75.7	24.7
limiting SEs *prior* ILP	81.2	19.2
limiting SEs *after* ILP	**82.0**	**17.1**

The Tab. 1 provides additional insights into the structure of SED errors. The AUC measure for call-signs (CS) was only about 70%. By analysing the SED results we found that for the test data the algorithm predicted 2131 distinct call-signs (with different scores naturally) although the test data contain just 308 distinct values. This observation motivated the second experiment where we incorporated the knowledge about the expected set of semantic entities into the SED process.

SED incorporating prior information. The SLU can profit from additional information about the state or situation of the dialog and its context. In our case the SED can exploit the additional knowledge about the simulation environment – for example the number of aircrafts shown on the radar and their call-signs.

To simulate the influence of prior information we extracted the set S of all possible semantic interpretations from the test data. Then we limited the generated set of SEs to be the subset of S. We observed that only some SE types are specific to the given simulation scenario, so that we limited the values of the following SE types only: call-sign (limited to 308 unique values found in test data), navigation point (70), frequency (50) and runway number (3).

We compared two possible ways of limiting the set of generated semantic entities according to the situation: (1) limit the SEs *prior* to ILP step, and (2) prune the invalid SEs in the disambiguated set $\mathcal{F}^*$ generated by the ILP (i.e. limiting *after* the ILP step).

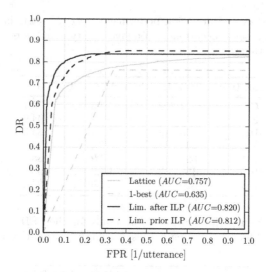

Fig. 1. ROC curves for semantic entity detection from the top hypothesis (1-best), unconstrained lattice and for two methods for limiting the set of all possible SEs

The overall effect of incorporating the situation-based knowledge into the SED process is shown in Tab. 2. It is obvious that by limiting the set of possible SEs the SED performance increases. It is caused by the fact that the number of falsely detected SE is reduced. More interesting is the fact that the second method (limiting SEs after the ILP step) performs better (2% absolute reduction in *EER*). This is illustrated on Fig. 1 where the solid line represents limiting the SEs after the ILP and the dashed line before the ILP step of SED. According to this plot the detection rate for the second method is significantly higher while considering the low *FPR* values (up to ∼0.2 false positives per utterance).

7   Conclusion

We presented a method for utilization of expert knowledge in the SLU module by using the semantic entity detection algorithm. We also showed that the performance can be increased by adopting the method which limits the output set of possible semantic entities. By using this approach the equal error rate of semantic entity detection in the ATC domain decreases from 24.7% for generic SED to 17.1% for SED which uses the knowledge about the context of the dialog.

In addition the presented method for incorporating situation-awareness into a SED allows to dynamically change the set of all possible semantic entities and the SED can be adapted in real-time to a new situation. Although the adaptation is performed by using the simple pruning of the set of all possible values, the pruning can be performed using the uncertain hypotheses from the SED module and the pruning is generally allowed by the ability of SED to process uncertain ASR lattices and produce SED output with assigned posterior probabilities.

Acknowledgements. This research was supported by the Technology Agency of the Czech Republic, project No. TA01030476. Access to computing and storage facilities owned by parties and projects contributing to the National Grid Infrastructure MetaCentrum, (project No. LM2010005), is greatly appreciated.

References

1. Allauzen, C., Riley, M., Schalkwyk, J.: OpenFst: A general and efficient weighted finite-state transducer library. Implementation and Application of Automata 4783, 11–23 (2007)
2. Can, D., Saraclar, M.: Lattice Indexing for Spoken Term Detection. IEEE Transactions on Audio, Speech and Language Processing 19(8), 2338–2347 (2011)
3. Hakkani-Tür, D., Béchet, F., Riccardi, G., Tur, G.: Beyond ASR 1-best: Using word confusion networks in spoken language understanding. Computer Speech & Language 20(4), 495–514 (2006)
4. He, Y., Young, S.: Hidden vector state model for hierarchical semantic parsing. In: Proceedings of IEEE International Conference on Acoustics, Speech, and Signal Processing, vol. 1, pp. 268–271 (2003)
5. Henderson, N., Gašić, M., Thomson, B., Tsiakoulis, P., Yu, K., Young, S.: Discriminative Spoken Language Understanding Using Word Confusion Networks. In: 2012 IEEE Spoken Language Technology Workshop (SLT), pp. 176–181 (2012)
6. Jurčíček, F., Švec, J., Zahradil, J., Jelínek, L.: Use of negative examples in training the HVS semantic model. Text, Speech and Dialogue 4188, 605–612 (2006)
7. Mohri, M., Moreno, P., Weinstein, E.: Factor automata of automata and applications. Implementation and Application of Automata 4783, 168–179 (2007)
8. Mohri, M., Pereira, F.C.N., Riley, M.: Weighted finite-state transducers in speech recognition. Computer Speech & Language 16(1), 69–88 (2002)
9. Povey, D., Hannemann, M., Boulianne, G., Burget, L., Ghoshal, A., Janda, M., Karafiát, M., Kombrink, S., Motlíček, P., Qian, Y., Riedhammer, K., Veselý, K., Vu, N.T.: Generating Exact Lattices in the WFST Framework. In: IEEE International Conference on Acoustics Speech and Signal Processing, Kyoto, Japan, vol. 213850, pp. 4213–4216. IEEE, Kyoto (2012)
10. Pražák, A., Psutka, J.V., Hoidekr, J., Kanis, J., Müller, L., Psutka, J.: Automatic online subtitling of the Czech parliament meetings. Text, Speech and Dialogue 4188, 501–508 (2006)
11. Šmídl, L.: Air traffic control communication corpus. Published in LINDAT/CLARING repository, available under CC BY-NC-ND 3.0 (2012), http://hdl.handle.net/11858/00-097C-0000-0001-CCA1-0
12. Švec, J., Ircing, P., Šmídl, L.: Semantic entity detection from multiple ASR hypotheses within the WFST framework. In: ASRU 2013: IEEE Workshop on Automatic Speech Recognition and Understanding, pp. 84–89. IEEE, Olomouc (December 2013)
13. Švec, J., Šmídl, L., Ircing, P.: Hierarchical Discriminative Model for Spoken Language Understanding. In: Proceedings of IEEE International Conference on Acoustics, Speech, and Signal Processing, pp. 8322–8326. IEEE, Vancouver (2013)

Simplified Simultaneous Perturbation Stochastic Approximation for the Optimization of Free Decoding Parameters

Aleksei Romanenko[1], Alexander Zatvornitsky[2], and Ivan Medennikov[1,3]

[1] ITMO University, Saint-Petersburg, Russia
[2] Speech Technology Center, Saint-Petersburg, Russia
[3] Saint-Petersburg State University, Saint-Petersburg, Russia
183460@niuitmo.ru,
zatvornitskiy@speechpro.com,
ipmsbor@yandex.ru

Abstract. This paper deals with automatic optimization of free decoding parameters. We propose using a Simplified Simultaneous Perturbation Stochastic Approximation algorithm to optimize these parameters. This method provides a significant reduction in computational and labor costs. We also demonstrate that the proposed method successfully copes with the optimization of parameters for a specific target real-time factor, for all the databases we tested.

Keywords: Simplified Simultaneous Perturbation Stochastic Approximation, SPSA, decoding parameter, real-time factor, RTF, speech recognition.

1 Introduction

The balance of accuracy and speed of automatic speech recognition depends on the solution of a number of related tasks, such as:

— optimization of the acoustic model;
— optimization of the language model;
— optimization of a large set of free decoding parameters.

Optimization of both the acoustic model and the language model in automatic speech recognition for large vocabularies is a well-known task [1]. In contrast, the problem of optimizing free decoding parameters is still often solved manually or by using grid search (i.e. searching for values in a grid with a specified step). The task is complicated by the fact that each parameter can have a different impact on the accuracy of speech recognition and/or the expected decoding time. Moreover, each new domain requires searching for new optimal decoding parameters every time we change the training data. Lastly, changing hardware configuration also requires adjustment of optimal decoding parameters.

A. Ronzhin et al. (Eds.): SPECOM 2014, LNAI 8773, pp. 402–409, 2014.

Typically, the search for optimal decoding parameters that satisfy the constraints of the real-time factor and at the same time provide high recognition accuracy is a very time-consuming task.

In this paper, we present a Simplified Simultaneous Perturbation Stochastic Approximation for optimizing free decoding parameters. The proposed method significantly reduces computational costs in compared to [2], and the reduction is even greater compared to grid search. In contrast to [3] and [4], Simplified SPSA takes into account the real-time factor, which is of vital importance for the design of an ASR system. The proposed method also requires lower computational costs than [1] and [2] for finding the optimal accuracy corresponding to a specific real-time factor. We introduce a penalty function, which is used to achieve a balance between recognition accuracy and decoding time. Then we demonstrate that this method provides robust and fast results. We present results obtained on three speech databases comprising spontaneous and read speech.

2   Simultaneous Perturbation Stochastic Approximation (SPSA)

Let us start by describing the standard form of the SPSA algorithm [5]. We denote the vector of free decoding parameters as θ. Let $\hat{\theta}_k$ denote the estimate for θ at the kth iteration. Then the algorithm has the standard form:

$$\hat{\theta}_{k+1} = \hat{\theta}_k - a_k \hat{g}_k(\hat{\theta}_k) \tag{1}$$

where $\hat{g}_k(\cdot)$ is an estimate for the gradient at the kth iteration. The gain sequence a_k satisfies certain well-known conditions [6], these conditions are necessary for the convergence of the algorithm. a_k is calculated as:

$$a_k = a/(A + k + 1)^\alpha \tag{2}$$

In order to determine the "simultaneous perturbation" we perturb each $\hat{\theta}_k$ with a vector of mutually independent, mean-zero random variables Δ_k satisfying the conditions given in [6]. Usually, Δ_k is taken as symmetrically Bernoulli distributed. A positive scalar is calculated as follows:

$$c_k = c/(k + 1)^\gamma \tag{3}$$

This positive scalar and mean-zero random variables are multiplied to obtain two new parameter tuples:

$$\hat{\theta}_k^+ = \hat{\theta}_k + c_k \Delta_k \tag{4}$$

$$\hat{\theta}_k^- = \hat{\theta}_k - c_k \Delta_k \tag{5}$$

Using (2) and (3) gain sequences a_k and c_k, SPSA and Kiefer-Wolfowitz finite-difference-based SA (FDSA) [7] achieve the same level of statistical accuracy for a given number of iterations, but SPSA requires p times fewer measurements of the loss function (p is a number of free decoding parameters that are being optimized).

The estimate of the gradient $\hat{g}_k(\cdot)$ is calculated from the values of the loss function $L(\cdot)$, as:

$$\hat{g}_k(\hat{\theta}_k) = \begin{bmatrix} L(\hat{\theta}_k^+) - L(\hat{\theta}_k^-) \Big/ 2c_k\Delta_{k1} \\ \vdots \\ L(\hat{\theta}_k^+) - L(\hat{\theta}_k^-) \Big/ 2c_k\Delta_{kp} \end{bmatrix} \tag{6}$$

The values of the non negative coefficients a, c, A, α and γ can be chosen according to the guidelines given in [6].

3   Simplified SPSA

The standard algorithm is designed so that a_k and c_k decrease with increasing k. If a_k causes a deterioration of the objective value, the optimal solution must stay at $\hat{\theta}_k$ and at the next iteration obtain the estimation of the loss function with a new a_k according to (2). Without an appropriate step size, the optimal solution will stay at $\hat{\theta}_k$ forever, which significantly slows down the rate of convergence of the algorithm [8]. This problem is illustrated in Fig. 1. The optimal solution is obviously located at $\hat{\theta}_k^+$. But the standard step size provides transition to $\hat{\theta}_{k+1}$, where we are faced with the problem described above. If we assume that the $\hat{\theta}_k^+$ point is obtained using an appropriate step size, then we can take $\hat{\theta}_k^+$ as the outcome of the current iteration.

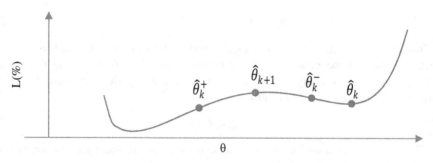

Fig. 1. The search process of the standard SPSA

According to the assumption above, SPSA takes the following form:

$$\hat{\theta}_{k+1} = \begin{cases} \hat{\theta}_k^+, if\ L(\hat{\theta}_k^+) < L(\hat{\theta}_k^-)\ and\ L(\hat{\theta}_k^+) < L(\hat{\theta}_k); \\ \hat{\theta}_k^-, if\ L(\hat{\theta}_k^-) < L(\hat{\theta}_k^+)\ and\ L(\hat{\theta}_k^-) < L(\hat{\theta}_k); \\ \hat{\theta}_k, in\ all\ other\ cases. \end{cases} \tag{7}$$

Moreover, if the parameter vector did not change at the current iteration, it means that the algorithm is close to the optimal point. In order to increase the convergence rate, it is necessary to reduce the coefficient c_k using the equation $c = c/1.5$.

The initial value of the parameter c must be chosen so that the coefficient c_k could converge to a certain minimum value in an expected number of iterations, giving the distance between the vectors of parameters $\hat{\theta}_k^+$ and $\hat{\theta}_k^-$ such that $\left| L(\hat{\theta}_k^+) - L(\hat{\theta}_k^-) \right| > 0$.

To take the decoding speed into account, we will calculate the loss function, penalizing it by the corresponding value of RTF (real-time factor). Then the loss function takes the form:

$$L(\cdot) = L(\cdot) + RTF \tag{8}$$

This function provides the tradeoff between the real-time factor and the accuracy of speech recognition.

The algorithm obtains an optimal solution, but this solution does not satisfy the desired real-time factor. We propose increasing/decreasing the parameters stepwise to change the speed of automatic speech recognition, in order to achieve the desired real-time factor. The step size and a set of parameters are specific for each decoder.

4 Setup

For the experiments we used three databases:

— Database A: recordings of read speech prepared by a collaborating speaker, the topic is sports, 1:06h, 5257 words, maximum accuracy obtained by manual parameter tuning is 92.505 at RTF= 0.357;
— Database B: recordings of telephone conversations (spontaneous speech), 0:49h, 2828 words, maximum accuracy obtained by manual parameter tuning is 62.694 at RTF= 0.253;
— Database C: recordings of internet broadcasts, webinars and podcasts, 0:40h, 3013 words, maximum accuracy obtained by manual parameter tuning is 62.297 at RTF= 0.864.

For each of these databases we have a corresponding language and acoustic model [9,10]. We are tuning the following parameters:

— max_hyp_num – maximal number of hypotheses;
— thr_common – common threshold;
— lm_scale –factor of the weight of any edge of the graph;
— wd_add –addition to the weight of the edge of the graph.

Speech recognition was carried out by the ASR system developed at Speech Technology Center Ltd. All experiments were performed on a workstation with an Intel Core i5 Desktop Processor with 4 physical cores, and 32 GB of RAM.

5   Experiment

We performed several tests for each of the databases with different target real-time factors. Table 1 shows the results obtained by the algorithm, and further improved by selecting the parameters that affect the decoding speed.

Table 1. Accuracy and real-time factor results on all databases, for the Simplified SPSA

database	objective RTF	initial indicators		output indicators		#iterations	#runs of decoder
		Acc	RTF	Acc	RTF		
A	0.1	91.021	0.115	92.505	0.090	22	42
A	0.3			92.581	0.154	23	43
A	0.5			92.619	0.321	25	45
B	0.1	50.636	0.309	60.962	0.074	22	42
B	0.2			62.023	0.178	21	41
B	0.3			62.553	0.273	22	42
C	0.5	47.063	0.823	60.438	0.499	25	45
C	0.7			61.401	0.679	25	45
C	0.9			61.998	0.892	26	46

In all the tests for all the databases the proposed method showed high efficiency. It managed to approach to the optimal values obtained manually, and sometimes exceeded them. All the results are within the confidence interval. Figures 2 and 3 show the results for databases A and C. We can see that a considerable improvement of Acc and RTF occurs already at the early iterations. After the twentieth iteration, the algorithm is aimed at selecting a specific target real-time factor.

6   Conclusions

In this paper, we demonstrated an effective method of optimizing free decoding parameters, which enabled us to obtain the optimum for a specific target real-time factor. The method can be applied to finding the optimal parameters for a specific target factor for all the databases we tested. All our results are within the confidence interval so they can be considered optimal. In practice, this approach allows us to obtain the parameters better than by grid search, and at the same time at a lower computational cost.

We are confident that the proposed method can be used for other decoders to optimize free decoding parameters in terms of a specific target real-time factor. To do that, it is necessary to form the parameter vector, and the subset of parameters that influence the speed of speech recognition.

Acknowledgements. This work was partially financially supported by the Government of the Russian Federation, Grant 074-U01.

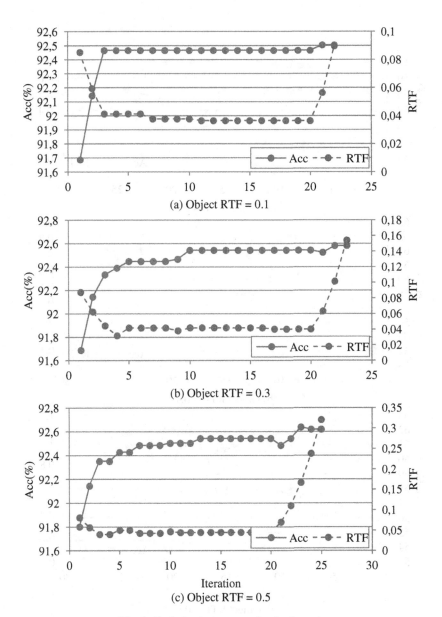

(a) Object RTF = 0.1

(b) Object RTF = 0.3

Iteration
(c) Object RTF = 0.5

Fig. 2. Optimization runs on the database A

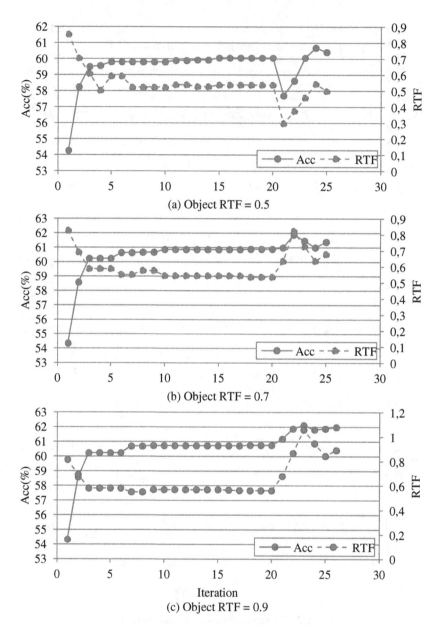

(a) Object RTF = 0.5

(b) Object RTF = 0.7

Iteration
(c) Object RTF = 0.9

Fig. 3. Optimization runs on the database C

References

1. Stein, D., Schwenninger, J., Stadtschnitzer, M.: Simultaneous perturbation stochastic approximation for automatic speech recognition. In: Proc. of the INTERSPEECH, Lyon, France, August 25-29, pp. 622–626 (2013)
2. El Hannani, A., Hain, T.: Automatic optimization of speech decoder parameters. Signal Processing Letters 17(1), 95–98 (2010), doi:10.1109/LSP.2009.2033967
3. Mak, B., Ko, T.: Automatic estimation of decoding parameters using large-margin iterative linear programming. In: Proc. of the INTERSPEECH, Brighton, United Kingdom, September 6-10, pp. 1219–1222 (2009)
4. Kacur, J., Korosi, J.: An accuracy optimization of a dialog ASR system utilizing evolutional strategies. In: Proc. of the ISPA, Istanbul, Turkey, September 27-29, pp. 180–184 (2007)
5. Spall, J.C.: Multivariate stochastic approximation using a simultaneous perturbation gradient approximation. IEEE Transactions on Automatic Control 37(3), 332–341 (1992), doi:10.1109/9.119632
6. Spall, J.C.: Implementation of the simultaneous perturbation algorithm for stochastic optimization. IEEE Transactions on Aerospace and Electronic Systems 34(3), 817–823 (1998), doi:10.1109/7.705889
7. Kiefer, J., Wolfowitz, J.: Stochastic Estimation of the Maximum of a Regression Function. Ann. Math. Stat. 23(3), 462–466 (1952)
8. Yue, X.: Improved Simultaneous Perturbation Stochastic Approximation and Its Application in Reinforcement Learning. In: Proc. of the International Conference on Computer Science and Software Engineering, Wuhan, Hubei, December 12-14, vol. 1, pp. 329–332 (2008)
9. Korenevsky, M., Bulusheva, A., Levin, K.: Unknown Words Modeling in Training and Using Language Models for Russian LVCSR System. In: Proc. of the SPECOM, Kazan, Russia, September 27-30, pp. 144–150 (2011)
10. Yurkov, P., Korenevsky, M., Levin, K.: An Improvement of robustness to speech loudness change for an ASR system based on LC-RC features. In: Proc. of the SPECOM, Kazan, Russia, September 27-30, pp. 62–66 (2011)

Speaker Detection Using Phoneme Specific Hidden Markov Models

Edvin Pakoci, Nikša Jakovljević, Branislav Popović, Dragiša Mišković,
and Darko Pekar

Faculty of Technical Sciences, University of Novi Sad, Serbia
{edvin.pakoci,darko.pekar}@alfanum.co.rs,
{jakovnik,bpopovic,dragisa}@uns.ac.rs

Abstract. The paper presents a speaker detection system based on phoneme specific hidden Markov model in combination with Gaussian mixture model. Our motivation stems from the fact that the phoneme specific HMM system can model temporal variations and provides possibility to ponder the scores of specific phonemes as well as efficient pruning. The performance of the system has been evaluated on speech database which contains utterances in Serbian from 250 speakers (10 of them being the target speakers). The proposed model is compared to a system based on Gaussian mixture model - universal background model, and showed a significant improvement in detection performance.

Keywords: Speaker detection, Hidden Markov models, Gaussian mixture models.

1 Introduction

Nowadays, when the amount of available multimedia data is huge and rapidly growing, it is becoming vital to classify such data automatically, in order to speed up data search. One of the interesting areas in this process is automatic speaker detection and indexing in audio stream, which corresponds to the task of speaker recognition. Traditionally, there are two basic approaches in speaker recognition: verification and identification. Speaker verification (or speaker authentication) is a binary decision problem, determining whether or not an unknown voice belongs to the particular (claimed) speaker. Speaker identification is the task of choosing an unknown speaker from the predefined set of speakers, who has the voice closest to the unknown voice. Speaker detection is the task of detecting one or more specific speakers (target speakers) in an audio stream [1]. If the number of target speakers is negligible compared to the total number of speakers presented in the data, the detection task is similar to the verification task, i.e. the task is to decide whether the speech segment belongs to the one of target speakers. On the other hand, if only target speakers are included in the data to be searched, or if they represent the majority, the detection task can be treated as an identification task [1].

The paper investigates the use of phoneme models in a speaker detection task. Previous experiments showed that the best system based on Gaussian mixture models (GMMs) outperforms the systems based on Hidden Markov models

A. Ronzhin et al. (Eds.): SPECOM 2014, LNAI 8773, pp. 410–417, 2014.

(HMMs), due to the ability of the GMM to better exploit the training data and a poor HMM parameters estimation [2]. While identical front ends were used, no gain in performance was achieved by the use of temporal information captured in the HMMs. Nonetheless, the HMM based systems that incorporate the knowledge about phonemes or phoneme classes outperform the conventional GMM based systems [3], especially in case where there is channel mismatch between training and testing data. Individual phonemes carry various amounts of speaker discriminating capability, and they each show different levels of performance, depending on the level of adaptation used to build the phoneme-specific target models [4]. Unlike the phoneme-based systems, the conventional speaker detection as well as speaker recognition systems rely on short-term spectral and prosodic features extracted from speech, e.g. [5–7]. These features are often unable to capture long-term speaker characteristic, even when they are expanded with their first and second order derivatives [8].

GMM in combination with universal background model (GMM-UBM) is a referent speaker identification system used in this paper. It has become a dominant modeling approach in speaker recognition applications [9]. The proposed HMM-GMM system uses phonetic information for creating the model of a speaker. Our motivation stems from the fact that the HMM system allows standard pruning procedures (pruning is more efficient in case of phonetic models) and the possibility to ponder the specific phonemes. This is an important advantage, having in mind the differences in reliability of log-likelihood rates for different phonemes (e.g. the log likelihood rates for vowels are much more reliable than the log-likelihood rates for plosives). We combine short-term spectral features with phoneme information, using the continuous speech recognition system described in [10], in order to improve the accuracy of our speaker identification system. Hidden Markov model toolkit (HTK) is used for speaker adaptation [11], while the rest of the system was built from scratch. The results are provided for both context-dependent and context independent phonetic models.

The paper is organized as follows. Section 2 provides the detailed description of the referent and proposed HMM-GMM system, as well as database used for performance evaluation. Section 3 gives the results of our experiments. Section 4 contains conclusions based on considerations from the previous sections.

2   Experimental Setup

All of the systems analyzed in this paper have the same front-end. Our feature vectors include 12 Mel-frequency cepstral coefficients, normalized energy and their first and second order derivatives, which are extracted on 30 ms frames with a 10 ms shift.

The referent system is GMM-UBM model where both the target speaker model and the universal background model (UBM) are based on GMMs with diagonal covariance matrices. The UBM is trained using the EM algorithm and the speech data from a large number of speakers (in this paper more than 400 speakers and 12 hours of speech). Maximum likelihood linear regression (MLLR)

[11] of the mean vectors is used to adapt the UBM for a target speaker. In the recognition phase, models for silence and noise are used to remove non-speech segments from the test sequence. The remaining speech frames are used in scoring procedures, where the logarithm of likelihood ratio of the target model and the UBM is computed for each frame. The final score for a test utterance is calculated by averaging the log-likelihood ratios on some portion of the best scored frames. There are 2 variants of a system based on the GMM-UBM used in this paper, which differ only in the number of Gaussians. The one containing 400 Gaussians will be referred as "GMM 400" and the other containing 800 Gaussians will be referred as "GMM 800".

The main difference between the proposed HMM-GMM system and the baseline system is in the way of modeling target speaker, i.e. in the proposed model each phoneme is represented with one or more HMMs. The number of HMM states is proportional to the average duration of the phoneme instances in the training set, and the number of Gaussians per state is estimated using the cross-validation procedure described in [13]. Since each phoneme corresponds to many phones, three different phoneme modeling units have been examined: monophones, biphones and triphones. The monophone model is the most general one, since it includes many phonemes which can be acoustically significantly different. In order to reduce these within-class variations, context dependent models (biphones and triphones) are introduced. Specifically, triphone model takes into consideration both (left and right) contexts, and biphone model takes only closer one. In case of triphone models, tree based clustering procedure was used to tie similar states, such that the total number of states is 1000. Low decoding computational complexity is the main reason for this small number of different HMM states in a model. It is important to note that a set of phoneme specific HMMs was built for each gender separately, in order to improve phoneme recognition accuracy.

To enroll target speaker adaptation based on MLLR is applied. Only mean vectors are adapted, leaving variances unchanged. Gender dependent model with higher likelihood on training data for a given speaker was used as an initial model in the adaptation procedure. Both supervised and unsupervised adaptation procedures were performed, since the assumption was that besides audio data, their transcriptions could also be known. The enrolment procedure consists of 3 adaptations, one (the first one) with global transformation and two with regression tree based transformations [11]. The regression tree consists of 128 leaves and about 1000 observations were used per each transformation matrix. In the case of unsupervised adaptation, the procedure is almost the same as the previous one, but it has an additional step in which phonetic (unfortunately erroneous) transcriptions of training data are automatically generated using speech recognition module. It is important to note that the speaker enrollment procedures are the same for all HMM variations which differ in phoneme modeling units.

The decoding procedure is the same for all HMM-GMM variations. It starts with Viterbi decoding with unconstrained language model (it allows transitions from any phoneme, silence and noise model, into any phoneme, silence and noise model) followed by scoring with UBM system (in this case "GMM 400"). After that, for each frame, the log-likelihood ratio of the target model and the UBM is computed, and all non-speech segments, as well as segments corresponding to the sequence of phonemes without any vowel are discarded from further scoring.

Besides capturing temporal information, as opposed to the baseline GMM-UBM approach, additional motive for phonetic approach was the ability to assign different weights to different groups of phonemes. Although we could not completely rely on the phonetic recognition results, the system at least recognized the correct group of phonemes (vowels, nasals, fricatives, stops...) which turned out to be very useful. Assigning different weights to different groups of phonemes improved the results significantly, compared to the average metric computed over the whole utterance. Postprocessing performs one additional task. It discards desired percentage of the worst scores from the results. Since our tests were performed on recordings which included both target speaker and imposter (or two imposters), it was perfectly reasonable to try this approach. All the mentioned coefficients (phoneme weights and percentage of utterance to be discarded), were carefully trained and optimized in order to maximize accuracy.

The speech corpus used in this paper is based on the speech corpora described in [14], where the utterances in original corpora are combined in the way that each audio file contains utterances of two different speakers with minimum duration of 30 s per speaker. On the other hand, the data intended for training speaker specific model contains only 30 s of speech of a single speaker. The database encompasses voices of 250 different speakers, where only 10 of them are target speakers (7 male and 3 female). The test data contains about 15 hours of audio recordings split into about 160 files, but only 50 of them contains voices of target speakers. The full spectrum speech data from "S70W100s120", "AN_Books" and "AN_Broadcast Speech" [14] is filtered and re-sampled to 8 kHz to reproduce telephone channel data.

3   Experimental Results

Figure 1 shows detection error trade-off (DET) curves of the baseline systems. Using 50 % of the best scoring frames resulted in performance gain for both baseline systems. Since the difference in the performance between "GMM 800 top 50" and "GMM 400 top 50" is negligible, the GMM-UBM models with more than 800 Gaussians were out of consideration. The "GMM 800 top 50" system was used as the referent one for the all HMM-GMM-UBM systems. The speaker scoring for both systems was performed only on the detected speech frames by averaging log likelihood ratios in 2 variants. In the first variant all speech frames were used ("all") and in the second variant only 50 % of the best scoring frames were used ("top 50").

Figure 2 shows DET curves for HMM-GMM systems with different level of phoneme model generalizations when both audio data and their transcriptions are used in speaker adaptation . Using scores obtained on all valid speech frames significantly deteriorates system performance, which was expected, since the test

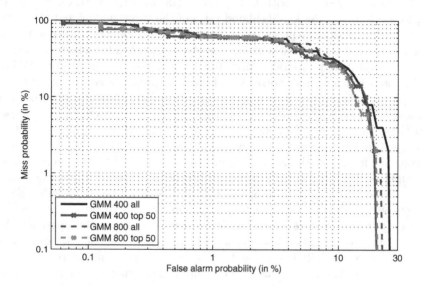

Fig. 1. DET curve for GMM-UBM systems

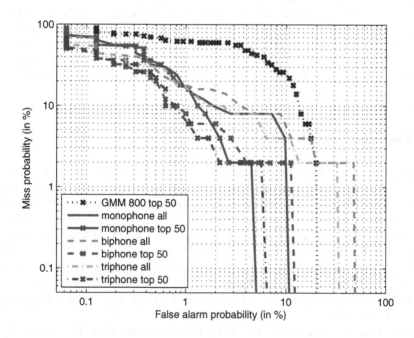

Fig. 2. DET curve for HMM-GMM systems if both audio data and their transcriptions are used in speaker adaptation

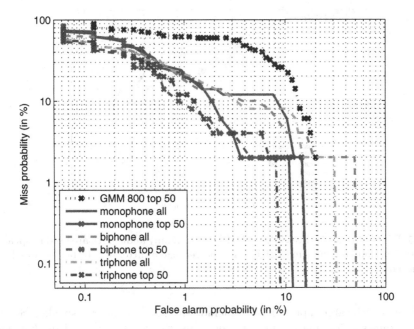

Fig. 3. DET curve for HMM-GMM-UBM systems if only audio data are used in speaker adaptation

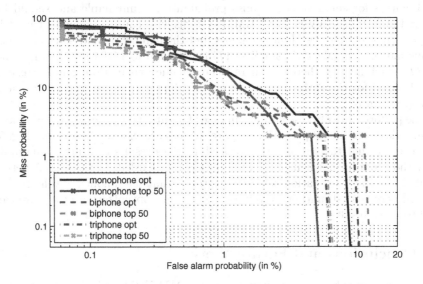

Fig. 4. DET curve for HMM-GMM-UBM systems if both audio data and their transcriptions are used in speaker adaptation, and the phoneme weights and percentage of utterance to be discarded are optimized

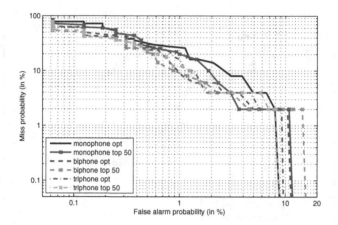

Fig. 5. DET curve for HMM-GMM-UBM systems if only audio data are used in speaker adaptation, and the phoneme weights and percentage of utterance to be discarded are optimized

utterances with target speaker voice include the voice of another speaker. Scores on the frames belonging to imposter decrease the total score and in that way mask the target speaker. One can see that the all HMM-GMM systems outperforms the baseline system ("GMM 800 top 50"). Since the test set has only 50 audio files containing target speaker, resolution of miss probability is 2 %, thus DET curves for small values of miss probability are unreliable and should be ignored in further analysis. Both HMM systems with context dependent models outperform the system with monophones, but the number of Gaussians in monophone model is significantly smaller (1716 compared to 14404 for biphones and 12732 for triphones), therefore there is no reliable explanation. Similar results are obtained for the HMM-GMM systems if adaptation is based only on audio data (see Fig. 3).

The performance of these systems in case of additional phoneme weighting and automatic discarding of potential imposter frames are shown in Fig. 4 and Fig. 5. One can see that the optimization procedure gives results that are comparable with those obtained when 50 % of frames are discarded. We expected better results, but small validation set used for the parameter (phoneme weights and discard percent) estimation as well as evolutionary optimization procedure can lead to these results.

4   Conclusions and Future Work

This paper presents a comparison between GMM-UBM and phoneme specific HMM based speaker detection systems. The proposed HMM based systems outperform GMM-UBM systems, since they use phonetic informations to filter frames log-likelihood ratios (exclude unreliable frames or segments from scoring).

Context dependent HMMs show a slightly better performances than the context independent ones, which means that the longer matching between unknown sequence and mode reduce classification errors. The proposed model should be tested on the larger database containing utterances in different languages.

Acknowledgements. This research work has been supported by the Ministry of Education, Science and Technological Development of the Republic of Serbia, and it has been realized as a part of the research project TR 32035.

References

1. Beigi, H.: Fundamentals of Speaker Recognition. Springer (2011)
2. Auckenthaler, R., Parris, E., Carey, M.: Improving a GMM speaker verification system by phonetic weighting. In: IEEE International Conference on Acoustics, Speech and Signal Processing (ICASSP 1999), vol. 1, pp. 313–316. Phoenix, Arizona (1999)
3. Kajarekar, S., Hermansky, H.: Speaker verification based on broad phonetic categories. In: A Speaker Odyssey - The Speaker Recognition Workshop (2001)
4. Hansen, E., Slyh, R., Anderson, T.: Speaker recognition using phoneme-specific GMMs. In: ODYSSEY 2004-The Speaker and Language Recognition Workshop, pp. 179–184 (2004)
5. Dunn, R., Reynolds, D., Quatieri, T.: Approaches to speaker detection and tracking in conversational speech. Digit. Signal Process. 10, 93–112 (2000)
6. Kinnunen, T., Li, H.: An Overview of Text-Independent Speaker Recognition: From Features to Supervectors. Speech Commun 52, 12–40 (2010)
7. Scheffer, N., Ferrer, L., Graciarena, M., Kajarekar, S., Shriberg, E., Stolcke, A.: The SRI NIST 2010 Speaker Recognition Evaluation System. In: IEEE International Conference on Acoustics, Speech and Signal Processing (ICASSP 2011), pp. 5292–5295. Prague, Czech Republic (2011)
8. Antal, M.: Phonetic Speaker Recognition. In: 7th International Conference COMMUNICATIONS, pp. 67–72 (2008)
9. Reynolds, D., Quatieri, T., Dunn, R.: Speaker Verification Using Adapted Gaussian Mixture Models. Digit. Signal Process. 10, 19–41 (2000)
10. Delić, V., Sečujski, M., Jakovljević, N., Janev, M., Obradović, R., Pekar, D.: Speech Technologies for Serbian and Kindred South Slavic Languages. In: Advances in Speech Recognition, pp. 141–165 (2010)
11. Young, S.J., Evermann, G., Gales, M.J.F., Hain, T., Kershaw, D., Moore, G., Odell, J., Ollason, D., Povey, D., Valtchev, V., Woodland, P.C.: The HTK Book, version 3.4 (2006)
12. Gales, M., Young, S.: The Application of Hidden Markov Models in Speech Recognition. Foundations and Trends in Signal Processing 1(3), 195–304 (2007)
13. Jakovljević, N., Miškovic, D., Janev, M., Sečujski, M., Delić, V.: Comparison of Linear Discriminant Analysis Approaches in Automatic Speech Recognition. Elektronika Ir Elektrotechnika 19(7), 76–79 (2013)
14. Delić, V., Sečujski, M., Jakovljević, N., Pekar, D., Mišković, D., Popović, B., Ostrogonac, S., Bojanić, M., Knežević, D.: Speech and language resources within speech recognition and synthesis systems for serbian and kindred south slavic languages. In: Železný, M., Habernal, I., Ronzhin, A. (eds.) SPECOM 2013. LNCS, vol. 8113, pp. 319–326. Springer, Heidelberg (2013)

Speaking Rate Estimation Based on Deep Neural Networks

Natalia Tomashenko[1,2] and Yuri Khokhlov[1]

[1] Speech Technology Center, Saint-Petersburg, Russia
www.speechpro.ru
[2] ITMO University, Saint-Petersburg, Russia
{tomashenko-n,khokhlov}@speechpro.com

Abstract. In this paper we propose a method for estimating speaking rate by means of Deep Neural Networks (DNN). The proposed approach is used for speaking rate adaptation of an automatic speech recognition system. The adaptation is performed by changing step in front-end feature processing according to the estimations of speaking rate. Experiments show that adaptation results using the proposed DNN-based speaking rate estimator are better than the results of adaptation using the speaking rate estimator based on the recognition results.

Keywords: speaking rate, speaking rate adaptation, speaking rate estimation, speech recognition, ASR, variable step, DNN.

1 Introduction

Speaking rate is one of significant sources of speech variability. In the past it was shown [1]-[12] that variations in speaking rate can degrade recognition performance in automatic speech recognition (ASR) systems. This effect is typically more significant for fast speech than for slow [1][5], that is, the higher the speaking rate, the higher the error rate in ASR systems. Fast speech is different from normal or slow speech in several aspects [5], such as acoustic-phonetic and phonological characteristics.

Many methods for compensating the effects of speaking rate variability were proposed in the literature [1][5][6][8][9][10]. They include: modification of HMM transition probabilities [6] and modeling of phone duration; intra-word transformations using special rules for transforming phones depending on phonetic context and lexical stress [6]; rate-dependent phone sets [6]; speaking rate dependent (or adapted) acoustic models [1][8][9]; temporal wrapping in front-end processing, such as the continuous frame rate normalization (CFRN) technique [10]; variable frame rate (VFR) analysis [11]; etc.

A reliable estimation of speaking rate is often needed in order to adapt the ASR system to variations in speaking rate. Existing rate of speech (ROS) estimators can be characterized by two properties: (1) the metric (or measure) and (2) the duration of the speech segment on which ROS is estimated (for example, per speaker, per utterance, per word, etc.). The most common speech rate metrics are: word rate [6] (number of words per minute), phone (or syllable) rate. Normalization and phone duration percentile [6] are used for more accurate and robust estimations. All these measures are

A. Ronzhin et al. (Eds.): SPECOM 2014, LNAI 8773, pp. 418–424, 2014.

based on linguistic information. They can be calculated from segmentation (if reference transcriptions are available) or from the recognizer output. These approaches give reliable estimations of speaking rate in case of high quality segmentation. When the accuracy of the ASR system is low, then other methods are to be used. An alternative approach is to directly estimate speaking rate from the speech signal. An example of a signal-based measure is the mrate measure [2], which incorporates multiple energy-based estimators. In [3] Gaussian Mixture Models (GMM) were trained to estimate speech rate categories. In the same work, an ANN model was used as a mapping function from output likelihoods of these GMMs to continuous estimation of the speaking rate.

In this work we investigate a novel approach to speaking rate estimation based on Deep Neural Networks (DNNs). DNNs have recently been used with great success in automatic speech recognition tasks [13], and it is interesting to explore their application to the speaking rate estimation problem.

2   Speaking Rate Estimation

As mentioned before, one of the most common ways to measure ROS is calculating the number of phones per second. There are several variations of this formula [1], such as the Inverse of Mean Duration (IMD), where the total number of phones in the unit is divided by the total duration of the unit in seconds; or the Mean of Rates (MR) formula. These measures do not take into account the fact that mean durations of different phones and triphones in the database may vary a lot. To get more accurate estimations, we use normalization on the average length of triphones, computed from the training database. Thus the measure of speaking rate (or ROS) is defined as follows:

$$\rho = \frac{n}{\sum_{i=1}^{n} l(i)/\bar{l}(i)}, \tag{1}$$

where n is the number of phones in the unit; $l(i)$ is the actual duration of the triphone i in the unit; $\bar{l}(i)$ is the expected (mean) duration of triphone i, estimated from the training database.

An important question is at which level this formula should be calculated. These levels include per speaker, per utterance or per word calculation. The choice depends on the task and the type of speech. In [10] it was found that per utterance adaptation to speaking rate is more effective than per speaker adaptation for broadcast transcription tasks. In conversational speech, fluctuations in speech rate may be very high within one utterance, and per word ROS estimation may be more appropriate [6].

An example of how speech rate may vary from word to word in spontaneous conversation is shown in Figure 1. We can see than even within one short utterance speaking rate fluctuations are high.

A more detailed analysis of changes in the speaking rate is presented in Figure 2, where normalized histograms for relative differences in speaking rate between two adjacent words are shown. These histograms are calculated on a database of conversational telephone Russian speech. The relative difference is calculated for every pair of adjacent words in the database that satisfies following conditions: (1) the pause between

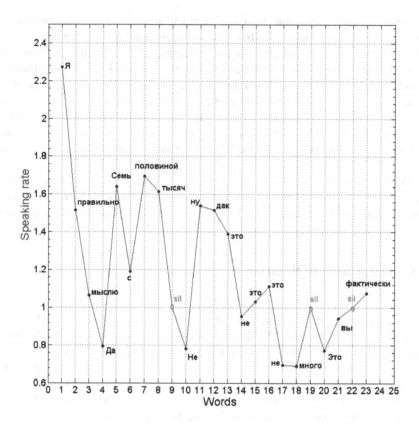

Fig. 1. An example of speaking rate estimation calculated for a spontaneous speech fragment

the two words does not exceed 250 ms; (2) the number of phones in these words is not smaller than a chosen threshold (1, 3 or 5 phones in our experiments). The relative difference $\Delta\rho$ in the speaking rate for two words with ROS ρ_1 and ρ_2 is calculated as follows:

$$\Delta\rho = \frac{2|\rho_1 - \rho_2|}{|\rho_1 + \rho_2|} \tag{2}$$

Mean and standard deviation statistics for relative difference $\Delta\rho$ in the speaking rate for two adjacent words are given in Table 1. We can see from Figure 1 and Table 1 that speaking rate is more stable for long words than for short ones. Note that ROS estimation for short words is less reliable than for long ones.

Based on the ROS estimation described above, we formed three groups, corresponding to slow, medium and fast speaking rate:

$$\text{ROS group} = \begin{cases} slow, & \text{if } \rho < 0.91 \\ medium, & \text{if } 0.91 \leq \rho \leq 1.11 \\ fast, & \text{if } \rho > 1.11 \end{cases} \tag{3}$$

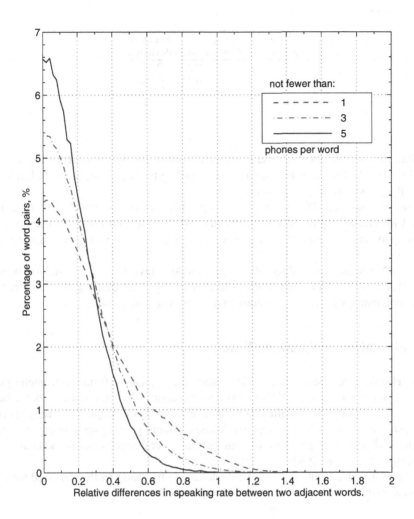

Fig. 2. Normalized histograms for relative differences in speaking rate between two adjacent words

3   DNN for ROS Estimation (ROS-DNN)

For the sake of simplicity, we train the DNN to classify each frame of speech into one of four classes: (1) slow, (2) medium, (3) fast speech or (4) silence. This classification may be extended further, since speaking rate is a continuous measure.

The training database was segmented into the four classes as follows. First, phone segmentation based on text transcripts was performed for each sentence in the training

Table 1. Mean and standard deviation statistics for relative difference $\Delta\rho$ in the speaking rate for two adjacent words

Minimum number of phones per word	Mean	Standard deviation
1	0.320	0.257
3	0.247	0.196
5	0.196	0.153

database. Second, ROS was estimated for each word in the segmented database, and the word was marked as slow, medium or fast according to its ROS value (as in Equation (3)); all pauses were marked as silence.

Thus, we had four DNN targets. The input features for the DNN were 13Δ and $13\Delta\Delta$ Mel-frequency cepstrum coefficients (MFCCs) spliced into 31 frames (±15), resulting in 806-dimensional feature vectors. These features indicated the speaking rate dynamic.

The DNN system used three 1000-neuron hidden layers and one 4-neuron output layer. The DNN system was trained with layer-by-layer pre-training using the frame-level cross entropy criterion. The output layer was a soft-max layer.

4   Adaptation to Speaking Rate

Many HMM ASR systems have a fixed step size, typically 10 ms, in frontend processing. But it was shown in [10,11,14] that this approach is not optimal, as the best choice of frame rate may be affected by speaking rate. For example, for steady speech segments we can use a longer step size, while for rapidly changing segments the step should be shorter. This phenomenon was used in several approaches for adaptation to speaking rate, such as CFRN and VFR.

We performed adaptation to speaking rate simply by changing the step used for feature processing, based on the ROS estimation.

5   Experimental Results

We evaluated the proposed algorithm on a database of spontaneous conversational telephone Russian speech.

The DNN acoustic model for the ASR system was trained on approximately 270 hours of speech data. A subset from this training database was used to train ROS-DNN. Input features for training DNN acoustic models are 13-dimensional MFCC, spliced into 31 frames (±15), resulting in 403-dimensional feature vectors. The same context length was used when processing input features for training ROS-DNN models. The DNN acoustic model had six hidden layers each with 1000 nodes and logistic activation, and an output layer with softmax activation. The output layer of the DNN acoustic model had a dimension of approximately 10K.

Table 2. Speech rate adaptation resuls for different ROS estimators: (1) the proposed approach based on using DNN models; (2) ground truth estimation based on ideal segmentation; (3) segmentation using texts derived from the recognizer

| | Baseline | | Rate-Adapted | |
| | | DNN | Segmentation | |
			Original transcripts	Texts from recognizer output
WER, %	38.3	37.4	37.0	37.6
Correcr, %	66.1	67.2	67.1	67.1

Experiments were conducted on approximately 300 recordings of conversational telephone speech. The total number of words in the test set was 3K.

We performed adaptation to speaking rate by changing step depending on ROS. We used a simple scheme for changing step: fast - 7.5 ms; medium - 9.4 ms; and slow - 10 ms.

A 200K vocabulary and a 3-gram language model were used in evaluation.

The performance results are shown in Table 2. The three columns on the right correspond to Word Error Rate (WER) results after adaptation based on three ROS estimators: (1) using DNN; (2) using phone segmentation as the ground truth estimation, and (3) estimation derived from the force alignment of recognition results.

We can see that adaptation based on all estimators leads to improved recognition performance: (1) 2.3% relative WER reduction for ROS-DNN, (2) 3.4% relative WER reduction for ROS based on phone segmentation, and (3) 1.8% relative WER reduction for ROS based on recognition results. Note that the acoustic models were trained with a fixed step (10 ms), and retraining them with rate-dependent step may improve results.

6   Conclusions

In this paper we propose a novel method for ROS estimation for the purpose of speaking rate adaptation. The proposed approach is based on training a DNN model on targets representing slow, medium and fast speech. Experiments with speaking rate adaptation show that our method of ROS estimation gives an improvement over unadapted baseline models. Moreover, the results of adaptation using the ROS-DNN estimator are better than the results of adaptation using the ROS estimator based on the recognition results. The advantage of this approach is that it does not require additional decoding passes.

This work presents only preliminary results of using DNNs for the task of speaking rate estimation. We believe that these results may be further improved by two modifications: first, by re-training acoustic models with a rate-dependent step; second, by using more groups for rate categorization or treating speaking rate as a continuous measure.

Acknowledgements. This work was partially financially supported by the Government of the Russian Federation, Grant 074-U01.

References

1. Mirghafori, N., Fosler, E., Morgan, N.: Towards robustness to fast speech in ASR. In: Proc. of the IEEE International Conference in Acoustics, Speech, and Signal Processing, ICASSP 1996, pp. 335–338 (1996)
2. Morgan, N., Fosler-Lussier, E.: Combining multiple estimators of speaking rate. In: Proc. of the IEEE International Conference In Acoustics, Speech, and Signal Processing, ICASSP-1996, pp. 729–732 (1998)
3. Faltlhauser, R., Pfau, T., Ruske, G.: On-line speaking rate estimation using gaussian mixture models. In: Proc. of the IEEE International Conference In Acoustics, Speech, and Signal Processing, ICASSP 2000, pp. 1355–1358 (2000)
4. Pfau, T., Ruske, G.: Estimating the speaking rate by vowel detection. In: Proc. of the IEEE International Conference In Acoustics, Speech and Signal Processing, ICASSP 1998, pp. 945–948 (1998)
5. Mirghafori, N., Foster, E., Morgan, N.: Fast speakers in large vocabulary continuous speech recognition: analysis & antidotes. In: Proc. of the EUROSPEECH, pp. 491–494 (1995)
6. Siegler, M.A.: Measuring and compensating for the effects of speech rate in large vocabulary continuous speech recognition (PhD Thesis). Carnegie Mellon University, Pittsburgh (1995)
7. Wrede, B., Fink, G.A., Sagerer, G.: An investigation of modelling aspects for rate-dependent speech recognition. In: Proc. of the INTERSPEECH, pp. 2527–2530 (2001)
8. Ban, S.M., Kim, H.S.: Speaking rate dependent multiple acoustic models using continuous frame rate normalization. In: Proc. of the Signal & Information Processing Association Annual Summit and Conference (APSIPA ASC), Asia-Pacific, pp. 1–4 (2012)
9. Nanjo, H., Kato, K., Kawahara, T.: Speaking rate dependent acoustic modeling for spontaneous lecture speech recognition. In: Proc. of the INTERSPEECH, pp. 2531–2534 (2001)
10. Chu, S.M., Povey, D.: Speaking rate adaptation using continuous frame rate normalization. In: Proc. of the IEEE International Conference in Acoustics Speech and Signal Processing (ICASSP), pp. 4306–4309 (2010)
11. Zhu, Q., Alwan, A.: On the use of variable frame rate analysis in speech recognition. In: Proc. of the 2000 IEEE International Conference in Acoustics Speech and Signal Processing (ICASSP 2000), pp. 1783–1786 (2000)
12. Benzeghiba, M., De Mori, R., Deroo, O., Dupont, S., Erbes, T., Jouvet, D., ... Wellekens, C. Automatic speech recognition and speech variability: A review. Speech Communication 49(10), 763–786 (2007)
13. Hinton, G., Deng, L., Yu, D., Dahl, G.E., Mohamed, A.R., Jaitly, N., ... Kingsbury, B.: Deep neural networks for acoustic modeling in speech recognition: The shared views of four research groups. Signal Processing Magazine 29(6), 82–97 (2012)
14. You, H., Zhu, Q., Alwan, A.: Entropy-based variable frame rate analysis of speech signals and its application to ASR. In: Proc. of the IEEE International Conference on In Acoustics, Speech, and Signal Processing – ICASSP 2004, vol. 1, pp. 549–552 (May 2004)

Speech Rhythmic Patterns of the Slavic Languages

Vsevolod Potapov

Lomonosov Moscow State University, Moscow, Russia
RKPotapova@yandex.ru

Abstract. The comparative experimental acoustic study of the subjective and objective characteristics of the rhythmic organization of speech was carried out on the material from three Slavic languages, i.e. Czech, Bulgarian and Russian. The present study has supported the validity of the hypothesis on the existence of a hierarchy of factors that determine the rhythmic patterns in the Slavic languages. The results of the acoustic analysis have revealed the phonetic specificity of RS and RPS, which is determined by the phonetic structure of stress in RS, realized in the studied languages by different means: definite combinations of prosodic features of vowels at the RS boundaries in Czech speech, a dynamic component in Bulgarian and a spectral as well as a temporal component in Russian.

Keywords: Rhythm; rhythmic structure; syntagma; rhythmic patterns; segmentation; hierarchy of factors.

1 Introduction

Rhythm is an important manifestation of the specific peculiarities of the perceptive and acoustic (prosodic, in particular) speech structure in various forms of speech production [5,11, etc.]. In the present study, rhythm of spoken prose is not understood as a rigidly fixed sequence of particular speech segments and the auditory perception of this sequence, which is characteristic for the verse rhythm [2,13,16, etc.], but as the specific distribution of these segments (e.g., of sounds, syllables, rhythmic groups and so on) in time as well as their phonetic (qualitative and quantitative) expression (see also: [6]). Such an approach to the rhythm of speech or the spoken language realized text makes the problem particularly complex and requiring thorough examination.

The comparative experimental acoustic study of the subjective and objective characteristics of the rhythmic organization of speech was carried out on the material from three related languages, i.e. Czech, Bulgarian and Russian; the experimental material included journalistic texts[1] (newspaper articles, papers and talks on various cultural, economic and political subjects) as well as scientific and technical texts (technical documentation, manuals etc.) read by native speakers of the languages in question; part of the research done was the first attempt at a comparative study of the rhythmic patterns of Czech utterances taken from journalistic, technical and fiction prose texts; besides the auditory analysis of prosodic characteristics (fundamental frequency, duration and

---

[1] The style of journalistic articles (= political essay style) is characterized by the presence of social and political terms and by being logical, emotional, evaluative and agitating.

A. Ronzhin et al. (Eds.): SPECOM 2014, LNAI 8773, pp. 425–434, 2014.

intensity), the study of rhythmic patterns in the three languages included spectral analysis of stressed vowels; the processing of experimental data obtained involved statistical means; the spectral analysis of stressed vowels was carried out by means of computer program Sound Forge (Sony Creative Software); the proposed description of rhythmic patterns of speech is the first one to use not only phonetic data but also data obtained as a result of a grammatical parsing of rhythmic units.

In the description of the rhythmic patterns of utterances the basic unit was defined as a rhythmic structure (RS)[2], understood as one or several words (both notional and auxiliary) united by a single word stress [10]. Unlike the related term phonetic word, the term rhythmic structure emphasizes the fact that the given unit belongs to the system of rhythmic units and allows to present it as a structurally organized sound and syllabic complex [14,15]. In the last few years linguists have been particularly interested in studying rhythmic units and the analysis of the details has proved the rightness of using rhythmic structures as basic units of rhythm, because they convey a certain meaning and at the same time carry certain prosodic information. Rhythmic structures are realized relatively discretely within utterances and can be isolated from the context; they can function independently (as a word-phrase) on one side and act as part of a connected text on the other, performing certain rhythmic and semantic functions. In speech communication, RS are both units of speech production and speech perception [7,8].

The syntagma[3], understood as "a phonetic unity, expressing single notion in the process of speech-thinking" [12], was taken as a larger unit on which the analysis of the speech material was based. Many phoneticians believe that a syntagma is a unit which is both semantic and formal in character, one of its most important characteristics being the ability of forming an intonation and semantic unity. Within a single syntagma there can be one or several RS expressing well-formed semantic notions that can be identified both by the auditors and at the level of acoustic experiments. Among the main parameters characterizing the syntagma we considered the number of RS and syllables within a syntagma, the order of RS in it, which reflect various types of *rhythmic patterns of syntagmas* (RPS).

The main assumption underlying our research was that closely related languages may be characterized by different means of the phonetic structuring of speech rhythm, which is not only related to the specific prosody of the languages in question, but also to the specific grammar of the latter. Besides the above main assumption we formulated some minor assumptions of a less general character. Thus we assumed that the structuring principle does not only underlie the organo-genetic, systemic and dialectal phonetic phenomena, but also the stylistic differentiating phenomena at the level of structural and rhythmic organization of speech. Furthermore, we believed that, as compared to Czech,

---

[2] For example, 3/1. The numerator of this fraction corresponds with the number of syllables of the RS (classes), whereas the denominator indicates the localization of the stressed syllable within the RS (types).

[3] In linguistics, a syntagma is an elementary constituent segment within a text. Such a segment can be a phoneme, a word, a grammatical phrase, a sentence, or an event within a larger narrative structure, depending on the level of analysis. Syntagmatic analysis involves the study of relationships (rules of combination) among syntagmas (see: [3])

Russian and Bulgarian have more features in common in their rhythmic organization (due to, e.g., various stress patterns, the reduction of unstressed vowels and so on).

Detailed study and understanding of various conceptions of rhythm has made it possible to conclude that at present works based on a comparative study of closely related languages are of great theoretical and practical value [4,6, etc.] because it is in closely related languages that we find "imaginary similarities" [9] that are more difficult of overcoming than "inconspicuous similarities" in unrelated languages.

Modern experimental speech studies have supported the presence of rhythm in spoken language. Rhythm is a result of a combination of physiological factors of speech production, of the specificity of the sound and syllable inventories and of the whole phonetic structure as such. The rhythm of prose interpreted here as a distribution in time of specific qualitative and quantitative features of various phonetic units is considered to be an intrinsically organized hierarchic structure. The basic level in the hierarchy of rhythmic segmentation of speech (the syllable rhythm level) is directly related to the level of syntagmatic and phrase rhythm, which in its turn is related to semantics and syntax. The rhythmic component is organically included in intonation. All levels are closely related and form a wholesome structure.

When studying the rhythm of speech, it is possible to use various basic units, depending on the character of stress patterns in different languages, different understanding of rhythmic segmentation and approaches to the problem in question (whether it is phonetic, physiological or any other). As mentioned above, in the present study we used RS as a basic unit.

2 Methods, Analysis and Results

In the course of the study, test texts (forty texts for each language) were recorded in an echo-free chamber by native speakers with a normative manner of pronunciation (15 speakers for each of the languages in question). In three months' time after the recording the same subjects were used for the auditory analysis of the texts and were asked to listen to the whole recorded material, to correct pronunciation mistakes made and to read once more the same texts but correctly. The next stage of the auditory analysis envisaged identification of stressed syllables and segmentation of spoken texts into minimal speech fragments, i.e. sequences of words united by a single stress. The auditory analysis was carried out on the individual basis binaurally and repeatedly according to the two programs: a) recording of the current phrases of the texts and their subsequent segmentation into RS and syntagmas; b) segmentation of the reproduced recording into minimal speech fragments, united by a single stress, relying on the text typed without capitals, punctuation marks and spaces between words, i.e. as a continuous string of letters.

Regarding the number of syllables in RS, we have found that two- and three-syllable RS are predominant in Czech texts, two-, four- and five-syllable RS in Bulgarian texts, and two-, three- and four-syllable RS in Russian texts.

As regards the most frequent structures, journalistic, scientific and technical texts differ from fiction prose (in the former the number of RS with more than three components is bigger than in the latter), Czech was found to have a more specific distribution of RS when compared to Russian and Bulgarian, and a more contrasting distribution of RS in terms of their frequencies for the two types of text (journalistic, scientific and technical on one side, and fiction prose on the other); for Bulgarian this distribution was found to be less contrasting.

The comparison of the rhythmic patterns of syntagmas (RPS) with due account of the RS specificity has shown the following: in Czech the most frequent RPS consist of two RS(3/1 3/3; 4/1 3/1; 2/1 4/1 and so on), of three RS and four RS (3/1 3/1 3/1; 3/1 4/1 6/1; 2/1 3/2 4/1 and so on). In Bulgarian the picture is different; the very type of RPS becomes different in syntagmas consisting of two RS, while in syntagmas consisting of three RS the pattern is like in Czech (2/1 3/1 2/2; 3/2 3/1 2/1; 4/2 4/3 4/3 and so on). In Russian, among the most frequent RPS we find those consisting of two RS (3/2 2/1; 3/2 3/1; 3/3 3/2 etc.) and of three RS (2/1 3/1 3/2; 2/1 3/2, 5/3; 2/1 1/1 5/2 etc.).

The least frequent syntaqmas in Czech are those consisting of nine RS, in Bulgarian those of eleven and twelve RS, in Russian those of nine, ten and twelve RS.

Regarding the number of syllables in syntagmas, we have found that in Czech two-RS syntagmas the average number of syllables is 7.6 and in three-RS syntagmas 10. In Bulgarian the figures are 7 and 12.6, in Russian 7 and 9.9 respectively. In the languages in question two-RS syntagmas are prevailing. Russian and Bulgarian are characterized by a greater frequency of three-RS syntagmas. Therefore in these three languages two- and three- component RPS can be considered the nucleus and the other RPS the periphery of the rhythmic structure.

Another point of interest was to see whether there were any trends in location of RS at the beginning and at the end of syntagmas. We proceeded from the assumption that rhythmic specificity of languages is determined not only by the predominant classes and types of RS, but also by their preferential location in syntagmas in which the beginning and the end (the first two and the last two RS) are presumably marked positions. The data obtained allow to present a Czech syntagma in the following schematic way:

$$3/1 \; 2/1 \ldots n/n \ldots 2/1 \; 3/1$$

A Bulgarian syntagma can be represented as follows:

$$n/2 \; (n/3; n/1) \; n/2 \; (n/3; n/1) \ldots n/n \ldots n/3 \; (n/2; n/1) \; n/3 \; (n/2; n/1)$$

The corresponding pattern for a Russian syntagma looks as follows:

$$n/2 \; (n/3; n/1) \; n/3 \; (n/2; n/1) \ldots n/n \ldots n/2 \; (n/3; n/1) \; n/2 \; (n/1; n/3)$$

The above considerations allow us to assume that the rhythmical structure of a language is determined, to a large extent, by its grammar. The variety of RS in analytic languages is the result of a wide use of combinations of auxiliary words and the notional ones, which supports our data for Bulgarian, the grammar of which is characterized by the analytic type of inclinations of nouns and pronouns. For synthetic languages like Russian, the specificity of RS is primarily explained by the variety of flexion forms in combination with conjunctions, propositions and so on. We have nearly the same picture in Czech, too. Therefore, the rhythmic peculiarities of languages do not only depend on their prosodic factors but also on the specificity of their grammars.

Another of our objectives was to see if there were any changes in timing, fundamental frequency and intensity within RS and RPS in the three languages considered. The following parameters were analyzed: duration (absolute total duration of RS, relative normalized total duration of RS, absolute vowel duration in RS, relative vowel duration in RS, mean vowel duration in syntagmas and so on); intensity (total intensity of vowels and sonorants in RS, maximum intensity of vowels and sonorants in RS); fundamental frequency (mean values of fundamental frequency for vowels and sonorants within RS, the range of fundamental frequency within RS, the range of fundamental frequency within syntagmas, the ratio of the fundamental frequencies for vowels at the boundaries between RS and others).

The analysis has revealed that in the flow of Czech speech RS are marked at the beginning and at the end of the structure but by various prosodic means: a positive or negative interval in the intonation at the boundaries of RS (in 75% of the cases regarding of all types of boundaries), a decrease in intensity at the end of RS (76%) and an increase in the duration of the final vowel or sonorant in RS (50%). There are two regularly marked positions in Czech, viz. the initial and the final ones. These positions seem to constitute a prosodic framework which is perceived aurally.

In Czech scientific and technical texts as well as in fiction prose realization of syntagmas is further characterized, as a rule, by an equally intensive markedness of syllables. The values of fundamental frequency tend to be monotonous. We also considered the timing of RS and of stressed vowels in RS. It should be noted that duration, fundamental frequency and intensity of RS in scientific and technical texts vary in a more narrow range than in fiction prose.

For Bulgarian RS we have established two types of features, common for the various types of texts and specific ones. In the first case we have a stable acoustic markedness of the stressed vowel by all prosodic means, but in the first place by duration and intensity, while in the second one we have a different contribution of these means. A greater dynamic range on stressed vowels of RS and a greater duration difference between stressed and unstressed vowels in RS make journalistic texts sound more expressive than scientific and technical texts. This is also supported by a wide range of changes in fundamental frequency (110 semitones for newspaper articles and 15 semitones for scientific and technical texts).

Comparison of the total duration of each RS within a syntagma has revealed the absence of RS isochronism in Bulgarian, which is a striking contrast to Czech. Bulgarian is also characterized by a greater degree of intonation variance and a wider intonation range than Czech. Stress patterns are also different in the two languages; in Bulgarian the maximally stressed vowels are those that bear primary stress. RS stress patterns are different in the two languages, too; in Bulgarian the RS stress is maximum in value and coincides with the lexical stress in a syllable bearing primary stress, while in Czech it is observed on the transition segment from the final vowel of one RS to the initial vowel of the subsequent RS. As already mentioned above, Czech speech flow is characterized by a prosodic markedness of the beginning and the end of RS; in Bulgarian regular prosodic features of this type are not observed.

It can be stated that for the two types of texts prosodic markedness is characterized by the same trend: greater markedness of RS in newspaper articles as compared to scientific and technical texts.

Regarding RS within syntagmas in spoken Russian, their duration varies considerably and depends, to a great extent, on the number of syllables in RS. This factor determines the total duration of RS to a greater extent than the position.

Comparison of the prosodic characteristics of RS in the three languages was carried out taking into account the following parameters: duration of all vowels in the syntagma (in percent), average duration of vowels, total duration of RS, number of vowels and syllables per unit of time, mean syllable duration, total intensity of RS, range of fundamental frequency across the syntagma, interval between fundamental frequency at the boundary between RS, and others.

In terms of total duration of vowels in the syntagma, the three languages are characterized by the following figures (see Table 1).

Table 1. Total duration of vowels and consonants in the syntagma (in %)

	Duration of vowels	Duration of consonants
Bulgarian	36	64
Russian	43	57
Czech	48	52

These data show that in the languages in question vowels account for a less share of the total speech flow than consonants. The minimum vowel duration is found in Bulgarian and the maximum one in Czech while Russian is somewhere in an intermediate position in this respect. Czech is characterized by the smallest ratio of the vowel to consonant duration.

Concerning average vowel duration, we can say that Russian has the highest values of this parameter (average $\overline{t_v} = 80$ ms). Bulgarian and Czech do not differ in this respect (average $\overline{t_v} = 60$ ms). In other words, spoken Russian is the slowest of the three.

Comparison of mean syllable duration reveals that the maximum mean value of syllable duration is found in Russian (average $\overline{t_s} = 205$ ms) and the minimum one in Bulgarian (average $\overline{t_s} = 137$ ms) while in Czech this parameter is intermediate in value (average $\overline{t_s} = 160$ ms). These data show that the average rate of spoken Russian amounts to approximately 5 syllables per second, of Bulgarian to 7 and of Czech to 6 syllables per second respectively. We may say that Bulgarian speech is the fastest and Russian speech the slowest, Czech being in an intermediate position in this respect.

As regards the intensity of stressed vowels in RS, Russian differs from the other two languages, the latter having a lower intensity of stressed vowels than the former. This testifies to a higher energy level of spoken Russian.

The three languages differ in terms of fundamental frequency, too. Across the phrase it varies in a wider range in Russian (up to 8 semitones), and in a more narrow range (up to 3 semitones) in Czech, Bulgarian being here in the intermediate position with values of up to 5 semitones.

For each sample of spoken texts the average total duration of RS was calculated, the average figures being $\overline{t_{\sum RS}} = 654, 550$ and 517 ms, respectively for Russian, Czech and Bulgarian. The average duration of RS varies from minimum in Czech to maximum in Russian. The values of average RS duration in Czech and Bulgarian are similar and not so high as in Russian, which enables us to state that the fragmentation of Czech and Bulgarian speech into RS is more detailed than in Russian.

Comparing RS in the languages concerned has made it possible to characterize spoken Czech as having a relatively narrow intonation range, with a minimum of changes in speech melody, a moderate level of energy content, a detailed fragmentation of syntagmas into RS (up to 7), a moderate speech rate and a shift of the 'gravity centre' in pronunciation onto the phonologically long vowels and sonorants, which leaves the impression of a rhythmic syncope. Spoken Bulgarian can be characterized as having a moderate intonation range, moderate changes in the intonation curve, moderate energy content, uniform fragmentation of syntagmas into RS (on the average 5 RS in a syntagma), a fast speech rate and reliance in terms of timing on consonants. The corresponding parameters obtained for Russian show that compared to Bulgarian and Czech, Russian speech is characterized by a maximum intonation range, a considerable amount of changes in the intonation curve, maximum energy content, uniform fragmentation of syntagmas into RS (on the average, from 5 to 7 RS per syntagma), a slow speech rate, the duration of consonants and vowels being nearly the same.

Each of the languages has certain acoustic features that make it possible to identify RS in the speech flow. Both vowels and consonants at the RS boundaries are characterized by definite acoustic features. In Russian, duration can be regarded as a parameter having the greatest information content in terms of the speech flow segmentation into RS. Maximum intensity and the rate of fundamental frequency changes can be regarded as complementary in this respect. In Czech which relies heavily on vowels and sonorants, duration is also an informative parameter. The duration of sonorants at the final position in RS considerably exceeds that at the beginning of RS before a vowel. Similar results were obtained in the acoustic segmentation of Bulgarian speech: duration, rate of fundamental frequency changes and intensity have been found to be indicative of RS boundaries.

The description of stressed vowels in RS would have been incomplete if their spectral characteristics had not been considered. The more so since prosodic features alone cannot determine the stress of a vowel. Therefore we thought it necessary to undertake a comparative analysis of stressed vowels in the languages in question. To obtain a more detailed description of the phonetic realization of RS, some fragments of the test texts were analyzed spectrally by means of computer program Sound Forge (Sony Creative Software). The results for Czech have shown differences for phonologically long and short stressed vowels. Thus, for example, average F1 and F2 of stressed vowels and average F1 and F2 of the corresponding phonologically long vowels differed not only quantitatively but also qualitatively. For example, the distribution of average F1 and F2 of phonologically long vowels shows that their articulation tends to be more frontal. In Czech post-stress and stressed vowels (outside the factor of phonological length) do not differ qualitatively.

For the Bulgarian vocalism the comparison was carried out on a different basis; we analyzed the spectra of stressed and corresponding unstressed vowels. The results have shown that unstressed vowels are closer than the stressed ones. Their articulation is characterized by a smaller jaw opening and restricted advance of the tongue to the front. Unstressed vowels in Bulgarian differ from the stressed ones both quantitatively and qualitatively. The spectra reveal a fuller realization of stressed vowels compared to unstressed ones as the latter are characterized by a considerable articulatory reduction in terms of both quantity and quality. As regards Russian, the results obtained with a special device for formant analysis have supported data obtained earlier by other researchers: stressed vowels are characterized by specific qualitative features.

The results obtained give us an insight into the nature of accent in the languages in question and therefore, into their specific rhythmic organization. Thus in Czech the qualitative characteristics of stressed and unstressed vowels in RS do not differ, they are characterized by the same degree of tenseness and the same duration. This is not true of the phonologically long vowels that are marked both quantitatively and qualitatively. On the whole, such a distribution affects the rhythmic organization of Czech which is characterized by the absence of vowel reduction, the identity of qualitative and quantitative characteristics of stressed and unstressed vowels and the markedness of phonologically long vowels. Such a spectral and temporal structure of vowels in Czech words together with the psychological fixation of the speaker and the listener on the first syllable of the word explain the specific rhythm of Czech speech which is in sharp contrast to that of Bulgarian and Russian where stressed and unstressed vowels differ considerably both qualitatively and quantitatively, phonologically long vowels are lacking and stress is free and mobile.

In conclusion we would like to underline the fact that modern typological language studies are characterized by the three main directions of search for universalities, for types and for individual specificity. The present study was carried out along the lines of this concept to solve the above mentioned tasks. We considered RS as a basic universal feature of rhythm serving as a link between languages with free and fixed stress.

The auditory analysis of journalistic, scientific and technical texts as well as that of fiction prose has revealed the specific features of the rhythmic structure of spoken Czech, Bulgarian and Russian. In terms of RS, no striking stylistic differences have been found within individual languages. We can only conclude that different types of texts are characterized by regrouping of RS classes and types. The study has provided another proof of the regularity observed earlier by other researchers that in Slavic languages there is a predominance of two-syllable RS with the stress on the first syllable. We have shown that three- and four-syllable RS are also quite frequent in the languages under consideration. The bulk of all RS is represented by those that contain from two to four syllables. As regards the number of RS per syntagma, we can conclude that in the three languages the nucleus is represented by syntagmas with three RS, while those containing only one RS or more than three lie on the periphery.

The frequency of RS with respect to their morphological composition is governed by certain laws intrinsic, for example, to Slavic languages. In this respect it is crucial whether the language is synthetic or analytical, because this fact determines the structure of RS and, consequently, the specific rhythm of utterances. Differences in style may also affect the prevailing grammatical composition of RS. The latter factor does not exert, however, as considerable an influence as the language grammar does.

The results of the acoustic analysis have revealed the phonetic specificity of RS and RPS, which is determined by the phonetic structure of stress in RS, realized in the studied languages by different means: definite combinations of prosodic features of vowels at the RS boundaries in Czech speech, a dynamic component in Bulgarian and a spectral as well as a temporal component in Russian. All these features are responsible for specific combinations of qualitative and quantitative parameters that shape the rhythm of spoken prose in the languages considered. RS are identified not only on the basis of stress but also on the basis of the acoustic features of boundaries between RS that are present in the speech flow but frequently deny identification because they are weakly expressed acoustically.

3   Conclusion

From the point of view of an integral perception of rhythm in Czech, it can be represented as a dot-and-dash line where dots correspond to equally stressed vowels (syllables) and dashes to specifically emphasized sounds (syllables) that are a result of phonological length, wide vowels, syllable-forming sonorants and RS final position. The corresponding picture of Bulgarian speech rhythm will be a dotted line where dots represent vowels (syllables) with a minimum quantitative expression. Russian speech which is characterized by a longer duration of vowels (syllables) can be represented as a dash line or a solid wave-like curve. The assumption of a greater similarity of Bulgarian and Russian as opposed to Czech with respect to a number of parameters has been supported by experimental phonetic data.

Therefore, the present study has supported the validity of the hypothesis on the existence of a hierarchy of factors that determine the rhythmic organization of utterances: the underlying factor is found in stress, followed by grammar which affects the speech rhythm indirectly, through various combinations of parts of speech, forming proclitics and enclitics, and finally by stylistic peculiarities though the latter exert but a weak influence on rhythm.

The specific tasks of modern studies, related to the comparative analysis of RS classes and types (i. e. classes of RS are based on the number of syllables, types of RS on the localization of the stressed syllable within RS) as well as of RPS types in languages, their prosodic markedness and perceptive specificity, allow to solve the main problem of determining the prosodic organization of rhythm in the contrasting aspect. It should be noted that in some cases in sufficiently developed rhythmic conceptions impede the perception mechanisms. The point is that word perception and decision-making about their meaning may go by two ways. The first way can be described as follows: each segment in the chain of sounds is consequently identified by the listeners with some phoneme. In this case every the segment elements should contain phonetic information sufficient for such phonemic identification. There can be another way when the listener relies, for example, on the rhythmic structure rather than on the segment units. If this is so, the rhythmic structure becomes the basis for word recognition process. Such a situation is most frequently observed when articulation is incomplete, primarily in colloquial speech and the listener tries to guess the meaning of words relying on their integral properties.

Acknowledgments. The survey is being carried out with the support of the Ministry of Education and Science of the Russian Federation in the framework of the project No. 34.1254.2014K at Moscow State Linguistic University (scientific head of the project R.K. Potapova).

References

1. Dauer, R.M.: Stress-timing and syllable-timing reanalyzed. Journal of Phonetics II, 51–62 (1983)
2. Lehiste, I.: Rhythm of poetry, rhythm of prose. In: Fromkin, V.A. (ed.) Phonetic Linguistics (Essays in honor of Peter Ladefoged), Orlando, pp. 145–155 (1985)
3. Middleton, R.: Studying popular music. Open University Press, Philadelphia (1990/2002)
4. Nikolaeva, T.M.: Frazovaya intonatsiya slavyanskikh yazykov. Nauka, Moskva (1977)
5. Pike, K.L.: Practical phonetics of rhythm waves. Phonetica 8, 9–30 (1962)
6. Potapov, V.V.: Dynamik und Statik des sprachlichen Rhythmus: Eine vergleichende Studie zum slavischen und germanischen Sprachraum. Blau Verlag, Kln (2001)
7. Potapova, R.K., Potapov, V.V.: Kommunikative Sprechttigkeit: Ruland und Deutschland im Vergleich. Blau Verlag, Kln (2011)
8. Potapova, R.K., Potapov, V.V.: Rechevaya kommunikatsiya: Ot zvuka k vyskazyvaniyu. Yazyki slavyanskikh kul'tur, Moskva (2012)
9. Reformatsky, A.A.: Fonologicheskie etyudy. Nauka, Moskva (1975)
10. Shvedova, N.Y. (red.): Russkaya grammatika. Nauka, Moskva (1980)
11. Strangert, E.: Swedish speech rhythm in a cross-language perspective. Ume Universitet, Stokholm (1985)
12. Scherba, L.V.: Fonetika frantsuzskogo yazyka. 7th ed. Vysshaya shkola, Moskva (1963)
13. Zlatoustova, L.V.: O edinitse ritma stikha i prozy. In: Zvegintsev, V.A (red.) Aktual'nye voprosy strukturnoy i prikladnoy lingvistiki. Izd-vo Mosk. universiteta, Moskva, 61–75 (1980)
14. Zlatoustova, L.V.: Foneticheskie edinitsy russkoy rechi. Isd-vo Mosk. universiteta, Moskva (1981)
15. Zlatoustova, L.V.: Universalii v prosodicheskoy organizatsii teksta (na materiale slavyanskikh, germanskikh i romanskikh yazykov). In: Vestnik Mosk. universiteta. Ser. 9. Filologiya. 4, 69–78 (1983)
16. Zlatoustova, L.V.: Rol' frazovykh aktsentov v organizatsii zvuchaschego stikha. In: Russkoe stikhoslozhenie. Traditsii i problemy razvitiya. Nauka, Moskva, 49–60 (1985)

State Level Control for Acoustic Model Training

German Chernykh[1], Maxim Korenevsky[2], Kirill Levin[2],
Irina Ponomareva[2], and Natalia Tomashenko[2,3]

[1] Dept. of Physics, Saint-Petersburg State University, Saint-Petersburg, Russia
chernykh@gc7511.spb.edu
[2] Speech Technology Center, Saint-Petersburg, Russia
{korenevsky,levin,ponomareva}@speechpro.com
[3] Dept. of Speech Information Systems, ITMO University, Saint-Petersburg, Russia
{tomashenko-n}@speechpro.com

Abstract. We propose a method for controlling Gaussian mixture splitting in HMM states during the training of acoustic models. The method is based on introducing special criteria of mixture quality in every state. These criteria are calculated over a separate part of the speech database. We back up states before splitting and revert to saved copies of the states whose criteria values have decreased, which makes it possible to optimize the number of Gaussians in the GMMs of the states and to prevent overfitting. The models obtained by such training demonstrate improved recognition rate with a significantly smaller number of Gaussians per state.

Keywords: acoustic modeling, GMM-HMM models, Gaussian splitting.

1 Introduction

Despite the considerable advances achieved in automatic speech recognition (ASR) in the past few years due to widespread use of deep learning [1] and particularly context-dependent deep neural networks (CD-DNN) [2] for acoustic modeling, hidden Markov models [3] based on Gaussian mixtures (GMM-HMM) continue to be one of the key tools in the development of ASR systems. Many of the most effective methods of speaker [4] and environment [5] adaptation are designed specifically for GMM-HMMs. Tied states of previously trained triphone GMM-HMM models are used as targets in the training of modern CD-DNN systems. This clearly demonstrates that the development of methods for more effective GMM-HMM training is still an important issue.

The well-known Baum-Welch algorithm [7] is the most widespread method of training HMMs with Gaussian mixtures in states (GMM-HMM). The Baum-Welch method is a special case of the more general EM-algorithm [8]. An iteration of the algorithm consist of an alternation of two kinds of stages: accumulation of statistics and updating of model parameters. After each two such stages the likelihood of models over the training data is guaranteed not to decrease and thus approaches a (at least) local maximum. Traditionally, several iterations of

A. Ronzhin et al. (Eds.): SPECOM 2014, LNAI 8773, pp. 435–442, 2014.
© Springer International Publishing Switzerland 2014

the Baum-Welch method in turn alternate with the procedure of splitting the states GMMs. When the GMM in a given HMM state is split, the Gaussian with the largest weight is divided into a pair of Gaussians to increase the accuracy of feature density approximation in this state. The parameters of the split GMMs are further refined during the successive Baum-Welch iterations.

The issue of proper selection of the number of GMM components is of great practical importance. Setting the number of Gaussians a priori too small may result in poor discrimination power of the obtained distributions, while if the number of Gaussians trained on a limited dataset is too large, this may lead to overfitting, which in turn results in poor recognition on previously unseen data. Moreover, unwarranted increase in the size of the GMMs reduces the speed of their likelihood calculation, which slows down the entire recognition system. In the literature we find several ways to optimize the number of Gaussians in GMMs, which are usually based on information criteria such as the Bayesian Information Criterion (BIC), Akaike Information Criterion (AIC) etc. [9]. But these approaches are not always stable and are more applicable to the simpler task of single distribution approximation using GMM, or to GMM-HMM training according to the Viterbi algorithm (when the boundaries of HMM states are considered as fixed and are set beforehand). Likelihood-based control of GMM-splitting can also be applied for Viterbi training, similarly to how it is done when constructing a decision tree for states tying [10], [11]. In this case splitting stops when the increase in the state log-likelihood over state-assigned data caused by splitting becomes smaller than a predefined threshold, however the threshold itself is set empirically. Nonetheless, the most common way to control the number of Gaussians in the HMM states for Baum-Welch training is to run the recognition process with the current models repeatedly on some speech data that are not included in the training sample and are usually called the (cross-) validation set. The configuration of the states GMMs that provides the best recognition accuracy on the cross-validation set is considered optimal and is not split anymore. However, this approach is laborious and noticeably slows down the entire training of GMM-HMM models.

This paper proposes an alternative way to control the number of Gaussians in HMM states. It also uses the idea of cross-validation, but it is integrated with the Baum-Welch method and so does not require repeated recognition runs with the models that are currently being trained. The method is based on the use of special criteria calculated on the cross-validation set. An increase in these criteria signifies an improvement of the models. When the criteria start to decrease, it serves as a signal for terminating the splitting of GMMs. A special feature of the proposed criteria is that they a calculated not only for the entire set of models but also for every separate HMM state. If, after the latest split, a state criterion has decreased during successive Baum-Welch iterations, then this state is reversed to the copy of the GMM backed up before split. Such detailed control makes it possible to stop splitting for every state at the right time. This prevents model overfitting and makes the models as "light" as possible but with better generalization capabilities.

The rest of the paper is organized as follows. The proposed criteria of state GMM quality are discussed in Section 2. Section 3 describes the algorithm for GMM splitting and rollback in detail. Experiments that confirm the advantages of the proposed method are described in Section 4. General conclusions and possible future directions are discussed in Section 5.

2 Training Quality Control Criteria

Before proceeding with the description of the proposed criteria, let us note that all the experiments described below use not the conventional Bawm-Welch method but its modification, namely the so-called "exact-match" algorithm, which is widely used in discriminative HMM training [12]. This method has an intermediate position between the conventional Baum-Welch and the Viterbi algorithm, because it applies the Forward-Backward (FB) algorithm not to the whole sequence of utterance phones but to each phone separately (in discriminative training, the FB algorithm is applied to each edge of phone lattices). That means that in order to use this method, phone labelling has to be done prior to training, which limits its applicability to some extent. On the other hand, this method is much faster and, provided that the labeling is sufficiently exact, it is more stable than conventional Baum-Welch training.

Since Baum-Welch training is designed to maximize model likelihood on the training data, the most natural criteria of quality for the obtained models should be based on likelihood or log-likelihood values. Log-likelihood adds up over time, so the quality of the models for a given utterance may be characterized by averaged likelihood per frame: $C_i = L_i/T_i$. Here L_i stands for the accumulated log-likelihood of the i-th utterance while T_i stands for its duration. To describe the quality of the models on the entire dataset we can use the following criteria:

$$C = \frac{1}{N} \sum_{i=1}^{N} C_i = \frac{1}{N} \sum_{i=1}^{N} \frac{L_i}{T_i}, \tag{1}$$

or

$$\overline{C} = \frac{\sum_{i=1}^{N} L_i}{\sum_{i=1}^{N} T_i}, \tag{2}$$

where N is the total number of utterances. Our experiments show that the criterion C, which "pays more attention" to separate utterances, behaves a little better when the dataset is unhomogeneous, so it is used for all the results below.

We will now describe the criterion used in the proposed approach for assessing the quality of GMMs in the states. For every state s within the state sequence of the composite HMM of a given utterance, we construct the trajectory of the log-likelihoods of this state on the corresponding observation sequence:

$$L_i^s(t) = \log p(x_i(t)|s),$$

where $x_i(t)$ is an observation (feature) vector in the time frame t of the i-th utterance, and $p(x|s)$ is a probability density function of observations in the state s. Note that since the "exact match" algorithm is used, these values are considered only in the time intervals which contain phones comprising the state s. On the other intervals we can set $L_i^s(t) = -\infty$. After that we find all local maximum points from this sequence $\hat{t}_1^s, \ldots, \hat{t}_{M(s,i)}^s$, where $M(s, i)$ is the total number of local maxima for the state s in the i-th utterance, and average all log-likelihoods in the found points over the whole data set:

$$C(s) = \frac{\sum_{i=1}^{N} \sum_{k=1}^{M(s,i)} L_i^s\left(\hat{t}_k^s\right)}{\sum_{i=1}^{N} M(s, i)}. \tag{3}$$

The derived value $C(s)$ can be treated as an average of the upper envelope of the state log-likelihood trajectory, and it is the proposed criterion of GMM training quality for a given state s.

3   The Strategy of GMM Splitting in HMM States

As has already been mentioned, during HMM model training, Baum-Welch method iterations traditionally alternate with the splitting of GMMs in HMM states. This results in increasing the number of free HMM parameters but can potentially improve their recognition accuracy. We propose a strategy of gradual GMM splitting based on tracking state-level quality criteria (3) over the cross-validation set as well as backing up states before splitting and reverting them to saved GMMs if the criteria decrease during successive Baum-Welch iterations. The formal description of the proposed algorithm is as follows:

Sequential GMM splitting algorithm with state-level accuracy control

1. Save the current value C of the global criterion (1) calculated during previous Baum-Welch iterations over the cross-validation set;
2. For every state s of HMM models: create its backup copy $s' := s$ and save the current value of its individual criterion (3): $C(s') := C(s)$.
3. For every state s of HMM models: split it and increase the number of Gaussians by 1: $s := Split(s, 1)$;
4. Perform a predefined number of Baum-Welch iterations on the training data along with the calculation of the new value C_{new} of the global criterion (1) and the new values $C(s)$ of individual criteria (3);
5. For every state s of the HMM models: if the new value of criterion (3) is smaller than the saved one, i.e. $C(s) < C(s')$, then revert to the saved copy of this state: $s := s'$, $C(s) := C(s')$.
6. If the new value of the global criterion is smaller than the saved one or exceeds it by less than a predefined threshold, i.e. $C_{new} - C < \varepsilon$, then stop training. Otherwise, go to step 1.

This algorithm assumes that several Baum-Welch iterations have already been performed and the initial values of the criteria C and $C(s)$ for every state s have already been calculated prior to the start of the algorithm. We emphasize once again that all the criteria we use are calculated over not the training but the cross-validation set, in order to control and prevent model overfitting.

4 Experiments

For our experiments we used the Russian LVCSR system developed by Speech Technology Center Ltd (www.speechpro.com). This is a tandem system, and it uses acoustic features based on LC-RC posteriors [13] for GMM-HMM training. LC-RC context vectors are calculated with CMN, performed in log-mel-spectral domain by means of exponential smoothing. The context (left and right) and merger neural networks all have 1000 neurons in one hidden layer and 163 target nodes, which correspond to 54 HMMs of Russian phonemes (with 3 states per phoneme) and one state of the silence model. State posteriors from the merger networks are log-transformed, and the PCA transform with dimensionality reduction to 55 is applied. These 55-dimensional features are used for HMM training.

The experiments were performed on the Russian part of the SpeechDat(E) speech corpus [14], which consists of phone-recorded utterances comprising phonetically balanced sentences, words, phrases, numbers and number sequences. One set of experiments was carried out over the entire training dataset (about 67 hrs) and another one was carried out over only a random 15% (about 10 hrs) sample of it to simulate data deficiency. In both cases the proposed approach to state-level cross-validation control was compared to the conventional approach when all GMMs in states are split in parallel and no rollback is done. Recognition tests were performed using a 12.5K vocabulary and without any language model (to estimate the accuracy gain from the acoustic modelling only).

The results of training over both the entire dataset and its 15% part are shown in Table 1. The notation $\overline{N}_g$ stands for the average number of Gaussians per state in the final models. The table shows that the proposed approach demonstrates considerable improvements over the traditional approach; the improvements are more pronounced for the limited training data. For the entire dataset, the proposed approach decreases WER by 2.1% (6.1% relative), whereas for the small training set the WER reduction is 11.8% (26.1% relative). In addition, our approach provides this accuracy at a substantially smaller average number of Gaussians per state (2.1–3.1 vs. 11). Moreover, state-level control of GMM splitting makes it possible to attain almost the same accuracy for the 15% training sample as for the entire training set and even to exceed the accuracy obtained by the conventional approach on the entire training set.

Table 1. Recognition results with the models trained on two datasets

	Entire dataset		15% sample	
Training method	WER, %	$\overline{N}_g$	WER, %	$\overline{N}_g$
Conventional	34.3	11	45.2	11
Proposed	32.2	3.2	33.4	2.1

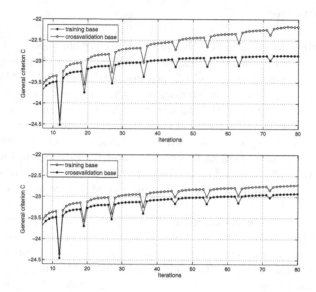

Fig. 1. Dynamics of the global criterion C for training on the entire SpeechDat(E) dataset (67 hrs). *Top:* conventional HMM training. *Bottom:* the proposed algorithm with state-level splitting control.

The dynamics of the global criterion C during the Baum-Welch iterations for each of the four versions of the training procedure are shown in Figures 1 and 2. The periodic "drops" in criterion values correspond to the splitting moments when there is a perturbation of previously trained models. The black markers represent the values of C calculated for the cross-validation part of the dataset; the white markers represent those for the training part. The divergence between the graphs obtained from the training and cross-validation parts by conventional training indicates the presence of an overfitting effect. A slight overfitting effect is observed even when training is performed on the entire dataset (the top graph in Figure 1) and is much more noticeable if there is a limited amount of training data (the top graph in Figure 2), which leads to a strong increase in recognition error rate. By contrast, when the proposed method is used (the bottom graphs in Figures 1 and 2), the criteria C grow almost in parallel for both training and cross-validation parts, which indicates an absence of overfitting.

To demonstrate that the proposed criteria are indeed indicative of model training quality, we provide word recognition accuracies obtained by using intermediate acoustic models just before every split. The results are presented in Table 2.

It can be observed that during training the dynamics of the recognition accuracy are almost the same as those of the proposed global criterion on cross-validation data, shown in Figure 2. For the conventional training the accuracy

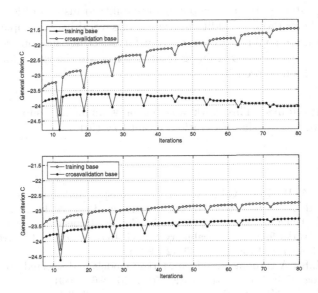

Fig. 2. Dynamics of the global criterion C for training on the 15% sample of the SpeechDat(E) dataset (10 hrs). *Top:* conventional HMM training. *Bottom:* the proposed algorithm with state-level splitting control.

Table 2. Recognition accuracy while training on 15% sample

Number of splits	2	3	4	5	6	7	8	9	10
Conventional training	63.2	63.8	63.3	61.1	59.9	58.2	56.5	55.7	54.8
Proposed training		65.5	65.5	65.7	65.9	66.0	66.0	66.5	66.5	66.6

decreases after 3 splits (which indicates overfitting), while for the proposed approach the accuracy increases monotonously in parallel with the criterion value.

5 Conclusions

We propose an effective approach to training acoustic models that controls GMM splits at the HMM state level by using criteria calculated on the cross-validation part of the speech dataset. The results we obtained demonstrate that the use of the proposed method improves the quality of HMM models (in terms of recognition accuracy) and makes them less complex thanks to an optimal selection of the number of Gaussians in the HMM states.

The proposed criteria are shown to be effective in preventing model overfitting and optimizing HMM complexity, but there are many other ways of introducing a measure that can provide a decision on whether to split the GMM in a given HMM state further or to stop splitting. As an alternative it is possible to try to use state posteriors (state occupancy probabilities) instead of log-likelihoods for deriving the criteria. In addition, the use of several backup copies of states, along with a more sophisticated algorithm for selecting the copy for rollback, will probably provide better training results. These are the issues for the future development of our approach.

Acknowledgements. This work was partially financially supported by the Government of the Russian Federation, Grant 074-U01.

References

1. Mohamed, A.-R., Dahl, G.E., Hinton, G.: Acoustic Modeling using Deep Belief Networks. IEEE Trans. Audio, Speech & Language Proc. 20(1), 14–22 (2012)
2. Dahl, G.E., Dong, Y., Deng, L., Acero, A.: Context-Dependent Pre-Trained Deep Neural Networks for Large-Vocabulary Speech Recognition. IEEE Trans. Audio, Speech & Language Proc. 20(1), 30–42 (2012)
3. Rabiner, L.R.: A tutorial on hidden Markov models and selected applications in speech recognition. Proc. of the IEEE 77(2), 257–286 (1989)
4. Giuliani, D., De Mori, R.: Speaker adaptation, pp. 363–404. Academic Press Inc., London (1998) R. De Mori ed.
5. Gales, M.J.F., Young, S.J.: HMM recognition in noise using parallel model combination. In: Proc. of the EuroSpeech, Berlin, Germany, September 22-25, pp. 837–840 (1993)
6. Mohri, M., Pereira, F., Riley, M.: Speech Recognition with Weighted Finite-State Transducers. In: Benesty, J., Sondhi, M.M., Huang, Y.A. (eds.) Springer Handbook of Speech Processing, pp. 559–584. Springer (2008)
7. Bilmes, J.A.: A Gentle Tutorial of the EM Algorithm and its Application to Parameter Estimation for Gaussian Mixture and Hidden Markov Models. Technical report TR-97-021, International Computer Science Institute, Berkley (1998)
8. Dempster, A.P., Laird, N.M., Rubin, D.B.: Maximum Likelihood from Incomplete Data via the EM Algorithm. J. Royal Statistical Society, Series B, 39(1), 1–38 (1977)
9. Steele, R.J., Raftery, A.E.: Performance of Bayesian Model Selection Criteria for Gaussian Mixture Models. Technical report TR-559, University of Washington, Dept. of Statistics (2009)
10. Odell, J.J.: The Use of Context in Large Vocabulary Speech Recognition (PhD Thesis), Cambridge: Cambridge University (1995)
11. Tatarnikova, M., Tampel, I., Oparin, I., Khokhlov, Y.: Building Acoustic Models for Large Vocabulary Continuous Speech Recognizer for Russian. In: Proc. of the SpeCom, St. Petersburg, Russia, June 26-29, pp. 83–87 (2006)
12. Povey, D.: Discriminative training for large vocabulary speech recognition (PhD thesis), Cambridge: Cambridge University (2003)
13. Yurkov, P., Korenevsky, M., Levin, K.: An Improvement of Robustness to Speech Loudness Change for an ASR System Based on LC-RC Features. In: Proc. of the SpeCom., Kazan, Russia, September 27-30, pp. 62–66 (2011)
14. Van den Heuvel, H., et al.: SpeechDat-E: Five Eastern European Speech Databases for Voice-Operated Teleservices Completed. In: Proc. of the InterSpeech, Aalborg, Denmark, September 3-7, pp. 2059–2062 (2001)

Structural Model and Behavior Scenarios of Information Navigation Mobile Robot

Maria Prischepa and Victor Budkov

SPIIRAS, 39, 14th line, St. Petersburg, 199178, Russia
{prischepa,budkov}@iias.spb.su

Abstract. In this paper behavior scenarios of information navigation mobile robot with multimodal interface during user service are discussed. The schemes of possible locations of a user and the robot in several functioning modes are described. Selection of the current scenario of robot behavior is based on the type of service providing during interaction and on the preceding user-robot dialogue history.

Keywords: Robot behavior, interaction scenarios, user personification, inquiry, navigation, multimodal interfaces.

1   Introduction

Stationary self-service robots, including ATMs, terminals, payment services, information kiosks, equipped with means of processing and output of audio-visual information are widely distributed in shopping malls, banks, transport hubs and other crowded places. The main requirement for the user interface of these systems is the availability of people with different skills and abilities [1, 2]. That is, human-computer interaction should be simple and easy so that the user is able to control the device intuitively without prior preparation and training [3, 4].

At the same time, the information reference services are developed [5, 6] on the basis of the ambient intelligent space concept that analyzes user behavior by non-contact sensors. However, so far there are only a few prototypes of such intellectual spaces: meeting room, class room, hospital room, etc [7, 8, 6]. One of the problems linked with the implementation of the intellectual space is the creation of a distributed sensor network as well as computing resources [9].

Another issue of inquiry systems is the use of self-service mobile personal devices. In particular, in museums the widespread personal mobile guides provide the user with context-sensitive information based on radio frequency identification technology. These solutions are easy to implement and do not re-quire large expenses. However, the optimal selection of screen size, weight and other ergonomic characteristics plays an important role in the development of mobile personal systems.

More attention is now given to the development of queuing systems with multimodal user interfaces, which use analysis of speech, gestures, and graphical user interface, three-dimensional model of a human head with a strong articulation of

A. Ronzhin et al. (Eds.): SPECOM 2014, LNAI 8773, pp. 443–450, 2014.

speech, facial expressions and other natural modalities of communication for interpersonal communication [10, 11].

Nowadays, one of the promising directions of development of information and self-service systems is the development of mobile robot that provides services to users in a given service area [12]. Because of their mobility, such systems are able to handle more users than the fixed systems. Moreover, mobile systems are not so limited in size as personal mobile guides, so the resources necessary to equip the user interface can be increased. However, when you create a mobile self-service system new unexplored aspects of human-computer interaction arise [13, 14]. Among others, there are issues of traffic safety, selection of the robot position in relation to the user in the course of providing services and the implementation of the user interface to deal with the mobility of a user and the robot.

The paper is organized as follows. Section 2 discusses the developed structural model of the information navigation mobile robot. The general schemes of positions of user and robot during interaction are described in Section 3. Scenarios of robot behavior during interaction are presented in Section 4. Section 5 presents experiments and results.

2   Structural Model of Information Navigation Mobile Robot

First we give a formal statement of the task about information services that mobile robots are provide. Let $U=(u_1, u_2,...,u_i,...,u_I)$ is a set of users, $R=(r_1, r_2,...,r_j,...,r_J)$ is a set of mobile systems on the specified service area, Z is a database of the service area with set of objects $O=(o_1, o_2,..., o_n,..., o_N)$, and information about this objects is supplied during system operation. Then a maintenance task may be formulated as follows. Considering features of location of objects and possible routes through the territory, it is necessary to provide a dialog between a user u_i and the robot r_j, as well as robot's accompaniment of the user to a required object o_n with safe and comfortable distance for interaction. Figure 1 shows the structural model of the mobile robot, which includes the basic blocks for realization of robot's interaction with the user and movement within the service area.

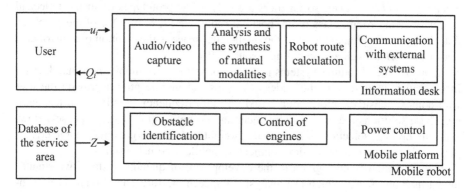

Fig. 1. Structural model of the mobile robot

Description of the service area contains the following set of basic components required for calculation of movement routes: $Z=<M, K, H>$, where M is a topological map of the territory with marked static and dynamic obstacles, K is coordinates of entrance to objects from the set O, H is data about the routes, dialogues and users.

In this task the complexity of constructing a dialogue is related to the mobility of both parties: the user and the informational robot. Moreover, data about a user u_i are defined by robot r_j, in the observation area of which this user was detected. Therefore, information model of user is characterized by the following parameters: $u_{ij}=<X_{ij},C_{ij},$ $S_{ij}, H_{ij}, B_i>$, where X_{ij} is a user location area, C_{ij} is coordinates of user, S_{ij} is a user speed, H_{ij} – coordinates of the center of the user's face, B_i is user biometric characteristics collected during interaction with the mobile robot.

To form the database of reference data about the objects their models are described by the following features: $o_n=<K_n, P_n, A_n, E_n, G_n>$, where K_n is coordinates of the entrance to the object o_n; P_n is a description of services provided by this object that are needed for training acoustic, language, and dialog models for speech/multimodal user interface; A_n is a media representation of an object that is used by robot in advertisement mode; G_n is a additional information about the object (work hours, phone), required for the functioning of the mobile robot.

Technical equipment of the robot can be divided into two main groups: 1) mobile platform providing the motion of the complex and obstacles detection during the moving along the route; 2) information desk, which displays multimedia data about objects based on the multimodal interface. Therefore, the model of the mobile robot contains parameters the values of which are generated by sensors embedded in mobile platform, and by capture devices embedded in the information desk. It also contains the parameters calculated during the dialogue with the user: $r_j=<C_j, S_j, f_j, V_j, U_j, D_j, W>$, where C_j is coordinates of the robot, S_j is a robot's speed, f_j corresponds to a functioning mode, V_j is sensors data, U_j is a set of users in robot's observation area, D_j is additional parameters (charge status and other embedded hardware) required for the operation of the mobile robot, W is a allocation data and mode of operation of all service robots in the area.

In this model the functioning mode is chosen from the set $f=(f_D, f_E, f_A, f_P,)$, where f_D corresponds to the dialogue; f_E is escorting; f_A is advertisement; f_P is turn to a base. The result of interaction between robot r_j and a user u_i is provision of a service Q, which includes output of information about the object o_n and/or escorting to the object located on the service territory Z: $Q(u_i)=f(r_j, Z, o_n)$. The navigation issues connected with the calculation of the optimal route are not considered in this work. Our research was focused on problem of interaction between robot and user during service.

There are three areas where the user may be located near the robot: observation area x_{search}, escorting area x_{escort}, interaction area x_{dialog}. User presence in one of these areas is defined on the basis of the following logical rules:

$$X_{ij}\left(d_{ij}, \alpha_{ij}, E_n \right) = \begin{cases} x_{search}, & d_{ij} < d_{search\_max} \wedge \alpha_{ij} < \alpha_{search\_max}, \\ x_{escort}, & d < d_{escort\_max} \wedge \alpha_{ij} < \alpha_{escort\_max}, \\ x_{dialog}, & d < d_{dialog\_max} \wedge \alpha_{ij} < \alpha_{dialog\_max}. \end{cases}$$

where Xij is a user location area, d_{ij} is a distance between the user and the robot, α_{ij} is a angle of deviation of user from the center of the robot, E_n is messages of speech recognition system, d_{search_max} is a maximum distance for users search, d_{dialog_max} is a maximum distance, at which dialogue with the user is possible, d_{escort_max} is a maximum distance in the escorting mode, α_{search_max} is a maximum angle for search, α_{dialog_max} is a maximum angle of deviation of user from the center of the robot during the dialogue, α_{escort_max} is a maximum angle of deviation of user from the center of the robot during the escorting. If these rules are not satisfied, it is assumed that the analyzed object is not a user.

3   Positions of User and Robot During Interaction

The schemes of possible location of a user and the robot in several functioning modes are presented in Figure 2. The interaction zone of the robot is marked by dotted line. During the dialogue the distance d to a user should be less than the $d_{dialogue\_max}$ and the angle $\propto$ of user deviation from normal to robot center should be less than the angle $\propto_{dialogue\_max}$. To save value of the angle $\propto$ the robot turns in direction to a user.

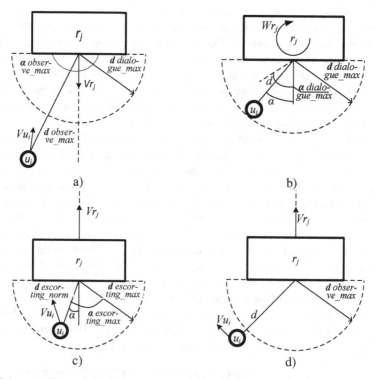

Fig. 2. Schemes of user and robot movements during the key stages of interactions: a) a user enters to the interaction zone of the robot, which moved in the advertising mode on a given route; b) the robot informs the user with the adjustment of robot position to the user direction; c) the robot escorts the user to the object of interest by a given route d) the user leaves the interaction zone of the robot

During the escorting a user can be located near the robot but moves with varying speed. In order to provide safety of interaction and more freedom in motion of a user the interaction zone is increased during the escorting. So, during the escorting the distance d to a user should be less than $d_{escorting\_max}$ and angle $\propto$ of deviation user from normal of robot center should be less than $\propto_{escorting\_max}$. Moving along the route to the object selected by a user the robot changes its own speed in order to save a value of the distance d equal to $d_{escorting\_norm}$.

Now several stages of the interaction between the robot and a user and scenario of the current working mode selection will be discussed. Figure 2 shows positions of a user and the robot in the different working mode. The mobile robot moving by a route in advertising mode carries out the search of a user located in a zone limited by the distance d_{observ_max} from the robot and the angle $\propto_{observ\_max}$. The user detection and tracking are performed by the video monitoring technology developed early [8, 11]. In case the user keeps staying in his/her position in the observation zone longer than $\tau_{attract}$ the robot changes its own place in order to let the user get into the interaction zone limited by the distance $d_{dialogue\_max}$ from the robot and the angle $\propto_{dialogue\_max}$. The size of dialogue zone is selected taking into account the constraints of audio localization technologies, possibility to use touch screen and safety of interaction. After correcting the position the robot turns into the dialogue working mode. During the dialogue the robot estimates the user position and correct own direction by turning to the user face.

After a user requests for escorting to a specified location, the robot turns into escorting mode (Figure 2c). In this mode, a user has more freedom in the selection of position relative to the robot, but he should stay not farther than the distance $d_{escorting\_max}$ to the robot. The preferred distance is maintained by adjusting the speed and direction of motion of the robot. If the user move away from the robot at the distance more than d_{observ_max} (Figure 2d), it is considered that user left the interaction area and the robot turns into standby mode.

4   Scenarios of Robot Behavior During Interaction

Figure 3 shows a functioning diagram of the robot behavior and multimodal data processing during the interaction with a user. After appearance of a user in the interaction region, the determination of its position in relation to the robot is carried out. The robot checks the value of distance $d_{dialogue\_max}$ and angle $\propto_{dialogue\_max}$ and according to the mode corrects its own position relative to the user.

If the mobile robot is in the inquiry mode, and the angle towards to the user is greater than the angle $\propto_{dialogue\_max}$, then the robot turns towards the user, so that the user enters in audio localization zone of voice request. When voice request is processed, the output multimedia data for response is compiled according to the level of external noise. If the robot is in a noisy area, the system's response to a user request will be output via several interfaces by speech synthesis and graphical display.

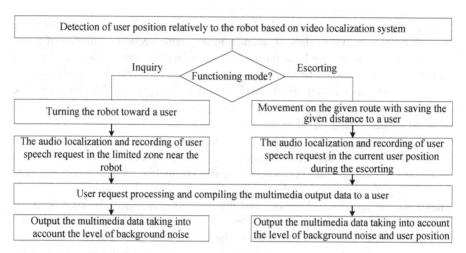

Fig. 3. Functioning diagram of robot behavior and multimodal data processing

In escorting mode, the values of distance $d_{escorting\_max}$ and angle $\propto_{escorting\_max}$ are verified too. In this mode the user can be located on either side of the robot, so the size of escorting zone is extended in comparison to the dialogue zone. The main aim of this mode is the movement on the given route and maintain the certain distance from a user, which should not go far than the distance $d_{escorting\_max}$. During escorting the audio localization is performed in the current position of user face detection by video tracking system. In the case of appearance of the user voice request it is processed and then the multimedia data is outputted taking into account the user's position and noisiness of the environment.

5   Experiments

For an experimental test of the robot, a shopping center database with 83 objects arranged of the service territory was developed. Boundaries of objects, exits and passageways between them were marked on a map. During the interaction with the user, its location and the selected object are indicated on the map. The route calculation to the required subject was carried out using the algorithm of type A*. When configuring the speech recognition system, a template of user query was built. It consists of 76 elements of the set $object_name_list, 7 elements of $service_name_list, 230 elements of $goods_name_list, 10 elements of $where_buy and 9 elements of $where_find. During the experiments it was found out that the majority (60%) of users prefer not to mention the object's specific name, but to use the category of goods or services, and to choose an object only after a list of all satisfying objects is displayed. About 40% of users make requests without introductory words ("where", "how to get"), but use one word or name ("shoes", "cafe", "Kids"). The percentage of requests processed incorrectly was about 15%.

Also during the research a sociological survey was conducted in order to identify additional requirements for ergonomics and functions of the information navigation robot. About 30 respondents aged from 20 to 60 years were interviewed. The obtained results allowed us to make the several conclusions about the preferences of users. Most important issues were related to: 1) height of robot: a) <150 cm; б) 150 cm; в) >150 cm; 2) distance of the robot interaction: a) <50 cm; б) 50 cm; в) >50 cm; 3) distance of interaction in the escorting mode: a) <50 cm; б) 50 cm; в) >50 cm; 4) means for data input: a) sensory menus; б) touch keyboard; в) voice input; г) gestural input; 5) means of information output: a) monitor output; б) audio synthesis; в) an avatar a "talking head"; г) avatar, which capable to gesticulate; 6) synthesized voice of robot: a) manlike; б) womanlike; в) childlike; г) «mechanical». Figure 4 presents the distribution histograms of responses of men and women.

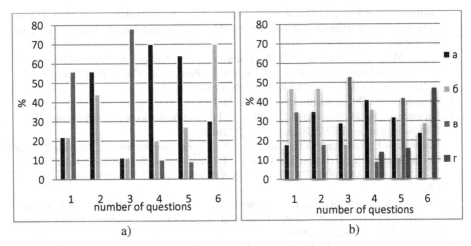

a)   b)

Fig. 4. Analysis of the user preference about information mobile robot: a) men; b) women

The main differences in the preferences are related to the height of the robot and its voice. Most of interviewed men (56%) prefer higher information systems (height> 150 cm, the answer is "c"), in contrast to women who have given their preference for average height (the answer is "b", height 150 cm). A "mechanical" voice was chosen by 47% of women, while men (70%) prefer a womanlike voice. According to the research, interaction distance with the robot in informing and escorting mode is recommended to be greater than 50 cm. According to the respondents, the most convenient means of input is the sensory menus (41% of women and 70% of men), and the most convenient output means is a "talking head" avatar and graphics output at the monitor. The received data will be used for the development of a prototype mobile robot for public places provided an effective human-computer interaction.

6   Conclusions

The solutions for the test-bed model of mobile information and navigation robot with a multimodal interface is proposed. The structural model of the mobile robot built on the basis of two systems responsible for the analysis of complex movement, taking into account obstacles on the route, as well as for the implementation of a multimodal interface providing a natural dialogue with the user and display multimedia data objects of interest. The multimodal mobile robot is a prototype of wide range of information and self-service systems located in business centers, airports, exhibition centers, medical centers, malls, museums, transport hubs and other public places.

Acknowledgements. The work is supported by RFBR (12-08-01261, 12-08-01167).

References

1. Budkov, V., Prischepa, M., Ronzhin, A.: Dialog Model Development of a Mobile Information and Reference Robot. Pattern Recognition and Image Analysis, Pleiades Publishing 21(3), 458–461 (2011)
2. Foster, M.E., Giuliani, M., Knoll, A.: Comparing Objective and Subjective Measures of Usability in a Human-Robot Dialogue System. In: Proc. of the 47th Annual Meeting of the ACL and the 4th IJCNLP of the AFNLP, pp. 879–887 (2009)
3. Breazeal, C.L.: Designing Sociable Robots. MIT Press (2002)
4. Nieuwenhuisen, M., Stuckler, J., Behnke, S.: Intuitive Multimodal Interaction for Service Robots. In: Proc. of HRI 2010, pp. 177–178 (2010)
5. Ronzhin, A.L., Saveliev, A.I., Budkov, V.Y.: Context-Aware Mobile Applications for Communication in Intelligent Environment. In: Andreev, S., Balandin, S., Koucheryavy, Y. (eds.) NEW2AN/ruSMART 2012. LNCS, vol. 7469, pp. 307–315. Springer, Heidelberg (2012)
6. Yusupov, R.M., Ronzhin, A.L., Prischepa, M., Ronzhin, A.L.: Models and Hardware-Software Solutions for Automatic Control of Intelligent Hall. Automation and Remote Control 72(7), 1389–1397 (2010)
7. Omologo, M., Svaizer, P., Brutti, A., Cristoforetti, L.: Speaker Localization in CHIL Lectures: Evaluation Criteria and Results. In: Renals, S., Bengio, S. (eds.) MLMI 2005. LNCS, vol. 3869, pp. 476–487. Springer, Heidelberg (2006)
8. Ronzhin, A., Karpov, A., Kipyatkova, I., Železný, M.: Client and Speech Detection System for Intelligent Infokiosk. In: Sojka, P., Horák, A., Kopeček, I., Pala, K. (eds.) TSD 2010. LNCS, vol. 6231, pp. 560–567. Springer, Heidelberg (2010)
9. Ronzhin, A., Budkov, V.: Speaker Turn Detection Based on Multimodal Situation Analysis. In: Železný, M., Habernal, I., Ronzhin, A. (eds.) SPECOM 2013. LNCS, vol. 8113, pp. 302–309. Springer, Heidelberg (2013)
10. Prischepa, M.V.: Development of the user profile based on the psychological aspects of human interaction with the informational mobile robot. SPIIRAS Proceedings 21, 56–70 (2012)
11. Kobozeva, I.M., Sidorov, G., Zimmerling, A.V.: Module for Dialog Management in the Interaction System Between User and Mobile Robotic Guide. SPIIRAS Proceedings 33, 186–206 (2014)
12. Lee, J.K., Breazeal, C.: Human Social Response Toward Humanoid Robot's Head and Facial Features. In: Proc. of CHI 2010, pp. 4237–4242 (2010)
13. Ronzhin, A.L., Karpov, A.A.: Multimodal Interfaces: Main Principles and Cognitive Aspects. SPIIRAS Proceedings 3, 300–319 (2006)
14. Ronzhin, A.L., Karpov, A.A., Kagirov, I.A.: Peculiarities of Distant Recording and Processing of Speech in Self-services Automatons. Information Control Systems 42, 32–38 (2009)

Study of Morphological Factors of Factored Language Models for Russian ASR

Irina Kipyatkova[1] and Alexey Karpov[1,2]

[1] St. Petersburg Institute for Informatics and Automation of RAS
SPIIRAS, St. Petersburg, 199178, Russia
[2] ITMO University, 49 Kronverkskiy av., St. Petersburg, 197101, Russia
{kipyatkova,karpov}@iias.spb.su

Abstract. In the paper, we describe a research of factored language model (FLM) for Russian speech recognition. We used FLM at N-best list rescoring stage. Optimization of the FLM parameters was carried out by means of Genetic Algorithm. The best models used four factors: lemma, morphological tag, stem, and word. Experiments on large vocabulary continuous Russian speech recognition showed a relative WER reduction of 8% when FLM was interpolated with the baseline 3-gram model.

Keywords: Factored language models, automatic speech recognition, Russian speech.

1 Introduction

One of the problems of automatic speech recognition (ASR) of Russian is tied with inflective nature of Russian. Words in Russian can inflect for a number of syntactic features: case, number, gender etc. New words with similar meaning can be created by adding single or multiple prefixes, suffixes and endings to a stem, or also by modifying a stem itself [1]. This results in increasing vocabulary size and perplexity of language models (LMs).

The most widely used language models are statistical n-gram models, which estimate the probability of appearance of a word sequence in a text. Rich morphology of Russian leads to increasing the perplexity of n-gram models. In [2], it was shown that changing the vocabulary size from 100K to 400K words increases the English model perplexity by 5.8% relatively, while the Russian model perplexity increases by as much as 39.5%.

An alternative to n-gram LMs is a factored language model (FLM) that for the first time was introduced in order to deal with morphologically rich Arabic language [3]. Then it was used for many other morphologically rich languages. This model incorporates various word features (factors), and a word is considered as a vector of k factors: $w_i = (f_i^1, f_i^2, ..., f_i^k)$. Factors of a given word can be word, morphological class, stem, root, and other grammatical features. Also some statistic or semantic information can be used as factors. Probabilistic language model is constructed over sets of the factors.

A. Ronzhin et al. (Eds.): SPECOM 2014, LNAI 8773, pp. 451–458, 2014.

2   Related Work

In [4], factored language model was incorporated at different stages of speech recognition: N-best list rescoring and recognition stage. Recognition results showed an improvement of word error rate (WER) by 0.8-1.3% with the FLM used for N-best rescoring task depending on the test speech corpus; and usage of FLM at speech recognition gave additional improving of WER by 0.5%.

FLM was applied for lattice rescoring in [5]. For speech recognition HTK toolkit was used. The decoder generated a lattice of 100 best alternatives for each test sentence using a word-based bigram LM with 5K vocabulary. Then the lattice was rescored with various morpheme-based and factored language models. Word recognition accuracy obtained with the baseline model was 91.60%, and the usage of FLM increased word recognition accuracy up to 92.92%.

In [6], morpheme-based trigram LM for Estonian was used for N-best list generating. Vocabulary of the language model consisted of 60K word particles. Then obtained morpheme sequences were reconstructed to word sequences. Factored language model, which used words and their part-of-speech (POS) tags, was applied to rescore N-best hypotheses. A relative WER improvement of 7.3% was obtained on a large vocabulary speech recognition task.

In [7], FLM was used for code-switching speech. The following factors were analyzed: words, POS tags, open class words, and open class word clusters. FLM was used at the speech decoding stage. For this purpose BioKIT speech decoder was extended to support such models. Experiments on recognition of Mandarin-English code-switching speech showed relative reduction of mixed error rate by up to 3.4%.

In [8], FLM was combined with recurrent neural network for Mandarin-English code-switching language modeling task. The combined LM gave a relative improvement of 32.7% comparing to the baseline 3-gram model.

An application of FLMs for Russian speech recognition is described in [9, 10]. FLM was trained on the text corpus containing 10M words with vocabulary size of about 100K words. FLMs were created using the following factors: word, lemma, morphological tag, POS, and gender-number-person factor. TreeTagger tool [11] was used for obtaining the factors. Investigation of influence of different factors and backoff paths on perplexity and WER was carried out. FLM was used for rescoring 500-best list. Evaluation experiments showed that FLM allows to achieve 4.0% WER relative reduction, and 6.9% relative reduction was obtained when FLM was interpolated with the baseline 3-gram model.

Another study of FLM for Russian speech recognition is presented in [12]. For FLMs creation, five factors were used: word, its lemma, stem, POS, and morphological tag. Four models with the word plus one of the other factors were created using Witten-Bell discounting method. FLMs were used for N-best list rescoring. Relative WER reduction of 5% was obtained after interpolation of the baseline 3-gram LM with FLM.

In [13], FLM was used to take into account word dependencies in a sentence. This model included the main words (heads) of word dependency in addition to the words. The authors used such processing stages as POS tagging, dependency parsing and hypotheses rescoring with FLM. Experiments were performed on parts of Russian National Corpora and have shown that only one of mixed models showed slightly better results than the baseline 3-gram model. The best word recognition accuracy was 91.77%, that was 1.26% better than results obtained with the baseline model.

3   Idea of Factored Language Models

When developing FLM it is necessary to choose an appropriate set of factors and to find the best statistical model over these factors [14]. In FLM, there is no obvious way of backing-off path [2]. In word n-gram modeling backing-off is performed by dropping first the most distant word, followed by the second most distant word, and so on until the unigram language model is used. This process is illustrated in Figure 1 (a). In FLM, any factor can be dropped at each step of backing-off, and it is not obvious, which factor to drop first. In this case, several backoff paths are possible, that results in a backoff graph. An example of backoff graph is presented on Figure 1(b). The graph shows all possible single step backoff paths, where exactly one variable is dropped per backoff step.

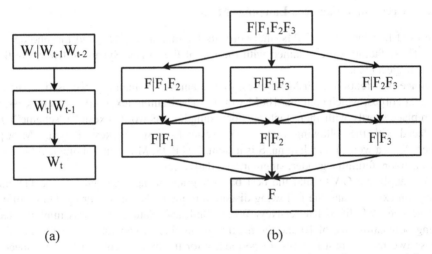

(a)   (b)

Fig. 1. Backoff trees for n-gram and FLM: (a) backoff path for a 3-gram language model over words; (b) backoff graph with three parent variables F_1, F_2, F_3

In order to choose the best factor set and backoff path, linguistic knowledge or data-driven techniques can be applied. In [4], it was shown that automatic method, which uses Genetic Algorithms (GAs) for optimization of the factor set, backoff path, and smoothing techniques, performs better than manual search in terms of perplexity. The goal of this method is to find the parameter combination that creates FLMs with a low perplexity on unseen test data [14].

4   Russian Language Modeling for ASR

4.1   Baseline Language Model

For the language model creation, we collected and automatically processed a Russian text corpus of a number of on-line newspapers. This corpus was collected from recent news published on freely available Internet sites of on-line Russian newspapers (www.ng.ru, www.smi.ru, www.lenta.ru, www.gazeta.ru, www.interfax.ru, ria.ru) for the years 2006-2013. The procedure of preliminary text processing and normalization is described in [15, 16]. The size of the corpus after text normalization and deletion of doubling and short (<5 words) sentences is over 350M words, and it has above 1M unique word-forms.

For the statistical text analysis, we used the SRI Language Modeling Toolkit (SRILM) [17]. We created 3-gram language models with different vocabulary sizes, and the best speech recognition results were obtained with 150K vocabulary [18]. Perplexity of the baseline model is 553. So this vocabulary was chosen for further experiments with N-best list rescoring.

4.2   Creation of Factored Language Model

We used five factors in FLMs: the word, its lemma, stem, POS, and morphological tag. These factors were obtained with the use of the "VisualSynan" software by the AOT project [19].

Since the creation of FLM requires a large amount of memory, we used a part of the text corpus, which contains 100M words. The training text corpus was processed to replace words with their factors. For example, the word 'схеме' ("scheme") is replaced with the following vector: {W-схеме: L-схема: S-схем: P-сущ: M-вс}, where W is a word, L is a lemma, S is a stem, P is POS, M is a morphological tag that means noun, feminine gender, singular, and dative case.

We apply the GA to find the best backoff graph using mentioned above factors, time context of 2, and the following discounting methods: Good-Turing, Unmodified Kneser-Ney, Modified Kneser-Ney, Witten-Bell, and Natural. GA was implemented using population size of 10 and the maximum number of generation equal to 20. We chose two models best in terms of perplexity for the experiments on Russian speech recognition. Both models used four factors: lemma, morphological tag, stem, word, and three discounting methods on different stages of backing-off: Unmodified Kneser-Ney, Modified Kneser-Ney, and Witten-Bell. Backoff graph for the first model (FLM 1) is presented on Figure 2; backoff graph for the second model (FLM 2) is presented in Figure 3. In the figures, a digit after factor symbol denotes a time context.

Values of perplexity of the baseline 3-gram and factored models are presented in Table 1. Perplexity is given with two different normalizations: counting all input tokens (PPL) and excluding end-of-sentence tags (PPL1).

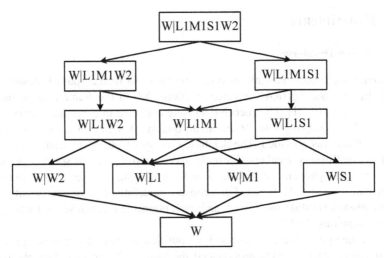

Fig. 2. Backoff graph for FLM 1

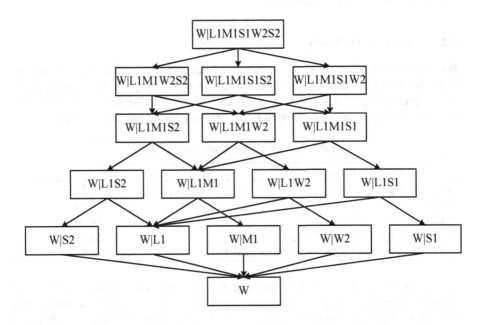

Fig. 3. Backoff graph for FLM 2

Table 1. Perplexity of created language models

Language model	PPL	PPL1
Baseline 3-gram	553	878
FLM 1	589	975
FLM 2	618	1027

5   Experiments

5.1   Speech Databases

For training the speech recognition system we used our own corpus of spoken Russian speech Euronounce-SPIIRAS, created in 2008-2009 in the framework of the Euro-Nounce project [20, 21]. The speech data were collected in clean acoustic conditions, with 44.1 kHz sampling rate, 16-bit audio quality. A signal-to-noise ratio (SNR) at least 35-40 dB was provided. The database consists of 16,350 utterances pronounced by 50 native Russian speakers (25 male and 25 female). Each speaker pronounced more than 300 phonetically-balanced and meaningful phrases. Total duration of speech data is about 21 hours. For acoustic modeling, continuous density Hidden Markov models (HMM) were used, and each phoneme (speech sound) was modeled by one continuous HMM.

To test the system we used a speech corpus that contains 500 phrases pronounced by 5 speakers (each speaker pronounced the same 100 phrases). The phrases were taken from the materials of the on-line newspaper «Фонтанка.ru» (www.fontanka.ru) that was not used in the training data.

5.2   Experimental Results

For speech recognition we used Julius ver. 4.2 decoder [22]. In our previous experiments we found out that usage of 20-best list for rescoring gives better results [12]. So, we produced a 20-best list, oracle WER for this N-best list was 16.63%. We carried out its rescoring using developed FLMs. The results are presented in Table 2.

Table 2. WER obtained with different LMs

Language model	WER, %
Baseline 3-gram	26.54
FLM 1	27.94
FLM 2	28.56
FLM 1 interpolated with the baseline model	**24.53**
FLM 2 interpolated with the baseline model	24.74

The use of FLMs for N-best list rescoring did not lead to improving speech recognition results. It may be caused that for FLM creation we used a smaller corpus than for the baseline model. Therefore we made a linear interpolation of FLMs with the baseline model. The best result was obtained with FLM 1 interpolated with the baseline 3-gram model, WER was equal to 24.53%.

6   Conclusion

FLMs allow including additional information in language model for ASR task. For morphologically rich inflective languages it seems to be useful to include some morphological features for words in the language model. In this paper, we have studied an application of FLMs for N-best list rescoring for Russian speech recognition. Tuning the model's parameters was made by means of the Genetic algorithm. Experiments on continuous Russian speech recognition were conducted using the best (in terms of perplexity) FLM interpolated with the 3-gram model. They showed the relative WER reduction of 8% with respect to the baseline model. In further research, we plan to investigate FLMs with other factors, for example, word ending, part of sentence, and other linguistic factors.

Acknowledgments. This research is supported by the Russian Foundation for Basic Research (project No. 12-08-01265), the Russian Humanitarian Scientific Foundation (project No. 12-04-12062), the Government of Russian Federation (Grant 074-U01), and the Committee on Science and Higher Education of the Administration of St. Petersburg.

References

1. Nouza, J., Zdansky, J., Cerva, P., Silovsky, J.: Challenges in speech processing of Slavic languages (Case studies in speech recognition of Czech and Slovak). In: Esposito, A., Campbell, N., Vogel, C., Hussain, A., Nijholt, A. (eds.) Second COST 2102. LNCS, vol. 5967, pp. 225–241. Springer, Heidelberg (2010)
2. Whittaker, E.W.D., Woodland, P.C.: Language modelling for Russian and English using words and classes. Computer Speech and Language 17, 87–104 (2000)
3. Bilmes, J.A., Kirchhoff, K.: Factored language models and generalized parallel backoff. In: Proceedings of Conference of the North American Chapter of the Association for Computational Linguistics on Human Language Technology, Stroudsburg, PA, USA, vol. 2, pp. 4–6 (2003)
4. Vergyri, D., Kirchhoff, K., Duh, K., Stolcke, A.: Morphology-Based Language Modeling for Arabic Speech Recognition. In: Proceedings of ICSLP 2004, pp. 2245–2248 (2004)
5. Tachbelie, M.Y., Teferra Abate, S., Menzel, W.: Morpheme-based language modeling for Amharic speech recognition. In: Proceedings of the 4th Language and Technology Conference, LTC 2009, Posnan, Poland, pp. 114–118 (2009)
6. Alumae, T.: Sentence-adapted factored language model for transcribing Estonian speech. In: Proceedings of ICASSP 2006, Toulouse, France, pp. 429–432 (2006)
7. Adel, H., Kirchhof, K., Telaar, D., Vu, N.T., Schlippe, T., Schultz, T.: Features for factores language models for code-switching speech. In: Proceedings of 4th International Workshop on Spoken Language Technologies for Under-resourced Languages (SLTU 2014), St. Petersburg, Russia, pp. 32–38 (2014)
8. Adel, H., Vu, N.T., Schultz, T.: Combination of Recurrent Neural Networks and Factored Language Models for Code-Switching Language Modeling. In: Proceedings of the 51st Annual Meeting of the Association for Computational Linguistics (ACL 2013), Sofia, Bulgaria (2013)
9. Vazhenina, D., Markov, K.: Evaluation of advanced language modelling techniques for Russian LVCSR. In: Železný, M., Habernal, I., Ronzhin, A. (eds.) SPECOM 2013. LNCS, vol. 8113, pp. 124–131. Springer, Heidelberg (2013)

10. Vazhenina, D., Markov, K.: Factored Language Modeling for Russian LVCSR. In: Proceedings of International Joint Conference on Awareness Science and Technology & Ubi-Media Computing, Aizu-Wakamatsu city, Japan, pp. 205–210 (2013)
11. Schmid, H.: Probabilistic part-of-speech tagging using decision trees. In: Proceedings of the International Conference on New Methods of Language Processing, Manchester, UK, pp. 44–49 (1994)
12. Kipyatkova, I., Verkhodanova, V., Karpov, A.: Rescoring N-best lists for Russian speech recognition using factored language models. In: Proceedings of 4th International Workshop on Spoken Language Technologies for Under-resourced Languages (SLTU-2014), St. Petersburg, Russia, pp. 81–86 (2014)
13. Zulkarneev, M., Satunovsky, P., Shamraev, N.: The use of d-gram language model for speech recognition in Russian. In: Železný, M., Habernal, I., Ronzhin, A. (eds.) SPECOM 2013. LNCS, vol. 8113, pp. 362–366. Springer, Heidelberg (2013)
14. Kirchhoff, K., Bilmes, J., Duh, K.: Factored Language Models Tutorial. Tech. Report UWEETR-2007-0003, Dept. of EE, U. Washington (2007)
15. Karpov, A., Markov, K., Kipyatkova, I., Vazhenina, D., Ronzhin, A.: Large vocabulary Russian speech recognition using syntactico-statistical language modeling. Speech Communication 56, 213–228 (2014)
16. Kipyatkova, I.S., Karpov, A.A.: Development and Research of a Statistical Russian Language Model. SPIIRAS Proceedings 12, 35–49 (2010) (in Rus.)
17. Stolcke, A., Zheng, J., Wang, W., Abrash, V.: SRILM at Sixteen: Update and Outlook. In: Proceedings of IEEE Automatic Speech Recognition and Understanding Workshop ASRU 2011, Waikoloa, Hawaii, USA (2011)
18. Kipyatkova, I., Karpov, A.: Lexicon Size and Language Model Order Optimization for Russian LVCSR. In: Železný, M., Habernal, I., Ronzhin, A. (eds.) SPECOM 2013. LNCS, vol. 8113, pp. 219–226. Springer, Heidelberg (2013)
19. Sokirko, A.: Morphological modules on the website www.aot.ru. In: Proceedings of "Dialogue-2004", Protvino, Russia, pp. 559–564 (2004) (in Rus.)
20. Jokisch, O., Wagner, A., Sabo, R., Jaeckel, R., Cylwik, N., Rusko, M., Ronzhin, A., Hoffmann, R.: Multilingual speech data collection for the assessment of pronunciation and prosody in a language learning system. In: Proceedings of SPECOM 2009, St. Petersburg, Russia, pp. 515–520 (2009)
21. Karpov, A., Kipyatkova, I., Ronzhin, A.: Very Large Vocabulary ASR for Spoken Russian with Syntactic and Morphemic Analysis. In: Proceedings of Interspeech 2011, Florence, Italy, pp. 3161–3164 (2011)
22. Lee, A., Kawahara, T.: Recent Development of Open-Source Speech Recognition Engine Julius. In: Proceedings of Asia-Pacific Signal and Information Processing Association Annual Summit and Conference (APSIPA ASC 2009), Sapporo, Japan, pp.131–137 (2009)

The Use of Speech Technology in Computer Assisted Language Learning Systems

Ekaterina Krasnova[1] and Elena Bulgakova[2]

[1] Speech Technology Center, Krasutskogo str. 4,
196084 St. Peterburg, Russia
[2] ITMO University, Kronverkskiy av. 49,
197101 St. Peterburg, Russia
{krasnova,bulgakova}@speechpro.com

Abstract. The article deals with the ways of application of automatic speech recognition (ASR) and Text-to-Speech (TTS) technology to Computer Assisted Language Learning (CALL) systems. Speech technology can be effectively used for such methodological purposes as pronunciation training, drilling communication skills, checking students' vocabulary and training listening comprehension skills. Despite some limitations, it is now possible to apply different types of speech technology to teaching which is effective for simplification of teaching process realization. Integration of ASR to a CALL system developed by Speech Technology Center is presented in the article.

Keywords: Speech technology, automatic speech recognition, text-to-speech, computer assisted language learning.

1   Introduction

Speech technology, including ASR and speech synthesis (TTS), occupies an important place in IT. Speech technology can be applied to formal and individual education, much of which can now be conducted via the Internet (e-learning). Speech technology is particularly well suited to CALL systems; such systems are currently in great demand world-wide.

Accessibility and flexibility are CALL's primary advantages over traditional classroom learning. Though, now CALL does not keep up learning with a teacher in some methodological delicacies that can be obtained only by a real teacher. That is why CALL is a fast emerging field at the present time.

The integration of advanced speech technology to CALL systems offers great methodological opportunities. We will dwell the question why to integrate speech technology into CALL for the reason that it was discussed in a number of previous papers (for example, [1, 2]).

Speech technology has been implemented to CALL quite recently [3]. For this reason, and because of some technical constraints [4], they are far from being completely applied to most CALL systems. In 1996, when scientists and educators were actively considering the question of speech technology use in CALL, the following limitations

A. Ronzhin et al. (Eds.): SPECOM 2014, LNAI 8773, pp. 459–466, 2014.

for ASR in terms of using it in CALL were identified: task definition (complexity, vocabulary size), acoustic models (speaker dependent, independent, or adapted), input quality (noise levels, microphone, sound card), input modality (discrete or continuous input). These critical issues presented a formidable challenging [5].

Many different types of speech technology are now available, and the general level of computer science development now allows nearly all of them to be effectively integrated CALL.

Nevertheless, there are still very few automated language learning systems that take all the advantages of speech technologies in all their diversity.

In this article, we describe methods for meeting functional and methodological objectives of CALL systems with the aid of ASR and TTS. The methods described feature Speech Technology Center solutions, as well as a CALL system that is now being developed by Speech Technology Center.

2   The Use of ASR in CALL Systems

There are different types of automatic speech recognition: recognition of voice commands, key word recognition, continuous speech recognition. All these types can be applied for CALL-systems to accomplish various functional and methodological purposes.

2.1   Recognition of Voice Commands

Recognition of voice commands is a type of discrete speech (separate words) recognition. The core of this technology is that the system responds to a separately pronounced word or collocation that is fixed in a short preset vocabulary. Applicability of this type of ASR is limited to the predefined vocabulary. At the same time this limitation provides very high level of recognition quality.

The technology of recognition of voice commands is applicable to accomplish the methodological purpose of training and checking learner's vocabulary: there should be some predefined vocabulary that contains the foreign words a learner needs to memorize to pass some part of a teaching course.

Still, the main field of ASR application in aid of teaching a foreign language is pronunciation training or CAPT (Computer Assisted Pronunciation Training). The main difference between CAPT-applied speech recognition systems and usual ARS systems is the possibility to recognize accent speech of non-native speakers that CAPT-applied ASR systems should have. Usual ASR systems that are supposed to recognize the speech of native speakers can be only partly applicable for the purposes of foreign language learning and only on advanced levels of learning whereas pronunciation training is required on beginning level. Besides, usual ASR systems cannot distinguish sounds of a native and a foreign language that are similar, for example, between English aspirated alveolar [t] and Russian dental dorsal [t]. In this case tailored feedback cannot be provided and there is not an opportunity to correct learner's pronunciation in a proper level.

2.2   Key Word Recognition

Key word recognition lies in recognition of certain fragments of continuous speech. In such a case the system does not need to transcribe the whole utterance produced; it is enough to recognize only certain words to response. This technology is applicable for CALL systems to train learner's communicative skills: key word recognition may be used in exercises that present question-answer communications. For instance, the exercise is a dialogue, in which there is some question given by the system and a learner should give an oral answer. The next question that the system is supposed to ask depends on the learner's answer: next question is selected by the system from several options. These are question-answer communications that are made as graphs because further path of user-system interaction is based on some data that is got from the user [6]. The most vivid example of this operation principle is training compound questions (fig. 1). Even if a learner has given a complete sentence as an answer, the system can choose the next question and consequently line up the further path of interaction.

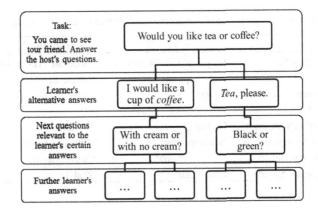

Fig. 1. Example of using key word recognition technology in a training exercise. The key words are in italic.

2.3   Continuous Speech Recognition

Application of continuous speech recognition technology for CALL systems is the most complicated. Nevertheless it offers the greatest methodological opportunities in foreign language learning.

Continuous speech recognition is exercised on large vocabulary (Large Vocabulary Continuous Speech Recognition (LVCSR)). The technology is based on acoustic and language models. Acoustic models are speech sounds patterns the input speech signal is compared with. In LVCSR systems acoustic models are usually correspond to acoustic events, for instance, allophones (monophones, diphones or triphones) and presented with the aid of hidden Markov process [7-9]. Language model is a compulsory part of ASR systems. There are some grammar and semantic links between words. Language model provides information about probability of different sequences of words in a language. Using language model helps to reduce search space and to disambiguate when choosing from several near-value acoustic hypothesis (for example, in Russian it helps to recognize correctly the case of a word).

Application of continuous speech recognition for CALL provides complete automatic analysis of an utterance produced by a learner (in the terms of presence or absence of grammar mistakes as well). Then the text recognized in such a manner is analyzed by parsers, thus a learner can train the use of morphological and syntactic rules of a foreign language [10].

Continuous speech recognition quality is provided by the special modules for estimation of quality and the module for voice activity detection that detaches voice and nonvoice fragments in a sound flow. Therefore, continuous speech recognition system is quite effective and is applicable for methodological purposes of CALL.

K. B. Egan [3] presented relevant differences and similarities of LVCSR and language learning speech qualities (table 1) to determine the challenges of integration continuous speech recognition to CALL.

Table 1. Comparison of variables, LVCSR and language learning [3]

Variables	LVCSR	Language Learning
Vocabulary Size	Large (20k-100k words)	Moderate (1k-5k words)
Speaker's Disposition	Noncooperative	Cooperative
Recording Environment	Noisy	Noiseless
Speaker's Proficiency	Native	Nonnative[*]
Speech Assessment	Not important	Very Important[*]
Speaking Style	Conversational	Conversational
Recognition Speed	Real Time	Real Time

Therefore, there are two main problems: nonnative speech and importance of speech assessment in language learning – the issues that are not supposed in LVCSR.

The problem of nonnative speech was also raised by G. Levow and M. B. Olsen: ASR in CALL must be able to recognize accent speech [11]. Now technical facilities and Internet opportunities allows developers to collect a proper accent speech database and train acoustic models.

The second problem is speech assessment. Certainly, assessment is inherent part of any teaching situation, in language learning it is necessary to assess speaking in a foreign language. Assessment of pronunciation at the segmental level is realizable by means of discrete speech, for instance, by comparing a learner's utterance with a sample by certain parameters. To realize assessment of learner's speaking at higher language levels (for example, syntax) the other natural language processing

---

[*] These two variables are critical for language learning ASR and are harder to deal with than in traditional LVCSR [3].

algorithms such as parsing and natural language understanding need to be integrated. Anyway speech assessment is an issue that still needs work towards.

The question of interpretation of the recognition result for a user is also related to the range of users a CALL system is developed for. For wide audience the feedback should be presented in as much as possible common and vivid form. ASR result can be given as "right"/"wrong" or as "correct"/"incorrect"; using of a point system or percentage appears to be effectless. Also there should be some comments and instructions on errors typical for certain language speakers. If a CALL system is developed for linguistics students there may be some power spectrums, fundamental frequency variation spectrums etc. as a feedback. Not only teachers but also students themselves could compare ASR results with some standard utterances produced by a foreign language native speaker. It has been established by studies that such a feedback is successful in self-teaching [4, 12].

3   The Use of TTS In CALL Systems

Previously, when speech technology was considered in terms of application to CALL, the emphasis was on ASR as the most applicable technology to process learner's speech [13]. In language learning perception and comprehension of foreign speech is also extremely important. TTS can be applied for CALL for this purpose as long as TTS quality on the most spoken languages is pretty high.

TTS for the Russian language developed by Speech Technology Center is based on Unit Selection method. According to this method units of different size (allophones, sequences of allophones, sentences) are selected from a large speech database [14-16]. Today this technology makes possible to reach the highest speech naturalness. According to Paul Taylor [14] who is one of the founders of Unit Selection technology, whereas this technology is comparable to the others (there is also formant speech synthesis, articulatory synthesis, HMM-based synthesis etc.) in intelligibility of synthesized speech, Unit Selection method leaves them behind in naturalness of synthesized speech.

TTS technology can be used for methodological purposes, for example, to create exercises that suppose a dictation in a foreign language. These exercises are necessary for training listening skills. Nevertheless, efficiency of TTS-supported dictation may be disputed. Automatically synthesized speech not always sounds completely naturally and can be distinguished from real speech. In this light it would be correct to use recordings of human speech to exclude possible errors and omissions that can undermine foreign speech learner's perception. However, it has been established by studies that dictation by synthesized speech is more efficient on the first stage of learning because it is more intelligible than human speech [17].

For the purposes of pronunciation training the technology of macro synthesis is applicable. This technology provides more natural sounding and do not make any distortion of speech signal. It is useful in creating exercises in which a learner should repeat and try to imitate sound of a foreign language. In macro synthesis continuous speech fragments are linked at the level of separate words and even phrases. But only separate and frequent speech fragments can be pronounced perfectly with the aid of this type of speech synthesis.

Application of TTS to a CALL system allows to add to a service new teaching material that needs to be sounded and there is no need to record human speech.

4   Developing a CALL System: Language Trainer Project

Now a CALL system is being developed by Speech Technology Center. The project is called "Language Trainer".

The Language Trainer is developed as an intelligent software solution dealing with mastering foreign languages listening and speaking skills. The system provides for computer assisted learning 9 languages: English, German, Russian, French, Spanish, Portuguese, Italian, Hindi and Japanese. The system is designed in such way that each language speaker can learn the other 8 languages because of the possibility to switch the interface into each of 9 supported languages. Each of 9 languages courses consists of 30 lessons. The basis of each lesson is a grammar topic and a conversational topic. The topics of all 30 lessons are connected by the plot. Certainly, there are test in each lesson. At the present stage of the system development there are grammar and vocabulary tests. The intelligence of Language Trainer is provided by expert system that forms learning strategy in terms of the obtained result.

As this is the first real attempt of creating a large-scale intelligent computer assisted languages learning system in Russia, speech technology is used in Language Trainer partially at the present stage. For example, one type of vocabulary tests is supported by limited-vocabulary type of ASR. There are 300 words in basic vocabulary of the Language Trainer (according to the course structure: 30 lessons, each contains 10 new words on a certain conversational topic), thus the size of predefined ASR vocabulary is 300 words. This provides very high efficiency of recognition. The result of user's utterance recognition is compared with an orthographic sample whereby the correctness is estimated. Therefore, there are traditional and ASR supported vocabulary tests in Language Trainer.

Preliminary inquiry of 100 testers that was conducted after beta testing the demonstrated high level of user satisfaction with presence of ASR supported exercises in Language Trainer (fig. 2). The reasons the testers named are presented at the table 2.

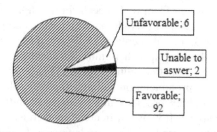

Fig. 2. User satisfaction with presence of ASR supported exercises in Language Trainer

Table 2. Comparison of variables, LVCSR and language learning

Report	Reasons
Favorable	High quality of recognition
	Diverse activity when doing exercises
	Less time spent to do an exercise
	Absence of discomfort when speaking that often presents in case of class-room training
Unfavorable	Inconvenience when doing exercises if someone else is in the room

As far as the basic version of Language Trainer is designed for a wide range of users and operation principle is based on comparing with orthography, ASR supported test results are presented in a simple way: "correct"/"incorrect". Detailed reports on ASR supported vocabulary tests are supposed to be added at later stages of the system development (now there are detailed reports only in grammar exercises which are not ASR supported). It will be achieved by comparing a user's utterance with a sound sample.

At later stages, when more exercises of different types will be added, speech technology will be implemented to the system more extensively according to the concepts and observations presented in this article.

5   Conclusion

As we can see speech technology can be applied for CALL systems in many different ways. Efficacy of ASR and TTS implementation to CALL lies firstly in simplifying purposes related to learning itself. This helps to perform teacher's functions to a certain degree which in makes foreign languages learning more freely available.

In this article we described different ways of speech technology implementation to CALL and the ways of overcome some technical limitations which is possible now due to high current level of speech technology quality and general technological development.

It is important that in the article we paid attention to TTS in terms of integration to CALL as long as in previous papers on the subject usually focused on ASR in this regard. Now high quality of TTS on the most spoken languages allows to implement it to CALL systems.

All the concepts presents in the article are useful for creating effective up-to-date CALL systems through more extensive use of speech technology.

Language Trainer being developed by Speech Technology Center at the moment can set an example of implementation of speech technology to CALL.

Generally, it is indubious that implementation of speech technology to the educatory process appreciably raises accessibility of education the whole world aims for nowadays.

Acknowledgments. This work was partially financially supported by the Government of the Russian Federation, Grant 074-U01.

References

1. Bernstein, J., Cohen, M., Murveit, H., Rtischev, D., Weintraub, M.: Automatic Evaluation and Training in English Pronunciation. In: International Conference on Spoken Language Processing (ICSLP), pp. 1185–1188 (1990)
2. Ehsani, F., Knodt, E.: Speech Technology in Computer-Aided Language Learning: Strengths and Limitations of a New Call Paradigm. Language Learning & Technology 2(1), 54–73 (1998)
3. Egan, K.B.: Speaking: A Critical Skill and Challenge. CALICO 16(3), 277–293 (1999)
4. Dodigovic, M.: Artificial Intelligence in Second Language Learning: Raising Error Awareness. Multilingual Matters, Toronto (2005)
5. Bernstein, J., Franco, H.: Speech Recognition by Computer. In: Lass, N.J. (ed.) Principles of Experimental Phonetics. Mosby, St. Louis (1996)
6. Khitrov, M.V.: Speech Recognition in Personnel Control Systems. Security Director 7, 38–41 (2012)
7. Young, S.J.: A Review of Large-vocabulary Continuous Speech Recognition. IEEE Signal Processing Magazine 8(5), 45–57 (1996)
8. Jelinek, F.: Statistical Methods for Speech Recognition. MIT Press, Cambridge (1998)
9. Rabiner, L.R.: A Tutorial on Hidden Markov Models and Selected Applications in Speech Recognition. IEEE 77, 257–286 (1989)
10. Cucchiarini, C., Neri, A., Strik, H.: Oral Proficiency Training in Dutch L2: The Contribution of ASR-based corrective feedback. Speech Communication 51, 853–863 (2009)
11. Levow, G., Olsen, M.B.: Modeling the Language Assessment Process and Result: Proposed Architecture for an Automatic Oral Proficiency Assessment. In: Computer-mediated Language Assessment and Evaluation in Natural Language Processing Workshop, pp. 24–31 (1999)
12. Stanley, T., Hacioglu, K.: Improving L1-Specific Phonological Error Diagnosis in Computer Assisted Pronunciation Training. In: Interspeech 2012 (2012), http://interspeech2012. org/accepted-abstract.html?id=555 (retrieved May 23, 2014)
13. Eskenazi, M.: An Overview of Spoken Language Technology for Education. Speech Communication 51, 832–844 (2009)
14. Taylor, P.: Text-to-Speech Synthesis. Cambridge University Press, Cambridge (2009)
15. Black, A.W., Hunt, A.J.: Unit Selection in a Concatenative Speech Synthesis Using a Large Speech Database. In: ICASSP, vol. 1, pp. 373–376 (1996)
16. Vepa, J.: Join Cost for Unit Selection Speech Synthesis. PhD thesis, Edinburgh (2004)
17. Pellegrini, T.T., Costa, A., Trancoso, I.: Less Errors with TTS? A Dictation Experiment with Foreign Language Learners. In: Interspeech 2012 (2012), http://www.inesc-id.pt/pt/indicadores/Ficheiros/8340.pdf (Retrieved May 23, 2014)

Using Random Forests for Prosodic Break Prediction Based on Automatic Speech Labeling

Olga Khomitsevich[1,2], Pavel Chistikov[1,2], and Dmitriy Zakharov[2]

[1] National Research University of Information Technologies, Mechanics and Optics
49 Kronverkskiy pr., Saint-Petersburg, Russia, 197101
{khomitsevich,chistikov}@speechpro.com
http://en.ifmo.ru
[2] Speech Technology Center Ltd.
4 Krasutskogo st., Saint-Petersburg, Russia, 196084
zakharov-d@speechpro.com
http://speechpro.com

Abstract. In this paper we present a system for automatically predicting prosodic breaks in synthesized speech using the Random Forests classifier. In our experiments the classifier is trained on a large dataset consisting of audiobooks, which is automatically labeled with phone, word, and pause labels. To provide part of speech (POS) tags in the text, a rule-based POS tagger is used. We use crossvalidation in order to be able to examine not only the results for a specific subset of data but also the systems reliability across the dataset. The experimental results demonstrate that the system shows good and consistent results on the audiobook database; the results are poorer and less robust on a smaller database of read speech even though part of that database was labeled manually.

Keywords: Phrasal breaks, prosodic breaks, prosodic boundaries, pauses, speech synthesis, TTS, text-to-speech, statistical models, Random Forests.

1 Introduction

Predicting prosodic breaks in text is an important part of Text-to-Speech (TTS) technology. Break placement methods often used in TTS systems include rule-based systems [1,2] as well as systems based on machine learning [3–6], employed either for punctuation-free text chunks or for all sentences. In this paper, we propose a system that uses a Random Forests (RF) classifier. We experiment with training such a system on large English speech databases. Because we mostly rely on automatic speech markup to find the positions of breaks in our speech datasets, we deal only with positions that contain a pause, and ignore prosodic breaks not accompanied by a pause. Using automatic labeling enables us to use large speech databases to train and test our system.

A. Ronzhin et al. (Eds.): SPECOM 2014, LNAI 8773, pp. 467–474, 2014.
© Springer International Publishing Switzerland 2014

2 Statistical Methods for Prosodic Break Detection

2.1 Classifiers for Break Detection

Machine learning methods are a common way of solving the problem of break detection and pause placement. Usually a speech or text dataset is used with prosodic break positions marked in the text or in the labels of the sound files; the input features of the classifier typically include Part of Speech (POS) tags as well as the number of words in the sentence and other features. The classifier classifies each word juncture as one containing a break or no break. A number of different classifiers have been used for this task over the years. For instance, [3] uses Hidden Markov Models (HMM); the authors of [4] opt for Memory-Based Learning (MBL); [5] uses Classification and Regression Trees (CART) to predict pause duration; [6] uses Minimum Error-rate Training (MERT), etc. In this paper, we propose using the Random Forests classifier, described in the next section.

2.2 The Random Forests Classifier

In this paper, we use the Random Forests classifier [7] to predict break positions in the text. This classifier was used in our previous work on predicting breaks in Russian. We compared this classifier to the CART classifier and found it to give a (slightly) more accurate result and to be more flexible and easier to tune than CART (see [8] for further details). Its disadvantage compared to CART is that it cannot be efficiently used for predicting break duration, since only break/non-break decisions are made; in this paper, we deal only with break positions and not break durations.

The Random Forests classifier is a machine learning method for solving classification and regression tasks. This method operates by using decision trees, which are built during model training on a random subset of the training data. The output of RF is the mode of the output of the classes of individual trees.

Advantages of the RF classifier include the good quality of the model [9], the ability to deal with large amounts of data and a huge number of features, easy paralleling and scalability. A disadvantage of the Random Forests classifier is the large size of the resulting model, especially when it is trained on a large volume of data. This makes it difficult to use in real-time TTS systems.

3 Description of the System

3.1 Classification Parameters

We used a five-word window when training our system, that is, we computed the classification features for the current word, two words before and after current word. The features we used were the following:

- Presence of a punctuation mark after the word and the type of punctuation (comma, colon, etc);

- Whether the word is capitalized;
- Number of words and number of syllables in the sentence;
- Number of words and syllables between the current juncture and the previous break (both absolute and normalized by the total number of words or syllables in the sentence), and between the current juncture and the end of the sentence;
- Part of speech of the word.

The RF classifier we used contained 100 trees and the probabilistic value was calculated by dividing the number of trees classifying the target class by the total number of trees. Each tree was built on the basis of 60% of randomized training data, which prevented the data from being dependent on noise in the training set.

3.2 Part-of-Speech Tagging

Part of speech (POS) tag sequences are commonly used as a predictor of break positions in text. The assumption is that the sequence of POS tags reflects the syntactic structure of a sentence, which is one of the major factors determining prosodic phrasing. Statistical or rule-based algorithms can be used for POS tagging. Statistical methods use n-grams or other means to predict the POS of a word in text (for instance, [10]). Another way is to use manually composed rules that predict a words POS based on its context. The disadvantage of this method is the time and effort involved in constructing the rules, as well as the difficulty of taking into account the possible instances of ambiguity found in the data. However, machine learning methods also have their disadvantages: a model trained on a large dataset is usually large and the classifier may work too slowly for real-time applications; the corpora used for training classifiers are usually labeled automatically and contain many tagging errors, which leads to errors of POS prediction [11]; the decisions the classifier makes are often unreliable, and are difficult to correct unless we want to combine the statistical tagger with manual rules [12].

To avoid these problems, we opted for a rule-based POS tagger that is more flexible and easier to correct. The tagger is based on two lexicons of POS tags, one for homonyms (words with more than one possible tag) and one for non-homonyms (words with only one unambiguous tag). The lexicons were constructed from a large POS-tagged database (the OANC database [13]); the database was found to contain many tagging errors, which were manually corrected in the lexicons. The lexicons use 36 POS tags. Then about 600 rules were constructed manually and semi-automatically to disambiguate between homonymous words with different POS tags.

A test conducted on a 10k word text sample (literary text) gave the accuracy of POS tagging as 97%. The majority of the errors stem from the remaining errors in the POS lexicon that we were unable to fully eliminate, to the presence of unknown words (so far we make no attempt to predict the POS of an unknown word; all unknown words are classified as nouns, or as proper nouns if capitalized), and to homonymy resolution errors.

4   Experiments

4.1   The Databases

We used two types of data for the experiments. The first dataset consisted of eight audiobooks read by a single professional female speaker. The audiobooks are part of the Blizzard Challenge 2013 database, which was made available for research purposes after the 2013 competition [14]. We will refer to this dataset as the Blizzard data. This dataset comprised 73 hours of speech (without pauses), the corresponding text consisted of over 850k words. All this dataset was labeled fully automatically. The original large files were automatically segmented into sentences, based on the textual information (punctuation, etc) and the presence of corresponding pauses in speech. Each sentence was stored in a separate file. This yielded over 37k sentences (files) in total. In the experiments, sentence boundaries were treated as known (since in a TTS system they are usually determined during the text normalization stage), and only intra-sentential breaks were examined (i.e. the breaks inside each individual sound file).

The sentences were automatically labeled with phones, words and pauses. Since no manual prosodic labeling took place, we can only rely on pauses as markers of prosodic phrasing. In our experiments, we tried setting different thresholds of pause length for predicting breaks: we either took into account all breaks longer than 1ms (virtually all pauses in the dataset) or only those longer than 100ms. Our hypothesis was that longer pauses are associated with major prosodic breaks in the sentence, and that those will be easier to predict using a classifier. They are also less likely to have been produced incorrectly as a result of an automatic labeling error. In our Blizzard dataset, there are about 68000 breaks with the duration of over 1 ms, and about 59000 breaks over 100ms.

Our second dataset was a dataset consisting of speech recorded by a professional female speaker for use in TTS Unit Selection. We will refer to it as the TTS data. This was a database of read speech consisting of separate sentences: 140k words in 11k sentences, comprising 15.5 hours of speech (without pauses), about 10000 breaks over 1ms and 8000 breaks over 100ms. This dataset was automatically labeled using the same procedure as with the Blizzard data, the difference being that the sound files and corresponding text files were already segmented into sentences to begin with. However, in a portion of the dataset comprising 2.2 hours of speech without pauses (about 3000 sentences with 22k words, about 2100 breaks over 1ms and 1200 breaks over 100ms), the automatic labeling was manually corrected and errors were largely eliminated, including errors in pause markup. We experimented with training our system both on the whole TTS dataset and on the manually corrected part only. Again, different thresholds of pause length were considered.

4.2   Experimental Procedure

To make the experimental results more objective, and also to compare the validity of results on the different datasets that we had, we opted for a 10-fold crossvalidation procedure to test our model. The procedure was organized in the following way: the dataset was randomly divided into ten separate parts of an equal size. Then each 10% part was used to evaluate the quality of the model that was trained over the rest of the data (the remaining 90% of the dataset). Finally, the mean quality measures (recall, precision, F-score, etc.) and their confidence intervals were obtained from the results of all the cycles.

4.3 Results

Tables 1-3 demonstrate the results of our experiments with predicting phrasal breaks in our datasets. Table 1 shows the results for the Blizzard dataset, Table 2 the results for the TTS dataset, and Table 3 the results for the part of the TTS dataset in which the automatic labeling was manually corrected by expert linguists. The results are given for all pauses in the dataset (pauses with 1 ms duration and longer), and for the relatively major breaks (pauses over 100ms long). Each result is compared to the baseline result, which is produced by a rule-based algorithm of break detection. This algorithm employs about 70 local context rules to predict breaks from punctuation, POS tags, etc.

Table 1. Break prediction results for the Blizzard dataset

	1ms threshold	Baseline for 1ms	100ms threshold	Baseline for 100ms
Junctures corr.	$94.43 \pm 0.20\%$	$92.11 \pm 0.29\%$	$95.38 \pm 0.26\%$	$92.73 \pm 0.29\%$
Breaks corr.	$68.38 \pm 1.35\%$	$67.22 \pm 1.52\%$	$74.28 \pm 2.38\%$	$73.45 \pm 1.47\%$
False Alarm	$28.87 \pm 2.92\%$	$53.10 \pm 3.06\%$	$31.56 \pm 2.90\%$	$63.82 \pm 4.13\%$
False Reject.	$31.62 \pm 1.35\%$	$32.78 \pm 1.52\%$	$25.72 \pm 2.38\%$	$26.55 \pm 1.47\%$
Recall	$68.38 \pm 1.35\%$	$67.22 \pm 1.52\%$	$74.28 \pm 2.38\%$	$73.45 \pm 1.47\%$
Precision	$70.32 \pm 2.08\%$	$55.87 \pm 1.53\%$	$70.19 \pm 1.79\%$	$53.51 \pm 1.68\%$
F-score	$69.33 \pm 1.23\%$	$61.02 \pm 1.29\%$	$72.17 \pm 1.46\%$	$61.91 \pm 1.35\%$

As measures for testing model quality, we use Junctures Correct (the percentage of junctures, or word pairs, that were correctly identified as containing a break or no break); Breaks Correct (the percentage of breaks present in the data that were correctly identified); False Alarm and False Rejection Errors (the percentage of breaks that were incorrectly inserted or incorrectly deleted, respectively); and the Recall, Precision, and F-score measures calculated based on the error count.

The results show that the RF classifier does better than the baseline system in all experimental conditions. The best results for the F-score are achieved when training the classifier on the Blizzard database with a 100ms threshold. It should be noted that generally better results are achieved when the system is trained to detect breaks larger than 100ms. Longer pauses are normally associated with more major breaks, e.g. between syntactic clauses; it appears that they are easier to predict, compared to small breaks that possibly depend more on meaning, the speakers attitude to the text, and other more subjective factors.

Table 2. Break prediction results for the TTS dataset (all)

	1ms threshold	Baseline for 1ms	100ms threshold	Baseline for 100ms
Junctures corr.	95.05 ± 0.43%	93.91 ± 0.58%	96.04 ± 0.46%	94.50 ± 0.68%
Breaks corr.	62.64 ± 3.62%	61.55 ± 4.56%	66.68 ± 3.9%	69.39 ± 4.79%
False Alarm	25.66 ± 4.37%	39.29 ± 6.53%	30.46 ± 4.56%	57.29 ± 10.52%
False Reject.	37.36 ± 3.62%	38.45 ± 4.56%	33.32 ± 3.92%	30.61 ± 4.79%
Recall	62.64 ± 3.62%	61.55 ± 4.56%	66.68 ± 3.92%	69.39 ± 4.79%
Precision	70.96 ± 3.76%	61.06 ± 4.39%	68.65 ± 3.36%	54.81 ± 5.21%
F-score	66.53 ± 3.11%	61.29 ± 3.80%	67.64 ± 2.95%	61.24 ± 4.50%

Table 3. Break prediction results for the TTS dataset (hand-labeled part)

	1ms threshold	Baseline for 1ms	100ms threshold	Baseline for 100ms
Junctures corr.	92.79 ± 1.80%	91.75 ± 1.69%	95.80 ± 0.72%	95.04 ± 1.61%
Breaks corr.	60.55 ± 11.15%	49.02 ± 10.43%	69.89 ± 10.46%	71.68 ± 12.20%
False Alarm	19.35 ± 9.17%	15.81 ± 9.26%	29.86 ± 13.79%	41.55 ± 17.81%
False Reject.	39.45 ± 11.15%	50.98 ± 10.43%	30.11 ± 10.46%	28.32 ± 12.20%
Recall	60.55 ± 11.15%	49.02 ± 10.43%	69.89 ± 10.46%	71.68 ± 12.20%
Precision	75.88 ± 8.02%	75.71 ± 11.39%	70.16 ± 11.07%	63.44 ± 10.34%
F-score	67.27 ± 7.30%	59.44 ± 9.65%	69.98 ± 9.33%	67.24 ± 8.97%

The classifier also yields a better result in terms of balance of false alarm (FA) and and false rejection (FR) type errors (this is achieved by means of adjusting the pause probability decision of the classifier). The baseline algorithm makes a lot of FA erros under most conditions, which is probably due to the fact that in this algorithm, pauses are nearly always used after punctuation marks, which is not the case with real pauses in any of the datasets. One instance when the rule-based break prediction algorithm does nearly as well as the classifier is on the hand-labeled subset of the TTS data, when only breaks longer than 100ms are dealt with. This may mean that it is easier to model relatively major phrasal breaks by manual rules, and also that hand-checking the labeling does eliminate some errors in pause labels and perhaps helps underscore the difference between major and minor breaks.

The crossvalidation technique clearly shows the importance of the amount of data for training the classifier. The results for the large Blizzard database have a small confidence interval, but it increases substantially when the smaller TTS dataset is used, and especially when only the hand-labeled subset is used.

We also conducted an experiment to compute the usefulness of the features used by the classifier. This measure was calculated based on the classification results that are achieved using only a single feature. Such an operation was performed for each feature from the set, and the results were then compared to each other. The most reliable predicting feature by far was punctuation after the current word, followed by the POS tag of the following word. This is intuitively understandable, since punctuation marks and function words such as conjunctions normally signal breaks between syntactic constituents, which in turn are often accompanied by a prosodic break. This is also the principle which is used most frequently in our baseline rule-based system.

5 Discussion

In comparison with other break detection systems based on machine learning, our system shows an average result; for instance, [3] achieves up to 91.1% correct junctures and the F-score of up to 71.9; [4] reports the F-score of 74.4 on the same data. However, these systems use databases hand-labeled with prosodic breaks, while we use an automatically labeled dataset for most of the experiments; the manually labeled dataset that we have proves too small for training a reliable classification model. Errors of automatic labeling result in wrongly identified pauses when parts of words are labeled as a pause, as well as in skipped pauses when pauses are labeled as speech. Additionally, hesitation pauses may be labeled as prosodic breaks, though there are not many of them in our material (audiobooks). Nevertheless, the results demonstrate that an automatically labeled dataset can be used for break prediction with good results.

It should be noted that all models that use classifiers to predict breaks from POS sequences have the drawback of being very local: they only take into account a small window of POS tags. A way to deal with that would be to include the information from a syntactic parser, which we leave for future research. Another difficulty is that the automatic testing procedure treats the breaks marked in the testing set as the only possible standard and any differences from the break positions as errors. In reality, there are usually multiple ways of segmenting a sentence into prosodic phrases. So the number of errors that the testing procedure reports is only an approximation to how good the classifier really is. It also cannot control the fact that some sentences may have too many pauses while others will have too few; the FA/FR correlation shows the overall number of breaks predicted by the system, but not how they are distributed in individual sentences. For this reason, a better testing technique might be a listening or reading test performed by native speakers or experts, which would rate the correctness of pausing in the text. The development of such a technique will be a matter of future work.

6 Conclusions

The paper presented the results of an experiment in predicting phrasal breaks in text using a Random Forests classifier. We use a rule-based POS tagger to obtain POS tags for training the model, and an automatic markup system to label the dataset with pauses. We demonstrate that using a very large dataset for training the classifier improves its results, even if the data is labeled automatically. It is also easier to model only break positions where a pause larger than 100ms is present, rather than all automatically predicted pauses. Crossvalidation shows that the size of the training dataset has a clear impact on the robustness of the system. The results of the classifier improve on a rule-based baseline model of break placement.

Acknowledgment. We thank the organizers of the Blizzard Challenge 2013 for making available the competition database. This work was partially financially supported by the Government of the Russian Federation, Grant 074-U01.

References

1. Atterer M.: Assigning Prosodic Structure for Speech Synthesis: A Rule-based Approach. In: Speech Prosody 2002, pp. 147–150 (2002)
2. Khomitsevich, O., Solomennik, M.: Automatic pause placement in a Russian TTS system. In: Computational Linguistics and Intellectual Technologies, vol. 9, pp. 531–537. RGGU, Moscow (2010) (in Russian)
3. Black, A.W., Taylor, P.: Assigning phrase breaks from part-of-speech sequences. Computer Speech & Language 12(2), 99–117 (1998)
4. Busser B., Daelemans W., Bosch A.V.D.: Predicting phrase breaks with memory-based learning. In: 4th ISCA Tutorial and Research Workshop on Speech Synthesis, pp. 29–34 (2001)
5. Parlikar A., Black A.W.: Modeling Pause-Duration for Style-Specific Speech Synthesis. In: Interspeech 2012, pp. 446–449 (2012)
6. Parlikar A., Black A.W.: Minimum Error Rate Training for Phrasing in Speech Synthesis. In: 8th ISCA Speech Synthesis Workshop, pp. 13–17 (2013)
7. Breiman L., Cutler A.: Random Forests,
   http://www.stat.berkeley.edu/breiman/RandomForests/cc_home.htm
8. Chistikov, P., Khomitsevich, O.: Improving prosodic break detection in a Russian TTS system. In: Železný, M., Habernal, I., Ronzhin, A. (eds.) SPECOM 2013. LNCS, vol. 8113, pp. 181–188. Springer, Heidelberg (2013)
9. Caruana, R., Niculescu-Mizil, A.: An Empirical Comparison of Supervised Learning Algorithms Using Different Performance Metrics. In: 23rd International Conference on Machine Learning, pp. 161–168 (2006)
10. Giménez, J., Márquez, L.: Svmtool: A general pos tagger generator based on support vector machines. In: 4th International Conference on Language Resources and Evaluation, pp. 43–46 (2004)
11. Manning, C.D.: Part-of-Speech Tagging from 97% to 100%: Is It Time for Some Linguistics? In: Gelbukh, A.F. (ed.) CICLing 2011, Part I. LNCS, vol. 6608, pp. 171–189. Springer, Heidelberg (2011)
12. Sun, M.: Bellegarda J.R.: Improved pos tagging for text-to-speech synthesis. In: IEEE International Conference ICASSP 2011, pp. 5384–5387 (2011)
13. Ide N., Suderman K.: The American National Corpus First Release. In: 4th International Conference on Language Resources and Evaluation, pp. 1681–1684 (2004)
14. King S., Karaiskos V.: The Blizzard Challenge 2013. In: Blizzard Challenge 2013 Workshop (2013)

Vulnerability of Voice Verification Systems to Spoofing Attacks by TTS Voices Based on Automatically Labeled Telephone Speech

Vadim Shchemelinin[1,2], Mariia Topchina[2], and Konstantin Simonchik[2]

[1] National Research University of Information Technologies, Mechanics and Optics,
St.Petersburg, Russia
www.ifmo.ru
[2] Speech Technology Center Limited, St.Petersburg, Russia
www.speechpro.com
{shchemelinin,topchina,simonchik}@speechpro.com

Abstract. This paper explores the robustness of a text-dependent voice verification system against spoofing attacks that use synthesized speech based on automatically labeled telephone speech. Our experiments show that when manual labeling is not used in creating the synthesized voice, and the voice is based on telephone speech rather than studio recordings, False Acceptance error rate decreases significantly compared to high-quality synthesized speech.

Keywords: spoofing, speech synthesis, unit selection, HMM, speaker recognition.

1   Introduction

Information technology plays an increasingly large role in today's world, and different authentication methods are used for restricting access to informational resources, including voice biometrics. Examples of using speaker recognition systems include internet banking systems, customer identification during a call to a call center, as well as passive identification of a possible criminal using a preset "blacklist" [1]. Due to the importance of the information that needs to be protected, requirements for biometric systems are high, including robustness against potential breakins and other attacks. Robustness of the basic technology of voice biometrics has greatly improved in recent years. For instance, the latest NIST SRE 2012 competition [2] showed that the EER of text-independent speaker recognition systems is down to 1.5-2% in various conditions. However, the vulnerability of these systems to spoofing attacks is still underexplored and needs serious examination.

For this reason, a new direction of spoofing [3,4,5], and anti-spoofing in voice biometric system has recently appeared. Different spoofing methods were examined. For example, [6] describes methods based on "Replay attack", "Cut and paste", "Handkerchief tampering" and "Nasalization tampering". However, spoofing using text-to-speech synthesis based on the target speakers voice remains one of the most successful spoofing methods. [7] examines the method of spoofing which is performed using a

A. Ronzhin et al. (Eds.): SPECOM 2014, LNAI 8773, pp. 475–481, 2014.

hybrid TTS method that combines Unit Selection and HMM. The likelihood of false acceptance when using high-quality speech synthesis and a speech database recorded with studio quality can reach 98%.

This paper explores the robustness of a text-dependent verification system against spoofing based on the method described in [7] using a synthesized voice based on automatically labeled "free" speech recorded in the telephone channel. This attack scenario does not require expert knowledge for preparing a synthesized voice and is more likely to be implemented by criminals.

The aim of our research is to find out how strongly False Acceptance (FA) error rate will decrease if the perpetrator cannot access an expert for speech database labeling, and if the database is recorded in the telephone channel.

2   The Voice Verification System

A typical scenario of the functioning of a text-dependent verification system is shown in figure 1. The user connects to the text-dependent verification system and inputs his or her unique ID. The system sends a passphrase for the user to pronounce. The user pronounces the passphrase, the system compares it to the model recorded during user registration and makes the decision whether the user should be allowed or denied access.

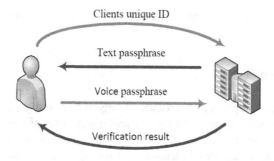

Fig. 1. The process of text-dependent verification

In our experiments we used i-vector based speaker recognition system [8,9].

We used special signal preprocessing module, which included energy based voice activity detection, clipping [10], pulse and multi-tonal detection. The front-end computes 13 mel-frequency cepstral coefficients, as well as the first and second derivatives, to yield a 39 dimensional vector per frame. The derivatives are estimated over a 5-frame context. To obtain these coefficients, speech samples are pre-emphasized, divided into 22ms window frames with a fixed shift of 11ms, and each frame is subsequently multiplied by a Hamming window function.

We also applied a cepstral mean subtraction (CMS) and did not apply Feature Warping [11] for the cepstral coefficients.

We used a gender-independent universal background model (UBM) with 512 - component gaussian mixture model (GMM), obtained by standard ML-training on the telephone part of the NIST's SRE 1998-2010 datasets (all languages, both genders) [12], [13].

In our study we used more than 4000 training speakers in total. We also used a diagonal, not a full-covariance GMM UBM.

The i-vector extractor was trained on more than 60000 telephone and microphone recordings from the NIST 1998-2010 comprising more than 4000 speakers' voices.

The main expression defining the factor analysis of the GMM parameters with the aim of lowering data dimensionality is given below:

$$\mu = m + T\omega + \epsilon,$$

where μ is the supervector of the GMM parameters of the speaker model,
m is the supervector of the UBM parameters,
T is the matrix defining the basis in the reduced feature space,
ω is the i-vector in the reduced feature space, $\omega \in N(0, 1)$,
ϵ is the error vector.
LDA matrix was trained on the same data from the NIST 1998-2010.

3   The Method of Spoofing the Verification System

We chose to model a spoofing attach method based on a TTS (Text-to-Speech) system developed by Speech Technology Center Ltd (STC) [14]. [15] demonstrates that when the synthesized voice is built using 8 minutes of free speech recorded in a studio environment and manually labeled, the spoofer can achieve 44% likelihood of false acceptance (Table 1).

Table 1. FA verification error for spoofing the verification system based on different length of high quality speech with professional labeling (amount of free speech used for passphrase synthesis)

Length of speech data for TTS	FA for threshold in calibration EER point	FA for threshold in calibration $FA = 1\%$ point
1 minute	12.7%	1.5%
3 minutes	34.9%	7.9%
8 minutes	44.4%	19.1%
30 minutes	55.6%	23.8%
4 hours	100%	98.4%

In our experiment we used automatic database labeling, which includes $F0$ period labeling and phone labeling. $F0$ labeling is done by means of the autocorrelation method of $F0$ calculation with preliminary filtering and postprocessing for more precise labeling of $F0$ periods. Low frequency filtering is used to lower the $F0$ detection error by deleting components higher than 500Hz from the signal. High frequency filtering is used to detect the fragments that have no $F0$ (nonvocalized phones).

Phone labeling is done automatically using automatic speech recognition (ASR) modules based on Hidden Markov Models (HMM). The labeling is based on forced alignment of the transcription and the signal. It involves three steps:

1. Building acoustic models of monophones, since monophones are best suited for this task.
2. Obtaining the "ideal" labeling that exactly matches the required transcription, and the "real" labeling that more closely matches the recording.
3. Automatic correction of the obtained phone labels based on the $F0$ labeling.

The process of automatically building a TTS voice is described in detail in [16].

The spoofing attack scheme modeled in this paper is demonstrated in Figure 2. The attack is based on creating a TTS voice based on previously recorded free speech of a verification system user and its automatic segmentation. In the process of text-prompted verification, the text of the passphrase is received and it is then synthesized with the users voice by the spoofing system.

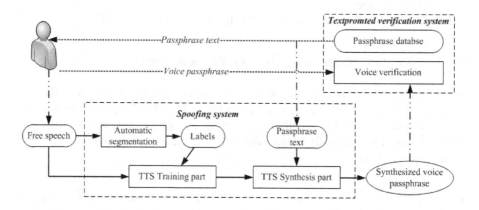

Fig. 2. Scheme of spoofing a text-prompted verification system using TTS technology

As previously recorded free speech we used a Russian phone speech database with 5 speakers whose voices were used for creating a TTS system. Examples of passphrases include: "2014 year", "City of Ekaterinburg, Railway Station street, 22, Railway Station"; "pay three roubles and publish an ad in the bulletin", etc. It is important to note that the recorded phrases were not included in the TTS database. In total, 95 phrases by different speakers were recorded.

The verifications system thresholds were calibrated using a YOHO speech database [17] consisting of 138 speakers (male and female) each of whom pronounced a "Combination lock" phrases of the form "36-24-36", with about 1.5-2 seconds of pure speech. Only one passphrase was used for enrollment and one for the verification. Two verification system thresholds were set:

1. A threshold based on Equal Error Rate (EER), so-called $ThresholdEER$. EER was estimated as 4% on the YOHO database.

2. A threshold with the likelihood of false acceptance not higher than 1% (*Threshold FA*). This threshold is usually used in systems where it is necessary to provide maximum defense against criminal access.

Then, for each speaker, attempts to access the system were made using a TTS voice that was created using the speech material of this speaker. The length of speech material used for creating the TTS voice varied from 1 minute to 8 minutes of speech. The experimental results are presented in Figure 3.

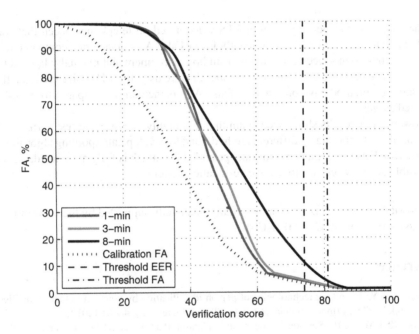

Fig. 3. FA diagrams for spoofing the verification system with a TTS voice based on different durations of telephone speech with automatic labeling (amount of free speech used for passphrase synthesis)

In Table 2, for different verification system thresholds, presented comparisons of the *FA* values obtained with automatic labeling of free speech with the results showed by [7], where free speech was labeled manually by experts.

As can be seen from the table, if automatically labeled telephone speech is used in TTS, the False Acceptance error rate is strongly decreased.

4 Conclusions

We analyzed the vulnerability of state-of-the-art verification methods against spoofing using a hybrid TTS system based on automatically labeled speech. As demonstrated

Table 2. FA verification error for spoofing the verification system based on different length of high quality speech with professional and automatic labeling (amount of free speech used for passphrase synthesis)

	FA for $ThresholdEER$		FA for $ThresholdFA$	
Length of speech data for TTS	Expert labeling	Automatic labeling	Expert labeling	Automatic labeling
1 minute	12.7%	1.1%	1.5%	1.1%
3 minutes	34.9%	4.6%	7.9%	1.8%
8 minutes	44.4%	10.8%	19.1%	4.5%

by the experiments, spoofing using a TTS voice based on telephone speech that was labeled automatically yields a significantly lower False Acceptance rate compared to a TTS voice based on speech recorded in a studio environment and manually labeled by experts. For instance, when 8 minutes of speech were used for TTS voice creation, the new spoofing method gave only a 10% False Acceptance error, compared to the 44% obtained earlier.

However, our results show once again that it is highly necessary to test verification systems against spoofing by different methods, and to develop anti-spoofing algorithms. Even a 10% False Acceptance error rate, provided the attack is fully automated, makes it possible to easily break into a voice verification system.

Acknowledgments. This work was partially financially supported by the Government of Russian Federation, Grant 074-U01.

References

1. Matveev, Y.: Biometric technologies of person identification by voice and other modalities, Vestnik MGTU. Priborostroenie. Biometric Technologies 3(3), 46–61 (2012)
2. The NIST Year 2012 Speaker Recognition Evaluation Plan, http://www.nist.gov/itl/iad/mig/upload/NIST_SRE12_evalplan-v17-r1.pdf
3. Wu, Z., Kinnunen, T., Chng, E.S., Li, H., Ambikairajah, E.: A Study on spoofing attack in state-of-the-art speaker verification: the telephone speech case. In: Proc. of the APSIPA ASC, Hollywood, USA, pp. 1–5 (December 2012)
4. Wu, Z., Kinnunen, T., Chng, E.S., Li, H.: Speaker verification system against two different voice conversion techniques in spoofing attacks, Technical report (2013), http://www3.ntu.edu.sg/home/wuzz/
5. Kinnunen, T., Wu, Z., Lee, K.A., Sedlak, F., Chng, E.S., Li, H.: Vulnerability of Speaker Verification Systems Against Voice Conversion Spoofing Attacks: the Case of Telephone Speech. In: Proc. of the ICASSP, Kyoto, Japan, pp. 4401–4404 (March 2012)
6. Villalba, E., Lleida, E.: Speaker verification performance degradation against spoofing and tampering attacks. In: Proc. of the FALA 2010 Workshop, pp. 131–134 (2010)
7. Shchemelinin, V., Simonchik, K.: Examining Vulnerability of Voice Verification Systems to Spoofing Attacks by Means of a TTS System. In: Železný, M., Habernal, I., Ronzhin, A. (eds.) SPECOM 2013. LNCS, vol. 8113, pp. 132–137. Springer, Heidelberg (2013)
8. Kenny, P.: Bayesian speaker verification with heavy tailed priors. In: Proc. of the Odyssey Speaker and Language Recognition Workshop, Brno, Czech Republic (June 2010)

9. Simonchik, K., Pekhovsky, T., Shulipa, A., Afanasyev, A.: Supervized Mixture of PLDA Models for Cross-Channel Speaker Verification. In: Proc. of the 13th Annual Conference of the International Speech Communication Association, Interspeech 2012, Portland, Oregon, USA, September 9-13 (2012)
10. Aleinik, S., Matveev, Y., Raev, A.: Method of evaluation of speech signal clipping level. Scientific and Technical Journal of Information Technologies, Mechanics and Optics 79(3), 79–83 (2012)
11. Pelecanos, J., Sridharan, S.: Feature warping for robust speaker verication. In: Proc. of the Speaker Odyssey, the Speaker Recognition Workshop, Crete, Greece (2001)
12. Matveev, Y., Simonchik, K.: The speaker identification system for the NIST SRE 2010. In: Proc. of the 20th International Conference on Computer Graphics and Vision, GraphiCon 2010, St. Petersburg, Russia, September 20-24, pp. 315–319 (2010)
13. Kozlov, A., Kudashev, O., Matveev, Y., Pekhovsky, T., Simonchik, K., Shulipa, A.: Speaker recognition system for the NIST SRE 2012. SPIIRAS Proceedings 25(2), 350–370 (2012)
14. Chistikov, P., Korolkov, E.: Data-driven Speech Parameter Generation for Russian Text-to-Speech System. Computational Linguistics and Intellectual Technologies. In: Annual International Conference "Dialogue", pp. 103–111 (2012)
15. Simonchik, K., Shchemelinn, V.: "STC SPOOFING" Database for Text-Dependent Speaker Recognition Evaluation. In: Proc. of SLTU-2014 Workshop, St. Petersburg, Russia, May 14-16, pp. 221–224 (2014)
16. Solomennik, A., Chistikov, P., Rybin, S., Talanov, A., Tomashenko, N.: Automation of New Voice Creation Procedure For a Russian TTS System. Vestnik MGTU. Priborostroenie, "Biometric Technologies" 2, 29–32 (2013)
17. "YOHO Speaker Verification" database, Joseph Campbell and Alan Higgins, `http://www.ldc.upenn.edu/Catalog/catalogEntry.jsp?catalogId=LDC94S16`

Author Index